HUMAN LIBERTY
AND
FREEDOM OF SPEECH

HUMAN LIBERTY

AND

FREEDOM OF SPEECH

C. Edwin Baker

New York   *Oxford*
OXFORD UNIVERSITY PRESS
1989

Oxford University Press

Oxford   New York   Toronto
Delhi   Bombay   Calcutta   Madras   Karachi
Petaling Jaya   Singapore   Hong Kong   Tokyo
Nairobi   Dar es Salaam   Cape Town
Melbourne   Auckland

and associated companies in
Berlin   Ibadan

Copyright © 1989 by Oxford University Press, Inc.

Published by Oxford University Press, Inc.,
200 Madison Avenue, New York, New York 10016

Oxford is a registered trademark of Oxford University Press

Library of Congress Cataloging-in-Publication Data
Baker, C. Edwin.
    Human liberty and freedom of speech / C. Edwin Baker.
       p.   cm.
    Bibliography: p.
    Includes index.
    ISBN 0-19-505777-5
    1. Freedom of speech—United States.   I. Title.
KF4772.B35   1989
342.73'0853—dc19
[347.302853]

9 8 7 6 5 4 3 2 1

Printed in the United States of America
on acid-free paper

For my parents
ERNESTINE MAGAGNA BAKER
and
FALCON OLERO BAKER

Preface

In the fourth grade, when my parents suggested that I join them in converting to the Episcopal Church, I invoked the First Amendment in defense of my right to remain a Southern Baptist. (Not until much later did I learn that the First Amendment only limited government, not parents.) That episode began the genesis of this book. In a segregated Kentucky public high school where students were punished for writing a letter in support of boys at another southern school who wore long hair, I wrote my main tenth grade paper defending the Supreme Court's desegregation decisions and arguing for freedom of speech. I had found, read, and been totally persuaded by John Stuart Mill's *On Liberty.*

College study of modern theorists such as Freud, Marx, and Manneheim and of psychological notions such as cognitive dissonance and processes of selective observation and retention undermined my intellectual confidence in Mill's theory. At the same time, observations of the irrationality of "educated" people's reasoning in justifying the Vietnam war undermined my belief in the effectiveness of free speech in practice. (What—other than psychological theories—could explain how a former Dean of Yale Law School could argue in the fall of 1969 that opponents of the war in Vietnam had never offered *any* alternatives to the administration's policies?) But the discussions and experiences surrounding my participation in political events—McCarthy's presidential campaign, tear-gas and police riots in the streets of Chicago at the 1968 Democratic Convention, a nine-day occupation of a research lab at Stanford the following spring, or People's Park demonstrations at Berkeley—increasingly led to a belief in the importance of individual liberty as well as structural change as fundamental both for a good society and, more to the point, for progressive change. Key to much of "radical" resistance of this period was the attempt to act in ways that were themselves more legitimate (and also more honest and open) than the practices and forces we were opposing. These undergraduate experiences led directly to my understanding of free speech as an aspect of practice that would be part of a more valid civic order and a practice that would help achieve democratic, progressive change—notions that Chapter 5 tries to systematize.

My law studies also figure prominently in the book's development. A major reason that I began teaching law in 1972 immediately after graduation was to have time to finish my third year law school paper, written under Thomas Emerson who, in addition to being the country's foremost First Amendment scholar, was also the professor whose personal and intellectual integrity stood out as most exemplary of all my law school teachers. This third year paper already contained versions of Chapters 1, 2, 3, 4, and 5 of this book. And I had also by then, partly on the basis of my study of Max Weber under David Trubek, began work on the material that became Chapter 9.

In addition to people previously thanked in articles that have been revised to become the center of this book, this personal history helps show the tremendous debt this book owes to the guidance and tolerance of my parents, the stimulation of my undergraduate professors, particularly Charles Drekmeier, Yosel Rogat, and Barton Bernstein, and to constant discussions with many student and ex-student radicals, people such as David Harris and Paul Ruppert, whose integrity, critical intelligence, and constant questioning provided the best of educations. Still, the result is a very "liberal" theory—liberal, however, when the key to liberalism is seen to be its potentially and historically "revolutionary" normative content, which centers on achieving maximum human liberation and equal respect for each person—not liberalism's more historically variable and, now, arguably regressive social theory and institutional content.

This book encompasses edited and revised versions of articles on the First Amendment published in *Iowa Law Review, U.C.L.A. Law Review, University of Southern California Law Review, University of Miami Law Review,* and *Northwestern Law Review.* Chapter 9 also includes sections drawn from an article on property and liberty published in the *University of Pennsylvania Law Review.* Some material that is new to this book has benefited from comments at a faculty seminar at Harvard Law School and a symposium on the First Amendment at Cardozo Law School and at the James Madison Days Symposium in Madisonville, Kentucky. Kent Greenawalt offered helpful and challenging comments on Chapter 3's discussion of coercion. I received valuable typing assistance from Debbie Neary. Carol Sanger, Simon Roberts, and editors and outside reviewers at Oxford University Press made very helpful editorial suggestions. And I have benefited, although I am sure the final product shows this less than many would wish, from constant discussions with law teachers and other friends and from published commentary and criticisms of my prior articles.

New York   C.E.B.
January 1989

Contents

I

THEORY

Introduction

Despite nearly universal acclaim for the value of free speech, little agreement exists concerning its scope. Do rock concerts, cigarette ads, pornography, libelous statements, racial slurs, coercive threats, incitements to crime, political lies, and commercial fraud constitute "speech" or expression covered by the notion of free speech? Are draft-card burnings, picketing, hair styles, and nude dancing forms of expressive conduct that should be treated as speech? Do group boycotts, intimate consensual sexual activity, parades, and sit-ins constitute "peaceable assemblies" (or speech) for constitutional purposes? By exploring several possible rationales for freedom of speech, and defending one, this book will address the issue of coverage.

I will conclude that a "marketplace of ideas" theory is the dominant rationale given for freedom of speech and that it is not persuasive. In its place, I will elaborate and defend a second rationale that also ubiquitously appears in the cases. The defense of this second, "liberty" theory will show its superiority to various versions of the currently dominant marketplace interpretation. This second rationale will provide a firm foundation for a somewhat different, and generally more extensive, realm of free expression.

Part I elaborates and evaluates these rationales. Chapters 1 and 2 analyze marketplace of ideas theories, beginning with the most prominent, "classic" model, best described by John Stuart Mill. Chapter 3 elaborates and defends the liberty model. Chapter 4 develops the implications of the liberty model for expressive *conduct*. Part I ends with a speculative chapter that considers the relationship between the liberty theory, the process of change, and visions of democracy. Overall, Part I concludes that the classic marketplace of ideas theory depends on implausible assumptions for its coherence. It shows that the market failure version of the marketplace of ideas theory is unworkable, dangerous, and inconsistent with a reasonable interpretation of the purpose of the first amendment. Likewise, the political speech theory either succumbs to the criticisms of the marketplace theories or cannot justifiably be limited to political speech. Although the Court consistently has used and proclaimed the classic marketplace of ideas theory and though most modern reformist proposals recommend a market failure theory, Part I argues that the liberty theory provides the most coherent understanding of the first amendment. Adoption of this theory, which delineates a realm of individual liberty roughly corresponding to noncoercive, nonviolent action, would have major, salutary implications for judicial elaboration of the first amendment.

Often the classic marketplace of ideas theory and the liberty theory reach similar conclusions concerning coverage and protection. Even then, there is pragmatic merit in getting the grounds of judgment right. Moreover, Part I examines in passing numerous situations where the two theories diverge. Part II applies the liberty theory in two areas where existing doctrine is particularly muddled. Chapters 6, 7, and 8 argue for an "absolutist," liberty approach to time, place, and manner regulations. Chapter 9 looks at liberty in the commercial sector and concludes that commercial speech should not receive protection. Chapters 10 and 11 argue that the press clause is a structural provision that has a fourth-estate function. Although it serves liberty instrumentally, this structural theory is independent of but congruent with the liberty theory of the rest of the book. These chapters conclude, on the one hand, that the independence of the press should be much more protected than current doctrine recognizes but, on the other, that this protection is consistent with considerable governmental structural regulation, even with guild socialism for the press. Finally, recognizing that the book exhibits a particular style of constitutional interpretation, I briefly describe and defend this approach to interpretation.

The classic marketplace of ideas model argues that the truth (or the best perspectives or solutions) can be discovered through robust debate, free from governmental interference. Defending this theory in *On Liberty*,[1] John Stuart Mill argued that three situations are possible: (1) if heretical opinion contains the truth and we silence it, we lose the chance of exchanging truth for error; (2) if received and contesting opinions each hold part of the truth, their clash in open discussion provides the best means to discover the truth in each; (3) even if the heretical view is wholly false and the orthodoxy contains the whole truth, there is a danger that the received truth, unless debated and challenged, will be held in the manner of prejudice or dead dogma, its meaning forgotten or enfeebled, and, therefore, this truth will be inefficacious for good.[2] Moreover, without free speech, totally false heretical opinions, which could not survive open discussion, will not disappear. Instead, driven underground, these opinions will smolder, their fallacies protected from exposure and opposition.[3] According to this marketplace of ideas theory, the value of speech lies not in the liberty interests of individual speakers but in the societal benefits derived from unimpeded discussion.[4] This social gain from unimpeded discussion is so great, and any loss from allowing speech is so small, that society should not tolerate any restraint on the verbal search for truth.

Real-world conditions prevent the completely laissez-faire economic market—praised as a social means to facilitate the optimal allocation and production of goods—from achieving the socially desired results. Similarly, critics of the classic marketplace of ideas theory point to factors that prevent it from successfully facilitating the discovery of truth or from generating proper social perspectives and decisions.[5] Because of oligopolistic control of the media, lack of access for disfavored or impoverished groups, overwhelmingly pervasive participation by favored groups, techniques of behavior manipulation, irrational responses to propaganda, and the nonexistence of value-free, objective truth, the marketplace of ideas fails to achieve optimal results. Therefore, advocates of the market failure model conclude that sensitive state intervention in the speech arena, just as in the economic arena, is sometimes necessary to correct for these failures.[6] Broadly based, effective, if not equal access to the marketplace of ideas must be guaranteed if freedom of speech is to promote socially desirable perspectives and decisions.

The liberty model holds that the free speech clause protects not a marketplace, but rather an arena of individual liberty from certain types of governmental restrictions. Speech or other self-expressive conduct is protected not as a means to achieve a collective good but because of its value to the individual. The liberty theory justifies protection of expression because of the way the protected conduct fosters individuals' self-realization and self-determination without improperly interfering with the legitimate claims of others. Of course, the liberty theory must specify what conduct is protected. I investigate the nature of speech—its uses and how it typically affects the world—and review generally accepted notions of the values of activities protected by the first amendment. I then argue that the constitutional protection of free speech bars certain governmental restrictions on noncoercive, nonviolent, substantively valued conduct, including nonverbal conduct. In this liberty interpretation, first amendment protections of speech, assembly, and free exercise of religion are merely different markers bounding a single realm of liberty of self-expression and self-determination. Although each concept provides illumination, the concept of protected speech most clearly delineates its scope.[7] Finally, the broadened scope of protection required by the liberty theory cures major inadequacies of the marketplace of ideas as a social process for finding or creating societal "truth." The liberty model thereby provides protection for a progressive process of change.

1

The Classic Marketplace
of Ideas Theory

THE THEORY AND ITS ASSUMPTIONS

> And though all the winds of doctrine were let loose to play upon the earth, so
> Truth be in the field, we do injuriously, by licensing and prohibiting to mis-
> doubt her strength. Let her and Falsehood grapple: who ever knew Truth put
> to the worst, in a free and open encounter.[1]

John Milton's imagery received possibly its best elaboration by John Stuart Mill,
whose arguments are summarized in the Introduction. According to this classic
theory, truth is discovered through its competition with falsehood. But why bet
that truth will be the consistent or even the usual winner? It is not self-evident
that this would happen. It would, however, given certain crucial assumptions,
all found in Mill's *On Liberty*. A clear understanding of the classic theory
requires knowledge of the assumptions on which it relies and clarity as to how
those assumptions are necessary for the theory's persuasive force.

First, truth must be "objective" or "discoverable." Truth is able to outshine
falsity in debate or discussion only if truth is there to be seen. Discussion that
compares verbal claims to "reality" might be expected to determine which
claims are more accurate.[2] Thus, if truth is objective, if there is a reality to which
the claims can be compared, debate might be expected eventually to show the
errors of falsehood and, thereby, lead to its rejection.

Instead, if truth is subjective, if it is chosen or created, an adequate theory
must explain why and how the usually unequal advocacy of various viewpoints
leads to the "best choice." Why does protecting speech freedom from state regulation provide a proper or legitimate process of choice or creation? Why not
protect people's freedom to engage in "experimental" practices as a means for
choosing their preferred truth? Or regulate speech in a manner that results in
greater equality of opportunities to create our truths? Each practice, including
free speech, predictably leads to or creates different truths. The classic theory
does not explain why the ones created by free speech would be best. These problems go away, however, if there is only one objective truth to discover.

Second, the classic theory does and must assume that people are basically
rational. People must possess the capacity correctly to perceive truth or reality.

6

This rationality assumption has two aspects. For the rationality assumption to hold, a person's personal history or position in society must not control the manner in which he or she perceives or understands the world. If people's perceptions are social creations, and if people's social experiences are radically different, they will radically differ in how they see and understand the world. Mere discussion would be inadequate for eliminating these differences in experience and position and, therefore, inadequate for discovering either objective truth or the uniformly "best" perspectives. Perceptions of truth would vary. Reason employed in discussion might accomplish something but could not provide an Archimedean point from which to gain an unbiased insight into reality. The dominance of one perception over another would depend, at least in part, on arbitrary social circumstances and power relations among social groups.

In addition, for the rationality assumption to hold, people's rational faculties must enable them to sort through the form and frequency of message presentation to evaluate the core truth in the messages. Otherwise, the marketplace of ideas would only promote acceptance of those perspectives that were most effectively packaged and promoted.

The value of a properly working marketplace of ideas follows from a third set of interrelated assumptions. The discovery of truth must be desirable—for example, because truth provides the best basis for action and, thereby, uniformly promotes human interests. If "objective" truth provides the best basis of action, then as humanity progressively finds more truth, the diversity of practice as well as of opinion[3] should gradually narrow. Cultural pluralism should progressively diminish. Moreover, truth would provide the basis for resolving value conflicts. For objective truth to be the proper basis of action implies that people's real interests do not conflict. In contrast, if truth is not objective or is not the best basis of action, there could be intractable value conflicts. Then the value of the marketplace of ideas would be unclear. Whether robust debate is useful would depend on whether it advanced or obstructed the interests of the group one favors or the group that "ought" to prevail.

Given the marketplace of ideas theory's assumptions about the objective nature of truth, the rational capabilities of humans, and the unity of the real aims of people,[4] the presentation of conflicting arguments and insights can be expected to aid people in discovering truth. In contrast, regulation of speech would only undermine the discovery and recognition of truth and impede wise, well-founded decision making.

JUDICIAL ADOPTION

The marketplace of ideas theory consistently dominates the Supreme Court's discussions of freedom of speech.[5] Marketplace imagery ("competition of ideas," the value of "robust debate") pervades judicial opinions and provides justification for the courts' first amendment "tests." A brief review of three prominent tests and several doctrinal contexts illustrates this judicial reliance on the classic marketplace theory.

Holmes and Brandeis grounded the clear and present danger test[6] on the classic marketplace model: "[T]he ultimate good desired is better reached by free trade in ideas . . . [T]he best test of truth is the power of the thought to get itself accepted in the competition of the market."[7] Likewise, "freedom to think as you will and to speak as you think are means indispensable to the discovery and spread of political truth."[8] Like Mill, Holmes and Brandeis talk glowingly about the *discovery* of truth and the "power of reason as applied through public discussion."[9]

The logic of their clear and present danger test derives directly from the marketplace of ideas theory. Since speech is normally the means relied on to eliminate error, suppression should not be allowed unless the danger of speech is "clear." Otherwise, as Brandeis indicated, suppression is likely to perpetuate error and be based on irrational fear, like the fear of witches exhibited by men when they burned women.[10] More important, it must be "present"—because if "there is opportunity for full discussion" or "if there be time to expose through discussion the falsehood and fallacies . . . the remedy to be applied is more speech."[11] If the danger is not "present," the gravity of the evil and the probability of its occurrence[12] must be irrelevant. Given faith in reason and discussion, if people choose the presumed evil after hearing both sides, that supposed evil must now be assumed to be the best—or the best we have yet discovered. Thus, "if in the long run the beliefs expressed in proletarian dictatorship are destined to be accepted . . . the only meaning of free speech is that they should be given their chance and have their way."[13] In other words, protection must be given to speech *as long as* the marketplace continues to operate. "Harms" resulting from speech cannot justify suppression as long as the harm results from people being convinced by the robust debate. (If the "right" side failed to participate, these nonparticipants, not those spreading the supposedly evil counsel, are at fault. The government acts improperly if it restricts those who do participate in the debate.)

Indeed, the development of the clear and present danger test by Holmes and Brandeis merely repeats insights made in the classic formulation of the marketplace of ideas theory. John Stuart Mill had already noted that

> [E]ven opinions lose their immunity when the circumstances in which they are expressed are such as to constitute their expression a positive instigation to some mischievous act. An opinion that corn dealers are starvers of the poor . . . ought to be unmolested when simply circulated through the press, but may justly incur punishment when delivered orally to an excited mob assembled before the house of a corn dealer, or when handed about among the same mob in the form of a placard.[14]

In *Roth v. United States*,[15] Justice Brennan denied obscenity constitutional protection precisely by identifying obscenity as that material that does not contribute to the marketplace of ideas. Many liberals quarrel with the factual descriptions, but they are crucial for the Court's conclusion that obscenity is "utterly without redeeming social importance."[16]

The Court in *Roth* recognized that "all *ideas* having even the slightest redeeming social importance . . . have full protection."[17] In regulating speech, the government must be neutral toward different ideas. Content discrimination amounts to forbidden censorship. Censorship is avoided only if all communications containing messages or conveying ideas are protected.[18] Brennan recognized that "the protection given speech and press was fashioned to assure unfettered interchange of ideas for the bringing about of political and social changes desired by the people."[19] Thus, an allegedly obscene communication has "redeeming social importance" and is not legally obscene if, but only if, the publication participates in the marketplace of ideas.[20] "[T]he First Amendment's basic guarantee is of freedom to advocate ideas, including unorthodox ideas, controversial ideas, even ideas hateful to the prevailing climate of opinion."[21]

The Court, in rejecting two obvious objections to its analysis, further highlights its reliance on the marketplace theory. First is an issue raised by Justice Douglas when he asks:

> When the Court today speaks of "social value," does it mean a "value" to the majority? Why is not a minority "value" cognizable? . . . [I]f the communication is of value to the masochistic community or to others of the deviant community, how can it be said to be "utterly without redeeming social importance"? "Redeeming" to whom? "Importance" to whom?[22]

Douglas finds "social value" not in the masochistic material's contribution to the pursuit of truth in the marketplace of ideas, but in its contribution to "the needs of this group."[23] Douglas could have further argued that people's willingness to pay money for the material proves that the material has some value. Any obscenity that sells has "social value."

To avoid Douglas' constitutional conclusion without rejecting his accurate factual observations, the Court must interpret "social value" from the perspective of the marketplace theory. The Court can plausibly conclude that the willingness to pay only indicates the value of obscenity for the entertainment "needs of the group." "Real" literature's redeeming social value in the marketplace of ideas follows from its insights into or its advocacy of ways of life and not from its mere use *within* a way of life. It has value because it presents information or argument, even if ineloquent, relevant to ideas, not merely because it is part of a practice that embodies certain ideas. In contrast to real literature, the "value" of hard-core pornography, according to Professor Frederick Schauer with whom the Court implicitly agrees, is as a sex aid. Schauer argues that obscenity is excluded from first amendment protection not because "it has a physical effect, but [because] it has nothing else."[24] This understanding of obscenity and the Court's emphasis on the marketplace of ideas are implicit in the Court's argument that "to equate the free and robust exchange of ideas and political debate with commercial exploitation of obscene material demeans the grand conception of the First Amendment."[25] Despite liberal protests that hard-core pornography provides relevant information, most would agree with the Court's assessment that it contributes little to the marketplace of ideas.[26] Defenders of pornography may do well to follow Douglas and find the constitutionally relevant value in the freedom "to enjoy" obscenity rather than in the operation of a marketplace of ideas.

Second, the Court, following the logic of the marketplace theory, often says that speech is protected because of its role in "bringing about political and social

change"—or its role in supporting some, and undermining other, social practices. Yet obscenity is clearly political. Major arguments for banning obscenity
are either that it reinforces certain (objectionable) social practices or that it contributes to (undesirable) social change.[27] Some claim that obscenity leads to violent sex crimes. Most would agree that its use affects the moral or cultural tone
of the community. Forceful analyses argue that pornography contributes to or
reinforces the subordination of women.[28] Of course, this debate is two-sided.
Obscenity has also been argued to serve positive, even feminist, values.[29]

Despite these (negative or positive) contributions to bringing about social or
political change, the Court's reliance on the marketplace theory explains its
refusal to protect obscenity. Use of obscenity, like engagement in any activity,
can influence people's attitudes and ideas. In the marketplace of ideas theory,
however, speech must bring about change by the (at least partly) rational process
of convincing people of ideas or opinions. The marketplace theory only protects
influence that results from the listener or reader understanding and assimilating
the speaker's claims. Or, for example, in the case of art and music, assimilating
some broader aspect of the communication, not merely engaging in an activity,
must be key to the influence. Thus, the marketplace theory denies protection to
pornography because of the conclusion that pornography exercises influence in
a manner more similar to engaging in sexual activity than to hearing argument
and debate.

In *Paris Adult Theatre I v. Slaton*, Justice Brennan correctly objects that the
Burger Court's alteration of the "any redeeming social importance" criteria (the
Court replaced it with a standard of "serious literary, artistic, political, or sci-
entific value") "jeopardize[s] the analytic underpinnings of the entire scheme."[30]
The jeopardy results because now the government (eventually the courts) must
evaluate the worth of the speech, the importance or "seriousness" of the ideas.
At least in theory, the earlier approach required the government to be agnostic.
Once the material was found to have some intellectual content, it was protected.
Nevertheless, the new majority repeatedly reaffirms its allegiance to "the free
and robust exchange of ideas," "the unfettered interchange of ideas,"[31] the prohibition of state "control of reason and the intellect," and the protection of the
"communication of ideas."[32] It still relies on the marketplace of ideas theory
although its implicit instrumentalist balancing of interests waters down protection, only providing for speech whose contribution to the marketplace is
"serious."

The Court's constitutional analysis of defamation also invokes Mill's marketplace of ideas theory to justify its conclusion. In *New York Times v. Sullivan*,[33] the Court found, at least in the case of defamation of public figures, that
the first amendment protects the speaker unless the false, defamatory statement
is made "with knowledge that it was false or with reckless disregard of whether
it was false or not."[34] It explained that the first amendment "was fashioned to
assure unfettered interchange of ideas," and emphasized the Constitutional faith
"in the power of reason as applied through public debate."[35] The Court quoted
Mill for the practical point that erroneous statements are continuously and inevitably made, even in good faith, during discussion.[36] On this basis, it recognized
that erroneous statements must be protected to provide the breathing space

needed for robust debate in the marketplace of ideas. The Court also cites Mill's argument that falsehoods can have value—they can serve a useful function by bringing about "the clear perception and livelier impression of truth, produced by its collision with error."[37]

Still, marketplace logic does not require that all defamation be protected. It only need protect people who are engaged in some search for truth or "any exposition of ideas."[38] The *New York Times* rule fully covers speech that stems from honest participation in the marketplace of information and ideas.[39] But it need not protect those who are unconcerned with the truth of their statements. As Brennan later explained, the "calculated falsehood. . . [is] no essential part of any exposition of ideas, and [is] of such slight social value as a step to truth" that it does not enjoy constitutional protection.[40]

Recent cases have developed a not-yet-complete complex of rules to cover defamatory injuries to nonpublic figures.[41] Despite abandoning the full reach of marketplace logic in favor of an explicit legislative-like balancing, the Court continues to emphasize the marketplace theory in explaining the role and value of speech. For example, in *Gertz v. Robert Welch, Inc.*,[42] Justice Powell opens his discussion of the first amendment by noting that we depend for the correction of pernicious opinions "on the competition of other ideas."[43] "[F]*alse* statements of fact," which Powell distinguishes from ideas, have "no constitutional value," because they do not "materially advanc[e] society's interest in uninhibited, robust, and wide-open debate on public issues."[44] Still, false statements of fact are sometimes protected because they are "inevitable in free debate."[45] Thus, although it does not provide the *New York Times'* degree of protection to speakers who defame nonpublic figures, the Court's analysis retains *New York Times'* reliance on the classic marketplace of ideas theory of speech.[46]

The marketplace theory assumes that unrestrained speech aids listeners in finding truth and, thus, promotes wise decision making. The Court has recently recognized that commercial advertising and corporate political speech can serve this function as well as traditionally protected speech. Specifically relying on the public's or the consumer's interest in the "free flow of commercial information" as a means to promote "intelligent and informed" economic decisions, the Burger Court has extended first amendment protection to commercial speech.[47] The Court reasoned that a commercial advertisement that merely proposes a commercial transaction is not "so removed from any 'exposition of ideas' . . . that it lacks all protection."[48] Likewise, in a severely criticized decision,[49] a 5–4 majority invalidated a state's restriction on the political speech of a (nonmedia) business corporation.[50] A dissent argued that the law did not restrict any speech that reflected individual choice; rather the restriction on corporate political speech could promote individual control over expression.[51] The majority rejected the dissent's emphasis on self-expression, self-realization and self-fulfillment in favor of the marketplace theory. It argued, for example, that the source was irrelevant to "the inherent worth of the speech in terms of its capacity for informing the public."[52]

The logic of its "tests" illustrates judicial reliance on the classic marketplace of ideas model. Other doctrinal examples could be given. The Court's increasing practice, however, is to eviscerate first amendment protection by means of deferential balancing. Here, again, the Court consistently invokes the marketplace theory. A prominent early example is *Dennis v. United States*,[53] upholding the Smith Act. Only the dissenters were willing to trust the marketplace to reveal "the ugliness of Communism."[54] However, even the plurality recognized that "the basis of the First Amendment is the hypothesis that speech can rebut speech... [and] free debate of ideas will result in the wisest governmental policies."[55]

Later discussion will show that marketplace of ideas notions are not the only strains to be heard in the Court's first amendment chorus. Some Court opinions and a few doctrinal areas suggest the "liberty theory." Individual justices clearly adopt the liberty theory in at least some situations. The marketplace theory, however, surely dominates both rhetorically and conceptually. Its rejection as the basis of first amendment protection of speech would have major practical implications.

FAILURE OF ASSUMPTIONS

At least within the academic world, the assumptions on which the classic marketplace of ideas theory rests are almost universally rejected. Here, I briefly note the rejection of each and consider some implications, especially the undermining of the plausibility of the belief that the marketplace leads to truth, or even to the best or most desirable decision. In the next section, I consider the possibility of defending the marketplace of ideas without these assumptions.

First, truth is not objective.* Even in the natural sciences, the presumed sanctuary of objectively verifiable truth, those values to which scientists personally give allegiance provide necessary criteria for judging between competing theories.[57] Criteria for choice of paradigms include the theory's ability to provide answers to currently pressing questions, its usefulness in suggesting applications or new investigatable problems, and its simplicity or aesthetic appeal. Newly accepted paradigms or theories usually fail to do some of what the old theory did, but do more of what we now "value" most. But no objective scale compares that which only the new theory does to that which only the old theory could do. Thus, which theory provides the most insight or knowledge depends on how we value what each does, not on any objective measurement. The choice between theories is not a matter of objective truth but of pragmatic or "value" considerations.

This rejection of objective truth can also be seen in the modern scholar's unwillingness to believe in Platonic forms or intelligible essences. Instead, knowledge is dependent on the way people's interests, needs, and experiences lead them to slice and categorize an expanding mass of sense data. Or, taking

---

*In the end, I would argue that there is truth and that reason is relevant to our understanding of it. But truth's human, practice-based nature means that we create it as well as find it and that it is variable and multidimensional.[56] These qualities of truth relate to why we cannot expect a marketplace of ideas to be adequate for understanding.

interactive practices rather than individual perceptions as the starting point, the same rejection of objective truth is seen in modern hermeneutic theories, which recognize that there is no meaning "there" except an interpreted meaning and that any understanding reflects in part both the experiences and the interests brought by the interpreter. The diversity and conflict in people's social interests, needs, and experiences may explain why social life has a greater number of, and more constant conflict among, competing paradigms than is usually the case within a "science." Even if "rational" debate can play some role in advancing understanding within a given social or scientific paradigm, discussion is often insufficient by itself to determine the choice among different paradigms. This sense of the inevitable inadequacy (but not failure) of discussion results, in part, precisely because the value-oriented criteria—interests, desires, or aesthetics—which guide the development of perceptions, appear ungrounded, incapable of objective demonstration.[58]*

The adequacy of the marketplace of ideas must be reconsidered once the assumption of objective truth is replaced with the view that people individually and collectively choose or create rather than "discover" their perspectives, understandings, and truths. First, it is not clear that the marketplace of ideas is the only, the primary, or the best realm in which to create truth. Do we not, and should we not, create truth by our activities? Second, assuming that speech and debate play a significant role, it is clear that in any process of creation, the conditions of creation will affect the results. The defense of an *unrestricted* marketplace of ideas must either show that it can be expected to lead to the "best" creations (with some criteria for "best") or show that it is itself a proper process in that results are "best" merely because they flow from this process. More generally, the issue becomes: What conditions can we expect to lead to the best choices?

An evaluation of the marketplace may depend on whether different people are advantaged by the choice or creation of the same truth or understanding. Certainly, if a single objective truth exists, its discovery presumably advantages everyone. Thus, assuming public availability of the discovery, it would not matter who made the discovery. Likewise, even if truth is created, as long as a unity of interest exists, differential contributions by various people or groups to its creation may be unimportant. If, instead, groups have divergent interests, the marketplace of ideas (and other activities that might be protected) presumably will lead to the "best" or "proper" or "progressive" understanding *only if* the marketplace favors those groups or interests who should be favored or if it "properly" distributes influence among various people or groups such that optimal compromises are reached. It is not clear that an unregulated marketplace meets either standard. For example, some argue for regulation that would create

---

*This rejection of objective truth does not necessarily mean that everything is "up for grabs," that unguided subjectivity and relativism prevail. My latter constructive argument will claim that we do accept the free development of people's humanity as a value.[59] I will argue that this value provides an initial basis from which something can be said about differing paradigms; and it leads to strong conclusions concerning some appropriate features of the process of developing or creating knowledge. I might even argue, but not here, that this value of free development of people's humanity has been progressively unfolding in human history.[60]

more or less equal access for all groups to the marketplace.[61] Herbert Marcuse went further and concluded that in present historical circumstances the market-place of ideas would work properly only if the rich and powerful were completely excluded and access were limited to progressive, leftist elements.[62]

The classic marketplace of ideas theory assumed rationality as well as truth. It relied on reason in two ways. First, the theory assumed that people's reason enables them to comprehend a set reality and test assertions or propositions against that reality. Alternative interpretations of people's relation to the world, for example, those emphasizing people's dependence on "sense data" rather than direct access to reality, also assume that reason allows people to grasp invariant truths. Second, the classic theory assumed that people use reason to avoid or unmask distortions in perceptions of reality that imbalances in message presentations might otherwise cause. In other words, reason enables people to find the truth that the theory assumes to exist.

Modern social theory also undermines confidence in the marketplace's reliance on assumptions of rationality. Its first reliance is immediately undermined once one rejects the assumption of objective truth. People cannot use reason to comprehend a set reality because no set reality exists for people to discover. Moreover, modern social theory often rejects reason as the primary determinant of what people conclude to be true. Instead, understanding exists within "language games" or social practices, which seem infinitely various. Our conceptions reflect forms of life rather than reason applied in a metaphorical marketplace of ideas—although speech within this marketplace may be an important, but not necessarily an especially privileged, practice that affects our conceptions.

The sociology of knowledge radicalizes the above point. People's perspectives and understanding are greatly influenced, if not determined, by their experiences and their interests, both of which reflect their different locations in an historically specific socioeconomic structure.[63] Two implications of the sociology of knowledge should be relatively uncontroversial. First, dialogue cannot completely eliminate conflicts and divergences between people's perspectives as long as the social structure causes people to have very different experiences and conflicting interests. Social change—changes in the family, social, economic, or political order—will have greater impact on people's divergent notions of "truth" than will any marketplace of ideas. Second, robust discussion will be insufficient (although not irrelevant) for achieving appropriate understandings since it is at best one determinant of understanding. A progressive development of understanding will depend as much on new experiences and changes in everyday practices as on discussion. Restrictions on experience-generating conduct are just as likely as restrictions on robust debate to stunt this process. Therefore, the goal of advancing truth or better choices does not explain treating the marketplace of ideas as more deserving of constitutional protection than expressive, experience-producing conduct. Any process of progressive development of understanding—the equivalent of the classic model's search for truth—will depend on the existence of a realm in which people can have new or changed experiences. Of course, not all experience-generating conduct can receive constitutional protection. Still, this analysis suggests the desirability of protecting a realm of conduct and everyday activity beyond mere discussion.

The classic model is dependent on rationality in a second way. People must be able to use their rational capacities in order to eliminate distortion caused by the form and frequency of message presentation and to find the core of relevant information or argument. This view of people's reasoning capacities cannot be accepted. It is equally inconsistent with psychoanalytic and behavioral theories. People consistently respond to emotional or "irrational" appeals. "Subconscious" repressions, phobias, or desires influence people's assimilation of messages. Stimulus-response mechanisms and processes of selective attention and retention influence understanding or perspectives.

Psychoanalytic considerations emphasize that understanding is a holistic phenomenon that cannot be completely circumscribed by reason and dialogue. Behavioral theory partially explains at the level of the individual what the sociology of knowledge observes at the level of the group—that people maintain particular perspectives even when presented with divergent information. Effective rewards lead people to adopt particular perspectives irrespective of their relation to truth, wisdom, or the progressive interests of humanity. The perspectives that are reinforced will vary depending on the person's social position as well as the stimuli applied. The psychological technique of selective attention and retention, as well as the insights of cognitive dissonance and balance theories, suggest *how* people preserve perspectives consistent with their personal interests.

These psychological insights, extensively relied on by advertisers and propagandists,[64] should eviscerate faith in the ability of the marketplace of ideas to lead to the "best" truths or understandings. Even if some understandings are better than others, there is no reason to expect these to be discovered in the marketplace of ideas. Instead, understandings will depend on the form and quantity of inputs, on the mechanisms by which people process these inputs, and on people's interests and experiences. Without the assurance of rationality as the dominant means by which people evaluate competing viewpoints, robust debate cannot, in itself, be expected to lead to the best perspectives.[65]

Diminished confidence in people's rationality leaves the quality of conclusions reached in robust debate apparently dependent on the quality of inputs or on conditions that would increase confidence in less rational processes. Inputs undoubtedly affect results. No one seriously suggests, however, that the existing distribution of access opportunities is apportioned in accordance with the intelligent or wise contributions each person or group can make to a "best" understanding of the world. Moreover, incredible inequalities of opportunity to use the marketplace also undermine claims that the robust debate provides a "fair" or otherwise justifiable process for regulating the struggle between opposing groups.[66] Reliance on the marketplace of ideas appears improperly biased in favor of presently dominant groups. These groups have greater access to the marketplace. In addition, these dominant groups can legally restrict opportunities for subordinant groups to develop patterns of conduct in which new ideas would appear plausible.[67]

The classic marketplace of ideas theory's obvious dependence on incorrect assumptions makes the theory's power and popularity quite curious.[68] Some cynics have suggested that really its popularity is primarily limited to writers, academics, and other intellectuals who have a professional interest in supporting faith in rational discussion and the intellectual pursuit of knowledge.[69] Alternatively, sociology of knowledge principles suggest that the theory's popularity can best be understood after considering whose interests this marketplace theory promotes. Since so much modern communication takes place through mass media, the interests the media serves merit examination.*

Two relatively clear results of modern social science research are: (1) that "the most common effect of mass communication is to reinforce its audience's pre-existing interests, attitudes, and behavior";[70] and (2) that "the media appear to be extremely effective in creating new opinions," possibly because "the audiences have no existing opinions to be guarded by the conscious or subconscious play of selective exposure, selective retention, or selective perception."[71] Only in changing people's existing conceptions—the normal goal of critics of the status quo—do the media regularly falter.[72] Since the mass media primarily reinforce existing views or create views where none existed, people are likely to conclude that the marketplace is working. It would appear that way to those who previously held the views that are reinforced, those who hold the new views created by the media, and those who wanted these views reinforced or created. These groups include almost everyone except critics of the status quo.

Since mass media are inherently least effective in changing existing perspectives, a bias in favor of the status quo results even if everyone has equal input. The bias is magnified by the nature or source of inputs. The three main determinants of media views are: a mass audience that must be willing to buy (or, at least, receive) the communication;† the present power elites, who usually own or manage the media; and the corporations and dominant economic groups, whose advertisements largely finance the media.[73] These overlapping groups seldom radically oppose status quo perspectives.[74] Usually they want either to reinforce existing attitudes or, occasionally, to stimulate new views, such as desires for a business' new products. Thus, the market predictably appears to be successful to influential elements in society: (1) participation counts—the marketplace effectively responds to most participation, which is usually their participation; and (2) the process works—it usually validates views held by these influential groups. Since the unregulated marketplace of ideas usually promotes the dominant groups' interests and reflects their view of reality, their experience confirms their self-serving belief that in this marketplace of ideas, "the ideas best for society will find the most takers."[75]

Dissidents may perceive the situation differently. Their views are least likely

---

*An additional point not developed here is the self-interest of the media or its owners or workers in promoting support for any principles of free speech that would leave them free to pursue their economic or professional interests as they wish. Obviously, to the extent that media exercise persuasive influence, this interest group is well situated to promote its favored values. Backlash against this situation is reflected in criticisms of the press as too powerful and irresponsible.

†Specialized media tap smaller audiences. Here, however, selective exposure is already working. These media are likely at best to deepen or marginally expand existing interests or inclinations.

to be presented by the media. When presented, since their views are most likely to challenge established views, their presentations are least likely to be effective. Two reactions to the ineffectiveness of their advocacy are plausible. Dissidents, if unwilling totally to reject the marketplace of ideas, could conclude that market failures exist and that the functioning of the market needs to be improved— possibly by government intervention.[76] Alternatively, dissidents could view the government as an instrument of dominant groups and perceive existing values as products of conscious or unconscious manipulations of these dominant groups. At least under current historical conditions, they will place little confidence in the power of mere speech or the workings of any marketplace of ideas.[77]

These observations concerning the ideological qualities of the marketplace theory show who it seems to favor and how it might look from different perspectives. The observations, however, have not shown whether critics or dominant groups should be favored. Unless either some processes or some perspectives can be understood as better or worse, criticisms or defenses of the marketplace of ideas could only have strategic relevance. This relativism that reduces the analysis to strategy seems wrong. Many people—in their everyday lives, maybe most people—believe that proper substantive evaluations can be made and defended. Many, including myself, would assert that these evaluations can be made on the basis of a fundamental long-range unity of human interests. However, nothing in this chapter's analysis shows that a marketplace of ideas would help us move toward this end.

Others make similar criticisms. Roberto Unger, for example, who at least in his early work maintains faith in some sort of long term basic unity of humanity and who also presents a vibrant defense of speculative thought, specifically argues that discussion itself is insufficient for reaching this better understanding. Improved understanding instead depends, he argues, on political action and social change.[78] If Unger is right, and if, as the classic marketplace model asserts, the first amendment protects a process for achieving improved understandings, then the question arises whether first amendment protection must extend to aspects of human action other than mere discussion.

REVISED ARGUMENT: DROPPING ASSUMPTIONS

Even if truth is not objective, even if people are not dominantly rational, even if their reasoning is greatly influenced by everything from childhood experiences to current social circumstances, people still must make decisions, reach conclusions, take action. Surely they can do this better with than without information. A free marketplace of ideas systematically contributes, even if only marginally, to reaching the wisest or best or most useful or most desired conclusions. As is often said in elitist circles about democracy, the issue in respect to free speech is: "compared to what?" This revised defense of free speech asserts that even if truth is chosen and even if the classic model had an overblown faith in our reason, we still can have greatest confidence in our choices if all views have their say. Suppression necessarily restricts presentation of information that we might have used or of ideas that we might have wished to adopt. Free speech may not be great, but suppression can only distort. Limitations on speech will deepen our admitted irrationality and increase the probability of deleterious conclusions. Speech does help us identify our errors. Given the fallibility of human judgment, we are best off with freedom of speech.[79]

In an important article, Benjamin Duval presented a version of this revised argument.[80] Duval claims that his defense of free speech rests only on the premise of the fallibility of human judgment.[81] Since uncertainty is ever present, only acts that implicitly acknowledge uncertainty and human fallibility are justifiable. "But any act which cuts off the possibility of modifying normative judgments implicitly asserts that the normative judgments upon which it is based are certain, and such an act is therefore inconsistent with the recognition of uncertainty. For only through modification of beliefs can error ever be corrected. . . . Since communication is necessary to modify beliefs, its suppression is inconsistent with a recognition of the uncertainty of normative judgments."[82]

The revised argument claims both historical and logical support. Historically, as Mill argued, suppression often delayed the development of perspectives that we now value. We now often affirm and rely on values and views that the "best of men" once suppressed. For all we know, suppression may have entirely prevented the development of valuable perspectives or routes of human development. Once we drop the assumption of timeless, ever-present objective truth and see history, like life, as a project in which we cannot go back, we see that the loss caused by suppression may be irretrievable.

Logically, the assumptions of objective truth and rationality allow for an analytically neater portrayal of the virtues of the marketplace of ideas. We can, however, drop these assumptions and still reasonably conclude that an unregulated marketplace of ideas is our best bet. Censorship inevitably impedes the development and acceptance of some perspectives that we would adopt as useful. Conversely, freedom of speech will predictably lead to some new insights and preferable choices. Surely, we would be better off, wiser, initially to allow the expression and, then, to decide which perspectives to adopt. Surely, burying our heads in the sand cannot be useful. The marketplace is as justifiable on the basis of nonobjective conceptions of truth and realistic notions of people's capacity to reason as it is on the classic model's untenable assumptions.

This revised argument fails. I will argue that its historical assertions are inadequate for their purposes. That it is unable to explain the criteria it uses to justify its claims. And that its logic is unpersuasive. Examples illustrate that a contrary conclusion is equally plausible. Thus, the argument for openness cannot rest *merely* on the assumption of our fallibility or of the usefulness of unrestricted speech.

The revised argument asserts that history both demonstrates our fallibility and shows us the error of suppression. At least the second part of this claim must rely on unestablished factual assumptions as well as undefended evaluative claims. First, consider the factual assumptions (to the extent that they are separable from the evaluative claims). History is difficult to read. Even though, as Mill points out, "we" now regret some suppressions, we may have benefited greatly from others. And are there not some cases, for example, Nazi propaganda before the Hitler takeover where, if suppression had occurred, it might have benefited the world?*

Even if our historical assessments show that past suppressions have been, overall, a mistake, that result may merely reflect the identity of the people doing the suppression. There is little reason to expect that past (or present) authoritarian rulers, whose interests were (and are) often contrary to those of their subjects, would engage in "wise" suppressions. But liberal, modern democracies might do a "better" job (particularly from the perspective of the whole). They may make marginal mistakes both in what they choose to suppress and what they permit. Overall, however, democratic regimes may primarily use suppression to prevent significant harms. Thus, the historically observed evil of suppression may be primarily the evil of nondemocratic regimes, not of suppression *per se.* By itself, past experience just does not provide any easy empirical basis to predict what stance will produce results that we like.

Even if we could confidently predict the *consequences* of suppression, these effects still must be evaluated. Evaluated on what basis? Proponents of this revised argument frequently predict that the marketplace will lead to results that are "in fact" wiser, or more useful, or preferable. Often these predictions rely, without overt acknowledgment, on an "objective" view of wisdom or utility. The revised argument then becomes subject to all the criticisms of the classic model's reliance on an objective notion of truth. If its proponents really abandon this objectivist assumption, they must explain their favorable characterization of the results of free speech. Why would these results be more useful than those from some alternative regime? The revised argument needs criteria for usefulness. Suppression and nonsuppression lead to different results. But why is one better?

This critique may seem to surrender to an unproductive relativism. A major project of modern social theory has been its search for an alternative that assumes neither pure objectivity nor mere relativism.[83] Pragmatic conceptions of truth, which see truth as existing within human practices and involve our striving for the best or wisest or most useful conclusions, probably represent the dominant modern view of truth.[84] Possibly the revised argument for the marketplace of ideas hopes to rely on some such pragmatic conception of truth.† Nevertheless, the nature or use or justification of this pragmatic conception must be explained in a manner that shows why it is likely to be furthered by an unregulated marketplace of ideas. For example, if the pragmatic conception of truth relates to the use of knowledge, the questions of use for whom, for which of their purposes, for what portion of their life, all become relevant—but the revised argument leaves them unanswered.[85] (Clearly, suppression will be more useful than free speech for some purposes and at some times.)

Thus, the evaluation of the marketplace of ideas must use the "right" prag-

---

*I neither claim nor believe that this would have been the most effective strategy of opposition to Nazism—only that history has not ruled out the possibility that it might have been effective.[86]

†Eventually I will tentatively accept a version of this view of truth—but only after a long excursion that threads its way through the liberty theory of free speech.

matic criteria—whether of truth, correctness, efficiency, usefulness. Otherwise, the criteria will not provide relevant guidance as to whether or what speech should be protected. And criteria like "useful" or "efficient" are certainly no less contested than criteria like "truthful" or "accurate." "Useful" or "efficient" have no inherent content. They become meaningful only when related to specific values.[87] If the evaluation of the marketplace of ideas or the notion of truth that it generates is made on the basis of values, which apparently it must be, then the identification of what values or whose values becomes crucial. But neither the revised argument nor Duval's reliance on human fallibility provide guidance. Neither gives any basis to identify what is to count as useful. Nor whose values are to count. Is the relevant group the elect, the masses, the educated, the worst off, the powerful, the democratic whole? Should the relevant values be those of the people who would choose to suppress? The values of the oppressed? "Our" present values? The values of the type of people we would be if an alternative choice about suppression had been made? The values of the next generation? True or humane values?

Clearly there is no "neutral" or "objective" way to evaluate the consequences of suppression. Thus, what do we say to those who disagree with our evaluation? Presumably, our answer can be no more persuasive than the arguments for the value premises embodied in the evaluation. Later I will claim that defensible value premises are those historical or practice-based criteria that are consistent with respect for people's autonomy and equality—and that this formulation provides some guidance as to the appropriate process of truth creation as well as to certain appropriate constraints on that process.[88] But nothing in the revised argument, as presented here, has shown why particular criteria for evaluation of the results of an unregulated marketplace of ideas are appropriate. Nor has it shown that the marketplace of ideas would promote *any* conception of best results. Thus, the revised argument has presented no reasons to expect that an unregulated marketplace of ideas, as opposed to some other process, will lead to results that we should or would treat as "best."

Put aside for a moment the question of evaluative standards. Consider only the logic of the revised argument. Why should we expect better results from non-suppression than from carefully (or democratically) chosen suppressions? The revised argument asserts that considering more alternatives cannot hurt and may help. But we know that sometimes more speech does hurt—that is usually why it is suppressed. Additional speech, racist speech, for example, may be divisive as well as painful. Or the added speech may divert us from more significant issues that need greater attention. Or it may destructively manipulate consciousness or enflame and poison emotions, leading to aggression, violence, and other evils. Or it may provide information, military information, for example, that is helpful to those who would do evil. Or the added speech may be a means used by a powerful group to dominate discussion so that its views improperly prevail.

Predictably, nonsuppression will lead to results that would be more useful for some purposes (and for some people) while suppression would be more useful for others. There is no reason to think that everyone would prefer the results of nonsuppression. (In economic jargon, nonsuppression is unlikely to be pareto superior to suppression.) But unless everyone would prefer it, the revised claim for nonsuppression will be persuasive only in respect to some purposes or some people. Thus, without guidance as to which purposes or which people we should favor, or an argument that whoever the market favors should be favored, the logic of the revised argument appears inadequate.

Thus, without additional premises, neither history nor logic demonstrate that suppression is necessarily objectionable. It is hardly clear that our best bet is always to choose nonsuppression. Several examples illustrate the point. First, legal restrictions on the expenditure of immense individual or corporate wealth to engage in campaign speech certainly suppresses speech and presumably constrains the free marketplace of ideas. But many people think such constraints on speech could result in pragmatically better, more just, political decisions. Second, the currently dominant legal view in the United States is that *Beauharnais v. Illinois* (upholding a conviction on group libel charge) is no longer good law.[89] Our current, apparently "pro" free speech view protects racist speech. In contrast, the probably dominant view among Western democracies is that racial hate literature can cause the most serious harms to society and should be outlawed.[90] Third, many liberals think that people should be free to purchase and consume alcoholic beverages, cigarettes, or even cocaine and that people should certainly be free to discuss the merits and demerits of using these drugs. However, even many of these advocates of freedom still conclude that commercial advertising by corporations that sell the drugs and profit from their abuse is more likely to deter than to promote wise decision making. More radically, others plausibly argue that the promotion of our materialistic consumer society by commercial, market-driven, "hidden persuaders" is inimical to wise or useful social practices and that we could devise intelligent and useful limitations on these advertising practices. Fourth, quite diverse groups conclude that suppression of pornography would have beneficial effects—even if they disagree about what these effects are. Fifth, government agencies sometimes mandate nondisclosure of information to protect privacy or promote sensitive planning. This mandated secrecy often seems desirable even though it restricts the availability of information in the marketplace of ideas. And the examples could be continued.

Of course, no one favors total suppression of speech. That is not the issue. Democratic governments only suppress speech when at least a colorable argument indicates that nonsuppression will result in some serious harm. The above examples illustrate very plausible reasons to expect that particular, carefully formulated limitations on speech could be socially useful.* Without some independent reason to have confidence in the marketplace of ideas as a process, it seems that suppression, even though it might turn out to be a mistake, could be justified. The danger of losses caused by improper suppression can be outweighed by the danger of losses caused by failure to suppress.

The claim that our fallibility requires a policy of free speech has been implicitly met. Freedom of speech may help expose error. But it may also do the opposite. Guaranteeing freedom of speech may result in new errors or even thwart

---

*Note that some of these restrictions would be acceptable on some theories of freedom of speech. Which ones will depend on the specific content of that theory.

efforts to identify and avoid some errors—errors of racism, sexism, capitalism, consumerism, incivility. Moreover, errors (e.g., about what is useful or desirable or wise or true) are harmful, but are not the only harms. Speech too can injure. We still must act despite our fallibility. Fallibility gives grounds for caution. Whether we choose either free speech or suppression our choice may be wrong. And either choice could help entrench error—as has been precisely the point of certain arguments to restrict free speech, for example, the arguments to restrict unlimited campaign expenditures, pornography, or speech of groups (presumably, communists) that would deny intellectual and political freedom. Certainly given the possibility that speech can help entrench error, our fallibility by itself provides inadequate reason to allow speech.

After dropping the assumptions of objective truth and human rationality on which the classic marketplace of ideas rests, neither logic nor history nor our fallibility provides obvious grounds for continued faith in the marketplace. The answer to: "as compared to what?" is: "whatever seems wisest." Our fallibility does not provide an adequate reason to rely blindly on the marketplace of ideas. Better that we cautiously try to achieve good results and determine what complex of rules best aids in disentrenching error. Thus, if reasons for confidence in the consequences of free speech exist, they must lie elsewhere.

DIALOGIC AND PARTICIPATORY IDEALS

Much of the continuing appeal of the marketplace of ideas theory surely reflects this ubiquitous, but often unexamined and ultimately unpersuasive, view that restrictions necessarily increase the likelihood of entrenching error and, in any event, more speech cannot hurt. Nevertheless, part of the theory's popular appeal may piggyback on its closeness to other, deeper insights, which merit comment even if, in the end, they too fail to justify the traditional theory.

The earlier critique of the classic marketplace of ideas theory focused on the actual circumstances of human life. Our limited rationality and the absence of objective truth undermined any basis for confidence that the marketplace would lead to wisdom. This critique did not consider the merits of the theory as an assertion of human aspirations. Arguably, people ought to interact on the basis of agreements and conclusions that are or could be subjected to discursive presentation and challenge.[91] We often try to act in accord with this ideal and we often honor those efforts. As an aspiration, this view describes one aspect of how we would like to be as humans. The notion of the marketplace of ideas could be seen as an attempt to describe or embody this aspiration. In an important respect this aspiration resonates with the revised argument for the marketplace theory described in the last section. Both can dispense with the assumptions of truth and rationality underlying the classic marketplace of ideas, although for somewhat different reasons—the revised argument because it claims that the assumptions presumably are not needed and the aspiration because it (merely) asserts an ideal, not a description contaminated by the reality of our limited rationality. In any event, the aspiration implicity asserts that people ought to try to create the circumstances under which dialogic interaction will be increasingly authoritative and will increasingly serve our interests.

The aspiration of dialogic interaction purportedly justifies dropping the classic marketplace of ideas' untenable assumptions but still accepting its version of the scope of freedom of speech. This result has at least three problems. First, as an aspiration, a regulative ideal, the argument provides a goal or standard but does not tell us how to act under circumstances where the conditions do not exist for that ideal to be met. Surely, to assume that those conditions already exist would be misguided. The issue set by the aspiration is, in part, how do we move toward conditions in which our dialogic interaction is properly authoritative? Nothing in the argument so far, although I will advance such an argument in Chapter 5, gives any reason to think that present protection of people's exercise of freedom of speech is crucial for moving toward this aspiration. Second, as will be noted further below, the scope of protection under this aspirational ideal may not be the same as the scope of protection under the marketplace theory. Certainly, the scope of protection will be unclear until this ideal is further specified—which leads to the third problem with the argument as currently elaborated. The discussion above presented this dialogic ideal as a plausible human aspiration but it neither explained why it is an appropriate aspiration nor indicated what commitments are implicit in the ideal. Does the ideal require protection of some large range of expressive *conduct* as a precondition of "uncoerced dialogue" or only a smaller range of *speech* that is part of that dialogue? Without clarification and persuasive argument in respect to these points, it will not be clear whether the aspiration presents a persuasive justification for freedom of speech. Nor will it be clear what the precise scope of the ideal is. Thus, this aspiration may account for some intuitive appeal of marketplace theories. However, at this point more elaboration and justification of the aspiration is required before it can lead to any conclusions concerning freedom of speech.

Faith in the marketplace of ideas may also gain appeal due to its closeness to another, more defensible justification. This alternative may follow even if, arguably, particularly if, we reject or remain skeptical about the notion of objective truth and if we recognize that, at best, our reason is limited and frequently distorted. We still could maintain that anyone who wanted to participate in the creation or search for the best or wisest practices and perspectives should be permitted to do so to the extent that she is able. We might even maintain that a purpose of government is to promote this capability. Each person's input deserves respect. Of course, direct conflicts between people's different attempted or proposed practices often require settlement or mediation—by law, for example. Arguably the best basis (if not always an adequate basis) for the claim that people ought to adhere to these settlements (that is, to law) is not that the adopted settlements are "true" or even that "wrong" settlements will necessarily be corrected. Rather, the best basis for justifying adherence is that people's input into these settlements and into the creation of their world was permitted and continues to be permitted. That is, both democracy and protection for individual liberty, including freedom of speech, may be prerequisites for legal legitimacy. Of course, the above is not argument—that will come in Chapters 2 and 3. The point here is that freedom of speech may be defensible, not because of the marketplace of ideas' supposed capacity to discover truth, but because freedom of speech embodies respect for the liberty or autonomy and responsibility of the participants.

This liberty-based defense of free speech, possibly like a better specified aspirational theory, subtly but dramatically redefines the practices meriting protection. Alexander Meiklejohn properly stated the requirement of the classic marketplace of ideas theory: "What is essential is not that everyone shall speak, but that everything worth saying shall be said."[92] Fulfillment of this marketplace requirement purportedly enabled reason to evaluate the different proposals to uncover truth. The revised argument critiqued in the last section did not challenge Meiklejohn's statement. But the liberty-based defense of the freedom of speech suggested here reverses priorities. What is important is not that everything worth saying be said—although as a policy goal, that might be nice, even if almost certainly unachievable. Rather, the important concern is that society deny no one the right to speak.

This analysis transforms the focus onto the liberty of the speaker. Regulations of the marketplace that do not restrict individual liberty would be acceptable. In contrast, those that do restrict individual liberty, like compelled speech, would be impermissible even if they appear not to interfere with, and even arguably promote, the marketplace. This perspective, however, is quite different from that of the classic marketplace of ideas theory.

2

Possible Modifications

POLITICAL SPEECH: AN ULTIMATELY UNPRINCIPLED LIMIT

Some prominent theorists argue that the first amendment should protect only "political speech" or speech that is a part of democratic self-government. Possibly because of the association of this political speech theory with a conservative political movement that became influential in the late 1970s and the 1980s as well as because of its consistency with currently popular process-oriented interpretations of the constitution, the theory has gained some currency in the courts and the academic community.

Nevertheless, the political speech theory of the first amendment has been subjected to persuasive criticisms and, at least in a pure form, has never been widely accepted. In summarizing his careful critique, Professor Steven Shiffrin emphasized that "a politically based approach to the first amendment abandons history, precedent, and important values in pursuit of a legitimacy that is founded on controversial question begging."[1] Others might add that the political speech theory abandons the language of the first amendment, which certainly suggests no such limitation. Here, however, my main concern is more specific: does the political speech theory offer a plausible alternative to the dominant marketplace of ideas theory?

Current scholarship contains two different, often intertwined, versions of the political speech theory, each with different premises. I will argue that the more influential version relies on the same premises as the marketplace of ideas theory; and that it merely amounts to an unprincipledly restricted formulation of the marketplace theory. This first version of the political speech theory, therefore, is subject to all the critiques the last chapter leveled against the marketplace theory. In contrast, the second, less dominant version of this political speech theory contains elements of an adequate first amendment theory. The problem with the second version is its inability to limit its logic to political speech. Nevertheless, both versions of the political theory build on some important pragmatic insights. These pragmatic insights may be relevant for designing an adequate legal structure for protecting the system of freedom of expression. They may also partially explain the real even if misguided popularity of the political speech theory of the first amendment.

Alexander Meiklejohn popularized the political speech theory. He forcefully argued that the first amendment absolutely prohibits abridgement of freedom of speech but claimed that freedom of speech, as protected by the first amendment, refers only to speech relevant to the self-governing process.[2]

Of course, the category of politically relevant speech could be narrow or broad. Over time, Meiklejohn, who influenced such major first amendment theorists as Harry Kalven[3] and, arguably, Justice William Brennan,[4] expanded his view of coverage. Eventually Meiklejohn concluded that this protected category must include all the arts, sciences, and humanities as well as any other expression that aids our capacity wisely and humanely to govern ourselves.[5] Indeed, once the insight that the personal is political is fully accepted, the category of politically relevant speech could be virtually unlimited—and any critique of the theory would rest on grounds other than its narrowness. Nevertheless, no first amendment commentator has yet taken the political speech theory that far. And, despite this tendency toward broadness, others, such as Judge Robert Bork, have argued that the protected category should include only a narrow category of explicitly political speech—which, for example, not only would exclude scientific or literary expression but also would not even count as political any "speech advocating forcible overthrow of the government or violation of the law."[6]

From a civil liberties perspective, a significant practical danger of the political speech theory is the availability of narrow conceptions of the political. In several recent cases, the defense of the speech claim has been left to Brennan's objection that the majority adopted too narrow a conception of public affairs— along with his assertion that the speech merited protection even if purely private.[7]

Justice Brennan is right. Any focus on political speech is likely to be abused. Whatever else would be said, I suspect that most people would characterize the speech and activities of leaders of the Communist Party as political. Surely, the prosecution of Communist Party leaders in *Dennis v. United States*[8] was an unambiguously political trial. Nevertheless, Justice Frankfurter exhibited the political speech theorists' willingness to grade speech into categories of greater and lesser constitutional value. Frankfurter concluded that "[o]n any scale of values which we have hitherto recognized, speech of [the sort for which the communist defendants were convicted] ranks low."[9]

Like the difference between lyric and vulgarity,[10] the identification of politically relevant speech depends on the eyes of the beholder. Thus, the gulf between Meiklejohn's broad and Bork's narrow conclusions concerning the proper scope of the political speech theory should be quite predictable. And this gulf illustrates possibly the most consistent, practical criticism of the theory—that the category of political or self-governing speech is undefinable.[11] More fundamental for present purposes, however, is another criticism—nonpolitical speech should be equally protected. All influential categorizations of political speech leave some speech, private gossip or libels, for example, outside the first amendment.[12]

Judge Bork's conclusions have been treated particularly harshly. Scholars have noted not only that "no justice on the Supreme Court has ever adopted anything close to Bork's theory of freedom of speech,"[13] but also that it is "quite probably the most narrowly confined protection of speech ever supported by a modern jurist or academic."[14] Reviewers also quickly point out fundamental logical flaws in Bork's main arguments.[15]

Bork's claim, apparently, is (1) that there must be a function of protected speech that distinguishes it from all other human activities—otherwise, the law could not be principled in protecting this speech and not protecting other activities; (2) that one "function of speech, its ability to deal explicitly and directly with politics and government, is different from any other form of human activity"; (3) therefore, "a principled judge" can only protect "explicitly and predominantly political speech."[16]

Bork's argument has obvious problems. First, it doesn't work. Many activities, for example, a vote, a bribe, or a political bombing or assassination, deal explicitly and directly with politics. (In addition, nonprotected, nonspeech activities such as an assassination can be politically *expressive* and often will be aimed at both communicating political sentiments and stimulating political discussion and reflection.) Thus, because political speech does not fulfill Bork's uniqueness criterion, his second proposition is wrong.

Bork also fails to explain why a principled interpretation of "speech" must exclude all speech except speech having some unique quality that distinguishes it from all other human conduct. A more likely possibility, which I will elaborate in Chapter 3, is that protection of speech may be constitutionally justified because of the combination of the values served by speech *and* the manner in which speech serves these values. Even this combination of values served and manner of service is neither universally present in speech nor unique to speech. Rather, the Constitution's specific identification of speech can be best understood in terms of the observation that this combination is paradigmatic of uses of speech. Still, if it is such a combination that particularly merits protection, then Bork's first proposition is also wrong.[17] Without either his first or second proposition, his argument collapses—a principled judge could hardly follow his advice.

Moreover, the constitutional focus on speech as the activity meriting protection may reflect history as much as logic or principle. Particular historical conflicts may have created the social and political importance of focusing on freedom of speech (and, even more so, on freedom of the press). Likewise, the related, historically embedded consciousness may have contributed to the intellectual tendency to adopt this focus. If the best defense of the constitutional right depends on speech's paradigmatic quality of both serving basic values and serving them in a particular manner, the issue of the appropriate scope of protection is left open. For example, what is the appropriate constitutional response, first, to speech that does not exhibit this combination and, second, to nonspeech conduct that does?—questions to which I will return in Chapters 3 and 4.

Meiklejohn and his followers cannot be faulted with either Bork's narrow elaboration or his peculiar defense of the political speech theory. The central claim of Meiklejohn's more appealing and more influential political speech theory is that free speech is essential to the self-governing democratic process. Given this claim and given our constitutionally affirmed commitment to democracy, constitutional protection of political speech apparently follows as a corollary. Therefore, a thorough examination of the political speech interpretation of the first amendment might usefully begin with this claim.

Two quite different arguments support the claim that free speech is essential to democracy. And these two arguments lead to the two different versions of the political speech theory. Probably the most ubiquitous argument is that robust debate about public issues, that is, unabridged freedom of speech, is necessary in order for the people, the governors, to engage in the "discovery and spread of political truth." Or, if "truth" seems to imply too much objectivity, a slightly reformulated argument would be that unabridged freedom of speech provides our best hope for reaching wise and desirable (or desired) political conclusions. According to this first argument, the value of free speech is instrumental and lies in the results, the truth or wisdom, that the free debate about public issues is expected to advance in a democracy.[19]

Meiklejohn's discussion often suggests this first version of the political speech theory—the version that values speech for its role in the political search for truth or practical wisdom. This version, for example, presumably maintains that for the political process to find and spread truth, all views must be presented. This claim echoes Meiklejohn's conclusion that "what is essential is not that everyone shall speak, but that everything worth saying shall be said."[20] The expectation that unabridged speech leads to the best or wisest results also provides a possible explanation for Meiklejohn's assertion that "the principle of free speech springs from the *necessities* of the program of self-government."[21] As he explains, otherwise, "the result must be ill-considered, ill-balanced planning for the general good."[22] Meiklejohn also argues that *the search for and sharing of truth* is a preeminent interest or need of a self-governing people.[23]

This extrapolation of free speech from the premise of democracy clearly embraces the marketplace of ideas theory—except that this derivation requires the marketplace of ideas only for the political arena. Therefore, this version of the political speech theory can stand no better than the marketplace theory, which it duplicates. If it relies on assumptions concerning reason and objective truth, it would be faced with the same critique as the classic marketplace theory that relied on these assumptions. Alternatively, these marketplace assumptions could be dropped—both Bork and Meiklejohn drop them.[24] Then, however, the political speech theory has the same difficulties as the marketplace theory when the revised marketplace theory abandons these assumptions. Without these particular assumptions concerning truth and rationality, the analysis no longer convincingly explains why the results of the political process that protects speech will be any better than the results would be if speech were intelligently and purposefully restricted.

A second version of the political speech theory rests on very different premises. Freedom of speech could be implicit in democratic self-government because this freedom is part of the very definition or meaning of self-government. This version does not require faith that free speech will promote truth, wisdom, or any other theoretically predicted result. Instead, an adequate basis for according status to the "results" of free speech is the abstract propriety of the process. In fact, most democrats view at least some political decisions as (temporarily) authoritative, although not necessarily right or wise, merely because these decisions result from an acceptable process. This theory of free speech asserts that the acceptable process is self-government that includes free speech as a constitutive element.

Still, this version of the political speech theory is not without difficulties. The key step is to show that free speech is indeed essential if the political process is to be acceptable; and this step must be made without relying on any marketplace of ideas assumption that free speech leads to results that are presumptively right or wise.

The conclusion that freedom of speech is an integral aspect of democracy feels right. Nevertheless, the explanation for this conclusion is not immediately clear. For example, as an explanation, consider the following three-part claim. First, democracy implies that the people engage in, or at least have the opportunity to engage in, the choice of policies. Second, for policies to be self-chosen, the governors, that is, the people, must be presented with all viewpoints, all alternatives. Third, this condition can only be, but can be, achieved by guaranteeing freedom of political speech.

This three-part claim fails. Surely, the second point is wrong. Decision-makers never hear nor consider all viewpoints. All decisions are made in at least partial ignorance. The existence of democracy cannot depend on full information. Much information does not presently exist—even information that we know how, at some expense, to develop. Democracy, moreover, does not imply that everyone devote their energies toward assimilating all "relevant" information. It does not even imply the general availability of the information that does exist. For example, most people consider self-government possible even if some members are unwilling to disclose their ideas or to reveal important information to others in the group. Self-government arguably even implies the collective power to restrict the circulation of some information. Of course, the consequences of either self-chosen silence or governmentally imposed restrictions on information are sometimes undesirable—even disastrous. But even if "official secrets acts" or "privacy acts" or recognition of a "right to remain silent" or delays in publishing minutes of Federal Reserve Board meetings or the confidentiality of judicial or jury deliberations are inconsistent with a fully "open society," few people would consider all of these limitations as inherently inconsistent with the notion of democracy. Obviously, both the empirical assumptions and the normative arguments favoring various restrictions on information flows are contested. Nevertheless, the existence of government power to repeal laws restricting the flow of information satisfies typical conceptions of democracy.

A plausible conception of democracy is that it consists simply in the majority's "power of choice." And the power of choice can, of course, be exercised in ignorance. It does not imply the impossible, full and free information. It does not even imply the absence of consciously imposed restrictions on information. More likely, the power of choice only implies the right of voters to rely on whatever information or misinformation they happen to have. The only freedom of speech that is "essential" is the right to say "yes" or "no" in a vote and, maybe, the right to make proposals to be voted on. The attempt to deduce any more extensive free speech logically from a notion of democracy identified with the power of people to make political choices fails.

The above argument may embody too shallow a conception of democracy.

More substantive conceptions abound. Some common conceptions of democracy identify democracy with the substance of rule—rule in the interest of the people.[25] Even those conceptions that merely emphasize process may include more than the mere right to vote or the exercise of choice. These fuller conceptions of democracy often include, as key elements, limits on the majority's unadorned power of choice. They may rule out certain choices, for example, choices to limit liberty or deny people's equality. Brandeis, immediately before his impassioned invocation of "the power of reason as applied through public discussion," asserted that "those who won our independence . . . valued liberty both *as an end* and as a means."[26] Free speech may be valued not so much, as in the first version of the political speech theory, for how it helps self-government achieve wise results—that is, as a means. Rather, within a suitably rich conception of democracy, free speech may be valued as a key element of the activity of self-government, an activity which in turn is valued as an end.

At times Meiklejohn appears to adopt this view that the relation between free speech and self-government is one of meaning rather than of service. He even rejects "the Miltonian faith that in a fair fight between truth and error, truth is sure to win"—a faith he finds "hard to reconcile . . . with the sheer stupidity of the policies of this nation." Instead, Meiklejohn argues that "'the people need free speech' because they have decided . . . to govern themselves."[27] But why do they need free speech if it can lead, as Meiklejohn suggests, to "sheer stupidity"? Apparently self-governors need free speech not because it leads to good results, but because free speech is part of what Meiklejohn means by "governing themselves."[28]

As noted, merely thinking of democracy as a process does not show that free speech must be an element. To definitionally include free speech in democracy requires reliance on more substantive value considerations. For example, acceptance of Brandeis' suggestion that liberty be valued as an end would help explain both the value of self-government and its relation to free speech. A democratic process might best be understood as an attempt to embody liberty, that is, self-choice, in a realm where collective decision making is necessary if people are to engage in self-determination. If so, then this value, liberty, should also be used as the guide for understanding the appropriate elements of that democratic process. In making collective decisions, people should be as unrestrained as possible, not because this form of the process necessarily leads to the wisest decisions, but because the process is an attempt to embody this fundamental value of liberty in the sphere of necessarily collective decisions. A theory of democracy centered on the fundamental status of liberty (as well as of equality)[29] argues that the political sphere itself is justifiable only if that sphere is consistent with liberty and embodies respect for liberty. Liberty, not democracy, is fundamental.

Intuitively it seems plausible to base the argument for democracy on the fundamental status of liberty. The most obvious reason to view democracy as fundamental is the importance we place on freedom. This pervasive vision of democracy also provides an explanation for why freedom of political speech must be an element of democracy. If, however, democracy is justified specifically because democracy embodies liberty in the sphere of its operation, an important additional conclusion seems to follow. From the perspective of valuing liberty, there is no reason to think that legal restrictions on liberty or, more specifically, on freedom of speech, are more acceptable within the nonpolitical than in the political sphere. The fundamental status of liberty would imply that the political sphere is only justified when it *respects* as well as embodies liberty. If particular values justify the political sphere, those values should likewise provide the basis for limits on that political sphere. Thus, it turns out that probably the most persuasive argument for treating freedom of "political" speech as a necessary and protected element of democracy also shows that freedom of "nonpolitical" speech ought to receive the same protection. Both freedom of political speech and freedom of other speech embody the same value—respect for individual liberty.

Two alternative, mutually reinforcing analyses support the intuitive claim that recognition of a fundamental status for liberty implies democracy. First, note that many aspects of our world are and could only be the product of collective decisions or collective consensus. For example, all communication requires some degree of consensus concerning language. Legal rules are similar. Allocations of decision-making authority among people require and depend on collective practices and collective decisions often embodied in property laws or other legal or customary practices. Even the collective "nondecision" to allow anarchy or force to reign in some sphere often amounts to a collectively accepted and often consciously adopted practice.[30] Clearly, the existence of such collectively effective and accepted practices is inevitable. Moreover, different possible practices make contributions to the pursuit of different values and significantly influence who we are as persons. Liberty presumably must include the opportunity for involvement in the choice of, or responsible acceptance and affirmation of, those elements of our world that are matters of human creation and that are important for a person's self-definition and self-realization. This notion of liberty, combined with the obvious fact that many of these elements are necessarily a matter of collective practice, choice, or consensus, means that liberty must permit involvement in this collective process, presumably in a manner that permits a like involvement by others—in other words, respect for liberty implies some type of democracy. Thus, although liberty "under law" often refers to somewhat individualized decision making within apparent zones of autonomy, a more complete notion of self-determination must include a right to participate in the many necessarily collective decisions. Agents capable of self-determination and having equal claims to engage in self-determination would have a right to democracy.

The above analysis concluded that liberty implies democracy as a process for specifying and implementing people's choices. Alternatively, if people specially value their participation in the process of determining who they are, then democracy is also implied as one of the essential activities of free people. On either view, narrowing the possibility of democratic political activity would be a narrowing of what it means to be a free person. This could be justified only on a few grounds. For example, if liberty is fundamental, presumably a restriction on political choice could be justified if the choice directly or purposefully conflicted with another's liberty or, maybe, with equality. Thus, this reason to value politics and, hence, democracy as a central element of a notion of being human also implies constitutional limits on democracy.

Note that both defenses of democracy treat liberty (and equality)[31] as basic; democracy only follows as a necessary implication. The deduced element, however, can only properly extend so far as is consistent with its premises. Specifically, the scope of democratic decision making must be limited to decisions that are consistent with respect for liberty (and equality). If liberty and not democracy is fundamental, and even more so if freedom of political speech is viewed as an element of democracy precisely because recognizing it as an element better makes democracy an embodiment of liberty, then limiting constitutional protection to political speech would be unprincipled.

A possible counterargument could claim that liberty in respect to self-government and, therefore, freedom of political speech, is special in some relevant sense. Because of this "specialness," political speech and self-government should be valued differently if not more highly than liberty or freedom of speech in general. For example, consider the following argument: Citizens of a democracy are both governors and governed. As governors, citizens must be free in deciding what limits on our freedom are appropriate. As governed, we necessarily accept limits on freedom that we legislate and enforce as governors. Speech about laws is fundamental to the determination of what behavior will be allowed; other speech is merely among the many multifarious activities that are or are not allowed.[32]

The most obvious problem is that this argument does not explain why liberty in respect to making laws is important unless liberty in general is important. This objection, however, may miss the key claim. The main point, I think, is that only speech about laws is a part of the system's self-correction mechanism. The argument for special protection of political speech admits, of course, that any specific restriction on nonpolitical speech may also be objectionable. Those limits on nonpolitical speech are, however, no different from any restrictions on people's freedom. Many laws are misguided. The proper response is to change them. Laws restricting political speech, however, are different. According to analyses such as those suggested in Justice Stone's Caroline Products footnote[33] or more recently elaborated by Dean John Hart Ely,[34] restrictions on political speech involve a more basic evil—they impede the correction of error and thereby undermine the system that justifies the other restrictions. Political speech serves as the corrective mechanism for the system of laws as a whole.

This "self-corrective mechanism" argument may seem quite persuasive. But on close examination it turns out to rely fundamentally on a classic marketplace of ideas theory, although restricted to the political realm. Even though we admit that we (and the political order) are fallible, why would we think that free speech rather than selective suppression would best lead to identification and correction of errors? In order to have confidence that the protection of political speech contributes to self-*correction* as opposed to mere change, "unimpeded" political speech must be assumed to lead, at least in the long run, to *better* decisions. Presumably, the presence or absence of various restrictions, for example, restrictions on corporate political speech,[35] will affect the content of political change—but how do we know that the absence of restrictions on the corporate political speech will lead to *better* decisions? The explanation apparently must rely on faith in a marketplace of ideas theory. Otherwise, might we not conclude that political interventions of powerful corporations could corrupt the democratic process? Thus, this reliance on speech as a self-correction mechanism as an explanation for special protection of political speech is subject to all the critiques of the marketplace theories already made.

There is, however, another possible basis for the self-correction argument. If the democratic political process is premised on being an embodiment of liberty, then people would have a basic claim to participate freely in revisions of current political conclusions. This right would reflect more their liberty than any necessary expectation that their choices will correct objective error. But, as noted, if this is the premise, than the same justification in respect for liberty that exists for the political speech applies to other speech. The notion of process that makes liberty central relies on a value that then cannot be limited to the political sphere.

Recognizing the centrality of liberty also deepens another criticism of the political speech theory. Line drawing between political and nonpolitical speech seemed nearly impossible. Meiklejohn eventually greatly expanded the range of communications that he considered relevant to our decision making as governors.[36] He continued, however, to distinguish collective decisions—his favorite image was the town meeting—from individual decisions. But the appropriateness of a line as well as its content depend on the reasons for it. If self-determination is the appropriate lens, the distinction between political and nonpolitical does not just blur—it disappears. Both "private," individual decisions and "public," collective decisions are inherent aspects of humans engaging in self-determination. Both affect an individual's world. Both may and often do reflect civic values as well self-interested concerns. In these ways the personal and the "private" are inherently political. Broadly conceived, politics is merely the label we give to the dialogue and the struggle concerning both group and individual decisions. Given the self-determination rationale for valuing democracy, there is no principled basis for making the distinction. No line identifying political speech can be drawn.

This concludes the critique of the political speech theory. Still, the notion that political speech is at the core of the first amendment has undeniable appeal—although whether this is only true for the probable majority of readers who I expect are quite interested in politics, I am not sure. Unless this appeal is understood, nagging doubts about the theoretical critique will persist. My suggestion is that although there are no abstract justifications for greater protection of political speech, several pragmatic considerations arguably explain a more intense focus on political speech and the special appeal of arguments for its protection.

First, within the broad scope of speech that ought to receive constitutional protection, the government may more often be interested in suppressing political speech than the other, arguably nonpolitical speech. Thus, first amendment protection may be more frequently needed for political speech than for any other type. Political speech would, therefore, likely appear central—or, at least, would be at the center of judicial attention.

Second, the government's decisions to suppress political speech may be systematically less justified than their other decisions to suppress. Those in power—whether they be political, religious, or economic elites—are likely to be least attentive to the need to protect expression that challenges their authority, upsets their preferred status quo, or interferes with their reforms. Their immediate political self-interest and their policy commitments are likely to distort their own judgment about the wisdom of suppression more in respect to political speech than other speech. Suppression of dissident political views is likely to be the most common and most vigorously pursued form of censorship. Thus, this may be the context where government is least trustworthy and objectionable censorship most likely. Therefore, even if political censorship is no greater an interference with fundamental liberty than any other censorship, suppression of political speech may properly make the greatest claim on our attention—that is, be our "central" practical concern.

The problem of government's distorted or self-interested judgments is even more acute because the scope of properly protected liberty includes some but not all expressive activity. Determining whether specific activities fall within the protected realm often will be difficult or controversial. As an interested party, the government should be least trusted in making those determinations regarding political speech.

An example will illustrate this point. Assume that telling manipulative "lies"—intentionally deceptive, knowingly false, statements of facts as a means for getting others to behave other than they would otherwise—is not included within the realm of protected expression but that protected expression includes unintentional falsehoods, metaphor, and hyperbole in the strong expression of opinion or perspective. Government (and juries) may be more biased and more prone to inaccurately characterize (their opponents') statements as conscious lies in the "political" than in the "private" realm. People habitually see the claims of their political opponents as false and often attribute bad motives, that is, a readiness to lie, to these opponents.

History, observation and, for many of us, self-reflection confirm this tendency. During World War I, for instance, people were convicted and punished on the basis of the obvious falsity and maliciousness of their assertion that the "government is for the profiteers."[37] Given this tendency to attribute the worst to political opponents, the only way to effectively protect the political speech that should be protected may be to adopt broad prophylactic rules against government interference. Given the heightened likelihood of mistaken findings, arguably we should not allow the law to reach "knowing falsehoods" in the political sphere, even if these falsehoods did not theoretically merit protection.[38] Thus, even if the same theoretical rationale for claiming a fundamental status applies to both political and nonpolitical speech, these pragmatic considerations argue for greater doctrinal protection for political speech and make political speech appear central or special.

A third consideration can be added. Many aspects of modern social life conform to a currently popular, reduced view of politics as merely the continued pursuit of private interest by means of government power. Fortunately, another, also widely held, deeply rooted, traditional view of politics challenges this reduced view. This second, more traditional conception sees politics as involving people's civic concern with the general good. Many aspects of our political institutions, including the ban on selling votes and on paying bribes and the public–regarding trappings of political advocacy, elections, and voting, call on people when acting in the political sphere to adopt this broader perspective, a concern for the public good and for collective value definition. In practice, people's political activities and their political speech sometimes do and sometimes do not correspond to this civic conception of politics. When it does correspond, however, the political speech exhibits altruistic or, in the economic terminology, "public good" qualities that distinguish it from a lot of private speech. This type of speech has value for the community as a whole beyond its value to the speaker and consequently ought to be specially nurtured.

Those political activists whose political speech authorities most often want to suppress seldom view their own speech and their other political activities as merely or even primarily "private goods." Typically, these activists are political dissidents who view their speech and their politics as attempts to gain solidarity with others and as civic-oriented, altruistic attempts to create a better society. Given our collective need for more people to take up the interest of the whole, to adopt the perspective of the general good, and to protect us from "the greatest menace to freedom [—] an inert people,"[39] we should especially value people engaged in political speech. Our institutions should encourage their activity. Whether or not specific political speakers are misguided, their civic orientation makes them particularly inappropriate people to punish.[40] Objectionable pursuit of private interest makes a much better candidate for punishment.

This "public good" quality of political speech also suggests a reason for predicting that the struggle over political speech would be central in the actual development of the first amendment. Those whom the government wishes to punish for their political speech often present a high visibility cause. Supporters are likely to exist. Issues can often be framed in terms of principle. Frequently significant elites can be stimulated to sympathize with and support even those victims of governmental suppression with whom they disagree.[41] This attitude contrasts with a typically lesser public sympathy for those whose misguided asocial conduct appears calculated to advance purely private interests.[42]

On the other hand, the "public harms" allegedly caused by unwise political speech may also intensify the self-righteous feelings on the other side. Suppression seems especially justifiable because the "evil" speech is not just a private wrong to another individual but a "public bad" that may cause harm to the whole community. (Sometimes I think political entrepreneurs find it easier to arouse emotions in support of laws against racist speech than to legislate against more intractable, economic, and power-based forms of racial discrimination. Frequent conservative, establishment support for limitations on racist speech suggests that observers ought to compare the likely class impact of this response with possible alternative legislative or societal attacks on racism.)

Thus, this "public good" quality of political speech may help explain the popularity of the political speech theory. Whether it justifies the theory is a different question. First, this public good quality of political speech certainly does not uniquely identify political speech or distinguish it from "private" speech. Often political speech narrowly advances private interests. In contrast, often private speech contributes to the social or cultural development of a decent society. The "public good" qualities of educating a child or promoting the arts are often noted.

Second, if the argument for special protection is only that it will promote the general welfare by providing us with more of a valued "public good," the argument views the first amendment less as a protector of individual rights against intolerant majorities than as a welfare-maximizing device. Usually we are content to allow the political process to make decisions both generally about welfare maximization and specifically about the need to purchase public goods. Thus, although the first amendment might be merely a rule utilitarian attempt to advance the general welfare, this rule utilitarian interpretation contrasts with an equally popular and, I argue, more profound view—the view that the first amendment recognizes individual rights that limit the manner in which the collective pursues the general welfare. Surely, the choice between (or combination of) these utilitarian and individual rights perspectives requires further argument. Certainly, nothing in the invocation of democracy suggests that the reason for protecting speech must be the rule utilitarian argument. In fact, the perspective that values democracy as an end and not merely as a means would suggest the priority of the individual rights interpretation.

In any event, looked at in their entirety, these pragmatic considerations only show that greater vigilance may be needed in respect to political speech, not that the constitution guarantees superior status to political speech.

This review of the political speech theory of the first amendment has led to several important observations. First, advocates of this theory typically rely on a basically marketplace of ideas rationale for protecting speech, although they then unjustifiably only apply this rationale to speech that relates to self-government. Since this version of the political speech theory is merely a restricted version of the marketplace theory, it is subject to all the last chapter's criticisms of the marketplace theory.

Second, sometimes proponents offer an alternative, more definitional version of the political speech theory. This version asserts that freedom of speech is central to an acceptable political process. The force of this version, however, turns out to depend on acceptance of a particular conception of an acceptable political sphere, namely, a conception that justifies the political sphere as a partial embodiment of individual liberty. Closer examination shows that this emphasis on liberty cannot be limited to valuing liberty in the political sphere. Thus, this second version of the political speech theory cannot finally justify treating political and nonpolitical speech differently. Moreover, this second version of the political speech theory calls for protection of somewhat different categories of expressive conduct than the classic marketplace theory. This difference reflects the emphasis on people's freedom to participate as opposed to the concern in the marketplace version that people obtain the information that leads to the best conclusions.

Third, even though no abstract grounds justify treating political speech as more important or more meriting of constitutional protection, various pragmatic considerations help explain why conflicts over restrictions on political speech often dominate popular attention and may be "central" in the legal development of first amendment protection. Political speech could be at the core of the legal and popular battle even though not uniquely at the core of the value, the value being individual liberty.

Fourth, these pragmatic considerations suggest that more extensive prophylactic rules may be necessary in the political arena than in other contexts to provide effective protection for the same theoretically justified realm of speech freedom. These pragmatic considerations may also help explain the coexistence of seemingly conflicting dicta in the case law. Sometimes judicial dicta assert that political speech is at the core of the first amendment. Other dicta indicate that the first amendment protects all types of speech and that distinctions between political speech and other speech are impermissible.[43] Each set of dicta provides an appropriate response to a different issue. The first set, which typically occurs in cases involving political speech, underlines the especially important need for constitutional protection in the political sphere.[44] The second set recognizes that no principled justification for protecting freedom of speech would distinguish political speech from speech on other subjects or in contexts that are not overtly political. This second set of dicta underlines the conclusion that nonpolitical speech, to the extent that such a category can be conceptualized, equally represents a properly protected aspect of individual liberty.

THE MARKET FAILURE MODEL

Adam Smith's invisible hand does not always produce the results desired in the marketplace of goods. The unreality of the assumptions underlying a perfectly functioning economic market results in various forms of "market failures" that require state intervention to achieve efficient allocations or desired distributions. Likewise, critics of the classic marketplace of ideas theory often base their critiques either on the failure of the assumptions concerning truth and rationality described and criticized in Chapter 1 or specifically on failures of the economic market, such as those caused by the monopolization of communication channels or by the difficulties of organizing participation by large, usually dispersed, often poor interest groups. These critics then advocate repair—various forms of governmental intervention to improve the functioning of the marketplace of ideas. The critics differ, however, as to the specific solutions proposed—differences that relate to the particular problem or market failure that the critic has identified.

The Reform Proposals

To clarify the content of the market failure model(s) I will outline the major frameworks of possible reform, analyze the assumptions justifying each, and give a few examples of specific reform proposals. Reforms generally fit into one of four frameworks: (1) correct failures of economic markets to the extent possible without restricting anyone's speech freedom; (2) guarantee all viewpoints adequate, but not necessarily equal, access to the marketplace of ideas; (3) guarantee all *viewpoints* equal access to the marketplace of ideas (e.g., equal time for each candidate); or (4) guarantee all *individuals* equal access. (I should note that implementing many proposals suggested by the first two approaches would be compatible with, but not necessarily required by, the liberty theory of the first amendment advanced in Chapter 3.)

The first approach to reform argues that failures of the economic market require government intervention when these market failures cause inefficient or distorted allocations of resources to speech activities. Misallocations may be caused, for example, by monopolization or by the difficulty that racial, sexual, or ethnic groups, consumers, the poor, environmentalists, and other large, unorganized groups have, due to organization costs and freeloading, in achieving efficient levels of advocacy.

Although based on free market economic theory, this analysis typically has a progressive political thrust. The extreme concentration of ownership of major mass media in the United States,[45] as well as the large corporate advertisers' power implicitly to set norms for acceptability of form and content and sometimes to control specific publication or broadcast decisions,[46] and the typically less organized status of those outside the existing power structure are among the factors that predictably cause these market failures to reinforce corporate power and the status quo. Reformist critics often propose invigorated enforcement of anti-trust laws or subsidies for advocacy by poor or difficult-to-organize groups.[47] These proposals, justified by economic efficiency concerns, do not require or imply any particular theory of free speech. Moreover, typically these reform proposals do not conflict with any significant first amendment theory. Thus, this economic market failure theory and the corresponding reform proposals, although of great social and political significance, are not directly relevant to the subject of this book and will not be further considered.

The assumptions of the second reform framework, which requires guaranteeing adequate, but not equal, presentation of all (serious?) viewpoints, are very similar to those of the classic model. In *On Liberty*, Mill recommended that we search for devices to assure the forceful presentation of viewpoints that, without our positive efforts, would not be adequately presented.[48] Like the classic model, this second, reformist approach must assume that reason dominates in human inquiry. That is, it must assume that people will use their intellect to find the core of insight, if any, in each message. Otherwise, people's conclusions will be controlled by the form and frequency of inputs. Consequentially, this reformist approach merely argues that the government should alleviate any blockage of meaningful access opportunities for particular viewpoints by guaranteeing adequate access to the marketplace.[49]

As a basis for reform, this second approach could be implemented by providing subsidies to under-represented viewpoints. Such subsidies, mandated by this version of the market failure theory, usually present no problems from the perspective of other first amendment theories. Of course, the serious practical problem with this approach as a constitutional standard rather than as a legislative policy is the difficulty of determining what constitutes an adequate or meaningful presentation opportunity.

A first amendment interpretation that requires only that each view receive an adequate presentation points to an interesting aspect of, and possibly an objection to, both this second market failure framework and the classic market model. Given a conclusion that some expression of a viewpoint suffices to assure its proper evaluation, a restraint on the speech of some individuals would not obstruct the search for truth as long as others who hold similar views are allowed to speak. Thus, any governmental restraint on speech, as long as the message was adequately presented by someone, would be unobjectionable—unless the objection is grounded on some rule utilitarian conclusion that any governmental power to suppress supposedly adequately presented views would be too often misapplied. Nevertheless, many commentators and courts object to such restraints because they interfere with an individual's right to express herself as she chooses. When they do object, despite their marketplace rhetoric, they often reveal an underlying concern with individual liberty that apparently supersedes their concern merely for the workings of the marketplace.[50]

The third reform possibility, *equal access for all viewpoints*, presents virtually insurmountable practical problems relating to the identification of different viewpoints. For example, critics of the Federal Communications Commission's Fairness Doctrine have noted that the Doctrine's requirement of a "fair" presentation of all sides of an issue is utterly manipulatable by whoever is empowered to decide what issue has been discussed and what constitutes relevantly different viewpoints concerning that issue.[51] Defining what constitutes a different viewpoint is an inherently value-loaded task.

Nevertheless, the general objective of this third reform agenda makes sense if "objective" truth (or a best or correct solution) exists but if people's rational faculties are too feeble to avoid or neutralize distortions caused by inequalities in the opportunities available to competing propagandists. Equalizing the presentation opportunities for each potentially true or wise viewpoint (in contrast to equalizing the opportunity for each speaker) enables each contrasting viewpoint equally to use quantity and packaging to neutralize the other's distortions. People's real but limited rational faculties should then suffice to allow them to pick out the true (or best) position from among the equally effectively presented viewpoints. In other words, this reform approach relies on the classic model's truth assumption but rejects the second aspect of the classics model's rationality assumption, that people are able to sift through the form and frequency of message presentation to evaluate the core notions.[52]

Among the few serious attempts to engage in reform in the manner implied by this third approach might be the provision for equal funding of all political candidates or of each political party. Arguably, these proposals attempt, at least in the context of political campaigns, to accomplish this goal of providing for equality of each viewpoint, each candidate or party being a proxy for a different viewpoint. (Or, if passing some threshold level of support provides evidence that a candidate is potentially the best choice, that is, that the candidate might win if presentation opportunities were equalized, then the state might assure equal resources only to candidates who meet this threshold requirement.)[53]

Equal access for all individuals is the fourth and most logical version of the market failure theory. A new, more defensible assumption replaces each of the classic model's faulty assumptions. First, this approach assumes that truth may be chosen or created rather than being objective and discovered. Second, reason exists but is not assumed routinely to control or dominate people's response to debate. Instead, people normally cannot divorce their understanding from their individual and group histories and their experiences in a particular social location. Moreover, packaging, quantity, and context affect people's responses to messages. Third, this approach assumes that people may have different needs and groups may have conflicting interests. Whether or not these conflicts are permanent, social choices ought to respond fairly to the differences.

Given these alternative assumptions, success in debate provides evidence of the merit of particular proposals or perspectives only if the debate is "fair." Cut adrift from the logic that explained how competition within the marketplace of ideas advances truth, and instead assuming that truth is created or chosen, at least in part, on the basis of inputs into the marketplace, the democratic notion provides a possible solution: The marketplace works if and only if all people are equally able to participate in making or influencing the choice. Moreover, providing each person a roughly equal opportunity to generate equal quantities of carefully packaged messages increases the role of reason. This equality helps neutralize the advantage that packaging and repetition presently give to well-financed perspectives.

At first, the failure of the classic model's assumptions appeared to make faith in the marketplace of ideas incoherent. The interpretation of the marketplace of ideas in this fourth reform approach suggests, however, that the purpose of the market is to provide legitimate scope for differing, often conflicting, interests or subjective truths rather than to promote the discovery of objective truth. This reformed marketplace theory follows from a conception of fairness or from a democratic notion that equal individual influence gives legitimate scope for differing interests. The marketplace of ideas seems perfectly coherent as long as people have equal opportunities (e.g., equal resources) for participating. Each person gets to make an equal contribution to creating truth.

Reliance on this equality standard rather than on existing wealth to control opportunities for speech is far from the norm in our basically capitalistic society. The arena in which we most commonly claim to adopt the equality standard is the political sphere—we proclaim a "one person, one vote" standard. Likewise, in holding the poll tax and property qualifications for the vote unconstitutional, the Supreme Court has concluded that wealth should not affect one's right to vote even though wealth or other unequally distributed tokens or personal attributes are assumed to be acceptable criteria for allocating most other goods.[54] Thus, equality for individual input is arguably most appropriate for speech that relates to what are perceived as political decisions, that is, collective decisions that will affect the rights as well as the values of the members of the collective.[55]

To achieve rough equality of opportunity for individual input requires either a combination of subsidies and restrictions or a method of making speech a free good—making any amount of communication the speaker desires costless to the speaker. I know of no specific proposal to fully implement the fourth market failure theory even in the limited sphere of politics. Nevertheless, some campaign reform proposals, for example, giving every person (not just candidates) an equal amount of government money to spend on election campaigns, can be interpreted as a partial move toward such an egalitarian system.[56]

Evaluation

The differing assumptions of each version of the market failure theory lead to differing critiques. Thus, some critiques will apply uniquely to only one version. For example, the second version of the market failure theory, requiring *adequate* access for all viewpoints, relies on the classic marketplace of ideas' rationality assumption—that is, as long as all views are presented, people will have the capacity to recognize or choose the best view. And the third version, requiring equal access for all viewpoints, relies on the classic model's truth assumption— if no viewpoint can rely on greater access to manipulate people's reason, people will gravitate to the best or true views that were originally held by only a few. Each reformulation is subject to the criticisms of the specific assumption of the classic model on which it relies. In the remainder of this chapter, however, I will develop more general points. I will first consider criticisms that apply to all versions (possibly with differing force). Then, I will note serious practical difficulties with the fourth version of the market failure theory, guaranteeing equal access for all individuals. This equal access argument merits special attention since, by reversing each of the classic model's assumptions, it may appear to escape all the theoretical criticisms directed against the classic model.

The two most fundamental objections to the market failure theories of the first amendment do not relate to their internal logic. Rather, these objections depend on the persuasiveness of alternative theories of freedom of speech and of equality.

First, the market failure theories are inappropriate first amendment standards if another theory provides a better interpretation of the scope and role of the first amendment. The force of this objection will depend on the appeal of the alternative. Thus, the force of this objection is left for the reader to consider in relation to liberty theory of the first amendment developed in the next three chapters.

The contrast with the liberty theory is sharpened because the market failure theories often require interference with some people's freedom of speech, interference that the liberty theory asserts is unacceptable. For example, fully implementing equality of access for either viewpoints or individuals could not be achieved without specifically limiting some people's use of their resources or talents for expressive purposes. Thus, this first objection to the market failure theories starkly poses the question of whether equalizing "real opportunities" to speak, unquestionably a policy goal worthy of pursuit to some degree and by some means, justifies restricting speech or other basic forms of personal liberty.

Invocation of notions of equality undoubtedly gives the market failure theories much of their appeal. Nevertheless, my second objection relates to the conception of equality on which a constitutionally based market failure theory must rely. In particular, this objection claims that its conception of equality misleads first amendment theory into sacrificing liberty. Rather than requiring the sacrifice of liberty, an appropriate constitutional conception of equality will be consistent with a liberty-based interpretation of the first amendment. Equality, moreover, ought to be seen as having a separate constitutional basis—for example, in the equal protection clause of the fourteenth amendment.

Elsewhere I have argued that a single ethical principle, equal respect for people as autonomous agents pursuing meaning, self-definition, and fulfillment, underlies justifiable collective interaction.[57] Government respect for, and treatment of, individuals as equals is necessary to morally justify legal obligation.[58] Respect for autonomous agents as equals requires a concern for people's liberty (for restrictions on liberty disrespect a person's autonomy as a moral agent) as well as for people's opportunities (which implies some concern with the distribution of opportunities, with equality). Moreover, although respect for people as equals places definite limits on the choices of democratic systems (e.g., it rules out invidious discrimination) and requires provision for some minimal levels of some goods, and although it suggests some degree of equalizing of conditions as a meritorious policy goal, equality of respect does not require any particular level of substantive equality. Since the same ethical principle requires collective concern both for individual liberty and for the distribution of resources, these two values, equality and liberty, properly interpreted or formulated in light of this single ethical principle, will not be incompatible.[59]

Both conceptually and in our constitutional system, the two values, liberty and equality, do different work. The first amendment provides the best constitutional text for basing a properly delineated, protected realm of liberty. Other constitutional texts, particularly the equal protection clause, provide the best basis for recognizing the equality claims. For example, respecting people as equals, although consistent with considerable economic inequality, may require that certain "merit goods" be provided up to a certain level.[60]

Thus, if "merit goods" properly include some opportunity to communicate one's views to a large audience, the fourteenth amendment's equal protection clause, not some market failure version of the first amendment, would provide the proper constitutional base for the argument. And, fortunately, this equal protection analysis, which only argues for *guarantees* of minimal levels of the "merit goods," avoids both the problem of restrictions on liberty and the serious practical difficulties, identified below, that make application of the market failure model objectionable. Moreover, even if not required by a fundamental or constitutional principle of equality, a society could conclude as a matter of policy that presently disadvantaged groups or individuals or viewpoints should have more adequate access to society's channels of communication. As long as the society accomplished this policy of promoting access by subsidies or similar means rather than by restrictions on liberty or improper discrimination, the society could pursue this egalitarian policy without violating constitutionally protected liberty.

The above comments reflect possible external criticisms of market failure theories—that they improperly sacrifice liberty that should be fundamental and they rely on an out-of-place and inappropriately formulated equality ideal. In addition, as a constitutional standard, the market failure theory is also subject to internal critiques.

Any correction of market failures requires criteria to guide governmental intervention. If adequate access for all viewpoints is the goal, any lack of criteria for "adequacy" undermines the legitimacy of government regulation. No one has even suggested plausible operational or objective criteria. Theoretically, "adequacy" most probably means sufficient for people to recognize any truth or wisdom in the viewpoint. Sufficient access will have been granted when, but not until, people recognize all the truth or wisdom in a viewpoint.

In practice, application of this standard inevitably will be influenced by people's assumptions concerning the truth of the viewpoint. For example, when David Paul O'Brien publicly burned his draft card in protest of our military involvement in Vietnam, he likely disagreed with most governmental officials and judges concerning whether the American public had been "adequately" exposed to anti-war messages. More generally, given the lack of objective standards of adequacy, leaving it to the government (or the courts) to determine when the presentation of a view has been adequate essentially allows the government to determine the truth or nontruth of the view. By deciding whether a presentation has been adequate, the government implicitly determines what is the correct resolution of the marketplace debate—or, more bluntly, the government defines truth. If a purpose of the first amendment is to protect unpopular ideas that may eventually triumph over the majority's established dogma, allowing the government to determine adequacy of access stands the first amendment on its head.

Moreover, the impossibility of specifying objective, operational criteria for identifying a properly functioning market will arise in each of the marketplace theories. Substituting "equality" for "adequate access" offers only slight help. Equality for viewpoints leaves open the crucial but inevitably subjective task of defining what counts as a different viewpoint. Even the notion of equality for individuals, no matter whether it is conceived as referring to opportunity, actual speech, or real influence turns out to be a theoretically elusive and practically manipulatable standard.

Justice Harlan's concurrence in *United States v. O'Brien*,[61] the draft-card-burning case, illustrates some of these problems. Harlan agreed that a person's constitutional right to have her view adequately presented to the public might justify violating an otherwise valid law, but only if the violation were necessary to present that view.[62] Presumably, Harlan and David O'Brien "only" disagreed over whether other "adequate" opportunities for presenting O'Brien's view were available. No criteria exist for making this determination. Differing determinations by Harlan and O'Brien are predictable—and illustrate two dangers of using makeshift criteria. Harlan's response corresponded to what must be expected of judges or other governmental officials. Judges drawn almost exclusively from the dominant classes in society will normally find that dissidents have had adequate opportunity. From any mainstream perspective, the dissidents will be seen to have lost in the debate only because their position is ultimately unpersuasive. Thus, without objective criteria of adequacy, this market failure approach is likely to systematically fail to provide for really effective expression by dissidents.

O'Brien, of course, disagreed about the adequacy of opportunities to present antiwar messages. His disagreement raises an additional problem with market failure conceptions of the first amendment—the predictable responses that this constitutional interpretation calls forth. O'Brien "knew" that reason confirmed his position, that the war was wrong. Thus, given that a properly functioning marketplace would lead to the right conclusion, he also "knew" that the market must have failed. The public and the politicians must not have adequately heard the right views and, therefore, his fundamental constitutional right to have those views adequately expressed had been violated. Either because violation of this right, until corrected, ends the legitimacy of his obligation to obey the laws of the state or because, as Harlan suggested, the constitution properly protects taking the steps required to vindicate or realize this first amendment right, O'Brien and the other dissenters are justified in breaking otherwise valid laws while doing what is necessary to achieve a properly functioning marketplace of ideas.

Given human psychology, the logic of these instrumentalist market failure theories is even more far reaching. Law breaking or violence cannot be expected to stop with O'Brien's protest. Major disputes usually produce at least two sides that firmly believe in the truth of their position. *Any* success on one side will appear to the other side to indicate a market failure and justify an increasingly forceful response. The combination of necessarily subjectively identified market failures, strongly held beliefs, and a right to a properly functioning marketplace easily leads to a logic of escalating use of increasingly extreme, possibly violent, means. Normally illegal activities appear necessary and justified to correct for the denial of the actor's right to a properly functioning marketplace of ideas.

This move toward violence applies specifically to market failure models of the first amendment. "[W]hen men have realized that time has upset many fighting faiths," and *if* they can accept the classic marketplace of ideas theory, despite their firm belief in their own ideas, "they may come to believe even more . . . that the ultimate good desired is better reached by free trade in ideas."[64] If, in contrast, a person recognizes that the marketplace frequently needs correction, she must decide between two plausible alternatives. In any given situation, should she set aside her fighting faith because she knows she is fallible or should she take effective action to correct for the apparent blockage of the free trade in ideas? Realizing that time has upset many fighting faiths does not help a person determine whether a market failure or her own error is preventing her firmly held views from prevailing.

Thus, we have the two serious practical problems with market failure theories. First, if the state determines adequacy, the adequacy standard will usually favor the status quo. Second, this instrumentalist conception of fundamental rights, which is implicit in market failure theories, inherently tends toward justifying violent or otherwise objectionable conduct.

Despite these practical problems, the theoretical merit of the market failure theories deserves attention. The one version that avoided all the criticized assumptions of the classic marketplace of ideas theory is the individual-equality-of-access approach. Reversal of the classic theory's assumptions combined with the premise that no one has a superior claim to define truth arguably leads to this approach. Truth is not so much found through reason as it is created on the "fair" basis of the equal individual input. But careful examination of the equality of access model shows fundamental flaws. First, the apparent clarity of its equality standard is deceptive. Second, the approach leads to objectionable or, at least, questionable results. Third, these objectionable results reflect the ultimate unpersuasiveness of the justifications offered for the equal access standard.

Equality of access to the marketplace of ideas turns out to be a vague, open-ended standard. Communication is ubiquitous. Almost all activities undertaken in a context where a second person will be aware of the activity communicate something. Everyday "performances" are inherently communicative. Thus, the equality standard arguably leads to requiring equality of resources for all publicly performed activities. I will not belabor the point that, as an interpretation of the first amendment, this resource allocation requirement would shock most people. If the arguments for strict equality are sound enough, possibly people could be persuaded. Equality of resources or equality of opportunities to engage in publicly performed activities, however, does not meet the need for clarity. Neither operational nor even theoretically objective criteria exist for identifying this sort of equality. Moreover, any attempt to achieve this equality would aggravate the other problems noted below.

The equality standard is also unclear because it is uncertain whether the sought after equality should refer to opportunities for input or opportunities for influence or actual input or actual influence.[65] If truth is chosen or created and if people diverge in their conclusions about what should be created, equality would apparently require that each person *be able* to exercise equal influence. That is, some people may not be as interested in influence as others—therefore, real equality of opportunity may be the right standard. But since the same expenditure of money enables different people, because of their different skills and connections, to exercise different degrees of influence, an equality of influence standard would require that the "naturally" influential be allowed even less resources for communication purposes than the noninfluential.

This is a curious constitutional standard. Some degree of specialization in being opinion leaders or information spreaders does not seem so unjust. Most people would assume that it is desirable, not objectionable, to allow people with integrity and wisdom and experience, arguably the "naturally" influential people, to exercise greater noncoercive influence. In fact, if the marketplace of ideas is not to further merely random changes, those attuned to the needs for change ought to exercise greater influence. Hence, forced equality seems crazy. The constitution should not prevent people from seeking the advice of the "elders." And although this problem is greatest for the most extreme versions of equality of influence standards, any interpretation of the equality standard generates a number of parallel objections.

The only way that the state could equalize the amount that both rich and poor can speak is to employ a combination of subsidies and legal restrictions or to make speech a free good, costless for everyone. Either approach raises numerous problems. First, the restrictions in the subsidy-restriction approach will inevitably impose severe restraints on liberty. The constitutional provision that apparently protects individual freedom from state abridgement would now be seen to require that abridgement. Of course, the strangeness of the result is not itself an objection. I postpone until the next chapter the argument that this liberty should be the heart of the first amendment.

Second, the intensity of people's desire to speak or communicate (at any given level) varies; it is not apparent that providing for two people to do the same thing, when their desire to do it differs, actually treats them equally.

Third, whether one utilizes subsidies for the poor or a universally "free good" approach, the resulting equality involves an inefficient use of resources, that is, often those who are subsidized will be relatively uninterested in speech and would have preferred to use the resources for other purposes. Moreover, the rich may disvalue the restrictions on their expression more than they would disvalue a direct transfer to the poor of an amount of their wealth that the poor would value more than the poor value the restrictions on the speech of the rich. In other words, there could easily be policies that both the rich and poor would prefer to this enforced equality in communications. Not that these standard economic efficiency arguments against regulation are conclusive—often they are not—but the predictably inefficient or wasteful use of resources necessary to achieve this form of equality should make its achievement questionable as a mandate of constitutional law.[66]

Fourth, if one justification for the first amendment lies in its contribution to the proper or wise or desired formulation of community values and improved collective decision making, guaranteeing equality of access makes little sense. Both the subsidy-restriction and the free good approach promote expression of weakly held viewpoints as compared to strongly held viewpoints, thereby preventing the marketplace of ideas from accurately reflecting the collective values or perspectives of the community.

In summary, it is usually desirable and progressive to change rules or policies or institutional arrangements in a manner that provides the poor and the unorganized increased access to channels of communication and to politics as well as to all other realms of life. A properly formulated, constitutionally based, notion of equality may even require that everyone have some minimum level of access opportunities. Nevertheless, all the market failure theories should be rejected as first amendment doctrine. Marketplace-of-ideas-based arguments for providing either "adequate" or equal access for all "viewpoints," the second and third market failure theories, rely on assumptions rejected in the earlier analysis of the classic marketplace model; moreover, they generate serious practical problems.

Only equality of individual opportunities for communication relies on plausible theoretical assumptions. This equality standard, however, is unworkable; it cannot be coherently defined. Moreover, on any plausible definition, it requires state intervention of tremendous scope—an unlikely mandate to draw from the first amendment. This equality standard is also objectionable as it leads to very inefficient uses of resources and to serious distortions in the representation of community values or perspectives. These practical problems occur because this equality standard relies on and treats as fundamental a misconceived conception of equality—a conception that mandates specific equalities in allocations or outcomes rather than politically chosen outcomes premised on a structure that provides for equality of respect.[67] But the most important objection to this equality standard is that it improperly subordinates liberty. The next three chapters will argue that an understanding and defense of this notion of liberty are key to a persuasive interpretation of the first amendment.

3

The Liberty Theory

My thesis is that the first amendment protects a broad realm of nonviolent, non-coercive, expressive activity. The method for determining the scope of protection proceeds, first, by considering the purposes or values served by protected speech. Violent and coercive activities, however, also can serve these same values. Thus, I conclude that constitutional protection of speech is justified not merely because of the values served by speech but because freedom of speech serves these values in a particular, humanly acceptable manner, that is, nonviolently and noncoercively. Describing these methods is the second step of the analysis. Then, I argue in Chapter 4 that when nonverbal expressive conduct advances the same values in a relevantly similar manner, the nonverbal conduct should also be viewed as speech and should receive protection.

FIRST AMENDMENT VALUES OR PURPOSES

In the marketplace theories, a single value justified and defined the scope of protection. These theories protected speech as a means of discovering truth or reaching the "best" societal or individual decision. This focus is too limited. Professor Thomas Emerson, probably America's most thoughtful and influential first amendment scholar, finds first amendment freedom essential for furthering four values: (1) individual self-fulfillment, (2) advancement of knowledge and discovery of truth, (3) participation in decision making by all members of the society (which is "particularly significant for political decisions" but "embraces the right to participate in the building of the whole culture") and (4) achievement of a "more adaptable and hence stable community."[1]

Emerson's list, which synthesizes his extensive review of the literature supporting freedom of speech, provides a helpful starting point. From a perspective I will defend later, two values from Emerson's list, the first, self-fulfillment, and the third, participation in change, are key. These values of self-fulfillment and participation in change impose somewhat different requirements on a satisfactory theory. The emphasis on "self" in self-fulfillment requires the theory to delineate a realm of individual liberty that allows for self-realization. The participation-in-change value requires the theory to specify and protect activities essential to a broadly democratic, participatory process of change.[2] Together the two imply a notion of freedom oriented toward self-realization and self-determination.

Emerson's second and fourth values are derivative. Given that truth is chosen or created, not discovered, advancement of knowledge and discovery of truth are merely aspects of participation in change. Also, a country achieves a "more flexible and thereby more stable community" by providing for individual self-fulfillment and allowing the disgruntled and the visionaries to participate in change. In other words, the second and fourth values, although certainly important in their own right, are predictably promoted by guaranteeing the individual liberties suggested by the first and third values. Henceforth, I will refer to individual self-fulfillment and participation in change, or self-realization and self-determination, as the key first amendment values.

Why should these two values receive constitutional protection? To some extent, I am content to follow Emerson and merely claim that constitutional protection for speech as a manifestation of these (two) values is and has been our historically developed commitment and has been urged by numerous theorists who have discussed freedom of speech. Still, it may be useful here to suggest one possible account of this commitment and the propriety of respecting these rights.

Note, first, that constitutional provisions, especially those providing for individual rights, limit majoritarian, presumably welfare-advancing or collective self-definitional, decision making. In fact, the notion of a right is that the right claimant, whether an individual or group, should be able to override the preferred outcome of the party against whom the right is asserted.[3]

Second, note that the assertion of a right involves a relation to another. The assertion is a claim addressed to another and a claim that the other ought to defer to the claimant in some manner. But why should the other defer? And if the other is the society as a whole that would, except for the recognition of the right, be acting to promote the welfare or self-definition of the whole, why should it defer? Presumably the reason for deference must in some sense relate to the content of the relationship of the party making the assertion and the party who is addressed.

Third, given that the question is: Why the whole should be limited in its welfare-advancing or self-definitional activities, it also makes sense to ask why the whole should be engaged in such activities in the first place. Three slightly different responses to these questions all lead to roughly the same conclusion concerning first amendment rights.

The issue can be approached either at the general level of whether anything is implied in the very activity of addressing claims to another, the more specific level of what is implied in the context of claims made between the political whole and its members, or the most historically specific level of such claims made in the context of our society with its particular and historically contingent commitments.

Assertions of particular claims on another may involve implicit reference to specific aspects of the relationship that justify obedience or deference to the particular request of that specific person. Still, any claim addressed to the other must implicitly treat the other as autonomous, as a being capable of acceding to or rejecting the claim—otherwise the address amounts at most to an instrumentalist threat of application of force. Moreover, if the claimant is seriously addressing rather than merely manipulating the other, the claimant must assume that the other ought to be able to make an appropriate or proper decision about his or her response—that is, the claimant must assume that the other's decision making ought not be distorted and that the other ought not be subject to domination. Thus, the practice of addressing claims to others arguably implies respect for the other as an equal or nondominated autonomous agent. If these comments are right, it seems such respect will be a common foundational feature of many moral practices and, in particular, will be involved in communicative interaction to the extent that such interaction involves each speaker in implicitly making claims that the other should accept the truth of what she says, the truthfulness or sincerity of her saying it, and the rightness of her assertions concerning normative standards or directives for behavior.[4]

From the perspective of the political order the analysis is similar. Collective groups, for example, states, have norms that they claim or assert members have an obligation to obey. They claim the obligation to obey the laws is a matter of legitimacy, not merely force. As noted above, such an assertion must be premised on a relation to the other. Specifically, the assertion must appeal to some aspect of the relationship that justifies the claim that the other should accede. It would be inconsistent with the practice of addressing appeals to others for the collective to expect the other to accede if the other was not being treated with respect as an autonomous agent—that is, as one to whom claims are properly addressed. And it would be implausible to expect the other to accede to a specific claim or practice that the other does not favor unless the overall practice—that is, the legal order—treats the other as intrinsically significant as other members of the collective, for example, as significant as those favored by the particular norm being asserted. In other words, reasoned justification of legal obligation may require respect for rights of equality and autonomy and democratic participation.

Elaboration of this core insight of social contract doctrines helps explain both the propriety of, and proper limits on, collective self-definitional or welfare-maximizing decision making. First, the practices of democratic decision making or welfare maximization policies can often be understood as properly implementing equal respect for persons as autonomous agents. Although some people may be more advantaged or disadvantaged by any particular decision or policy, at least the abstract or formal claim of both democratic decision making and utilitarianism is that their procedures do not imply distinctions between the worth of persons but that they do provide a method for choosing collective norms, which are the only alternative to interactions based on raw force. For example, utilitarian theory argues for fulfilling as many of people's desires as possible, weighting the desires (or preferences) of each person equally. Democratic decision making gives each person the same potential say in results, a say that properly would represent the person's autonomous choice or commitment. Thus, democratic decision making manifests, or at least is consistent with, respect for people's autonomy and equality. This respect is important given that its presence is crucial for redeeming the implicit claim that the resulting norms are obligatory.

But if this respect for people's equality and autonomy is crucial, then any collective decision, norm, or practice that denies this equality or autonomy is inconsistent with a necessary aspect of the claim for accepting or according legitimacy to the collective's practices and decisions. This observation leads to the conclusion that the group has no authority to act in ways that deny a person's equality or, for the purposes of this book the more relevant consideration, a person's autonomy. Hence, the same basic considerations crucial for justifying legal obligation both justify collective democratic decision making and require limits on it. Fundamental constitutional restraints on democratic choice are the result.

Historically, not all societies have exhibited the view that these premises of respect for individual autonomy and equality are necessary for a justifiable legal order or for legal obligation. Despite whatever desirable features exist in these societies, from our present perspective, their denial of these premises reflects objectionable hierarchy, closure, and their structural distortion of the possibility of communicative action and discursive will formation. Even putting aside the universalistic aspect of these evaluations, the assumption that respect for people's equality and autonomy is fundamental may still provide the best explanation for the basic commitments of actual liberal democratic states. In other words, we could start with the various commitments that we do in fact seem to accept—democracy, for example. That commitment can surely be explained in various possible ways. Still, as suggested above, a quite persuasive account of that commitment is that it embodies even more fundamental commitments— that is, the commitment to democracy is an implication of the more basic commitment of respect for individual equality and liberty.

This account of democracy as secondary also provides a logical explanation of constitutionalism— that is, of foundational restraints on democracy. The normally accepted account of our constitutionalism is that it protects certain rights even from majority override. In other words, this account treats certain values— human dignity, respect for individuals equality and autonomy—as fundamental and directs that democracy must operate within the constraint of respect for these values. Moreover, many alternative accounts of democracy or of other basic, accepted features of our society as well as interpretations of cultural and legal texts, when discursively pressed, will also seem best defended from perspectives that assume respect for equality and liberty as basic.

Thus, from any of three different perspectives—the abstract nature of communicative action aimed at agreement, the abstract justification of legal obligation, or the historically contingent accounting for legal obligation and the institutional order of our liberal democratic society—we have an account of the legal order or of the collective whole that commits it to respect individual autonomy or a realm of individual liberty that serves the values of self-fulfillment and participation in change. Moreover, this account of the foundational status of this realm of liberty would help explain why utilitarian balancing does not justify limiting first amendment rights.

Of course, other accounts of cultural texts, institutional arrangements, and social practices are possible. And the above argument is surely not as complete as its importance calls for. Nevertheless, without trying to develop further this justification for the centrality of these two values, below I will merely rely on the widely accepted conclusion that *individual self-fulfillment and participation in change are fundamental purposes of the first amendment.*

USES OF SPEECH

Any listing of uses of speech will reflect the perspective and concerns or goals of the examiner. Since there is no limit to possible perspectives and concerns, no natural, stable, or complete categorization is possible. Nevertheless, some consideration of various uses will show something about our unreflective understanding of speech and will exhibit the arbitrariness of too narrow a conception of uses. This examination will also suggest multifarious ways in which speech contributes to the key first amendment values of self-realization and self-fulfillment. Finally, it will suggest further generalizations concerning why and when speech merits special constitutional protection.

A prominent, insightful article by Professor Thomas Scanlon illustrates the common trap of adopting a narrow vision of the uses of speech and writing. Scanlon argued that the acts protected by a doctrine of freedom of expression will be some proper subset of acts of expression, which he defines as "any act that is intended by its agent to communicate to one or more persons some proposition or attitude."[5] Scanlon is right that "acts of expression" as he defines it is "an extremely broad class" and unfortunately he is also probably correct that "almost everyone would agree" that all protected acts of expression will fit into this class.[6] Nevertheless, speech and writing have significant uses that do not fit Scanlon's classification and I will argue that protection should not be limited to this class.

Our tendency to accept Scanlon's emphasis on *acts intended to communicate some proposition or attitude* illustrates the dominance of a marketplace of ideas theory in his and our thinking. But this categorization of protected acts of expression is inadequate in three respects.

First, inclusion of only acts intended to communicate facts or attitudes to others excludes many uses of speech. People continually speak or write without intending any other person to hear their speech or see their writing. These "solitary" uses of speech—to record by keeping a diary, to organize by outlining or cataloging, to understand by problem solving, to amuse or relax by singing or making up a story, to perform a duty by praying, or to direct one's own behavior by writing oneself a note—contribute to self-fulfillment and often to individual or social change. Of course, the government may be less interested in controlling these "solitary" uses of speech than it is in controlling acts of communication, but, if so, this lesser interest relates to a lesser need of protection, not to the proper scope of the first amendment. Moreover, the government sometimes does attempt to control or regulate these solitary uses of speech. For example, the government might try to control some of these solitary uses if it wishes to punish or disempower a prisoner; or if, as in Orwell's *1984*,[7] the government believes that the person's solitary speech is an aspect of, or contributes to, a person's ability or will to resist the government; or if society wants to promote a morality that would be offended by making and viewing, or writing and reading, pornography all within the confines of a person's home;[8] or decides that religious purity must be maintained in the community; or if the government fears that a person's solitary problem solving might lead to dangerous new knowledge or capabilities, like nuclear weapon or genetic research, that the government wants to control or suppress.

Second, many interactive uses of speech—for example, story telling or singing or ceremonial enactments are activities that sometimes have a primary purpose of entertaining or engaging in group activity or diverting the other, a child, for example, from pain or anguish, rather than promoting insight—are better described as the speaker intending to do something.[9] Attempting to force such uses of speech into the category of communicating propositions or attitudes is a possible perspective but generally seems misleading and strained. As Wittgenstein remarked, "the paradox disappears only if we make a radical break with the idea that language always functions in one way, always serves the same purpose: to convey thoughts—which may be about houses, pains, good and evil, or anything else you please."[10]

Third, the notion that a prerequisite of protection is that the speech contain propositions or attitudes directed toward listeners duplicates the marketplace model's emphasis on content as being the important consideration. In contrast, the first amendment values of self-fulfillment and popular participation in change emphasize the speech's *source* in the self, and make the choice of the speech by the self the crucial factor in justifying protection. If, for example, there were good reasons not to view the speech of a corporation as representing the choices of any relevant people within the corporation (an issue to which I will return), then the liberty theory would not protect the speech while the marketplace of ideas theory would, given that the corporate speech communicated facts or values.

In any attempt to describe an alternative to Scanlon's categorization, Wittgenstein's warning should be kept in mind. He wrote:

> But how many kinds of sentence are there? Say assertion, question, and command?—There are countless kinds: *countless different kinds of use of what we call "symbols," "words," "sentences."* And this multiplicity is not something fixed, given once for all; but new types of language, new language-games, as we may say, come into existence, and others become obsolete and get forgotten. . . . Here the term "language-*game*" is meant to bring into prominence the fact that *the speaking of language is part of an activity, or of a form of life. . . .*[11]

Moreover, Wittgenstein could have further observed that the listings or categorizations of uses of language only occur within particular language games, within particular contexts. Here, in this chapter, the task is to find characterizations of uses of language or of forms of life that provide insight into the scope of first amendment protection, not to develop a comprehensive catalogue. This particular task suggests prominence for two categories, self-expressive uses and creative uses. These two uses cut across the communicative/noncommunicative dichotomy and closely correlate with the key first amendment values of self-fulfillment and participation in change.

To engage voluntarily in a speech act is to engage in self-definition or expression. A war protestor may explain that when she chants "Stop This War Now" at a demonstration, she does so without any expectation that her speech will affect the continuance of war or even that it will successfully communicate anything to people in power. Rather, she participates and chants to define herself publicly, partly to define herself to herself, as in opposition to the war. This war protestor provides a dramatic illustration of the importance of this self-expressive use of speech, independent of any expected communication to others, for self-fulfillment or self-realization. More broadly, any time a person engages in chosen, meaningful conduct, whether public or private, the conduct usually expresses and further defines the actor's identity and contributes to his or her self-realization.

Speech is not merely expressive but also can be creative. Most dramatically, the Bible reports: "And God *said*, 'Let there be light;' and there was light."[12] For six days God spoke and named things and by these means created the world. Hannah Arendt claims that, to the ancient Greeks,

> [T]hought was secondary to speech, but speech and action were considered coeval and coequal, of the same rank and the same kind; and ... finding the right words at the right moment, quite apart from the information or communication they may convey, is action. Only sheer violence is mute, and for this reason violence alone can never be great.[13]

And, Arendt argued, "to act. . . means to take an initiative, to begin."[14] Through speech and action new worlds are created—"new" because action, which "may proceed from nowhere," "acts upon beings who are capable of their own actions," and thus "action and reaction among men never move in a closed circle."[15]

The practice of the poet parallels Arendt's description of the Greek emphasis on the creative use of speech. A poem, which "should not mean [b]ut be,"[16] requires no project but instead a "flicker of the soul."[17] Gaston Bachelard, a modern French philosopher, describes the poetic image as "a new being in our language, expressing us by making us what it expresses. . . . Here expression creates being. . . . Through this creativeness the imagining consciousness proves to be, very simply but very purely, an origin."[18]

Although the Bible, the Greeks, and the poets may seem to be rather esoteric authority, more mundane practices equally illustrate the creative use of language. Activities in which the creative use of language is particularly prominent include: (1) making up new rules for a game or practice, as well as the language embodying the new rules; (2) coining a word, forming a new verbal image; (3) writing a poem or a play; (4) "creating" or planning a new strategy; (5) verbally but privately formulating an analysis to "discover" new relationships or possibilities, or problem solving and developing new capabilities in oneself; (6) persuading someone and thereby changing future practice; (7) teaching or developing new capabilities in another; (8) engaging in a dialogue through which both participants gain insights neither possessed before; (9) adopting verbal practices that embody any of the above and thereby creating a new environment. The creative aspect, the new aspect of the world that results, varies in these examples.

But in each case either the speaker or the listener or both possess something new—new images, new capacities, new opportunities, new amusements—that did not exist before and that were created by people's speech. Often the new creation will influence subsequent behavior. And in each case the creation has changed the social world, the world of meanings, opportunities, and restraints, in which people live.

Although the overlap of categorizations is great, self-expressive and creative uses of speech more fully and uniformly promote the two key first amendment values, self-fulfillment and participation in both societal decision making and culture building, than does speech that communicates propositions and attitudes.

First, many *solitary uses* of speech clearly contribute to self-fulfillment. These solitary uses can also contribute to social change. A person's self-analysis of her own character or her design of a plan intended to advance some goal, or her prayer, as well as a person's engagement in singing or drawing, or creating and reading or viewing literature or obscenity for private enjoyment or enrichment, can all be solitary uses of speech that, by empowering or changing or defining the person, can affect the individual's interactions with others and, thereby, change or modify the culture.

Second, communications not specifically intended to communicate propositions or attitudes of the speaker— such as story telling merely meant to entertain the listener, or singing intended merely to show the accomplishments of the singer, or group singing or a ritual performed with words that possibly is intended to maintain group identity or develop group solidarity—may both contribute to self-fulfillment and affect the culture.

Third, the category of self-expressive and creative uses of speech properly excludes some uses that do not promote the key first amendment values but that would be included in Scanlon's marketplace definition. Initially, the broad category of self-expressive acts might appear to include all communications. Nevertheless, to the extent that speech is involuntary, is not chosen by the speaker, the speech act does not involve the *self*-realization or *self*-fulfillment of the speaker. Focusing on the self-expressive uses of speech directs the inquiry toward the responsible source, not the content, of the speech. For example, once a person is employed to say what she does, the speech usually represents not her own self-expression but, at best, the expression of the employer. And if, as I argue in Chapter 9, either competitive market forces or legal requirements force a business enterprise to be profit oriented and to select its speech accordingly, then the enterprise's speech is also not self-chosen. If these claims are right, then from the perspective of protecting self-expressive speech, commercial advertising should not be constitutionally protected despite its communication of propositions, attitudes, or information.

HOW SPEECH OPERATES

The first amendment could not possibly protect all the manifold self-expressive activities, some of which involve violence or coercion, that further an individual's conception of self-fulfillment or that contribute to change. The logic of constitutionally protecting speech relates to combining common-sense notions concerning the importance of speech for furthering certain values and similar notions concerning the method by which speech usually advances those values. In fact, in the next chapter I will argue that the first amendment protects non-verbal, creative, and self-expressive activities when these activities advance first amendment values in a manner relevantly similar to how speech normally advances these values. In this section, however, the concern is to determine what methods or manner of using speech deserve constitutional protection.

Speech, unlike other behavior, is seldom thought of as physically violent or destructive—the shrill voice breaking a glass is an aberrant example not typical of our normal notions of speech use. Similarly, the use of high decibel levels of sound to interfere physically with another's activities belies our characteristic image of speech. Few urge constitutional protection for sheer noise that merely disrupts a meeting.[19]

The childhood denial "sticks and stones may break my bones but names will never hurt me" overstates the insight. All sorts of speech can harm others. Normally, however, speech differs from most other harm-producing conduct in the way it causes harm. Both the amiable interchange that leads to replacing old with new friendships (consider the tort of alienation of affection) and the destructive interpersonal interchange create "harmful" effects by influencing the mind and emotions—the perceptions, feelings, beliefs or understandings—of the listener or, sometimes, of the speaker. Governments' frequent attempts to suppress highly offensive or dangerously persuasive speech typically involve an understandable desire to prevent identifiable harms—harms that are likewise created by the speaker's influence on the mind or emotions of the listener.

Seldom does the government restrict liberty without at least plausible grounds to conclude that the unrestricted behavior could cause some type of harm. Prevention of harm commonly justifies legal restraints. But if the Constitution limits the government's power to restrict people's liberty, then some harms or, at least, some methods of causing harms must not suffice to justify legal restrictions on some harm-causing behavior. This conclusion cannot be controversial. Laws attempt to promote the general good. The Constitution restricts legal choices. These restrictions on law making can only mean that some harm-causing conduct is protected.[20] Thus, under existing doctrine, harms caused by speech normally do not justify a restriction on speech, while harms that result from invading another's area of decision authority (e.g., destruction of another's property or coercing another's behavior) normally justify outlawing the intruding conduct.

Justifications for protecting harm-causing expressive conduct are obviously controversial. Above I argued that the collective must respect the equality and autonomy of individuals. This respect requires limiting the collective's decision-making authority, limits that arguably leave people with the right to cause harms by certain means (speech-caused harms) but not by others. This claim needs elaboration to show how respect for autonomy distinguishes the different methods of causing harms.

The key quality distinguishing most harms caused by protected speech acts from most harms caused by unprotected activities is that speech-caused harms typically occur only to the extent that people "mentally" adopt perceptions or attitudes. Two observations deserve emphasis. First, the speaker's harm-causing speech does not itself interfere with another person's legitimate decision-making authority. At least, this follows as long as the other has no right to decide what the speaker should say or believe. And this assumption that the other has no right to control a person's speech is a necessary consequence of our respecting people's autonomy. Second, outlawing acts of the speaker in order to protect people from harms that result because the listener adopts certain perceptions or attitudes disrespects the responsibility and freedom of the listener.

Both observations follow from our typical concept of the person, which identifies a person, at least in part, with the person's perceptions and feelings. We generally hold a person responsible for actions that are based on the opinions or perceptions the person accepts. In fact, respecting the listener's integrity as an individual normally requires treating the listener as responsible for her conduct unless she has been coerced or forced into the activity.

This perspective on protecting speech suggests the uses that do not merit protection. Of course, care ought to be taken to avoid finding categories of unprotected speech too easily—the fact that speech can cause harm makes for an ever-present possibility of powerful even if unreflective appeals claiming that a particular "harmful" use of speech must fit into some exception to the principle that speech is protected. Nevertheless, the respect-for-autonomy rationale for protecting speech does not apply if the speaker coerces the other or if the speaker physically or otherwise improperly interferes with the other's rights. "When [the listener] does something because of threats, the will of [the threatener] is operating or predominant."[21]

Thus, determining what speech can be banned requires an ability to identify coercive speech.[22] Arguably, a reason for focusing on speech as a specially protected liberty relates to the implicit recognition that speech behavior is normally noncoercive. Speech typically depends for its power on increasing the speaker's own awareness or on the voluntary acceptance of listeners. Nevertheless, some speech can be coercive. But identification of coercive categories of speech requires great care. People constantly invoke loosely formulated or inappropriately broad notions of coercion to justify regulation of various behavior, including speech, of which they disapprove. The inevitable misapplication of this liberty approach to freedom of speech will most likely involve expansive, imprecise notions of coercion—while meaningful limits on government's authority to restrict speech will require a narrow, precise, and defensible concept of coercion that is clearly distinguished from the broader notion of harm. Thus, a digression on the concept of coercion and of threats, an important subclass of coercive acts that must be distinguished from offers or warnings, will clarify the permissible scope of restrictions on speech acts.

In general, a person coercively influences another if (1) she restricts the other to options that are worse than the other had a moral or legitimate right to expect or (2) she employs means that she had no right to use for changing the threatened person's options.[23] Less relevant for the present discussion, socially constructed contexts, as opposed to the acts of a specific person, can coerce a person if that context leaves a person with options worse than the person has a moral or legitimate right to expect. For example, a person who would not have taken religiously unacceptable employment except for a need for minimal subsistence income is properly characterized as being "coerced" into accepting this "wage slavery" if people in her society had a right to expect guarantees of minimal subsistence. The claim of coercion will often be a "contested" claim, with the dispute being, at least implicitly, whether people in her society do have such a right.

Later, examples will clarify the abstract formulation of coercion. Note initially, however, that in the present formulation, coercion relates not to the severity or effectiveness of the pressure or influence applied to a person but to the impropriety of the form of pressure. This formulation requires some method of determining the relevant benchmark of options to which the person has a moral or legitimate right and it requires an identification of improper means. Thus, for present purposes, I have rejected reliance on a more positivist conception of coercion that would use the "normal or expected course of events" or "options to which one has a legal right" as the benchmark for determining whether the person has been made worse off. Using "options that one has a moral or legitimate right to expect" as the benchmark more overtly requires reference to normative considerations.

Of course, either a positivist or normative conception of coercion is possible. People will disagree about which is most useful—as well as about which is most prevalent in "ordinary" discourse. Nevertheless, the normative conception is necessary as long as coercion is used as a critical principle in evaluating either individual actions or the legal and social order. Thus, the following discussion should not be viewed as an attempt to identify the essentially or logically correct notion of coercion but as an elaboration of a conception that hopefully best embodies the features relevant for the discussion of freedom of speech.

Three considerations show the inadequacy of the positivist reliance on normalcy or legality as benchmarks for identifying coercion. First, to play a critical role, coercion must refer to *improper* interferences with another's choices. If the normal conditions are morally objectionable, then a person's reliance on this state of affairs in influencing another's behavior can be coercive. A slave can properly criticize the slave owner's "offer" to allow her to work in the house rather than in the field as coercive—assuming that the slave would not have accepted the offer under just conditions. Certainly, the slave can view herself as coerced when she accepts the offer. A positivist view that this is not coercive because the offer improves the slave's condition, given the existing state of affairs, accepts as a given precisely the condition that the person who calls the offer and the situation "coercive" asserts cannot be accepted.

Second, normality cannot be crucial for defining the benchmark if people have a right to change the normal order. Although many activities that deviate from or change existing practices will be impermissible and coercive, any right to participate in change suggests that other non-normal practices must be viewed as acceptable just as noncoercive and (prohibitable) coercive pressure must be distinguished. For example, if a landlord normally has allowed the tenant to stay without paying rent, to demand that the tenant start paying should not be viewed as coercive *unless* other morally relevant facts show that the tenant had a right to stay without paying or that the landlord did not have a right to demand rent. Similarly, a member of a voluntary association is not being coercive when she applies pressure on existing members by stating that she will change the existing situation (by dropping out of the association) unless the organization adopts certain changes that lead the organization to better conform to her values, possibly to accept members no matter what their race (or the opposite). The key to the conclusion that this pressure is not coercive is the assumption either that in a morally acceptable society a person could not be barred from dropping out of such association when the association does not conform to her values or that, if a morally acceptable society could either allow or not allow such a right, that her society in fact grants her such a right. (This argument assumes that the legitimacy of a society will require that some rights be recognized while leaving many issues to collective choice or practice.)

Third, to the extent that the propriety of outlawing behavior (e.g., speech) turns on whether the behavior is coercive, reliance on law to specify the benchmark would be circular. Suppose Joe tells the Senator that he will continue his protests until the Senator supports the Equal Rights Amendment. And assume that the law can only prohibit coercive protests. Are Joe's protests coercive and, thus, subject to prohibition? The analysis is obviously circular if an answer "yes, the protests are coercive" follows specifically because the protests are legally prohibited. That is, they would be coercive and subject to prohibition because they are prohibited.

This circularity point should not be misunderstood. Often a "threat" will be coercive because of a benchmark established by law. The coerciveness of Theo's statement to Vickie, I will cut and sell the flowers unless you plant a tree, should depend on whether the law has assigned Theo the relevant rights in respect to the flowers. The legal order could either have or not have so assigned the rights. The speech analysis is different because of the implicit underlying normative assumption that respect for individual autonomy requires that rights to speak be assigned to the speaker unless the speech is in some special sense coercive rather than being a manifestation of autonomy. Thus, if freedom of speech is to perform its constitutional (or theoretical) role as a critical principle, the speech's illegality cannot support the view that it is coercive. Only an independent demonstration that the speech is inconsistent with another's autonomy or is not intrinsic to the speakers's autonomy would show that it can properly be outlawed as coercive.

The explanation for the special status of speech rights helps show why speech may be, but why it normally is not, coercive. A person's speech could be coercive of, or an improper interference with, or an injury to others if society could and did give others authority over the speaker's speech—that is, if society could provide that a particular expression by a speaker violates someone else's right to have that expression not spoken. As noted, clearly society can and does choose to create many different types of property rights, that is, it chooses different ways to allocate decision-making authority. Nevertheless, respect for the integrity and autonomy of the individual usually requires, at least for the most part, giving each person at least veto power over the use of her own body, which is the normative premise that connects such disparate principles as the thirteenth amendment's prohibition of involuntary servitude with the right of a woman to seek an abortion.

Similarly, this premise of respect for autonomy leads to the same conclusion concerning a person's control of her own speech. Respect for people as autonomous agents implies that people should be viewed as responsible for, and given maximal liberty in, choosing how to use their bodies and minds to develop and express themselves; and should be given an equal right to try to influence the nature of their collective worlds. Such respect is belied unless each person has a right to decide on and employ speech—and possibly other noncoercive conduct—for realizing substantive values and visions.

The key ethical postulate is that respect for individual integrity and autonomy requires the recognition that a person has the right to use speech to develop herself or to influence or interact with others in a manner that corresponds to her values. At least, this is the ethical postulate of respect for the ethically autonomous individual that this book argues is and should be the foundation of first amendment freedom of speech. Granted this ethical postulate, and since the concept of coercion only has a place within some such ethical order, the use of speech (normally) ought not to be viewed as coercive—even if the person's expression, for example, her racist or sexist speech, reflects and perpetuates an unjust order and affirms or promotes a much more stunted view of the person. Likewise, this same premise, which views people as agents who can either reject or accept views that they hear, implies that a person's speech cannot normally be viewed as improperly interfering with a listener's or third party's proper realm of decision-making authority.

Nevertheless, some speech practices are or can be coercive and, therefore, properly subject to prohibition. Speech used to influence another person may be coercive if the speaker manifestly disrespects and attempts to undermine the other person's will and the integrity of the other person's mental processes. Both the concept of coercion and the rationale for protecting speech draw from the same ethical requirement that the integrity and autonomy of the individual moral agent must be respected. Coercive speech acts typically disregard the ethical principle that, in interactions with others, the actor ought to respect the other's autonomy and integrity as a person. Likewise, the political morality summed up by the first amendment requires governmental respect for individual autonomy. Thus, the first amendment calls for protection of speech that manifests or contributes to the speaker's values or visions—speech which furthers the two key first amendment values of self-fulfillment and participation in change—as long as the speech does not involve violence to or coercion of another.[24] This leaves three types of speech properly subject to legal control: First, there is speech involved in an actual or attempted taking of, or physical injury to, another's person or property. Neither the leader of the bank robbers who only gives orders or the person who says to an associate "shoot him" is protected because her only activity was to engage in speech. Second, there is speech not chosen by the speaker and which, therefore, cannot be attributed to the speaker's manifestation of her substantive values. Chapter 9 will argue that this characterization applies to a properly delineated category of commercial speech. Third, there is speech designed to disrespect and distort the integrity of another's mental processes or autonomy. This encompasses coercive speech, a category that will be further considered here.

This abstract formulation of the third category must be tested in the context of concrete issues. The theory should explain why speech activities such as fraud,[25] perjury, blackmail, espionage, and treason are unprotected. Here, for illustrative purposes, I will focus on only two: (1) blackmail, because of its similarity to presumably protected activities, including whistle blowing (public exposure of others' misdeeds); and (2) espionage, because of its relation to frequently raised first amendment issues concerning the political role of protected speech.

Blackmail, Whistle Blowing, and Coercion

Consider two situations: First, Jane says to Dick, "I will tell the public or the police what you are about to do (or did) unless you give me $1,000." Second, Kira says to Kevin, "I will tell the public or the police if you proceed (or unless you return the money to its owner)." In both cases the speaker "warns" the listener that he will be harmed by public exposure unless he modifies his planned course of action. Moreover, in both cases the speaker may have a right to expose the other. She may have a right to "ruin" the other by informing the public that he is an actual or incipient robber, rapist, or whatever.

The purpose of the "threat" as well as the latter public exposure, if it occurs, differs crucially in the two cases. In the blackmail situation, the response Jane wants from Dick is unrelated to the facts that she might expose. She may have no personal, substantive concern with whether Dick has done or proceeds to do the act she threatens to expose. Jane merely uses her threat of exposure instrumentally to gain some general control over Dick. She has designed her speech as a means to undermine the other's autonomy and get him to act in a manner she chooses. Jane in a sense attempts to make Dick a puppet of her will. Although a speaker has an autonomy-based claim to use her speech to embody and advance her substantive values, for example, by exposure, a speaker has no autonomy claim to power over another. Since in the blackmail situation her values are furthered *only* through gaining power over another, the speech is unprotected.

In contrast, in the second situation, Kira's precise concern is with the act that she threatens to expose. Her speech is designed less to use special knowledge to gain power over the listener than to stop the very activity that could give her this special power.[26] Moreover, the listener's requested response may provide a substitute means that better furthers the same values the speaker would be pursuing by exposure. Thus, the threat is not *merely* an instrumental means of gaining power over the other. Whistle blowing, but not blackmailing, involves using speech directly to make the world correspond to the speaker's substantive values rather than merely to increase the speaker's wealth (or area of decision-making domination) and does so without disrespecting the listener's integrity. Therefore, the whistle blowing threat is a form of action-inducing conduct that directly relates to the first amendment theme of protecting individual liberty. Despite the speaker's intended effect on the listener, the law cannot treat the speech as coercive because the speech involves merely the speaker's exercise of her autonomy in the pursuit of her substantive values.

The above example further illustrates the difference between a liberty theory of the first amendment and most marketplace theories. Marketplace theories typically focus on the content of the speech—that is, whether the expression makes assertions of facts or values that could have relevance to the listener's thinking or decision making. In both whistle blowing and blackmail, the "threat" equally communicates information about the speaker's future plans. Moreover, in both cases the threatened exposure is relevant to the listener as well as to some broader public. In this sense, both arguably communicate information and should be protected.

On the other hand, in both cases the speech is, like other possible action, conduct by means of which the speaker hopes to do something—alter the other's behavior. In both cases, the speaker attempts to apply pressure to get the listener to change his behavior. Moreover, the speaker tries to obtain the change by pressure—not persuasion or conversion. The speaker does not try to change the listener's values or perceptions or capabilities; she only changes the listener's knowledge about the speaker's planned conduct. Thus, possibly both communications would be unprotected as action rather than protected as expression that is part of a marketplace of ideas.

In contrast, for the liberty theory of the first amendment, whether or not the speaker communicates information is not crucial. Speech—stories, song, or other forms of verbally reaching out—that offers a friend comfort and sympathy or diverts the friend from agony is an activity that changes the speaker's and listener's world even if no particular information is communicated. Rather, the liberty theory focuses on the nature of the speaker's acts. The speaker's *method* of having an effect on the world is crucial.

Even if the effect of the act on the other is the same, its point or purpose is quite different when the volleyball player trips over another person's sand castle than when she kicks it down. The character of different threats can similarly differ.

Sometimes the "threat" seeks the listener's help in pursuing the same values that the speaker's threatened exposure itself would further. In these cases, the listener's compliance changes the substantive significance to the speaker of the speaker's threatened exposure. In a sense, the speaker "explains" that her values require her threatened actions, for example, exposure of the listener's intended behavior and that she believes the behavior should only occur, if at all, when publicly exposed. Other times, the effect of the threatened exposure on the listener does not reflect the speaker's direct pursuit of her own values. In these cases, the listener's compliance with the speaker's "request" would not affect the value to the speaker of the threatened exposure. For example, for a blackmailer, since exposure usually has no relation to her substantive values, it is equally without substantive value whether or not the listener does as requested. Rather than being the speaker's pursuit of her own values, the threat *merely* reflects her use of her resources (e.g., a capacity to expose) to gain power over the other. Thus, although the informative content of the speech and its effect on the listener may be similar in these two cases, the manner in which the speaker pursues her ends differs. The liberty model assumes that people must be able to use speech as part of the activity of pursuing or implementing their substantive values. The effect on others occurs because of this pursuit in the whistle-blowing case, and, therefore, this manner of affecting others should be a protected aspect of the speaker's liberty.

Despite my assumption that these conclusions concerning whistle blowing and blackmail depend on the liberty theory, Professor Kent Greenawalt reaches very similar conclusions although he assumes that the first amendment primarily applies to assertions of fact and value.[27] This focus on assertions of fact and value is much more resonant with marketplace of ideas theories than with the liberty theory. Possibly it would be best merely to accept the relative congruence as evidence of the correctness of the conclusions. Still, despite his claims, my tentative view is that Professor Greenawalt's analysis really implicitly relies, or needs to rely, more on an individual liberty or autonomy analysis than he realizes.

Greenawalt contrasts assertions of fact and value with situation altering utterances—and assumes that the reasons for protecting speech apply primarily to the first category. This approach makes sense from the perspective of marketplace of ideas theories. Assertions of fact and value constitute expression to be tested, debated, and revised in the marketplace while situation-altering utterances are more a matter of action—doing something. In contrast, from the perspective of individual liberty or autonomy, Greenawalt's assumption is wrong— the first amendment should generally protect people's expressive activities that alter the world in which they live. According to the liberty theory, an important aspect of the right of free speech is to change the world. The relevant issue relates to *how* the speaker alters the situation—she or he cannot do so in a coercive manner or by invasions of other people's realm of decision-making authority.

Implicitly, Greenawalt may agree. His development of a strangely narrow concept of situation-altering speech roughly corresponds to the liberty theory's category of unprotected means. Nevertheless, I will suggest that his development of the notion of situation altering is itself internally confused precisely because of its tie to the marketplace of ideas focus on assertions of fact and value rather than the liberty theory's focus on coercion.

Consider the following paradigm situation: *A* tells *B*, "I will do X unless you do Y." According to Greenawalt, sometimes this will be a warning threat, which is not situation altering and is covered by the free speech principle and sometimes it will be a manipulative threat not so covered. It is a presumptively protected warning threat when *A* intends to do X unless *B* does Y, even in the absence of having made the statement. *A* would go to town to get paint, unless someone gives her paint, even in the absence of the threat: "I'll go to town to get paint unless you give me some paint." In this case, Greenawalt says that for *A* to do X, go to town to get some paint, is a "natural" response to *B*'s failure to give her paint and that for *A* to communicate this merely communicates a fact. In most of Greenawalt's examples of warning threats, when *A* would have done X anyway, the reason *A* gives *B* an "option" is that *A* doing X and *B* doing Y will be alternative, although not necessarily equally effective or desirable, methods of furthering *A*'s substantive values. For example, *A*'s desire to end corruption is furthered either by *B*'s refraining from corrupt acts or by *A*'s exposing *B*'s corruption. *A*'s desire that *B* end a secretive extramarital relation is advanced either by telling *B*'s spouse or by *B* stopping. Thus, those threats that I argue are noncoercive and protected (e.g., whistle blowing) are roughly equivalent to

Greenawalt's protected, warning threats, which merely communicate the speaker's "natural response."

In contrast, sometimes A will do X only because of having made the threat of doing X and only to make good on the threat. This constitutes, in Greenawalt's terminology, an "unnatural" response and involves a "manipulative threat." According to Greenawalt, only these manipulative threats are situation altering. A is likely to engage in the unnatural act only because of having made the threat. Thus, unlike warning threats, which only give the listener information about the world she faces, the manipulative threat itself actually changes that world.

I agree both that Greenawalt's category of "manipulative threats" are situation altering and that these threats should normally be unprotected. Inevitably, manipulative threats will correspond to my category of instrumental threats designed solely to gain power over the person threatened. Nevertheless, Greenawalt's explanation for why manipulative threats and only manipulative threats should be unprotected is strained.

Greenawalt's conception of situation altering is very constricted. A situation is comprised of many aspects including: perceptions and expectations (which A changes when whistle blowing or making a protected "warning threat"), capacities for action or thought (which A can change by teaching B or which dialogue can change for both A and B), the likelihood of a person's engaging in a certain behavior (which A changes in respect to B's behavior by making a protected, warning threat), opportunities for enjoyment or for other activities (which A may create, to use a different type of example, by writing and publishing a popular song or story or instruction manual), emotions (which A can change in B by offering verbal comfort or distractions), as well as the likelihood that the listener will be faced with particular behavior of the speaker (which A can change by threatening an unnatural act, that is, by making a manipulative threat.) *In each case*, the speech changes the world. In at least a reasonably plausible interpretation of the term, the speech alters the situation. If only the manipulative threat should be unprotected speech, this is not because it is the only speech that is situation altering but because it is the only speech that uses an unprotected means to accomplish the alteration.

Thus, since protected speech alters situations, situation altering cannot be key—unless Greenawalt's narrow definition of situation altering can be defended. Moreover, unprotected manipulative threats almost always assert or communicate both values (the speaker's desires) and facts (e.g., the speaker's plans).[28] If reasons for protecting expression apply primarily to assertions of fact and value, Greenawalt needs an explanation for why the added fact that the speech is situation altering should mean that these assertions of facts and values do not count under the rationale for protecting speech. In other words, Greenawalt's key categories, threats of natural responses and threats of unnatural responses, correspond respectively to properly protected and properly unprotected speech; but the analytic devices suggested by marketplace theories—distinguishing assertions of facts and values from situation altering utterances—do not lead to or explain these categories.

Greenawalt's categories can, however, be explained. The reason for denying protection to a manipulative threat is not that it does not assert facts and values

—it does. Nor that it is situation altering—lots of protected speech is. Rather, the relevant difference lies in the coercive manner in which the manipulative threat alters the situation. Individual liberty does not extend to this manner of altering situations—does not extend to merely instrumentally valued acts aimed at subverting the autonomy of others.

An additional ambiguity in Greenawalt's analysis further illustrates the inadequacy of its roots in a marketplace of ideas perspective. Protection of assertions of fact or value makes analysis of some situations difficult. Should the speech be protected when it communicates an intent to engage in a natural response unless the listener adopts an entirely unrelated response—for example, paying money? My concern is how to treat, and whether to distinguish, the following two types of threats made by a person who personally disapproves of corruption and is inclined to report any corruption of which she is aware. She might say: "I will report your corruption unless you stop"; or "I will report your corruption unless you pay me $100."

The liberty theory would treat the two differently. The appropriate characterization of a stated willingness to change a natural course of conduct on condition that the listener makes a desired response is dependent on the relation between the desired response and the values implicit in the speaker's "natural" course of conduct. In both cases above, I assume that the speaker substantively opposes corruption and that the threatened exposure would further this value. From the speaker's perspective, for the listener to stop engaging in corruption substitutes for the exposure, with both serving the same value. The threat of exposure does not involve the speaker trying to gain power over the listener except in respect to advancing the specific substantive values that the speaker could properly advance with her own speech without applying pressure on the listener. This correspondence between the listener's response and the exposure is reflected in the fact that for the listener to stop engaging in corruption changes (i.e., reduces) the value to the speaker of the exposure she had threatened.

In contrast, in the second situation, the listener paying $100 does not advance the speaker's substantive interest in stopping corruption. The payment does not change the value of exposure to the speaker. Thus, in this case the speaker uses the possibility of nonexposure purely instrumentally, that is, to gain power over the listener. Although a person's use of his or her resources to gain power over a listener is often perfectly proper (market exchanges are not intrinsically evil), respect for individual autonomy does not require protection of purely instrumental attempts to gain power over others.

Greenawalt reaches the same conclusion. Although he notes that the communication about the natural response is an assertion of fact, he concludes that a situation-altering element predominates because the aim is to get the listener to act in a way that will lead the speaker to forgo her natural response—which, however, is also true of protected warning threats—and because here the expressed willingness to forgo the natural response is manipulative.[29] Moreover, this conclusion is supported by Greenawalt's conclusion that offers and agreements are normally situation altering and, therefore, unprotected[30]—a conclusion that, at least as Greenawalt broadly states it, would be rejected by a liberty theory.[31]

Nevertheless, despite Greenawalt's agreement with the conclusion reached by the liberty theory, it is not clear that his general approach unambiguously supports his conclusion. First, the speaker who says, "I will tell unless you pay me," only communicates current plans and makes the listener aware of her willingness, which presumably existed prior to and independently of the communication, to modify those "natural" plans for a desired response. Thus, the speaker merely asserts facts and, except for the listener's new perception of available options, does not alter in any way the listener's situation.

Another way to see how the situation has not been changed is to note that even if the speaker who naturally reports corruption had not made the statement, "I will report unless you give me $100," the listener, who knows of the speaker's typical natural response, may say: "I will pay you $100 not to report my corruption." The same situation has been arrived at without the speaker having altered the situation by her speech. Thus, in the situation where she does speak, the speech merely informs the other of the speaker's disposition to accept money in exchange for a certain forbearance. Surely, here, assertions of fact and value predominate.[32] This does not involve, as Greenawalt says of manipulative threats, "the creation of prospective harmful consequences in order to achieve one's objective."[33]

In other words, if I read him correctly, Greenawalt agrees with the liberty theory that the threat "I'll engage in my natural act unless you pay me $100" is not protected. Nevertheless, both the statement about the natural act and the one about a disposition to forgo in exchange for money appear to be mere assertions of fact and, therefore, Greenawalt should argue that the statement is protected. Moreover, the speaker is not creating harmful consequences for the listener *by means of her speech*—thus, again, Greenawalt should not find the speech to be situation altering. That is, his analysis opposes his conclusion.

The problem, I think, lies in the inadequacy of the categories of communicating something versus doing something that are deeply embedded in the marketplace-of-ideas theory of speech. From the liberty perspective, almost any speech can be, as informative speech is often intended to be, situation altering. Still, both the warning of a natural response and the statement of a willingness to forgo a natural response[34] also seem genuinely communicative of information[35]—and, on a marketplace theory, should be protected. The real objection, if there is one, to the threat "I'll tell unless you pay" relates to the speaker's purely instrumental attempt to use the threat as a means to gain power over the other. Although a speaker has a general autonomy claim in respect to pursuing her substantive values by exposing facts about the world, she does not have any general claim to be able to exercise power over others. Greenawalt's conclusion, so hard to explain on his own terms, may reflect his implicit agreement with the liberty theory that *the way* speech changes the world is crucial.[36]

Espionage

Espionage—at least secret transmission to a foreign nation of information relating to the security of this nation—presents, for me, a difficult issue. The speaker uses speech (or writing) to change the world in a desired fashion. Creative uses of speech usually should be protected. Moreover, the effect of espionage may be the same as the properly protected act of publishing classified, previously secret, information in a newspaper.[37] The foreign enemy may find the newspaper publication as useful as the secret deliveries of information to its agents. And normally a speaker's choice of audience, or its size, should not affect the speaker's first amendment rights. Speech directed toward a large audience, no audience, or a small, carefully selected audience, may equally contribute to the speaker's self-fulfillment or participation in change.

Professor Emerson takes as a key reason for denying protection that "espionage [takes] place in the context of action"; that espionage usually "consists in conveying information concerning military secrets and would fall within the system of military operations" and always "involves aiding a foreign country." Therefore, he concludes, even if espionage is "expression," it "is not that form of domestic, civilian expression that is embraced within the system of freedom of expression."[38] Emerson's readers may be inclined to agree but still wish for more of an explanation for why the first amendment does not protect foreign-oriented, military-related expression.

An analogy will clarify the picture. Individuals as well as the press constantly communicate information that they think ought to be public and could be used for proper purposes. Frequently, these communicators are aware that the information may also be used for improper purposes—but that does not and should not make them responsible for the improper use. Normally, the first amendment should protect publishing the layout and security system of a bank even though the publisher knows that a bank robber might use this information in a robbery attempt. Alternatively, in the context of carrying out a bank robbery, one participant's sole role might be to inform associates about the bank's security and layout. This individual's only participation in the bank robbery would be this informative speech, but her speech would be part of the attempt to employ illegal force to invade and steal another's property. If a robbery resulted, this participant would not be constitutionally protected.[39]

Significant aspects of the relations between nations involve both the threatened and actual use of violent force. First amendment liberty does not protect a person's knowing attempt to aid either another person or a country in the application of violent force. Engaging in military-related espionage resembles supplying plans to fellow bank robbers. The effect, which also might result from a newspaper article, is not sufficient to characterize the behavior. The first amendment should not protect espionage only because, and only to the extent that, the prosecuting country can reasonably conclude that information gathered through espionage increases the coercive power of another country and because the purpose of the criminalized activity is to have that effect. The first amendment extends protection until the person's speech becomes merely the person's method of involvement in a coercive or violent project. Espionage often is such a project.

Thus, Emerson's basic conclusion seems correct—but this focus on protected liberty versus unprotected coercion suggests that the first amendment places greater limits on permissible definitions of espionage than are apparent in Emerson's conclusory categorization.[40] Moreover, this focus would protect speech that is currently outlawed by federal law, which prohibits giving information that could be injurious to the security of the United States (even if the information could also be valuable for purposes of public debate and decision making within the United States) not only when it is given to enemy agents but also when given to any unauthorized party, including the press.[41]

Although my focus in this and other sections has been on the speaker, communications are also used for many diverse purposes by the listener. Without analyzing these uses, I merely assume for now that the broad categories of listener's uses will resemble speaker's uses and will be protected to the same extent. Nevertheless, differing first amendment theories will each have a characteristic justification for, and interpretation of, listeners' rights. A brief digression on these interpretations and the different constitutional conclusions that different theories support may help clarify my analysis.

In the classic marketplace model, the listener's formal right is equal to the speaker's. The government must not interfere with communications between a willing speaker and willing listener. This conclusion, which mostly corresponds to the case law holdings,[42] is also implied by the liberty theory.

Nevertheless, the rationale of the classic marketplace model's protection is the interest in the listener's receipt of information. The first amendment provides protection so that people will have the information they need for the thoughtful pursuit of truth or for intelligent decision making. Given this rationale, the argument easily collapses into a market failure theory that would recognize affirmative claims to get "needed" information that otherwise would not be readily available. In the market failure version, listeners would have an independent right to know, which presumably could be asserted against an unwilling speaker, against the government, or against a government restraint of an unprotected speaker.[43] This market failure analysis will raise problems that are similar to those described in Chapter 2, problems that would include the necessity to balance the interest in the production and receipt of information against other legitimate governmental interests. Moreover, any right to receive information would create conflicts with liberty, for example, the desire to remain silent, and with informational privacy.

The liberty theory does not assume that the first amendment could or should presume to guarantee adequate information. Rather, it protects nonviolent and noncoercive methods of obtaining as well as imparting information. The listener, like the speaker, uses speech for self-realization or to promote change. These uses provide the basis of the listener's constitutional right. But the listener does not have a general claim for societal informational allocations—for example, for the "wealth" that corresponds to unencumbered access to any desired information.[44] The listener cannot demand that a person speak who is unwilling to. Moreover, *if* the government can, consistent with the required respect for liberty, restrict someone's speech—for example, the speech of a prisoner or of the government's file clerk who possesses confidential personnel records or of a commercial corporation—the listener has no affirmative constitutional right to override the restriction.[45] Although a listener's right to receive information would advance the worth of the listener's liberty, it does so in roughly the same way as any allocation of resources to the listener—allocations that the first amendment also does not mandate.

Within the liberty theory, the listener does, however, have a right to demand that the government not prohibit the listener from receiving or using otherwise available information. Either restrictions aimed at the listener's receipt or (non-commercial) use of information must be defended as not really interfering with the listener's self-realizing activities—a consideration that may explain part of the first amendment basis of copyright law's "fair use" exception.[47] Or restrictions must be justified by some special characteristic of the listener—for example, the government often claims, and *might* be able to show, that children or prisoners or soldiers have diminished constitutional rights.

Thus, from the perspective of the liberty theory, both speakers and listeners have separate constitutional claims. However, if in the particular context the restricted party does not have a valid constitutional claim, the effect of the restriction on the other party—for example, a listener's access to information or a speaker's access to an audience—does not justify a challenge to the regulation. The constitutional analysis must first determine specifically who the law restricts—the speaker or the listener. The lack of the marketplace's instrumental objective means that only a right of persons specifically restricted justify invalidating the restriction.

Press reporting of criminal trials provides an obvious context for applying this analysis. The press, as listener, may have no first amendment access right to restricted information. Even a contrary view, if based on reasoning that treats the courtroom, like the streets and parks, as an arena historically held in trust for particular first amendment activities, is less a general listener's right to information claim than a time, place, and manner type argument,[47] which will be discussed in Chapter 8. However, if the press "hears," the government cannot prohibit the speaker's use (the press's publication) of the restricted information.[48]

Likewise, if commercial speech were unprotected, the government could prohibit the druggist from advertising its prices but, as Justice Rehnquist pointed out, the state could not and did not prohibit the consumer from hearing or receiving price information. The information that the druggist could not place in an advertisement could be reported to the consumer by newspapers or consumer guides, for example.[49] This example should suggest how the speaker and listener have separate, even if normally overlapping, liberty claims. The constitutional analysis must always focus on whether the party whom the law restricts has a constitutionally based liberty claim that is infringed.

This focus on each participant's liberty interest and on the values of self-fulfillment and participation in cultural change alters, and sometimes simplifies, the analysis of some traditional first amendment issues. For example, as noted in Chapter 1, marketplace of ideas theories do not provide a convincing justification for protecting obscenity. Pornography may have more to do with ribald entertainment than with robust debate. If pornography degrades sexual intimacy or contributes to the subordination of women it does so more by being an undesirable activity and a corrupting experience, not by being an argument. From the perspective of the liberty theory, however, pornographic communications, or even pornographic materials produced and pursued by a solitary individual, contribute—whether in a good or bad fashion—to building the culture. As

Douglas pointed out, materials that most people view as pornographic may play an important role in some people's self-fulfillment and self-expression. Even if obscene publications do not contribute to the marketplace of ideas, they promote these key first amendment values. Therefore, the first amendment should protect the listener's or reader's interest in obscenity.[50]

Complicated problems remain. This chapter, however, should have clarified the general approach to determining what and why speech should receive constitutional protection.[51] Speech is protected because, without disrespecting the autonomy of other persons, it promotes both the speaker's self-fulfillment and the speaker's ability to participate in change. This leads to the conclusion that, as long as speech represents the freely chosen expression of the speaker, depends for its power on the free acceptance of the listener, and is not used in the context of a violent or coercive activity, freedom of speech represents a charter of liberty for noncoercive action.

4

Protection of Action

Literalism loses force when virtually all commentators concede that the first amendment does not protect all speech. If literalism is rejected and some speech is not protected, then an obvious possibility is that some nonverbal activity should be protected. If some speech is not like speech, some nonspeech may be like it—that is, it may be relevantly similar to speech from the perspective of the reasons for protecting speech and for distinguishing protected from unprotected speech. Thus, unsurprisingly, both courts and scholars recognize that some nonverbal behavior, like flying a red flag,[1] should be protected. Still, no agreement exists on criteria for identifying protected nonverbal behavior.

I think, however, that a persuasive argument for protection of conduct could be made by showing that: (1) the conduct is expressive and furthers key first amendment values; (2) it promotes first amendment values in a manner relevantly similar to the way protected verbal conduct promotes these values; (3) its protection is essential for an adequate realization of these values; and (4) principled lines or doctrines can identify both the appropriately protected conduct and the appropriate forms of protection. My discussion will attempt to meet these four requirements.

THE INADEQUATE EXPRESSION-ACTION DICHOTOMY

Professor Emerson's approach to delineating the scope of protection relies on a fundamental distinction between "expression" and "action,"[2] a categorization that "must be guided by consideration of whether the conduct partakes of the essential qualities of expression or action, that is, whether expression or action is the dominant element."[3] Emerson gives little specific guidance as to these "essential qualities" other than to explain that "[t]he concept of expression must be related to the fundamental purposes of the system [of freedom of expression] and the dynamics of its operation."[4]

If Emerson's approach meets the four criteria suggested above, my present inquiry can come to an end. Unfortunately, neither common sense nor the purposes of the system of freedom of expression work to distinguish between the "essential qualities" of expression and action. Clearly, the four central values of the first amendment set forth by Emerson, or the two key ones, self-fulfillment

70

and participation in change, can be, and frequently are, furthered by many types of conduct—including violent, coercive action that is properly subject to collective control. The assassination of either the President or an abusive lover can be expressive and contribute to change. Thus, in themselves, these purposes of the system cannot distinguish protected expression from unprotected action.

Common sense operates less to divide the world of behavior objectively between expression and action than to indicate the perspective of the person doing the dividing. If the distinction is between "expressing" and "doing," most conduct falls into both categories. Most consciously undertaken actions are at least self-expressive; and many—a political assassination, a hair style, a knife placed behind another's back—can be primarily intended to communicate something to others. Contrarily, verbal conduct usually does something. A speaker may be described as composing a poem, commanding the troops, testing the student, creating a mood, threatening an enemy, or making a promise or contract.[5] The observer can choose to focus on either what is done (other than expressing) or what is expressed. The choice of focus will usually be both purposeful and subjective. Either cultural or personal idiosyncrasy, values or whims or habits, or purposes of the description, but not logic or objective analysis, will determine the choice.[6] Sometimes a person might "give comfort" to a friend or to an enemy (of the state). The comfort could consist of various types of conduct—delivering a speech on domestic or foreign radio, providing medical supplies or medical attention, giving sanctuary. In each case, the activity could be viewed as expressive or as doing something. If the constitution protects expression but not action, the determination of which element dominates in acts that "give comfort to an enemy" will likely depend on whether the interpreter believes the acts should be protected, not on the essential nature of the conduct as expression or action. Thus, neither purposes of the first amendment nor common-sense identification of essential qualities work to distinguish expression and action.

In addition to not working, there are other objections. Since both verbal and nonverbal conduct advance first amendment values, the purpose of the distinction is unclear. Moreover, only an extremely crabbed reading of other clauses of the first amendment will be consistent with implementing an expression-action dichotomy. If religion plays a significant role in a person's life, its *free exercise* normally will require doing or abstaining from certain conduct. Likewise, people typically assemble and associate to multiply their power and to do something.[7]

Even if Emerson's "expression-action" dichotomy is not very helpful, his highly perceptive analyses of concrete situations are. These analyses, however, frequently appear to make a different distinction: whether or not the conduct is, or is intended to be, coercive or physically injurious to another. All Emerson's examples of unprotected conduct, "action," involve coercion or injury to or physical interference with another person or damage to physical property. These unprotected acts cause harm in a manner quite different from the way protected conduct causes harm. The harm "caused" by protected conduct typically results from the assimilation of messages by, and sometimes from the subsequent actions of, an independent agent, the listener.

For example, Emerson says about meetings and assemblies:

> [A]ll nonverbal [as well as verbal] conduct that is an integral part of assembly
> would normally be considered "expression.".... On the other hand, the use of
> physical force or violence, against person or property, would be considered
> "action." . . . Disruption of a meeting by moving about *or making noise* must
> also be counted as "action."[8]

These examples illustrate that speaking (if speaking includes loud, disruptive
chanting and yelling) can be "action" and that active conduct can be "expression." Protected nonverbal conduct may consist of doing things—setting up the
meeting hall, climbing onto the podium, gathering together and occupying space.
The unprotected loud disruptive chanting may be expressive and may further
some people's self-fulfillment or promote change. Neither the abstract character
of the behavior nor the key first amendment values guide Emerson's categorization. Rather, the most apparent distinction is that "action" involves coercive
or physically interfering conduct.

Expressive political protests sometimes involve acts of physical obstruction
or property damage like lying down in front of troop trains, blocking traffic in a
city, or pouring blood over files. Emerson argues that these must be considered
"action" and that to characterize them as "expression" would destroy the distinction between "expression" and "action."[9] Neither the physical activity nor
the motives of the actor distinguish these "action" cases from draft-card burning, which Emerson characterizes as expression. Rather, Emerson classifies the
first examples of civil disobedience as "action" because the "[c]ivil disobedience
attempts to achieve results through a kind of *coercion or pressure.*"[10]* However,
burning a draft card, unlike failing to carry one,[11] does not involve coercing or
directly injuring or physically obstructing any person or government activity.
This fact apparently explains why Emerson concludes that the expression element clearly predominates in draft-card burning.[12]

Emerson finds "a fundamental difference between most labor picketing and
most nonlabor picketing."[13] He points out that the "labor picket line is . . . not
so much a rational appeal to persuasion as a signal for the application of immediate and enormous economic leverage, based upon an already prepared position."[14] Labor and nonlabor picketing may involve the same physical acts, but
the context is dramatically different. Nonlabor picketing is typically "directed
much more to the general public than to their own members. . . . [It] is a call to
reason, not the application of *economic coercion*, and as such must be classified
as expression."[15] How the conduct achieves the actor's desired results is crucial.
The nonlabor picketing may inform people, may change public opinion, and this
may result in the public bringing pressure on people to change their behavior.
Still, none of these activities, including, it seems, the pressure involved in people's decisions not to associate, interferes with anyone's rights. As the liberty
theory makes clear, pressure is not the equivalent of coercion. Thus, although a
marketplace of ideas theory could not justify protecting action aimed at achiev-

---

*Emerson does not sharply distinguish between pressure and coercion, although some
behavior that he would protect, like the refusal to associate involved in nonlabor boycotts,
clearly involves pressure.

ing change not through persuasion but through pressure created by "'threats' of 'social ostracism, vilification, and traduction,'"[16] Emerson is right that the first amendment should protect both speech and noncoercive conduct that induces this public response.[17] Even though public pressure is a "very powerful weapon," the Court properly protects such pressure.

Although the issues examined above deserve more careful analysis, in each case Emerson would protect the expressive conduct unless it was coercive or a physical interference. This interpretation of Emerson's examples suggests a surprisingly broad scope of protection. Emerson's examples indicate that the relevant question is *how the conduct advances the key first amendment values.* Expressive conduct that advances the actor's values should be protected unless it is "coercive," physically injurious, or intended to be improperly obstructionist. Unfortunately, application of this maxim is difficult, but giving it systematic, operational content must be attempted.

INTERFERENCE WITH THE RIGHTS OF OTHERS

The logic of Emerson's examples suggests John Stuart Mill's conclusions concerning liberty in general (as opposed to Mill's special defense of freedom of speech). Mill argued:

> [T]he sole end for which mankind are warranted, individually or collectively, in interfering with the liberty of action of any of their number is self-protection. . . . [T]he only purpose for which power can be rightfully exercised over any member of a civilized community, against his will, is to prevent harm to others. . . . The only part of the conduct of anyone for which he is amenable to society is that which concerns others.[18]

Despite the widespread appeal of Mill's argument, it lacks criteria for determining when a person's behavior "harms" others or when a person's manner of acting "concerns others." If "feeling harmed" or having one's interactions with others unfavorably "affected" count as criteria for "harm" or for being properly "concerned," then any action, no matter how privately undertaken, can be of concern to others, can harm others. Both the racist insult and telling the end of the movie can harm the listener. Libel or winning the listener's romantic affections can harm a third party. In fact, any speech that influences a listener can cause harm to a third party who does not like the change in the listener. Moreover, given that a person's private as well as public activities influence, develop, or "change" that person's personality or capacities or inclinations, and given that a person's personality and capacities affect that person's interactions with others, a person's private, solitary activities can cause frustration of others' desires (i.e., may "harm" them). Even a person's private yoga exercises or obscenity readings contribute to the culture and affect interpersonal relations in ways that may lessen some people's opportunities to realize their desires. If any expressive conduct is to be protected against plausible legislative judgments that a prohibition would promote the general welfare, harm to others cannot be the touchstone. Any general argument for protecting a realm of liberty must show that either certain harms or certain ways of causing harms cannot justify certain restrictions on liberty.

The last chapter argued that neither law nor custom could adequately define the benchmark for identifying coercive threats. They likewise do not provide an adequate guide for distinguishing prohibitable from unprohibitable harms. Law and custom are inadequate guides precisely because they do not provide critical principles. Even if both Mill and Emerson failed to develop the needed critical principles, they both recognized the need for such principles to delineate limits on the proper use of law and to define a proper realm of protected liberty. To construct useful critical principles, two distinctions are needed.

Rules that directly prevent a person from fulfilling her desires can be divided into two categories.[19] First are rules that restrict a person's liberty by giving to another the opportunity or decision authority the person wants for herself. For example, Tony's desire to drive this car may be frustrated by the rules that make Pat the owner. I will call these "allocation rules." Second are rules that deny a certain decision authority or opportunity to all people—at least, until the rule is changed. For example, a law might say that no one shall possess pornography. I will call these "general prohibitions."

The distinction between allocation rules and general prohibitions is likely to be unfamiliar—and must be carefully distinguished from the more familiar, but for first amendment purposes, less important distinction between criminal and civil law. Both criminal and civil laws protect allocations—"this is Pat's car." Likewise, either criminal or civil laws can be used to enforce a general prohibition—possession of pornography could make a person either civilly or criminally liable. Forbidding theft is an allocation rule to the extent that the owner can give the object to the would-be thief. Likewise, laws against murder or nonconsensual sex are allocation rules while laws against suicide, statutory rape, or fornication are general prohibitions.

Mechanical, conceptual distinctions will necessarily fail to reflect life's fluid circumstances. They will therefore necessarily fail to be unambiguous embodiments of value premises. Nevertheless, the distinction between allocation rules and general prohibitions highlights a feature of rules that is particularly relevant from a perspective that emphasizes liberty. Although a specific individual may be equally prevented from engaging in a desired act because of a lack of resources (a consequence of allocation rules) or because of a general prohibition of the activity, the two types of rules have dramatically different relations to liberty. Allocation rules do not eliminate individual decision-making authority. Either they allow a person to undertake a desired act or, to the extent that the activity involves another person or resources allocated to another person, allocation rules allow the person to undertake the act if the person receives cooperation or authorization from the other—Pat can let Tony drive the car.

Two people cannot simultaneously engage in mutually exclusive uses of space or objects. This inherent possibility of conflict—a problem engendered by the inherent limit on available resources (scarcity)—creates the *necessity* of at least customary or implicit allocation rules or practices to determine where authority resides. Allocation rules can grant decision-making authority on numerous bases. The allocation can be to anyone strong enough to undertake the act, to the first-come, to the person with the greatest need, or to a person who has received by gift or purchase or devise an exclusive, transferable right to make a large set of decisions relating to some object. Even anarchy (no rules) is an allocation rule of a sort. Allocation rules do not eliminate decision-making authority or liberty; they merely locate it. All allocation rules serve some values more than others and different allocation rules will serve different values and benefit different people. Still, the inevitability of some allocation practices means that restrictions on choice resulting from allocation rules are an inherent feature of social life. From a formal perspective—that is, treating the decision-making authority as the same in whosever hands it is—allocation rules do not limit liberty. Even substantively, this type of limit on liberty is inherent for life in a social world.

The formal concept of liberty value embodied in the first amendment places few restrictions on the state's power to choose among allocation rules. The state is always deciding to give property or opportunities to one person rather than another. It must do so since it inevitably must determine the content of property, tort, or contract rules. Only two significant first amendment constraints on state choice of allocation rules exist. First, only rarely and in limited contexts can the state give one person an original right to decide what another person must do or say or not say.[20] Second, in some contexts (e.g., in respect to public forums) the state may be obliged to respect some neutrality criteria[21] in making allocations that promote private parties' opportunity or ability to express themselves. The state also may be required to guarantee some minimum level of opportunity for expressive activities, but, like most constraints placed on the state's choice among allocation rules, this allocation requirement may be best derived from the fourteenth amendment notion that the state must treat and respect people as equals.[22]

General prohibitions are more problematic from a perspective of liberty. They do not allocate decision-making authority but deny authority to all individuals as individuals. General prohibitions say: "No one (or everyone) shall do X"—for example, no one shall read pornography, pollute the air, commit suicide, fix prices, engage in sodomy, create a fire hazard, or advocate communism. This form of restriction is frequently more objectionable than the form imposed by allocation rules. Unlike allocation rules, there is no logical necessity for general prohibitions. Rather than say, "no one can do 'X'," it is always possible to identify someone who gets to decide whether to do 'X.' By excluding everyone from making certain decisions, general prohibitions limit individual choice more than allocation rules do. If liberty is thought of as a pie containing all possible individual choices, allocation rules divide the pie, while general prohibitions typically reduce the size of the pie—although the majority presumably finds this reduced pie sweeter than the larger one.

General prohibitions let the majority directly control minorities. Allocation rules allow both the majority and minority to use whatever resources they have in ways they desire. Allocation rules define the decision-making authority that people bring to both egotistic projects and interpersonal cooperation, while general prohibitions restrict both individual and cooperative initiatives. Some general prohibitions ban substantively valued behavior, unnecessarily restricting opportunities for self-fulfilling activities. Moreover, by completely denying the opportunity to engage in novel or disapproved activities in which new logics or perspectives or values could gain coherence, general prohibitions can drastically limit the possibility of popular participation in change. In other words, general prohibitions unnecessarily and purposively restrict conduct that may be self-expressive and, therefore, unnecessarily limit opportunities for self-realization and self-determination. For these reasons, I conclude that many general prohibitions violate the first amendment.

Even if the point of the first amendment is to prohibit unnecessary restraints on self-expressive behavior, the argument above needs further elaboration. Even if general prohibitions, unlike allocation rules, are an avoidable type of restraint on liberty, society may conclude that they are "necessary," or at least useful, for creating the type of world that society as a whole wants. This amounts to a claim about substantive liberty and self-determination. Achievement of some aims requires group action, for example, group norms. Prohibitions on air pollution are only one of many general prohibitions that help create a favored type of world.

Before rebutting typical justifications for general prohibitions, I want more directly to explain their objectionable nature.

First, as noted earlier, respect for individual liberty and for autonomous self-determination calls both for collective, democratic decision making and for limits on that decision making. Some constitutive aspects of the social world and some human projects necessarily reflect collective practices or decisions. Choice or acceptance of these features of the social world by means of majority-rule-based processes provides for potentially equal input from people and respects people's appropriate interest in self-determination. Other aspects of the social world could reflect either certain collective rules (e.g., general prohibitions) or individual choices within some constitutive framework (e.g., within a framework of allocation rules). In the latter cases, individual choice leads to creation of a collective world by means of the summation of individually chosen practices, which amounts to a form of "behavioral voting." In the right contexts, this behavioral voting is preferable to majority rule procedures from the perspective of respect for liberty. Majorities can simply reject minorities' preferred outcomes. Loser's preferences need not be embodied in final results at all. In contrast, behavioral voting results in a collective world that by summing everyone's chosen practices reflects each person's contribution. It thereby arguably gives greater respect and more equal respect to people's different values and choices. Also, participation in creating the society by doing things, practicing one's values, and changing only in response to persuasive arguments or new conditions, manifests an arguably better, more vital image of people and a more meaningful involvement in self-determination and self-realization. This preference for behavioral voting reflects a preference for decentralization to the smallest unit capable of properly taking into account the relevant concerns and deciding the issue. General prohibitions are objectionable to the extent that they unnecessarily limit this initiative. Still, general prohibitions will sometimes be necessary, I will argue, because sometimes reliance on individual behavior will not be responsive to the values at stake.

A second way of seeing the objection to general prohibitions is also premised on respect for individual liberty. General prohibitions operate by restricting, not allocating, choice. General prohibitions typically involve saying that people should not use themselves or their resources in an activity that they would choose. To the extent that the collective order is premised on respect for people's autonomy as choosing agents, a desire to accomplish collective goals by restricting people's liberty should generally be an impermissible means.

Any law inevitably and properly makes some forms of life easier, others harder. No laws are neutral between different forms of life. People acting as lawmakers as well as individually are properly concerned with other people's welfare. They should choose laws that encourage and make it easier for others to act "wisely" and that allocate resources in ways that promote favored forms of life. Nevertheless, respect for liberty requires limits on the means by which laws promote favored values. Laws should "encourage" collectively preferred choices rather than bar dissident choices. The general principle is that in justifying laws, limits on individual liberty should not count as an aspect of the collective good and limits on a person's expression of his or her substantive values should not be treated as an appropriate means. Laws should not be aimed at supplanting individual choice or commitment. Allocation rules can seldom be charged with these offenses. General prohibitions often can. The problem with general prohibitions is that they operate the second way—they are aimed at barring choices, not at promoting or encouraging collectively preferred choices. Moreover, general prohibitions often embody the majority's preference to limit people's liberty—to treat the limit not only as a means but as itself an end. This is simply inconsistent with protection of individual expressive liberty.

This critique of general prohibitions must be hedged. A large category is justifiable. To explain this point, I must first distinguish two ways of valuing behavior, instrumentally and substantively—a distinction already suggested in the earlier discussion of coercive threats.

An actor may or may not positively value a specific aspect of behavior that others find offensive. The person who chooses to read pornography, unless she is a Supreme Court Justice,[23] presumably values this "polluting" activity. (The term "polluting" can be used to refer to any activity that affects the social or physical environment in ways that some people find offensive.) In contrast, owners of a steel plant or an automobile that emits exhaust pollutants normally do not value polluting the air per se. Polluting the air is an undesired consequence, a subsidiary result, of the activity that they do value—making steel or driving a car.

Pornography and air pollution illustrate the possibility that the polluter can value a polluting activity either substantively or instrumentally. Since prohibiting the activity forecloses the possibility of anyone undertaking it, if the activity is substantively valued, the prohibition wholly prevents a specific form of self-fulfillment or self-realization. But, if the polluting activity is only instrumentally valued, prohibiting the pollution potentially operates more like an allocation rule. That is, even with polluting behavior prohibited, the person (if she has sufficient resources) typically can still engage in the aspect of the activity that she substantively values—only the cost or difficulty of the valued activity may have increased. (At least, this is true unless the polluting activity is a technically necessary condition for the substantively valued activity.)

Reconsideration of key objections to general prohibitions shows that they do not apply to prohibitions of instrumentally valued activities. All general prohibitions are directed at behavior that the ruling group disvalues, that it views as a cost. The issue is *whether counting these costs of the behavior is appropriate* in justifying the legal rule. If the majority respects individual liberty, its negative evaluation of someone's behavior should not count as a reason to restrict it if the actor views the behavior as self-expressive, substantively valued; the majority would be saying that the person was only free to act in ways that they, the majority, thought was valuable. In contrast, this disrespect does not exist if the general prohibition applies only to instrumentally valued practices. In this second case, the majority is not claiming to override the actor's own values about her own behavior but rather can be better understood to be saying that the restricted person does not have a right to use as a means resources for which she does not pay the cost.

In addition, behavioral voting makes least sense in respect to people's behavior that is not expressing their values. The decentralization argument for behavioral voting recognizes that a person's behavior externalizes certain costs on to the community. Without adequate sentiments of solidarity or market type incentives, an actor is unlikely in her decision making fully to take into account other people's dislike of her chosen expressive behavior. Nevertheless, liberty concerns suggest rejecting decision making at the larger collective level, where all preferences presumably could be considered. Collective decision making would predictably consider the majority's preferences to restrict the actor's liberty as a reason for its decision. Then, the prohibition would embody a judgment that the collective wants to achieve its goals by forbidding dissident behavior, by forbidding actions based on the dissenter's values. In other words, when the individual substantively values the desired behavior, allowing the majority to say "no" allows it to suppress the dissident's own values and the dissident's desire (or willingness) to create the world in a particular way. More respectful of liberty would be to allow the majority to create the world by their behavioral voting combined with that of the dissident minority. When, however, the desired behavior is instrumentally valued, for the majority to say " no" amounts to a resource allocation. The "no" need imply nothing about the dissident's value choice but only about costs unrelated to the dissident's values that the dissident imposes on others. In this case, people's capacity to engage in self-determination may require group decision making. General prohibitions may provide the best way to properly account for all legitimate concerns.

Characterization of conduct as instrumentally or substantively valued is tricky. Given the importance of the categories in this discussion, these unfortunately manipulatable terms need more attention. Instrumentally valued behavior, as used here, refers to a distinguishable component or aspect that the actor treats as a means and does not value in itself. For example, the auto owner can distinguish emitting pollutants from driving the car—and usually values the first only instrumentally.

Public concern will occasionally focus on an aspect of the actor's behavior that is recognizably distinguishable from, but technically necessary for, the aspects the actor substantively values. In these cases, a prohibition on the instrumentally valued aspects may arguably be best characterized as a general prohibition on substantively valued behavior—that is, this is its necessary effect. On the one hand, the prohibition operates no differently from an allocation rule that leaves the actor without sufficient resources or the particular resources needed to engage in the desired activity. On the other hand, unlike allocation rules but like general prohibitions, the rule completely and necessarily bars the substantively valued behavior; and, usually, those proposing the rule will know of this effect even if they are not motivated by it. I find the appropriate conclusion from the perspective of equal respect for individual liberty and autonomy to be uncertain. Where feasible, I think, respect for liberty should require the community to allow this behavior—but since the actor cannot claim a first amendment expressive right to the merely instrumentally valued aspect, the community should be able to charge the actor for the negative value of this instrumental, "polluting" aspect. Respect for liberty requires, however, that the community not count as a cost those aspects that it negatively values but that the actor substantively values.

The basic claim is that general prohibitions on substantively valued, expressive behavior violate the first amendment. These laws prohibit expressive behavior. The expressive behavior serves the same values and operates in the same manner that justifies first amendment protection of verbal expression. Sometimes application of this principle will be difficult. Gray-area line drawing based on generalizations will sometimes be necessary. In the auto pollution situation, few people will substantively value air pollutants. If other feasible technologies exist that permit driving without air pollution, prohibiting the pollution "only" increases the cost of driving—an instrumental burden typical of many imposed by allocation rules. A prohibition in effect merely allocates wealth in a democratically chosen manner. But if no feasible alternative exists, the people desiring to drive can argue in principle that their driving ought to be permitted if they pay the cost of these nonsubstantively valued, polluting aspects of their behavior.

A further example may help illustrate the importance of the substantive/instrumental distinction. A rule prohibiting extended families from living together would prevent these families from realizing the substantive value they find in this physical association.[24] In contrast, requirements that housing have a certain floor space per occupant, have adequate parking space, fire protection services, etc., usually only impose added costs, instrumental burdens, on realizing the substantive values relating to living arrangements.[25] Like allocation rules in general, these instrumental burdens may prevent some people, usually the poor, from realizing their substantive values. Still, the liberty-based critique of general prohibitions would hold only the first rule—prohibiting extended families from living together—to be an unconstitutional abridgement of substantively valued, expressive conduct.

Application of this distinction between prohibiting the realization of substantive values and imposing instrumental burdens may be difficult. Although a large group (a family, fraternity, or retirement community) may substantively value living together, their desire normally does not require living together at a particular place. A geographic division that only allows fraternities in certain areas might increase total community satisfaction while, at worst, only making it somewhat more expensive for particular groups to realize their values.[26] Assuming that housing opportunities for all groups are actually made available by the jurisdiction responsible for zoning, geographic limits on living arrangements would only instrumentally burden individuals—unless people substantively valued living in a particular house or community or type of community, for example, an integrated community. If they did value the specific location or community, the geographical exclusion could thwart the group's substantive values.[27] Most often, however, this value placed on the particular place or community will relate to the person's historical attachments, which suggests a partial explanation for pre-existing use exemptions from many zoning rules.

This discussion of general prohibitions has implicitly assumed a background of private property and regulation of private decision making. Obviously, government decisions about the use of public property can operate like a general prohibition—that is, the collective decision prevails. Public control (ownership) of resources, however, is often useful and sometimes necessary to embody and carry out many of people's substantive values. Seldom will public ownership be for the purpose of preventing individual choices; rather, usually it will be to use certain resources to promote various values. With this thought in mind, most issues raised by public property are left to the discussion of time, place, and manner regulations in Chapters 6, 7, and 8. Generally, however, first amendment doctrine in this context will serve the same objective served by the objection to general prohibitions in respect to privately owned resources. It will identify cases where a challenged regulation improperly advances public purposes by deliberately or unnecessarily restricting liberty.

This public property context, moreover, will be rich with problems implicating the instrumental/substantive value distinction. For example, although sleep as well as camping are often substantively valued, a law prohibiting sleeping in certain places only restricts a normally instrumentally valued aspect of sleeping or camping. Sleeping in Lafayette Park in front of the White House, for instance, may make seeing the Capital or going to Congress to lobby easier or cheaper. But sleeping there is seldom an essential element of the substantively valued conduct. The situation changes, however, when the sleep is intended as public expression that dramatizes and to an extent embodies the plight in which Presidential policies have left the homeless.[28] The location of the sleep could be an aspect of substantively valued, expressive conduct, that is, protected speech. Then, the propriety of the prohibition must depend on the principles that control the government's decisions regulating speech on public property.

Putting aside the public property context, when a general prohibition applies to substantively valued behavior, generally it unconstitutionally abridges freedom of speech or expression. This conclusion derives from two observations: (1) substantively valued conduct is inherently expressive and clearly contributes to the two key first amendment values of self-fulfillment and participation in change; (2) general prohibitions forbid behavior that promotes first amendment values in the same manner as protected speech—that is, in a noncoercive manner. In fact, from the perspective of individual liberty, the evil of the government's imposition of general prohibitions is curiously parallel to the evil of private parties' coercive acts. Imposition of general prohibitions enables those in power to make use of others (if the rule requires specified conduct) or avoid the bother of others (if it forbids specified activities). In this way, general prohibitions, like coercive acts, treat others as means. General prohibitions also unnecessarily restrict individual liberty, and thereby, like coercive acts, disrespect individual autonomy.

Allocation rules and notions of private coercion intertwine in a different way. Allocation rules help provide the baseline needed to distinguish coercion from pressure, influence, offers, persuasion. They define and then forbid invasions of a person's realm of decision-making authority. Coercion involves subverting a person's autonomy by invading or threatening to invade the victim's decision-making authority. Coercion, therefore, implies an allocation rule that it violates or threatens to violate. Allocation rules are part of the "grammar" of coercion.

General prohibitions restrict expressive conduct that operates noncoercively to advance self-fulfillment and popular participation in change. Still, before leaving my claim that general prohibitions of substantively valued conduct are unconstitutional abridgements of first amendment rights, justifications typically offered for general prohibitions must be rejected. These justifications normally take one of three forms. General prohibitions are valued and should be permitted because they: (1) define and help form a community; (2) result from a valuable group process of choice; (3) promote efficiency or welfare maximization.

General prohibitions (or general requirements) sometimes help constitute communities. A religious community may partially define itself by rules that prohibit smoking, drinking, working on certain days, or fighting in unjust wars or rules that require praying, wearing certain clothes, engaging in various rituals, or performing certain types of service. A social or voluntary political association may require that all members do or believe certain things—for example, vote for the candidate selected in the primary or boycott products of unacceptable firms. The mores of a community may obligate a person to love one's brother or sister, or parents, or spouse, or neighbor. Moreover, even the most direct beneficiary of certain obligations may lack authority either to demand or excuse compliance. A sibling may be obligated to help her sister even in times when the sister would release the sibling from the obligation or even disclaim needing help. A member may have a duty to follow an association's political line without anyone having the authority to release the person from the obligation. In other words, sometimes the obligations defining a family, a religious community, or a voluntary association take the form of general prohibitions or requirements rather than allocation rules. Moreover, many customs and conventions that make up our society require, prohibit, or structure behavior in ways that people are supposed to conform to. In fact, speech itself, conversation, depends on some degree of conformance to language rules that are in many respects more like general prohibitions than allocation rules—although our poetic power to transform the language makes language also like an allocation.

The value of these rules and practices that help form and define communities and relationships must be recognized. Nevertheless, their value as well as legitimacy often relates to the permissibility of noncompliance. The rules and practices' continued existence and often their origin will lie in individuals' voluntarily adopted practices or in their voluntarily chosen allegiance to the group defined by these rules. Spontaneous enforcement by expressions of approval or disapproval, by continuance or withdrawal of association, by comprehension or incomprehension of language usually will be adequate to maintain these community-defining practices. When these voluntary, noncoercive methods of enforcement are not adequate, respect for people's liberty often means that the rules or practices should no longer be maintained. By contrast, the state could enforce obedience to rules that define both individuals and the community.[29] This enforcement would involve the state in partially but coercively attempting to define who a person is. Such a practice clearly disrespects individual autonomy.[30] Since self-defining obligations can and often do exist within the *voluntary* practices of people, state enforcement with the consequent disrespect of people's autonomy requires a justification beyond the mere observation that most people value these rules. No obvious justification exists, except possibly the claim that state enforcement promotes welfare maximization, that is, that enforcement satisfies more desires, either due to a marginal reduction of deviation from the popularly favored community-defining practices or due to the symbol of state enforcement, than it thwarts. This efficiency claim is a version of the third argument and will be considered below.

Second, people sometimes value the group process of formulating rules. Positive value may inhere in dialogue—the process of identifying and understanding issues, in resolving or compromising conflicts, and, finally, in expressing group unity through reaching agreement. Republican politics is a high ideal. Moreover, the group process may improve the quality of the resulting decisions. Nevertheless, even if these process values can be realized in governmental decision making, it is not obvious that they justify government decision making about general prohibitions. People can realize the significant participatory process values in the governmental arena while choosing allocation rules and formulating public policies and programs, activities which involve the community in determining what type of community will exist but are not aimed at limiting individual autonomy. In contrast, group decision making concerning general prohibitions or requirements, such as deciding what books to read, may be a valuable exercise for a study group precisely because of its voluntary nature. Only then is this decision-making process a noncoercive method of individual or group self-definition. Social pluralism may require the existence of opportunities for voluntary associations to create general prohibitions or requirements; but this valuable pluralism could itself be coercively destroyed if the state could create and enforce general prohibitions or requirements.

These observations do not deny that some positive process value could exist in any community decision making. This value is a consideration that could contribute to utilitarian arguments for allowing political decisions to impose general prohibitions. From a liberty perspective, the relative voluntariness of private associations and the less liberty-denying quality of allocation rules and public projects explain why realizing process values has justificatory significance in these contexts. But from this liberty perspective, the possibility of realizing these positive process values should not justify denials of liberty. Thus, only utilitarian or efficiency arguments for general prohibitions remain. They must now be considered.

The efficiency argument notes that people who substantively desire to act in a manner that others find offensive often would agree to abandon the offensive behavior and accept a restraint on their liberty if paid an amount that those offended would be willing to pay. Those opposed to air or pornographic pollution might be willing to pay the polluters an amount that the polluters would be willing to accept for ceasing their pollution. However, difficulties and expenses in negotiating and carrying out the transactions often prevent these beneficial agreements from being reached. A general prohibition could provide a solution. Although burdening some, a general prohibition could increase the general level of preference satisfaction as measured by the market criterion of willingness to pay—or, if more defensible, some other criterion could be used within the same basic analysis. In other words, general prohibitions may correct for "market failures" and be efficient.

Three objections are commonly raised against the efficiency justification for general prohibitions. First, the inefficiencies of predictable abuses by the majority of a power to adopt general prohibitions may significantly outweigh any efficiency gains that result from their "proper" use. Abuses occur because often the majority has no incentive to avoid imposing general prohibitions even when the benefit to it is less than the cost to those restricted. An additional cost that political decision-makers often ignore is the dissatisfaction generated among those who believe, and often properly believe, that the majority uses general prohibitions to impose its values and increase its own well-being by improperly restricting the liberty of minorities. Particularly when this demoralization cost is added, a rule utilitarian could plausibly conclude that the danger of abuse outweighs the potential for gain.[31] Of course, this argument loses force if the beneficiaries of the rule adequately compensate those who are restricted. Compensation, however, virtually never occurs in these situations and, given the numbers of people who could claim to be injured, is unlikely to be an administratively feasible response. The rule utilitarian's fears would also not apply if those restricted favor the restriction, seemingly a paradoxical but not that unusual a situation. A person sometimes engages in particular conduct only to maximize her interests given her assumption that others also engage in the behavior. For example, a person may prefer that no one pick the flowers in the park but, given that other people are picking them, decide to pick some. In other words, the efficiency argument is persuasive for general prohibitions properly designed to avoid the typical prisoner's dilemma problem—although, when this is really the case, a liberty-based objection is unlikely. In the final analysis, even if a strict rule utilitarian (or slippery slope) argument against general prohibitions cannot be dismissed, the better utilitarian argument may only require care and circumspection in their adoption.[32] Hence, this rule utilitarian analysis provides only weak support for a comprehensive constitutional ban on general prohibitions of substantively valued conduct. Because it does not reject the efficiency standard, it cannot persuasively oppose balancing as the appropriate constitutional approach.

Second, efficiency does not justify violating people's rights.[33] Of course, if all rights are based on positive law, this point does not provide a ground for objecting to any legal rule. To avoid circularity, a conception of rights independent of positive law is required. Inevitably, such a nonpositivist conception will only be partial. Some rights or constraints on the positive creation of rights may be implied by the existence of a justifiable legal order, but certainly most aspects of people's rights are culturally relative and can properly be determined positively.[34] The present objection to efficiency requires a demonstration that general prohibitions of substantively valued, expressive conduct violate people's rights. Essentially, the demonstration merely repeats the earlier claims for the liberty theory of the first amendment. Here, I will only restate some of the key points.

Initially, note that these general prohibitions thwart people's self-expression and people's personal and social creativity. The rules directly impinge on realizing these two central values of the first amendment. Moreover, unlike allocation rules, which necessarily exist and merely influence people's values and their opportunities to pursue their values, state-enforced general prohibitions can entirely eliminate the legal possibility of some people acting in accord with their substantive values.* Moreover, these effects are purposeful. Again, unlike most allocation rules, general prohibitions are designed specifically to prevent people from engaging in the conduct. Often, the purpose involves hostility to and a desire to suppress people's value choices. If, as argued earlier, state action must respect individual autonomy, general prohibitions of substantively valued behavior are objectionable because they violate this required respect. General efficiency concerns do not justify these means any more than they justify torture.

Third, efficiency or welfare maximization conclusions are particularly incoherent justifications for certain types of decisions. Efficiency refers to effectiveness in promoting some goal, but the goal must be independently supplied. In welfare analysis, this goal is usually described as "satisfying preferences." Efficiency calculations must presuppose, but cannot justify, some particular set of tastes or desires, usually the existing set, as the ones to be satisfied.[35] Until some set of preferences is assumed, efficiency has no evaluative criteria. But if *change* is to be subject to human choice, if human self-determination is possible, then a central issue is determining which preferences are best. Efficiency analysis can provide information about the possibilities of realizing different preferences, but it has no criteria for guiding the choice of preferences. No intrinsic quality of existing tastes justifies treating their fulfillment as always being the dominant

---

*Although the distribution of wealth is not a central concern of the first amendment, note that the liberty concern can be reformulated in distributional terms. If wealth is treated as authority to make various decisions, freedom from general prohibitions provides a minimum guarantee of some "wealth" to each individual. General prohibitions (or requirements) could strip people of virtually all valued wealth (i.e., authority to make desired decisions about their own or others' conduct) except for the value of their political rights (i.e., the right to participate in choosing general prohibitions).

concern. Rather, beliefs like John Stuart Mill's faith in people as progressive beings,[36] suggest that people can sometimes evaluate the merit of change not in terms of whether it fulfills existing tastes but whether it improves the type of people we are. As Professor Tribe has argued, the major choices facing us as a people are those that will determine who and what we will be.[37] Human integrity and responsibility require that people be free to decide (or participate in deciding) what or who they will be.

Thus, when evaluating the process of change, it is a logical mistake to evaluate choices merely in terms of how well they satisfy existing preferences. Rather, a person must either evaluate change in terms of the legitimacy of the process or substantively evaluate the political and ethical content of the change. This substantive evaluation of the content of change corresponds to many people's practice of subjecting their attitudes and activities to ethical or political criticism. Practical reason or judgment, not efficiency or instrumental reason, provide the bases for evaluation. Efficiency analysis is largely irrelevant because it takes as given the primary issues in dispute—the appropriate set of preferences and the distribution of influence. As for the legitimacy of the decision-making process, that is, of "normal" politics, the key issues concern what types of inputs are proper and how the process itself can be designed to respect our equality and liberty while promoting our humanity and strengthening community. As for inputs, nothing about existing preferences makes them particularly appropriate bases for answering questions about what we should become. Rather, these questions suggest the need for dialogue and experiments and attempts to understand alternative, new logics. Contrary to assumptions of the efficiency analysis, the legitimacy of the process requires it to exclude or restrict the role of some preferences, for example, liberty or equality-denying preferences as well as any preference that reflects and maintains the injustices of the existing order. But if the earlier description of general prohibitions is correct, often they will restrict the development of experimental logics and reflect preferences for denying liberty. Thus, viewing politics as a process of self-determination suggests efficiency justifications are inappropriate because the desires for general prohibitions are not proper inputs and the prohibitions are liberty denying output that partially close the process.

Possibly, the limited role of efficiency analysis in considering the questions of what process of change makes sense and what particular changes are justified helps explain the intuitive view that the first amendment should (absolutely?) protect a process of change from limitations justified merely by utilitarian calculations (i.e., balancing). General prohibitions may increase the satisfaction of existing preferences but hinder the creation of a better society by impending people's development of "better" preferences. Of course, this logical irrelevance of efficiency arguments for justifying general prohibitions should not be surprising if the state is justified in adopting utility maximization as state policy only because and only when necessary to carry out the state's obligation to treat all members as deserving equal respect as autonomous moral beings. Efficiency is important only after the liberty of autonomous beings, particularly the right of self-determination, has been given priority.

One added consideration points to why general prohibitions are objectionable. We need, and sometimes have had, progressive change. The legal structuring of the process of change ought to protect those elements that could be progressive and which, without protection, would be restricted. Identifying progressive elements is, of course, difficult. However, barring general prohibitions of substantively valued conduct increases the chances of protecting progressive elements. These general prohibitions consistently suppress value realization that is contrary to majority or status-quo values. Popular sentiment is likely to support precisely those general prohibitions that attempt to suppress progressive practices conflicting with current regressive orientations. Of course, the dominant existing orientations may be the preferable or progressive ones. But if the democratic faith is sound, we should expect that it is best to leave people free to affirm or deny existing orientations. Respect for the first amendment is an unpersuasive explanation for the decline of Rome.

Closely related to the need for progressive change is a concern of critical theorists such as Roberto Unger and Jurgen Habermas. They argue that the confidence we should have in our judgments depends on the extent to which these shared values are formed under circumstances of nondomination.[38] Since general prohibitions characteristically involve dominating minorities on the basis of current majority interests and values, general prohibitions undermine the legitimacy of the very values they promote. Contrarily, by banning general prohibitions of substantively valued conduct, we decrease majoritarian domination and increase the basis for confidence in relying in practice on the shared judgments that do exist. By allowing minorities to live their values even when the present majority finds the behavior offensive, society protects an important process for peaceful change of tastes and values while decreasing the conditions of domination.

Interestingly, these three abstract criticisms of efficiency justifications for general prohibitions duplicate traditional defenses of first amendment rights. Typical attempts to justify prohibitions on specific expressive activity rely on: (1) predictions that the expressive activity will lead to future violations of allocation rules—for example, the anarchist advocacy creates a clear and present danger of lawlessness; pornography leads to sex crimes; (2) conclusions that the activity will affect the actors, observers, or third parties in detrimental ways, thereby corrupting the cultural climate and negatively affecting friendships and interpersonal relations—for example, public sales or use of obscenity and public use of vulgar language undermine the desired moral tone of the community; racial hate propaganda inflicts emotional injury on people, undermines civility, distorts reasoning, and creates unwelcome tensions; publication of unsavory, libelous information damages valued reputations or invades areas of sensitive privacy; harassing remarks cause emotional distress and pain; (3) outright disapproval of the values or attitudes expressed—for example, some majorities are appalled by the disrespectful or unpatriotic attitudes expressed by sexist speech, flag burning, wearing long hair, or draft-card burning.

Well-developed defenses of free speech meet each claim. First, the traditional objection to the "bad tendency test" for restricting speech is that the state can forbid the advocated act, which is usually a violation of an allocation rule, but cannot prohibit the speech using a general prohibition. This objection parallels criminal law and due process notions which, except in exceptional circumstances, are offended by taking away a person's liberty because of what a person might do in the future. Of course, like preventive detention, speech restrictions based on the "bad tendency test" may maximize preference satisfaction; they may be efficient legal rules. The classic responses rely on the same objections to efficiency as developed above. The bad tendency test will be abused or, like laws prohibiting obscenity or marijuana, cannot be effectively enforced and, thus, will not be efficient in practice. More fundamentally, civil libertarians assert that, even if efficient, restrictions on speech based on the speech's tendency to lead to objectionable behavior are impermissible because they violate rights of individual liberty that society must recognize. Society must restrict itself to forbidding the objectionable act, not the individual's expression of dissent that might lead someone else to act.

The other two arguments for restricting people's noncoercive expression focus on the expression's bad consequences for individuals and society and its embodiment of offensive values. Both could be viewed as efficiency arguments: The majority would prefer to avoid the expressive activities' predicted effects on people's personality and behavior or to avoid injuries that individuals experience due to the expression. Traditional first amendment analyses reject these arguments on grounds that parallel the reasons to reject efficiency justifications of general prohibitions: (1) Allowing even justifiable restrictions on expression will lead to acceptance of improper suppression. (2) The majority must respect individuals' choices about their own values and not force them to falsify their values. (3) The state must permit people to speak to express themselves and make their contribution to changing their world even if some people find the speech harmful or distasteful. Both the second and third points, of course, are straightforward applications of the principle that the state must respect people's integrity and autonomy.

One final comment about the discussion of extending first amendment protection to substantively valued, expressive *conduct* may be appropriate. Obviously, a person could agree that this conduct should be constitutionally protected without agreeing that it should be protected as an interpretation of freedom of speech. Whether this chapter's liberty analysis would provide appropriate content to ninth amendment rights retained by the people or to a substantive notion of due process—or even whether there is any proper substantive content for the concept of due process—will not be considered here. Clearly, some commentators and judicial opinions suggest that due process provides the best home for these liberty arguments—and I have no desire to reject that possibility. Still, one example may illustrate some reasons to pause before pursuing that route.

From the perspective sketched here, laws prohibiting sexual interaction between consenting adults present an easy issue. People often consider their sexual conduct as among their most self-expressive activities. Sexual conduct can be fundamentally expressive of a person's own nature and values. It can also be a complex, profound form of communication. General prohibitions against forms of this conduct are surely censorship of self-expression and communication. These general prohibitions try to preserve an existing normative order that the majority purportedly supports by outlawing expressive conduct, which constitutes "behavioral voting," that could lead to both cultural change and to new ideas or logics. These laws unconstitutionally abridge an intimate, powerful, fundamental form of speech.[39]

This conclusion is direct and obvious, using the first amendment analysis developed in this chapter. The key is seeing the first amendment as protecting a realm of liberty against invasion by a majority on the basis of its restrictive views of proper conduct, views that likely reflect values of the dominant culture.

Substantive due process, as frequently formulated, seems to respond to quite different concerns. In his concurrence in *Griswold v. Connecticut*,[40] a case that struck down a state's "general prohibition" on the use of contraceptives, Justice Goldberg relied on due process as well as ninth amendment arguments. Quoting earlier judicial authority, he said that the due process inquiry requires the judge "to look to the 'traditions and [collective] conscience of our people' to determine whether a principle is so rooted [there] as to be ranked as fundamental.'"[41] This version of due process theory seems to affirm rather than limit majority or mainstream values.* Thus, even though the issue was not raised by the case, it should be no surprise that the three concurring opinions in *Griswold*, each relying on due process principles, all went out of their way explicitly to say that laws forbidding fornication and homosexuality are constitutional.[42] Justice Harlan's concurrence referred back to an earlier opinion in which he argued that "laws forbidding adultery, fornication, and homosexual practices . . . form a pattern so deeply pressed into the substance of our social life that any Constitutional doctrine in this area must build on that basis."[43] This conclusion seems right given the traditional formulation of due process.

The only opinion upholding the constitutional challenge in *Griswold* that found it unnecessary to make this concession—or speak to the point—was Justice Douglas' majority opinion. Although some read Douglas' opinion to rest on a right of privacy created by the overlapping penumbras of privacy found in various amendments, the better reading finds Douglas' opinion based on the zone of privacy created by the first amendment. Douglas' brief references to other amendments show how each creates its own, independent, although sometimes mutually reinforcing, zone of privacy. This reading explains both why most of Douglas' opinion discusses first amendment cases and why he concludes by asserting that the case deals with an "association"—a right that Douglas had already emphasized is a protected penumbra of the first amendment. Douglas has elsewhere made clear his view that the first amendment protects not only communications directed at discovering universal truths but also sexual expression that satisfies the expressive needs and tastes of the most eccentric minorities.[44] Thus, if *Griswold* was for Douglas a first amendment case, he could be expected to extend his reasoning to cover fornication and homosexuality. The first amendment protects the dissident. But this extension hardly corresponds to substantive due process's preservation of tradition—at least until we recognize governmental respect for liberty as the bedrock of our tradition.

---

*Of course, if one looks deeply enough, respect for liberty may be deeply rooted in our political and ethical culture despite the many "traditional" abridgements.

THE MARKETPLACE OF IDEAS REVISITED

One should not too quickly dismiss an analysis that has dominated informed opinion as completely as the marketplace of ideas theory has. In Chapter 1, I criticized the marketplace of ideas as a method of discovering truth or arriving at the "best" perceptions or values. Confidence in its effectiveness for achieving these goals seemed dependent on several invalid assumptions. Here, my inquiry considers whether protecting a broader range of expressive conduct, more specifically, whether forbidding general prohibitions of substantively valued conduct, blunts the criticisms of the classic marketplace of ideas model. If it does, this contribution could only provide added support for this chapter's broad interpretation.

Protecting substantively valued conduct from abridgement by general prohibitions makes important contributions. It makes the hope that people will be able to make the "best" choices in some marketplace of ideas more plausible for at least four reasons. First, the classic model assumes that truth is discovered or found. To the extent that reality is created, the acceptability of the first amendment theory depends on the manner in which it provides for this creation. The theory must be concerned with questions of who and how. Equality of opportunity to create reality provides a possible standard. Since all conduct, not merely speech, contributes to this creation process, equality of opportunity would require a regime of strict equality of all resources and skills—a regime as unnecessary as it is inconceivable. Lack of sufficient "wealth" is only one limit on people's opportunities. Ruling groups often use general prohibitions to entirely suppress opportunities for certain choices. This use of power can be more oppressive and usually is less justified than are limits on dissident opportunities caused by inequality of resource distribution—at least, if the inequality results from defensible policies, if the inequality is not too extreme, and if a minimum level opportunity is guaranteed. Clearly, barring state-imposed prohibitions of substantively valued conduct greatly increases opportunities for minorities to develop new logics and new realities—the notion that replaces objective truth. This broadened liberty eliminates a major method by which ruling groups prevent peaceful challenges to the existing orthodoxies. Thus, a ban on these general prohibitions seems necessary, whether or not sufficient, to provide adequately for opportunities to create new realities. This expansion of dissident opportunities should provide a basis for some greater confidence in the acceptability of any resulting order—and, thus, greater confidence in the process of creating truth.

Second, a ban on these general prohibitions makes the process of creating realities much more democratic. Many people have neither the resources, skills, nor interest to participate in a rational discursive or political search for the best societal decisions. Most people do have an interest in their own life and their relations with others. Most have sufficient skill (and, in the liberty model, they also have the right) to pursue their own visions and values. Only by disallowing general prohibitions can everyone, by their choice of activities, participate in the behavioral debate and in building the culture.

Third, people's liberty to live their values provides for the possibility that at present, or always, pluralism best meets human needs and goals. Moreover, by allowing this pluralism, change can occur by people living, and finding others to join in living, a set of values. Thus, peaceful, gradual change will have space and opportunity to develop.

Fourth, protecting greater liberty of action breaches the status-quo bias of the marketplace of ideas. Even without considering the consequences of an elite, monopolistic, corporate structure of ownership, mass communications as a medium apparently are more effective in reinforcing the status quo than in stimulating criticism. Face-to-face verbal communication and existing forms of reason also typically reflect people's experiences in the existing order. Of course, various economic or social groups experience and evaluate the existing order from radically different perspectives. Still, that existing order is likely to dominate people's logic and perceptions when they consider alternatives. As long as the ruling groups control the content of the existing order, calls to base decisions on dialogue will be inadequately progressive. By protecting dissident, substantively valued, expressive conduct, the first amendment restricts the power of political elites to legally limit experiences—thereby restricting the power of the status-quo-oriented forces. More important, protecting this expressive conduct protects the possibility of developing new loci of experience that potentially can falsify the existing, dominant perspectives. This first-amendment-protected method of change requires neither violence nor approval of dominant societal groups. Just as in the classic market model's conception of speech, the power of new perspectives depends on their voluntary acceptance by people. However, protection of new, nonverbal practices has the crucial advantage of allowing dissidents to make a new perspective available in an experiential form in which its logic might be coherent. Thus, the broader protection overcomes some of the status-quo bias of mere verbal debate.[45]

This revised theory replaces both the doubtful assumptions of the classic marketplace of ideas theory and its hope for a basically rational discovery of timeless truth with a defense of the legitimacy of a social process of choice. The legitimacy of the process must be defended on at least one of two grounds: It follows because all people have a basic right to participate in the individual and social processes of self-determination. Or it follows because a "better" individual and collective expression of humanity can be expected as a consequence of the increased opportunity of each person freely to participate. If either ground is persuasive, it would justify protecting people's liberty to engage in substantively valued conduct. Both grounds imply that eliminating or weakening existing structures of domination that influence or distort people's choices[46] improves the process of developing and expressing values.

The main merit of the market failure version of the first amendment was its concern with reducing domination. Unfortunately, the market failure theory's focus on equality of speech opportunities—usually, equality of access to channels of mass communication—belies the fact that only general economic equality would even plausibly suffice to implement the approach. Because of this theoretical confusion, the market failure theorists fail to realize that providing considerable equality of access to communication channels may be less central to dismantling the existing structures of domination than banning existing restrictions, general prohibitions, on liberty. This confusion illustrates the market failure theory's more basic problem: It merges the concepts of equality and liberty. Although both concepts are fundamental, they provide separate guidance for describing a just social order.

In addition to highlighting these mistakes of the market failure theory, the liberty approach avoids the problems which engulf that theory. The liberty theory avoids offering the false hope that dissenting positions without a real basis in experience can be discursively shown to be best. Instead, the liberty theory manifests a deep, democratic faith in people by providing for a more realistic method of change from "the bottom up." The liberty model protects noncoercive uses of speech and forbids enforcement of general prohibitions of substantively valued, expressive behavior. These standards are clearer, less subjective criteria for limiting government action than those provided by the market failure model. Also, because it guarantees a realm of liberty rather than a properly functioning market, people can correct for perceived infringements of the guarantee by violating only the "improper restriction" on liberty. This should be more appealing than the endless, destructive cycle of possibly violent actions needed to get the "proper results" that opposing sides could find necessary to remedy perceived infringements of a constitutionally guaranteed marketplace of ideas. Thus, the liberty model provides for a process of public decision making and a search for, or creation of, truth that avoids the problems and improper assumptions of both market models.

5

The Process of Change

Most first amendment theorists agree that a central function of rights protected by the first amendment is to contribute to a legitimate, democratic process for achieving needed change.[1] In order to defend first amendment rights on this basis, a theorist must explain how the first amendment rights delineated by such a theory make this contribution to needed change. Unfortunately, the explanation is seldom given. Its absence leaves a crucial gap in first amendment theory. This chapter attempts to fill the gap by proposing a theory of the process of needed or "progressive" democratic change and showing how the rights identified by the liberty theory are crucial to this process.[2]

A subsidiary purpose is to critique the currently dominant understanding of the process of change. This understanding assumes that in this process, people's ends are entirely separate from the means they use to achieve change. This view, which recognizes the constant possibility of "good" ends justifying otherwise "bad" means, will be called the independence thesis. My claim will be that the perspective embodied in this dominant, independence thesis not only leads to inadequacies in legal theory, but also reflects and helps perpetuate existing societal contradictions, thus obstructing rather than facilitating social change.

This chapter offers an alternative to the independence thesis. My claim is that means and ends are better viewed as necessarily united in the process of change: the unity thesis. If correct, this claim is of vital importance for all those interested in progressive change as well as for first amendment theorists.

Considerable ambiguity exists in the notion, often presented as a hackneyed slogan or dismissed as romantic naivete, that means determine ends. The first section of this chapter clarifies what is meant by the unity thesis and its alternative, the thesis that ends are independent of means. Since this inquiry into the unity and independence theses relates specifically to the context of change, this section will also offer thoughts about what amounts to change and some suggestions about how change can be evaluated.

The second section explores the ideological and experiential reasons for the appeal of the independence thesis, and the fundamental role this thesis plays in liberal social and normative theory. Next, the third section reviews theoretical considerations that support an interpretation of our experience consistent with the unity thesis. These considerations help show errors of the independence thesis and, in part, suggest content of needed change. The fourth section reviews practical considerations that support the unity thesis. It also undertakes a brief historical investigation that indicates that reliance on objectionable means is misguided. Finally, the last section further elucidates the relation of the process of progressive change and the rights protected by the liberty theory of the first amendment.

EVALUATING ENDS AND MEANS

The unity thesis proposes that in the historical process of social change, ends and means cannot be sharply separate. The means people use shape and limit the ends people achieve. More important, it also claims that the ends achieved normally embody the value framework implicit in the means used. That is, people can achieve "good" change only by using "good" means.

People often fail to examine the unity thesis carefully. The cynical or "hard-nosed" pragmatist quickly dismisses the thesis as a romantic illusion. Conversely, others think it obviously true "that the means employed determine the nature of the ends produced."[3] Some of these divergent initial reactions—quick dismissals and uncritical acceptances—may trade on ambiguities in the unity thesis. An initial problem may be to understand the claims that are really at issue.

"Ends" refers both to results (or events) and to values. "Results" suggests a causal analysis, while "values" suggests an analysis focused on human meaning. An initial inquiry is whether the claim embodied in the unity thesis involves an analysis of either type.

In a causal framework, results or ends flow naturally from the means. In the continuing stream of life, labeling some events as means and others as ends often appears artificial. Nevertheless, causal connections between labeled events appears obvious—means apparently do determine the content of the ends. But these causal connections constitute a very trivial version of unity. Any interesting version of the unity thesis must be with the normative correspondence or normative transference of means to ends. But nothing about the causal connectedness of means to ends implies that their normative attributes correspond.

If the concern is correspondence of normative content, perhaps the focus should be on human evaluation or meaning. Unity would follow if a person's normative evaluation of the end were equivalent to the sum of the person's normative evaluations of the means. The maxim that two wrongs do not make a right or that two false statements do not combine to make a truthful statement illustrate this form of unity. Unfortunately, this defense of the unity thesis is also misdirected. It ignores the dimensions of time and change. Given a temporal analysis, ends appear not as the evaluative sum of means but as separate events, as distinguishable consequences that are subject to separate evaluation. Thus, an evaluative summation cannot be the basis of the unity thesis. The thesis must involve something other than either rigid causality or narrow evaluative logic.

Presumably the unity thesis must involve elements both of temporal sequence, that is, something like causality, and of evaluation or meaning. Nevertheless, unity is implausible if based on a simple combination of the two elements. If a person can place any value she wants on an event,[4] she necessarily can place inconsistent values on the causally connected ends and means. Moreover, evaluative freedom means that people who agree in the evaluation of particular means can disagree in their evaluation of resulting ends. When they do, then necessarily for at least some of them, unity would not exist.

Still, the unity thesis's claim must be that either our actual evaluation or the appropriate evaluation of ends and means will be such that only good means will lead to good results. Such a claim runs into the problem mentioned in the last paragraph—evaluative freedom necessarily leads to possible falsification of the unity thesis. This problem, combined with the common experience that sometimes a good and important end seems to require objectionable means, may indicate that a meaningful version of the unity thesis is both logically and experientially implausible. Nevertheless, those who accept something like the unity thesis cannot be blind to these arguments. Thus, their claim must be somewhat different from what this reasoning suggests.

A different tack is to treat the unity thesis more as a perspective and an interpretation than an analytic or objective historical claim. This more plausible account views the unity thesis as an interpretive possibility and an experiential tendency. The claims are that in important respects we are better off to the extent we see and interpret events through the lens of the unity thesis, and that events will usually correspond to this thesis and will correspond more often than a person would expect if he or she had not adopted this lens. If so, the maxim opens up more insight and leads to better practice than does the independence thesis.[5] As an interpretative perspective, the unity thesis is related to how we should and often do view ourselves and the world, as well as a claim about tendencies in events.

If the unity and the independence theses are to be understood as perspectives, as claims about interpretative possibilities and experiential tendencies, a number of questions immediately are suggested. Why and when do we or should we adopt one or the other perspective? Which perspective gives us the most useful insight into interpreting events, interpreting history? How does adopting one or the other perspective affect behavior—that is, what are the consequences of adopting one or the other perspective? Seeing the theses as alternative perspectives rather than rigid claims about the essential qualitative nature of causally related events also suggests that the claim for the truth of unity thesis will not be absolute. Rather the thesis claims to describe empirical tendencies and evaluative insights. Even as thus limited, the thesis concerning the unity of means and ends could be generally right, generally misguided, or appropriately applicable in only certain contexts.

Theorists sometimes divide conduct into two broad categories: (1) symbolic or communicative action and interaction; and (2) strategic, instrumental, or purposive-rational action.[6] This distinction between communicative action and instrumental action suggests several hypotheses and raises further issues concerning their relationship.

A plausible hypothesis is that the relationship of ends and means will vary depending on which type of action dominates. The normative quality of means may transfer to the normative quality of the ends more routinely if communicative action dominates. For example, when the positive normative qualities of honesty, accuracy, and respect characterize initial interactions, we might expect some transference to any continuation of the interaction or any resulting agreement. In contrast, in the realm of instrumental or purposive-rational action, a single person will often differ sharply in her evaluation of means and ends. For example, some work as well as many instrumental, manipulative actions will be objectionable or otherwise distasteful, yet the reward or outcome may be morally unobjectionable, or even desirable. A second hypothesis is that evaluatively important aspects of social change will depend on the relative dominance of communicative action or instrumental action in the process of change. For example, I will argue that market practices, paradigm examples of instrumental action, reliably produce only commodity ends. In addition, the distinction between these two types of action raises more general questions concerning their relationship: for example, whether their relative prominence varies historically; whether one always prevails in cases of conflict; and whether either is dependent upon the other.

Several tentative, speculative claims may help illuminate these issues. First, both types of action are necessary for human existence. No society could or should eliminate either communicative action and purposive-rational action or work. Second, the general relation between the two types of action has varied historically. In some premodern societies, for example, symbolic or communicative action arguably dominated or controlled and guided purposive-rational or instrumental action. According to usual interpretations, feudal society was structured by hierarchical, traditional authority patterns, with work being a matter of craft, skill, and traditionally defined roles controlled by established relations between people. In this world, as may also be true of tribal cultures, symbolic or communicative action controls. But the closed, hierarchical, traditional structure of society prevented the development of participatory, egalitarian practices as a basis for the symbolic or communicative interaction. As a result, this pervasive structure distorted communicative interaction during this period. That is, communicative action was neither fully self-conscious nor democratically based.

The revolutionary aspect of the modern period lies in the increasing separation of the two types of action and in the tendency of purposive-rational or instrumental action to destroy or dominate the realm of communicative or symbolic action.[7] The modern period is increasingly dominated by instrumentally oriented market and bureaucratic practices that treat wealth and efficiency as goals that properly dominate all other concerns. Max Weber's study of the seemingly irreversible "rationalization" of the world describes this process of change between these two periods.[8]

This historical trend could have consequences even for our view of the first amendment. For example, the historically increasing prominence of instrumental action might lead to an increasing unwillingness or inability to offer noninstrumental justifications for communicative or symbolic actions, such as symbolic protest. First amendment rights would increasingly be perceived as relevant only to the extent that they are rights to "effective speech."[9] Moreover, politics would seem to be less a matter of "practical" or ethical discourse and more a matter of either administration or strategic action designed by the actors to gain greater shares of available resources.[10]

A liberated, postmodern period would see another revolutionary reversal. Symbolic or communicative interaction would again dominate, but this time not within a closed, hierarchical structure. Rather, the universalism of the modern period would be retained, and the communicative or symbolic action would be increasingly based on conscious choice, free of traditional, structural domination. Discursive will formation based on communicative action would dominate purposive-rational action or work in a manner that: (a) excludes coercive, manipulative, or degrading means that are contrary to the values of equality, respect, and autonomy that characterize undistorted communicative action; and (b) makes the choice of both ends and means a matter of undistorted, free communication, that is, of democracy.[11] This hypothetical postmodern world broadly corresponds to the content of presently needed, progressive change. That is, the needed change is to reverse the current dominance of purposive-rational action and establish the social and political supremacy of undistorted symbolic interaction. This dominance of communicative action arguably would lead to both means and ends that are consistent with the values implicit in communicative action itself. If it did, means and ends would exhibit a degree and form of unity that would be central to their moral significance.

This sketch of a hypothesized historical dialectic and the corresponding claim concerning presently needed change may have moved too fast. Some preliminary consideration both of how to evaluate the adequacy of a process of change and, even more basically, what should count as change is needed.

The appropriate measure of the process of change will turn significantly on whether the independence thesis or the unity thesis is (or is properly assumed to be) true. If ends and means are separate, the adequacy of a process for achieving progressive (or nonprogressive) change will depend simply on the process's instrumental effectiveness. If united, adequacy will depend on the congruence of the process and the *needed* changes. This congruence, however, would be recognizable only with knowledge of the proper ends or with noninstrumentalist reasons to accept the results of or values implicit in a particular process. (Note that the unity thesis implicitly asserts there could be no "value neutral," pure process theory of the first amendment.)

An evaluation also presupposes an understanding of what counts as change. The inquiry here and for purposes of an adequate first amendment theory arguably requires a notion of fundamental or at least meaningful social change relevant to our historical circumstances. Although any attempt to define these concepts will be controversial, some notion of what counts is necessary for further analysis. I assume that mere change in the ruling elite, or even a change in the composition and ideology of that elite combined with a change in the legal ownership of resources, would not in itself amount to significant social change. Rather, from a democratic perspective "only changes in daily life make a substantial difference. . . . [B]eside them the overthrows of political superstructures remain superficial. . . . Political changes, those which modify the government and the economic structure (the relations of production), have human interest only inasmuch as they change daily life."[12] For example, whether or which state bureaucrats or capitalist managers control a person's work life may make little difference in what the person does, in how she relates to or controls her activities, or in the security or benefits she receives. Given this notion of change, much apparently political but really tactical conduct relates at best to achieving intermediate goals that may not result in meaningful social change. Even successful major strategic efforts by revolutionary parties to replace political leaders will not necessarily result in fundamental change, whereas implementation of seemingly more mundane but innovative value-based practices consistently do. Therefore, it becomes important not to tie first amendment protections to the merely tactical at the expense of the more truly political.

Although a theory explaining the process of all significant social change, good and bad, would be interesting, this chapter's inquiry into the role of the first amendment in protecting a "desirable" process of change does not need a theory of such breadth. It merely requires a theory of the process of progressive change for our historical period—a theory of change that our society needs or, perhaps, of the change that it wants. Even this narrower inquiry requires, however, that the theory be evaluative as well as descriptive. It must be able to identify needed or progressive change.

The value-laden task of abstractly determining the proper goals of change might be avoided if we could conclude that progressive change is what results from an identifiable "proper" process.[13] For example, progressive change might be whatever change is produced by the continued exercise of first amendment rights. Thus, Holmes could suggest that if in the long run, presumably after a complete presentation of alternative views, the dominant forces of the community accept the beliefs expressed in a proletarian dictatorship, so be it.[14] This view treats the *process* as the relevant concern.

This process "definition" treats progressive change in a manner quite analogous to the way some economists treat economic efficiency or welfare and some pluralist political scientists describe the public interest. Each analysis presumably responds to whatever individualistic inputs (preferences) that actually exist and can make themselves felt or heard.[15] And although each analysis has a similar allure, including a superficial claim to value neutrality, each also has similar problems. Their focus solely on process is inadequate. Since different processes stimulate and respond to different inputs and achieve different ends, any choice of process necessarily implicates and should depend on value considerations. And at least if the value content of the process itself and its outcomes can differ, the relevance of first amendment rights to needed political or social change will apparently depend on an evaluation of predicted outcomes. A theory of the first amendment predicated on its desirable contribution to the process of change must show that first amendment rights, either alone or in combination with other practices such as majority rule, representative democracy, federalism, or guaranteed provision for certain of people's substantive needs, can contribute to progressive change that our society needs.[16]

The traditional marketplace of ideas theory claims to satisfy this requirement. The theory asserts that truth is a proper guide to how we should organize society and that first amendment protection of speech, that is, the free trade of ideas, will move us toward truth. However, Chapter 1 showed that this theory depends on assumptions about the nature of truth and human rationality that are fundamentally flawed. Thus, this solution must be rejected.

In contrast to the marketplace of ideas defense of a process, the "radical" who proclaims the necessity of violent revolution claims to identify at least some necessary substantive elements of needed change, even if only a radical redistribution of power. Implicitly, this radical asserts that exercise of first amendment rights necessarily is inadequate for achieving needed social change. This pessimism may reflect the conclusion that violent means are inherently necessary (and could be effective) and that the first amendment does not protect these necessary violent means. Alternatively, even if first amendment protected activities are in theory adequate to achieve the needed change, the radical could argue that in practice the state will not permit their effective use. American history shows radical political or labor dissidents' basic civil liberties continually subjected to legal restrictions and state-sponsored illegal violent suppressions. This history belies any hope that dominant power elites will permit real scope for nonviolent, expressive, presumably first-amendment-protected, means that could actually lead to fundamental change. The radical also points to the consistent willingness of the United States to use violent and illegal means to suppress democratic progressive change anywhere in the world if the change threatens certain established interests—a pattern dramatically illustrated by the U.S.-backed overthrow of Allende in Chile in 1973 or our consistent military interventions in Central America. Thus, on one or the other ground, the radical claims that desired progressive change can (only) be achieved by instrumental, even though objectionable, means that are justified only by the ends.

This chapter criticizes this radical's theoretical argument, which reduces to the independence thesis. Moreover, I argue that the radical's quite realistic doubts about the actual opportunity to use first amendment rights is an admission of defeat.[17] I argue that the obvious alternative—violent, revolutionary action—cannot produce the needed, progressive change. To make these arguments, this chapter defends the unity thesis. To the extent that this thesis is correct, normatively defensible behavioral practices, especially including first amendment rights, will be central to achieving desirable or progressive change. Although I have not yet discussed the specific content of needed change, the issue will be postponed for the moment to first examine and critique the independence thesis on which, as noted above, the proponent of violent revolution relies. This diversion will prove useful for the later, more affirmative discussions.

THE IDEOLOGICAL AND EXPERIENTIAL BASIS OF THE INDEPENDENCE THESIS

The unity thesis, the belief that the means used determine the ends produced, enjoys a long history.[18] But so does the independence thesis, the claim that ends are independent of the means, and the independence thesis clearly predominates in modern thought. This thesis sees power as instrumental: With power, one can implement any end; without it, one can achieve nothing.[19] Force may be inadequate for directly achieving some ends—for example, force may not by itself be sufficient to create desirable or democratic relations between people. Still, obtaining power is a necessary, if not sufficient, means to accomplish ends. Thus, many radicals argue that unless the left seizes state power and takes control of the means of violence, any attempt to realize democratic ends will be suppressed.[20] They implicitly agree with C. Wright Mills that "[a]ll politics is a struggle for power; the ultimate kind of power is violence."[21] Therefore, the first task of those interested in implementing democratic, socialist ends is to obtain instrumental power and to seize state power. This radical argument merely particularizes the more general thesis that ends are independent of instrumentally effective means.

Two features of this radical argument are particularly important. First, it equivocates between the broad claim that instrumental means can produce any end and the narrower claim that the left must control instrumental force in order to prevent others from frustrating its attempts to realize radical goals. This narrower claim reflects realistic pessimism about the willingness of the right to cede power peacefully and democratically and is consistent with the common observation that violence can be destructive although not creative.[22]

Second, the independence thesis does not distinguish various related, but different, phenomena such as violence, strength, and power. This reductionism reflects an uncritical acceptance of instrumentalism. It may, moreover, blur our understanding of the process of change. Hannah Arendt argued that these phenomena are so different that violence and power should be treated as opposites: violence is instrumental, depends on implements, and can only be destructive; whereas power is an end itself, depends on consent, and is creative.[23] An important feature of Hitler's Nazism and of Stalin's Bolshevism was their heavy reliance on violence to destroy much of the traditional community, leaving many people isolated and therefore powerless.[24] In the following discussion, "violence" refers to instrumental activities that destroy or injure the objects against which they are directed. "Strength" refers to the capacity of an individual to act autonomously and resist manipulation and domination by others. "Power" refers to the capacity of people to act in concert to create and maintain practices or institutions.[25]

The independence thesis is even more central to liberalism or, more specifically, the worst elements in liberalism. The *assumption* of independence of ends and means is a central strand in liberal social thought. The felt but false[26] *experience* of their independence is a major and fundamentally alienating aspect of modern society. Neither of these two points is obvious. Their development below helps both to explain the appeal and expose the flaws of the independence thesis, to explain typical intellectual resistance to the unity thesis, and to show why progressive change requires action that embodies the values it attempts to realize. Specifically, in developing these points I argue that liberalism contains contradictory oppressive and liberating impulses and that human progress requires realization of the liberating impulses while transforming the social conditions that presently link the liberating and oppressive impulses. Furthermore,

I argue that oppressive aspects of liberalism relate to a deeply embedded experiential and intellectual acceptance of the independence thesis.

Liberalism is an elusive label. Its various elements are broad enough to encompass most elements of "modernism." In this country's politics, it clearly encompasses most values and views of both "conservative" Republicans and "progressive" Democrats. My usage requires clarification. As used here, liberalism has normative, institutional, and theoretical content. The key *normative content*, which is the most fundamental and persistent aspect of liberalism, exalts the values of human equality, self-determination, and self-realization—that is, of equality and liberty. Historically, the *institutional content* of liberalism has included capitalist economic forms, bureaucratic organizational forms, and, at its best, democratic political forms. The *theoretical content* attempts to explain and justify liberal institutions in terms of liberal values, and sometimes to explain and justify liberal values themselves. This theoretical component faces the ultimately impossible task of showing that the fundamental value of liberty or autonomy is consistent with a social structure that in reality controls and limits human choice. I argue below that the key element of the prevailing, although unsuccessful, explanation is the assumption that ends are independent of means.

Progress within *liberal thought* requires first exposing contradictions between liberalism's institutions and its values and then recommending appropriate reform or transformation of those institutions. In this sense, John Stuart Mill's flirtations with socialism and welfare programs carried on the liberal tradition more profoundly than did Herbert Spencer's atomistic, competitive individualism, which by the time he wrote was no longer liberal even if these same views had been liberal and progressive as an attack on feudalism and aristocracy during earlier centuries. Likewise, progress within *liberal practice* requires establishing better institutional embodiments of basic liberal values. From this perspective, many self-proclaimed radical critics of liberalism turn out to be the true modern liberals.

The modern world has seen the rise of instrumental rationality, which is solely concerned with effective means, and the simultaneous decline of substantive or value rationality.[27] Liberal thought often treats substantive values not as matters of reason at all but as merely arbitrary individual preferences.[28] It even reverses the traditional view of public discourse as a realm of value debate. Value issues are increasingly removed from public discussion while technical rationality becomes the central public concern. Although less frequently noticed, this distinction between substantive values and instrumental reason also implies the separability of ends and means. Only if means are independent of ends can commentators isolate and evaluate instrumental action or reason solely in terms of its effectiveness or efficiency in achieving exogenous ends. Instead, if means and ends are not separate, we must normatively evaluate action for its congruence with ends.

This assumed independence of ends and means influences our view of the world. For example, this assumption encourages the view that the market is merely a relatively efficient means to satisfy people's subjective preferences; or the view that bureaucratic organizations ideally are merely efficient structures of advancing organizational goals. Likewise, only the assumption of the independence of ends and means permits the belief that a social scientist can describe the world from a neutral perspective and that the "descriptive" perspective chosen does not itself implicate important value choices. Most important, only the independence thesis allows the democrat or the liberal to leave questions of means to the technocrats or policy scientists.

The independence thesis is also key to the theoretical content of liberalism. First, liberal social theory maintains that people often have no real choice of means. Ambitious individuals or organizations will search for, and successful individuals and organizations will find and employ, the most efficient means. A Darwin-like competitive struggle for survival will cause those who employ the most efficient means to prevail. For example, given market competition, the enterprise that does not find and adopt the most efficient means will be unable to reproduce or replace its means of production and, therefore, will face eventual bankruptcy. In this way, properly functioning capital markets control the choice of means employed by market enterprises.* Second, a central normative value and empirical assumption of liberalism is that people should be and are "free" to choose their ends. If structure and circumstance dictate the means people employ, choice of ends or values is possible only if the chosen ends are separate from the dictated means. Thus, liberal theory must endorse the premise of separability in order to make its social theory that treats means as dictated consistent with its normative content that treats ends as subject to free choice.

The writings of Hobbes and Weber, two magisterial theorists of the liberal order, illustrate the dependence of liberal theory on the independence thesis. Their writings show liberal social theory resting on "logical" arguments for the basically empirical claim that context, that is, circumstance and structure, normally dictates the choice of means.

In one of his most famous passages, Hobbes writes:

> I put for a general inclination of all mankind, a perpetual and restless desire of power after power, that ceaseth only in death. And the cause of this, is not always that a man hopes for a more intensive delight, than he has already attained to; or that he cannot be content with a moderate power: but because he cannot assure the power and means to live well, which he hath present, without the acquisition of more.[29]

According to this view, *no matter what a person's ends*, and no matter whether the person would be content with moderate delights, *the desire to maintain one's present level of well-being dictates a constant search for ever more efficient or more extensive means.* Power for Hobbes is a means unrelated to any particular end, but to the accomplishment of ends in general: "The power of a man, (to take it universally,) is his present means, to obtain some future apparent good."[30] Two features of Hobbes' account are particularly significant here. First, in this portrayal, people may not naturally want more and more and they are

---

*This point and others made here about the nature of market-oriented institutions will be further developed in Chapter 9 and will be central to one of its arguments concerning commercial speech.

presumably free to choose their ends, but they are nevertheless forced constantly to pursue efficient means and more power. Second, his account thereby implies a world in which ends and means are separate.[31]

Weber describes a similar world. He argues that a monocratically organized bureaucracy is "capable of attaining the highest degree of efficiency and is in this sense formally the most rational known means of carrying out imperative control over human beings."[32] He concludes that the development of an organized bureaucracy "makes 'revolution,' in the sense of the forceful creation of entirely new formations of authority, more and more impossible."[33] Escape from the bureaucracy is "normally possible only by creating an organization . . . which is equally subject to bureaucratization."[34] According to Weber, this "process of rationalization" is "man's destiny, against which it is useless to rebel and which no regime can avoid."[35] Yet this mandated selection of bureaucratically efficient means apparently does not entirely control people's ends. Indeed, the contribution of efficient means to the advancement of people's multifarious ends is what makes escape as undesirable as it is impossible. "[T]he material fate of the masses depends upon the continuous and correct functioning of the ever more bureaucratic organizations of private capitalism, and the idea of eliminating them becomes more and more utopian."[36]

Weber makes a similar argument regarding capitalist markets, which, along with bureaucracies, propel the historical process of rationalization. Competitive markets force enterprises to employ efficient means in the economic realm in order to successfully reproduce spent capital and avoid bankruptcy. Both Marxist and conservative economists basically concur in this aspect of Weber's analysis. The manner in which competition mandates the choice of efficient means is a key reason for the conservative economist to glorify the market: it efficiently fulfills human desires.[37] The Marxist sees the same compelled structural logic but argues that market relations of production are exploitative and the dictated behavior is alienating.[38]

Hobbes' and Weber's similar depictions of a structurally enforced orientation toward efficient or effective instrumental means is consistent with the possibility of human liberty only if ends are independent of means. Weber often acknowledges, some say despairingly recognizes, the problematic character of this assumed independence. Even though Weber considers the process of rationalization essential for the welfare of the masses and, thus, apparently essential for the realization of their ends, he also sees its more somber consequences. For example, Weber states that bureaucratic domination leads to the "dominance of a spirit of formalistic impersonality: . . . without hatred or passion, and hence without affection or enthusiasm."[39] "Bureaucracy develops the more perfectly, the more it is 'dehumanized,' the more completely it succeeds in eliminating from official business love, hatred, and all purely personal, irrational, and emotional elements which escape calculation."[40] Likewise, the other instrument of rationalization, the market, "is fundamentally alien to any type of fraternal relationship."[41] "The private enterprise system transforms into objects of 'labor market transactions' even those personal . . . relations which actually exist in the capitalist enterprise."[42]

Weber's observations imply that the structurally dictated means do have major value consequences, that they do affect which ends are realized. Specifically, they are well suited for serving certain instrumental and commodity ends. Thus, the independence of ends and means required by liberal normative theory would not appear to be empirically false under circumstances in which all of people's actual ends have an object or commodity nature. Likewise, the independence thesis would appear plausible as long as the analysis focuses only on ends that do have a commodity nature—as opposed to ends involving social development, participation, or relationships between people. In a typical commodity transaction, the buyer is concerned solely with the object of the trade and not with the sellers's past means. Similarly, the seller is unconcerned with the buyer's future use of the object. If all ends have this commodity nature, then only the instrumental effectiveness of the process of producing or reaching these ends would be relevant. However, this restricted view of ends ignores relations between people, excludes all forms of human interaction that are valued in themselves.

Many fields of academic study as well as many aspects of popular culture tend toward this commodity-oriented view of ends. For example, John Rawls implicitly fell into this view when he wrote: "Now obviously no one can obtain everything he wants; the mere existence of other persons prevents this."[43] Although Rawls later retracted the main implication of this statement,[44] this restricted view of people's ends plays an unfortunately key role in his argument.* Likewise, despite the efforts of better economists to avoid such simplification, economic analyses also typically assume a commodity orientation. This commodity-oriented view helps explain economists' tendency both to adopt theoretical constructs that assume that people view their own welfare as independent of others' welfare (i.e., assumption of independence of utility functions) and to be concerned primarily with market exchanges rather than to value relationships, including the quality of market relations.[46]

Although this commodity view of ends sometimes seems absurdly narrow, it is implied by the thesis that ends are independent of means. And, as noted above, this independence thesis in turn is crucial for reconciling liberal social theory (which emphasizes and explains the impossibility of escape from the efficiency and primacy of bureaucracies and capitalist markets) with liberal normative theory (which emphasizes the primacy of individual choice or freedom). Thus, this commodity view of ends reflects the struggle of liberal social theory to canonize an interpretation of human ends that justifies liberal institutions and reconciles these institutions with liberal normative theory.

Moreover, liberal social institutions generate experiences and promote val-

---

*Rawls argued that just principles for evaluating basic societal institutions that allocate primary goods are those that a person stripped of all information about herself and her society would choose for the allocation of "primary goods." Since principles that maximize some allocative goal in respect to primary goods will have consequences for other types of "goods," the rationality of the Rawlsian choice of allocative principles that only considers primary goods must depend on people's good life being unaffected by anything except the allocation of primary goods. To the extent that this effectively ignores "relational goods," the rationality of Rawls' argument for his principles of justice appears heavily dependent on people having solely commodity-oriented ends.[45]

ues that appear to confirm the independence thesis. Thus, the assumption that people's ends have a commodity nature increasingly corresponds to reality as market relations and bureaucratic practices spread into ever more realms of life and as market forces promote increased commodity orientations. As Weber observed, "[w]here the market is allowed to follow its own autonomous tendencies, its participants do not look toward the persons of each other but only toward the commodity."[47] Yet this reality is never fully realized. The market's and the bureaucracy's effect of devaluing human interaction, of devaluing both the actor's history and her participation, encourages resistance to extensions of market commodity relations and the false picture of humanity that such an extension reinforces.[48] Thus, despite the heroic effort of liberal social theory and the power of liberal institutions, in the end, neither can make the independence thesis true. And without the thesis, the theoretical efficiency-based justifications for liberal institutions likewise fail.

THE FAILURE OF THE INDEPENDENCE THESIS

Although liberal social theory assumes it, and liberal institutions reinforce the experience of it, the thesis that ends are normatively independent of the means is wrong. The following discussion defends this claim and in the process suggests certain key objectives of needed change.

In the bureaucratic and market contexts briefly examined above, means appear to be independent of commodity ends. For example, a person can condemn exploitative child labor while positively valuing the attractiveness and usefulness of furniture that these youth produce. Because commodity relations pervade liberal society, experience appears to confirm the thesis that a person properly sees ends independent of means. Nevertheless, more thorough consideration shows a unity between the nature of ends and means in this society.

The competitive aspects of liberal society mandate the choice of instrumentally efficient means. This institutional mandate systematically treats everything and everyone involved in the process of production, exchange, or administration as raw material for advancing structurally determined ends, specifically the ends of profit or instrumental power. That is, these institutions treat their means, including the people involved, as commodities that lack any intrinsic value. The process systematically duplicates this commodity nature of its means in its commodity-ends. As Weber noted, the market and the bureaucracy systematically subvert those ends that are inconsistent with these institutions' instrumental nature. Thus, the first confirmation of the unity thesis is that in a market society, instrumental means only realize ends in their own image.

Corresponding to this identity is a second sense in which these ends and means are united. Neither the ends nor the means of the competitive market process reflect rationally considered value choices of the participants. As noted, the structure mandates the choice of efficient means. Likewise, a combination of the market enforced profit orientation, the technical capacities of the enterprise, and the profit opportunities generated by the expected responses of consumers determine the ends that the market enterprises produce. The enterprise's ends and means are alike in being dictated by the structure rather than by the producers' value choices. Thus, unity exists in the means and ends both being outside the control of the participants.[49]

People's lived experience provides a third confirmation of the unity thesis. Although liberal institutions assertedly separate means and ends, people properly experience their activities·as their lives and, in this sense, as their ends. When their daily activities are viewed as central to their lives, people's ubiquitous productive activities must be relevant as ends as well as means. In other words, means and ends are the same. This reality of unity manifests itself within liberal institutions of markets and bureaucracies as alienation—which is precisely the experience of lack of unity between a person's values or choices and the person's activities, characterized as either ends or means.

In contrast, imagined or partially existing alternatives to these key liberal institutions would also exhibit a unity, although a different unity, of ends and means. These possible practices or institutions, for example, those that intentionally emphasize interpersonal relations and participatory practices, would implicitly assume an intrinsic connection between ends and practice. The human, cooperative or self-realizing valuation of labor inputs that is possible in participatory practices allows this process to use noncommodity means and achieve noncommodity ends, at least in terms of the work experience. But like in the existing order, the different means within these imagined alternatives would correspond to its different ends. Moreover, the alternative could manifest unity by treating both its means and its ends as subject to either individual value choice or uncoerced value agreement. Thus, the alternative also illustrates the unity thesis.

The three confirmations of the unity thesis produce a seeming paradox. At one level, existing market and bureaucratic structures produce experiences that reflect the assumption that ends are independent of means. The economic structure separates the commodity ends that people produce from the actual producer's control, values, and, usually, ownership. Economic practices encourage people to separate their presumably positive evaluations of the commodity ends from their often negative evaluations of the means, that is, of their work. Thus, this economic order creates the experience of an independence of means and ends. Nevertheless, from the different and arguably more fundamental perspective of the relation between structure and experience, the thesis that means determine ends is confirmed. From this perspective, the experienced truth of the independence thesis in fact illustrates its falsity. Its instrumentalist assumptions concerning means are reproduced in people's everyday experiences of being mere instruments. Alienated practice produces alienated experience. Ends and means are unified both in being outside people's control and in being commodity–like.

The unity thesis identifies problems with the liberal order, thereby providing guidance as to the needed content of change. Social institutions ought to reflect and serve rather than limit people's needs, desires, and values. Institutions that restrict people's ends to those that conform to a commodity orientation are inconsistent with the liberal normative value of self-realization. Both theory and experience teach that many important human ends do not have a commodity nature. Personal relations, and sometimes productive or political projects, embody ends that analysis cannot reduce to a commodity form.[50] People value participation in itself, not merely as a means. Moreover, liberal institutions are equally inconsistent with the liberal normative value of self- determination. Left to their own devices, that is, unless politically controlled, liberal institutions are not within human control. The market pressures that generate "needs" for commodity goods are independent of human choice. In contrast, human self-determination requires that institutional forces be guided and controlled by undistorted communicative interaction free of domination.[51] In other words, the unity perspective identifies three ways in which modern liberal society's institutional structure is inadequate. It restricts the ends that are realizable. It divorces people's lives (at least, the that portion during which they are being used as means) from their values, thereby encouraging an alienated experience of disunity between their own ends and their lives. And it restricts the extent that people's lives, their values, and the activities in which they are used as productive means are subject to their own value choices. Each inadequacy points toward an element of needed change. These institutions should be transformed so that they better serve a broader range of needs (specifically better serve noncommodity needs); so that the process of serving needs is itself more a manifestation of people's values; and so that the process allows for human choice and self-determination.

The above discussion argued that the unity thesis provides the more powerful perspective in relation to key liberal institutions—markets and bureaucracies. Although liberal normative theory most requires the independence thesis in this context, here independence is at best an illusion obscuring the possibility of an alternative in which the actual unity would be affirming rather than alienating. Still, the insightfulness of the unity thesis for understanding these institutions and for pointing toward the need for institutional change may not be generalizable to other issues. The unity thesis is not necessarily transferable to understanding the *process* of fundamentally changing that society. Machiavelli may be right that criteria of action, criteria of right and wrong, that properly apply within an established order cannot apply to the "prince" who establishes that order.[52] The application of the unity thesis to the context of progressive change is undertaken in the next section. Still, to the extent that the above discussion convincingly described the independence thesis' ideological role in justifying liberal institutions, its deeply embedded place in modern life, and its tendency to distort our understanding of our experience, this discussion should undermine any unreflective confidence in the insightfulness of independence thesis in other contexts.

The unity thesis emphasizes the importance of people's practices being themselves valued and fulfilling. Arguably all activities should be of a sort that can be substantively valued. However, society clearly cannot do without instrumentalist activities, without work. Even most utopian visionaries concede that some of these activities will not be intrinsically enjoyable. Thus, something more must be said about the notion of a unity of means and ends as both description and objective.

The discussion of liberal institutions argued that, within them, the requirements of instrumental action largely control both means and ends. Both human self-determination and the realization of people's more specific ends require reversing instrumental action's present domination of individual value choice and of communicative action aimed at consensus. People need to experience their activities and interactions (the means) as manifestations of their values (the ends). Only activities controlled by and consistent with either undistorted communication or, where appropriate, individual value choice can provide this experience. For example, to the extent that the content of work is outside the worker's control, or involves the manipulation of others, or disrespects others, the existing order does not provide the participants with the experience of their activities being subjected to and controlled by themselves or by undistorted communication. Certainly, existing institutions are inadequate for achieving interpersonal and democratic ends. Thus, progress requires the transformation of social institutions that generate the experience of separation of ends and means. But this transformation cannot imply the elimination of instrumental action. Rather, if instrumental action is freely undertaken *and* is consistent with the norms of communicative action, if it embodies rather then contradicts values accepted in communicative action, then even if unpleasant, as work can be, the instrumental action is not alienated or separate from human choice but represents a form of unity. The progressive ideal, from the perspective of the unity thesis, must be to subordinate instrumental action and not use it in any way that undermines, distorts, or destroys communicative action oriented toward consensus.

This concept of needed change corresponds to the image of system evolution presented by several modern dialectical theorists. For example, Jurgen Habermas argues that the modern age has experienced economically produced value as the key scarce resource,[53] and that liberal institutions might be adequate to provide for this need. In contrast, the thematic scarce resource in postmodern societies, as currently envisioned, will be the supply of motivation and meaning. Providing for this need will require replacing or transforming existing institutions. Habermas suggests that the most hopeful of the possible consequences of this historical development would be that "the social integration of internal nature . . . [would be] accomplished discursively, [and] principles of participation could come to the fore in many areas of social life."[54] In other words, the needed change is for symbolic or communicative action and interaction to come to prevail over instrumental action.

When communicative action dominates, unity not only exists but is for the first time experienced. In this sense unity becomes the goal of change. A further claim will be defended in the next section—that unity also describes the proper means of change. Instrumental action suffices to produce commodity ends. But only symbolic and communicative action can produce structures in which these forms of action control. Progressive change today depends on using means that reflect or embody the desired ends. Achieving this change presently depends on employing communicative action and action subordinated to communicative action rather than relying on mere instrumental action. If correct, this conclusion has major implications for political activists as well as for first amendment theorists.

Of course, a caveat must be recognized. The thesis that the nature and normative quality of the means used will control or be congruent with the nature and normative quality of the ends achieved is, at best, a claim about a tendency or a useful perspective. That it is only a tendency and a useful perspective follows logically as long as people can disagree about the proper evaluation of means and ends. More fundamentally, it follows from the inevitably unpredictable consequences of any action and the variability of potential human response—facts no one in this nuclear age should forget. A stronger claim would imply that people could completely master their destinies. Only religious faith could sustain such absolutism.

THE UNITY OF ENDS AND MEANS IN THE PROCESS OF CHANGE

A central goal of progressive social change is to eliminate those market and bureaucratic practices that both assume and create the experience of a separation of ends and means and to end the dominance of instrumental action.[55] An obvious hypothesis is that people cannot eliminate the separation through actions that rely on it. Nevertheless, many "revolutionaries" who support the goals of ending the dominance of instrumental action and eliminating or transforming existing market and bureaucratic institutions conclude that this goal requires the seizure of state power, probably by violent means, thereby affording an opportunity to implement an end to alienated practices. Other radicals reject this conclusion of the "revolutionaries" and emphasize that using coercive means to eliminate objectionable practices contradicts the objective of integrating actual practice and human values. In response, the advocate of revolutionary seizure of state power observes that contradictions are an intrinsic aspect of our condition, a fact the realistic activist must be aware of while aiming at transcendence. Activists cannot transcend contradictions by ignoring them. Unappealing instrumental means are necessary in these circumstances.

Despite the force of this argument, its conclusion is wrong. Professor Sholomo Avineri argues that "Marx's theory of *praxis* easily suggested to him that such a revolutionary *praxis* will substantially determine the nature of future society. A revolutionary movement based on terror, intimidation and blackmail will ultimately produce a society based on these methods as well."[56] Marx was basically right. Although claims about the relevant relation of means and ends cannot be made with logical or causal certainty, the following comments offer suggestive support for the hypothesis that the separation of ends and means cannot be eliminated by actions that rely on it.

First, if the earlier analysis of liberal theory is correct,[57] the "revolutionaries' analysis adopts precisely the worst features of liberal social theory. A key radical aim is to transcend social structures that separate or alienate ends from human means. In contrast, western liberal social theory claims that, to reach the separately identified goal, rationalized structures usually mandate the choice of (often objectionable) means.[58] When the "revolutionary" accepts this entirely instrumentalist theory, he* implicitly concedes the impossibility of the radical aim to integrate ends and means, values and practice. If this liberal social theory must be accepted, how can the revolution ever transcend it? This dilemma suggests that a truly radical analysis would describe practices that directly undermine the social basis of this premise of liberal social theory. Possibly, the revolutionary's violent project is not really radical at all.

Second, the hope of successfully using destructive instrumental means to transform society depends on eventually achieving the desired end, and subsequently abandoning the objectionable means. The metaphoric postrevolutionary withering away of the state exemplifies this type of hoped for eventuality. In disquieting ways, these revolutionary hopes parallel the hope that a person can achieve salvation in commodities rather than meaningful activity. Just as commodities never fulfill the succession of desire after desire, the utopian ends of revolution constantly recede while the means that they seem to justify continue. In both contexts, the everyday experience of life as a constant process of becoming rather than as a matter of achieving contentment undermines this hope that future ends will eventually justify present means. Means do not so much *achieve* as *form* the actual content of everyday life.

Third, the revolutionaries' use of normatively offensive means encourages several predictable behavioral responses. Because people have a psychological need to reduce dissonance, they are inclined to establish a congruence between their practices, ways of perceiving, and ends or values. Thus, a revolutionary leader who has relied on violent, hierarchical, or otherwise "bad" means is likely to reduce dissonance by assuming the desirability, or at least the inevitability, of using these means to achieve "good" ends. Moreover, the revolutionaries' success places in power people who may be well intended and dedicated, but whose personal experience has taught them that destructive instrumental practices are the most successful way of responding to threatening circumstances. Given these experiences and the improbability of any society in which threatening circumstances, real or apparent, are not of concern, reliance on instrumental, violent means will continue to appear necessary.

Fourth, the content of change may depend on the role played in the process of change by the two types of action previously discussed: instrumental or purposive-rational action, and communicative or symbolic action.[60] Instrumental means obviously can change the world. The purest form of instrumental action—violence—can destroy existing structures, both material structures and patterns of human interactions. Other forms of instrumental action are well suited for constructing or producing material forms. For example, instrumental action dominates in commodity production. Instrumental or purposive-rational action, however, may be incapable of creating new, less distorted, and more democratic patterns of communicative interaction and control—and these are precisely the changes that are most crucial today. The needed new patterns of communicative interaction and control and the corresponding increased human

---

*The use of "he" flags the possibility that this instrumentalist aspect of liberal thought is presently more identified with the thought of men than of women.[59]

capacities are most likely to result precisely from new embodiments of such new patterns in people's symbolic and communicative interactions and from changes in their consensual arrangements. That is, the change requires means that embody the needed ends.

Struggle is, of course, necessary. However, the instrumentalist notion that some people can force other people to interact as equals who respect each other is dubious. Reliance on instrumental force at best achieves a reversal of the dominant party. It is ill-suited to achieve the dominance of egalitarian, communicative interaction. However, other forms of struggle, resistance, and creation are possible. Principled refusal to cooperate except as equals may be the most direct and successful method to overcome elite opposition and resistance to needed change. In this scenario, force appears impotent—it can destroy but cannot achieve cooperation or interaction. In contrast, only new practices and patterns of interaction seem capable of increasing people's capacities to comprehend others' viewpoints, to formulate their own viewpoints, to see alternatives, and, most relevantly here, to embody values in action while respecting the equality of others. In stark contrast to instrumental action, symbolic and communicative interaction and consensus-based cooperation appear perfectly suited for creating new human capacities and new patterns of human interaction and for extending democratic control.[61]

This distinction between the different types of changes resulting from these two types of action closely parallels Hannah Arendt's claims that violence, a paradigm of instrumental action that separates ends and means, can destroy power but never create it, and that violence is by its nature mute.[62] Likewise, the distinction reflects Jurgen Habermas' conclusion:

> The substance of domination is not dissolved by the power of technical control. . . . The irrationality of domination . . . could be mastered only by the development of a political decision-making process tied to the principle of general discussion free from domination. Our only hope for the rationalization of the power structure lies in conditions that favor political power for thought developing through dialogue.[63]

The revolutionary might accept the claim that violence cannot create power or eliminate domination. This "radical" could still argue that the initial task of the process of change must be to destroy the old, objectionable institutions, and that instrumental "bad" means can most effectively serve this "destructive" end. The alternative perspective of the unity thesis sees it differently. The radical's objectionable means may not really move us forward at all. In place of the hierarchical, instrumental institutions of the old order, these instrumental means leave a similar hierarchical, instrumental organization that was the means of the overthrow. The radical has conceded that Weber was right: Escape is achieved only by employing equally hierarchical, efficient bureaucratic structures.[64] The revolutionary struggle, so costly in human terms, leaves the good objectives of the "revolution" unfulfilled. Arguably, these objectives cannot be fulfilled except through communicative interactions that would constitute a democratization of social institutions and a unification of practice and liberal ends.[65] Thus, the only possible gain of an instrumentalist, violent overthrow is an increased likelihood that the new regime will allow the "real" revolution to begin. Yet even this potential gain will be unlikely for various reasons, including factors mentioned above. Experiences and necessary rationalizations of a successful revolutionary group encourage it to find continued use of instrumental or violent means acceptable and perhaps necessary. In destroying the old order, violence may also destroy institutional protections for popularly chosen experiments and practices.[66] Moreover, the new regime's successful takeover probably means that it is more powerful and effective than the replaced regime, a fact that bodes ill for the prospect of increased popular control. Ultimately, for these objectionable means to contribute to progressive change, some of these predictable effects of the "revolutionary" process must not occur. Only then could we even hope that, *after* the use of destructive instrumental means, real progress could begin—a rather implausible line of empirical assumptions to justify destructive, inhumane practices.

History is the obvious field on which to test a theory concerning the relation of ends and means in the process of change. The broad issue is to what extent and in what ways the process of becoming controls what societies, as well as persons, become. A full presentation would trace how the content of fundamental change in each historical period related to the process of change in that period.[67] Here a more limited investigation will suffice to test my basic claim: that when the process of change depends on the use of objectionable instrumental means such as violence, the outcome will neither realize the liberal values of autonomy and self-determination nor be democratic and egalitarian. Instead the outcome will at best be a more instrumentalist, hierarchical, centralized regime. Thus, in the modern period, successful use of these means predictably lead to either capitalism or state capitalism. In contrast, truly progressive change would require mass participation in democratizing and transforming existing institutions. Or would require large-scale refusals to cooperate with existing institutions combined with popular involvement in creating new institutions that incorporate democratic, egalitarian values. In other words, progressive change requires that the process embody the values implicit in the ends sought.

Before turning to the historical account, however, one consideration deserves special emphasis. There are certainly historical examples of successful, progressive revolutions that used violent, instrumentalist means to create capitalist or bureaucratic states. These examples are consistent with the thesis that use of these means is both unnecessary and, in fact, adverse to leftists' present attempts to move beyond capitalism. The unity thesis would predict that these violent means would be successful in producing capitalist or bureaucratic states precisely because these states, like the means used, maintain the dominance of instrumental rationality and the experience of the separation of the ends and means. And although these states could be progressive advances beyond the feudal or colonial regimes that they replace, the change needed today is different.

The obvious initial issue for the historical investigation is whether violent, revolutionary seizure of state power has ever produced democratic, socialist, or otherwise "liberated" societies that represent revolutionary advances beyond liberal capitalism. This investigation poses a number of problems. First, clearly, people strongly disagree about the proper characterization of Russia, China, and various other countries such as Cuba, Cambodia, Vietnam, and Nicaragua, that have experienced violent, leftist seizures of state power. Nevertheless, to continue the discussion without undertaking a full-fledged and inevitably inconclusive historical investigation, I will rely on characterizations that I find most persuasive. And although there are some variations in characterizations, some of these states are best described as embodying a bureaucratized state capitalism; others, despite some positive achievements, also have not created effective, socialist, democratic societies. Finally, attribution of result to means is complicated by the inevitable mixture of means used during the revolution.

Second, attribution of historical cause and effect is inherently controversial and value laden. Moreover, historical time and change never stop. Even if the unity thesis is basically insightful, to what extent should we expect events (that is, further practices or "means") subsequent to the Russian and Chinese revolutions to have more impact on the existing states than do the past revolutions? Possibly the discussion below should be understood as at best opening up possibilities for seeing and understanding historical change rather than as "proving" any thesis.

Third, it would be out of place as well as beyond my ability to undertake here a comprehensive account of even a few past revolutions. Instead, the following historical discussion relies primarily on an account of the French, Russian, and Chinese revolutions given by Theda Skocpol in her highly respected book *States and Social Revolutions*.[68]

Many aspects of Professor Skocpol's analysis support the thesis of a strong connection between the content of revolutionary means and revolutionary outcomes. She also emphasized, however, that the available means are mostly structurally determined—claiming that decisions and ideological orientations of revolutionary leaders have virtually no relevance to revolutionary outcomes.[69] Skocpol argues that the French, Russian, and Chinese revolutions developed under similar structural conditions. Each country's economy was dependent on underdeveloped agrarian production. Additionally, each state's governmental leadership sought to increase state revenue or national productivity—increases necessary to meet the political elite's goal of more effective military competition with rival nation states. In each case, the government's efforts generated opposition from the economically dominant classes who probably have to pay these bills. Loss of support for the state leadership followed from the regime's international ineffectiveness and the disaffection of the economically dominant classes. Under these circumstances, each old regime collapsed in the face of peasant revolts.[70] Finally, in all three countries, the circumstances that lead to the collapse also made building armies and more potent administrations the key initial task after the revolution.[71] Each revolution spawned a leadership that effectively used organized coercion to set up a larger, more centralized, and more effective state administration.[72]

In many respects these revolutions support Weber's thesis of a historical movement toward increased rationalization and bureaucratic domination from which escape is impossible since any revolutionary regime must rely upon an administrative structure at least as rationalized as that of the old regime.[73] Nevertheless, Skocpol identifies two problems with Weber's thesis: its failure to explain adequately the specific variations in the French, Russian, and Chinese revolutionary outcomes; and its failure to explain the outcome in postrevolutionary China, where, to some extent, less bureaucratic domination and greater popular control and participation in decision making occurred.[74]*

On closer examination, the congruence between Skocpol's historical account and Weber's thesis occurs only in those areas where Weber's thesis and the unity thesis overlap, while the unity thesis corresponds to the deviations from Weberian predictions that Skocpol observes. Both theses predict that revolutions or processes of change that rely on instrumentalist means will lead to more efficiently organized, bureaucratized, or rationalized, new regimes. For Weber, this expectation follows simply because the historical movement toward increased instrumental rationality permits no escape. The historical process merely represents the evolutionary survival of the fittest society. Therefore, any successful revolution inevitably must rely on these means. For the unity thesis, this expectation follows because instrumentalist means predictably lead to instrumentalist, bureaucratic outcomes. But according to the unity thesis, other outcomes, reflecting noninstrumentalist means, are theoretically possible.

The unity thesis explains why China partially deviated from Weber's model. Unlike the French or the Russians, the Chinese Communists, after their purge from the Kuomintang in 1928, became the first set of revolutionary state builders whose only option during the revolutionary struggle was to "persuade" peasants to volunteer soldiers, supporters, and supplies.[75] The Chinese Communists developed an unusual method. The army engaged in political education and productive activities and generally tried to practice the ends of the revolution as a means of mobilizing the peasantry and gaining its cooperation.[76] Also unlike the French and Russian revolutions, the Chinese revolution resulted in a remarkable degree of decentralization of decision making, a relatively egalitarian distribution of material wealth, the improvement of local welfare through the use of local agricultural surplus, and a greater control by committees than by bureaucratic hierarchies.[77] These differing outcomes in China parallel the different form of the Chinese revolutionary struggle. The progressive aspects of China's new regime were essentially an extension of their method of revolution.

Nevertheless, China's postrevolutionary development has not been unwavering. To the extent the Chinese revolution depended on the use of organized coercion and violence, the unity thesis would suggest that its desirable deviation from an instrumental, bureaucratic, hierarchical result would be only partial and possibly temporary, unless popular pressure and mass involvement could continue the revolution with an ever increasing use of methods that integrate means with desired outcomes.

Skocpol notes that in the mid–1950s China appeared on the verge of becom-

---

*Events since Skocpol wrote may change the appropriate characterization of China. As noted above, it may be inappropriate to attribute those changes to practices that occurred during the revolution. This underlines that the unity and independence theses can at best be insightful interpretive devices.

ing, institutionally, a carbon copy of the Stalinist system.[78] But after 1957, "through hard-fought debates, a tentative new leadership consensus emerged."[79] Surprisingly, Skocpol pictures here a more "voluntarist," consciously chosen route of development than her main arguments would suggest possible. This result is predictable, however, on the basis of the unity thesis. Participatory, democratic, value-integrated means should result in outcomes that embody the consciously formulated ends of the participants. Therefore, this particular route of development would be more "voluntarist" in the sense that the ends could correspond to people's choices.[80] As Skocpol describes it, the particular strategic position of the Chinese Communists led them to adopt means that in turn led to outcomes that more accurately embodied their objectives.[81] In contrast, the French and Russian revolutionaries adopted the most efficient available instrumental means, a choice apparently dictated by their circumstances.[82] Again, according to the unity thesis, when the structure effectively controls the choice of means, whether or not people could have refused or avoided its dictates, the structure, and not the revolutionaries' program, will control the outcomes. Those outcomes will correspond to the content of the means in important ways. Thus, the unity thesis explains the different outcome of the Chinese revolution. The Chinese revolutionaries' ability to steer away from Stalinism reflects capacities for egalitarian and participatory value-implementing action that they developed during their revolution and further reflects means, such as "hard-fought debates," that they later used in extending their revolution.

Of course, these broad observations prove little. Even if in retrospect the ends and means of historical change have congruent value content, the plausibility of the unity thesis depends on the relation's being more than a mere chance correlation. Thus, confidence in the thesis presupposes some understanding of why outcomes, or the never-ending succession of outcomes, are connected with means.

Skocpol's study illustrates the main practical explanations that were presented earlier in this section. She notes that the process of obtaining political dominance leaves a legacy of learned skills and capacities that continue to be the new regime's most reliable and, therefore, most frequently utilized means of further action.[83] If the new regime obtained dominance through organized coercion and violence, those means normally will continue to be the most available instruments for furthering the leadership's goals and interests after the revolution.

For example, post-revolutionary Russia was faced with choosing between two development strategies: inducing increased peasant production in return for low-priced manufactured goods or coercively collectivizing and exploiting the peasantry in order to support heavy industry. The revolution's legacy of political and organizational means made the second, Stalinist solution the only feasible choice.[84] This solution relied on "mobilizing urban-based Party and worker teams to go out into the politically hostile countryside to seize grain from and reorganize the peasant communities, [which] was exactly the kind of activity that had led to victories for the same men in the recent heroic past."[85] The strikingly different results of the Chinese revolution, at least in the 1960s and 1970s, relate to the distinctive political capacities developed and practiced by the Chinese Communists in their rise to power.[86] The Chinese revolution did not use violence to destroy all community-based organizational power in the countryside. Instead, it had developed local political institutions that both increased and democratized power within local communities.

A second reason to expect a connection between the method of overthrowing an old order and the practices within the new order is that the process of change reinforces notions of the proper and permissible ways to advance ends. Skocpol suggests that revolutionary ideologies, such as Jacobinism or Marxism-Leninism, help provide justifications for the employment of "unlimited means to achieve ultimate political ends on earth."[87] The revolutionaries' experience of using objectionable means to further important but never fully achieved goals reinforces their tendency to view particular instrumentalist, dehumanized responses as justified on the basis of forever receding ends.[88]

Furthermore, unless revolutions perceived as politically "correct" occur in all countries at once, real or apparent external threats as well as internal needs will apparently justify postponing the adoption of practices that themselves embody desired ends. This justification will appear particularly persuasive to a leadership that perceives instrumentalist, hierarchical practices to be the only effective means of furthering revolutionary ends. And since this leadership would perceive itself as necessary to implement these revolutionary ends, these ends will also appear to justify the leadership's use of instrumental practices to maintain its own position of dominance.

The revolutionaries' experience of forever receding ends justifying objectionable instrumental means is not unique. Liberal market societies justify dehumanized work experiences and instrumental relations on the basis of the forever receding satisfaction promised by consumer goods, fame, or power. The "revolutionaries'" purportedly radical analysis merely echos liberal social theory in accepting the independence thesis. Implementation of this misguided analysis frustrates their revolutionary aims in the same way that liberal market societies and bureaucratic regimes frustrate liberal values. This revolutionary strategy fails because it accepts a misguided aspect of liberal social theory as its guide.

A hierarchical system, whether of capitalist managers or revolutionary state builders, may be capable of accomplishing many useful instrumentalist ends. Nevertheless, few actual examples exist of those in power willingly offering freedom to subordinated groups who have the capacity to accept it but who had not effectively demanded it. Moreover, historical changes in what would count as an advance in freedom and changes in the structures of domination may make it even more difficult for today's capitalist than, for example, for yesterday's feudal lord or slave owner effectively to offer freedom, and more difficult for today's worker than for yesterday's serf or slave to accept freedom. Many past structures of domination, based on specific legal relations between the subordinate and the master, permitted the individual owners in individual cases to eliminate the domination. The slave could be legally freed. In contrast, in the modern world, the dominated already have formal freedom. It is unclear now what the dominant party can give directly. Of course, the dominant party could, but often does not, avoid concerted and often illegal action directed at further disempowering the subordinate party. Despite market pressures to engage in it, managers or owners could, for example, avoid illegal union busting. But "good will" of the "master" neither prevented nor ended legal slavery. Today absence of good will may be even less of the problem and its presence may provide even less of a possible solution to the evils of modern alienating, subordinating institutions. Rather, today the key to advances in liberation may be mass participation in liberating practices and in the creation of new, democratic institutions. The presence of opportunities to participate in these practices could be crucial to progressive change. The first amendment, for example, could become relevant to the extent that its formal guarantees actually protect participation in these liberating practices.

Skocpol's speculations concerning the conditions for a *future* revolutionary transformation of advanced industrial nations superficially appear quite anomalous given her analysis of earlier revolutions. These earlier revolutions depended on two crucial factors: intense pressure on the existing regime from escalating international military competition; and a political conflict between the state organization and the dominant economic classes. Furthermore, these two factors occurred in a world undergoing an *uneven* transformation to capitalism.[89] In contrast, Skocpol suggests that a social revolution in an advanced industrial nation would depend not on international competition and military pressures, but would require an easing of international military rivalries coupled with roughly *simultaneous* progress of democratic movements in all advanced countries.[90] Moreover, unlike earlier "cataclysmic" revolutions, she suggests this modern revolution would "flow gradually . . . out of a long series of 'non-reformist reforms,' accomplished by mass-based political movements struggling to democratize every major institution."[91] Finally, at least in tone, she appears to credit this future revolutionary process with a self-consciousness about its struggle for democratization,[92] although she severely criticizes the voluntaristic pretensions of past revolutionary leaders either to have contributed importantly to the earlier revolutions or even to have known or desired the outcomes.[93]

Despite the divergence of her hopes and predictions for the future from her descriptions of past social revolutions, Skocpol's focus on structure holds constant. She investigates both the structural features that determined the forms of past revolutions and those that would determine the necessary form of a successful future revolutionary process. In particular, she argues that the implausibility of "modern states disintegrat[ing] as administrative-coercive organizations without destroying societies at the same time"[94] requires the revolutionary process that she projects.

The unity thesis makes sense of Skocpol's analysis. Skocpol views these projected revolutions as differing in both process and outcome from those she has studied. The earlier revolutions led, with some apparent, progressive differences in the case of China, to increased hierarchy, centralization, and capacity to apply instrumental force. In contrast, her projected revolution would democratize all social institutions. Earlier revolutions used centralization and instrumental, violent, coercive techniques to seize and consolidate power and resulted in instrumentalist, centralized regimes. Skocpol's projected successful future revolution in advanced industrial states would rely on means that are less instrumental, less violent, more value-embodying, and more democratic; and those means would achieve more egalitarian and democratic ends.[95] Thus, the unity thesis corresponds both to her description of past social revolutions—instrumental, centralizing, and hierarchical both in means and results. And it corresponds to the relation of the ends and means in her projected future revolution. Moreover, the unity thesis justifies Skocpol's otherwise unexplained assumption that the revolutionary means she speculates are structurally necessary could lead for the first time to a "true democratization." It supports her assumption that this revolution would be unlike past revolutions, which have "not conformed to Marx's ... moral vision" and which, even where they "have expropriated domestic capitalist classes in the name of socialist ideals, have hardly resulted to date in ... prosperous, democratic communist societies."[96] Finally, given that one aspect of progressive social change is greater human self-determination, the unity thesis helps explains Skocpol's view of how this change could occur. If the nature of the means determines the nature of the ends, Skocpol is right to conclude that greater political self-awareness combined with value-embodying political activities are necessary as means and would lead to more self-determination. As the unity thesis asserts, greater self-determination results from practices that directly embody the actor's ends rather than from instrumental practices that maintain the experience of separation.

Skocpol implies the following analysis: (1) Different outcomes require the use of different means. (2) These different means are available under different structural conditions. (3) The progressive changes needed in modern, advanced industrial states are different from the progressive changes needed by earlier societies that underwent revolutions. (4) Therefore, modern states require different revolutionary means if they are to advance. The missing link in this progressive dialectic would be supplied if structural conditions in these modern states allowed for the different means. Specifically, progressive change would be possible if liberal, capitalist states offered institutional structures and normative conceptions that allowed for and encouraged the use of more democratic, value-integrated means.[97] Providing for democratic change is consistently seen as a major function of the first amendment.[98] Accordingly, the question is whether an effectively institutionalized first amendment would provide this missing link.

THE LIBERTY THEORY OF THE FIRST AMENDMENT AND THE MEANS NEEDED FOR PROGRESSIVE CHANGE

The dominant theory of the first amendment, the marketplace of ideas theory, focuses on expression intended to communicate a proposition or attitude that potentially can become a part of some debate. This theory does not provide adequate scope for the means needed for fundamental, progressive change.[99] First, since existing structures of domination distort people's values and perceptions, mere appeals to rationality are predictably inadequate to move us forward. At a minimum, for better values and new, more democratic, egalitarian perspectives to seem coherent, these values and perspectives must be grounded in new, possibly experimental practices that do not embody the existing structures of domination. Second, progressive change requires not only communication, but the development and exercise of power, the power to create new forms as well as the strength to resist existing structures.[100] Third, given that change requires using means that embody the desired ends, people must do more than talk; they must act in ways that embody their values. Failure to recognize value-based action as a necessary aspect of the process of change would be similar to concluding that a person whose religion placed stringent demands on behavior could adequately engage in the "free exercise" of religion if the law absolutely protected beliefs but gave little or no protection to action.[101] For needed change as for free exercise, value-based action is central.

These objections do not apply to the liberty theory of the first amendment. Although this theory is premised on respect for autonomy rather than on the societal need for an adequate process of change, it encompasses practices that could constitute a process of legitimate and progressive change. It justifies protection for political action that embodies people's values to a much greater extent than does the generally accepted marketplace of ideas theory. But to emphasize the relevance of the rights defined by the liberty theory, a final review of the process of change is necessary.

This chapter assumes that reliance on nonhierarchical, noninstrumental means for progressive change is a historical possibility. If the argument concerning the relation of means and ends is right, only this possibility permits advancement of the key liberal values of increased human autonomy and self-determination, and the attainment of a less alienated, more democratic society. But this possibility and, therefore, the relevance of the unity thesis, depend on the incorrectness of Weber's view that escape from the process of rationalization is impossible.

The unity thesis suggests the outlines of a framework of escape. During most of their life activities, for example, during work, the market and the hierarchical bureaucracy deny people the institutionally defined sources of value, such as commodities or instrumentally achieved outcomes. Moreover, people increasingly find that continued striving for more and more of these institutionally defined ends is itself unsatisfying and unfulfilling. Once people realize that the engines of rationalization, the market and the bureaucracy, fail to provide for central human needs, escape will appear desirable. Escape actually begins as people no longer accept or cooperate with the demand for instrumental behavior. The social dominance of alienated means crumbles as people refuse to act on the premise that alienated means are necessary for or capable of producing desired results. At the same time, for escape to be successful, people must create alternative forms or practices that institutionalize value-integrated approaches to the world. Since the power of the instrumentalist institutions depend in large part on consent, at least the consent implicit in participation, these steps, by eliminating that consent, break the sway of instrumentalism and bureaucratic domination.[102]

This outline ignores the possibility that the existing regime may counterattack. Instrumental means may be inherently incapable of creating egalitarian social relations and humane institutions, but they are capable of being destructive. Even as the power of the old institutions crumbles, the agents or beneficiaries of this old order may continue to be able and willing to use instruments of violence or organized coercion to destroy the new forms. Several possible conditions would help limit the effectiveness of these repressive means. Such favorable conditions include: (1) the availability of nonalienated methods to restrain the old order's use of violence or coercion, methods such as effective legal protection both of behavior that implements substantive values and of expressive behavior that exposes and protests the old order's unjust use of violence or coercion; (2) the unavailability of the instruments of violence, a factor that suggests the wisdom of disarmament and of creating and institutionalizing nonviolent approaches to dispute resolution; (3) the breakdown of the apparatus of organized coercion either due to the refusal of those in physical control of the instruments of violence to apply them as ordered, implying an effective withdrawal of consent, or due to a failure of cooperation or coordination within the hierarchical command structure; and (4) the increasing strength or power of those who have rejected the old order so that they are able to resist, be unaffected by, or, at least, be uncontrolled by those using instrumental means. Since each factor would reduce the instrumental effectiveness but not the cost of organized violence to those whose calculations or values are primarily instrumental, the presence of any of them would also decrease the utility and, therefore, the likelihood of the use of organized violence.

This view of the process of escape suggests that the structural preconditions for successful progressive change include: (1) opportunities to develop and practice alternative forms of life, and (2) restraints on the destructive use of instrumental, coercive means. Effectively maintained constitutional rights to engage in these new, alternative forms, such as Chapter 4's description of a constitutional ban on general prohibitions that restrict new experimental practices disliked by the majority, could help provide both the needed opportunities for change and some of the necessary restraints on governmental use of organized coercion. In other words, the rights covered by the liberty theory of the first amendment could provide some of the structural preconditions for progressive change.*

A dialectic analysis can easily sketch this vision of escape from the "iron cage" of instrumental rationality. Progress, or synthesis, depends on the base, the material practices of societal reproduction, generating a superstructure, including a set of values, a culture, and a legal order, that turns back on and transforms the base from which it arose. Evolutionary development beyond the modern age, the age of instrumentalism embodied in the hierarchical structures of bureaucracies and capitalist markets, depends on: (1) the existence of superstructure values of liberalism—equality, self-determination, and autonomy—values that embody liberalism's progressive impulses and at one time provided an apparent justification for replacing feudal practices with liberalism's instrumentalist institutions; and (2) the institutionalization of these superstructure values in order to protect people's struggles to further realize these values. This institutionalization could be accomplished through effective social and legal pro-

---

*A caveat to this claim is required because current constitutional doctrines fail to protect freedom of expression from distortion by private power centers, in particular from corporate economic power that limits worker freedom.[103]

tection of the first amendment liberty to engage in new practices and through the guarantee of the material resources necessary to allow large numbers of people to engage in self-constitutive political activities. Progress results from people engaging in popularly chosen, self-realizing, value-integrated practices that oppose, transform, or replace the alienating institutions. Thus, a crucial movement in this historical dialectic is the creation of adequate popular or institutional protections for the liberal values of autonomy and choice, in particular, protections for activities that embody people's substantive values. Protection of these activities, which integrate ends and means, is crucial for escape, for progress. In sum, the various elements of liberalism institute a key historical stage. Even while its instrumentalist institutions, at key points, block emancipation, it also generates both the human capacities, the values, and the value embodying institutions that are needed for human emancipation.

This dialectic parallels the picture of progressive evolution outlined by Jurgen Habermas. He lists "two series of initial conditions for evolutionary learning processes of society": (1) challenges presented by unresolved system problems, and (2) "new learning levels . . . already . . . achieved in world views . . . but not yet incorporated into action systems."[104] The first condition is satisfied by the failure of liberal institutions—the market and the bureaucracy—to meet human needs, particularly the needs for equality, participation, and self-determination, that are themselves to some extent the historical product of the dominant institutions of the liberal order. This system depends on consent. Dysfunction occurs to the extent that it fails to provide for the needs that the system itself makes prominent. Thus, the conflict between liberal normative theory and the liberal institutions of the modern social order presents unresolved system problems. Liberal normative theory satisfies the second condition. The required new learning level is a reflective, democratic, discursive justificatory process controlled by free and equal agents.[105] This is precisely the form of communicative interaction that the liberal world view promises, but which our institutional practices deny.

Habermas argues that a solution to the system crisis requires "(a) attempts to loosen up the existing form of social integration by embodying in new institutions the rationality structure already developed in world views, and (b) a milieu favorable to the stabilization of successful attempts."[106] Habermas' analysis, like the above description of the preconditions for escape from the Weberian process of rationalization, suggests the central importance of first amendment rights. According to the liberty theory, the first amendment mandates that government pass no laws and adopt no practices that "abridge" substantively valued expressive conduct, and that government not limit people's opportunities to join together in voluntary associations in order to implement value-based practices. By actually protecting these constitutional rights, the social order allows for practices that could "loosen up" society. In addition, by protecting these practices from legal prohibition and from illegal private interference, effective first amendment rights help stabilize successful attempts to change the old order.[107]

Thus, corresponding to these prerequisites of progressive change is a rough outline of the elements of first amendment liberty. First, broad popular participation in the process of change must be protected. In particular, first amendment rights must protect means of participation that are unified with the ends sought to be achieved. That is, it must protect people in both expressing and living their values.[108] Second, first amendment rights must protect people's right to join and act together to generate power and create new structures and practices that embody alternative normative perspectives and new forms of reason.[109] Third, these first two points also imply protection for individually valued practices even when these practices outstrip existing collective preferences. In other words, welfare maximization must not be recognized as an adequate justification to restrict these value-based practices. This protection contributes to progressive social change by preventing people's existing preferences, which inevitably embody distortions that reflect the injustices of existing structures of domination,[110] from legally justifying prohibitions on attempts to create new, undistorted alternatives. Finally, the first amendment does not need to protect even expressive political practices that are violent and coercive. The process of real progressive change must be basically nonviolent and noncoercive. This conclusion follows if, as has been argued, an important aspect of progressive change is to overcome the experience of the separation of ends and means, and if this can be accomplished only by means that are consistent with the actor's values and that respect people's worth.

These four requirements that first amendment protection must satisfy to provide adequately for progressive change correspond almost exactly to those rights identified by the liberty theory of the first amendment as developed in Chapters 3 and 4. For example, the liberty theory protects self-expressive and creative conduct that involves people in living their values. It protects voluntary associations that promote and implement people's values as well as associations primarily engaged in communicating messages. Given its emphasis on individual autonomy, the liberty theory protects nonviolent, noncoercive practices even if they are not welfare maximizing, but does not protect violent or coercive practices even if they are.

In contrast, the marketplace of ideas theory has little use for even value-based, self-expressive conduct that is not intended to communicate some proposition to others. It typically protects only associations principally engaged in communicating messages. Given that the value of the marketplace is basically instrumental, the marketplace theory provides little reason to protect conduct that is not welfare maximizing. Marketplace theorists are typically prone to balancing, often protecting theoretically covered communications no more than is necessary for promoting the general welfare.[111] Finally, marketplace theory can sometimes justify protecting even violent or coercive action if this action is necessary for achieving effective communication.[112] Thus, given the theory of progressive change proposed herein, implementing the liberty theory of the first amendment at each point at which it diverges from the marketplace of ideas theory better promotes progressive change.

If the primary function of the first amendment lies in its political role, in its contribution to society's ability to decide on and implement needed change, then a derivation of the content of first amendment liberties depends on understanding the process of progressive change. This chapter proposes a theory of change, a theory that rejects much of the conventional wisdom shared by liberal social theorists and many self-proclaimed "revolutionaries." From the perspective of this theory of change, I describe the necessary scope of the first amendment.

Alternatively, the liberty theory developed in Chapters 3 and 4 argues that the primary function of the first amendment is to protect those elements of individual liberty and autonomy that a political order must respect if it is to claim legitimacy. This individual rights interpretation identifies the *same* content for first amendment rights as does this chapter's focus on the needed content of change. This initially surprising duplication in results, however, is explicable, given two assumptions: First, that a focus on individual rights successfully identifies the content of first amendment rights that would be appropriate for a just, liberated society.[113] And, second, that the normative content of outcomes normally correspond to the normative qualities of the means of change. This second assumption implies that the expressive and self-determinative practices permitted by a society committed to individual liberty and autonomy are also the practices necessary for achieving that society.[114] In other words, the identity of the content of first amendment rights derived from these radically divergent foci follows from this chapter's key thesis: The ends of the process of change are embodied in the means. The correctness of this thesis vindicates John Stuart Mill's belief in the connection between liberty and the permanent interests of humans as progressive beings.[115]

II

APPLICATIONS

6

Time, Place, and Manner Regulations: Unreasoned Reasonableness

The constitutionality of regulating the time, place, and manner of assemblies and regulating the physical components of expressive conduct depends on the "reasonableness" of a particular restriction. This conclusion, with its overt acceptance of balancing expressive freedom against other interests, is possibly the most universally accepted tenet of first amendment doctrine.[1] If, as I will argue, this balancing approach is neither necessary nor desirable, its ready acceptance needs some explanation. This chapter offers, but then critiques, such an explanation; it also tentatively defends an alternative, "absolutist" approach. Chapter 7 explores this alternative in the context of a particular issue—*i.e.*, I criticize the almost unchallenged acceptance of the constitutionality of "reasonably" drawn, mandatory parade permit requirements. Then, Chapter 8 describes and defends a set of general principles that interpret and elaborate the term "abridge."[2] It illustrates the type of reasoning that should substitute for balancing and the reasonableness standard.

I must make a preliminarily note about terminology. No significant proponent of an "absolutist" approach claims that all legal restrictions on people's freedom of speech or assembly are automatically unconstitutional. For example, restrictions on assembly that result from trespass laws' protection of private property are not necessarily unconstitutional. Instead, absolutist approaches focus on and give sensible force to the terms "abridge," "freedom," and, sometimes, "speech" or "peaceable assembly." This focus avoids the need to discuss reasonableness or to engage in a quagmire of ad hoc, case-by-case, weighing of competing considerations that is thought to be unavoidable in this context.[3] Absolutism does not embody an indefensible literalism in constitutional interpretation.[4] Instead, I will argue, this interpretive approach gives better focus and more guidance to the analysis of key constitutional issues than does the reasonableness or balancing approach.

THE APPEAL OF REASONABLENESS

Common observations seem to lead irresistibly to the conclusion that balancing is necessary. Certainly, the government cannot guarantee the right to speak or assemble at any time or place or in any manner that some individuals might desire. Trespass laws that protect private control of certain property and other rules that promote the government's effective use of public property for public purposes are essential for the well-being of community life. Two individuals or two groups often want to make incompatible uses of a particular area at a particular time. Legal rules will allow one to prevail and these rules necessarily limit the other's freedom. And if both want to use the property for first amendment purposes, restriction of someone's speech or assembly activities is logically compelled. Even if the government stays out of the fray, it effectively restricts the first amendment rights of the strategically weaker party. Thus, restrictions on time and place and manner are intrinsic to the context of competing, often conflicting, demands for space or facilities. The issue is allocation of scarce resources, not censorship.

This problem of resource allocation is unavoidable. Not only should the government develop some Robert's Rules[5] to determine which first amendment use should prevail at a given time and place, but sometimes the law also should permit an owner, whether a private party or the government, to use its property for nonspeech purposes. We presumably do not want to turn people's homes or society's fire stations, jails, or office buildings into forums in which anyone may freely engage in first amendment expression. From these relatively incontestable observations the conclusion apparently follows that the Constitution must allow reasonable restrictions, judged roughly by balancing first amendment concerns against other social values.[6]

Although the above conclusion seems inevitable, it is not. Instead, it reflects particular but problematic ways of looking at the issue. Three interrelated conceptual props support the existing doctrinal emphasis on balancing and reasonableness. All three contribute to a strongly ingrained, habitual manner of thinking about the constitutionality of regulations of assemblies and parades. First, most *doctrinal* first amendment analyses emphasize individual rights, thought of in terms of what a person has a right to do, rather than emphasize what the person has a right to expect of others, particularly the government. This emphasis on the right "to do" leads to a focus on objective effects. Second, most analyses reflect a mainstream *ideology*. It favors the status quo, middle class values, order, and the priority of private over public life. Third, the dominant marketplace of ideas *theory* of the function of first amendment guarantees favors balancing. Although doctrine, ideology, and first amendment theory are not independent, looking at each separately will uncover the deep-rooted but possibly flawed supports of the dominant reasonableness, balancing approach to freedom of assembly.

DOCTRINE[7]

Typical ways of thinking about the first amendment may underlie the view that reasonable, content neutral restrictions—that is, abridgements—are necessary.

Our common usage continually treats the "first amendment" as an adjective that applies to certain "individual rights" to do or not do various things. "She has a first amendment right to speak." In contrast, the text of the first amendment does not explicitly guarantee any individual rights or freedom. Rather, it is aimed at laws and lawmaking. The first amendment directs the government or, more specifically, Congress, not to pass certain types of laws, those that abridge the freedom: "Congress shall *make no law* . . . abridging the freedom . . . or the right. . . ." Thus, a law against tresspass can negatively "affect" the demonstrator's right to speak but arguably is not a law directed at "abridging" speech.

The focus on lawmaking and the exercise of government power does not necessarily require different conclusions than does a focus on individual rights. Nevertheless, the choice of focus or starting points emphasizes different concerns and these can lead analyses in different directions. First, the focus on a constitutional restraint on lawmaking tends toward a consideration of *the type of laws* that are prohibited. The focus on rights more easily leads to consideration of *the effect of the law* on people's activities.* Second, the focus on lawmaking leads more easily to developing interpretations of the constitutional prohibition that are relevant for lawmakers to whom the first amendment is addressed, rather than interpretations primarily relevant to the courts. Third, the implausibility of an absolutist reading of the first amendment follows from the conclusion that *a right* to speak or assemble could not be absolute. An absolutist reading becomes plausible if, instead, the first amendment "absolutely" directs the government not to pass certain types of laws or, more broadly, not to exercise power in certain ways or for certain purposes.

Earlier it was observed that when one group's assembly would conflict with the assembly of others, people *could not* have an unlimited right to assemble. Moreover, when a right to assemble would conflict with legitimate private property rights or with the proper functioning of government, it was suggested that people *should not* have an absolute right to assemble. Since some restrictions on the right, presumably reasonable restrictions or accommodations, are necessary and proper, this customary focus on the individual right almost forces acceptance of a reasonableness standard. In contrast, the focus on what the government can or cannot do emphasizes the need to interpret "abridge."[8] For example, possibly this term prohibits all laws (and maybe other *governmental* decisions), but *only* laws (and decisions), that are specifically directed toward assemblies (or speech), that have a purpose to restrict assemblies, *or* that deny to people who want to assemble resources that the Constitution mandates that government make available.[9]† Viewed as a specific restraint on government

---

*This distinction blurs if we understand the right as a right to be free of certain types of laws or the prohibited types of laws to be laws that have particular effects.

†Although the first amendment focuses on lawmaking, it only prohibits laws directed at certain "things." A theory of the first amendment must identify these "things." Partly with this issue in mind, I will continue to use "first amendment" as an adjective. Nevertheless, when it makes a difference, as it does for the issues discussed here and in the next two chapters, my approach focuses on lawmaking or, at least, on government decisions. Admittedly, this lawmaking focus embodies a more direct emphasis on formal than on substantive freedom—one that eventually will require some value-based defense.

rather than as a guaranteed individual right of assembly, the first amendment can be interpreted as absolute.[10]

Somewhat less ingrained than commentators conventional focus on rights, but equally problematic, is a tendency to draw a rigid doctrinal line between speech and conduct. Courts often treat conduct as, at best, "speech-plus," which receives less protection than pure speech. Moreover, courts and commentators tend to value the conduct, the assemblies and associations, the picketing and parades, only because and, thus, only to the extent that they facilitate speech, which remains the primary focus. The first amendment, however, certainly does not suggest this dichotomy. The first amendment explicitly protects assemblies, an activity that obviously involves more than verbal conduct. In fact, the dichotomy even disembodies speech itself—which is necessarily a physical activity that takes place at specific times and places and can interfere with other activities.[11]

If accepted, the speech-conduct dichotomy ignores constitutional language. It immediately relegates assemblies, which are obviously conduct, to a lesser constitutional status than speech.[12] Moreover, the only nonphysical aspect of speech is content. This suggests that content regulations are the only regulations of "pure" speech—or are the only regulations "purely" of speech. Thus, if only nonphysical or nonconduct elements receive significant constitutional protection, the dichotomy easily leads to the claim that the central concern of the first amendment is (discriminatory) content regulation. But this claim should be controversial—even though the censorship quality of content regulation is unquestionably improper.

An alternative view might consider opportunities for engaging in expressive activities as an equally key, constitutionally mandated concern. Any law directed at prohibiting or restricting these activities would be problematic. But acceptance of the speech-conduct dichotomy effectively entrenches the controversial content focus into our conceptual apparatus. Dropping this dichotomy forces a more explicit consideration of the types of regulation that the first amendment permits or prohibits.

IDEOLOGY

A reasonableness, balancing analysis requires judgments that typically exhibit unstated and often unrecognized biases. The systematic support these biases give to established interests may contribute to the widespread appeal of the analysis and, therefore, may partially explain its prevalence. Making these biases explicit opens the analysis to criticism.

An evaluation that considers the reasonableness of a regulation or a balance that considers its merits and demerits will necessarily rely on someone's subjective, relatively unconstrained judgments. And for legal purposes, the relevant subjective judgments are usually those of legislative, executive, or judicial decision-makers, not the dissident who thinks the regulation is "totally unreasonable!" The inquiry into reasonableness typically claims to compare the cost and benefits, the pro's and con's, of the regulation against the result that would be achieved either without any regulation or with alternative regulations pursuing the given end(s). This inquiry requires three types of very subjective judgments. To determine the reasonableness of a regulation, the decision-maker first must consider (which usually means, must formulate) any other, possibly less restrictive, means to achieve her ends. Second, she must guess what the consequence will be of having the proposed regulation as compared to not regulating or adopting the best alternative regulation. Third, she must value, must place some "weight" on, these hypothetical consequences.

Determining reasonableness normally depends on these three inevitably subjective tasks of envisioning alternatives, predicting consequences, and then evaluating these predicted consequences. Each task gives renewed opportunity for mainstream assumptions and values to influence reasoning and to appear to justify decisions to limit dissent. First, envisioning workable alternatives requires use of a seldom-encouraged creative imagination. Few people are good at coming up with novel alternatives unless they have some type of subjective incentive to succeed—which is unlikely when the decision-maker is personally likely to disfavor the speech she is trying to imagine how to protect. Second, for those satisfied with the status quo, the extent to which the restricted expressive activities are likely to occur and the degree to which these activities will have negative consequences often appear greater than they would be in fact. Finally, those consequences that actually would occur often appear to be more objectionable, worse, than they actually would be.

Not only is the reasonableness standard very subjective, its tilt is likely to be in a particular direction. Both practical and theoretical considerations suggest that the subjectivity will be conservatively biased in favor of upholding regulations of assembly. At different points in its application, the reasonableness standard gives an undue role either to elites who benefit from the status quo, to a bureaucratic apparatus that has an occupational concern with order, or to those members of the general public[13] who place particular value on order and the status quo. Both the predispositions of decision-makers and the context in which they make decisions combine to encourage conservative decisions. City council members, park commissioners, university administrators, police chiefs, and other legislative and executive decision-makers have the initial, often unreviewed responsibility to apply the constitutional standards. They, as well as the judges who occasionally review their decisions, frequently have relatively elite, conservative backgrounds. They also often have vested interests in maintaining many elements of the existing social and political order, which has placed them in positions of authority. Possibly most important, their day-to-day routine involves responding, often politically, to the demands and desires of the potentially vocal, often complaining public. These officials' primary occupational responsibility is to maintain order, prevent or respond to unexpected or unwanted events, and ration and conserve scarce public resources while maintaining their own positions of authority. This combination of responsibilities and a daily routine of responding to complaints and handling "problems" predictably leads to a very restrictive view of the desirability and reasonableness of dissenting, disruptive activities—a theoretical prediction that many activists and reformers find confirmed in their actual attempts to have bureaucracies

adopt or enforce less restrictive rules and policies. For example, despite the lobbying and participation in rule-making proceedings by groups such as local chapters of the American Civil Liberties Union and the National Lawyers Guild, the
dynamics of the political process result in most parade ordinances having textual provisions that are arguably "unreasonable" and clearly unconstitutional.
And these dynamics usually result in only loose, but often discriminatory
enforcement. Better results, however, are unlikely as long as constitutional standards tell the pressured official little more than, "do what you think makes
sense." Given their responsibilities, the pressures of their role, as well as their
likely predispositions, "no" will seem to be the reasonable response. The reasonableness standard is unlikely to effectively constrain officials to favor dissent
or even to treat it evenhandedly.

These observations about the incentives and pressures felt by government
decision-makers are commonplace. The observations become important, however, if some or most of these public decision-makers, from the level of police
officer to legislator, generally try to respect people's rights and to follow constitutional mandates. Given this assumption, the problem with the reasonableness
standard is that it fails to offer helpful guidance. Rather it almost calls for decision-makers to rely on assumptions, perceptions, and values that are systematically biased in favor of restraint and order. Thus, restrictions on expression
follow not merely from the pressures on and dispositions of the decision-makers
but from these factors combined with the inadequacies of the reasonableness
standard. Constitutional theorists and judicial creators of doctrine must share
with front-line decision-makers the blame for the government's constant tendency to burden, restrain, or suppress dissent.

The above points considered how "reasonableness" would predictably operate in practice. The most plausible, most common, theoretical interpretations of
the reasonableness standard and the balancing approach are also systemically
oriented toward the status quo. Balancing analyses most commonly and most
logically employ some version of a utilitarian or public welfare standard.* Likewise, "reasonable" suggests a concern for what most people, or for what the conventional, educated, intelligent, "typical" person after being prodded into
acknowledging the importance of liberty, would find acceptable. Both the utilitarian and the reasonable person foci systematically favor the status quo and
mainstream or dominant values. Utilitarianism (or, at least, most versions of it)
takes as given existing preferences, which reflect and partially define the status
quo. The utilitarian evaluation of a regulation becomes a matter of how well the

* Obviously, this standard is not necessarily part of a balancing analysis. A balancer, for
example, could give special weight to first amendment "values" beyond whatever a utilitarian
calculation would yield—that is, the balancer could place a first amendment thumb on the
scales. This balancing could even be based on critical theories that discounted some conventional or distorted concerns and recognized peoples' "real interests." Nevertheless, examples of
this critical balancing are rare, and some prominent attempts are, in my view, more dangerous
than successful.[14] Moreover, because of the intellectual difficulties of, and the predictable contextual deterrents to, applying critical, protective balancing analysis, its application by the relevant decision-makers is very unlikely. Thus, even if theoretically defensible, a balancing
approach would not be a very promising legal instrument with which to pursue critical
objectives.

regulation satisfies existing preferences—a rather dubious standard for protecting dissent. In fact, utilitarianism, or at least existing preferences, is an inherently inadequate standard with which to evaluate the need for or merit in or "benefit" of dissent from the existing order.[15]

"Reasonableness" may be even more biased. Unlike utilitarianism, reasonableness is so much a matter of the dominant viewpoint that it may not even acknowledge the propriety of counting either the dissidents' values or their preferences concerning what opportunities society ought to make available to people for expressing or communicating their dissenting views. The dissident's preferences, which in the utilitarian balance may receive some recognition in a compromise that best promotes the mix of preferences, are more likely ignored as unreasonable in the reasonableness analysis. But both standards are standards perfectly designed to avoid surprising, sometimes radical, conclusions.

FIRST AMENDMENT THEORY

The marketplace of ideas theory—the view that wise counsels will prevail over false ones in the clash of free public debate and "that the best test of truth is the power of the thought to get itself accepted in the competition of the market"[16]— has dominated scholarly and judicial thinking about the first amendment.[17] This theory allows the conclusion that reasonable time, place, and manner restrictions do not "abridge" the right of peaceable assembly or the freedom of speech.

In the classic version of the marketplace of ideas theory frequently embraced by the Court, progress toward truth only requires that no view be censored. Of course, some views—those of the poor and the unorganized—may have less entry into the marketplace. The classic version nevertheless argues that the truth will eventually prevail as long as it has some access. As long as the correct view enters into the debate, people eventually will see its wisdom. Thus, the only real cause for fear is censorship. In the context of assemblies and parades, the prohibition on censorship may require that the courts prevent local governments from unequally cutting off access to the streets. Since the streets sometimes are the only mass "media" available to poor groups, possibly the courts should also prevent local governments from totally denying access to the streets for expressive purposes. But most even-handed, noncontent regulation of the streets would be unproblematic.

A reformist marketplace theory recognizes that debate in the marketplace will be influenced by people's ability to participate. This reformist theory argues that a properly operating marketplace can break down. Typical versions of the theory suggest that guaranteeing effective access best prevents these breakdowns. Thus, the market failure version of the marketplace of ideas theory might require, for example, that the government waive permit or user fees for those poor groups that otherwise would be unable to engage in these expressive activities. But even granted special concern for the poor, reasonable, noncensorial, content-neutral restrictions that leave adequate alternative communication outlets available would presumably not interfere with the effective operation of the marketplace of ideas. Any view that any significant group of people would want to discuss or present could be discussed or presented. "Reasonable" opportunities to assemble or parade should suffice if, as the courts continually imply, the rights of assembly and association are valued merely as necessary adjuncts of speech in the marketplace of ideas.[18] Of course, any time, place, or manner restriction will have some unpredictable effect on the quantity and mix of expression. But so do tax laws, housing patterns, and any other law or social practice that affects resource allocations and values. The quantity and mix of expression are not major concerns of the marketplace theory. The issue is only whether the restriction limits the effective operation of the marketplace of ideas. So long as the system allows "everything worth saying [to] be said," speech is adequately protected.[19]

Despite the dominance of marketplace of ideas theories, an individual liberty or self-realization, self-determination interpretation of the first amendment has never been entirely eliminated in scholarly or judicial thinking. This liberty or individual autonomy theory dramatically changes the analysis of "reasonable" regulations of assemblies. The issue shifts to whether the restriction limits substantively valued, expressive behavior.

A focus on individual liberty dissolves many anomalies in the traditional justification for the protection of assemblies. It simultaneously raises concerns about many "reasonable" restrictions. First, the focus on liberty draws attention to the fact that time, place, and manner regulations often prohibit the specific activity in which people want to engage. For example, many parade permit systems bar spontaneous or leaderless marches or assemblies—even though participants may specifically value this format. More generally, whenever the time or the place or the manner of the expression is central to the intended meaning of a person's expression, a time, place, or manner regulation could prohibit the specific, substantially valued, expressive activity. Thus, from the liberty perspective, these regulations can abridge the protected freedom.

In a marketplace theory, carefully run assemblies can obviously be important for debate—for the formulation and presentation of ideas. The function of parades and large demonstrations is less clear. Thoughtful debate seldom occurs in parades and often is not present in large rallies.[20] In an unfortunate opinion, employing reasoning clearly dominated by this marketplace of ideas perspective, the Canadian Supreme Court argued:

> Demonstrations are not a form of speech but of collective action. They are of the nature of a display of force rather than of an appeal to reason; their inarticulateness prevents them from becoming a part of language and reaching the level of discourse.[21]

Unsurprisingly, the Canadian Court rejected the constitutional claims of the demonstrators.

The number of those who will rally and parade in support of a particular viewpoint has no relevance to identifying truth in its struggle with falsehood. Numbers do not make the viewpoint correct. Thus, from the classic marketplace of ideas perspective, limiting the size of a demonstration should not interfere with the relevant speech. At best, the large demonstration can serve a market-place function by gaining attention that makes a broader public aware that a certain viewpoint exists and that it ought to be considered.[22] Much more limited means, however, can usually serve this "notice" function. Therefore, under the classic marketplace theory, courts should uphold limits on the number of people participating in an assembly, parade, or demonstration, or limits on the time of a gathering. These legal limitations would not, at least not significantly, restrict the operation of the constitutionally protected marketplace of ideas.

The size of support (or type of support) could be relevant to wise political decision making—a possibility that suggests a political rather than an objective notion of truth. A larger, louder, longer demonstration might show a greater level of support for a viewpoint. Thus, time, place, or manner regulations could interfere with the communication of this politically relevant fact. Nevertheless, even this "political truth" version of marketplace theory should treat time, place, and manner restrictions as only instrumentally burdening, not as abridging people's rights. These regulations cannot be relevantly distinguished from the distribution of wealth, the concentration of media ownership, and innumerable other legal restrictions, all of which create similar "interferences" with the expression of the level of support. Restrictions on assembly do not prevent people from using other means—paid advertisements, petitions, many small demonstrations—to communicate the size and degree of support for a particular position. Content-neutral time, place, and manner regulations also do not prohibit the communication of any specific message, although as a practical matter they, like all rule structures, differentially influence the effectiveness of communications. Time, place, and manner regulations are merely one of many burdens on communications that leave people free to pursue their notions of truth within the set of opportunities that the existing rule structure makes available. Without a standard for the amount or manner of influence that each person must be permitted to exercise, and as long as the same rules apply to all groups or viewpoints, there is no basis to conclude that a particular set of time, place, and manner regulations upsets the proper working of the marketplace of ideas, and, thereby, abridges the first amendment.[23]

In contrast, from an individual liberty perspective, limits on numbers of participants or the time or duration of assemblies can abridge the right. These limits constitute a total rejection of, rather than a marginal burden on, the first amendment right of each person who is told that she cannot participate because the maximum size has been reached or is told that she cannot continue to participate because the allowed time has passed. From the liberty perspective, each person has an independent right to participate. Furthermore, if the person considers being assembled at particular times or remaining assembled for a long period to be appropriate or necessary for living and expressing her values, time limits can also violate her right. Although the instrumental contribution of a demonstration to a marketplace of ideas may decrease after a period of time, a person's liberty may continue to be at stake in the same way after several hours as it was at the beginning. A round-the-clock vigil may be necessary for a person to express, live, and implement her values.

The liberty perspective also provides a fuller understanding and recognition of the role and value of the right of assembly. A marketplace of ideas perspective views the right as merely an adjunct to, an important support for, people's right to communicate.[24] Communication, however, is only one aspect of assembly. People assemble and associate in order to generate and exercise power and to do things that are valued in themselves. People may assemble in order to experience an exhilarating sense of solidarity, power, and self-actualization. An assembly can embody the extraordinary as a way to challenge and change the ordinary and the routine.[25] If, as the liberty theory asserts, these roles of assembly justify constitutional protection, the marketplace of ideas theory would be wrong about which regulations seriously interfere with the right and, therefore, are "reasonable." If the aspects of assembly that renounce and challenge existing routines by being unreasonable from orthodox perspectives merit protection, then even the reasonableness of the "reasonableness" criterion needs reevaluation. The "reasonableness" of a restriction cannot sensibly lie in the desirability of suppressing precisely those aspects of the assembly that justify constitutional protection.

The problem with reasonableness is that often it reflects the majority's judgment that a particular, participant-valued, peaceable exercise of liberty is itself undesirable. For example, the reasonableness of a regulation might consist of its capacity to restrict the extraordinariness of the demonstration or the demonstrator's capacity or opportunity to do things, to generate power nonviolently, or to refuse to acknowledge the legitimacy of established authorities. These limitations can be reasonable given mainstream preconceptions and a marketplace of ideas perspective.

In contrast, if, as the liberty theory assumes, individuals have a fundamental right to assemble peaceably in ways that realize their values, the method and objective of analysis change. The majority's dislike of those values or the peaceable practices that embody the values may make the regulation seem reasonable. It would not count, however, as a justification for restricting or disfavoring the expressive conduct. From the perspective of the liberty theory, reason only supports the regulation if the regulation does not prevent the valued expressive activity or if it applies solely to nonprotected conduct—for example, if it prohibits assemblies that violate the rights of others or that are nonpeaceable or coercive.[26] Rather than evaluate to determine whether the regulation promotes maximization of preferences, the evaluation should determine if the regulation respects individual liberty.

The liberty theory affirms the widely accepted notion that the function of constitutional rights, and more specifically the role of the right of assembly, is to protect self-expressive, nonviolent, noncoercive conduct from majority norms or political balancing and even to permit people to be offensive, annoying, or challenging to dominant norms—that is, to permit people to be unreasonable. Challenges to existing values and decisions to embody and express dissident values are precisely the choices and activities that cannot be properly evaluated by summations of existing preferences. Balancing is not helpful. The constitutional right of assembly ought to protect activities that are *unreasonable* from the perspective of the existing order.

SUMMARY

The virtually universal acceptance of balancing or reasonableness criteria in the evaluation of time, place, and manner regulations reflects the view that fundamentally these regulations present only a question of resource allocation and that first amendment activity cannot legitimately claim an absolute right to priority in resource use. Given the "unbeatable proposition" that "you cannot have two parades on the same corner at the same time,"[27] some allocative decisions are logically compelled. This practical need to allocate resources supposedly shows that any absolutist interpretation is untenable.[28]

Common ways of thinking about the first amendment as a guarantee of individual rights, the dominance of status quo orientations, and the generally accepted marketplace of ideas theory of the first amendment all contribute to the acceptance of reasonableness and balancing criteria. In each case, this section has offered an alternative to these conventional features of our first amendment thinking. Before further developing this liberty-theory-based alternative, it may be appropriate to warn against one additional way in which typical styles of legal thinking improperly favor a reasonableness standard and militate against a more absolutist approach.

The lawyerly technique of imagining worst case scenarios and then proceeding to base analyses on the need to prevent it, no matter how unlikely, has been frequently noted—and often criticized. This attention to detail and to worst-case possibilities is very valuable for some purposes. For example, this lawyerly care may be useful in considering contingencies in contractual planning; here, lawyer time is the only significant cost associated with taking account of the contingencies. Lawyers or judges, however, also commonly use this technique to defend challenged time, place, and manner regulations. First, they describe some outlandish, offensive, or otherwise costly behavior that the challenged regulation prohibits. Then, they imply that without the regulation we may be inundated with the offensive behavior. Here, where liberty is at stake, this ingrained habit can produce unnecessary and unwarranted conservativism in a weighing or balancing analysis.

The rhetorical power of this worst case scenario does not correspond to its reasoned persuasiveness. Often the state could regulate imagined worst cases with clearly constitutional rules. When these "less restrictive alternatives" are available, the worst-case scenario has operated in the argument simply as a scare technique. Sometimes, however, a less restrictive alternative will not exist. For example, one will not exist if the first amendment specifically protects the behavior that is offensive. Still, the hypothesis of an inundation of the offensive behavior is usually implausible. These worst-case scenarios usually predict an improbable series of worst cases. How often will thousands of people be so incensed that they will want to take to the streets and block traffic as a means to protest current problems? How often are people actually going to deliver a political message in the town center while locked in a nude, sexual embrace?—a possibility that the Court imagined and then feared.[29] To provide for greater liberty we should permit the predictably occasional offensive uses of that liberty.

The proponent of "reasonable" regulation has a further response. She can appropriately argue that once the law permits the offensive behavior, under some circumstances, the "offensive" behavior may become widespread.[30] The implications of this observation, however, are ambiguous. Rather than providing a reason for enforcing restrictions, the observation could reflect the positive value of protecting liberty. This conclusion should follow in at least two different scenarios.

First, the circumstances in which the offensive behavior is widely adopted, for example, the circumstances in which thousands of people will routinely occupy the streets in protest, will often be precisely the circumstances in which the status quo is not responsive to the real concerns or needs of large numbers of people. In these situations, society needs to have the status quo disrupted. Many of us need to be shaken up even if this means being inconvenienced or offended. In retrospect, many people conclude that the times of the great depression, the civil rights struggles against segregation, our involvement in Vietnam, and, of course, the period preceding the American revolution, were periods that merited widescale protest.

Second, sometimes when behavior that we now consider offensive becomes ubiquitous, the behavior will then seem acceptable and we will have become a different people. These results may be desirable— although this conclusion may depend on whether we adopt the perspective of the people we are now or of the people we will become if we do not enforce the restrictions.[31] Whether a sexual revolution, new family or work forms, or merely new dress and hair styles, the behavioral change suggests either that people's values and preferences have changed or that, in the past, their values had been suppressed. Of course, the future, transformed situation may continue to offend many—particularly those who presently advocate the restriction or regulation. Often, some people benefit from the suppression and, in any event, some people will not change as new norms develop. Nevertheless, whether a great increase in this "deviant" behavior represents a change in community values or a reduction of suppression or both, the increase in the behavior exposes the prior argument for regulation as at bottom a defense of the status quo. The regulation attempts to prevent people from creating a new status quo. It is a means for a present majority (or present power elite) to dominate a possible future majority. Seen in this light, the argument for the regulation seems less a matter of "reasonableness" and more a rejection of the first amendment rights of liberty and a repudiation of first amendment protection of the process of peaceful social change.[32]

Professor Mark Tushnet could recently look back on the debate between advocates of balancing and absolute protection of first amendment rights that occurred during the late 1960s and conclude that the absolutists clearly won.[33] Others have aptly noted that balancing analyses are so ingrained in all areas of constitutional law that we can hardly imagine an alternative.[34] Certainly, balancing in first amendment cases has been on the rise in the Supreme Court over the last ten or fifteen years. Although many of the greatest first amendment theorists of the 1950s and 1960s, Justices Douglas and Black, Professors Thomas Emerson and Alexander Mieklejohn, were absolutists, most of the current generation of first amendment scholars are balancers. As Judge Hans Linde has noted, often these balancers contemptuously dismiss absolutist approaches by mindlessly mischaracterizing them and merely assuming the propriety of balancing.[35] A few, however, like Professor Steven Shiffrin, offer thoughtful theoretical and illustrative arguments to show the superiority of an appropriate nonabsolutist approach.[36] Elsewhere I have, as have others, offered a theoretical response to these claims for balancing.[37] In the end, there may be serious objections to either approach. The question may turn out to be a practical one: Which style of thought best promotes human interests by aiding us in such tasks as identifying unnecessary and unwarranted repressions in the current order? The next two chapters argue that we would do better with the recommended absolutist approach, not just as argued in theory but as cashed out in practice.

7

Mandatory Parade Permits

RETHINKING THE ISSUE

During a single hour on the evening of July 8, 1939, approximately 26,000 people passed by an intersection in Manchester, New Hampshire. Included among those 26,000 were about eighty-eight Jehovah's Witnesses divided into four or five small groups. The people in each group walked single file and carried small staffs and signs. The only legally relevant difference between their conduct and that of the other 26,000 is that the Jehovah's Witnesses walked "in formation" in small, organized groups or "moving assemblies" in order to be expressive rather than singly or in groups in order to engage in shopping, business, travel or other similar pursuits. This single difference in what these people did, walking in an "assembly" that the first amendment presumably protects, turned out to be crucial. It made them guilty of a criminal offense. The law required these Jehovah's Witnesses, unlike all other people walking by the intersection that evening, to apply to the government for special permission and pay the government a special fee.[1]

Surely something is wrong with this result. The question of whether a person should have special rights or immunities because she is engaged in first amendment activities is difficult. Here, however, that is not the question. The Jehovah's Witnesses asked for no special rights. On the contrary, New Hampshire placed special restrictions on them specifically because they assembled, because they engaged in activity protected by the first amendment. This law, unanimously upheld by the United States Supreme Court in *Cox v. New Hampshire*,[2] stands constitutional commands on their heads.

Cox gave Supreme Court sanction to the now standard view that permit requirements are acceptable under the reasonable time, place, and manner rubric. Without citing any other case that had upheld the application of a permit system,[3] the Court found sufficient justification for the statute in two purposes asserted by the state. The permit requirement aided in policing—the city would have knowledge of when and where to assign police to cover the parade. The requirement also allowed the city to engage in scheduling to prevent conflicting parades or other conflicting uses of the streets. The Supreme Court noted that the state court had indicated that the city was required to grant the permit unless the parade would unduly disturb the public convenience.[4] Thus, the Court, presumably assuming that city officials could apply this standard in a content-neutral fashion, also implicitly approved the use of the permit system as a means to prevent unduly inconvenient parades.[5]

Despite the unanimity of the Court's decision, past history did not so unambiguously indicate the need for, or the acceptability of, permit requirements. The Jehovah's Witnesses' period in the courts during the 1930s and 1940s mirrored the Salvation Army's confrontation with the legal system fifty years earlier.[6] In the last quarter of the nineteenth century, local governments, often in an attempt to stop activities of the Salvation Army,[7] adopted ordinances that required permits for parades as well as for public meetings. Professor Glen Abernathy, however, reports that, with the exception of Massachusetts which followed Holmes' infamous decision in *Commonwealth v. Davis*,[8] state courts during this period all "held that parading peaceably and lawfully was a fundamental right of Americans and could not be abridged by the municipal requirement of a permit."[9] These early decisions objected not only to the discretion given to local officials but also to the permit requirement itself.[10] The obvious change between the late nineteenth century and the period fifty years later when courts readily accepted parade permit requirements presumably needs some justification or explanation.

Neither of two obvious, but opposing, explanations of the change from the earlier judicial invalidations of parade permit requirements to the more recent judicial approval can be completely ruled out. The increased urbanization and the modern use of the automobile may have changed conditions between the 1890s and the 1930s so that permit requirements became an increasingly reasonable method of responding to conflicting demands for use of the streets. Alternatively, the judicial change may have had nothing to do with parade permits becoming more needed and, thus, reasonable. Rather, it may have reflected a chance combination of intellectual (doctrinal) developments and social, historical conditions, possibly including an elite's increased fear of or distaste for dissent or disorder. For example, it may have partially reflected a generally increased recognition of the need for and acceptability of government regulation. Moreover, increased social and psychological pressures of modern urban life may have led many people, including the comparably elite groups from which judges are drawn, to find government regulation of public space increasingly acceptable. The new need may have related less to problems of traffic, policing, and resource allocation than to a desire to assert control over the disorderly activities of the riff-raff. Under this second explanation, the permit requirement may be as improper and unnecessary a restriction on individual's liberty now as it was in the 1890s.

Of the two explanations, the second seems more convincing. The first hypothesizes that judicial approval of permit schemes reflected legitimate needs for such schemes, but needs that arose only during the fifty years between the early invalidations and the later judicial approvals. This hypothesis is not supported by the circumstances of the first judicial approval of permit requirements. Modern traffic conditions do not explain why courts in the nineteenth century upheld permit requirements for "street meetings" and assemblies in the parks while at the same time invalidating the parade permit schemes. More important, the hypothesis is not supported by the circumstances of the enactment of permit requirements. For example, as noted, the original enactment of the permit requirements seemed to be aimed primarily at suppressing the expressive activities and assemblies of unpopular groups, particularly the Salvation Army.

The late nineteenth and early twentieth century cases suggest that the courts' evaluation of permit requirements did not turn on an ideologically neutral consideration of their necessity for maintaining order. Shortly after the courts of the late nineteenth century had struck down permit requirements for parades, the courts were faced with permit requirements for street meetings. Most courts upheld these permit requirements.[11] This contrasting result may seem surprising. For those accustomed to thinking in terms of the constitutional concept of assembly or, even more obviously, in terms of the marketplace of ideas emphasis on speech and deliberative discussion, meetings would seem to deserve more protection than the "moving assemblies" in which little rational debate can be expected. Several explanations for the courts' converse holdings are plausible.

Courts sometimes imply that parades differ from street (and park) assemblies in that parades involve people in the normal use of the streets, that is, for movement, while meetings obstruct this normal use. Therefore, possibly parades but not assemblies should be protected.[12] Nevertheless, this formalistic explanation sounds strained, as if it is rationalizing a conclusion reached for other reasons. Professor Abernathy marshalls considerable support for his claim that "the most plausible explanation" for the judicial preference for parades lies in the fact that the "'better type' of people participate in parades" but that "the street meeting is not customarily held by the 'better class' of citizens" who normally have or can hire private halls or land for their meetings.[13] If Abernathy is right, the courts' early approval of permit systems for street meetings depended less on the permit's contribution to traffic control or maintaining order, which would not distinguish them from parade permit requirements that courts invalidated, than on the judges' lesser concern for the people or views that these permit requirements burden.

Thus, both the original enactment of permit requirements and their initial judicial acceptance only in the context of outdoor meetings seem premised primarily on the local government's desire to suppress unpopular groups and on the lack of judicial sympathy for the groups who were significantly restricted. Likewise, there is little real reason to think that the courts' eventual approval of nondiscriminatory parade permit requirements related to the government's increased legitimate need for notice in order to provide for adequate policing,[14] traffic control,[15] or the prevention of violence initiated by those who wanted to parade.[16] Although permit requirements may sometimes actually serve these legitimate purposes,[17] which the Court invoked in *Cox,* these purposes certainly are an inadequate explanation for the modern courts' willingness to approve permit requirements for the small "parades" that occur on sidewalks and violate no traffic rules. Other explanations for the changed judicial response are needed.

The late nineteenth-century state courts' invalidation of permit requirements for parades relied on neither the first amendment nor similar provisions in state constitutions. Instead, the judicial attitude underlying these invalidations seems a part of these courts' general attempt to restrict legislative powers. Substantive due process was only one part of this phenomenon. When, in a period after the demise of *Lochner*,[18] federal courts were first presented with permit cases, this earlier, restrictive judicial attitude had changed dramatically, particularly in the federal courts. The Supreme Court had generally abandoned constitutional activism. In fact, a key point in the Court's reasoning in *West Coast Hotel*[19] for abandoning serious substantive due process review was echoed by the Court in *Cox* when it observed: "Civil liberties, as guaranteed by the Constitution, imply the existence of an organized society maintaining public order without which liberty itself would be lost in the excesses of unrestrained abuses."[20] This post-*Lochner* deferential posture dominated in 1941 when, turning to the then relatively undeveloped first amendment precedents, the Court found no arguments or precedents justifying invalidation of the permit requirement.[21] At least, it found no precedents requiring invalidation once it characterized the permit requirement as nondiscriminatory and reasonable. In addition to this general change in judicial attitudes, the Court could have observed that for roughly sixty years local governments had applied permit systems to at least some first amendment conduct—meetings in the streets and parks. This sixty-year "tradition" may have dispelled the notion, held by some of the earlier state judges who invalidated the parade permit requirements, that permit systems were inherently novel, offensive, and unnecessary restrictions on liberty. Thus, this general decline in judicial activism, combined with a recognition that, from a first amendment perspective, parades should not receive any greater protection than assemblies in the parks and streets, may have contributed to the courts' "new" view that the parade permit systems were reasonable.

Other considerations also support the view that doctrinal developments combined with increased sensitivity to problems of public order, not a real change in the social need for a permit system, explain the shift. The court's willingness to uphold the application of parade permit requirements in situations in which the paraders presented little in the way of traffic problems supports this thesis. The advent of the automobile would seem to have little consequence for the small numbers of people walking on the sidewalks in *Cox v. New Hampshire*. The same observation applies to the action of the Pennsylvania Superior Court that upheld a permit requirement as applied to the leader of a group of thirty or forty Jehovah's Witnesses.[22] The finding that a procession of this size would improperly disturb normal Saturday afternoon shopping must be the product of a very cautious, order-minded court. Neither the specific content of many later ordinances nor their judicially accepted application appears limited to situations in which the "paraders" would pose serious traffic problems.[23]

The lack of any clear need for the *parade* permits in these contexts parallels the late nineteenth-century courts' approval of permit requirements for *assemblies* in parks as well as on streets. This earlier approval was apparently independent of modern traffic problems and occurred before the courts were ready to hold that local needs justified parade permits. Both those early ordinances and those upheld more recently, however, require all fringe and dissident groups to go to the authorities, announce their plans, and seek permission before they exercise their "right" to engage in assembly and expressive group activity. The most plausible explanation of these new holdings is that modern courts overcame the earlier courts' concern that parade permit requirements would unduly burden acceptable groups while the modern courts joined the earlier courts in their willingness to restrain less orthodox groups.

This history, in which our judges initially found parade permit systems to be unnecessary and unacceptable restrictions on liberty, suggests the desirability of rethinking the parade and assembly permit issue. In the following portions of this chapter, I will first analyze mandatory parade permit requirements from the perspective of two alternative, dramatically different doctrinal approaches to time, place, and manner regulations: the dominant reasonableness standard, and an absolutist approach that centers on giving content to the concept of abridgement. Second, after this doctrinal discussion, I discuss the predictable real-world consequences of mandatory parade permit requirements—that is, I engage in a rough cost-benefit analysis. This "balancing" discussion serves several purposes. For those who will not budge from their allegiance to some version of balancing, this analysis could be the most useful part of my discussion; it might even persuade them to reject mandatory permit requirements as unreasonable. More generally, this analysis further develops points raised in the doctrinal discussion and illustrates the preferable consequences of the absolutist approach.

This exploration of the costs and benefits of a mandatory system requires comparison with some alternatives. I hypothesize that much of the persuasive force of claims that mandatory permit requirements are reasonable results from the normal impulse to compare mandatory permits with a totally anarchistic situation. Although anarchy is a possible alternative, there is no reason to rely on this comparison. Any permit or regulatory system that does not run afoul of the absolutist interpretation of the first amendment, and that at least partially serves the purposes presently served by mandatory permit systems, could provide an equally appropriate comparison. My strategy is to propose a voluntary permit system as the appropriate comparison. I argue that a voluntary system is permissible under the absolutist approach, thereby avoiding the serious interference with first amendment freedoms that result from a mandatory system. Then, I argue that a voluntary system adequately serves the permissible functions of the mandatory system. Thus, the comparison strongly suggests that, "on balance," mandatory systems provide little benefit at great cost to first amendment freedom. Nevertheless, the cost-benefit discussion turns out to be rather obviously inconclusive. This inconclusiveness finally forces a return to some of the value arguments that are central to the liberty theory of the first amendment.

THE THEORETICAL PERSPECTIVES

Endless disputes never resolve what regulations are "reasonable."[24] Still, many cities have ordinances similar to San Antonio's, which, except for a few narrow exemptions, requires parade permits for virtually any procession or assembly on outdoor public space.[25] The existence of these ordinances implies that many local lawmakers agree that mandatory permit requirements are reasonable. Lack of serious popular or academic outrage with the Court's unanimous decision in *Cox v. New Hampshire* also suggests that many people accept the Court's holding that the government can require people to obtain permits before they purposefully group themselves together in public areas. The fact that the permit process sometimes does serve legitimate functions usually mutes criticism under the reasonableness standard. Of course, courts invalidate some time, place, and manner regulations when less restrictive alternatives are arguably available. Nevertheless, a court would likely distinguish permit requirements from, for example, the unconstitutional attempt to prohibit door-to-door canvassing and leafletting on the street.[26] It could argue either that the permit requirement seems to lack a good alternative,[27] or, more emphatically, that unlike the invalidated regulations, the permit requirement does not appear to stop the protected activity. In any event, I assume that the presently dominant "reasonableness" standard can be interpreted—as it has been—to sanction many existing, narrowly drawn, content neutral, mandatory parade permit requirements.

A second, more absolutist approach radically departs from current orthodoxy. It would invalidate mandatory permit systems that apply to parades or assemblies in which the activity of each individual, taken separately, would be legal. Given that people have a right to talk and to walk on the streets, parks, and sidewalks, the sole factor that distinguishes the behavior for which the local government requires a permit is the group's "assembled" character. The government abridges freedom of assembly if it imposes restrictive requirements that turn on people's status of being assembled. *Cox* was wrongly decided.[28]

A defender of the mandatory permit ordinance might argue that such an ordinance is not directed solely at constitutionally protected assemblies. For example, presumably the permit requirement would apply to nonpeaceable as well as peaceable assemblies. Likewise, the constitutional status of parades, presumably covered by most ordinances, that are conducted as profit-making ventures of businesses, is not clear.[29] Assemblies protected by the first amendment are merely a subcategory of the activities covered by the ordinances. Thus, the ordinances are not discriminatorily directed at protected conduct.

This defense does not work. Of course, some assemblies will be a part of an activity that the government can prohibit. The first amendment does not protect these assemblies. Thus, restrictions directed generally at assemblies will *always* cover some unprotected conduct. But this observation should be irrelevant. A full protection theory requires that the government initially direct its restrictions at something other than expression or assembly. The government at most can only incidentally restrict people's first amendment activities and can only do so if it defines the evil behavior in terms other than their assembling or engaging in expression.

A more difficult issue for the absolutist approach is presented when a government regulation, although directed at the assembly, is not obviously restrictive. The government does not abridge freedom of assembly when it places appropriate conditions, sometimes including permit requirements, on the receipt of special benefits that the government makes available. The government can give the group that reserved the auditorium priority over the one that did not. The priority is conditioned on the reservation. The constitutionality of the conditions depends on the reason that the government imposes them or the function they serve—that is, on their purpose. And it depends on their being imposed only on "special benefits" rather than on an opportunity or resource to which people already have a right. Generally, conditions are appropriate only if they are necessary to make a special benefit available, to serve a purpose for which the benefit is made available, or in order to protect a public interest that the grant of the benefit would otherwise jeopardize.

The government could provide various special privileges to those engaged in first amendment protected conduct. For example, it could provide parade organizers with a "reservations" system that could reduce conflicts and provide for priority among planned parades or assemblies. The government could also make special efforts to provide police protection to the assembly or parade, or, if it wishes, the government could provide other facilities—special parking, first aid, toilets, water, or insurance. The government can also impose *appropriate* conditions on the receipt of these special benefits. For example, to *guarantee* some degree of police protection or provide various temporary facilities for people engaged in the parade or assembly, the government would need timely notification by the groups planning to march or assemble. Likewise, a "permit" system might provide the most convenient, obvious means for people who are planning an assembly or procession to reserve the use of particular streets or parks. Since these conditions enable the government to provide these benefits, an absolutist approach could uphold these *voluntary* notification or permit requirements. Such conditions do not abridge the freedom.

One of the most important but difficult questions for the absolutist analysis of permit systems is to determine what conditions a full protection theory would allow the government to place on the parader's right or privilege to violate normal traffic laws—for example, laws restricting pedestrians to sidewalks and cross-walks or requiring people to stop for red lights. Specifically, could the government require, as a condition of violating these rules, that the paraders provide advance notice, apply for a permit, or conform to conditions relating to route, size, and time? The constitutional analysis of this question will be controversial. Unlike *Cox* where the government placed a special restriction on people identified only by their exercise of a constitutional right, here those exercising their first amendment rights are claiming a special privilege. Certainly, imposing a permit requirement or other conditions in these circumstances could serve to facilitate traffic management and promote safety, particularly the safety of the paraders. Certainly, imposing these conditions as a means to secure public interests seems less obviously an abridgement of assembly than the blanket permit requirement upheld in *Cox*. In fact, many cities apparently hold precisely this view of when they legitimately can or need to require parade permits. They only require a permit if the assembly or procession "does not comply with normal and usual traffic regulation or control."[30] These ordinances certainly take an important step toward constitutionality. Nevertheless, I will argue that even these permit requirements are unconstitutional. To succeed, my argument must show that the opportunity to violate these normal traffic laws is, *in these circumstances*, a right, not a special benefit and, therefore, that the permit requirement is a (significant) restriction of the right.[31]

My claim is that the state cannot treat use of the streets for parades and assemblies as incompatible with their dedicated use. The opposing claim is that the state does have discretion as to how the streets can best be used to promote the general welfare and that it has expressed its conclusion in traffic laws. These traffic laws restrict without eliminating people's opportunity to use the streets. This opposing claim should be rejected. As much is implied by Justice Roberts' dictum in *Hague v. CIO*.[32] According to Roberts,

> the streets and parks . . . have immemorially been held in trust for the use of the public and, time out of mind, have been used for purposes of assembly, communicating thoughts between citizens, and discussing public questions. Such use of the streets and public places has, from ancient times, been a part of the privileges, immunities, rights, and liberties of citizens.[33]

Whether or not good legal history, Roberts' dictum is very accurate social and political history. All sorts of groups—patriotic and civic organizations, public schools, workers and strikers, the unemployed, religious groups, political parties, dissidents, neighborhoods holding block parties, circuses, and athletic running groups—have used and still continuously use the streets for parades and assemblies. Our political, economic, and cultural life would be radically impoverished without this use. Of course, these activities have always shared the streets with other activities, particularly the movement of people and goods from one location to another. The obvious question is how to intergrate these different uses. Are normal traffic laws always a permissible means? Two interrelated considerations support the conclusion that the government cannot constitutionally use traffic laws to restrict freedom of assembly. These considerations focus on the permissibility of the government making decisions in respect to the priority of different uses and on the nature and function of normal traffic laws.

Given people's historically and culturally rooted right to use the streets for expressive purposes as well as for transportation uses, the question becomes whether the government should be permitted to provide for transportation in a way that limits the constitutionally protected expressive use. A full protection, absolutist theory must answer that laws protecting the transportation function are unconstitutional if they stop valued, protected, expressive behavior.* Often, traffic regulations perform zoning-type functions and will be consistent with full protection for the valued expression. For example, assume that people have no right purposefully to maximize their disruptive effects, and assume a relatively small parade. In this case, laws or government practices that restrict the parade to the sidewalk or a portion of the roadway are consistent with each person's exercise of the right of assembly. A full protection theory must, however, prohibit any government decision to favor some activities over the constitutionally protected assembly of people who are in places where they have a general right

---

*I do not intend to downplay either the societal importance of traffic usage or even its possible constitutional basis. Rather, the claim is that the degree and type of burden on transportation or travel that results from fully protecting the first amendment conduct will only be the type of instrumental burden that we often find acceptable and that does not in any sense prevent the desired travel or make it illegal.

to be for expressive purposes. A further examination of the expressive aspects of parades and assemblies is needed before identifying cases where the traffic rules prohibit rather than merely zone expressive conduct. But where they do, the traffic rules unconstitutionally abridge freedom of assembly.

The normal and legitimate function of traffic laws should not lead to their being applied to restrict assemblies or parades. In people's everyday use of the streets for purposes of moving from one place to another, traffic laws ultimately function not to suppress desired activity but to facilitate it by basically zoning the activities[34]—requiring people to go in different directions on different sides of the street, requiring pedestrians to stay on sidewalks, or requiring alternating use of intersections. Although these traffic rules may instrumentally burden some people, they operate as a Roberts Rules of Order, as Professor Kalven proposed,[35] generally aiding and certainly not preventing people's desired activity of going from one place to another. The traffic rules usually operate less to favor some valued activities over others[36] than to facilitate everyone's safe and convenient use of the streets. This role of traffic laws should not be controversial.

The role of traffic regulations changes in an impermissible direction, however, when local officials apply them to prevent particular valued forms of parades and assemblies or to prohibit a person's participation in these events. Then, rather than facilitate various uses, enforcement of the traffic regulations favors traffic uses. At least in places where people have a general right to be and to engage in expressive activities, which presumably includes the streets and parks, the first amendment requires that the laws not give priority to the transportation function over expressive functions. Most communities agree. The traditional practice in almost all communities is to suspend traffic rules in favor of parades, although sometimes to require permits. Of course, since the streets are more continuously used for travel and transportation, legislators predictably and appropriately design the basic rules of the road with travel and transportation primarily in mind. Nevertheless, this focus of attention on traffic concerns does not show a conscious governmental decision to subordinate or sacrifice use of the streets for expressive purposes. Given either our social and cultural history or our first amendment values, it would be impermissible to assume any intent to subordinate expressive activities. The intended and appropriate function of traffic rules lies solely in their instrumental contribution to facilitating the various accepted uses of the street. Their "zoning" rationale no longer applies when the application of these traffic rules in the particular circumstances would undermine symbolic, advocacy, group-unifying, or other peaceable, substantively valued aspects of the parade or assembly. Still, rules properly designed with traffic in mind leave open the ever present possibility that a particular community at any time will apply them to suppress speech or assembly. Their application becomes unconstitutional precisely at this point.

A counterargument is that history and current practice show that the primary use of the streets is for transportation. Therefore, it is asserted, this use can legitimately claim priority. This is unconvincing. Doctrinally, the Court rejected this argument when it accepted Roberts' *Hague v. CIO* dicta that "the streets . . . have immemorially been held in trust" for these expressive uses; our society rejects it continually when it accepts use of the streets for parades and mass demonstrations. Moreover, the argument's logic is unsound. The observation that the streets are continuously used for transportation does not mean that transportation should be the priority use. The observation equally supports the alternative conclusion. The ever increasing use of the streets for transportation means that the vital use of the streets for expressive purposes should receive legal priority in order to prevent this constitutionally protected use from being squeezed out, or significantly limited, by the more routine transportation use. At most, the observation may explain why traffic laws are written with the transportation use primarily in mind. Thus, the observation is entirely consistent with a conclusion that the traffic rules should only control in transportation context. Both the present importance and the historical dedication of streets for use by parades and for other expressive activities support the conclusion that although the government can properly undertake to accommodate or promote the various uses of the streets, it must do so in a manner that does not restrict their use for expressive and assembly purposes. In other words, the Court was right in *Hague*. Given this conclusion, any condition on the use of the streets that prevents the exercise of first amendment rights is unconstitutional.

A ROUGH COST-BENEFIT ANALYSIS— OR REASONED ABSOLUTES

Many people, certainly the balancers, will not find these abstract doctrinal arguments very compelling. Mandatory parade permits seem reasonable and should be constitutional. Certainly, the government should be able to make permission to violate traffic laws dependent on receipt of a permit. Given the prevalence of these views, it may be useful to consider more specifically the possibility of doing without a mandatory parade permit system by examining costs and benefits. This investigation will argue that even balancers should reject existing legal doctrine.

Benefits of a Mandatory Permit System

Historically, the primary function of mandatory permit requirements was probably their overtly unconstitutional use to harass, control, or suppress expressive activities of unpopular groups. Other than this, the major announced functions of the permit requirement have been to provide notice that aids local governments in traffic planning and in assigning police to control traffic and prevent potential violence (and other illegal activities) either by the paraders or the audience.

In addition, the permit procedure usually gives local officials, normally the police department,[37] effective authority to reject applications on the basis of the local official's stated view that the time or route is inappropriate. This allocation of decision-making authority forces paraders to bargain with the police over the conditions under which the city will allow a march. In general, this bargaining process may be both desirable and permissible—the bargaining may usefully accommodate the interests of both sides, achieving more satisfactory social results. Nevertheless, the permit requirement gives the local governmental officials the upper hand in bargaining. This consequence can be described in terms of property or allocation rules. Mostly, private individuals decide when to engage in any particular, permissible activity on sidewalks and streets and in parks. The permit requirement effectively takes the legally recognized decision-making authority away from these people if they want to engage in certain first amendment protected conduct and transfers it to local officials. The rule effectively transfers "wealth" or power from the paraders, particularly from dissidents,[38] to government officials.

Thus, there are arguably three benefits of the mandatory permit system. First, the notice allows for better traffic planning and rational assignment of police, both of which in turn contribute to maintaining order and reducing traffic disruption. Second, the system helps eliminate scheduling conflicts. Third, it creates a bargaining process in which city officials clearly have the upper hand. In assessing these benefits, the issues include: the extent to which the constitutionally questionable aspects of the system actually contribute to these benefits; the actual importance or value of these benefits; and, in respect to the form of the induced bargaining, the legitimacy of characterizing the effect as a benefit.

The full-protection, absolutist approach recognizes that *the city may offer, although not require, parade permits.* As part of the offer the city could provide that the recipient of the permit would receive "reservations"; that is, the voluntary permit holder would, in the case of conflicting desires to use the space, have priority. In this respect, the system would resemble the way some city parks treat larger picnics—allowed without reservations but permitted to reserve space by means of a "permit." The city also could guarantee or promise special efforts to provide for the assignment of police officers to protect and facilitate the parade's operation. Finally, the city also could provide permit recipients with various additional supports, for example, special toilet facilities or a ban on parking along the parade route, for which advance city planning is crucial.

A properly designed *voluntary* permit system is likely to be well received by most groups that parade and normally could be expected to fulfill reasonably effectively the legitimate functions that the mandatory system serves. Even under existing mandatory permit systems, local officials consistently and, probably, accurately view the paraders themselves as a major beneficiary of the permit process.[39] Under a voluntary permit system, most organizers of parades, and certainly the organizers of the large parades or demonstrations that are planned well ahead of the actual event, should welcome the opportunity to receive the "reservations" and other guarantees that could come with a permit. Most parade and demonstration organizers would also want to cooperate with authorities, even in respect to choosing the time and route. Organizers usually want the parade to be viewed favorably. They could expect that cooperation promotes good public relations, reduces any antagonism that the parade might produce, and helps gain public support, for example, the support of the business community or the neighborhoods through which the parade will pass. Parade organizers to some extent usually share the city's proper concern with the "inconveniences" caused by the parade. At least in the normal case where the organizers are concerned with public relations, these "inconveniences" are "costs" that public reactions bring to bear on the organizers of the parade. The organizers have an incentive to "balance" popular antagonism to the parade caused by the inconveniences it imposes against any gains achieved either by their choice of an unpopular route or time or by their noncooperation. Finally, a voluntary permit system will place appropriate incentives on the government. Since the city will have the notice that aids policy planning if parade organizers use the voluntary system, the city has an incentive to make the permit system convenient, nonintimidating, and open. The bureaucracy will have an incentive to avoid red tape. A properly designed voluntary system that provides reservations and other special benefits to the parade organizers will predictably generate most of the useful information and cooperation that results from a mandatory system—and will do this while avoiding the great costs, discussed below in terms of first amendment freedoms, that a mandatory system creates. If this is right, the benefits attributable to a mandatory system will be slight.

If everyone would voluntarily apply, constitutional complaints about the mandatory system might seem insignificant—if everyone is happy to comply, what is wrong with making it mandatory? (Although the converse might also be asked.) Of course, even if everyone would voluntarily apply, invalidating the mandatory system could have important consequences. As noted, the mandatory quality reduces the pressure on the city to make the system convenient and gives a particular tilt to the bargaining interactions between city authorities and parade organizers. But, clearly, some paraders will not voluntarily apply. Even with a mandatory system, groups sometimes do not apply for permits—and occasionally are prosecuted. Presumably, even a well-designed voluntary system will result in some increase in nonuse. The point is not to show that rejection of the mandatory system will have no costs. Rather, this description of the voluntary system highlights the distortions caused by viewing the alternative to mandatory permits as a system without permits. Ignoring the potential of a well-designed voluntary system results in gross overestimation of the costs of giving full protection to the first amendment activity.

Other observations support the claim that the costs of changing to a voluntary system should be acceptable. First, local governments recognize that costs outweigh any gains in requiring permits for certain processions that are otherwise within the category for which their ordinances require permits. For example, most cities exempt funeral procession from their permit requirements.[40] Certainly, this exemption is "reasonable." Cities are surely right to conclude that to require a parade permit for funerals would be unseemly and offensive; that lengthy advance notice to the city will seldom be either important or feasible; and that even without a permit requirement, the city usually will know in advance which funerals require special preparations by the police and city officials.[41] But these observations about funerals apply more broadly.[42] At least for some other parades, such as relatively spontaneous politically oriented parades, requiring a permit would be offensive (at least to some people), requiring lengthy advance notice would not be feasible, and effective notice will exist even without the permit procedure. Moreover, for many small parades, advance notice will not really be particularly important to the city's interests. The organizer of most large parades for which effective advance notice would be useful will provide the notice under a well-designed voluntary permit system. Even if they do not, the leaflets and advertising designed to notify potential participants of the event will usually provide the police with adequate notice.[43]

Some cities already officially recognize that advance notice, although desirable, is not crucial. Many ordinances allow for waiver of the requirement that parade organizers apply for a permit some specific number of days in advance.[44] The Sacramento, California, ordinance[45] requires the city manager to issue a permit (presumably immediately on demand) for any parade that "is spontaneous or organized on short notice in response to an event of obvious importance" as long as the parade is of the type that could have received a permit if the organizers had gone through the permit application process.[46] Sacramento properly recognizes that the city should and can accept this added burden caused by the lack of early notification.

Although each city is unique, other cities' failure to take Sacramento's approach most likely does not reflect a careful assessment of the actual burden this waiver approach would impose on the city. Most probably they have not considered the alternative adopted by Sacramento. Moreover, many governing officials may lack an interest in providing any more opportunity for spontaneous parades than they believe is legally required under the "reasonableness" standard. Not everybody loves *every* parade. The implicit balancing of local officials may place a low or negative value on these spontaneous, political parades. Even if the police normally allow "spontaneous" parades to proceed, the permit requirement, by making the parade itself illegal, gives the police more options in choosing a response and the upper hand in any negotiations with the paraders. This gain in police flexibility, however, is illegitimate. It must be unacceptable to achieve government flexibility by making constitutionally protected conduct illegal. This method of gaining flexibility depends on giving the police arbitrary, censorial power over expression.

Any balancing analysis must also consider how much serious disruption would result *because* a few parades would take advantage of the voluntary scheme's option not to obtain a permit. The increased disruption is easily overestimated unless the analysis focuses precisely on the added disruption that results because of permit system being voluntary. I will assume that a permissible permit system cannot be used to restrict parades but rather can only be used as a means for the city to obtain notice and give priority, for example, in order to avoid conflicting parades. Given this assumption, the relevant "added disruption" is only the disruption that results from the authorities not receiving notice that they would have received under a mandatory scheme. There is reason to think this added disruption will be minimal. Under either system, some parades will not apply; but under either, police will still often know of these parades in advance. Moreover, many parades for which the authorities will not have notice will be of a size or nature that will not cause disruption. Finally, the same disruption will often occur whether or not the authorities receive notice. In each of these situations, a mandatory system would not help decrease disruption. The only situation where the mandatory system produces a gain is for the parade the police will not learn of under the voluntary system but that would apply under a mandatory system and is disruptive but would have been less so if the police had had advance notice—a likely small set. In other words, although some parades can be disruptive, a mandatory permit system may do little to decrease their disruption.

In practice, the mandatory permit system may even increase disruption. Again and again violence in the parade or demonstration context results from the police attempting to enforce the mandatory permit requirement against those who refused to, were unable to, were unaware of the need to, or had failed in their attempt to obtain a permit.[47] Professor Herbert Gutman describes how the famous Tompkins Square Riot of 1874 was a police riot that occurred as the police attempted to enforce their cancelation of a meeting permit.[48] The Walker Commission study of violence in Chicago during the 1968 Democratic National Convention found that the "clearing of demonstrators from Lincoln Park," for which a permit had been denied, "led directly to the violence. . . . [L]iterally, it forced the protestors into confrontation with police in Old Town and the adjacent residential neighborhoods."[49] In the south in the 1960s, police attacks on civil rights demonstrators who had been denied permits were a substantial cause of violence. Earlier in the century the same happened to meetings of socialists, unionists, and the unemployed.[50] Some of this violence should be attributed to the mandatory permit system or, at least, to enforcement of a mandatory system. Given this attribution, a plausible conclusion is that the net effect of the mandatory aspect of the permit system is to increase violence and disruption.

In addition to depending on predictions of consequences of a mandatory as compared to a voluntary permit system, a calculation of the benefits of a mandatory permit system will also depend on evaluating those consequences. The evaluation will be controversial. It is surely debatable whether or when nonviolent disruption should count as a cost or a benefit. People's capacity publicly and legally to create turmoil and impose costs on an unresponsive government and on the dominant society may be a valuable aspect of the right of assembly. Thus, possibly, some disruption should count as a social benefit. Similarly, should the effect of the mandatory permit process on the bargaining process between the paraders and the local authorities count as a cost or benefit? The mandatory and voluntary systems differ in how they allocate decisional authority with respect to the streets between private citizens and governmental officials. As in the case of all allocative decisions, whether a particular distribution should count as a cost or benefit will be a contested ethical or value issue. The mandatory system distributes "wealth" to those who want greater social control and away from those who want to parade, protest, or dissent. Of course, many local authorities view this as a benefit. But a proper interpretation of the first amendment may require the opposite evaluation. This difficulty in evaluating consequences again demonstrates that totaling the benefits of the mandatory system is inherently inconclusive. Still, on any calculation, the benefits do not seem very extensive.

Costs of a Mandatory Permit System

If the benefits of a mandatory permit system are often overestimated, conventional filters on thought also may cause its costs in terms of first amendment freedoms to be underestimated. Three types of costs occur. (1) Even the ideal mandatory system prohibits certain valuable types of expressive conduct. (2) It also has the effect of coercing behavorial expressions of ideological conformity or deference to government. (3) The abuses of the system are predictable and unavoidable and inevitably are directed primarily at unpopular groups.

The factor that makes a permit requirement an "abridgement" rather than just a "burden" on freedom of assembly is that it effectively makes some substantively valued and socially significant types of peaceable parades and assemblies illegal. Although sometimes waivable, most parade ordinances require that people apply for a permit some number of days before a proposed march. In contrast to the assumption implicit in these ordinances, people's expressive desires cannot be so routinized. All periods of our history have witnessed socially and politically important "spontaneous" demonstrations, assemblies, or marches. Marches and demonstrations frequently take place within a few days, often within a few hours, after people learn of objectionable acts committed by those in power.[51] Arrests of civil rights activists in the 1960s often brought immediate responses in the streets. During the Vietnam war, the announcement of a new, secret invasion of Cambodia by the United States military brought antiwar students out of university halls and into street assemblies and protests within hours. As the authors of the Sacramento parade ordinance apparently recognized, the typical requirement that permit applications be submitted days before the proposed event would legally bar these important expressions of dissent. This effective prohibition of spontaneous marches is a significant cost. A society committed to popular expression and involvement in public life must highly value the opportunity to engage in this type of immediate expression.

A second, closely related feature of most parade ordinances is in effect a content discrimination against certain expression. The ordinances assume that a march will have an identifiable leader, a group or person who organizes and controls the parade. These ordinances only allow the organizer or a representative who identifies the organizer or sponsoring group to secure a permit. Typically, ordinances require the permit applicant to identify a "parade marshall" who will be in charge and who has the responsibility and the capacity to control the march.* Although most political marches and demonstrations, as well as cultural or festive parades, fit the mold contemplated by these requirements, these assumptions of hierarchical structure do not always apply. For the government to make the rights of parade participants dependent on the acts of their leaders is itself an infringement on the participants' freedom.[52] Moreover, to assume that there will always be individuals or organizations in leadership roles is an ideological distortion of reality. (This particular distortion reflects the orderly world of legal or bureaucratic thinking, a world that constantly assumes the existence of some leader or representative with whom the lawyer or official can speak.) Basically, parade ordinances assume and, then, require organization, planning, and hierarchy. Sometimes refusal to fit this mold is a significant aspect

---

*Permit applications also usually ask for varied information, including the number of participants—although it is not clear whether, in practice, ability to answer these questions accurately is made a condition for getting a permit.

of the expression and value-based behavior of the demonstrating group. Hence, the permit requirement prohibits many assemblies or marches that express or embody spontaneity, flexibility, and an anarchistic or egalitarian organization and operates as a content discrimination against this speech. The requirement that parades, demonstrations, and other assemblies have leaders and representative agents overtly imposes mainstream values and, if enforced, clearly prohibits valuable exercises of the right of assembly.

Although not so unambiguously meriting constitutional protection, other types of assembly are also made illegal by a mandatory permit system. An established form of political and social protest is the surprise mass presence, accompanied by demands for a response, at the scene of the offensive government action or on the steps of government power. Even if demonstrators would be happy to persuade officials merely on the basis of reason, logic, or the rightness of their position, dissidents implicitly realize that class or cultural prejudice block or distort dialogue. And they recognize that their physical presence is a form of power that can sometimes pressure the authorities first into paying attention and then into making some response. Dissidents unabashedly and properly try peaceably but forcefully to impose pressure through the intimidation produced by numbers, solidarity, and the spotlight of their mass presence.[53]

Demonstrations designed to apply pressure and exercise power may also communicate information, publicize grievances, and at times be necessary to attract the attention of authorities. Still, this use of assembly for exercising power cannot be easily defended on the basis of a marketplace theory of the first amendment. An assembly's capacity to do things—particularly to apply pressure—does not fit well into a theory of first amendment rights centered on dialogue and rational persuasion.[54] Justice Jackson summed up this view when he treated the group nature of people's action as constituting an illegal conspiracy rather than a constitutionally protected association. Jackson argued that "[t]here is no constitutional right to 'gang up' on the Government."[55] Although later disavowing reliance on the marketplace of ideas theory, Professor Abernathy likewise observes that given "the argument that the interchange of ideas and opinions, especially on public questions, is the practice which the right of assembly is primarily designed to protect and encourage, one can readily see that many parades would not fall within the intent of the constitutional guarantee."[56]

The court's hesitation to conclude that a permit requirement abridges people's rights may reflect a similar hesitation to recognize a right to create power peacefully, a fear of the crowd,[57] and an inclination to follow a marketplace of ideas theory of the first amendment. Nevertheless, a key aspect of assembly is its capacity to generate power through the union of people. Beyond the general reasons to protect *expression*, from a liberty perspective, the primary additional reasons to protect *peaceable assembly and voluntary association* is that they are nonviolent methods of creating valued experiences, developing new perspectives, and generating the power necessary to do things. Except when people exercise this power coercively—that is, violate specific rights of others—the first amendment should protect the creation and exercise of this power.[58] As long as the pressure that the assembly imposes merely involves its unexpected, unannounced presence and the *assertion* by those assembled that their concerns should receive attention and their demands should be met, a liberty theory would protect the assembly as a noncoercive method of peaceably generating and exercising power.[59]

Guerrilla theater, although often painstakingly planned in advance, also frequently relies on the surprise of its unannounced staging for part of its impact. Whenever it depends on surprise or on flexible changes in locations and timing in order to find, attract, or confront its intended audience, this expressive form of assembly will conflict with rules contained in most permit systems. Again, the permit requirement would prohibit a valued and meaningful manner of peaceable assembly, thereby abridging the right.

A second cost in terms of rights of expression is often ignored but represents a serious conflict with first amendment values. The mandatory permit system requires that those assembling and parading must symbolically and practically bow to the very authorities that the paraders may strongly believe are, and that they may assert to be, unacceptable or even illegitimate. The mandatory permit ordinance requires paraders to go to these authorities, announce their plans, and request permission to exercise their rights. This requirement is very close to compelled symbolic affirmation of allegiance. When *Cox v. New Hampshire*[60] first upheld a permit requirement in 1941, compelled affirmations of support for our government appeared to be constitutional. The ruling precedent was a widely criticized decision that permitted compulsory flag salutes within the classrooms.[61] Two years after *Cox*, the Court observed that a "fixed star in our constitutional constellation . . . [forbids any government] official [to] force citizens to confess by word *or act* their faith" in any prescribed orthodoxy.[62] In a ruling extended in more recent cases to strike down other forms of compelled speech,[63] the Court proceeded to overrule the earlier decision that had upheld flag salutes. Importantly, the Court's refusal to tolerate statutes commanding compelled confessions of allegiance implicitly recognizes that the marketplace theory's concern that all ideas are expressed does not exhaust the force of the first amendment. These decisions indicate that, at least at times, the first amendment protects an aspect of people's liberty, namely, their freedom not to express support for, or deference to, their government.[64]

The Court's new reasoning could be extended to parade permit requirements. The compelled symbolic expression inherent in applying for permits has tormented many groups. Some conclude that in good conscience they cannot apply to the government for permission to exercise their rights and, therefore, must violate the permit requirements. Nevertheless, unlike the classroom compulsion, the compulsion in *Cox* never generated widespread popular or academic outcries. And the Court has not yet reconsidered this parallel violation of the integrity of people's expression.

This argument analogizing mandatory permit requirements to coerced speech should not be overread. The compelled flag salute had a key objectionable feature absent in the permit situation. It served no purpose other than obtaining the speaker's avowal of allegiance. The mandatory permit process has other arguably legitimate purposes. Presumably, the first amendment does not create a general right to receive all governmental benefits or opportunities without applying for a license or permit.[65] Neither a person's objections to the overall legitimacy of the government nor to the particular permit requirements give the person a general right to refuse to apply. Still, the objection to the mandatory *parade* permit system has a stronger basis. The parade permit requirement differs from many other permit requirements. Unlike many permit situations, in the parade context, the government requires the permit to do what people already have a right to do—not to receive a special benefit or privilege.[66] The parader's belief, arguably supported by the Constitution, that the government cannot abridge the freedom increases the offensiveness or "cost" of requiring a person to ask for the government's permission. The procedure forces the dissident implicitly to deny her (correct) belief concerning her right to dissent. To force the person to seek permission symbolically states that the right to parade exists at the pleasure of the government. Also unlike most other permit contexts, the offensiveness of the symbolism is even greater because the specific "unabridgeable" right in question is a right to protest and dissent from the government. The mandatory permit requirement systematically and routinely forces dissidents to acknowledge, by requiring them to act out, the authority and dominance of the very government against which they protest. To require the dissidents to obtain permission symbolically co-opts their protected dissent.

A third cost of the mandatory permit system may, in practice, be its greatest. Even if benign in theory, a mandatory permit system cannot be expected to be benign as an actual, operating system. Local authorities consistently have used and continue to use the permit requirement as a means to harass those whom they wish to harass. Although I cannot unambiguously prove the above claim, even an unsystematic reading of the case law suggests the prevalence of abuse. The courts frequently invalidate permit systems because they do not contain adequate standards or because the local government does not apply them uniformly.[67] Typical parties to litigation, presumably, representative of those who have had trouble obtaining a permit, are dissident political or religious groups— groups that local authorities often find objectionable.[68] Combined, these observations strongly suggest that permit requirements are used to harass nonneutrally selected targets. But the litigation likely represents only the iceberg's tip. Harassment can occur at various points. Local officials can engage in virtually nonreviewable harassment by merely refusing to cooperate in the permit granting process. They can give applicants an administrative runaround in obtaining forms or information needed for the permit application. They can delay action on particular permit applications.[69] Local governments also often place unnecessary conditions on the grant of a permit, refuse to grant one, or selectively enforce the law against those who do not have permits. The dissident's spontaneous action, the occasionally principled refusal to apply for a permit, or the uninformed failure to obtain a permit, may make the dissident disproportionately subject to selective enforcement. As noted earlier, some evidence suggests that local governments frequently adopted permit systems specifically in order to harass unpopular groups more effectively.[70] The present abuse of the system, however, does not depend on this historical fact. The opportunity for and likelihood of harassment results from the mere existence of a system in which unpopular groups must make timely and proper requests for permission to exercise their rights. Any realistic assessment of permit systems must take into account their inevitable and often unreviewable susceptibility to abuse by local officials.

A final cost of the mandatory permit system, or a benefit of a voluntary system, relates to the comparative dynamic effects of each. Local officials are charged with protecting the public interest, imagining and then preventing the worst conceivable scenario of events, responding to irritated residents, businesses, and commuters, conserving city resources, and pleasing political and often business elites. Parades, particularly parades by unpopular groups, can conflict with any or all of these charges. Thus, the incentives placed on the officials are obvious. The most typical and most understandable administrative response to people's desire to use public resources is to begin by saying "no." The intuitive question for these officials or administrators to ask is not, "Why should this activity be restricted?" but instead, "Why should it be allowed?" Local officials or administrators seldom find it obvious why an activity, often promoted by dissidents and certainly by people who will make more work for authorities, ought to occur here and now. Saying "yes" creates more trouble, more work, potential problems, and accompanying criticisms. The entire structure of the situation encourages local officials to limit parades and demonstrations of dissident and unpopular groups[71] and to discourage these groups by making the permit application process as onerous as possible. Forms can be difficult to obtain and fill out. Requirements can be strictly enforced. Difficulties with routes and times can be emphasized.

When officials are assigned the duty of managing public resources in the public interest and are told to accomplish this task by writing and enforcing "reasonable" restrictions, their natural constituencies are the general public, local elites, and other officials, both front line and higher level, with whom they interact. These constituencies are always ready to complain about unnecessary waste or about abusive or offensive use of public facilities—for example, use by dissidents. Moreover, the officials who are responsible for police, management, and clean-up functions may complain about the unnecessary problems, work, and costs that parades and assemblies cause. From the perspective of these constituencies, those people who wish to engage in first amendment protected conduct are often the problem.

Despite these pressures, local police and city officials are often remarkably helpful and conciliatory, whether because of respect for democratic, first amendment values, or because experience teaches that failure to be helpful eventually results in an increase in disruption and violence. Nevertheless, interaction dynamics frequently result in the more predictable, noncooperative, restrictive response by local officials to groups, particularly unpopular or dissident groups, who seek parade permits. In contrast, if the first amendment would allow only a voluntary permit system, the dynamics change. The assignment of these officials shifts from that of writing and enforcing restrictions to offering and providing benefits in order to gain the voluntary cooperation of those engaged in first amendment conduct. This legal change transforms both the constituency of and the relevant pressure on these officials. Since the effect of the voluntary permit system is to require the officials to secure the cooperation of those exercising first amendment rights through agreement rather than through imposition of conditions, such a system changes the dissidents from adversaries into one of the officials' key constituencies. Since the norm is the right to parade, to obtain the paraders' participation in the permit process, officials must present themselves as easily accessible, friendly, and helpful. The incentives would be to reduce red tape and other burdens on the exercise of rights.[72]

THE NATURE OF THE INCONCLUSIVENESS OF THE COST-BENEFIT ANALYSIS

The survey of the costs and benefits of a mandatory as compared to a voluntary permit system shows minimal benefits—some uncertain amount of reduction of traffic problems, an unclear net effect on violence and major disruption, and the greater capacity of authorities to dominate, control, or harass demonstrators (an ambiguous benefit). Costs of the mandatory system include the prohibition of certain types of substantively valued assemblies. The prohibited types of assemblies can and have significantly contributed to democratic progressive change. The prohibited types are also disproportionately employed by the dissident groups for whom constitutional protection is most necessary. Other costs of the permit systems include: the compelled symbolic statements that are implicit in the act of seeking permission from those whom the demonstrators may be repudiating; the unavoidable, predictable abuse of the system to harass and suppress both dissidents and other groups that are unpopular with the authorities or the mainstream community; and the allocation of decision-making authority in a manner that encourages police and local authorities to restrict rather than support the exercise of first amendment rights, thereby limiting public expressive activity and reducing popular involvement in the society's public and political life. These costs are clear and seem significant. Still, no evaluative standards force any particular assessment of either these costs or the possible benefits mentioned before. Persons with different perspectives can draw different conclusions from this rough outline of costs and benefits.

For the absolutist, the description of the minimal benefits of the mandatory parade permit systems is relevant primarily for demonstrating that absolute protection is feasible. For the balancer the problem is more complex. First, the careful balancer must identify the issue that the balancing is to resolve. The balance arguably relates not to the actual costs and benefits of any particular permit system but to the costs and benefits of the government's having the authority to enact this type of permit system. At this metalevel, the issue becomes the desirability of various types of limits on the government's decision-making authority. For this issue, the above summary of costs and benefits may have been too specific to be informative.

The opposite may also be the problem. The "reasonable accommodation" or balancing that most courts and commentators recommend as an approach to time, place, and manner regulations is more specific. The balancer attempts to evaluate the actual merits of specific rules in an identifiable context. For example, she might try to determine the predictable present costs of doing without a specific mandatory permit system in a particular, historically situated city and then compare these costs (the benefits of having the permit system) to the costs to freedom of expression of having that system. Sometimes the balancer even evaluates the justification for a particular application of a rule. For these analyses, this chapter's summary of costs and benefits may have been too general. Nevertheless, even this balancer should consider the categories developed here. She should examine the degree to which a voluntary permit system could achieve the goals of the permit system. She should note that laws specifically prohibiting people from intentionally interfering with others' movements can legally bar a significant amount of the feared disruption—and though these laws may not be effective in practice, when they are not, a permit system is also unlikely to have stopped the disruption. This balancer should also recognize that worst-case scenarios are most likely to occur precisely in those rare situations when society ought to be strongly diverted from life as normal and forced to face the problems that bring massive numbers of people into the streets. And she should note that these worst case situations are, in any event, unlikely to be controlled by means of permit requirements.

Once the balancer considers the costs in this way, she may conclude that the minimal benefits attributable to the *mandatory* permit requirement do not outweigh its costs. But again, this evaluation will necessarily depend not only on predictions concerning consequences but also on more basic value commitments. Thus, the conclusion that the balancer finally reaches will depend heavily on how she values normality in contrast to the right to dissent and to challenge the status quo. It will depend on whether the balancer favors enforced order over individual expression and peaceful conflict, on whether she prefers a less disrupted private life or a more robust public life.

People's preferences in relation to these value choices will also fundamentally influence their inclination to rely on a reasonableness or balancing standard or to apply more absolutist rules or principles that limit permissible regulations. The reasonableness standard—and the operation of many permit systems—give some consideration to both sides of these value dichotomies, although it tends to favor normality or order more than expression or conflict. Reasonableness is basically defined by the status quo. Something is reasonable only in relation to some standard and that standard is normally the existing order or, in some theories, the preferences or convenience of the majority.[73] Likewise, absolute rules against abridgement give both sides of the dichotomy some consideration. Protection of homeowner's property, recognition of government's right to dedicate property to particular public uses, and careful definitions of "peaceable" and of "abridge"—all provide some support for normalcy and order. The absolute prohibition on abridgement, however, gives special protection to the values of dissent, peaceable conflict, and public expression and disruption. And it restricts the evaluative role of existing preferences. Moreover, it gives protection when protection is most needed—when the majority finds suppression to be reasonable. An absolutist approach does not allow the concern for order or normalcy routinely to trump the dissidents' choices.

The same value premises could determine both whether mandatory permit requirements are acceptable within a balancing analysis and whether balancing

and the reasonableness standard itself are acceptable. Moreover, a proper interpretation of the first amendment speaks precisely to this value issue. The liberty
theory, which emphasizes the values of self-realization and self-determination
and respect for individual autonomy, can guide the implicit choices always present in characterizing facts or evaluating consequences of alternative approaches.
The constitutional status of the first amendment should mean, at least in part,
that some people's preferences to restrict other's liberty in order to produce
greater normalcy and order are not a proper basis for public policy. Self-realization requires that we protect value-based dissent and self-expressive peaceful
deviance. Self-determination necessitates the existence of a politics and a public
sphere in which people have a right to participate. Indeed, virtually all first
amendment theorists agree that the first amendment implies the importance of
a public sphere in which political debate and peaceful conflict occur. In other
words, a proper reading of the first amendment leads to weighting the costs of a
mandatory permit system more heavily than its benefits. But, the underlying
values embodied in the first amendment also suggest the propriety of an absolutist rather than a balancing approach to evaluating time, place, and manner
regulations of assemblies.

Social and political commentators frequently note and usually bemoan the
low level of popular interest in a vibrant public sphere. They decry people's low
participation even in voting, in contrast to most people's apparently intense
interest in a private sphere, which many of these commentators find overfilled
with mindless entertainment and wasteful material consumption. Here, I neither offer a remedy for this state of affairs, criticize people's present response to
their existing options, nor even argue that our society would be better if we were
different. Still, the observations already made do contribute to an explanation
for why "we" are the way we are. The incentives and obstacles embodied in
society's structure and the values and messages symbolically proclaimed by that
structure surely influence people's practices and preferences. Society's regulation
of assemblies is, of course, only one small part of this overall social structure.
Nevertheless, if these regulations are symptomatic, given the obstacles these
regulations create and the messages they symbolize, the extent of people's present orientation toward the private sphere should not be surprising. The preference for the private sphere may merely reflect the incentives provided by our
social structure. On the most literal level, the value priorities symbolically
embodied in a typical parade permit ordinance rank the private world of funerals first, normal commercial life (with which some ordinances do not allow
parades to interfere substantially[74]) second; and, to the extent that organizers
typically plan entertainment parades well in advance and that these parades are
predictably not subject to regulatory hassling, while political parades are often
quick, sometimes spontaneous, initiatives and are often subject to bureaucratic
roadblocks, the permit systems rank entertainment third, and politics fourth. Of
course, other interpretations of these ordinances are possible—explanations
could focus on the predictable problems different parades will normally cause.
More generally, however, the whole framework created by mandatory parade
permit requirements suggests a primary concern with order and a desire to rou-

tinize public life. Surely this symbolic aspect of mandatory parade permit systems is contrary to the spirit of a robust and free public life called for by all theories of the first amendment.

The democrat might claim that, if people want to favor private society, a democracy must allow them complete freedom to structure their society to conform to these preferences. The constitutional status of the first amendment's preference for liberty requires that that claim be rejected. Possibly the central justification both for providing a vital public sphere and constitutionally protecting liberty is that the legitimacy and desirability of existing preferences are subject to doubt. The notion of democracy, in which democracy is valued because and to the extent that it is an embodiment of respect for liberty, equality, and human dignity, assumes that people's existing preferences are *usually* the best available basis for policy choices. Promoting these preferences normally respects people's equality and furthers their liberty. But there should be two caveats—first, preferences to subordinate or deny other's liberty should not be respected for purposes of lawmaking; second, no preferences can be expected to be entirely free of objectionable distortions that reflect evils and blindnesses of the existing order. Reliance on democratic choice becomes illegitimate precisely to the extent that these choices and the preferences they reflect fail to respect the liberty, equality, and dignity of the individual. A choice to restrict first amendment rights is subject to this objection. Moreover, the propriety of relying on people's preferences is undermined to the extent that those existing preferences are not subject to challenge by dissident individuals or groups. Restrictions on first amendment rights or on a robust public sphere also leaves reliance on existing preferences subject to this objection. Provision for and protection of opportunities to challenge existing orthodoxies is the basis for the hoped-for spiral of increasing understanding and legitimacy, for the truth that the marketplace of ideas theorists hope will come from free debate, and for the legitimacy that the dialectic theorists hope will make reliance on existing preferences increasingly acceptable.[75] The legitimacy of our system—and, thus, the best interpretation of the first amendment—does not require that we force people into participation in a public sphere. But it does necessitate that society's structure encourage rather than discourage the flourishing of such participation. The legitimacy of our system and our reliance on democratic choice requires that we attempt to eliminate, not increase, the obstacles to participation in this public sphere. We must evaluate regulations with an eye toward possibilities for change, for dissent, and for liberty rather than merely for order. This orientation should influence how we value the costs and benefits both of specific regulations and of different approaches to evaluating them. If this view is correct, then the legitimacy of our system is best supported by an absolutist protection of freedom of assembly.

8

Absolute Protection: Tentative Principles

An absolutist approach to time, place, and manner regulations must determine which rules or government practices "abridge" freedom of speech or the right to assemble peaceably. Not all laws that have the effect of restricting some speech or assembly amount to an abridgement. For example, laws outlawing trespass on "private" property are not unconstitutional merely because of their restrictive effect on some expressive conduct. Whether an abridgement occurs depends on how the rule restricts freedom and whether restricting freedom should be understood as the rule's purpose.

The absolutist analysis does not balance the amount of abridgement or the size of the "effect" against the infringement's contribution to some public purpose. Even a challenged rule's failure to promote a public purpose only indirectly affects the conclusion about whether the rule is an abridgement—for example, by affecting the interpretation of the purpose of the rule or by violating a governmental duty not to gratuitously restrict expression. Likewise, the fact that, as compared to some imagined alternative, a law, such as the trespass law mentioned above, greatly "restricts" some people's opportunity to engage in speech or assembly does not by itself make the rule an abridgement. Evaluating the law's constitutionality requires a theory of the relevant freedom and an interpretation of the term "abridgement."

One strategy for developing the needed interpretation is to formulate, evaluate, and defend various principles considered as possible implementations of an understanding of the relevant freedom and of abridgement. The objective would not be to find a unique, nonoverlapping set of principles that completely embodies some underlying values such as liberty and autonomy or that completely implements the constitutional prohibition on abridgements. Rather, the proposed principles, while individually defensible, are merely attempts to give more operative meaning to the prohibition on laws that abridge freedom of peaceable assembly. The proposed principles are merely exemplary. They predictably will be both incomplete and overlapping. Entirely different, although presumably nonconflicting, principles would be possible. Nevertheless, the enterprise of examining these noncanonical principles is justified by the practical interest in having principles to provide guidance and the theoretical interest in advancing our understanding of the relevant values.

Both the practical and the theoretical facets of this project are important. Practically, as reasoned interpretations of the notion of abridgement and of the relevant freedom, the principles can serve as a useful alternative to reasonableness or balancing for the purpose of deciding cases. Even more important, these principles can provide lawmakers with relatively effective guidance in their decision-making as well as a relatively unambiguous standard for explaining and defending potentially unpopular decisions that protect speech or assembly. Theoretically, the reasoned development and defense of these principles become part of the task of developing an adequate theory. A beneficial practical side effect is that it can stimulate consideration of presently undeveloped approaches to problems. A common tendency of those adopting a reasonableness orientation is to view a convenient means for advancing an admittedly significant end as justified despite some arguably minor suppression of individual liberty. In contrast, the absolutist approach assumes that suppression is not an appropriate means of pursuing admittedly important ends. This premise encourages a different, more creative attitude that is attuned to formulating nonrepressive means to further our goals—an orientation illustrated by the last chapter's suggestion of "voluntary" permit systems.

Although the liberty theory calls for absolute protection for individual autonomy and although the proposed principles will be an attempt to embody this notion, several caveats should be kept in mind. First, in the end, any standards or principles worth defending must be "reasonable" in the sense that they are susceptible to a plausible, reasoned defense. This admission does not imply, however, acceptance of the balancer's typical methods of determining reasonableness or engaging in cost-benefit calculations. Second, the defense of the principles proposed below appears to claim that we can abstractly identify aspects of rules or practices that should lead us to understand them as abridgements of protected freedom. This claim might seem problematic. Various aspects of the human condition—ranging from the continuous pattern of historical change, to the importance and legitimacy of collective human self-determination, to the limits of human insight, and to the nature of language and human understanding—will prevent articulation of comprehensive, timeless principles.[1] At best, the enterprise of proposing, defending, and implementing these principles is a strategy for increasing our insight and improving our condition. Thus, its more appropriate, modest claim is to be a useful method of moving toward an ever receding reflective equilibrium.[2]

This Chapter tentatively evaluates six proposed principles that provide for a more absolutist approach to various regulations of particular, time, place and manner restrictions on assembly or speech. The six proposed rules or principles are:

1. The government cannot restrict assemblies or expressive conduct on the basis of content unless the content restriction does not prevent the exercise of the valued liberty *or* unless it is necessary to provide for the constitutionally permissible uses to which the government has dedicated some space or facilities.

2. Restrictive regulations specifically directed at assembly or expression are unconstitutional abridgements of these activities.
3. The government cannot restrict the use of government facilities in a manner that prohibits substantively valued first amendment conduct unless the conduct interferes with the constitutionally permissible purposes to which the government has dedicated the space or facilities.
4. Zoning, that is, regulations directed at the time, place, or manner of speech or assembly, is not an abridgement of freedom if its rationale is not hostility to protected liberty and if it does not prevent the exercise of the substantively valued liberty, for example, if ample equivalent channels or opportunities really exist. (This amounts to a caveat that further specifies the notion of "restriction" in the first three principles.)
5. a. People engaged in first amendment conduct have no right to interfere unnecessarily and intentionally with the activities of others.
   b. Nevertheless, the government cannot prohibit disruption that results merely from the number of people engaged in first amendment activity; in a place where they have a right to be, the government cannot favor or "accommodate" other activities by limiting the presence of people engaged in first amendment conduct.
6. In providing special benefits that make assembly or speech rights more effective, the government can impose procedural conditions as long as the purpose of the conditions is not to affect the content of the expression or to restrict first amendment conduct.

Although subject to some scholarly[3] and judicial criticism,[4] the first principle, which prohibits content discrimination except under specific conditions, is widely accepted.[5] The ban on content discrimination should apply in all but very limited circumstances—limited circumstances that are suggested by the other principles. For example, sometimes a content restriction implements the government's dedication of a particular place at particular times to specific uses. (See principle 3.) Thus, in courtrooms, judges appropriately make and enforce content distinctions both when they silence the audience and when they rule that lawyers' remarks are either out of order, improper, or irrelevant. More generally, at places where the public has no general right to be present for their own purpose or to use the specific resources for expressive purposes, and if only the permitted expression furthers the purposes for which the area is primarily used (see principle 3), the content discrimination would be permissible. Although these content discriminations limit protected freedom, they should be understood as aimed at positively promoting a specific activity rather than at suppressing unwanted expression. This distinction between promotion and suppression attempts to implement the notion that the government can affirmatively promote majoritarian visions of the good although it cannot do so by means of suppression of deviant visions.

The most controversial aspects of the principle prohibiting content discrimination raise issues identical to those posed by the second principle. Since the rationale for a broad interpretation of both principles is very similar, further development of the first principle can await discussion of the second. Here, one illustrative application of the first principle will show that this principle could produce dramatic consequences, not yet realized in case law.

Apparently since their origin in the last quarter of the nineteenth century,[6] parade permit ordinances have typically exempted funeral processions.[7] The no-content discrimination principle, which refuses to allow the government to distinguish labor picketing from other picketing,[8] should also treat this distinction as an invalid content discrimination.

A reasonableness analysis is likely to accept the existing regime of exemptions for funerals. Most people would find it totally unacceptable to apply to funeral processions the general requirement, typical of parade ordinances, that sponsors apply for the permit several weeks before the parade. A reasonableness analysis might justify the distinction between funerals and other processions on grounds unrelated to a governmental wish to discriminate between different speech. Policymakers might assume that funeral processions will be less disruptive of traffic and normal routines than some political demonstrations. They might expect that funeral processions are less likely to stir either observers or participants into riotous action. Thus, the evil of censorship might not be present and the reasonableness approach arguably could promote the general welfare by allowing this content discrimination.

Further consideration demonstrates, first, the questionableness and conventionality of the reasonableness analysis presented above and, second, the lack of necessity of permit requirements for any parades. First, the general assumption that funeral processions do not create the same problems created by other parades can be factually wrong. Since parade-based violence may most commonly either be initiated by the government or result from the government attempting forcibly to stop parades,[9] if funeral processions are less likely to become violent, this may be in part because government authorities are more likely to treat funeral processions with respect, as illustrated by their exemption from permit requirements. Nevertheless, historically, some of our largest, often very politically significant and occasionally terribly disruptive parades have been funeral processions held for political figures, labor martyrs, or cultural heros.[10] Certainly, these processions are potentially as disruptive as other marches. If funeral processions present the same problems as other parades, the reasonableness analysis presented above is inadequate to account for the exemptions. The most obvious additional consideration is that policymakers thought requiring a permit for the funeral procession would be very unseemly but were not similarly troubled by imposing the requirements on other parades, which were thought to be less intrinsically necessary. In other words, the exemption for funeral processions may be best explained merely by the government's lesser respect for, or lesser concern about burdening, other parades. Surely, such lesser regard for the expression is not a proper justification for discriminatorily restricting first amendment rights. Catching this evil is a central purpose of the no-content discrimination principle.

Even if the above explanation for the exemption is wrong, the funeral procession exemption violates the principle against content discrimination. This is the right result. Cities' ability to manage without permits for funeral processions indicates that the city could also manage without imposing permit requirements on other processions. Moreover, often real problems caused by parades can be met by content-neutral means. For example, if the manner of movement of people in typical funeral processions makes these processions nondisruptive, lawmakers could avoid the application of this principle by formulating noncontent distinctions that exempt all parades exhibiting that type of movement—thereby exempting both (most) funeral processions and any other, physically similar processions. This possibility illustrates how the no content discrimination principle not only provides protection for protected expressive activities, particularly the less favored activities most in need of protection, but also encourages the development of less restrictive means to serve the government's legitimate interests.

Given the range of laws that inevitably affect speech and assembly, "abridge" must be interpreted more narrowly than "affect." The first amendment prohibition on making laws that abridge the freedom can, however, sensibly be understood as prohibiting laws specifically directed at restricting the protected activities. This reading leads directly to the second principle: *Restrictive regulations specifically directed at assembly or expression are unconstitutional abridgements of these activities.*

This principle requires only that the government not specially disfavor activities protected by the first amendment—surely a reasonable requirement. Nevertheless, its implementation would often provide much more extensive protection of assemblies and expressive conduct than does current doctrine. For example, it would invalidate most prohibitions or burdens on parades, the issue discussed in the last chapter. Normally a person is free to enter even a crowded sidewalk and walk in the same direction as other people. A law that restricts this activity specifically when people consciously collect together for their "walk," that is, when they assemble, or that restricts this activity specifically when people engage in the activity for expressive reasons, is a restriction directed at assembly or expression. According to the second principle, this law "abridges" assembly or expression. Likewise, whether or not the government can generally prohibit burning a flag, a rule that specifically prohibits burning a flag as a means of expression* is impermissibly directed at expression.[11] In contrast to a rule that prohibits holding "objects" in a manner that blocks other people's views, a rule against hand-held signs or posters at school board meetings is obviously directed at restricting expression. Under the second principle, that rule too is unconstitutional.[12]

While the prohibition on restrictions directed at first amendment conduct has quite dramatic consequences, *this* principle never prevents the government from stopping activities that, independently of their expressive or group assembly aspects, cause some problem. First amendment conduct is permissibly subject indirectly to regulation when the nonexpressive aspects of the conduct "cause" an evil. A statute can directly regulate the nonexpressive aspect of blocking of an intersection, the fire, or interference with vision, even though the

---

*18 U.S.C. Sec. 700 prohibits "knowingly *casting contempt* upon any flag of the United States by publicly . . . burning . . . it." (Emphasis added.)

statute thereby restricts expressive conduct. The second principle merely means that a statute cannot directly identify the first amendment conduct as the prohibited evil.

Thus, at least under this principle, the Court properly upheld an ordinance that prohibited anyone "on . . . grounds adjacent to any building in which a school . . . is in session . . . [from] willfully . . . making . . . any noise or diversion which disturbs . . . such school session."[13] This noise ordinance, at least as written, does not discriminate against first amendment conduct. It apparently equally prohibits loud construction activity and loud protest demonstrations during school hours. Likewise, the government can protect the quiet of the home by requiring outsiders to respect no trespassing or no solicitation notices posted by the occupant, can raise revenue by generally taxing the sale of goods, or prevent littering by prohibiting littering. In contrast, the Court has struck down laws pursuing these goals by specifically regulating expressive activities. It has struck down a ban on door-to-door canvassing, a tax specifically on newspapers, and a ban on leafletting justified as a means to prevent litter.[14] Although narrower explanations can be given for these decisions, each decision illustrates a result required by the second principle.

Both the first and second principles are compatible with regulations that attack virtually any evil. Still, these principles' requirement that restrictions be formulated without reference to first amendment conduct would be unacceptable to an advocate of balancing. For example, although a noisy political demonstration and construction work might both cause the same interference with various public or private interests, a policymaker might reasonably conclude that in particular circumstances the construction work is sufficiently valuable that its negative aspects should be tolerated. This policymaker, however, might reach the opposite conclusion about first amendment conduct or about certain content-based categories of first amendment conduct. In these circumstances, application of the first or second principles could prevent the government from legislating welfare-maximizing distinctions. Likewise, these principles require rejection of finely tuned legislation based on empirical assumptions that people engaged in certain first amendment protected conduct are more likely to cause disruption and become involved in violence than are those engaged in other activities. (Of course, this result arguably is also required by the long accepted first amendment doctrine that a mere tendency of expressive conduct to cause violence, as opposed to a speaker's purposeful creation of a clear and present danger of violence, does not justify a law prohibiting the conduct.[15])

For example, the University of Oregon once proposed to prohibit people on campus possessing any "sticks and rigid handles . . . affixed to any hand held sign, placard, or banner"[16] and justified the proposal as a safety measure. The university did not suggest a more general, campus-wide ban on people possessing sticks and rigid handles, which presumably would also prohibit umbrellas from the rainy Oregon campus. Quite possibly, its proposed rule merely reflected the illegitimate view that expression ought to be regulated. Alternatively, its narrow proposal may have reflected a judgment concerning the importance of keeping people dry, the inconvenience of a wider ban to those with umbrellas (whom the university administrators may have perceived to be more consequential people than most demonstrators), or the greater likelihood that those carrying signs will use them for violent purposes. These value judgments may have been widely shared and the empirical assumptions may have been true—that is, the University's proposed discrimination may have been "reasonable." Still, the general premise of the liberty theory or other full protection theories is that these utilitarian considerations do not justify overriding first amendment claims.[17] The "preference for liberty" requires that, in this context, the government must devise methods to pursue its general welfare concerns without disfavoring first amendment conduct even if this results in some marginal utilitarian loss. Thus, the first two principles prohibit these "reasonable" discriminations.

The second principle implements several important constitutional values. First, it implies that the government ought to treat first amendment activities as being at least as valuable as other chosen activities—like carrying umbrellas. Second, by requiring that the law be written in more general or nonspeech terms, the principle gives the first amendment activities the advantage of having those who engage in the other restricted conduct as allies in opposing the law or at least in forcing a proper, fuller consideration of the restriction's merits. This prophylactic function of the second principle may be its most valuable aspect. A rule utilitarian might even conclude that this aspect adequately compensates for welfare losses that the principle occasionally causes. Finally, by requiring that the law focus on the evil to be prevented or the good obtained, the principle helps assure that the government's objective is oriented toward something other than suppression of assemblies or speech. The principle thwarts the common bureaucratic or legislative inclination to strike out at the most vulnerable and visible targets, expression and assembly. It forces the authorities more carefully to define and legislate against a specific evil.

The second principle would invalidate a law that specifically prohibited speaking or assembling in parks or on streets. Frequently, the Supreme Court avoids a direct ruling on the validity of this type of restraint. Nonuniform enforcement of such bans, discriminatory exceptions written into the statute, standardless provisions for administratively granting exceptions, or procedural inadequacies in the administration of the bans often provide easier bases for invalidation. Still, in a sense, the second principle merely extends by one step the first principle's prohibition of content discrimination. Combined, the principles provide that the government can discriminate neither among nor against first amendment expression. If the first principle is accepted, the similarity between the two principles suggests the acceptability of the nonutilitarian aspect of the second principle. Narrowly interpreted, the "no content discrimination" principle merely prevents the government from restricting one side in a public debate. Under this interpretation, the evil is viewpoint censorship. A broader interpretation of content neutrality prohibits the government from favoring expression or assembly oriented toward particular subjects, like labor disputes, as opposed to others.[18] This interpretation implements the notion that the government should not only refrain from restricting any side of the debate but also should not set the agenda of public debate. Even if the government, in its own communications, can affirmatively take one side, at least, it cannot set the agenda by ruling certain issues out of order. Nevertheless, even this argument does not apply readily to the third, broadest form of content discrimination. The government can with some plausibility claim that it neither takes sides nor sets the agenda when it only regulates because of the content's offensive form, not its message. For example, the government might ban nudity in films shown at drive-in theatres,[19] or ban "dirty" language on the radio[20] or on campus[21] or in the courthouse,[22] or ban all signs except those providing information about the occupant of the land where the sign is located.[23] Courts and commentators, however, often condemn these regulations for being unconstitutional content discriminations.

Sometimes the argument against discrimination may be that the medium is the message,[24] or that the medium is itself ideological. Usually, however, the main constitutional objection to these types of "content" discrimination is not viewpoint censorship. Rather, the argument is that, by allowing some speech, the government shows that speech, presumably including the prohibited speech, is compatible with the use of the area. Thus, the regulation unnecessarily restricts expressive liberty. The government can respond that welfare maximization justifies these content discriminations. This response is the same that the government often uses to justify noncontent-based restrictions on first amendment conduct. The government could claim that nonnude films or labor picketing, like umbrellas as compared to posters on sticks, is sufficiently valuable that it should be permitted in these locations even if it creates some problems. Not so valuable, however, is the prohibited expression—the nude films, the nonlabor picketing, or the posters on sticks at the University. These welfare-maximization arguments should be rejected, and should be equally denied whether implemented by a discrimination against particular content or against expression as a category.

Both the broad interpretation of the first principle's prohibition on content discrimination and the second principle's prohibition on restrictions directed at first amendment conduct, as well as the third principle's requirement that first amendment conduct be allowed if not incompatible with the normal or dedicated use of the government property, reflect the same value commitment. All three reject situation-by-situation cost-benefit or general-welfare analyses to justify restrictions on first amendment conduct. None object to the government's affirmative pursuit of collective goals but each prohibits the use of suppression as a means. All three protect people's use of space for expressive conduct against real or imagined cost-benefit analyses that favor more conventional uses. The judgment that, even if welfare maximizing, the government cannot favor residential labor picketing over residential nonlabor picketing is little different from the judgment, required by the second principle, that the government cannot prohibit all picketing or leafletting in a residential neighborhood given that it allows neighbors to stand on the sidewalks, make noise, hand each other small objects, and engage in similar forms of behavior.[25] The neighbors' or other observers' dislike of the leafletters and picketers, of their expressive activity, or of their specific messages, as well as fears of consequences resulting from people's responses to the expressive aspects of the conduct, are all impermissible bases on which to restrict communicative activity.[26] The first amendment activity cannot be treated as more of an evil than are the allowed uses.

The second principle only condemns laws that are specifically directed at first amendment conduct. For example, it would apply to a law banning leafletting or door-to-door canvassing but not the ordinance noted above prohibiting "the making of any noise or diversion which disturbs . . . [a] school session,"[27] or a law against sleeping in the park, even if these laws restricted first amendment protected expression. The latter laws, which are not directed at first amendment conduct, raise a different, but crucial issue. Legislators can write totally restrictive regulations without reference to speech or assembly. They can do this, for example, when they want to devote some space (or other resource) for purposes other than first amendment conduct. The possibility of these types of restrictions suggests two questions: first, despite the government's dedication of specific resources to these other functions, are there situations in which it must allow some use of the resources for first amendment conduct? Second, are there situations where the government cannot favor nonfirst amendment activities at the expense of first amendment activities? (Note that the second principle only prohibited discriminatorily disfavoring first amendment conduct.) The answer to each question should be and, precedent makes clear, is: yes. The Court has found laws not directed specifically at speech being unconstitutional as applied—and has frequently suggested this holding as a possibility even when it has not protected the expressive, sometimes symbolically expressive, conduct.[28] The specific inquiry here is: What scope must the government give first amendment activities and in what situations can the government not favor other activities?

Both courts and commentators have generally accepted the view of the plurality in *Hague v. CIO*[29] that streets and parks must be available for first amendment activities. Justice Roberts' much-quoted dictum argued:

> Wherever the title of streets and parks may rest, they have immemorially been held in trust for the use of the public and, time out of mind, have been used for purposes of assembly, communicating thoughts between citizens, and discussing public questions. Such use . . . has, from ancient times, been a part of the privileges, immunities, rights, and liberties of citizens.[30]

Although Roberts added a statement that suggests the reasonableness standard, arguing that the privilege "is not absolute," he also asserted that the privilege "must not, in the guise of regulation, be abridged or denied."[31] Roberts' approach suggests that even a law not written in terms of restrictions on speech and assembly, for example, a rule that people could only use streets for travel or, possibly, a rule against distributing to strangers on the street items that could become litter,[32] would be invalid as applied to first amendment activities. If so, then sometimes some facilities or public resources must be available for first amendment conduct.[33] But when the Constitution requires this availability is unclear. Doctrinally, the issue is whether the analysis must depend, as the Court and commentators generally suggest, on balancing and on the reasonableness of the restrictions as applied to the first amendment conduct or whether some general principles could provide the courts and lawmakers with better guidance.

In his 8–1 majority opinion in *Grayned v. City of Rockford*,[34] Justice Marshall announced an appropriate, relatively protective principle. He concluded that "[t]he crucial question is whether the manner of expression is basically incompatible with the normal activity of a particular place at a particular time."[35] Although Marshall also emphasized reasonableness and weighing of values,[36] his "crucial question" points to a much more precise issue. Still, difficult issues are left open. The Court's announced principle quite clearly protects nondisruptive, expressive conduct in places where people have a right to be—a conclusion that has a long judicial history.[37] But does the Court's question also mean that people have a right to further their first amendment activities by commandeering otherwise unused space or facilities from which the government normally barred them? Do people have a right to assemble, speak, or demonstrate in various government facilities when the facilities are temporarily not in use? If an office is only used by government employees on weekdays, with what would a weekend demonstration interfere? With the weekend quiet? With the days off of maintenance personnel and guards? With normal weekday use? What is "normal" use and "basically incompatible"? Although it still leaves difficult interpretative issues, an alternative formulation is: (3) *the government cannot restrict the use of government facilities in a manner that prohibits substantively valued first amendment conduct*[38] *unless the conduct interferes with the constitutionally permissible purposes to which the government has dedicated the space or facilities.*[39] Under this principle, the government cannot, for example, restrictively deny access for first amendment conduct even to facilities that would otherwise be off limits to the public unless the normal function of the facilities necessitates the denial.

This third principle accomplishes an important task in an increasingly governmentally "owned" or socialized society. On the one hand, it does not attempt to determine abstractly what resources must be available to people engaged in expressive conduct; it does not require that the government distribute, presumably either equally or on a basis of equal opportunity to all people in the society, some level of resources for use in expressive activities. The third principle also does not prevent the government from pursuing collectively chosen conceptions of the good.[40] On the other hand, as a practical matter, the principle provides assurance that modern government's increasing control over physical space and material resources does not operate to eliminate the space or opportunity needed for the exercise of first amendment liberties. The principle effectively guarantees space for dissent on the part of those who reject majority conceptions.

The third principle implicitly means that the government must exhibit at least a minimal concern for people's freedom of assembly and expression—a mandate surely consistent with the constitutional status of these expressive activities. Unnecessary restrictions on these freedoms are either evidence that the government has failed to exhibit this concern or evidence that, whatever the subjective motivation of the government decision-makers, the regulation should be understood to have an impermissible purpose to restrict the exercise of these freedoms. More generally, the third principle recognizes that the government's capacity to effectively pursue collective purposes requires that it be permitted to devote public resources to uses other than expression. Hence, the government's decisions to devote resources to various uses, assuming that the objective is not to restrict expression, should not be viewed as abridgements. In contrast, when regulations that restrict the expressive use of public resources are not necessary to further dedicated uses, they should be understood as withdrawing those resources from expressive uses, and, therefore, as abridgements of people's freedom. Basically, the third principle embodies a value-based interpretation of government policies. In practice, this interpretative method effectively mandates opportunities for expressive activities.

This third principle has surprisingly wide application.[41] For example, it provides a simple explanation for why a public library operates under more stringent constitutional requirements when it removes books from its shelves because of their content than when it purchases them because of their content.[42] The government's decisions to construct and maintain a library and to select certain books illustrates society's general authority to use resources for advancing goals it considers appropriate. The local community's policy of promoting particular concerns, as illustrated by the library's book selection and purchasing activities, is different from a policy of limiting or burdening people's access to dissident views. Assuming that removal of books is unnecessary for the contemplated use of the library—for example, assuming that overcrowded shelves do not make removal necessary—removing the books is an unnecessary restriction on the facility's use by those who want to engage in the first amendment activity of reading those books. The third principle distinguishes between the community's permissible attempt to promote its values by adopting a purchasing policy that makes "good" books available from its impermissible attempt to promote its values by removing books in order to make certain views less available. The third principle embodies the fundamental insight that the first amendment does not mandate governmental neutrality—the government can and should pursue democratically chosen goals—but that the first amendment does outlaw suppression of expression as a means for pursuing these goals. Under the assumed facts, nonremoval is fully compatible with any permissible uses of the library. It is only incompatible with the impermissible purpose of restricting the user's freedom. The legitimate purpose of using public resources to make available the government's favored books does not require removal. Thus, removal unnecessarily limits the resources available to support the exercise of first amendment rights.

The third principle provides the correct answer to many other issues. At least in communities where the climate restricts outdoor meetings during portions of the year, if the only hall suitable for large indoor meetings is a school auditorium or courtroom owned by the government, then a complete ban on public use of the hall intuitively seems objectionable. Even if there were private halls, the government should make its public hall available if, for example, the private owners discriminatorily permit only certain groups to use the private halls.* The third principle mandates at least these results. The government cannot deny use of its unused auditorium to private groups, even on an ideologically neutral basis, if the denial will prevent the occurrence of a peaceable assembly.

---

*Historically, governmental hostility to expression has gone much deeper than refusal to allow use of public facilities. Even private discrimination often occurred because of governmental pressure on private owners. The government effectively closed private halls to dissident groups.[43] Such governmental pressure is an independent constitutional violation.

Unanswered questions still remain, however. For example, can the government require payment for the use of its facilities and, if so, how much? Do private groups have the right to select among several unused public halls or can the government make the allocation?[44] The second question leads to the fourth principle. However, before considering it, an abbreviated discussion of the question of fees, although generally beyond the scope of this chapter,[45] could be suggestive.

Any full protection theory of freedom of assembly would not allow imposition of a fee on the exercise of the right. More generally, full protection theory should distinguish three situations. First, sometimes facilities that ordinarily would not be available to the group are made available to enable the group to engage in its desired expressive conduct. Here, the government should be permitted to charge the group the expense born by the government directly as a result of making the facilities available. The fee is for use of the facility, not the exercise of the right. Free use would amount to a special subsidy for the expressive conduct. Still, even here the government should not be permitted to charge if the specific context indicates that it is imposing the charge primarily in order to suppress expression.

Second, sometimes the government makes use of the facility widely available, does not discriminate against its use for expressive conduct, but generally imposes a charge on its use. Here, the mere fact that people are engaged in protected expressive activity does not give them a constitutional right to be exempt from the charge. The government is not required to make special "allocations" for expressive purposes. For example, the government could charge paraders the standard bridge toll or the political rally the standard charge for the exhibition hall.

Third, often the government allows people to make general, free use of an area—for example, parks and streets. Still, from the perspective of local governments, assemblies or parades may create special, greater than "normal," expenses. Estimates of the direct costs that parades or demonstrations impose on cities vary widely. In the late 1960s, a large two- day demonstration was estimated to cost Washington, D.C., over $1 million.[46] Ninety-seven events over a 10½ month period were estimated to cost another city $7 million.[47] In contrast, during the early 1980s, the police in several large cities reported that numerous events during a single month only cost a total of several thousand dollars.[48] In any case, some local governments want to charge fees to recover these costs and require the organizers of the parade or demonstration to buy expensive (and sometimes unattainable) insurance policies. Although these charges are increasingly common,[49] they should be impermissible. The paraders have merely exercised their rights in places where they have a right to be. If the government had special expenses, it was largely their own choice. The local government's decision to spend money to provide the parade with police services (or the state government's decision to make local governments liable under some circumstances for damages or injuries related to the parade) does not justify charging special fees to paraders. The local government seldom charges special fees to rush-hour traffic, late-night convenience stores, or afternoon strollers even if these activities impose extra costs on the city. Of course, the cities might perceive parades or demonstrations as unnecessary or special, and thus see the expenses as not "normal" governmental expenses for which it routinely pays out of general tax revenues. This view, although understandable, is unacceptable. Disfavoring expressive conduct in a place where people have a general right to be and where the government could not ban the expressive conduct is surely inconsistent with the conduct's constitutional status. At least in these places, first amendment conduct must be considered "normal" for purposes of determining what expenses the government should bear. To charge a special fee for those who engage in expressive activities is to suppress and discriminate against first amendment conduct—thereby violating both the second and third principles.[50]

Universal application of the third principle may seem disturbingly and unnecessarily broad. Does the principle require that private groups be permitted to commandeer any government facility for assembly or their other expressive purposes as long as their use of the facility does not directly conflict with its dedicated use? This requirement could impose arguably unnecessary costs on society. On this interpretation, the third principle apparently would require the government to allow non-interfering but possibly expensive use of facilities whenever some member of the public so requests. Facilities equally suitable for a proposed expressive use may be differentially expensive or dangerous to make available. "Reasonable accommodation" may seem a sufficient response. "Reasonable accommodation," however, is not a standard for decision making. At best, "reasonable" is a summary label for a decision-maker's operative reasons and is, at worst, a mask for caution, for acceptance of conventional practices, or for ideological or class discrimination. A useful constitutional analysis must identify the reasons for a decision and explain their appropriate role within the decision making.

Two lines of judicial pronouncements arguably point to conflicting answers to the question of when the government can limit where people engage in expressive conduct. But their reconciliation may lead to standards that avoid the "reasonableness" catch-all. In *Schneider v. State*,[51] the Court struck down a ban on leafletting. Speaking for the majority, Justice Roberts concluded that "one is not to have the exercise of his liberty of expression in appropriate places abridged on the plea that it may be exercised in some other place."[52] (Roberts' statement followed his observation that "the streets are natural and proper places for the dissemination of information and opinion."[53])

Arguably, Roberts' often quoted conclusion has not been uniformly followed. In *Young v. American Mini Theatres*,[54] the Supreme Court upheld zoning restrictions on the location of commercial screenings of sexually oriented adult pictures. The plurality noted that there was no claim that the regulation denied either exhibitors or viewers access to the market, or that it significantly restrained the market. It emphasized that "[t]he situation would be quite different if the ordinance had the effect of suppressing, or greatly restricting access to, lawful speech."[55] In *Heffron v. International Society for Krishna Consciousness*,[56] the Court, over vigorous dissents that claimed that the majority misapplied its own criteria, upheld a ban on the distribution at a state fair of any merchandise, including written material, except from fixed, licensed locations.[57] The Court, repeating what now appears to be the standard doctrine, stated as one of three criteria for approving time, place, and manner restrictions that the restriction must "leave open ample alternative channels for communication of the information,"[58] again implying that a restriction might be upheld on the plea that the expression, like the film screening in *Young*, can occur in some other place.

Possibly these later cases merely involve the current Court being less protective of speech in the time, place, manner context, now allowing alternatives to justify the restriction. That approach is consistent with the dominant marketplace of ideas theory, which objects merely to obstructions in the flow of information. Still, this analysis does not explain the continuing prevalence of the *Schneider* language. Moreover, a possible reconciliation of the cases has more provocative doctrinal implications. The two lines are consistent if the availability of alternative channels *does not justify* a controverted restriction (*Schneider*) but if the lack of alternative channels makes an otherwise permissible restriction impermissible (*Heffron* or *American Mini Theatres*). Together, the two statements mean that *the government must make channels available.* The availability of ample alternatives is a necessary (*Heffron*), but not sufficient (*Schneider*), condition for most time, place, or manner regulations.

The "necessary but not sufficient" analysis reconciles the Court's two lines of doctrine. Still, broadly applied, this reconciliation is doubtful. This elaboration of time, place, and manner doctrine is a strange place to announce a major affirmative duty of the government to assure that people have adequate channels of communication.* However, an alternative explanation of the Court's two lines of doctrine is possible. They could reflect two different ways that the government can abridge freedom, each with independent relevance.

As noted further below, sometimes people merely need some fungible time or place, some channel, to engage in their chosen expressive conduct; American Mini Theatre merely needed a location. Other times, people's particular chosen expressive conduct requires a particular time or place. In the first case, the time, place, or manner regulation would abridge their expressive freedom unless there are "ample alternative channels." Here, if obvious alternatives exist, they obviously provide for the need. In the second, the plea that points to some other place does not remedy the particular abridgement caused by the restriction. For example, to carry out their purposes, common forms of advocacy or proselytizing speech must reach their potential audience wherever that audience can be found.[59] These advocates cannot assume that their desired audience will search them out. The government's plea that the person can exercise her liberty in a different place is not responsive—the given place is crucial to the expressive activity of reaching that audience. Even though other channels may exist for reaching similar large audiences, a prohibition on leafletting in a particular place would abridge the first amendment activity of reaching the particular people present at that place at that time. Under this interpretation, the plea that the freedom could be exercised at another place should be rejected because these other places are not really alternatives. For example, the leafletters in *Heffron*

---

*This reconciliation, by requiring adequate channels, appears to adopt a form of the market failure theory discussed and rejected in Chapter 2 and generally rejected by the Court.

whom Brennan thought had inadequate alternatives surely could find *other* large crowds, but they could not adequately reach *these* fairgoers. And Brennan recognized that the possibility of the fairgoers searching out information at booths does not adequately protect the proselytizer's right to reach this potential audience.[60]

A single broad principle summarizes these considerations: (4) *Zoning, that is, regulations directed at the time, place, or manner of speech or assembly, is not an abridgement of freedom if its rationale is not hostility to protected liberty and if it does not prevent the exercise of the substantively valued liberty, for example, if ample equivalent channels or opportunities really exist.* This principle should be read as an exception to the first three principles. It interprets what they meant by a "restrictive" regulation. A crucial point here is that apparent alternatives are often not really adequate equivalents for a particular desired exercise of rights.

The adequacy of alternatives is easier to assess once the inquirer recognizes that speech and assembly have many different substantively valued uses. People engage in first amendment conduct for various purposes —for example, for advocacy and proselytizing, or as a symbolic expression for which the place or manner may be crucial to the expressive content, or as a form of commercial entertainment, or as a means for an on-going group to meet, deliberate, and interact. Whether a time, place, and manner restriction—that is, zoning— amounts to an abridgement or merely involves an instrumental burden on the substantively valued expressive activity often depends on the type of expressive activity. For example, since theatre owners presumably want to reach only those people interested enough to pay admission, their audience has some interest in seeking out the speech. For the theatre owners, location usually has importance only in relation to the owners' instrumental or commercial goals. The owners' interests are in obtaining a paying audience and reducing operating costs. The owners have no right to be exempt from general laws affecting these operating costs.[61] Thus, as long as the zoning restriction does not materially reduce the availability of adult theatres to the audience, a restriction on the theatres' location arguably does not limit, and therefore does not abridge, either the freedom of people to obtain this entertainment or the freedom of theater owners to show films protected by the first amendment. As Justice Powell argued, "[t]he communication involved here is not a kind in which the content or effectiveness of the message depends in some measure upon where or how it is conveyed."[62] In contrast, a rule that prohibits leafletting at the location where proselytizers expect an audience, or that prohibits picketing in the residential area where picketers consider the relevant audience to be, restricts the freedom of the proselytizers or picketers to communicate with particular, otherwise unavailable, passersby or residents.[63] Zoning the leafletting or picketing prohibits the valued expressive activity and amounts to an abridgement in a manner that the zoning of the theatre, assuming adequate available alternative locations, does not.

Determining whether zoning is proper on the basis of whether it prevents the exercise of a substantively valued liberty inevitably will be difficult and controversial. All restrictions that prevent first amendment activity at the place or in the manner desired "burden" both the person restricted and the protected activity. Restrictions on location presumably burdened the theatre owners who otherwise would not have litigated *American Mini Theatres*, the people who want to hold an assembly in the mayor's office because it would be more likely to attract media attention, and the people who find a particular city-owned auditorium most convenient for their meeting. This observation is often the first step in reaching the improper conclusion that, since all restrictions are burdensome and some must be permissible, "reasonableness" must be the criterion for determining constitutionality.

Rather than adopt the "reasonableness" criterion, the fourth principle focuses on interpreting "abridgement." In situations in which the first three principles would otherwise find an abridgement, the fourth principle asks whether the governmental restriction prohibits the *specific* activity that the person substantively values. This question, as opposed to the issue of burden, looks at people's formal liberty rather than the effectiveness with which a person is able to use that liberty.

Presumably an advocate or proselytizer substantively values the interaction between the speaker and any person willing to listen or to accept a pamphlet. This advocacy, this activity, should be protected. Of course, general rules not written in terms specifically discriminating against expression can properly restrict advocacy if necessary to carry out other social purposes. Respect for formal freedom does not require the government to provide means to reach an audience. It does not require free use of the mails, or guaranteed access to the airwaves or to houses that have posted bans on uninvited visitors or even to locations that will make a demonstration interesting to, and hence covered by, the broadcasters but that is otherwise not essential to demonstration. However, a different issue is raised by zoning directed specifically at expression or by limitations unnecessary given the place's dedicated use. If these regulations restrict access to the targeted audience, then they stop the substantively valued expression and, thus, abridge the expressive activity of advocacy. This zoning of advocacy violates formal freedom by entirely stopping a particular substantively valued expressive action. Although it does not stop all advocacy, it does halt the advocacy directed at the people at the zoned location. As the Court has recognized, protected freedom is abridged if the government prohibits advocacy on the streets[64] or knocking on the doors of dwelling places.[65]

In contrast, if a group of people plan a demonstration in the mayor's office (presumably after hours so that the demonstration arguably is not incompatible with the dedicated use) solely in order to gain a larger media audience[66] rather than because the office has particular relevance to the demonstrators' message,[67] they are not choosing the place because of its necessity for their own advocacy. Although media exposure may further their advocacy goals, the media coverage is not their expression, not their interaction with an audience, but is the media's expression. Their choice of location is solely for the instrumental goal of enlisting other private parties' (the news media's) aid and resources for reaching an audience with whom the demonstrators substantively wish to communicate. Of course, a restriction on this choice instrumentally burdens the dissemination of the group's message. But the restriction neither stops advocacy nor limits the expressive content of the demonstrator's activity.

Zoning's instrumental burden that reduces the group's ability to obtain media coverage should have the same constitutional status as does the denial of a constitutional guarantee of access to the air waves.[68] In both cases, legal rules limit the effectiveness or reach of people's speech but do not limit their freedom to engage in speech activities. Of course, people value the effectiveness of their speech, that is, the speech that reaches and then convinces an audience. But people also should and often do value the formal freedom independently from their capacity to reach an audience. Self-expressive speech is important to a person's identity whether or not it actually reaches and has an impact on an audience. Both the freedom to be self-expressive and the freedom *to try* to reach an audience are valuable, formal aspects of liberty. Zoning that prevents advocacy to a specific audience violates this formal freedom while zoning that only prevents instrumental use of resources in the attempt to enlist the aid of third parties, the media, is like an allocation rule that instrumentally burdens the substantive freedom. The first amendment serves an adequate and appropriate task, although not the only important task, if it enjoins restrictions on the formal liberty.

This distinction between formal and effective liberty also conforms to the view that the economic burden a zoning regulation places on theater owners is permissible—*assuming* that hostility to the expression was not the basis of the regulation. Likewise, this distinction explains why the city should normally be allowed to choose which of its auditoriums will be available for public meetings, again, assuming the city's choice does not reflect hostility to the expression. The city's choice might burden those going to the meeting but does not stop their substantively valued, expressive conduct. These inconveniences are more like the denial of subsidies to first amendment activities than like the prohibition of a desired assembly. Where a restriction only instrumentally burdens first amendment activity, it has not prohibited any substantively valued communicative interaction nor abridged the freedom.

This discussion critiqued rules that stop the advocate from reaching potential willing listeners in the places where these listeners are. There are other ways in which time, place, or manner regulations can directly prohibit people's substantively valued expressive activity. Sometimes the actor's central concern is her personal engagement in the self-expressive activity. Moreover, the location or manner of the expression may be integral to its content rather than being merely instrumentally relevant as a means to obtain media coverage or to apply pressure on others. Demonstrators may hope and expect that others will learn of their self-expression and be moved or awakened by it. But often they treat their self-expression and their unity as sufficient, vital concerns independent of their communication with outsiders. In these circumstances, a time, place, or manner regulation could directly prohibit, that is, abridge, the exercise of the first amendment right. For example, if demonstrators want to protest and remedy the alleged segregation of a library, their presence in the library may be integral to both what they want to *do* and what they want to communicate by their assembly. Their expression is their physical presence which constitutes an actual, if only temporary and, therefore, symbolic desegregation of the library. A content-neutral time, place, or manner regulation that prevented their presence would abridge their right of expression. Thus, in *Brown v. Louisiana*,[69] the Court properly emphasized the content of the demonstrators' expression, namely, that they were objecting to segregation of the library in which they were quietly present.[70]

The plurality's emphasis in *Brown* on the demonstrators' obvious desire to protest the segregation of the library leads to a possible objection to its analysis: the plurality *accepted* content discrimination of a sort.[71] A speaker's sincere conclusion that the location was essential to the meaning of her speech makes content relevant or, more precisely, makes relevant the combination of content and sincere attitudes about the location's relation to the content.* A quick comment could be that the government is not making content distinctions. It does not express approval or disapproval of any content, although it does allow some and deny others the opportunity on the basis of content. Still, the fourth principle provides the primary explanation for the propriety of this content distinction. Although this distinction specially *protects* specific speech, it is analogous to and at least as acceptable as the content distinction that specially restricts "adult" theatres. In both cases, the constitutional issue is whether the zoning restriction prohibits a person from engaging in particular, valued, first amendment conduct or manifests hostility toward the content of restricted speech. In *American Mini Theatres*, the Court concluded that the content-based zoning restriction on adult theaters did not prevent the substantively valued aspect of the first amendment conduct. Likewise the plurality in *Brown* reasoned that the government could not constitutionally apply even a generally valid restriction to the protestors' peaceful expressive conduct.[72] Since the restricted location was an integral part of the expressive meaning of their nondisruptive, peaceful assembly, other alternative channels would not be adequate. And since their expression does not interfere with the normal use of the facility, the first amendment should require that the government permit the expression. In contrast, others who wanted to engage in similar activities for expressive purposes unrelated to the library would be like the owners of adult theatres— they would presumably have ample alternatives and, therefore, a limitation would not abridge their rights. This difference is why the first amendment often should require certain "content-based" exceptions to time, place, or manner restrictions.

The fourth principle's zoning analysis also requires protection of those people who conclude that group, public, shelterless sleep in front of our country's lawmaking institutions is the most meaningful way both to manifest their own solidarity with the many who are without shelter and to demand that the government take some responsibility for the homeless. Their sleep on Lafayette Park in front of the White House is integral to the meaning of their expression. An unnecessary prohibition on this assembly abridges protected liberty, just as a prohibition on the proselytizer's leafletting abridges that freedom. Thus, contrary to the Court's conclusion in *Clark v. Community for Creative Non-Violence*,[73] since the demonstrators were in a place where people have a right to be and their presence was not incompatible with the dedicated use of the space, the government's ban on their behavior abridged their first amendment freedoms.

*There is a clear analogy to special claims under the free exercise of religion.

Likewise, a limit on the time length of their demonstration would only be permissible if neutrally applied and if necessary so that others could use the space for their first amendment conduct. A governmental rule against sleeping in the park "with intent to remain for a period of more than four hours" thwarted a person's commitment to engage in "a round-the-clock vigil protesting his treatment at the hands of the VA" in a park adjacent to the headquarters of the Veterans Administration.[74] The government's time-zoning prohibited a manner of expression that the protestor presumably saw as central to the content or meaning of his expression. Moreover, the protestor's conduct was consistent with the permitted uses of the property. Any interference with other uses that he caused was presumably acceptable since, under the four-hour rule, a succession of four-hour sleepers could keep the space occupied. Only the length of the intended sleep made it impermissible under the rule.[75] Under the absolutist liberty theory developed here, this application of time-zoning should be unconstitutional.

The government does, however, have a "reasonable" basis for the four-hour sleep rule. Unrestricted camping could wear down the central parks of Washington, D.C. The government also could reasonably conclude that other public uses of these park grounds are more valuable to the public. Despite the rule's reasonableness, the constitutional objection should prevail. These other, permitted uses create the same type of injury or problems as does the expressive conduct. The expressive use is compatible with the general uses of the park; all uses tend to wear down the park. First amendment protection of liberty means that the government cannot rely on its higher valuation of these other uses as a justification for prohibiting the specifically valued, expressive conduct.

Still, "zoning" against camping is valid as applied to most people. Even for those coming to the city for lobbying or other unquestionably expressive purposes, camping, especially camping specifically in Washington's central parks, would at most instrumentally contribute to, but would not be an integral part of, their expression. Of course, people do find camping in general to be a substantively valued, self-expressive experience—sort of like seeing "adult movies." But this generally valued experience usually does not depend on its occurrence at a specific location. The government is expected to administer public resources in a manner that promotes the public welfare and societal self-definition. Usually it should be permitted to do this by allocating only noncentral locations for camping or even to require people to use their own resources to obtain camping space. The liberty theorist only claims that the camping regulation is invalid when it operates to prohibit the substance of the expression or when there are not adequate alternatives for engaging in the expressive activity. Only then does the government's decision to favor other, potentially compatible uses become impermissible.

This analysis leaves the delicate problem of identifying those for whom camping at the specific place is protected expression. This practical difficulty may justify a number of not perfectly accurate presumptions. Proper recognition of the constitutional rights, however, means that the difficulty of making the distinction cannot justify denying the right.[76] If the government is unable to apply the distinction in practice, unprotected camping should be the beneficiary of its incapacity. Nevertheless, the Constitution presumably allows the government to prohibit "camping" in specific places as long as the place is not integral to the meaning of the camper's expression. The government could adopt and enforce a rule that embodies this distinction, taking to the jury any dispute as to whether the location was integral to expression.[77]

On the spot, ad hoc attempts by police to distinguish protected and unprotected camping would likely be burdensome to both the government and those who are properly engaged in first amendment expression. A voluntary permit system might be preferable to both.[78] The prospective campers could explain in their permit application how the location is integral to the content of their expression. If convinced, the government office would be required to issue the permit. Receipt of a permit would insulate the campers from arrest and prosecution for conduct covered by the permit. Under a voluntary permit system, however, protestors who did not apply for or were denied a permit could also engage in "expressive" camping. But in these cases, the police could independently evaluate the campers' claim that sleeping there is integral to their expression. If the police concluded otherwise, they could make the arrest and present the issue to the court. I suspect, however, that the interests of both police and demonstrators would encourage both the government's adoption and demonstrator's use of a voluntary permit system.* This permit system should be relatively successful in distinguishing camping that the government constitutionally can, from that which it cannot, zone out of the park.

Reliance on these absolutist principles as an alternative to "reasonableness" challenges the accepted understanding of a deeply rooted premise of first amendment theory. Usually liberal constitutional jurisprudence at least implicitly distinguishes liberty from the worth of liberty to an individual. Formal liberty contrasts with effective opportunities to exercise liberty.[80] People have a right to seek an abortion or search for an audience, but not a right to actually obtain an abortion or reach an audience. Most time, place, and manner regulations normally are thought only to raise questions of resource allocation, which affects opportunity or the worth of liberty to an individual. Moreover, this traditional analysis typically assumes a marketplace of ideas theory in which the liberty is only the right to communicate thoughts to another. Since the Constitution does not guarantee the effective exercise of a person's liberty, the only unconstitutional limitations are those that prohibit the exercise of the liberty itself, for example, the liberty to say particular things, or those limitations that show hostility to liberty by purposefully making its exercise more difficult. This tradition provides no obvious ground for striking down most time, place, and manner regulations. Here, the reasonableness standard could be merely a method of uncovering impermissible purposes. Or, although theoretically difficult to justify, it could be a minimal recognition that the availability of actual opportunities for exercising liberty has some constitutional relevance.

---

*If these expressive uses are rare, rather than a formalized permit system, an equivalent practice is likely to arise. Demonstrators are likely to seek preclearance which, when given, should insulate them from arrest.[79]

A less dominant, generally more progressive, "realist" strain in traditional thought rejects this distinction between the liberty and its worth or effective exercise. A person values actual opportunities, not abstract or formal rights. This perspective argues that the Constitution must protect the effective exercise of the liberty. Such a realist approach, however, must admit that effective exercise can only be protected to a reasonable degree. Unlike formal liberty, substantive exercises of liberty inevitably conflict. They require resources needed for other purposes. Thus, this "effects" orientation of the realist perspective concludes that the decision-maker must balance expressive liberty against other values or policies.

The absolutist, liberty approach developed in this section claims to identify more accurately the constitutional liberty at stake. It rejects aspects of both the traditional analyses. Although responsive to the realist's concern with the exercise of liberty, it rejects the realist's merger of liberty and its exercise. The first amendment claim never overrides the government's actual, conflicting use of its resources. The liberty theory also rejects the traditional formalists' conclusions about the limited content of the protected liberty. Instead, this liberty theory shows that content-neutral restrictions that apparently only zone or allocate resources sometimes should be understood to abridge the protected liberty itself. Abridgement occurs if two conditions are met. First, either the restriction must be specifically directed at protected expression or the protected expression must not interfere with dedicated uses of the place or facility. Second, the restriction must either prohibit conduct that is integral to the meaning of the actor's intended expression or eliminate expressive opportunities when adequate alternatives are not available.

Often in order to find an abridgement, this liberty approach must be able to identify a baseline of public resources that people normally have a right to use in their expressive activities. The principles described above help in this task. For example, in places where people are generally permitted to gather and talk, the first and second principles imply that a restriction on assembly or speech is not merely a failure to allocate resources to expressive purposes but a taking away of resources—that is, a penalty or abridgement. Even where people are not generally allowed or are only allowed for limited purposes, but where the expressive conduct is compatible with the normal uses of the space or facilities, the third principle requires that the place be potentially available for the expressive conduct. Nevertheless, an important caveat applies here as well as in places where people have a right to engage in expressive activities, that is, in places where the first, second, or third principle would protect the expressive activity. The controverted regulation can be upheld as not abridging expression if other facilities are available *and* if the change to another time or place or manner will not negatively affect the meaning of the expression or assembly *and* if the restrictive regulation is not adopted out of hostility to the regulated expression. To use terms developed in Chapter 4, the permissibility of the restriction may turn on whether the restriction prevents what the person wants substantively or only what she wants instrumentally. If the government unnecessarily restricts conduct that the person values substantively, the rule amounts to an unconstitutional "general prohibition." If, however, the government only restricts what the

182

Applications

person wants instrumentally, the rule would be a constitutional "allocation rule."

Traditional theory's failure to carefully identify "liberty" and "abridgments" in the context of streets and public facilities has an implicit ideological bias. This failure effectively treats even the formal liberty of the poor less favorably than that of the rich. Progressive reformers and their allies succeeded in enacting limits on campaign expenditures as a means to increase the equality and fairness of the political process. The Supreme Court invalidated this "reasonable" means of pursuing egalitarian, reformist ends.[81] The best justification for the Court's decision is that expenditure limitations directly prohibit protected expression. A conservative bias is evident in the Court's failure to devise equally absolute principles for invalidating time, place and manner regulations that directly prohibit expression in the streets. In contrast to those who can make very large electoral expenditures, often the poor depend on the use of the streets and other public facilities as the place for certain expressive activities. Protecting liberty only in the first situation seems discriminatory. This combination appears to favor formal liberty of the wealthy over equality, but to favor order over the formal liberty of the poor or the dissident.

Democrats also often bemoan the power of the press, which is increasingly dominated by a few people and a relatively narrow range of perspectives, to control the public agenda and to slant public debate. Still, legal regulations designed to restrict the power of these owners of the press and to open the press to wider participation are often thought to unconstitutionally abridge formal liberty even as they advance substantive liberty.[82] In contrast, the poor and dissident more democratically use public space for demonstrations that sometimes reorient public debate. Here, however, formal liberty as well as substantive liberty is ignored and status-quo conceptions of reasonableness justify limits on expressions. Preserving maximum expressive use of public space—particularly the streets and parks—offers a crucial opportunity for more popular, even if often more turbulent, participation in setting and pursuing a public agenda. Formalist doctrine deserves its bad name if it consistently favors not liberty but rather only favors liberty of the rich. The claim made in this chapter, however, is that this tilt toward the powerful is not inherent in a formalist or absolutist respect for liberty, which would be quite progressive, but, instead reflects elements of the dominant "reasonableness" analysis.

Implicit in the principles elaborated so far is the claim that even "reasonable" restrictions of assembly or speech that prohibit the valued aspect of any expressive conduct are normally unconstitutional. The "valued aspect" can be, for example, an advocate reaching a listener or the symbolic expression whose meaning is tied to a time or place or manner. In places where people have a right to be, the government cannot, for example, favor everyday traffic over first amendment assembly. Meaningful protection of liberty requires that people sometimes have a right to assemble even though their assembly inevitably interferes with other people or with other possible uses of the space. The present inquiry concerns the extent to which the government can limit expressive conduct that interferes with others. A principled, although an unfortunately subtle, distinction must be drawn between protected and unprotected ways that people's expressive conduct interferes with others' conduct. *(5a) People engaged in first amendment conduct have no right to interfere unnecessarily and intentionally with the activities of others. (5b) Nevertheless, the government cannot prohibit disruption that results merely from the number of people engaged in the first amendment activity; in a place where they have a right to be, the government cannot favor or "accommodate" other activities by limiting the presence of people engaged in first amendment conduct.*[83]

If expressive conduct is to receive any significant protection, interference with others cannot in itself justify limits. For example, the interference with others' movement or quiet relaxation that results from a large number of people assembled in a place where people have a right to be is normally inherent in a public exercise of the right of assembly. The fifth principle means that the government cannot choose to disfavor people's exercise of constitutional rights and favor the status quo by characterizing the first amendment activity as interfering with the other activities rather than vice versa.[84] For example, the government should not be permitted to reduce disruption by limiting the size of a demonstration. This limitation would mean that someone could lose her first amendment right, that is, her right to be present, because others are exercising their right or, even worse, because others prefer unprotected conduct.

Part (a) of the fifth principle does allow the government to outlaw a purposeful aspect of some demonstrations—namely, the strategic activity of disrupting everyday life by intentionally and *unnecessarily* interfering with the activities of others. (Unnecessary in the sense that everyone who wanted to assemble could have assembled or demonstrated at roughly that place without the interference occurring.) This principle denies protection to the small group locking arms in order to cordon off a street. In contrast, many interferences with other people's activities, even purposeful interferences, are a necessary result of exercising one's rights. (What constitutes "unnecessarily interfering" will be further explicated below.)

Even though this fifth principle protects some disruptive conduct, 5(a) may be too restrictive of the right of assembly. Moral responsibilities and historical conditions may often justify unnecessary, intentional interferences with others. Brandeis observed that "those who won our independence by revolution . . . did not exalt order at the cost of liberty."[85] These people, people who eventually demanded and ratified the first amendment, accepted the propriety of disruptive demonstrations. According to Pauline Maier, an historian writing about the period, colonial Americans commonly expressed the view that, in their words, "mobs and Tumults never happen but thro' oppression and a scandalous Abuse of Power."[86] People recognized that, by bringing people's feelings to the attention of public authorities, popular uprisings were "an evil . . . productive of good."[87] Occurring most often under free governments, these uprisings "could be interpreted as 'Symptoms of a strong and healthy Constitution.'"[88] Thus, Maier concluded that "popular uprisings benefited from a certain presumptive acceptability that was founded in part on colonial experience with mass action."[89] She even quotes "the conservative Thomas Hutchinson" as saying in 1768 that "[m]obs, a sort of them at least, are constitutional."[90]

This early history supports the plausibility of the relatively moderate claim that people should have the right to use the peaceful presence of their bodies to interfere nonviolently with others' everyday activities. When conditions and events so strongly offend people's political and ethical consciousness that they are moved to take nonviolent, disruptive steps, the situation has usually become one in which it is more important for the community to have its normal routines broken and people's everyday activities disrupted in order to awake the government and the community to this deep dissatisfaction, than it is for the community to avoid the inconveniences of the disruption.[91] This conclusion follows whether the protestors are right or wrong—although, historically, they have very often been right. When people feel compelled to engage in disruptive activity, the greatest need is for the government to respond appropriately to this dissatisfaction, not to suppress the dissidents.[92]

A properly formulated right of freedom of assembly would encourage and ease the process whereby people bring their dissatisfaction to the attention of the government and other members of the community.[93] Even if the dissidents forcibly and intentionally interfere with others' activities, to the extent that they can nonviolently accomplish this task of awakening the community, we should praise, and arguably the first amendment should protect, their nonviolent assembly and protest. Protecting this conduct becomes even more plausible once we conclude that the first amendment protects not so much a marketplace of ideas, but the liberty of people to engage in expressive conduct and to gather together in assemblies and associations to generate power and do things. Although the Constitution only protects people's right to assemble "peaceably," the nonviolent interference with others' activities described above does not involve any physical attack on, destruction of, or injury to people or property. This disruptive conduct falls within a very plausible interpretation of "peaceable."

Collective or mass behavior is often viewed as being irrational, fickle, violent, undirected, and contagious. Le Bon's classic, very influential, late nineteenth-century book, *The Crowd,* dramatically illustrates this view. For example, Le Bon argues: "Crowds are only powerful for destruction. Their rule is always tantamount to a barbarian phase.... In consequence of the purely destructive nature of their power crowds act like those microbes which hasten the dissolution of enfeebled or dead bodies."[94] This view is often encouraged by superficial newspaper accounts of group or gang behavior and is implicit in much popular thinking about crowd behavior. Even a prominent social psychology text suggests that collective behavior is "likely to be foolish, disgusting, or evil."[95]

Deeply ingrained in our culture, this view of crowds may influence the judicial tendency to restrict the range of assemblies that receive constitutional protection.[96] Nevertheless, historical studies consistently reject this negative vision of disruptive assemblies—usually described, depending on the commentator's value commitments, as either a "mob" or a "crowd." Increased historical awareness implicitly supports the propriety of protecting a broader range of assemblies. Historians apparently find that the "crowd" is usually quite rational in its choice of targets for the application of force.[97] Occasionally the assembled people purposefully destroy property. Still, these studies find that the crowd or mob seldom kill or injure people—in stark contrast to the behavior of governmental authorities who respond and who most often initiate any violence that occurs. In retrospect, the crowd's use of force and violence typically seems restrained. Even though crowds occasionally turn violent, legal restrictions could and should be limited to situations of actual or attempted violence. Constitutionally protected conduct receives no meaningful protection if the mere possibility that unprotected conduct may follow justifies restrictions.

People's assembling and occupying space in a manner such that their physical presence is intended maximally to interfere with other people's activity is certainly a nonviolent, plausibly a peaceable form of conduct that can express their values.[98] The conduct is an obvious example of people exercising power and doing something. The right of assembly ought to protect behavior having these general attributes. Although disruptive, this form of collective action is even more peaceable than forms of action that apparently seemed acceptable to many of the people most dedicated to liberty in colonial America. Finally, the disruptive conduct may be ethically justified and may contribute to a more just society. Nevertheless, the more persuasive development of a liberty theory of the first amendment would not interpret "peaceable" assembly to include such conduct.

There is a fundamental difficulty with recognizing a constitutional right to engage in intentional, unnecessary interference with legally permissible activities of another person. From a liberty perspective, any claim of a right to interfere with another person's liberty must be very problematic. Intentionally and unnecessarily interfering with another's activities as a means to achieve one's own objectives resembles coercion, discussed in Chapter 3. The disruptive activity attempts to make nonvoluntary use of another person. The demonstrator, *A*, is not merely making use of public resources, the street, for *A*'s purposes, but is intentionally using another person, *B* (to the extent that *B* needs or wants to be in the space occupied by *A*) for *A*'s purposes without *B*'s agreement. *A* uses *B* solely as a means for *A*'s purposes. For *A* to have this right restricts *B*'s liberty not merely as a necessary result of not disfavoring constitutionally protected expressive use of the street in the allocation of resources. Rather, this right accepts the propriety of *A*'s purpose to restrict *B*'s liberty. It treats as a fundamental principle *A*'s authorization to use *B* as an instrumental means with which to pursue *A*'s objectives. Whether or not this should be one of the many situations where society decides to allow instrumental use of one person by another, this result cannot follow solely from a first amendment theory premised on respect for individual autonomy.

The argument changes if the interference with other people is a normal, physical result of people's independently desired assembly. In this case, the interference is necessary if people are to engage in the assembly at the place and time they have chosen. The argument changes even if the necessary interference is *one* of the consequences that those assembling desire. In addition to its "reasonableness," there is a simple explanation for this conclusion. The converse, prohibiting the act of assembling—or leafletting or engaging in other recognized first amendment conduct—because the conduct interferes with other peoples' activities, stands first amendment protection on its head. Interference is always a two-way street. It is not the assembly that interferes with the passerby, but whoever is permitted to prevail that interferes with the other.[99] Protection of the assembly must follow as long as the government does not or cannot prefer nonexpressive activities in its allocation of public space.

Interference exists whenever there are conflicting uses of, or claims to use, resources. Labeling one use an interference implicitly recognizes the normative priority of the other use. To prohibit the people engaged in the protected activity of assembly from interfering with the activities of others abandons the notion that the first amendment bars the government from abridging freedom of speech and assembly. Whether or not laws must favor first amendment rights, at least the law cannot permissibly disfavor these rights. To forbid first amendment conduct because it interferes with the other conduct also permitted on the public space would allow behavior that has no particular constitutional significance to trump, to dominate, constitutionally protected behavior. This eliminates virtually all significance of constitutional protection. Even if the Constitution protected both parties' behavior so that both stood at the same level in the constitutional scheme, for example, if both were engaged in expressive conduct, and even if interference with one by the other were inevitable, a rule automatically favoring one type of conduct or expression would be unconstitutional discrimination. Constitutionally permissible solutions to conflicting uses are possible. Both parties could be permitted to try to use the space as best they can as long as they do not engage in violence against the other. Or the government could allow whoever got there first to use the space. Or, if otherwise preferable, it could provide some cuing or other relatively even-handed mechanism that did not obviously favor the status quo in assigning priority. It could employ the voluntary permit system described in the last chapter. To be constitutional, however, the government must either favor the constitutionally protected activities or allow the choices and actions of individuals, operating within some rule structure, to determine the prevailing conduct.

Two other common interpretations of the right of assembly would not require even this relatively minimal protection of peaceful assemblies that unavoidably interfere with other people. First, some courts and commentators have treated the right of assembly as only an appendage to the marketplace of ideas, an arena in which, as Alexander Meiklejohn argued, the important concern "is not that everyone shall get to speak, but that everything worth saying shall be said."[100] Only allowing an assembly of a "reasonable" size, time, and location should suffice to enable the demonstrators to make their point. And this theory could define reasonable as an assembly that does not seriously interfere with other uses of the streets, sidewalks, parks, or other public space. Everything worth saying could still be said. Second, if the right of assembly were a group right, rather than a right of an individual to be a part of a group, it could be argued that the group will have had its right to assemble recognized as long as it gets to hold an assembly, even if the state limits the assembly in a manner that prevents the participation of some individuals who want to participate.[101] The reasonable time or size limitations, justified as protecting the interests of other users of the space, would not necessarily abridge the *group*'s right to assemble and speak.

Neither argument for limiting the right to assemble is fully convincing on its own terms. If the effectiveness of the marketplace of ideas depends solely on the truth and persuasiveness of the viewpoints presented, even a demonstration burdened by reasonable regulation may adequately introduce the viewpoint into the marketplace of ideas and, therefore, the regulation would not interfere with that marketplace. Nevertheless, given a realistic assessment of the communication process, the larger crowd may be important in order to increase media coverage, thereby making the speech more audible. Or on less objective, more political assumptions about the nature of truth or the purposes of public debate, it is relevant that the larger crowd may express a more intense or larger measure of public support for the assembly's views. Likewise, on the group right theory, although the limitation on the assembly may not have prevented the group from exercising its right to assemble, the government's power to restrict the group's choice or manner of assembly narrows what the group can do. Thus, from the marketplace of ideas and the group right perspectives, the right of assembly is arguably inadequately recognized unless the first amendment protects people's choice of manner, of time and size and place, of assembly.[102]

In contrast to the debatable implications of the marketplace and group right theories, permitting these "reasonable" regulations is clearly inconsistent with the right of assembly if the right is recognized as an aspect of individual liberty. Any individual legally prevented from assembling has her liberty abridged. A "reasonable" regulation abridges the liberty and completely denies a person's right to assemble if the regulation prevents the person's participation in the assembly. The regulation abridges the person's right even if it embodies a "reasonable" accommodation of the assembly with the interests of other people whose activities otherwise would be more disrupted.

Given the liberty theory's absolutist premises, the frequency with which the right to assemble will actually result in interference with others or, more specifically, the cost of providing for the right, should be irrelevant to any justification of the right. Still, the possibility of frequent disruptions merits consideration. First, note that the implications of frequent disruption would be ambiguous. In fact, a high frequency of disruption may be less a reason to restrict the right and more an indication of the urgency of society's need to recognize rights of protest. Quoting an earlier speech delivered in England to Parliament, a colonial pamphleteer argued in 1764: "The People seldom or never assemble in any riotous or tumultuous Manner, unless when they are oppressed, or at least imagine they are oppressed. If the People should be mistaken . . . it is the Duty of the Magistrate to endeavor first to correct their Mistake by fair Means. . . . The only effectual Method to suppress Tumults will be, to enquire into the Causes, and to take such Measures as may be proper for removing those Causes."[103]

Moreover, the disruptions and costs properly attributable to full protection of the right are easily overestimated. For example, the state frequently asserts a particularly strong public interest in "reasonable" rules that prohibit blockage of passage ways, entrances, and exits or that protect against interference with pedestrians. A mass demonstration, however, is seldom so densely packed that a person cannot, slowly and possibly inconveniently, make her way through the crowd. *Except* when members of the crowd intentionally stop the movement of particular persons (which the state can prohibit consistently with principle 5a), nonparticipants may be slowed, inconvenienced, or intimidated by a crowd, but they are seldom stopped. Likewise, although a group of forty could *strategically* locate its members in order to block a major intersection, their conduct is unprotected. The only parades or assemblies whose size *necessitates* the blockage of streets to normal traffic will be much, much larger. The protected aspect of most demonstrations will only rarely stop vital movement. The normal interference will be minimal even though the assemblies or demonstrations have priority, that is, even if people have the right to assemble in a manner that leaves passageways, entrances, and exits in a crowded condition.

Occasionally, a small number of demonstrators block the movement of others as a conscious strategy of disruption. Narrowly framed laws can make this illegal. Broader laws that generally make blockage of passageways illegal should, however, be more troublesome. Authorities can too easily rely on laws relating to blockage of passageways or sidewalks as a pretext either to arrest, prosecute, or order dispersal of demonstrators even though there was no actual, serious blockage.[104] Given that circumstances often offer colorable, even if not persuasive, bases for invoking these laws, and given the pressures that encourage law enforcement officials to invoke the laws in order to harass or disperse unwanted demonstrations, the actual use of these laws may seldom correspond to the announced justifications for their existence. Often, these justifications will be merely rationalizations that overlay a fear of disorder, a deep-seated distaste for mass demonstrations, or a focused hostility to certain demonstrators. (Putting aside blockages that would not be protected under the fifth principle because the blockage was intentional and unnecessary, that is, was physically enforced, I suspect that most other arrests for blocking passageways involve blockages less severe than occur routinely as rush hour crowds stream out of subway exits in New York.)

The first amendment should protect the dissidents' call for a massive rally to bring the city's normal routine to a stop or their call for their supporters to fill the streets in order to stop traffic until the government responds to their demands. In the rare circumstances when this call receives a mass response, the interference with others is admittedly one purpose of many demonstrators. It is important, however, that this disruption is not a result of a few individuals strategically locating themselves in specific places to maximize the interference. It is not a case of people locking arms to stop other people's movement. The disruption occurs only as a necessary result of individual decisions of many people to be present at a place where they have a right to be. Their purpose is to engage in protest by means of their presence. The disruption reflects their individual response to the call for a massive demonstration. The large rally unites people in the exercise of their individual right to be present, their right to occupy space, and their right to proclaim and live their opposition to life continuing as usual. The demonstrators are not claiming a right to use other people as means but rather are claiming that they have as much right to occupy this space as do others. They are not claiming a right specifically to cause injuries to another person—as they might if they purposefully stopped an ambulance from getting an emergency patient to a hospital. But constitutional protection of individual rights requires that we accept the inevitable disruption that occurs when so many people want to make a statement by standing in protest. No individual can be identified as stopping the movement of others. In contrast to the frequent disruptions of traffic that we typically, although grumblingly accept at rush hour or during construction or after snow storms, we will seldom need, but should be willing, to bear the disruptions caused by people exercising their first amendment rights. Under the fifth principle, the disruption is a necessary and, therefore, protected result of the exercise of the right.

In many ways, the mass demonstration parallels the economic or social boycott,[105] a practice that has a long and respectable history. Many American colonists in the years immediately before our revolution viewed the boycott as an appropriate, nonviolent, legal form of group action or petition.[106] In both the demonstration and the boycott people combine into a group, an assembly or association, and they embody their expression of values in their practice. In both, people hope and expect that this form of expression will be disruptive and exert pressure to change. In both cases disruption results when each member of the group individually acts in a way that she clearly has a right to act but in a way contrary to the normal routine that others expect and on which, to some extent, others depend. Although in both the boycott and the mass demonstration, the possibility of placing pressure on others can be crucial to the motivation of the participants, their protest behavior is also in itself expressive, value-based conduct, *independent* of the pressure they impose. The boycotter affirms that under present conditions she considers purchases from or interactions with the boycotted party to be objectionable. The rally participant considers her participation, the protest symbolized by her presence, to be ethically and personally the right thing to do at this time.

In contrast to the mass rally or boycott that results in disruption, consider situations in which the expression completely depends on the disruption. When the method of expression depends on its effectiveness as an interference with others, the demonstrator's expression depends on the unwilling use of other people. This solely instrumental value of the interference with others contrasts with intrinsically intertwined and desired aspects of the group boycott or mass rally. First, the public communication is not treated as dependent on, although it may be enhanced by, the interference with other persons. Second, participation in the boycott or rally embodies a personal testament that is not dependent on interfering with others. Finally, the participants may apply pressure on others, or exercise a form of power over others, who otherwise would interact with the boycott participants or who would use the assembly space.

This third quality, pressuring others, in itself neither justifies nor forfeits constitutional protection. All societies permit some means of exercising power over other people.* The mass assembly is even less troublesome than most generally accepted means. The distribution of the capacity to impose pressure by means of physical presence is relatively egalitarian. The exercise of the power requires constant commitment and choice. Most important, although having opportunities to use instrumental means to apply pressure on others does not justify

---

*The use of money or property in exchange transactions, for example, involves an exercise of power that gets others to act in ways that they would not otherwise choose.[107]

constitutional protection, it also does not require denying protection. Since pressure that merely results from activities in which people otherwise have a right to engage cannot in itself justify abridging clearly protected freedom, these assemblies and boycotts should be protected.

The public communication and the personal testament involved in the boycott and rally occur through the decision to associate or not to associate as a means of expressing and living the actor's own values. Given that the instrumental aspect of applying pressure neither justifies protecting or requires prohibiting the behavior, even if people intentionally hold the mass rally in part to stop normal activities, as long as people's participation also involves these other, protected aspects of expression, these substantively valued aspects justify constitutional protection. As long as the participants apply pressure or accomplish this disruptive result as a normal consequence of each person engaging in expression by doing what she has a right to do, by being present or by not associating, their expression does not intrinsically rely on the use of the other person as a means. For this reason, their disruptive behavior is not constitutionally equivalent to the prohibitable act of trying to cordon off the street or lock arms to interfere with others.

This capacity of the mass assembly or boycott peaceably to create power, to apply the pressure of mass participation, is foreign to marketplace of ideas theories of the first amendment. It may be the feature of assemblies and associations that cause many liberal theorists and jurists consistently to downplay the right of assembly and to treat assembly as a subordinate aspect of a marketplace of ideas theory of free speech. In contrast, this capacity to generate power and to do or to refuse to do things is an element of the rationale for protection in a liberty theory.[108] A liberty theory requires that the government respect people's choices to do things, to live according to their values, and to participate in change. It treats the right of assembly seriously. People's right to join together, independent of any contribution to public debate, is an important aspect of the constitutional protection of the autonomy and liberty of the individual.

The practical consequences of this broader, liberty-based right of assembly are also likely to be desirable. The constitutional distinction between the necessary and unnecessary disruptive effects permits the state to restrict those people who attempt, by maximizing the frustration they can impose on others, to multiply their power quickly and out of proportion to their numbers. This distinction permits the state to limit a small group's capacity to exploit the many. In contrast, the value of protecting people who necessarily disrupt others with their assembly is threefold. First, since the disruption is in direct proportion to the numbers of people who participate, who engage in the boycott or take to the street, it is a very democratic means of expression and disruption. Second, constitutional protection removes from the hands of cautious officials the legal authority to use the inevitable disruption caused by any large rally or assembly as an excuse to harass and suppress the proponents of social, cultural, religious, or political change.[109] Third, the disruption itself may be valuable. A democracy profits when large numbers of people who are really outraged engage in joint, expressive activity that can have a material as well as expressive effect sufficient to force authorities to pay attention and respond.

A final principle underlines what should be obvious. Still, the principle is often ignored when officials try to justify restrictions on expressive conduct and, therefore, merits explicit attention. (6) *In providing special benefits that make assembly or speech rights more effective, the government can impose procedural conditions as long as the purpose of the conditions is not to affect the content of the expression or to restrict first amendment conduct.*

The last two clauses of the sixth principle merely implement the uncontroversial proposition that a governmental purpose to censor or to restrict the exercise of first amendment rights is improper. More generally, the principle embodies the notion that the government must be permitted to impose conditions relevant to making the benefits available. And in situations where the government chooses, rather than is constitutionally mandated, to make available the opportunity for the expressive conduct, the sixth principle permits conditions that protect governmental interests that otherwise would be threatened by physical aspects of the speech or assembly. Chapter 7's discussion and approval of voluntary permit systems has already illustrated this principle. Although the principle involves complexities that will only be considered briefly here, often they can be resolved by application of the first five principles. Thus, here I will make only a few minimal comments about the sixth.

Traditional analysis of constitutional theory's perennial right/privilege problem begins with the observation that the government must not restrict the exercise of a right. The difficulty is that often the government does not directly restrict the right. Instead, it conditions the receipt of some benefit on the nonexercise of the right. To achieve its proper goals, the government, like any other owner of resources and provider of benefits, should generally be able to impose conditions on the receipt of its resources. Thus, initially, the characterization of whether the government was conditioning the receipt of a benefit or restricting the exercise of a right, as well as whether it was pursuing a permissible goal, becomes crucial. In this context, a right defines the status quo so that conditions on the right make the person worse off (abridge the right) but a benefit or privilege is a gain from the status quo and, thus, a person is still better off (no abridgement) even if the benefit or privilege is dependent on meeting certain conditions.

The doctrine of unconstitutional conditions appears to sidestep the difficulty, which is unresolvable on strictly positivist terms, of distinguishing rights and privileges. It does so if certain conditions, presumably ones that constrain the exercise of a constitutional right, cannot be imposed even on the receipt of apparent privileges. This reading of the doctrine is, however, too broad. In fact, although each has serious problems, the right/privilege analysis and the unconstitutional condition doctrine are complementary rather than substitutes. Imposition of a condition (or restriction) directly on the exercise of a right is necessarily an impermissible abridgement. The theoretical difficulty is that the positive law of the state typically creates the standard, the status quo, that defines people's rights. If only positive law determines the standard, there is no standpoint from which to distinguish a right from a privilege. For example, does the individual's right to use a street for a parade become a privilege if the government first prohibits use of the streets for parade purposes (or for all but specific purposes) and then provides, as a special benefit, the privilege of having a parade on the street if the paraders meet certain content-neutral conditions? If the opportunity to use the street is constitutionally mandated, the answer is easy. The conditions are unconstitutional restrictions on the exercise of a right.

If the opportunity is merely a creation of positive law, the problem is more difficult. The government should be permitted to impose the condition unless the government is penalizing or its purpose is to burden the exercise of the right. The difficult problem is to understand what is meant by "purpose" and to characterize purposes in specific cases. This characterization should rely on notions of contextual purpose and common understandings to determine whether the positivist conditions are best understood as provision of special opportunities or attempts to undermine constitutional rights. If the second, then the conditions are unconstitutional for having the purpose of penalizing the exercise of the protected liberty.

The denial that the government can prohibit expressive, peaceable uses of the streets, a conclusion implicit in *Hague v. CIO*,[110] follows from either analysis. First, tradition and common understanding recognize that people have a general right, not a mere privilege, to use the streets for any peripatetic purpose and, in particular, for purposes of meeting, talking, and walking. Granted this tradition, regulations that interfere with this use should be seen as an unconstitutional restriction on a right. The right/privilege distinction is crucial for this analysis. Alternatively, given that access to the streets and parks is normally permitted, restrictions imposed on their use specifically for first amendment activities, as opposed to more general restrictions on their use, are best understood as having a purpose to restrict first amendment conduct and to favor private choices to do things other than engage in speech-making or assemblies. Under this interpretation, without determining whether the person has a general, nonpositive law right to be in the streets, the regulation should be seen as an unconstitutional condition. In either case, the restriction is impermissible.

Still, various government practices could aid people in their use of the streets for first amendment purposes. These benefits would normally be privileges. The sixth principle indicates, however, that the way these government practices operate or the reason the government grants these special benefits will determine whether the apparent offer of the privilege constitutes an unconstitutional condition.

Obviously this set of six principles is not perfect. They will not solve all problems. They interpret "abridgement" to encompass various situations: hostility to speech and assembly as compared to other individually chosen activities; gratuitous or merely administrative-convenience justified restrictions on expressive conduct; and attempts to suppress certain expressive content. "Abridge," however, does not include the state's affirmative attempts to promote its own goals. The crucial point is that popular use of the streets, public facilities, and public space is too important to be left to the conventional notions of reasonableness. Any current look around the world shows governments of all sorts attempting to repress or carefully channel popular demonstrations. From the perspective of those in power, this suppression inevitably appears reasonable. From their perspective, it often *is* reasonable. But these demonstrations, these popular uses of the streets, should also remind us of something else. The right to assemble in the streets, the "unreasonable" use of the streets, is a central and powerful democratic right. The democratic power of the people is much more secure to the extent that this right exists and is not throttled by dehabilitating administrative red tape and regulatory channeling. Principles of the sort suggested in this chapter and effective rights to parade and demonstrate as described in the last chapter are central to a democratic, politically active people.

9

Commercial Speech: A Problem in the Theory of Freedom

Judicial analysis of commercial speech has exhibited doctrinal flux and intellectual failure. When in 1942 the Court first considered the issue, in an opinion that Justice Douglas later described as "casual, almost offhand [and as] not surviv[ing] reflection,"[1] the Court in *Valentine v. Chrestensen*[2] denied all first amendment protection to "purely commercial advertising." For the next thirty-three years, this commercial speech exception continually eluded either theoretical justification[3] or precise definition.[4] During the later portion of this period, both academic[5] and judicial[6] criticism of the exception grew. Predictably, the situation was unstable. Finally, the Court changed course in two decisions in 1975 and 1976, *Bigelow v. Virginia*,[7] and *Virginia State Board of Pharmacy v. Virginia Citizens Consumer Council*.[8] It announced that it could find no justification for excluding commercial speech from first amendment protection and accordingly would henceforth treat commercial speech like other varieties of speech.[9]

As was convincingly shown by Professor Martin Redish, from the perspective of its possible value in the marketplace of ideas, commercial speech is no different in principle from other speech.[10] Traditional marketplace theory protects speech in order to spread information and promote discussion that are relevant to people's search for truth or their attempts to make wise decisions. Commercial speech serves these functions.

Certainly, commercial speech addresses the problems of everyday life. Consumption and purchasing are major sources of recreation and satisfaction. Many people devote more attention and care to private economic decisions than they do to political issues. Private economic decisions may be both more personally controllable and more relevant to a person's life, to self-expression and self-realization, than are most political issues. Advertising often provides information and arguments relevant to these decisions and, thus, is relevant for "achieving a materially satisfactory life." Practice in assimilating commercial speech also could help develop people's rational decision-making capabilities. In all these ways, commercial speech, probably to a greater extent than political speech, makes individual self-government more effective.[11]

"Private" economic decisions and, thus, commercial speech also affect the content and directions of change in our communities. First, private economic decisions immediately determine the appearance of our society. People's purchases largely determine what objects we are surrounded with, what industries are developed, what types of employment are available, and in what ways the environment will be exploited. Second, decisions about purchases strongly influence the value structure and empirical perspectives of individuals in the community.[12] Third, people's purchases affect the locus and distribution of power within a society— for example, they determine the economic demand for various resources and skills.

In sum, commercial speech appears just as important as other speech, and for the same reasons—for stimulating social change and contributing to a broadly conceptualized marketplace of ideas. Unsurprisingly, once the Court began protecting commercial speech, it consistently premised this result on its dominant marketplace of ideas theory of the first amendment.[13] Nevertheless, this chapter will describe the appropriate treatment of commercial speech under the liberty theory developed in this book—and the result will be quite different.

Moreover, this alternative evaluation may not be entirely out of line with the movement of the law. The new wisdom, embodied in the 1975 and 1976 decisions protecting drug price and abortion service advertising, did not entirely prevail. Despite lack of theoretical justification, the common-sense intuition remained that commercial speech is different from other speech and should not be protected. Some of our strongest champions of free speech, including Thomas Emerson[14] and Alexander Meiklejohn,[15] reject protection for commercial speech, a conclusion that should give pause to those civil libertarians who support the Court's new position. In any event, the Court's holdings proclaiming protection have unraveled.[16] In 1942 in *Valentine*, the Court had permitted the state to prohibit commercial advertising circulars even though the constitution protected the distribution of noncommercial leaflets.[17] Then the 1976 decision in *Virginia Board of Pharmacy* supposedly eliminated any "fragment of hope for the continuing validity of [*Valentine*'s] 'commercial speech' exception."[18] Five years later in *Metromedia, Inc. v. San Diego*,[19] the majority of the Court indicated that the state could bar commercial billboards even if political billboards were not banned[20]—a result hardly distinguishable from the result in *Valentine*. The backtracking continued. A key aspect of the decision in *Bigelow* and *Virginia Board of Pharmacy* was the view that the state had no interest, consistent with the first amendment, in denying consumers truthful, nonmisleading information that could be relevant for their decision making.[21] But inexplicably in 1980 the Court in *Central Hudson Gas v. Public Service Commission*[22] suggested that the state could prohibit an electric utility from engaging in presumably truthful, informative advertising if the prohibition was narrowly tailored to serve the state's interest in energy conservation. *Central Hudson* was followed by *Posadoas de Puerto Rico Associates v. Tourism Company*,[23] in which the Court upheld a prohibition on truthful advertising of casino gambling directed at the residents of Puerto Rico. The Court characterized the state interest as precisely an interest in restricting information that the government feared would be relevant to the listener's decision making—a state interest that from a marketplace of ideas perspective appears overtly and impermissibly paternalistic.

Thus, the Court now says that commercial speech is protected by the first amendment. But false or misleading commercial speech is not protected.[24] Truthful commercial speech suggesting criminal activity is not protected.[25] Prior restraints on commercial speech are allowed.[26] Time, place, and manner regulations that are impermissible for other speech are allowed. And if the state has an interest in people not being influenced by the content of commercial speech, paternalistic bars on the speech are allowed—at least, if the commercial speech provides truthful, relevant information about casino gambling or energy consumption, although the Court protects nonmisleading information about drug prices or lawyer services. None of the above restrictions would be upheld for noncommercial speech. In sum, the Court has retreated drastically from its claim in 1976 that "the notion of unprotected 'commercial speech' [has] all but passed from the scene."[27] Instead, the Court's requirement that the state pursue its aim with suitably narrow means provides doctrinal flexibility to strike down regulations of commercial speech that it finds sufficiently offensive. The Court can advance consumer protection by striking down industry-advocated restrictions on advertising, such as anti-competitive restrictions on advertising by lawyers or pharmacists, while upholding restrictions on commercial promotion of energy consumption or casino gambling—a policy distinction that seems admirable but has little to do with any plausible theory of the first amendment.

At this point, reconsideration of the entire treatment of commercial speech appears appropriate. Admittedly, entrenched precedents proclaim that the first amendment covers commercial speech. Still, this chapter provides a basis for reconsideration as well as a justification for the Court's more recent retreat. It does so by offering an analysis of commercial speech from the perspective of the liberty theory of the first amendment, a theory that had not been systematically articulated until after the Court had abandoned *Valentine*'s commercial speech exception.

This chapter offers two arguments that first amendment theory requires a complete denial of first amendment protection for commercial speech.[28]* Briefly, the first argument is as follows: The first amendment protects a person's use of speech to order and create the world in a desired way and as a tool for understanding and communicating about that world in ways he or she finds important. These uses are fundamental aspects of individual liberty and choice. However, in our present historical setting, commercial speech reflects market forces that require enterprises to be profit oriented. This forced profit orientation is not a manifestation of individual freedom or choice. Unlike the broad categories of protected speech, commercial speech does not represent an attempt to create or affect the world in a way that has any logical or intrinsic connection to anyone's substantive values or personal wishes. Rather, it is logically and intrinsically connected to the structurally enforced requirements of the market. Therefore, profit-motivated,[29] commercial speech should be denied protection. It lacks the crucial connections with individual liberty and self-realization that are central to justifications for the constitutional protection of speech, justifications that in turn define the proper scope of protection under the first amendment.

---

*Of course, much commercial speech is useful and should be allowed. The claim here is only that commercial speech should not receive *constitutional* protection.

The second argument will describe constitutionally relevant differences between expressive liberty and the uses of property within market exchanges. Market exchanges inherently involve people exercising purely instrumental power over each other. Although this behavior is often entirely unobjectionable, it is not basic to individual liberty and, therefore, should be subject to regulation. Commercial speech, as an integral aspect of this market process, should likewise be subject to regulation.

This second argument responds to an additional concern. The Court's recent embrace of commercial speech may merely reflect the failure to find a rationale for its exclusion from the category of protected speech. However, the embrace may reflect a more fundamental disenchantment. Judges and scholars have failed to justify the greater constitutional protection that the Supreme Court has given to individual or personal rights, as compared with property or economic rights, during the past forty years.[30] If extending protection to commercial speech was a response to this failure,[31] it may foreshadow an ominous shift either in the Supreme Court's deference toward governmental regulation of economic interests or in the Court's special solicitude for individual rights. Although this chapter focuses on commercial speech and first amendment theory, this second argument more directly and more abstractly shows that, from the perspective of individual liberty, market practices including commercial speech should be more subject to regulation than other behavior. It distinguishes constitutionally protected liberty rights from property rights.

The fundamental differences between the approach developed here and the analysis employed by the Court for the last ten years can usefully be summarized. First, the Court's reasoning has consistently relied on the marketplace of ideas theory of the first amendment.[32] This theory, criticized in Chapter 1, attributes the special constitutional status of speech to its instrumental role in seeking truth, recognizing universally agreed on values, and changing people's attitudes.[33] The ultimate purpose of protection under this view is to guarantee a proper distribution of the product, speech, to the consumer, a listener or reader. As the Court put it in a commercial speech case, "the inherent worth of the speech in terms of its capacity for informing the public does not depend upon the identity of the source."[34] In contrast, the liberty theory focuses on the speaker and the speaker's choice to speak, not the listener and the usefulness of the content. Second, the Court's analysis has relied heavily on balancing—in fact, virtually no one has suggested that commercial speech should really go as unregulated as other speech.[35] The usefulness of the commercial speech to the listener is relative and can be outweighed by other considerations. In contrast, this book has developed a definitional, absolutist interpretation that focuses on the speaker's liberty.

COMMERCIAL SPEECH AND INDIVIDUAL LIBERTY

Chapter 3 concluded that *as long as speech represents the freely chosen expression of the speaker while depending for its power on the understanding and response of the listener, freedom of speech represents a charter of liberty for noncoercive action.* Speech is both a person's most important political "tool" or instrument and the most democratic possible political practice. Everybody's speech counts. Speech implants the speaker's stamp on at least some small part of the social world and maintains that world—and while speech requires a common, plural world for its meaning and existence, the source of specific speech is in principle the individual.

It is worth reemphasizing that the crucial aspect of protected speech is its origin or source in a self. Because the speech noncoercively expresses the choices, values, commitments, or identity of the self, protection of speech respects that self's liberty or autonomy. Assuming that the power of speech follows only from listener's activity of assimilating it and responding, the fact that verbal activity is motivated by self-interest (or even selfish interest) is no reason to frown on or limit speech. Self-interest is, in fact, a normal and valuable aspect of speech.

This view of speech as an expression of the self seems ill suited for describing the profit-motivated speech of the marketplace of commodities, which intuitively does not seem to deserve the same status as the speech of the marketplace of the mind. However, to justify excluding this commercial speech from constitutional protection requires an explanation for why a "profit" motive is, in principle, any different from other self-interested motives, which are generally present in protected uses of speech and even provide part of the rationale for protecting speech.[36]

The Existing Economic and Social Order

To paraphrase Justice Holmes, constitutional results should not depend on the theories of either Herbert Spencer or Karl Marx.[37] Still, some conception of the social world, that is, some theory, is always implicit in legal decisions as well as in any words or concepts we use and in any distinctions we make. For example, the "obviousness" of legally relevant similarities or distinctions between situations will only exist because of widespread *agreement* about the importance of various features of the social world, and about the relation that legal disputes bear to these features. The "obviousness" can always be destroyed by finding or postulating a lack of agreement or an alien conception of the importance of those features of the social world. Moreover, a brief sketch of the social world as it exists in twentieth-century America is especially necessary in order to explain the historically relative distinction between profit-oriented speech and other speech.

All meaningful classifications of behavior rely on implied or explicit knowledge of the human world, knowledge normally grounded in historically specific social practices. Thus, the category "profit-oriented speech" gets its meaning in relation to the types of profit-oriented social practices to which it applies. The rational pursuit of "profits" has only been a ubiquitous social activity in certain historical periods and has, in different periods, taken different forms.[38] The meaning of "profit" as well as the characteristics of profit-oriented speech change as the forms of commerce change. Therefore, reference to *some conception* of the social economic order is implicit even in the identification of commercial speech. More important, any special constitutional treatment of "commercial speech" must depend on the presence or absence of certain characteristics of that speech. Identification of these characteristics must also rely on some conception of the social economic order. Since the purposes of the inquiry dictate those aspects of the social world that must be sketched, the present analysis focuses on those distinctions between commercial speech and noncommercial speech that are relevant for the realization of first amendment values.

A laissez-faire economic model could seem inadequate at a time when government regulation and intervention intrude into virtually every aspect of the economy. However, within the limits and structures maintained by government, a capitalist market process of allocation currently dominates the American economic system.[39] State involvement and regulation are not in themselves contrary to the centrality of profits as an organizing principle. At most, state regulation constitutes part of the constraining environment in which profit-oriented economic activity operates. Thus, even though the capitalist market model does not completely describe the economic world, market principles or structures constitute the behavioral paradigm of modern commerce. Moreover, this paradigm often either implicitly or explicitly provides the foundation for legal doctrine. Many contract, tort, and damage rules assume a market paradigm. Sometimes, the law even duplicates the competitive market's requirement of a profit orientation. The law's charge that corporate officers of the typical business enterprise not waste corporate assets implicitly requires a profit orientation. The defense to the charge of "wasting corporate assets," the claim of "business judgment," reflects the legal necessity of a profit orientation, even though law is such a blunt tool that few noncriminal corporate policies will be vulnerable to judicial challenge.[40]

In a possessive market society, where "value" represents commodity value or exchange value, an enterprise's failure to exploit its resources in the most efficient manner necessarily leads to a decrease in the value of these resources. The value of property or capital depends on its capacity to return a profit—to reproduce itself with a surplus. Unless the enterprise always strives to increase profits, to reproduce capital, the profit-making value of what it has at present may, because of competition, decrease and then disappear. For example, suppose that both Firms A and B produce a food for $12 and sell it for $13 and then Firm B changes to more efficient practices, producing for $10 and selling for $11. Assuming competition, unless Firm A also changes to new, more efficient practices, it will lose business or sell at a losing price—either of which eventually lead to bankruptcy and nonparticipation. If Firm A stops changing in accord with the requirements of a profit orientation while some other firms continue to change, Firm A will be unable to reproduce itself without a loss and the value of its capital will eventually decline to zero. As C. B. Macpherson has shown, systematic orientation by an enterprise within a possessive market society toward anything but profits will eventually result in its destruction.[41]

This analysis applies only to possessive market societies.* Within these soci-

---

*For example, people, say, farmers, who own their means of production and are largely self-sufficient, can continue to use economically "inefficient" techniques, possibly because they value the technique as serving a preferred quality of life, even if neighbors adopt more efficient means. The difference from the competitive market system is that these people do not depend on sales in a market to reproduce used-up means of production.

eties, the individual must strive for more and more, business must be oriented toward efficiency and profits. Rather than supplant the profit motive, "inefficient" governmental regulations merely impose side constraints to be integrated into the profit calculus. State regulation normally leads not to economic collapse of the firm but, like a technological factor, to additional costs that must be internalized by all similarly situated firms. Max Weber observes that "in a wholly capitalistic order of society an individual capitalistic enterprise which did not take advantage of its opportunities for profit making would be doomed to extinction."[42]

Particular social practices and institutional features make profit-oriented behavior necessary as well as possible.[43] Without competition and the existence of settled markets for productive inputs and outputs, *the economic structure* would not require or enforce such a profit-oriented stance.[44] In addition, only the development of modern accounting methods makes possible rational calculations concerning the profitability of various courses of action. Likewise, the profit orientation is significantly served by the separation of the enterprise from the household.*

The Distinction Between the Profit-Making Enterprise and the Household: Freedom of Choice

In the historical development of the West, as economic behavior became increasingly oriented toward the formally rational pursuit of profits, the household or consumption-oriented arenas of life became increasingly and more radically separated from the profit-making enterprise. Logically, the separation makes possible a more rational orientation toward profits.[46] Efficiency calculations could not be as easily made, risk could not be as well controlled, and profitability or unprofitability would be less evident without the legal and budgetary separation between the household and the business enterprise.[47]

Historically, this legal and budgetary separation (usually accompanied by physical separation as well) uniquely occurred in the West—and, scholars have argued, is integrally related to the rise of the capitalist industrial economy in the West.[48] Moreover, this separation affects the resulting forms of life which, like any structure of interaction, must be "valued," whether negatively or positively.[49] The separation allows and requires activity within the economically productive sphere of life to be increasingly divorced from the individual values of the actors[50] and, instead, to be instrumentally oriented toward the one structurally required goal—profits. The separation, combined with possessive market

---

*As used here, "enterprise" refers to the profit-oriented business enterprise. The "household" or "budgetary unit" refers to all areas of activity in which choice depends on the substantive values of the individual and the satisfaction of the chooser's desires. This distinction between the enterprise and the household parallels that between production and consumption. This usage reverses the Greek conception in that for these purposes the "political" sphere, as a realm in which values are expressed, debated, formulated, and pursued, constitutes a portion of the household. Of course, for other purposes, the political and household spheres should be distinguished—for example, in emphasizing public dialogue and the public formulation and justification of values within the public sphere.[45]Split Rings and Shear Plates

institutions, means that in the economic sphere actors have no choice but to pursue profits.

Accepting freedom as the standard, the constitutional issue is whether or not the action in this commercial sphere represents a manifestation of individual choice. Justice Douglas' conclusion was that "[c]orporate motives have no tinge of an individual's choice to associate."[51] Thus, he argued that the constitutional rights of the corporation-owned restaurant should be distinguished from the rights of a person in the home, or even those of the owner of the "classical country store . . . [which is] an extension, so to speak, of the home."[52] Douglas based the distinction on the character of the motivation attributable to the action. The corporate motives are purely commercial.[53] "[T]he corporate interest is in making money, not in protecting personal prejudices."[54] In the household, on the other hand, decisions reflect personal values or "prejudices,"[55] which is the basis for the constitutional protection of choice within this sphere. Or, in language echoing the themes of this book, Justice White, joined by Justices Brennan and Marshall, noted: "the use of communication as a means of self-expression, self-realization, and self-fulfillment, is not at all furthered by corporate speech. It is clear that communications of profit making corporations . . . do not represent a manifestation of freedom."[56]

In the social-economic world described above, market competition requires profit-oriented behavior at least for the enterprise that has been separated from the household[57]—a separation that enhances the instrumental rationality* of the enterprise. The obvious implication for commercial speech is that market competition firmly directs the enterprise's speech toward increasing profits. Ideally, the enterprise's profit calculations determine the content, form, and frequency of its commercial speech.

The key feature of this context, often ignored in the commentary on commercial speech, is that the profit orientation is *externally imposed* on the capitalist enterprise by the market. The enterprise has no general goal other than the instrumentally rational goal of increasing profits. Any other goal would detract from that rationality, would partially reintegrate the household and the enterprise, and would effect a merger of substantive and instrumental reason. *Given the household-enterprise separation, commercial speech is in fact and in principle independent of the speaker's decisions about the world or her investigations into its nature. Rather, the source of commercial speech lies in the structure of the competitive market.*

To conclude that no necessary or causal connection exists between the company's commercial speech and the personal beliefs of owners or workers is not to deny that a high correlation between speech and beliefs might be expected. Both psychological and structural factors promote a coalescence. People appar-

---

*Instrumental rationality is the form of reason that fits means to ends but is incapable of judging or evaluating ends. Professor Tribe has referred to it as *"that form of rationality which seeks to discriminate among alternative actions by assessing their comparative tendency to advance or to retard the achievement of the actor's goals or values."*[58] Weber distinguished the instrumentally rational orientation and the "value-rational" orientation: the latter involves the determination of action "by a conscious belief in the value for its own sake of some ethical, aesthetic, religious, or other form of behavior, independently of its prospects of success."[59]

ently have psychological tendencies to reduce dissonance between value contradictory behavior or attitudes.[60] A more balanced mental state will result if a person's beliefs correspond with her business speech or behavior. Reduction of dissonance can take the form of a person (consciously or unconsciously) increasing her personal acceptance of the values promoted and communicated by the enterprise. This form of dissonance reduction is particularly likely the more the economic actors view their involvement in the enterprise as voluntary. Moreover, this psychological effect might be expected on behaviorist grounds, given a reinforcement system within the enterprise that rewards manifestations of private belief in enterprise policy.[61]

Structurally, congruence may result from hiring the person who agrees with the enterprise's message or disagrees with it the least. Everything else being equal between two potential jobholders, if one agreed and the other disagreed with the values promoted by the enterprise, and if both placed some value on integrating beliefs with behavior, the one who agreed with the enterprise's values could be employed more cheaply than the other. Consequently, assuming the existence of job competition, that person would be the one hired. Widespread opposition to the enterprise's activities and speech might even incidently affect profitability calculations since higher wages may be necessary to attract needed employees. Nevertheless, in a capitalist market system, these profitability calculations still determine the speech.

Thus, the correspondence between private beliefs and the enterprise's speech do not justify attributing (or not attributing) the speech to the values of individuals.* The key consideration is that this correspondence is irrelevant to the speech that results; even if the correspondence were not present the commercial speech would be the same. The competitive market still induces the enterprise to consider the advocacy entirely from the technical perspective of sales and profit. *Thus, the domination of profit, a structurally required standard, breaks the intrinsic connection between speech and any vision, or attitude, or value of the individual or group engaged in advocacy.*

Human Self-Determination: The Rationale for Regulation

Even though commercial speech is not rooted in individual choice, regulation might be inappropriate if commercial speech were a neutral phenomenon, irrelevant to the major decisions facing us as individuals and collectives. Sometimes defenders of the market[62] claim that ever greater want satisfaction is a neutral or, more plausibly, an overriding and virtually universal value. Therefore, pursuit of profits and the corresponding commercial speech, both purportedly serv-

---

*In many situations there will be psychological and structural reasons to expect the person's speech to be as it is. But as long as the structure leaves this issue to individual choice, as long as our practices require attributing responsibility to the speaker, or as long as different choices are not structurally prevented, respect for individual autonomy means that these reasons are not a basis for denying that it is the person's speech. The claim here is that a market structure generates structurally determined speech in a manner much more independent of the person's values, however those values are formed.

ing the value of want satisfaction, merely promote a desired form of the social world. Profit maximization serves as the paradigm of rationality as well as the key to the system's dynamism. This system of coordination, it is argued, takes into account and adjusts all the conflicting values of the participants.[63] These market apologists further claim that the market takes individual and group preferences and predilections as given, promoting fulfillment of whatever preferences happen to exist.

Whether or not this description, if accurate, would justify first amendment protection for commercial speech,[64] the description is decidedly not accurate. In practice it fails for three main reasons: (1) preference satisfaction is not a neutral, universal, overriding value; (2) preference satisfaction is not uniformly served by free markets; and (3) most important, the market does not take preferences as given. Commercial speech not only helps mold the world, it molds the world in very particular ways.[65]

First, at least since Rousseau, ubiquitous cultural critics have pointed to evidence that neither happiness, nor a sense of freedom, nor any other important human goal closely correlates with a maximum satisfaction of market-stimulated desires.[66] Examination of major social institutions suggests that even our "other-directed" consumer society rejects giving an overriding voice to the goal of maximum want satisfaction. Contrary to the "logic" of the market, our most idealized educational practices assume that the primary criteria for the choice of which tastes and values to develop should be neither that they are easily stimulated nor that they are inexpensive to satisfy. Controversies concerning child-rearing practices also exemplify not only our great lack of knowledge about the effects of various practices but also lack of agreement as to how to evaluate those effects.[67] Often among the contested criteria are goodness, salvation, development of cultural or scientific sensitivities or capabilities, honesty—various virtues bearing no necessary relation to maximizing consumer satisfaction or even to happiness. Surely, human self-fulfillment, even happiness, are served by struggle, solidarity, initiative, skill development, honor, reverence, and a host of practices not dependent on, and sometimes undermined by, the domination of an instrumental orientation toward market-based wealth and profits.

Second, "market failures" often prevent the market from effectively serving even the goal of preference satisfaction. Many regulations of commercial speech—for example, mandatory disclosures or bans on misleading information or even bans on promotion of purchases of goods or services that have significant negative externalities[68] could sometimes reduce these market failures.

Third, an even more significant inadequacy of this defense of commercial speech, and one that applies even to perfectly functioning markets, is especially relevant here. The market does not take people's preferences as given. Too often simplistic accounts of the market misleadingly picture a static situation, thereby obscuring the process of change and development of values. The economic enterprise does not passively accept individual values as given. To increase profits, the enterprise attempts to create and manipulate values, an objective that is often the overriding purpose of commercial speech. While stimulating particular desires, some potential values or desires are necessarily ignored; others are undermined or distorted.

Popular critiques of planned obsolescence and modern America's Madison Avenue culture[69] are reflected in C.B. Macpherson's observation that "the market system . . . creates the wants which it satisfies."[70] Macpherson goes on to argue:

> There is no reason to expect that the wants and tastes which [the market] satisfies will reflect or permit that full development of the individual personality which is the liberal-democratic criterion of the good society.[71]

Speaking anthropomorphically, the competitive market directs commercial speech toward creating the world as "profit" requires. This profit-directed orientation has a number of implications. Profit requires a constant increase in our desires.[72] In addition, the particular desires stimulated share characteristic features—they must be desires for objects or services that can be sold by the enterprise. Preferably, purchases of the desired objects or services ought not lead to any lessening of desires nor impede the stimulation of tastes on which the sale of other products depends. With all other factors held constant, profit can most easily advance by stimulating the most cheaply aroused desires. "Profit" strives to create or reinforce certain images of humans useful for profit's purposes.[73] It thereby changes the social world in ways consistent with its needs. But how "profit" wants the world to be bears no necessary relation to how any individual wants it to be. No one need decide or even believe that the world is better if these desires are created. Allowing the dictates of profit to reign, allowing profit to "vote," is to depreciate human freedom.

An example may clarify the point. Compare the propaganda of a temperance league with the advertisements of a whiskey distilling and distributing company. At one level, the speech of each merely communicates messages on opposing sides of the same issue.[74] The freedom of all sides to present their views is, of course, basic to first amendment freedoms. In addition, often both side's messages relate to the source's self-interest. Nevertheless, a structural difference of a fundamental, qualitative sort does distinguish the two. Although people may belong to a temperance league for a wide variety of reasons, membership normally involves at least a public, and often a private, commitment to the substantive belief that less drinking would result in a better world. Listeners properly assume an uncoerced, intrinsic connection between the league's speech content and its members' values.

In contrast, neither the management, the owners, nor the workers of the distillery need have any belief in the facts or values communicated in its commercial advertisements. They could all be teetotalers who personally oppose the use of alcohol. No one associated with the whiskey company need believe that more drinking would make for a better world. The only necessary belief is that promoting the advocated activities will increase profits. The only necessary question about the speech is whether it is the most effective available means to increase profits. The failure to adopt the most profit-stimulating speech is a business mistake that is no different, in principle, from a failure to adopt an efficient productive technique or any other profit-promoting change. As the Court described the difference between these two contexts:

> The resources in the treasury of a business corporation . . . are not an indi-
> cation of popular support for the corporation's political ideas. They reflect
> instead the economically motivated decisions of investors and customers. . . .
> [In contrast,] [i]ndividuals who contribute to [Massachusetts Citizens for
> Life] are fully aware of its political purposes, and in fact contribute precisely
> because they support those purposes.[75]

Given the value consequences of commercial speech combined with its independence from anyone's values, human freedom requires a realm in which people can make value choices that control commercial speech. That realm can only
be a political sphere where people, not market forces, decide. The very purpose
of legal regulation, of political choice, is often to consider which values we want
to create and which we want to discourage—that is, to consider what type of
people do we want to be. The market's incapacity to embody this self-definitional dialogue makes a public or political sphere essential.

The market's substitute for this political process is the market defining people in a manner that serves profit. From the perspective of human self-determination, this market substitute is rightly subject to severe criticism.[76] Even if a
"value" gain would result from cutting down our greatest redwood forests and
replacing them with properly advertised plastic Disney trees, in their political
dialogues people can advance reasons against this move.[77]* We may want not to
become the type of beings who prefer convenient and profitable Disney forests
more than the redwoods and the wilderness.

Respect for people's autonomy requires a right to meaningful participation
in the processes that formulate the values through which people define themselves. This interest in participation in value formation may be what defines us
as political, not merely power-oriented, beings. And this interest is not limited
to determining the practices that will result in the most happiness. Certainly,
neither our legal-political structures and obligations nor our economic structures
can be adequately evaluated solely in terms of their contribution to the satisfaction of the endless stream of desires. Rather, the issues for political choice
extend more fundamentally to questions of fairness, justice, and individual and
collective self-definition, to determining the types of persons we want to be.
Since different economic forms tend to create different types of persons, any
defense of freedom as self-determination or any vision of the person as being
the subject of the human will, necessarily implies that people should have a right
to choose the content and determine the boundaries of the economic system.
Neither a concept of humanity that centers on self-determination nor the actual
state of existing social practices permits viewing the maximum creation and satisfaction of desires as a universally accepted or neutral value. The very values

---

*Note also that which values the market promotes is not random. The market is more likely
to produce advertising for a plastic Disney forest and redwood lumber than advertising to stimulate desires for solitude within the redwood forests, at least to the extent that potential advertisers are better able to capture the gain resulting from the increased desire for the former.

of respect for human autonomy and self-determination that require the first amendment necessitate that commercial speech be subject to collective, political control.

COUNTERARGUMENTS FAVORING PROTECTION

The argument has been that, given the sway of the profit motive, commercial speech contributes to the creation of a world that is not the product of individual choice. Two counterarguments seem particularly plausible but, in the end, are unpersuasive.

The Commercial Context Is Not Special

In many situations the value implications of instrumentally useful speech are contrary to the speaker's own personal values. In each situation, the person determines both costs and benefits of the instrumentally useful speech from the perspective of her values, and then freely adopts a chosen course of action. The politician, friend, or lover often finds herself in situations where expression in accord with her personal values has costs. Sometimes the person goes ahead and speaks in accordance with her own substantive values. Other times, with fingers crossed, the person speaks in ways contrary to her beliefs or values. This first counterargument assumes that the individuals comprising, managing, or owning the enterprise can similarly choose whether to follow the dictates of profit or their own personal values and assumes that these choices will determine what is said.[78]

This hypothesis must be considered within a specific historical and socioeconomic context. If competition effectively enforces or law requires profit-oriented behavior, the hypothesis of individual choice controlling outcomes must be rejected. Commonly, the legal obligation of corporate decision-makers is to pursue profits.[79] Although slippage predictably occurs, given their legal obligation to pursue profits, these decision-makers cannot properly attribute the enterprise's speech to their free choice. Rather, their claim must be that the speech reflects their cunning calculations.

More dramatically, since failure to pursue profits in our competitive market society results in a decrease or elimination of the "value" of the enterprise, even an "irrational" *attempt* to pursue these other values would soon come to an end.[80] In *Leviathan*, Thomas Hobbes demonstrated a precise understanding of this observation about competitive market societies. Hobbes saw that even though the individual may be "content with a moderate power," choice is not allowed; rather, he must have a "perpetual and restless desire of power after power," or ever more profit. Unless the individual continues to pursue profit, the value of the enterprise will diminish and he will be left without support. This explains why "he cannot assure the power and means to live well, which he hath present, without the acquisition of more."[81]

Finally, in most situations where a person chooses to speak in accordance with her values, her choice is added to everyone else's choice and this combination determines the overall message content that will be made available to the public. In contrast, a properly functioning market assures that if one person refuses or fails to head the directives of profit, not only will that person lose out, but the economic opportunity will be grabbed by someone else. The efficient practice will still occur; the same market-dictated commercial speech will be heard. Thus, choice is made irrelevant by the market structure in a way it is not within other contexts.

Commercial Speech Embodies People's Values

The second counterargument admits that commercial speech is value-laden, but argues that many persons do adopt the substantive values implicit in their commercial speech. According to the liberty theory of the first amendment, people should be free to speak in a manner that embodies their values. Therefore, commercial speech should be protected at least for those who want it. Even more, the liberty theory argues that the first amendment protects not only advocacy but also the expressive freedom to practice beliefs, unless those practices operate "coercively"[82] on others. Only such a broad, pluralistic view of the first amendment provides protection for the peaceful creation of societal alternatives and for democratic participation in change. Often the creation of revisionist or dissenting views requires a group or sect or community to provide stimulus, support, and a place to practice or utilize the revisionist views. The liberty theory of the free speech apparently implies that those who so desire should be free to sell as well as advertise in a manner that embodies their values. Nevertheless, closer examination shows that this argument also fails.

The liberty theory protects the speaker's expression of her values, allegiances, or "self." Commercial speech can certainly *advance* a speaker's interests in a variety of ways. But the question here is whether any of these ways amounts to *expressing* the speaker's values or, more specifically, expressing them in a manner that justifies coverage by the liberty theory. To determine this issue, it will help first to examine the different ways commercial speech advances the speaker's interests.

Four main possibilities potentially connect the commercial speech to the speaker's values. (1) Like any other advocate, the commercial speaker may value other people engaging in the substantive activity promoted by her commercial speech. The speaker may believe that we would have a better society if more people smoked cigarettes, used mouthwash, or purchased Hondas, just as she thinks we would be better off if more people had families, joined unions, or voted Republican. (2) The speaker may substantively value her commercial activity itself—that is, her productive activities, interactions with fellow workers and customers, or creation of advertisements. The speaker would then value the commercial speech because it increases her opportunity to engage in preferred activities. (3) The speaker may value the economic gain resulting from commercial transactions promoted by the commercial speech. Commercial speech helps the speaker make money. (4) The speaker may value her activity as in 2 above but value it specifically as a commercial, profit-oriented activity. Irrespective of the money received, paid employment can promote a person's self-esteem and a wholesome sense of being productive. The desire to make a productive social contribution can make engaging in an activity as a job different and substantively more valuable than engaging in the same activity as a hobby.

Assume, as has been argued, that the competitive market dictates the content of commercial speech. Then, even if a person values commercial speech in the first two ways, that is, values other people acting as the speech directs or values being better able to engage in her preferred commercial activities, the reason the speech occurs and, thus, the reason it advances these results is not that the speaker values them. Without any logical or determinative connection between the speaker's values and the content of the commercial speech, this commercial speech is not the speaker's expression of her values. In these circumstances, protection of the speaker's expression of her values cannot justify protection of the commercial speech.

Of course, this argument does not mean that speech with the same content as the commercial speech could not be an expression of the speaker's values. But regulation of the commercial speech is consistent with protecting the person's chosen speech. In his dissent in *Virginia Pharmacy Board v. Virginia Consumer Council,*[83] Justice Rhenquist argued that one reason the state could ban the commercial advertising is that, contrary to the majority's assumption, the law did not ban the circulation of price information. Consumer groups, for example, could publish it. If a person substantively values a world where more people drink or have accurate drug price information,[84] she can hand out leaflets providing the price information or tell her friends or write a book extolling the virtues of drink.[85] Likewise, a person who has adequate resources—which is always a limit on self-expression—can continue brewing whiskey or making pottery or mouthwash even if the prohibition on advertisements or sales makes the activity unprofitable.[86]

The third reason to value commercial speech is that the person values the profits to which the speech leads. However, this value, the desire to make a profit, is qualitatively different from other value commitments. The speaker's other allegiances represent commitments to either the speaker or listener engaging in behavior that is valued in itself—that is, represent substantive commitments. Making a sale in order to make a profit has only instrumental value.[87]* Of course, protected speech is often used instrumentally—to gain a result that the speaker values. But in these protected uses the speaker's instrumental and substantive values are intertwined—she substantively values advocated result. In contrast, commercial speech is doubly instrumental.[88] Not only is the speech used only as a tool to gain the profit, but the profit has no value itself except as an instrument to gain unrelated substantively valued results. Unlike instrumen-

---

*Although a person may express expertise or capabilities through effective instrumental activity, in these cases, the exercise of skill, not the instrumental goal, is the meaningful element. The skill itself can be exercised outside the commercial context and, therefore, is not prohibited merely by a prohibition on the commercial speech or activity—unless the skill is doing the activity in a commercial manner. That possibility will be discussed below as the fourth way to value commercial speech. There, the key point will be that if the value is in being commercially "skillful," the value does not require anything more than the right to act within the legally established commercial framework.

tal advocacy of valued ends, instrumental advocacy directed toward instrumentally valued profits does not express the speaker's substantive values. Since the first amendment protects the pursuit and living expression of people's substantive values, this self-expression rationale does not apply. Moreover, if the state is allowed to promote or protect any system of order, it must have power to regulate instrumentally valued activities.[89]

This instrumental/substantive distinction may be too facile. A person may substantively value successful engaging in instrumental activity. The sense of self in our society is frequently precarious and insecure. Comparison with others and social recognition serve to mold one's sense of personal identity. Many people find their affirmation and personal fulfillment in making money, making a profit, or being "successful" in their economic activities. Prominent social theorists have even correlated the historical development of western industrial capitalism with the spread of the attitude that economic success is evidence of personal worth.[90]

This "economic-success" notion of self-fulfillment may lead to a truncated notion of the self. Still, many people value profits not instrumentally because of contemplated uses of the money but substantively because making profits is itself considered good. This is a version of the fourth way of valuing commercial speech. The speaker values an activity specifically as a job or as a market-recognized productive activity. Whether this person values "making profits" or having the "productive job," prohibiting commercial speech seems to interfere with the activity that the speaker substantively values. Two further considerations, one discussed here and the other in the next section, meet this claim.

An opportunity to engage in an activity as a "job" requires not merely the use of the person's own skills and property but also necessitates a particular social world. Others must be willing and able to buy her product or service. Normally, however, a person has no right to have the particular social-economic world, the distribution of wealth, or the power over other people that is necessary to realize her values.[91] Chapter 4's distinction between allocative rules and general prohibitions made precisely this point.

Moreover, all collective choices increase some opportunities while restricting others. Collective choices affecting the availability of opportunities for employment and commercial gain are inevitable—*any* definition of property rights or any other legal rule has this effect. And these effects are desirable—self-determination requires the existence of collective choice concerning the constitutive framework of action. Thus, the substantive values a person places on profit making or on an activity as a "job" cannot give her a right to the result. More plausibly, these values justify allowing the person to try to realize the values within the economic structure made available by the legal or social order.

In sum, the first three ways in which commercial speech advances a person's interests do not show that the commercial speech involves the person's expression of her values. To the extent that the fourth way involves the person's expression of her values, the expression depends on the existence of a particular social-economic order. A person's autonomy or liberty claims cannot give her a right to demand any particular social-economic order and, therefore, does not provide her a constitutional basis to object to the regulation that prevents the existence of this order.

Beyond the conclusion that unrestricted commercial speech does not promote individual or human sovereignty, one further comment seems appropriate. Initially, it might seem that little is lost by reading the first amendment slightly more broadly than is theoretically justified. Therefore, without carefully considering the proper scope of freedom of speech, some first amendment commentators recommend including commercial speech within the first amendment. If commercial speech is not quite so valuable as other speech, their solution is merely to require weaker justifications for its regulation. But this approach is wrong.* Much is at stake. If the argument of this chapter is correct, including commercial speech represents not only intellectual confusion, it is directly at odds with the aim of the first amendment. It denigrates rather than affirms human liberty.

Persuasive critiques argue that commercial practices in a possessive market society operate to deny most people real freedom of choice in many significant decisions; that unregulated competitive markets operate to decrease both the totality and equality of human power to exercise human capacities; and that alternative socioeconomic structures would allow for a more just and more democratic society.[92] This chapter need not take a position on these claims since the argument is only that commercial speech and other market practices should be subject to democratic control, not that this democracy should choose to regulate. But certainly to the extent that these critiques are right, individual freedom could be increased by regulating value-laden market competition in accordance with the democratic choices. The concept of democracy might even require that these regulatory choices be made by the smallest subdivision of the polity capable of making and implementing them effectively. According to such an analysis, the commercial sphere should be marked off as especially appropriate for restructuring by the polity, not in order to maximize welfare but in order to expand freedom. Still, in regulating the commercial sphere, the first amendment mandates that the regulatory means not be inconsistent with respect for individual autonomy or liberty. If the arguments of this chapter are wrong, that would mean that the regulations must not touch commercial speech. But if the first amendment does not cover commercial speech, then the very value of individual liberty that the first amendment enshrines also requires that the political sphere have authority to regulate that speech.

COLLECTIVE CONTROL OVER "PROPERTY AS POWER": A MORE GENERAL ARGUMENT FOR REGULATING COMMERCIAL SPEECH

This section provides a less historically and empirically contingent, more general argument that commercial speech, as part of the system of commerce rather than the system of freedom of expression,[93] is subject to regulation.

*In addition to the point noted in the text, this approach of initially including all speech necessarily leads to balancing and the acceptance of weak justifications for some regulation, arguments that may have bad systemic consequences for the system of freedom of expression if they cannot be confined to the commercial speech context.

Where an activity is subject to regulation, so is the speech that is an integral part of the activity.* The bank robber who only gives orders, who "only" speaks, is still subject to criminal penalty. Our constitutional order has assumed, at least since the demise of *Lochner*, that commercial practices are subject to regulation. Thus, presumably the speech that is an integral part of the commerce should be also. The liberty theory, however, and the argument that the first amendment should protect expressive action, not just verbal conduct, might be thought to cast doubt on the basic premise—that commercial practices should be routinely subject to regulation. This section responds to this worry.

Two theses, taken together, provide the response. First, a person's use of property in an exchange differs fundamentally from other uses of property; similarly, people's interaction in a voluntary market exchange differs fundamentally from other, constitutionally protected forms of voluntary interaction. Second, these differences are relevant from the perspective of a defensible, formal conception of liberty.[95] Specifically, these differences show that it does not infringe liberty to regulate exchange and commercial practices, including commercial speech, oriented toward these exchanges,† while it does abridge liberty to regulate many other uses of property. This second thesis builds on a claim that exchange in our society essentially serves as an allocative device. I argue that exchanges should be subject to political control for the same reasons that allocations generally are.

Two observations suggest relevant differences between market exchanges and other, protected uses of property. First, for purposes of a market exchange, the owner values the property that she gives up only instrumentally, that is, for its "exchange-value." She uses the property solely as a means to influence or gain temporary power over another. When the government restricts these exchange-oriented practices, it only restricts people's opportunity to exercise power over others, not people's expression of their own values or their own autonomy.‡ By contrast, when the owner uses the property within her chosen activities, the owner values the use of the property itself or her activity that uses it. When the government restricts choices related to these "use-values," it restricts people's expression of their substantive values: it restricts their autonomy or liberty.

Second, exchanges are a means to achieve allocations. The purpose of exchange is to allow people to obtain goods or services from each other. Of course, the results of exchange may contribute to a person's substantive liberty in important ways: the person may value her use of the item that she obtains in

---

*Speech advocating an activity is not, however, part of the activity. The clear and present danger test for when advocacy of illegal action is unprotected might be viewed as an effort to distinguish "mere" advocacy from a criminal attempt, with speech then being unprotected because it is an integral part of the outlawed attempt.[94]

†Hereafter, references to regulating "exchange" or "the market" are intended, unless the context suggests otherwise, to include regulation of all the activities oriented toward exchanges—for example, production as well as commerce.

‡As used here, the notion of autonomy does not include one person's exercise of power over another or the person's use of the other's property. If it did, autonomy would not be a useful concept since then respect for one person's autonomy would amount to a restriction on the other person's. The present approach was also implicit, for example, in Chapter 3's argument that coercive speech should not be constitutionally protected.

the exchange. This contribution, however, occurs in the same way that any desirable allocation of resources contributes to liberty. Any allocative practice—for example, either national health insurance or medical care for the highest bidder, the right to walk across unused land or strict trespass laws—can contribute to substantive liberty by placing valued resources at a person's disposal. Moreover, any particular allocative practice blocks other allocations that some people desire. Society can, should, and often does evaluate the resulting allocation in terms of fairness, general welfare, and societal self-definition. Exchange is merely one allocative practice that achieves particular results. And exchange, like other allocative practices, depends on collectively recognized rules—for example, contract and property law or other similar forms of legal regulations. Therefore, regulation of exchange should be viewed as more like a collective decision concerning allocation than a restraint directed at a person's substantively valued activities. This is particularly true since regulation of exchange leaves a person free to engage in any chosen activity (except for further reallocations accomplished by certain exercises of power over others) as long as she has the needed resources. But having particular resources cannot be demanded on first amendment, autonomy grounds.

This view of exchange might be opposed. A counterargument emphasizes that liberty encompasses voluntary interaction, of which exchange is an important subcategory. Both parties "voluntarily" participate in the exchange. And even granted that the function of property within exchanges is to influence the behavior of the other person, all interactions involve people influencing each other.

This counterargument starts out right. Personal expressive liberty certainly extends beyond the opportunity to act alone. Liberty includes the opportunity to engage in interaction with others. The right of association is fundamental. A person's ability to understand herself, live her values, and satisfy her desires, regularly depends on securing the association and cooperation of others. Still, like uses of property, interactions can take various forms.

Adding the associational element does not, in the end, change the analysis. The use of property within personal-liberty-embodying interactions (protected) differs from exchange-oriented interactions (unprotected) in the same two ways that consumptive uses of property differ from exchange uses. First, in liberty-embodying interactions, participants value their use of property not as a means to exercise power over the other or to achieve a preferred allocation of resources. Rather, they value the use of property as an integral part of the valued activity. Illustrative are uses of property within the scope of freedom of association.[96] Each participant values the use of the hall for the meeting, the ball in the game, or the contraceptive for birth control, as well as valuing the substantive form of interaction with the other person or persons. Second, even if these liberty-embodying interactions sometimes involve manipulation or instrumental use of one person by the other, this instrumental exercise of power is not an essential or inevitable aspect of the interaction the way it is central to the very structure of market exchanges.

An essential aspect of market interactions is people's use of property to exercise power over others and to achieve allocations—neither of which are aspects of expressive liberty. In an exchange, each party conditions the availability of a resource on the other party doing something he or she would otherwise not choose to do—for example, the book owner would not give the student the book except for the ten dollars he offered. (Or if she would give it to him anyhow, as long as gifts are permitted, regulation of the market does not interfere with her choice.) This exercise of power is inherent in an exchange.

The potentially different nature of influence exerted in nonmarket interactions can be seen by contrasting them with market exchanges first from the perspective of the influencing party and then from the perspective of the influenced party, although, of course, each participant plays both roles.

Consider a person exercising influence in nonmarket interactions. The influencer, for example, the person trying to get the other to play tennis or attend the political demonstration, relies on a combination of factors in order to secure the other's voluntary response. These factors include the context of the interaction, the property that she makes available to be used in the interaction, and her personal qualities—for example, her personality, physical strength, intelligence, beauty, interactive skills, or persuasive skills.[97] Often, the interaction enhances her skills, knowledge, or other qualities. She typically values her own involvement. The influencer usually does not transfer or lose either the resources or personal qualities she commits to the interaction.[98] At most, she uses up the resources or her time. If she can use the property in her own activities, she should also be permitted to use it when her valued activities involve interactions with others. These uses increase the property's use-value for the owner. When the influencer substantively values the joint use, she does not treat the property merely as a means to induce the other to engage in otherwise unwanted action. The tennis player presumably values the joint activity and her use of the tennis balls, and is not making the balls available as a means to induce the other party to behave in ways she assumes the other would prefer not to behave.

An even more important difference relates to the perspective of the party influenced. Of course, whether payment or persuasion secures the influenced party's performance, the performance is in a sense voluntary. At least at the time it occurs, the influenced person believes she has gained from the interaction. Nevertheless, in one crucial respect the party influenced will view the two forms of securing her performance as strikingly different.

In a market exchange, the influenced person performs in order to secure the other's property or performance. Presumably, this person would have preferred to have already possessed this payment, thereby avoiding the necessity of her own performance. The influenced person acted only in order to change the existing allocation of resources. The prior owner has exercised power over her. This is not the experience of freedom. In contrast, in conversation, in play, in political or religious activity, in friendships and loving relationships, and in some forms of joint productive activity, the structure is always consistent with the influenced party viewing her response as itself desirable. In these situations, she is in a sense "empowered" by the existing allocation. She can view her associate, whether a friend, playmate, lover, or political or cultural ally, as offering a mutually valued association or offering engagement in a desired performance. Often, the interaction is more a mutual association than an exchange.

The exercise of power over others is therefore not inherent in the very *structure* of nonmarket interactions. This is not to deny that in practice these nonmarket interactions often have a dark underside. Too often, people experience their interpersonal or associative interactions as exchanges rather than unifications. They may experience their own performance as burdensome rather than as itself valuable, and view the offers of their allies, friends, or lover as manipulative exercises of power. Moreover, in practice, exchange-oriented activities often have bright undersides. Even if exchange activity is not an element of formal liberty, there is nothing necessarily evil about the mutual exercise of power involved in "voluntary" exchange. And the style of exchange activity sometimes makes the activity itself enjoyable. The point here is only that the instrumental or power-exercising element is inherent in exchange but not in the associative interaction.

Still, these nonmarket interactions and property uses differ in two interrelated ways from the market exchange. They differ, first, in the way each participant values the interaction itself and the use of the property that she brings to the interaction. Second, they differ in the way each participant experiences treating the other and being treated by the other. From the perspective of individual liberty, these differences are crucial. A requirement that government respect individual autonomy would mean that the government normally cannot restrict an individual in using herself or her property merely to express or embody her values. Restrictions directed at those interactions based on unity of values and at noninstrumental aspects of association would be directed at a person's liberty.

In contrast, no useful formal notion of liberty would include the idea that respect for a person's autonomy gives her a general right to exercise power over another, either to obtain the other's performance or to achieve a preferred distribution of resources. Respect for a person's use of herself or her property in expressing or embodying her values certainly does not require such a right. In market exchanges, however, the participants necessarily exercise power over each other.

There is another way to see this same point. Property rules serve various functions. They secure material resources people need for everyday life,[99] connect people with objects tied to their personhood,[100] provide means with which people can exercise power over others,[101] and allocate resources in a manner that promotes productive or meaningful uses. Recognition of rights in respect to one function does not necessarily require recognition of a right in the same person in respect to another. A camper may have a right to use a forest until a developer exercises his right to sell it for homesites. The state or the collectivity has the unavoidable, inherent responsibility to adopt the rules or practice that determine both the distribution of property for each of these functions, in particular, the distribution "for use" and the distribution "for power." The two allocations need not correspond. Once the various functions of property are disaggregated,[102] it is obvious that society's decision to adopt a particular distribution of property for individual use need not correspond to its view about the role or proper distribution of property as a means to exercise power over others.[103] Merely because the government recognizes unequal claims on wealth does not mean that it must also recognize a right of people to use this unequal wealth to exercise power over other people.

Perhaps the only justification for legal rules or social practices that distribute claims to material resources unequally is that such rules promote the general welfare by increasing the total wealth, or that they promote society's self-definition and its preferred forms of social relations.[104] This justification does not find any general merit in allowing people to have unequal power to exercise control over others. If society allows unequal distributions of wealth to exist only for various policy reasons, it should be legitimate for society to restrict those aspects of inequality that it finds socially undesirable—although expressive uses, unlike power uses, cannot properly be prohibited because they are viewed as undesirable. Particularly when society distributes property very unequally, any unrestricted right to engage in "voluntary" exchange or in exchanged-oriented activities like production or commercial speech can undermine the experience of liberty. This unrestricted right could also thwart collective decisions about the appropriate nature of society and further the domination of some people by others. These different roles of property suggest different standards with which to evaluate limitations on different aspects of the distribution of property. A useful notion of liberty relates to a person using whatever resources she has in her activities. Since there is no need to connect liberty with exercising power over others and since the allocation of property-for-power is properly within societal control, the society can properly regulate the use of property-as-power by regulating or blocking certain exchanges.

In summary, regulations of market exchanges and the activities oriented toward these exchanges typically promote plausible, even if contested, substantive conceptions of liberty. Thus, any argument that these regulations necessarily interfere with liberty must refer to a formal conception of liberty. But the above analysis shows that even a formal conception of liberty does not imply objections to regulation. The use of property in exchange involves an exercise of power over others. From the perspective of respecting people's expression of their substantive values, a limit on people's use of their property to exercise power over others is unlike limits on their use of property directly within self-realizing activities.

In addition, the regulation of exchange is most like a rule establishing a socially desired distribution of resources. The exchange is merely one of various collectively recognized means of obtaining resources necessary for substantively valued activities. Thus, collective control is proper whether we view exchange as a means to exercise power or as a means to secure desired resources. It is proper because exercising power over others is not an inherent aspect of liberty and because allocative or distributive rules are necessarily a matter for collective choice or acceptance.

The above analysis ignored one recurring argument. Many people substantively value the activity of work. Sometimes this may in part reflect a need to stave off boredom, but people also value work as self-expression, as meaningful activity. For many, work is more significant than any of our consumer society's consumptive activities as an expression of their identity and their substantive values. People define themselves through making productive or creative contributions to society, through exercising skills, and through having their skills and contributions recognized by others. The issue addressed here is whether this similarity between market-oriented activities and other substantively valued expressive activities means that they merit the same protection under the liberty theory.

People value their economic activities in various ways. In distinguishing income taxation from the violations of liberty implicit in forced labor,[105] I once argued:

> A person may (positively or negatively) value (1) the laboring activity, (2) the liberty to choose among various activities given the nature of the activity and the reward for performance, and (3) the reward itself. Taxation of earnings relates only to this third factor; and taxation is only one societal practice among a wide range of societal practices that determines the reward.[106]

Somewhat similar distinctions help justify the view that regulation of people's productive activities is not an infringement on their liberty, even though they may substantively value these activities.

Regulation, of course, cannot be equated with taxation. Regulation has a broader impact. For example, regulations sometimes define or establish qualifications for engaging in a business, mandatory terms for interactions between employer and employees, and impermissible or mandatory aspects of economic activities, including practices relating to safety, environmental effects, financial reserves, advertising, and competition. By requiring or prohibiting certain practices, economic regulations may seem more like forced labor than like taxation. But this similarity is superficial. Economic regulation differs significantly from forced labor in ways that show that it normally does not abridge individual liberty.

Usually, a significant number of people substantively value the specific requirement mandated by the economic regulation—like a safer workplace, a better physical environment, or less dictatorial, less discriminatory, more democratic employment relations. In contrast, usually even the person who substantively values the overall productive activity and objects to the regulation does not substantively value the prohibited feature, for example, the unsafe condition, the pollution, or the high price to the consumer.* Rather, the typical objection is to the regulation's effect on efficiency or profitability. Any gain from the regulation is said not to be not worth this cost. In these cases, the regulation merely operates like a tax, making the activity more expensive. Rather than prohibiting substantively valued behavior, the regulation should be seen as an allocation rule. It takes away wealth from some people—those who either like or would benefit from the prohibited practices—and advances the substantive values of others.

The analysis must be slightly different in the relatively rare case where the objector does substantively value the restricted activity. This narrow category, however, may be even smaller than suggested above in that often only the com-

---

*Occasionally an economic regulation, say, a workplace safety regulation, restricts an activity that the worker substantively values or requires an activity that she substantively disvalues. Even though this point does not change the analysis, it may be overstated. My guess is that a class bias leads many commentators to overestimate the frequency of this occurrence.[107]

mercial version of the activity is restricted. A person often is still free to engage in the activity on her own. For example, prohibitions on the unauthorized practice of law should not, and often do not, prevent a nonlawyer from offering *free* "legal" advice to friends.[108] As long as it does not, the regulation does not prohibit a substantively valued activity. Rather, the complaint can only be that the regulation affects the valued activity's profitability for those who do not have the required qualifications.

Regulations of market practices are typically intended to modify either people's use of property to exercise power over others, the user's externalization of costs, the distribution of wealth, or the preferences that the market processes generate. With the arguable exception of zoning, economic regulations seldom have as a purpose the prohibition or restriction of substantively valued activities. Even zoning is consistent with the first amendment when, as noted in Chapter 8, it only regulates the location of valued activities.

Thus, even though regulations prohibit or require particular behavior, in terms of their effect on activities that people substantively value, most regulations of market practices are more like taxes than like forced labor. Like taxes, they primarily affect the instrumentally valued economic reward accompanying market practices. Like taxes, they sometimes leave a person without the resources needed to engage in some substantively valued activity. But like taxes, these consequences are inherent in any economic order. Moreover, if a person values an activity itself, usually she may still engage in it if she is willing and able to forego an economic return.

The above argument moves too quickly. It is not only the miser, the confirmed haggler, and the empire builder who substantively value economic activities specifically as economic activities. Many people do. Restricting an activity to nonmarket contexts can change the quality of the activity. The argument also studiously ignores the degree that regulation can in practice restrict the actual opportunities to engage in a valued activity.

This point has already been answered. An individual who would substantively value a particular consumptive activity has no liberty-based right to be allocated sufficient resources to engage in it. Likewise, the individual who would substantively value engaging in a particular market-oriented activity has no liberty-based right to demand that the opportunity exist. In both cases, the state may decide to allocate resources in a manner that thwarts this individual's desires. The person's liberty-based right can only be to use resources or market opportunities that the allocative order makes available.

As has also been noted, the actual availability of particular market-oriented opportunities necessarily depends on collective choices. First, because other people's willingness and ability to pay is a crucial determinant of the content of economic opportunities, the existence of market opportunities depends on society's recognition of people's claims to resources. Second, collective practices or governmental choices, ranging from its property laws to its school curricula and immigration laws, affect the content of people's preferences; and consumers' money-backed preferences determine the existence of market opportunities. Thus, the existence and distribution of economic or market-oriented opportunities are created in part by collective, governmental decisions. Constitutional liberty is not abridged merely because regulations restrict some people's preferred economic opportunities.

Still, arguably the state should not act purposively to eliminate an opportunity.[109] Unlike opportunities denied merely due to lack of resources, regulation of exchange *purposively* blocks certain opportunities that some people may substantively value—for example, the opportunity to pollute, to discriminate, to be unsafe, or to practice a chosen profession. Surely, this blockage is inconsistent with respect for liberty. Given the resources and preferences that people do have, the government should not refuse to enforce people's agreements, prohibit their voluntary interactions, or regulate their productive practices.

This argument is also wrong. The aim of regulating market-oriented activities is not to restrict autonomy but to allocate resources and control exercises of power. Society must and justifiably can make choices about the distributive or allocative order. The inevitable effect and appropriate purpose of these choices is to create or favor the opportunity for some activities, which inevitably eliminates or disfavors others. Likewise, a workable formal notion of liberty does not require protection of exercises of power. A person can only claim a liberty right to engage in those exercises of power over others that the society permits. Because market exchanges involve each participant's exercise of power over the other, society must have the right to determine which exchanges will be permitted and which will be blocked in order to further alternative opportunities.

This section has offered a general argument that regulation of the market order is consistent with the concept of liberty. It thereby provides a second explanation for why regulating commercial speech is consistent with a liberty theory of the first amendment. Speech that is an integral part of these commercial practices, or speech that claims to be an integral part (for example, for purposes of claiming a tax deduction or claiming not to be a waste of corporate assets), should be treated as a regulatable part of system of commerce rather than part of the system of freedom of expression or of individual liberty.

POLITICAL SPEECH OF THE COMMERCIAL ENTERPRISE

Treating all the profit-oriented enterprise's communications as unprotected commercial speech may be unjustified. Corporations engage, for example, in "core" political speech. Private utility companies publicize the advantages of free enterprise and encourage opposition to public ownership of utilities.[110] Tobacco companies make massive expenditures or contributions to defeat state ballot measures regulating smoking. Other enterprises find political speech useful, presumably profitable.[111] Clearly this corporate political speech would be protected under a marketplace of ideas theory of the first amendment.

Fairness also seems to require that the first amendment protect the utility company's political speech since it protects the individual's advocacy of government ownership. Of course, business considerations may dictate the content of the company's political speech. "Investment" in political speech may even produce a higher rate of return than investment in production or product advertising. Still, the utility company's "political" speech appears qualitatively different from, for example, a shampoo advertisement. Courts have suggested a distinguishing criterion: commercial speech is speech that does no more than merely propose a private commercial transaction.[112]

Although "proposing a private commercial transaction" is a serviceable operational distinction, the theoretical question is whether the distinction has a principled justification. Such a justification is not obvious. The argument for denying protection to the shampoo or liquor ads was that the market determined the content of the advertisement.[113] This argument seems to apply without change to corporate political speech. The reasoning focuses only on whether the speech can be attributed to the choice of a free agent. The tobacco company's political speech is likely to be as market determined as its product advertisements.

"Private" political speakers exhibit either a broadly or narrowly *self-interested* motive. Their speech presumably represents their values. In contrast, the motivations structurally attributable to the source of "political commercial speech" show that this speech should be included within the category of commercial speech. Three motivational bases for business' "political" speech are plausible: (1) The speech may represent the management's market-oriented judgment that the political speech will advance the company's income, profits, or stability. (2) The speech may represent the management's own personal social and political beliefs. (3) The speech may be made by management in behalf of the stockholders or owners who personally favor the advocated political positions, whether because of their ideological beliefs or their economic self-interest.

The first motivational account conforms to the scenario presented in this chapter. The speech is merely an efficient means to advance profits. The market determines its content. Of course, as long as the company does not use fraudulent or unlawful means, pursuit of profits is often socially approved. Still, there can be good reasons for regulating this process. Profit maximization requires manipulating or creating values. The enterprise's determination of which values to promote does not depend on either individual or collective visions about what humanity should be but is instead based on the technical requirements of profit maximization. Thus, this chapter's liberty analysis applies. Human self-determination requires a sphere in which humans decide whether and when to allow the economic structure to generate value-laden speech. Permitting market-determined political speech is arguably corrupting, particularly to a sphere devoted to human self-determination, since this speech need not reflect anyone's substantive political views. In any event, the propriety of this market-dictated speech should be determined within the political realm.

Corporate apologists are unlikely to advance the second motivational account, which suggests that the speech merely represents the management's personal prejudices or values. Use of corporate funds to fulfill management's personal desires, rather than aid management in carrying out its fiduciary duties, is normally described as either taxable compensation[114] or illegal conversion.[115] Of course, the owner's or management's views often coalesce with the enterprise's profit-oriented speech. Mere coalescence, however, is not a basis for attributing the market-determined speech to the individual.

The sociological premise of this chapter has been that in developed capitalist economies the sphere of the household or of consumption is normally separated from that of the enterprise and the market. Possibly the most important function of modern corporate law is to formalize this separation.[116] But although separation generally corresponds to the existing order, it is never total. Where there is an incomplete separation or a partial merger of spheres, the corporate "political speech" is sometimes properly attributable to management's personal prejudices. When it is lawful to spend corporate funds in behalf of the management's (or owner's) personal political preferences and when such an attribution can properly be made, the corporate political speech should receive first amendment protection. Even in these cases, however, the law could require (e.g., for tax purposes) that the cost of the speech be characterized as income for those corporate actors who express themselves through the speech. The government's power to regulate commercial speech never gives it authority to ban speech because of its content nor to bar anyone from speaking as he or she chooses. Rather, the government only has authority to bar speech based on the source, that is, speech paid for and properly attributable to the commercial enterprise.[117]

The third motivational account, that the speech represents the *personal* values of the owners or stockholders, also denies any clear separation of the realm of personal values from the economic enterprise. Of course, sometimes the two are not separate. People often form associations to advance members' values and visions. Just as people form political parties and labor unions to advance various substantive goals, people sometimes use their resources to subsidize a productive enterprise's relative independence from the market. Both individuals whose low wages subsidize their chosen form of value-oriented market activities and the similar associative behavior of worker cooperatives and communes, quite clearly unite productive and personal values. These enterprises' effective integration of values into their productive activities make them more like voluntary associations in which, as the Supreme Court has recognized,[118] individual liberty is more at stake and, therefore, regulation is less permissible.

Modern business corporations, however, normally cannot be, and are not expected to be, oriented toward such associative value goals. The business corporation is primarily oriented toward profit maximization as well as some degree of investment and institutional security.[119] Thus, a declaration that its "political speech" is "personal" rather than "business"—that the corporation has designed the speech to advance specifically approved substantive ends of its owners or workers rather than the instrumental end of profit—would be inconsistent with the business' normal institutional role.

Still, if the owners or stockholders in fact approve and willingly pay for the substantive message, the message should be viewed as personal speech and should receive first amendment protection.[120] But corporate payment of the cost of the speech would then represent (taxable) income to those owners rather than a business expense of the corporation. Moreover, a requirement that *voluntary* contributions of owners or shareholders finance the corporate political speech would be an appropriate means for overcoming the presumption that expenditures are market oriented or "commercial." And unless the presumption is appropriately overcome, the government should be permitted to attribute the speech to the dictates of the market and, on that basis, should have authority to regulate or prohibit the commercial political speech.[121]

Both the importance and the difficulty of determining whether the source of an activity is the household or the enterprise, the sphere of personal choice or of business necessity, is embedded in our law. Tax laws, for example, allow deductions for business expenses but not for personal expenses or consumption. Difficult line-drawing problems occur precisely when the separation of the household and the enterprise is unclear or incomplete. For example, controversy over deductions for the office in the home or for "business" entertainment is notorious.

Existing statutory provisions reflect a long tradition of belief that the political activities of corporations can and should be regulated. Corporations achieved dominance over the political process in the late nineteenth century, particularly after the Pendleton Act of 1883 restricted the assessment of "contributions" from federal civil servants. In response, reformers between 1900 and 1920 successfully got Congress to pass the Tillman Act of 1907 and over thirty states to enact legislation prohibiting most corporate political expenditures, especially corporate contributions to candidates.[122]

The two most common justifications for the reform legislation were that: (1) if corporate contributions reflected the political views of management, management would be improperly "impos[ing] their political views upon a constituency of divergent convictions,"[123] that is, they would be forcing the stockholders to subsidize their views; and (2) if intended (as seemed consistently to be the case) solely to promote corporate profits, the contributions would corrupt the political process. In support of the second point, writers repeatedly emphasized that these corporate contributions were "not determined by political sentiments, principles, or party loyalty."[124] Passage of these laws represented people's attempts to exercise some control over their destiny, and the object of the laws was to create a political process that would reflect people's values and better enable people to exercise such control.[125] These justifications for regulation, of course, are precisely the values emphasized by the liberty theory of the first amendment.

Other statutory provisions likewise implicitly assume that corporate political speech is subject to regulation. These provisions rely on legally created devices to draw the difficult enterprise/household distinction. As noted above, business expenses are mostly tax deductible. Deductions for a business' grassroots lobbying for legislation or for any type of corporate support of political candidates are, however, disallowed even though this "political speech" may be as profit oriented as any other activity of the corporation.[126] Denying these deductions places a differentially greater burden on one specific component of the enterprise's various profit-directed activities—its political speech.[127] Specially burdening constitutionally protected speech would, of course, be unconstitutional.[128] This otherwise anomalous result makes sense only if our tax laws embody the assumption that the first amendment does not protect the discriminatorily burdened commercial political speech.

Statutory provisions also permit corporate-related political speech if the speech can properly be attributed to individual allegiances. Disallowing a tax deduction for corporate grassroots lobbying takes the money from (after-tax) profits. The effect is to charge the owners for the speech, thereby permitting the speech but only by first attributing the speech to the owners rather than to the business. Likewise, the legal structure of PACs (political action committees) permits corporate funds to be used for political contributions but (except for the corporation's statutory right to pay certain organizational costs of the PACs) only if the corporation's owners or employees first receive the money as income and then "voluntarily" return the money to a political fund.[129] This technique prohibits political speech by the enterprise *qua* enterprise—surely an impermissible effect if commercial "political" speech receives first amendment protection. But by allowing political speech that is properly attributed to individual's non-market-determined "personal" judgments, these laws implicitly recognize that limits on this individually chosen speech would be improper.[130]

In contrast to this legislative tradition, judicial holdings reflect confusion as to whether to follow the marketplace of ideas theory or the liberty theory. Relying entirely on the language and logic of the marketplace of ideas theory of the first amendment, a sharply divided Court in *First Nation Bank v. Bellotti*[131] struck down a regulation of corporate political speech. Justices White, Brennan, and Marshall's dissent emphasized the liberty theory. It noted that the corporate speech, which opposed a ballot measure relating to graduated income taxes, "do[es] not represent a manifestation of individual freedom or choice" and "does not further the self-expression of self-fulfillment of its shareholders the way that expenditures from them as individuals would."[132] Likewise, Justice Rehnquist's dissent echoed a theme of the early supporters of bans on corporate political contributions: that corporations are artificial entities that have no claim to constitutionally protected liberty.[133]

After the much criticized decision in *Bellotti*,[134] the Court four years later in *Federal Election Commission v. National Right to Work Committee*[135] reached the opposite conclusion. It ignored marketplace of ideas considerations in an opinion upholding a severe limitation on a corporate entities' opportunities to solicit funds for political speech. Although solicitation of contributions is protected expressive activity when done by individuals or nonprofit organizations,[136] the Court found the law justified by two purposes: to ensure "aggregations of wealth amassed by the special advantages which go with the corporate form . . . should not be converted to political 'war chests'" and "to protect the individuals who have paid money into a corporation from having that money used to support political candidates to whom they may by opposed."[137] Despite claiming consistency with *Bellotti*,[138] this unanimous decision clearly adopted the reasoning of the *Bellotti* dissents.

Thus, the continuing vitality of *Bellotti* and the general question of governmental power to regulate corporate political speech remain in doubt.[139] However, the real possibility of corporate control of the political process leaves no doubt about the importance of the issues. Legislative attempts to regulate corporate political expenditures have never been more than marginally effective but they apparently have slowed the flow of money from corporations to politicians and, thereby, reduced corporate influence somewhat. But after *Bellotti*, and even before in states without bans on corporate participation in electoral referendums, publicly admitted expenditures on referendums have been significant. Corporations have often enormously outspent other interests, frequently with telling results.[140] For example, in a 1979 public power referendum in Westchester County, New York, the Consolidated Edison Company of New York contributed $1,200,000 to defeat the proposal. This was almost 80 times the $16,000 spent by a citizens' group that provided the only organized support for the measure. Consolidated Edison's campaign overcame the measure's reported two-to-one initial public support, defeating the measure with 55 percent of the vote on election day.[141]

Also clear is the differing resolution of the issue under the marketplace of ideas and the liberty theories. An earlier advocate of legal control of corporate electoral influence observed that "[i]t is quite possible that people have no desire to be 'free' but they ought to be given at least an even chance for freedom if they wish it."[142] The analysis here agrees, arguing that human self-determination must include the power to legislate restrictions on the expression of the commercial enterprise.

CONCLUSION

Before leaving the issue of corporate speech, it is important to note that the argument here does not imply that all speech related to "economic" activities is unprotected. The commercial speech category is based on the historically relative, and necessarily incomplete, separation of the enterprise from the household or budgetary unit. Alternatively, the category can be based on the state's power to regulate the use of property to gain instrumental power over others and its power to regulate the speech that is an integral part of this use of property. Neither argument applies to some important activities related to the economic world, where speech can and often does address or manifest the values or visions of the speakers. Labor activities and organizations represent a clear example. Even demands for higher wages do not quite fit the profit-oriented model. The conditions of employment clearly involve substantive, although often self-interested, values of the worker. In a sense, labor's demands merge the household and the enterprise. Their demands are not mere attempts to exercise instrumental power. Often their requested and offered performances would establish substantively valued or disvalued aspects of an on-going association. Although the market may dictate employer's responses, labor's demands can be determined less by the market than by its own value decisions. Thus, despite the superficial symmetry of regulation of corporate and union speech,[143] both the political and the nonovertly political speech of workers and their unions should receive first amendment protection.[144] Only the enterprise speech rooted in the profit-oriented requirements of the market or in instrumental attempts to use property to exercise power over others fails in principle to exhibit individually chosen allegiance to personal values and, therefore, should be subject to regulation.

Like its relevance for showing the nonsymmetrical relation of corporate and union speech, this chapter's analysis has other implications that need further development. At present, the necessity of squaring first amendment doctrine with appropriate legal regulation of business warps the resulting first amendment theory. For example, Chapters 7 and 8 criticized the limited scope traditionally given to the first amendment freedom of assembly and the derivative freedom of association. (An association, it was suggested, is best seen as a form of assembly dispersed over time and space.) Often, assembly and association receive only instrumental protection as means of fully exercising the right to free speech. They are protected to enhance the distribution of speech in the market-place of ideas. However, the characteristics of assembly and association are intrinsically different from those of speech. Speech clarifies, explains, or per-suades. In assemblies and associations, humans join together to generate power. Typically, they associate to act or accomplish some aim by exercising their com-bined power. This activity of associating, as opposed to other acts that either individuals or groups can commit, should be protected as a basic aspect of lib-erty. But an important branch of law fails to recognize this point. People do little more than associate when they conspire. A conspiracy is essentially an associa-tion and is feared because of the power association brings.[145]* Of course, the law can prohibit criminal acts and criminal attempts. However, given that the underlying activity has already been criminalized, the conspiracy makes the mere fact of association an added crime.

One impediment to development of an associational right to "conspire" is a widely recognized need to regulate and even criminalize certain commercial agreements and joint activities. Unless these commercial associations are treated differently from other associations, any extension of the right of freedom of assembly and association to cover conspiracies should be resisted. Individual liberty is not advanced by granting these commercial associations the right to generate unregulated power. The governmental should have authority to protect politically adopted visions of proper market behavior.. The extension of first amendment rights to commercial associations would, for example, undermine the foundations of antitrust law. But a constitutionally persuasive distinction between commercial or profit-oriented associations and other associations would make this extension of the notion of freedom of association more plausible.

The constitutional propriety, not the merits, of state regulation of commer-cial speech has been the subject of this chapter. It claims to justify and clarify the instinctual notion that commercial speech is properly subject to regulation. The argument has been that, given existing economic structures, commercial speech is not a manifestation of the liberty of the speaker. Market determination breaks the connection between commercial speech and individual choice. More generally, when an owner uses property purely instrumentally to exercise power over others, that usage and the related commercial speech should be subject to legislative control. This is key to the difference between constitutionally unpro-tected property claims and constitutionally protected expression or liberty rights.

---

*An overt act is required, but this act can be perfectly legal. If the act comes close to being the crime, the actor and accomplices can be charged with an attempt.

10

Press Rights

Chapter 9 argued that competitive markets dictate the speech of commercial enterprises. For this reason, and more generally because the government should be permitted to regulate people's use of property to control other people's choices, Chapter 9 concluded that the speech of commercial enterprises is not a manifestation of individual liberty and should be subject to regulation. But these arguments may prove too much. Authors and journalists write, at least in part, for profit. Newspapers, magazines, publishing houses, the broadcasting industry, and the movie industry normally operate as profit-making businesses. These important sources of news, information, and first amendment protected entertainment are largely composed of profit-oriented enterprises. Yet any theoretical analysis that would deny first amendment protection to the press surely must be rejected. Certainly one fixed point in our constitutional thinking is that the first amendment protects the commercial press.[1] Thus, the problem of this chapter is set: Given the last chapter's critique of commercial speech, what justifies protection for and what is the nature of constitutional protection of the commercial press?

This chapter develops an instrumentalist argument for an interpretation of the press clause that is independent of the speech clause, an argument that recognizes special rights for the press and for occupants of press roles. I specifically examine and defend the "fourth estate" theory of the press, a theory recently made popular in legal circles by Justice Potter Stewart, who recalls Thomas Carlyle's report: "Burke said there were Three Estates in Parliament; but, in the Reporters' Gallery yonder, there sat a Fourth Estate more important far than they all."[2] Finally, of the various special rights often asserted on the press's behalf, I conclude that the fourth estate theory justifies only "defensive" constitutional rights, which despite their instrumentalist foundation should generally take an absolute form.

PRELIMINARY OBSERVATIONS

The last chapter's analysis is surprisingly insightful when applied to the press. It resonates both with popular critical evaluations of the press and, even more interestingly, with proposals to regulate the press sometimes supported even by first amendment theorists.

Other than the perennial accusation of ideological bias, possibly the primary charge leveled against the mass media is that their desire for profits dictates both the substantive content and artistic form of their expression. Sex and violence sell. Too often the communications industry neither supplies the public with quality material nor communicates what the writers, reporters, editors, producers, or station managers would want to tell us or show us if they had artistic and journalistic freedom. Instead, the bottom line dictates production of only the most marketable content reduced to the lowest common denominator of the target market. The conventional wisdom is that broadcasters are concerned with virtually nothing but the "ratings"—with what will sell.* Good writers lower their standards in order to write "popularly" and sell. Formula fiction writers admit that their writing is a hack job, the typewriter merely replacing the assembly line. The stock market measures the movie industry's success. Even if newspapers seldom make specific content decisions to mollify advertisers, a more general decision to increase sensationalism may be adopted to expand circulation.[4] Cheap, prepackaged filler replaces more expensive, local news reporting in increasingly chain-owned papers. In essence, the charge is that the communications media fail to carry out their function in a free society because of an overriding concern for profits.[5] This profit orientation undermines the informational and visionary roles of the press and prevents media content from reflecting real editorial choice and, thereby, from being a manifestation of freedom.

Profit concerns can have devastating consequences. Pressures to increase circulation have led to sensationalist stories supporting military actions. Similar pressures also contribute to the press' failure to report on drier, more complex domestic problems—such that "poverty" had to be discovered in the 1960s. Even when the media appears to be helping, profit concerns may result in catastrophic distortions. In the mid 1970s, a respected commentator observed that the need for sensational news caused even elite publications to misrepresent the nature of the world food crisis. And he argued that this misinformation creates such a misunderstanding that "informed" American opinion promoted ill-conceived governmental policies that exacerbated food shortage problems that could be successfully and humanely solved.[6] Careful consideration of the consequences of the press's market-induced pursuit of profit will not be pursued here. Such an investigation would show, however, that this pursuit directly contributes to inaction and wrong action, causing human misery of vast proportions.

This popular critique of the press duplicates the last chapter's analysis of commercial speech. Market pressures undermine the participants' freedom and leave the public with a largely market-determined product. Not surprisingly, the same conclusion reappears. Substantive freedom and human development require that people's decisions not be dictated by a structurally enforced pursuit of profit. This identity of the two critiques suggests that the analysis of commercial speech uncovered crucial variables.

---

*Or possibly even worse, or at least less democratically, the media want high "ratings" in the more profitable audiences—and, therefore, often ignore or discount the interests of the poor, the elderly, or other groups advertisers are less interested in.[3]

The critique of commercial speech also clarifies the logic of major proposals for reforming portions of the communications industry. The premise of reform is that separating decisions concerning speech content from the media's profit-oriented decisions could promote first amendment values. The most obvious way to accomplish this separation would be to regulate the media as "common carriers." As a common carrier, the broadcaster or publisher could not make decisions concerning content. Instead, the communications industry would be required to publish or broadcast submissions of private parties on a nondiscriminatory basis.[7] Or profit-induced private censorship could be reduced by other possible regulations such as the FCC's fairness doctrine, guaranteed media-access for political candidates, nondiscriminatory access for editorial advertising, or guaranteed free access to newspaper space under defined circumstances.[8] In each case, the reform is said to promote first amendment values as long as it expands the range of communications made available[9] and prohibits discrimination in access.[10] Only laws that restrict permissible communications, the reformers argue, would be constitutionally prohibited.

The intuitive plausibility of applying the common carrier argument appears to correlate with popular assessments of the independence of the media's expression from profit concerns. For example, newspapers are generally believed to be more intent on objective and relatively complete, even if opinionated, journalistic coverage while broadcasters are thought to be more concerned with packaging and "selling" entertainment to the public, which leads to the impoverishment of quality and a lack of diversity of content. Therefore, speech-promoting regulation of broadcasters is commonly accepted as more defensible than similar regulation of newspapers. Again, Chapter 9's analysis of market forces dictating speech content has identified the crucial concern that intuitively supports regulation.

Nevertheless, imposition of access requirements, much less a common carrier regime, on all commercial media surely should be unconstitutional. Thus, in *Miami Herald Publishing Co. v. Tornillo*,[11] the Court unanimously concluded that a right-to-reply statute abridged the first amendment rights of either the newspaper's editors or its owners. The question, then, is how the liberty theory justifies this result.

The liberty theory might justify protection if the press' speech choices, that is, its publications or broadcasts, are qualitatively freer from market dictates than is the speech of other commercial enterprises. Two structural features of the communications industry may produce that result. First is the manner in which and the extent to which profit concerns constrain message choices. The market forces both media and advertiser to supply products that the consumer wants or can be stimulated to want. But for the advertiser, this dictate requires those messages that best promote the advertiser's limited set of available products. In contrast, the media is free to present any message that some element of the public will purchase.[12] Precisely because the message is the media's product, the media retains considerable freedom in choosing message content. Thus, market constraints require the nuclear power industry or the casino to choose speech designed to lead the listener to one specific substantive conclusion, that nuclear energy is acceptable, maybe essential, or that gambling can be desirable.

In contrast, the news media's product is, in part, their judgment about appropriate content or vewpoint. Thus, a journal may be (equally?) able to editorialize for or against nuclear energy, for or against gambling.

Second, market constraints control the content of the media's speech less effectively if workers[13] or owners[14] are especially able to subsidize their speech choices by working for lower wages or accepting operating losses. Even if the cost of chosen communications is less than the monetary return, receipt of some revenue increases the opportunities for communications. As both preachers and politicians know, people are better able to continue their speech activities if they receive funds, payments for their product, that help pay for their speech activities. Characteristically, the evangelist or politician's message includes a request for monetary contributions to finance future speech activities. Similarly, a speaker or writer who can convince listeners or readers to purchase her speech has a method of financing her desire to communicate on a mass scale. Given the sizeable investments required for large-scale communications, market sales may provide the only viable way for any but the super-rich to communicate regularly to a large audience. An outsider will have no abstract criteria for determining whether the mass media's communications are the product of commercial demands or whether commercial activities merely support expressive values of those involved in industry. Thus, from the perspective of the liberty theory, the contribution of the commercial press to subsidizing people's individually chosen communications, as well as the difficulty in distinguishing that subsidizing function from the use of the commercial press to gain profits, suggests a rationale for protecting the press.

The above observations, however, do not clearly distinguish the press from other economic enterprises. In both, the person may substantively value her productive activities and the enterprise's market-oriented expression. Chapter 9 argued that a ban on commercial speech meant merely that the person could not attribute her speech to the economic enterprise, for example, for accounting or tax or compensation purposes. It argued that the person had no right to demand that commercial activities be unregulated in order to subsidize her expressive activities. Thus, the question remains, why should the commercial press be treated differently?

The difference could lie in the nature of their product. The press sells "expression" rather than cat food, beer, or piano tuning. The communications industry's product is unique. The industry produces, distributes, and sells products such as speech, print, or pictures. In contrast, other businesses do not sell "commercial speech" to the public. The advertisement is not the product that the enterprise markets; rather it is a meticulously concocted stimulant for the product sold. But, still, the obvious question is: Why does the production of this special product—speech (or print or pictures)—deserve special protection?[15]

A possible answer provided in the Constitution is that one specific industry, the press, has been singled out for constitutional protection. But, unfortunately, this is merely one interpretation of the press clause. For purposes of the first amendment, is "freedom of the press" granted to a certain type of institution or is it merely protection for people to write as well as speak? An answer depends on articulating and defending some theory of the press clause.

In sum, there are some reasons to think the argument of the last chapter should not apply to the press. Nevertheless, argument based on the claim that the market is less determinative of its speech is not particularly persuasive, as illustrated by the extent to which Chapter 9's market determination thesis has been central to the critique of the communications industry and to reform proposals. The emphasis on the unique product of the press returns us to looking for a theory that explains the constitutional relevance of its uniqueness.

RATIONALE FOR A SEPARATE INTERPRETATION OF THE PRESS CLAUSE

The problem of justifying protection of the commercial press under the liberty theory might be avoided if the press clause has an entirely different basis—if it is directed at protecting a particular institution rather than respecting individual autonomy.

Some commentators suggest that the religion clauses of the first amendment, which direct that "Congress shall make no law respecting an establishment of religion, or prohibiting the free exercise thereof," provide a helpful analogy.[16] Possibly, the prohibition on religious establishments bar the government from aiding religious *institutions* and endorsing membership in religious sects, while the free exercise guarantee may protect *individuals* engaged in practices required by conscience or religious belief. In the establishment clause, "religion" refers primarily to sects and institutions, while in the free exercise, "religion" refers to conscience.[17] In the first case, the concern is with the relations among institutions, possibly because of the effect these relations will have on people's membership in the political community[18] and, thus, on their liberty. In the second, the concern is directly with individual liberty. Analogously, freedom of speech, including written expression, protects fundamental individual liberties. Like the prohibition on religious establishments, freedom of the press is instrumentally justified and involves conclusions concerning the conditions under which the press can make appropriate contributions to society.

The analogy, however, is just that, an analogy. It does not explain why the press should receive special constitutional protection. Since the analogy does not address the purposes of the press clause, it leaves unexplained both the content of press freedom and the form of the required relation between the press and the government.

The language of the Constitution may provide clues. It specifies that the press receive protection from the government. The mandate is poorly designed to promote the public's interest in receiving high quality or large quantities of information, for these marketplace goals might best be promoted by various governmental interventions—including regulations that promote access.[19] Rather, the more obvious role of the guarantee is to protect a *nongovernmentally regulated* source of information, argument, and entertainment. But the question remains: Why should or why does the constitution protect the press as a source of nongovernmentally regulated communications?

Although not explicitly using a different analysis for the press clause, Justice

Brennan has explained the jurisprudential basis on which any differential constitutional protection for freedom of speech and freedom of the press[20] should rest. While arguing in dissent for a qualified press privilege to resist disclosure of "predecisional communications among editors,"[21] Brennan began by describing the grounds for absolute protection of freedom of speech, using language resonating with the liberty theory of the first amendment:

> Freedom of speech is itself an end because the human community is in large measure defined through speech; freedom of speech is therefore intrinsic to individual dignity. This is particularly so in a democracy like our own, in which *the autonomy of each individual is accorded equal and incommensurate respect.*[22]

But Brennan noted that the press did not and could not properly rest its arguments for an editorial privilege on the value of individual self-expression. Thus, he then discussed how the first amendment also "foster[s] the values of democratic self-government"[23] and is thereby "instrumental to the attainment of social ends."[24] Citing Professor Blasi's influential article, "The Checking Value of the First Amendment,"[25] Brennan focused his instrumentalist discussion primarily on the Court's prior decisions and statements that involve or refer to the press. He emphasized the central, instrumental role the press serves in "censor[ing] the state or expos[ing] its abuses."[26] Brennan's distinction between respect for the autonomy of the individual and the instrumental advancement of social ends provides the foundation for separate constitutional interpretations of the speech and press clauses.

Freedom of speech, of course, is often seen as both an end and a means. But to accord *incommensurate respect* to freedom based on individual autonomy is to imply that protection of this freedom should prevail over policies based on normal instrumental or utilitarian concerns. Thus, this value of freedom of speech as an end renders its value as a means, even if extremely important, redundant for purposes of justifying constitutional protection. Likewise, the "incommensurate" value of the freedom means that the justification for protection is not diminished in contexts where the expression has no instrumental value. Even the arguably welfare-diminishing aspects of subversive, defamatory, profane, racist, or pornographic speech should not justify limitation.[27] In contrast, if the sole foundation for particular constitutional rights are instrumental concerns—for instance, those relating to an *institution's* contribution to our welfare or freedom—then the appropriate form and extent of protection may be different and less than absolute. In these cases, protection should be fashioned to further that institution's instrumental role. Thus, Brennan's foundation provides an instrumental justification for a fourth estate or "checking function" theory of the press under which the press might make claims different from, and independent of, those grounded on a claim for respect of autonomy under the speech clause.

Special provision for this fourth estate role of the press is a particularly logical use of constitutional power. Of course, the fourth estate arguments are instrumentalist claims about the best way to advance the collective social welfare and normally, in a democratic society, the legislature is assumed to be the most appropriate governmental body to make social welfare judgments. Nevertheless, sometimes that is not the case. A branch of government should not be expected to make sound welfare or utilitarian evaluations as to the advantages of outsiders investigating the abuses and opposing the judgments of that branch. Leaving judgments about the contributions of press freedom to the political branches allows the fox to watch the door. A more sensible alternative is to set up a structure that protects authority of the press to engage in activities helpful for exposing abuses from limitation by the potential abuser. A key function of any "constitutive" plan is to allocate powers and set procedures rather than to make particular, outcome-oriented decisions.[28] Some allocations are designed to promote efficiency. Others are required by fundamental value premises such as respect for individual autonomy. Others perform a third function. The constitutional "separation of powers" into executive, legislative, and judicial branches and the provision for interaction of these institutions under the doctrine of "checks and balances" involve this third rationale. They are designed to decrease the likelihood of abuse of concentrated power. This purpose suggests the plausibility of interpreting the press clause as an instrumentally justified provision that functions to check abuses of governmental power.

The fourth estate theory of the press clause follows suggestions of Justice Stewart[29] and builds on Professor Blasi's elaboration of the checking function.[30] The reliance on Blasi's influential article requires some comment. Justice Brennan's citation of Blasi's article occurred among quotations referring to freedom of the press, in a dissenting opinion in which Brennan considered a claim for a special editorial privilege. Blasi, however, treats the checking value not as a basis for interpreting freedom of the press, but as a general component of first amendment theory.[31] Nevertheless, Blasi's own historical and theoretical observations support a different conclusion—that the elaboration of the checking function should focus on the press clause.

Reliance on the instrumentalist checking value predictably leads to interpretations that give inadequate scope to speech rights.[32] As developed by Blasi, it leads to interpretations of the speech clause that offer less protection than existing doctrine in areas such as libel, political expression by government employees, and press reports on criminal trials. For example, unlike advocates of strong protection of free speech, Blasi approves laws like the Hatch Act to the extent that it prohibits government employees from politicking on behalf of incumbents.[33]

This weak protection of speech follows naturally from Blasi's consistent employment of a balancing analysis and his use of the checking value to interpret the speech clause. In contrast, stronger protection of speech could be justified if the checking function and its related balancing were restricted to the press context.[34]

Blasi notes that the "concept of human autonomy is largely irreducible."[35] This irreducibility, combined with Brennan's "incommensurate respect,"[36] explains why those who espouse the liberty theory usually claim that individuals have an absolute right to engage in expression that is an aspect of human autonomy. In contrast, as is appropriate for instrumentalist values, Blasi recognizes

that the activities serving the checking value and not expressing human autonomy can properly be "balanced against competing regulatory interests" and can
be promoted incrementally.[37] Nevertheless, if the autonomy value and the
checking value are coexisting bases of the first amendment, they could be
meshed by either of two approaches.

First, they could be combined within a balancing analysis. Blasi views the
checking value as narrower in scope and possibly more important in constitutional interpretation than most other first amendment values. Of course, when
the various speech values overlap, they reinforce the argument for protection.
But they can also conflict.[38] A plausible calculus gives greatest constitutional protection to the more important or the more specific, narrowly defined values.
Either way, Blasi's calculus provides greatest protection to speech relevant to the
checking function. The checking function even helps justify restrictions on
speech that an autonomy theory would protect. Thus, the checking function
itself justifies restricting the political speech of government employees,[39] while
defamatory speech that does not serve the checking function and reports on
criminals trials not involving public officials receives less protection than at
present.[40] Rather than provide absolute protection on the basis of the autonomy
value, Blasi consistently applies to all speech the instrumentalist approach of the
checking function. This approach naturally assumes that all law is a compromise
between interests. Blasi states simply that "the process of formulating legal standards is one of accommodating competing interests rather than deriving standards from constitutive premises."[41]

A second, more plausible response to the different nature of the autonomy
value and the checking value is to give each a separate role. Then, even if the
courts absolutely protect speech rights on autonomy grounds, the checking value
need not be redundant in all instances. The checking value could usefully give
content to the press clause. The liberty or autonomy theory of free speech may
not protect commercial enterprises, leaving the problem of justifying protection
for the commercial press' "speech." Moreover, the liberty theory's demand for
absolute rights has little coherence, much less rationale, when applied to protection of institutions. Our concept of a person and the related notion of personal
autonomy provide the guide to specifying the content of absolute rights that protect a person's expression of identity. No similar concept explains the content
or form of institutional rights. Institutions are human constructs valued not in
themselves but for how they serve other values. Although some institutions may
serve very basic functions, they are inherently in need of instrumental justification. Thus, both the formulation and protection of rights of institutions could
properly proceed incrementally on the basis of "accommodating competing
interests."

This second approach argues that the constitutional relevance of the checking function is in justifying and interpreting press rights. This interpretation
reflects: (1) the checking function's instrumentalist content and reach; (2) the
necessarily instrumental basis of rights of institutions, such as the institutional
press; (3) the preeminent place of the press in serving the checking function; and
(4) the irrelevance of instrumental arguments for justifying fundamental individual liberty rights. Of course, private speakers also serve the checking func-

tion. Still, in our society, the role of the press in exposing abuses of power is likely to be central; think of Watergate or the Pentagon Papers and many local exposes. Blasi makes this point when he notes that, given the complexity of modern government, the checking function needs "well-organized, well-financed, professional critics to serve as a counterforce to government."[42] Moreover, the speech clause should provide adequate protection for the individuals' role in checking abuse. In contrast, although media enterprises are usually more powerful than single individuals, their operations usually depend on the continued cooperation of many individuals both within and outside the institutional boundary. This complexity leaves the institutional press particularly vulnerable to governmental manipulation or pressure that can undermine its independence. Consequently, the press may need special types of protection.

The press clause interpretation of the checking function builds on Blasi's basic insights. Not surprising, given the press's special need for protection, Blasi argues for some special press rights.[43] Moreover, both before and contemporaneously with the adoption of the first amendment, the checking function was primarily invoked in statements and arguments that referred to the press or that used press activities as their central example. Blasi reports that Wilkes emphasized the checking function inherent in the "liberty of the press"; Father of Candor attacked the doctrine of seditious libel and viewed exposure of bad government as possibly the greatest benefit of "the liberty of the press"; Junius emphasized the checking value within the "liberty of the press"; and a letter from the First Continental Congress to Quebec emphasized the checking role as a justification for "freedom of the press."[44] Similarly, modern Supreme Court reliance on the checking function as a first amendment value occurs in cases involving the press.[45] For example, in a classic statement, the Court argued:

> The Constitution specifically selected the press . . . to play an important role in the discussion of public affairs. Thus the press serves and was designed to serve as a powerful antidote to any abuses of power by governmental officials and as a constitutionally chosen means for keeping officials elected by the people responsible to all the people whom they were selected to serve.[46]

In sum, Blasi's careful development of the checking function is best read not as a general first amendment interest to be balanced, but as the doctrinal foundation for the press clause and special press rights.[47] As Justice Brennan implicitly concluded, Blasi's discussion of the importance of the press adds detail to Justice Stewart's earlier call for special constitutional protection for the fourth estate.[48]

The fourth estate theory is distinct from the liberty theory. Like the marketplace of ideas theories, it is not directly based on promoting the liberty of the speaker. But it is also unlike marketplace theories, which are concerned with the adequacy of the speech's *content* to give listeners the information and argument they need in their search for truth or agreement. Rather, the focus of the fourth estate theory is a *source* that the government does not control. Its basis is more a distrust of power than a faith in truth or rationality.[49] The mandate of the press clause is to protect a limited institutional realm of private production and distribution of information, opinion, and vision, of fact and fancy. Ideally, this press can, if needed, provide the information and rationale, and stimulate the motivation, for challenging or resisting government.

The fourth estate theory justifies protection of the press, even given Chapter 9's argument that freedom of speech does not justify protection of profit-oriented enterprises. Specifically, even if commercial, the press serves a constitutionally protected, instrumental purpose. In this interpretation, the definition of the press should include all those enterprises or organizations whose primary product finally delivered to the consumer is speech or print or picture, whether sold or given to the public. This definition would not include the whiskey company that advertises whiskey, since whiskey, not speech, is the product the company wants to deliver to the consumer. Of course, the advertiser could also serve the checking function. In fact, any activity protected from governmental regulation provides some counterbalance to governmental power. But expanding the definition of the press to include commercial advertisements is not necessary to assure production of substantial amounts of nongovernmentally controlled information or opinion, or to provide a counterbalance for governmental dogma. Chapter 9 concluded that human freedom would be increased if commercial speech were subject to collective control. Given this conclusion, a more normal definition of the press, which does not include the advertiser, is a more desirable formulation that still assures the press room to perform its constitutional role.

DEFENSIVE, OFFENSIVE, AND SPEECH RIGHTS

So far, the discussion of the fourth estate does not indicate whether the media should have any special rights over and above the speech rights of individuals. Mere differences in the theoretical foundations for the freedoms of speech and of press do not necessarily mean that the rights of the press and individual speakers differ. Different foundations could be merely different routes to the same point. Certainly the "weaker," instrumentalist justification of press freedom does not obviously require "special" press rights. And if the press should have special rights, their content is subject to controversy. For example, Justice Stewart, the most prominent judicial proponent of the view that the press is special, rejected the claim of many press advocates that the press has a special constitutional right of access to prisons or various other government facilities.[50] Only further elaboration of the fourth-estate role of the press can lay a proper foundation for an instrumental analysis of the propriety and content of press rights.

Controversy over whether special rights for the press do or should exist is common. Although the Court protected the speech of both the media and the private, nonmedia defendants in *New York Times v. Sullivan*,[51] disagreement inexplicably persisted concerning whether the first amendment provides any immunity for defamatory statements made by individuals.[52] Some argued that the constitutional limitations on state defamation laws derive from the need to protect the press' attempt to assure the "bold and vigorous prosecution of the public's business"[53] and therefore do not protect nonmedia speakers.[54] The Court, however, recently embraced the opposite conclusion,[55] namely, that the Constitution equally protects the defamatory communications of all speakers.[56]

Commentators also disagree about the implications of *Miami Herald Publishing Co. v. Tornillo*,[57] in which the Supreme Court struck down a right-to-reply statute, and *CBS v. Democratic National Committee*,[58] in which the Court rejected political advertisers' claim of a right of access to the media. According to some commentators, these cases recognize the superiority of the press's claim over the competing speech claims of those denied access.[59] According to others, the cases merely follow the traditional analysis that protects the expression of private entities from government interference, and reaffirm that the first amendment has never provided a right to effective speech.[60] Finally, one commentator even argues that the press clause requires government neutrality toward the press and, therefore, prohibits the government from giving the press any special right of access to information.[61] This commentator argues that the press clause is not only consistent with, but possibly requires, the denial of a reporter's testimonial privilege.[62] In sum, judges and commentators who agree the press clause has a special role radically disagree about its content. A more focused inquiry is needed.

Claims that the press clause guarantees special privileges or protection for the press appear in many contexts. Although many claims are not presently accepted by the Court, among the possible claims are: (1) the press has some constitutional right of access to information or facilities controlled or maintained by the government, such as a right to interview prisoners[63] or to be present at all criminal proceedings;[64] (2) reporters have a special right to violate some laws, such as trespass laws, in order to gain information and report a story;[65] (3) the press has a special right to make defamatory statements; (4) the press has greater constitutional protection against gag orders and other prior restraints than do other speakers;[66] (5) reporters have a special right not to appear before or not to answer certain questions posed by a grand jury;[67] (6) in civil suits, the press is privileged not to respond to "inquir[ies] into the state of mind of those who edit, produce, or publish, and into the editorial process,"[68] (7) the press receives special protection against searches and seizures by government, at least when it is not suspected of criminal activity;[69] and (8) the press is immune from restriction by either various generally applicable or special press-related regulations, for example, regulations designed to further general economic and social policies,[70] or to promote fairness or diversity in press communications.[71]

Generally, these claims can be characterized as either defensive rights, offensive rights, or speech rights. Defensive rights protect the institution (or reporters and press corps) from destruction, interference, or appropriation by government. They include testimonial privileges, protection against searches and seizures, and most protections against regulations that are directed particularly against the press. Offensive rights enable the press to function more effectively by giving the press enterprise or the reporters special opportunities to obtain information or materials that exist outside the institutional boundaries of the press. These rights include special rights of access to information or a privilege to engage in activities that break an otherwise valid law. Speech rights protect the press in communicating what it chooses. They include protection against gag orders, prior restraints, and defamation suits.

Distinctions between defensive and offensive rights are obviously somewhat conventional. Refusal to cooperate (e.g., let others look at your files) is defensive; a demand for the cooperation of others (e.g., let you on their property) is offensive. But how do we know whose files, whose property it is? Each characterization necessarily rests on our culturally (and legally) based understanding of institutional boundaries. In a society in which government files were viewed, in a sense, as the property of the press (or of the public), the institutional boundaries of the press would encompass much more than they do in ours. In such a society, a government official denying journalistic access to the files would be interfering with the internal operations of the press. The press' assertion of a right to block this government interference would be defensive. In contrast, our culture's conventional understanding of institutional borders imparts the intuitive understanding that government files in no sense belong to the press. Hence, in our society, since access would require cooperation from the government, the press could have at most an offensive right to the files.

The following discussion will consider arguments for these three types of proposed press rights. Relying heavily on the justifications for institutional protection of the press—(1) the need to preserve an independent entity that can expose government practices and abuses and (2) the importance of nongovernmentally controlled sources of information, opinion, perspective, and speech-based entertainment—I will conclude that the rationale of the press clause is persuasive only for defensive rights and equal, not special, speech rights.

Defensive Rights

To operate as a check on government, the press must have some independence from it. Such independence implies effective defense against government intrusions. This defense against hostile, manipulative, retaliatory, or merely appropriative action by government is vital for protecting the press's capacity to perform its checking and informative functions. Even well-intended regulations designed to further the government's conception of a properly functioning, responsible press, such as public access or right-to-reply rules, may undermine press independence. They would restrict the way the press packaged and conceptualized its message, its potential exposé. Likewise, government practices that are designed to address public concerns and that affect media and nonmedia alike can weaken the press's institutional integrity.

Other considerations support protection of defensive press rights. Defensive rights fit neatly into a constitutional framework that distributes decision-making power among various entities and specifies and guards their boundaries. Defensive rights merely police the boundary between government and the press. Thus, they operate in the way that principles of federalism or separation of powers provide some autonomy for various centers of governmental decision making or that individual rights protect individual autonomy from certain forms of government intrusion. Moreover, the instrumental analysis appropriate for defining institutional rights can more often lead to usefully clear rules in respect to defensive than to offensive rights. This is a very important systemic feature. Clear rules give greater guidance in individual cases and help avoid continual, inept, ad-hoc judicial evaluations of each controversy.

Protection of defensive rights is supportable for yet another pragmatic reason. People assert defensive rights in contexts that simplify the troublesome problem of identifying "the press." Defensive rights, like refusing to testify or not allowing a search of a press office, will usually be claimed at a time when the claimant is identifiably engaged in activities as a "press." Here, the task of identifying the press becomes plausible.[72] Of course, definitional problems remain: Does the in-house publication qualify? Does the one-shot pamphleteer qualify? Is the informant as well as the informed reporter protected? These questions are, however, addressable by reasoned arguments. In contrast, a person's claim to be the press when that person asserts an offensive right will often require speculations concerning inchoate motivations and unknown future behavior. When an individual claims an offensive privilege, such as access to a prison, it is difficult for the state and sometimes difficult even for the person seeking access—perhaps a young Doris Lessing, Truman Capote, or Alexander Solzhenitsyn[73]—to know whether the visit will move that person to write or lecture about it in the future.

Offensive Rights

Offensive rights are more problematic constitutionally. Clearly, a right to violate otherwise valid criminal laws could greatly aid the press in its investigative efforts. Supreme Court dicta,[74] however, have consistently echoed the holding of *Dietmann v. Time*,[75] that the first amendment does not "accord newsman immunity for torts or crimes committed during the course of newsgathering. The First Amendment is not a license to trespass, to steal, or to intrude."[76] Although states sometimes construe their common law to allow some trespasses by the press,[77] it is difficult to imagine that the press clause gives any general constitutional right to trespass—or steal—to gather news. Even if the press is analogized to a fourth branch of government, governmental trespasses (i.e., searches and seizures) are not a matter of constitutional right but, instead, are constitutionally restricted and subject to further statutory restriction. However useful to the press it would be to violate these laws, its institutional integrity simply does not depend on this behavior.[78]

More plausible are access claims. Undoubtedly, press access to information held by the government could be useful to the public, could help check abuses, and could eventually lead to better government. The issues are, first, whether the extent of this access should result from political choice or from constitutional mandate; and, second, whether the press should have greater rights than the public at large.

Access to government facilities or to governmentally held information would further the press's capacity to inform and expose. Having access as a matter of right rather than privilege may also be important for protecting the press from being subtly manipulated by, or falling into a cozy cooperation with, those whom it claims to watch. Nevertheless, constitutionally based access rights are not necessary for protecting the press's integrity. Their absence does not itself give the government a tool with which to frustrate the internal workings of the press. Because offensive rights do not maintain institutional autonomy or boundaries, neither a separation-of-powers nor a fourth-estate theory requires them.

Moreover, a constitutionally based right of access to information is not crucial for effective functioning of the press. Even if the press were granted access to government files or facilities, it would probably continue also to rely on independent sources of information. Government officials engaged in dangerous abuses are too likely to attempt, often successfully, to render unproductive any access designed to disclose their abuse. They will shred the relevant documents or stonewall the embarrassing requests for information.[79] Moreover, today's press has at its disposal potentially powerful weapons to use when the government denies legitimate requests for access. The press can report rumors of unseemly practices or conditions while publicly speculating about the reasons why the government denied access, thereby forcing the government to provide either access or a convincing justification for its denial. A strong, competent, and independent press should be able to work within any information environment.

The fourth estate or institutional integrity rationale for constitutional protection of the press leads to no obvious standards with which to evaluate access claims. Almost no access advocate argues that all government information and practice should be public. The press even argues that its own secrecy is sometimes essential,[80] thereby implicitly conceding the utility and propriety of some institutional secrecy claims.[81] Given the legitimacy of some secrecy in government, a judicially created right of access is likely to require continual adjudication of access claims without the benefit of clear standards for evaluation. Judges would have to determine and weigh the public interest in access relative to the public interest in keeping the relevant information confidential. These decisions would require analysis of a myriad of complex issues concerning both the scope and terms of access—issues that lawmakers found required drafting and passage of the lengthy Freedom of Information Act and the Privacy Acts, which respectively take up six and eleven dense pages in the U.S. Code and are then subject to extensive implementing regulations and interpretations.[82] This analysis involves the type of factually based policy judgments that arguably are least appropriate for constitutional resolution.

The proponent of a constitutional right of access to information could persist by arguing that the courts would gradually develop rules or guidelines for evaluating secrecy claims. The decisions would not necessarily be ad hoc. The courts could develop principles to distinguish contexts in which access could be denied or must be mandated, to categorize justifications for denials, and to evaluate the procedures and restrictions on which the government could condition access. The courts could provide for at least a constitutional minimum of access, leaving more extensive opening of government to the other branches. Rather than condemning this process as an unprincipled form of judicial policymaking, the access proponent would emphasize that constitutional theory explains that it is appropriate to engage in balancing in determining press rights since press rights, unlike autonomy-based speech rights, are inherently incremental.

Most significant, the access proponent would also emphasize the general rationale for constitutional protection of the press. The self-interest or limited perspective of the political branches lead them to give the press insufficient opportunities to check abuse or maximize welfare. This point applies with particular force to informational access claims. Governments, like most enterprises, have a virtually automatic impulse toward socially undesirable degrees of secrecy. Courts could usefully operate as an outside, more dispassionate evaluator of the real needs for secrecy, providing a useful check on the worst abuses while predictably not forcing too much openness.

This last argument may be misplaced. Courts are unlikely to order legislative bodies (in contrast to executive bodies) to disclose information.[83] If most access demands actually are directed at executive agencies, legislatures, like courts, are outsiders that should be able rationally to evaluate secrecy claims. Congress and state legislatures have, in recent times, responded to demands for access with a plethora of acts fostering freedom of information, open meetings, and open records. The political process may in fact work better here than in many other areas.[84]

Although a democratic society cannot allow government to operate in secret, sufficient openness generally should ensue from the pressure of an independent press, the demands of a politically active people, the legislative responses of democratic bodies, and the responsible decisions of officials. And in those cases where it does not, I wonder if constitutional access rights will be a real solution. As an undergraduate in the 1960s, I heard Senator William Fullbright argue that Congress and the American people should not accept any argument for our activities in Vietnam unless the argument was based on publicly disclosed information—that democracy demanded no less. The one time I met Vice-President Hubert Humphrey he argued that people like me should not question our policies in Vietnam—that these policies were clearly justified but the justification was based on information only available to people like him; that if we knew what he knew, we would agree and also would not want him to disclose the information. I agree with Senator Fullbright, but the question is how to achieve the needed openness. No judicially crafted, constitutional right of access is likely to require disclosure of the information to which Vice-President Humphrey referred (even if it existed). Remember the Court's close split on whether even to lift the *judicially* imposed prior restraint on the Pentagon Papers and then guess whether courts on their own would have mandated that a resistive executive branch grant a desirous press access to the documents. Courts consistently allow abridgement of relatively clear and absolute constitutional provisions in the context of foreign affairs and national security. Combine this willingness with the initial observation that any right of access would necessarily be very qualified and the conclusion quickly follows that courts would not require disclosure of Humphrey's secret information. Access to the needed information inevitably will depend on effective public political pressure, legislative decisions, and investigative efforts.

The arguments for and against particular offensive rights seem inconclusive. Despite the practical difficulties of formulating the rights, a person could reasonably conclude that some offensive rights are constitutionally mandated. Nevertheless, three considerations identified above point the other way. First, the lack of clear principles to guide the inherently empirically based policy judgments needed to give scope to offensive rights suggest that judicial protection of institutional integrity is both the more traditional and the more essential type of decision making for a court purporting to rely on constitutional premises. Second, an insufficient degree of legislative recognition of access claims does not seem as likely, as frightening, or as dangerous as the possibility of governmental actions that attack the internal workings of the press or stop the press from publishing what it chooses. Third, the strongest argument for the constitutional status of defensive rights—that they are implicit in the idea of separation of powers or necessary for the structural integrity of the press—does not apply to offensive rights.

My tentative conclusion reflects one additional consideration. A claimed right of access to information closely resembles contentions that the first amendment guarantees a right to effective speech. Chapter 2 argued that courts should not and do not recognize a first amendment right to effective speech, although the state ought to promote more egalitarian speech opportunities as a matter of policy. The access claim, like the effective speech claim, would require judicial action to promote "interests" assumed to be implicit in the first amendment. But the phrase "Congress . . . shall make no law *abridging* the freedom . . ." (emphasis added) suggests an intent merely to protect an individual or institution from governmental restraint or punishment in exercising its freedom. The first amendment does not mandate that the government assist in that exercise. This reading of the first amendment finds individuals' claims for a right of effective speech and press' claims for a right of access to governmentally held information equally unpersuasive as first amendment premises.

Special Speech Rights

Claims that the press has greater rights than private individuals to communicate information or opinion are unjustifiable. Only the broadest protection of individual rights of expression is consistent with the constitutionally required respect for individual autonomy and the relation of speech to self-fulfillment and self-determination. Any justifiably protected expression should be protected when engaged in by an individual. Certainly, any speech that serves the checking function or informational and visionary roles of the press also serve these individual autonomy values when spoken by the individual. Thus, *greater* protection for the press' speech is unreasonable.

The initial question raised in this chapter was: Why does the first amendment offer any protection for the speech of the commercial press? The instrumentalist, fourth-estate argument satisfied that concern, but it could never justify more protection for the press' speech than the autonomy-based arguments justify for an individual's speech. Indeed, all the social functions served by press communications[85] are also served when individuals communicate.[86] Only because the press is particularly vulnerable as an institution does it require special defensive rights protecting its independence and structural integrity. There are no similar grounds for permitting the press to say things forbidden for individuals. Any other conclusion would be quite odd: imagine it being illegal to say to another what you had just read in a newspaper.[87]

Certainly, there is no reason to give the press special rights to be free of gag orders or prior restraints on its speech. Gag orders usually prohibit the press from printing certain information relating to criminal trials. The Court has established an almost absolute prohibition on these gag orders.[88] It is difficult to find considerations that justify allowing the press to print this information that do not apply equally to individuals' right to talk. Gag orders applied to the witnesses, defendants, and attorneys because of their involvement in a case raise discrete issues unrelated to this discussion.[89] Even if permissible, these restrictions on trial participants, assuming that they also apply to the press when it is a party,[90] would not imply that the Constitution distinguishes between the press and individual speakers.

Should the press receive special protection when it makes defamatory statements? The probability of large jury awards in defamation suits, added to the high cost of defending the suit, could destroy the press or have a serious deterrent effect on press activities.[91] When addressing constitutional limits on libel laws, the Court commented that "[w]hether or not a newspaper can survive a succession of such judgments, the pall of fear and timidity imposed upon those who would give voice to public criticism is an atmosphere in which the First Amendment freedoms cannot survive."[92] Justices Black and Douglas went even farther and argued that the "the Federal Constitution . . . dealt with this deadly danger to the press in the only way possible . . .—by granting the press an absolute immunity."[93] Still, why should we not also worry about private individuals who will have to pay such awards? Obviously, from the perspective of the liberty theory we should.

An argument for special treatment of the press may reflect an implicit instrumentalist calculation that fear of jury awards will deter useful speech of the press more than of individuals. Moreover, even if equally deterred, the deterrence of useful exposes by the press might be a greater loss to society. The instrumentalist arguments, however, could cut the other way.

First, the very attention to profit and legal risks that could cause the press to be more "deterred" should result in a higher degree of compliance with the details of the legal rules. Therefore, appropriate prohibitions on defamation should have greater effectiveness in stopping objectionable, truly defamatory speech when applied to the press. The costs of enforcement, in the sense of wrongfully deterred speech, may be less per gain in objectionable defamations prevented when the law applies to the press rather than to individuals. Second, the press' larger audience means that its defamations are likely to cause greater injury than similar defamations by individuals.

Third, the instrumentalist calculus should include the rule's initially symbolic injuries. Privileging the press' defamatory speech permits actions that the law otherwise establishes as an illegal harm to the defamed person. Assuming that the first amendment permits the state to recognize this property interest in reputation, the special press right grants the press a privileged right to appropriate it. This amounts to a forced transfer of wealth to the press from defamed individuals. Moreover, it appears to put the press above the law. The net result is that the press is made out to be the villain, allowed casually to injure or destroy individuals through defamation or invasion of privacy.[94] Meanwhile, individual dignity, asserted protected by defamation law, is sacrificed.

In contrast, defensive rights merely impose constitutional constraints on the interaction of the press and the government. The press' exercise of defensive rights does not seem so directly to injure people and can more easily be cast as a claim of principle rather than special privilege. Thus, they are much less likely to have serious symbolic costs or to create resentment against the press.

In summary, the application of libel rules to the press is likely to result in more defamation prevention and remedial compensation per given expenditure of enforcement resources than would their application to individuals, while recognition of special press rights are likely to have hidden costs—to the press and the public—beyond the defamation injuries themselves.[95] Thus, instrumentalist justification for *special* press rights to defame is doubtful.[96] Note, however, that these points do not show whether or not the press should be held liable. Defamation law must still consider whether the purposes of and care taken by the speaker, the falsity of the speech, and the identity of the person injured, effect whether the first amendment protects the speech. But these questions should receive the same answer whether the defendant is a private individual or the press.

THE FORM OF PROTECTION

I have argued that various social interests justify interpreting press freedom to include certain "defensive rights." The instrumentalist nature of the argument suggests the theoretical legitimacy of a "balancing of interests" analysis. Still, the propriety of balancing, not to mention the form that it would take, remains to be discussed.

Critiques of balancing and arguments favoring an absolutist, line-drawing approach vary.[97] Sometimes, the absolutist argues that the fundamental nature or constitutive basis of the claimed right means that general societal welfare interests should not count as sufficient reasons to override the constitutional claim. Therefore, the absolutist concludes, utilitarian or instrumentalist balancing is inappropriate. Justice Brennan, for example, arguably adopted this analysis when he claimed that the "autonomy of each individual is accorded equal and incommensurate respect."[98] This analysis, of course, cannot follow from the instrumentalist argument developed here for press rights.

Pragmatic critiques of balancing stress its consequences for effective operation of our system of legal rights.[99] In the first instance, the Constitution addresses most of its directives to legislative and executive officials. Conscientious officials can most easily follow directives that are clearly and precisely formulated. Clarity should increase the effectiveness of the directives and, possibly, their degree of acceptance. Since constitutional provisions are less clear if interpreted as a set of interests to be balanced in each case, a balancing approach undermines these desirable objectives.

There is yet another pragmatically undesirable feature of ad hoc balancing.

The weighing of interests is especially subjective. Even in normal situations, the ad hoc balancing will most readily protect claims congruent with the values of the judge's social class, since the judge is apt to be persuaded that these values or interests are most weighty. But in times of conflict or perceived crisis, the times when defensive rights are most important,[100] dominant factions of society often feel threatened. They frequently respond by limiting the rights of those who appear to be connected with or contributing to the threat or crisis. The judges, who usually associate with the same dominant community, predictably conclude that these restrictions advance weighty interests. Consequently, their balancing is likely to lead to accordion-like protection: When the need for protection is small, the "constitutional interests" may be favored; but in times of turmoil when the need for first amendment protection is urgent, the "governmental interests" will seem greater—and protection collapses.

These pragmatic considerations suggest that because of systemic features of the legal order, ad hoc balancing will not provide effective protection. If the need is for "rules" whose application is less subjective, possibly the instrumentalist evaluations should only take place in the formulation of the rules, not the decisions of individual cases. Thus, these pragmatic considerations suggest a "metabalancing" that aims at instrumentally justified absolute rules.

As a possible result of metabalancing, consider the following two-part formulation: First, the government must not have a purpose either to lessen the capacity of the press to perform its special constitutional functions or to retaliate against the press for its performance of these functions. Second, the government has no right to appropriate the items, thoughts, or information that flow from the press's performance of its constitutionally protected role. This protection extends to press personnel as investigators and reporters of crime but, of course, does not cover their participation in crime or their taking evidence of the crime except for evidence, like photographs, that press personnel create themselves.

The first principle seems obvious—the government must not try to destroy or undermine the operations of the press. This principle derives from standard constitutional doctrine applicable to many doctrinal contexts. For example, even if the government can act in a way that has the *effect* of limiting speech opportunities or disproportionately burdening a racial minority, it cannot permissibly have this effect as its *purpose*. When the Court split on whether reporters should have a privilege not to divulge confidential sources to grand juries, all the Justices agreed that a prosecutor's use of the subpoena to harass or undermine the press would be unconstitutional.[101] Likewise, if President Nixon had proceeded with his plans to order licensing trouble for the *Washington Post*'s broadcast stations in retaliation for the *Post*'s exposes, he would clearly have violated the press clause.[102]

The second principle, which protects the legitimate work product of the press from government appropriation, embodies the concept of institutional autonomy. This protection does not give the press any special affirmative privilege to act or obtain information or resources. It merely prohibits government from requisitioning products that would not exist except for the proper activities of the press.

This principle would require a testimonial privilege that is similar in nature and rationale to other recognized testimonial privileges. When secrecy is important for the successful fulfillment of their social roles,[103] common law, statutory, or constitutional privileges often protect the confidential communications of lawyers, doctors, psychiatrists, and priests. In each case the scope of the privilege relates to the beneficial performance of the role. The protection of privilege extends to information or communications that often would not be generated and that the privileged party would not possess but for the confidentiality essential to that person's performance of a certain socially useful, socially sanctioned role. Denying the privilege would discourage socially important communications and, to that extent, would not even serve law enforcement concerns. Moreover, although the legitimate scope of these roles, and hence the privilege, do not extend to the professional's involvement in crime,[104] the privilege can be absolute within its relevant range.

All these general statements concerning privilege apply to the press' work product. The instrumental justification for protecting the work product follows from the belief that maintaining the integrity of the press promotes a better society and makes our liberty more secure. Depending on empirical factors, granting the privilege to the press might even better satisfy government's need to receive information about wrongdoing. The privilege should assist the press in gaining knowledge of wrongdoing. If the press then publishes the expose, the law enforcement agencies could benefit.[105]

If exceptions to the press' work product privilege are appropriate, as they are for other testimonial privileges, they cannot be identified by simple analogies to these other exceptions. Any exception must relate, in part, to the exception's effect on the particular social function served by privileging the communication. Since these functions differ, the propriety of each exception must be separately determined. For example, arguably the press' privilege, like many testimonial privileges, should not cover information about future crimes. But the analogy to other privileges is misleading. Most testimonial privileges relate to the need to promote a counseling relationship between the role holder, the priest or lawyer or psychiatrist, and a "client." Arguably, protecting communications concerning future crimes does not fit within the scope or further the rationale behind this counseling. Even if it did, the importance of stopping the crime may outweigh the importance of promoting this aspect of the counseling relationship.[106] Privileges for most professions, thus, do not protect communication about future crime.

A testimonial privilege for the press is premised on the need to promote an investigative role that provides information to the public, not the need to promote counseling about certain topics. This informative function blurs the importance of any distinction between communications about past, present, and future crimes. To the extent that the privilege helps the press obtain and then make available information about criminal activity, including government misconduct, the social gain from extending the privilege to information concerning future crime is arguably worth any possible weakening of law enforcement effectiveness.[107]

Of course, having a privilege does not imply that it will or should be used. A privilege to print the names of crime victims or announce the timing of a secret military action does not imply that a newspaper or broadcaster will routinely ignore the victim's privacy or the country's international security. Likewise, a legal privilege not to divulge confidential communications and sources, even when a future crime is involved, does not eliminate an ethical obligation to help stop evil practices. The newspaper may sometimes properly choose to betray its confidences. And not only ethics but economics could support this result. The newspaper could lose economically valuable goodwill if it gets a reputation in the community for abusing the privilege and failing to live up to common ethical standards.

Although suggestive, these comments are inadequate to demonstrate that the press' work product privilege should cover information about future crime. Rather, my claim is: (1) that the issue should be framed as an instrumental judgment reflecting how we ought to define the press role, and hence the boundary between press rights and government authority; and (2) that the answer will not necessarily duplicate privileges accorded other roles. Nevertheless, these comments do support an absolute version of the second principle, restated in the context of a testimonial privilege. Unless a member of the press appears to have engaged in criminal conduct—which may give her a fifth amendment privilege—she should not be required to answer questions about her investigations or her sources.

This proposal goes beyond the *qualified* testimonial privilege that the lawyers for the press advocated in *Branzburg v. Hayes* and that Justice Stewart accepted in his dissent.[108] Stewart did not even address arguments for an absolute, rather than a qualified, privilege, possibly because he took the relevant analogy to be demands made by legislative investigations for information concerning private associations protected by the first amendment.[109] This analogy is misleading. A testimonial privilege for the press rests on very different premises than the Court's grudgingly recognized limitations on legislative demands for information about voluntary associations' membership. The constitutional basis for these limits on legislative investigations is obscure. Although a complete analysis will not be attempted here, two lines of reasoning seem promising, and both avoid the ad hoc balancing typically attributed to these cases.

A first approach seems consistent with the case results.[110] It asks whether a plausible explanation of the legislative questioning is that it aids legislative policymaking. Alternatively, it asks, given the actual social context, the method of investigation, and the relation of the inquiry to proper government purposes actually being pursued, whether the only plausible explanation is that the legislature is punishing or intentionally hindering first amendment activities.[111] Although the first amendment does not guarantee either the association's effective speech or its secrecy, the first amendment does outlaw government action undertaken for the purpose of penalizing or stopping speech.[112]

An alternative approach goes beyond this analysis of purpose. It relies on the well-accepted doctrine that the government cannot impose burdens based on the exercise of constitutional rights.[113] By requiring a person to testify concerning the exercise of her constitutional rights, the state imposes a burden that exists only because of the exercise. This imposition is an impermissible penalty.[114] Granted, the capacity to demand disclosure is useful to the government. Nevertheless, perhaps something is wrong with government or the way it allocates costs when citizens will not voluntarily provide it with needed information. But even if we accept this unwillingness as a fact about modern life, still the government could be prohibited from requiring a person to report about her constitutionally protected activities when the substance of the report, not just the inconvenience of reporting, operates to make the exercise of the right more "costly."

In any event, protection from this legislative questioning is not analogous to a press testimonial privilege. First, the generally weak protection properly reflects the fact the legislative questioning and exposures do not directly abridge the autonomy-based speech or association rights. Even under the limelight, people can still choose to speak and associate. Thus, the absolutely protected autonomy rights are arguably not at stake. This situation contrasts dramatically with the context of the press claim of a testimonial privilege. The speech and press rights have different foundations—with the press' foundation in instrumentalist considerations being weaker. More relevantly, however, the compelled testimony has a different relation to each right. Compelled testimony can directly breach only the fourth estate's "institutional integrity." This is the reason why the analogy to compelled testimony concerning the membership of associations fails. The instrumentalist fourth estate rationale, on which Stewart properly premised his argument for a testimonial privilege,[115] is directly at stake when the press' institutional boarders are being breached. The integrity of the institution is being violated and its work product appropriated. Thus, this rationale should offer the press more protection than freedom of speech offers an individual when the individual's speech is not prohibited but is only being burdened.

This same fourth estate rationale also justifies protection of the press against some searches and seizures.[116] The issue breaks into two parts. First, what materials possessed by the press should potentially be available to the government? Second, what methods of obtaining this information does the Constitution permit?

The premise behind the testimonial privilege is that governmental authority to appropriate the legitimate product of the press' investigative efforts would improperly undermine the integrity and independence of the press. This premise should equally imply that the government should not search or enforce a subpoena for the press' work product. Unless the press has taken possession of material evidence in addition to the press' own pictures, notes, or recordings, it would possess nothing that the government has a right to obtain.

But sometimes the press may possess or be suspected of possessing evidence other than evidence that it has created. This changes the situation. The press' protected activities do not include taking possession of the evidence of a crime. To do so would actively interfere with law enforcement activities, and would be an "offensive right" that neither the citizen nor the press should have. Thus, the government should be permitted to wrest these materials from the press' possession. The question is, "how?"

A subpoena is always a proper means for the government to use when attempting to obtain material it has a right to see. But the danger that the press, faced with a subpoena, will destroy or deny the existence of evidence, is said to create a reasonable basis for the government to want to use an alternative procedure—a search of the press.

The press properly objects. Execution of a search warrant could seriously disrupt press operations. Moreover, the government may use this disruptive means as a legal shortcut to the subpoena route, thereby improperly externalizing the costs of its investigation onto the press. However, the gravest danger to a press intent on exposing government wrongdoing is that the governmental wrongdoer or her agents or supporters will ransack press files, destroying or taking important notes or documents and obtaining information that the wrongdoer could use in thwarting an exposé. These governmental searches can seriously threaten the checking function of the press.

Still, a complete prohibition on searches of press facilities seems unwarranted. If the government were a lawless monolith, no legal rule could provide the needed security. If it were uniformly law abiding, abuse would not be a worry. But it is neither. In this in-between situation, appropriately designed legal rules can reduce the danger of abusive press searches. These rules should limit warrant availability to discrete situations in which the danger of press abuse makes the government's need to search great, and in which a specific burden of proof imposed on the warrant-seeking officials reduces the risk of sham searches.

Tentatively, two responses to this context, two interpretations of the press clause, seem plausible. First, the press clause could bar searches unless the government presents a magistrate with strong grounds to believe that the press would destroy the evidence if subpoenaed. Alternatively, the bar could apply except when there are reasonable grounds to suspect that the press has gone beyond its information gathering and transmitting functions and has itself become involved in a crime.

The second response seems preferable. First, although a general assumption of lawfulness might properly be attributed to both the government and the press, searches should be allowed when abuse by government is least likely and abuse by the press is most likely. For the government, abuse is least likely when it can demonstrate, rather than merely assert, clearly proper grounds for its action. For the press, abuse is most likely when it has strongly self-interested reasons to prevent the government from obtaining evidence of a crime and when it has exhibited a disinclination to follow the law. Neither criterion is met by the government's mere assertion of the ever-present possibility that a generally law-abiding press (even if it illegally removed evidence in aid of its investigative and communicative activities) will destroy the evidence rather than turn it over if subpoenaed. Both, however, are met when the government can demonstrate adequate reasons to believe that the press itself, or people at the press who maintain control over the potential evidence, are involved in a criminal enterprise. Second, an inquiry focused on reasons to suspect past press involvement in crime may be more factual and less subjective than an attempt to predict its future actions. This greater factual content means that the second approach will be somewhat less likely to exhibit the accordion-like quality of contracting whenever times are tense and the authorities distrust the entity claiming the right. Thus, this interpretation would greatly limit the government's opportunity to obtain a warrant, while allowing it to obtain one when the reasons to trust the press to preserve and present the evidence are weakest.

A final speculative example can dramatize possible implications of the institutional integrity, fourth estate interpretation of the press clause. In an affidavit to the World Court, Edgar Chamorro, a former leader of the "contras" (a U.S. backed, arguably CIA-created, insurgency group that has been attempting to overthrow the government of Nicaragua), stated that he and others, under the direction of the CIA, used CIA funds to bribe nearly two dozen Honduran and Costa Rican journalists to report favorably about the "contras."[117]

An initial question is whether the government violates the first amendment by its activities involving foreigners outside U.S. territory.[118] Putting that issue aside, would governmental bribery of reporters to print slanted news violate the Constitution if it occurred in the United States? If the first amendment does not protect the press as an institution but only the right to speak or write as one chooses, this bribery might be constitutionally no different from the government's paying papers to print its propagandistic advertising. The overt result of the bribery, misinformation, differs little from the distortions that the government creates by its rather frequent, even if discreditable practice of issuing false or misleading press releases. Attempts by the government to influence the news, or even itself to publish its version of the news, are presumably constitutionally acceptable practices.[119] As in these permissible practices, bribery does not prohibit anyone's speech—and no one is forced to speech against her will. Finding a constitutional violation is difficult using an individual rights perspective.

From the perspective of a "fourth estate" interpretation, a different conclusion follows. The argument is the same as that for other "defensive rights." Secretly corrupting reporters and alienating their allegiance to their professional responsibilities and to their papers compromises the structural integrity of the entire institution. An independent press can doubt or believe, investigate or accept, the government's inaccurate press releases and its attempts at influence. As an autonomous body, the press is responsible for its own response. In contrast, the bribery directly subverts press independence. It goes beyond "influence" and breaches the institutional boundaries of the press, poisoning the constitutionally protected watchdog. For this reason, the practice should be unconstitutional.

Before concluding this chapter, a few comments about the general approach seem in order. Rather than describing existing law, I tried first to determine if there are persuasive arguments for recognizing the press as a constitutionally protected institution. There are. I then tried to determine what kinds of rights these arguments justified. Claims of special press rights can be classified as defensive rights (testimonial privileges, protection from search and seizures), offensive rights (rights to violate trespass laws, special access to information), and special speech rights. Only the arguments for defensive rights seemed convincing, although the arguments for offensive rights have considerable force, and the fourth estate argument justifies speech rights equivalent to those of private individuals.

Rather than guessing what content of these rights would garner majority support on the Court, the discussion considered what content is most defensible. Different conclusions and different balances are possible. For example, if legitimate government interests in obtaining information possessed by the media often seem quite weighty, it might be appropriate and, hopefully, not too counterproductive to allow appropriation of the press's work product in situations where predictable interferences with press operations are not too serious. Sources could still receive some protection and searches could still be limited. Case-by-case balancing or somewhat more structural resolutions, such as those suggested by Justice Stewart's dissents in *Zurcher v. Stanford Daily*[120] and *Branzburg*,[121] are possible. Nevertheless, the most persuasive elaboration of the rationale behind the press clause points to complete protection from forced government appropriation of the press's legitimate work product. Except when there is adequate reason to suspect press involvement in crime, this implies protection against searches of press offices and files as well as an absolute testimonial privilege.

11

Private Economic Threats to Press Freedom

Advertisers veto program content. Even after printing, publishers stop distribution of books that would offend allied elites. Profit concerns dominate media corporations. Networks and local broadcasters revamp broadcast news to reduce costs and maximize audience at the expense of information gathering and transmittal. Nonmedia-based corporations (companies not primarily engaged in journalism, e.g., railroads or tire companies) own large portions of the communications industry. Conglomerates increasingly monopolize media outlets. Owners of the remaining large, independent media outlets often share similar political and economic views.[1]

These are the facts and the trends. From the perspective of some conceptions of freedom, these economic forces and industrial structures threaten press freedom to an equal or greater extent than government does.[2] Rather than document these problems or analyze the merits of possible governmental or private responses, this chapter adopts a narrow focus and considers only the first amendment implications of possible responses.

FREEDOM FOR WHOM?

The special constitutional status of the press as an industry may suggest negative answers to two overlapping questions: First, does the press clause permit and, second, does it require, a government response to this private economic threat to freedom? The quick answer, allied with the fourth estate concept of the press, is that the private press should be powerful. Any governmental regulation contradicts the rationale for the industry's special constitutional status: maintenance of institutional autonomy to allow performance of the checking function and to provide a nongovernmentally controlled flow of information and opinion. This answer, I think, comes too quickly.

The only question traditionally assumed to be relevant for interpreting the first amendment's command that "Congress shall make no law . . . abridging the freedom . . . of the press" is: "freedom *from* what?" The obvious answer is, "freedom from the government." Nevertheless, a possible equally important question, forcefully raised in 1967 by Jerome Barron, is: "freedom of the press *for whom?*"[3] Three possibilities come immediately to mind: the public; the owners; the press professionals—that is, reporters, journalists, writers, editors and other people who make up a media enterprise. Leaving aside for now the explanation of why this second question is constitutionally relevant, I want to consider the claims that each group can make that the freedom ought to be theirs.

Freedom for the Public

The meaning of "freedom for the public" is unclear. The instrumentalist argument for special constitutional protection for the press emphasized that the press's rights are designed to benefit the public, to serve the public's interest in nongovernmentally regulated information and in checking abuses of power. The mere fact that an institution or practice is "for the public," however, does not necessarily mean that individual members of the public do or should have any legal right to obtain specific goods or opportunities from the institution. For example, without necessarily creating any enforceable rights in the public, the public's interest in liberty provides a primary justification for the constitutional separation of powers in government, the doctrine to which the "fourth estate" label is analogized. Likewise, presumably it is the public interest that justifies the policy of keeping military secrets.[4] Thus, the public's interest may provide the ultimate justification for press rights, but this fact would not imply that the public must have a legal right to have their views "presented" by the press or even a right to receive specific information from the press. The public might be best served by leaving editing to the editors.[5]

Alternatively, "freedom for the public" might mean the right of anyone to become a press professional or, if financially able, to own and operate a press outlet. This interpretation, though, merges with the second or third: freedom for the owners or for the press professionals.

Advocates most often claim that "freedom for the public" justifies public access rights. Thus, in upholding the governmentally created right of people who had been criticized on a broadcast to have access to the broadcasting facilities in order to make a reply, the Court said that "it is the right of the public . . . which is crucial."[6] The Court relied for its holding on the "paramount" "right of the viewers and listeners"[7] even though, I expect, those viewers and listeners are often not interested in these replies and would prefer material chosen by the "editors," that is, the programers.

Individuals desire access to the media for various noncommercial (as well as commercial) reasons: to respond to attacks on their reputation,[8] to exhibit their creative talents, to disseminate information, to maintain or further particular cultural, artistic, political, or moral perspectives, and to get elected. The public might gain from the increase in the diversity of presentations resulting from public access to the media. Alternatively, a multitude of tongues often produces babble. If less material resources and less professional talent are devoted to these broadcasts or if the views presented appeal to only a small subset of the population (i.e., if the presentations are really diverse), the audience for those media time slots or media outlets devoted to public access is likely to be exceedingly small, resulting in no significant change in what the public receives. Television's purported influence does not follow merely from being on the air but rather reflects the huge audience for its programming. If access programming does not attract viewers, increased "public forum" or "access" broadcasting, on some or all channels, would not equalize or diversify this influence.

Thus, whether and on what terms the public, or a particular segment of it, wants greater diversity than the media as a whole already provides, whether the programming should be offered, wanted or not, and whether the public would view it if offered, remain debated issues.[9] Whether access rights would benefit the public as a whole, as opposed to the inevitably few members of the public who exercised access rights, is doubtful.

In contrast, protection of press professionals from both the market and the government might be more beneficial to the public. For example, although public broadcasting[10] gathers only a limited audience, in comparison with public access programming, public broadcasting has well-developed, well-financed programs and schedules.[11] Market pressures presently induce commercial stations to broadcast profitable but sometimes economically inefficient,[12] lowest-common-denominator programming. Public broadcasting could partially cure this significant "market failure" in provision of television service. Certainly, if noncommercial media are to have any significant impact, a version of this form of organization is likely to be more appealing and more beneficial for most communities than would be a public forum or "Hyde Park" form of broadcast—although, particularly on cable, there may be room for both.[13]

The "freedom for the public" analysis has other faults. Public access conflicts with Chapter 10's instrumentalist, public-interest-based arguments for special press rights. These special press rights were intended to protect the institutional integrity of the private press and thereby assure the press' control of its own output.[14] Public access rights breach this institutional integrity.

Of course, the argument for access rights may rest on premises other than the notion that the freedom of the press is "for the public." Demands for access may be understood as assertions of individuals' right to effective speech. The "marketplace of ideas" fails adequately to perform its social functions in part because of the concentrated ownership of the media and the limited access available to disfavored or impoverished groups. Advocates of the market-failure theories discussed in Chapter 2 conclude that these social realities require state intervention in the speech arena, just as in the economic arena.[15]

The Supreme Court has rejected the market-failure interpretation of the speech clause.[16] Even if the Court were to recognize a right of effective speech as an aspect of free speech or equal protection, this right should create a claim against the government, not against private entities in the communications industry.[17] Government would have to provide people with at least some minimal level of opportunities to print or broadcast[18]—but this would not justify any restrictions placed on private presses.

In summary, although "freedom for the public" sounds good, it has little clear content. The public may benefit most by protecting some narrower group's freedom—for example, the freedom of the owners or the press professionals. The most common claim made under this rubric is that private parties ought to be able to gain access to media outlets. As a general principle, this public access policy may run counter to the public's interests. Even if a more narrowly tailored, statutory public access right is desirable, arguably this public benefit could and should result only from means that do not abridge the appropriate sphere of press autonomy. For example, 'the government could provide for public access to governmentally owned media outlets.

Freedom for the Press Professionals

Reporters, editors, writers, and other press personnel sometimes claim the protection of the press clause. Their ranks can provide diversity; their investigations and their judgment can expose abuses and provide for public needs. These professionals plausibly argue that the public interest justifying freedom of the press requires their protection. Moreover, as long as the question "freedom for whom?" is the sole focus, the worker's claim of freedom presumably would be directed at both the government and the owners of the press, either of which might want to censor content, prevent particular exposes, or punish attempted exercises of freedom.

A number of things follow if the press is identified with the press personnel so that freedom of the press means their freedom. First, legal rules protecting their freedom against abridgement by the press owners would be necessary for adequate legal protection of freedom of the press. Analogies exist. In part because of a belief that the protection contributes to an overall freer society, we have developed institutional and legal forms to maintain academic freedom in government-owned universities, to help protect employees from censorship by the owners in government-subsidized public broadcasting, and to protect student editors in student-managed school papers. These institutional arrangements could provide parallels for protecting the freedom of press personnel from abridgement by either private or government owners.[19] Second, if freedom of the press means freedom for the press professionals, it would raise all the legal issues implicit in the problem of maintaining worker freedom in either a capitalist or socialist state. A solution would suggest that freedom of the press is consistent with socialism. The absence of a solution would suggest that freedom of the press will be absent in both capitalist and socialist systems.

Interpreting freedom of the press as freedom of the press personnel is intuitively plausible. I suspect that most people—people not legally trained and thus not so concerned with emphasizing the first amendment's literal restraint only of "Congress"—understand freedom of the press to mean, at least in part, the protection of journalists and editors to say what they think, report what they see, and have some discretion in determining what needs investigation. This popular conception of freedom is violated when a multi-industry conglomerate orders its newspapers not to report on certain matters of important public interest. Certainly, many people think that freedom of the press is violated if a corporate owner fires a reporter or editor because that owner is embarrassed by the reporter's expose or editor's endorsement. Likewise, advertisers undermine freedom when they use their economic power to pressure stations or papers not to report important news stories or not to present certain perspectives.[20] The failure of popular magazines to report the known dangers of smoking while the magazines received significant revenue from cigarette advertisers hardly represents a triumph of press freedom.

A well-trained lawyer could quickly point out that the public's concept of freedom of the press is naive, that many members of the public also find violation of freedom of speech when an employer fires an employee because of her publicly expressed views. This public, the lawyer might say, merely fails to read the constitutional language, which specifically restrains "Congress" (or, as the more priestly lawyer explains, restrains "government").

Of course, often lawyerly responses are appropriate—but not always. Sometimes the public may be more perceptive about Constitutional values. For example, even if lawyers merely find no state action in each case, many nonlawyers can see a greater abridgement of freedom or denial of equality when a conglomerate fires an editor in order to suppress her speech or a business refuses to hire an employee because she is black then when an individual chooses her friends among persons holding particular political views or belonging to a particular race. This public might be ahead of the Court in intuiting that the rationale for finding "state action" and enforcing constitutional constraints often applies to the decisions of economic enterprises.[21] Likewise, arguably freedom of the press should connote protection of press personnel from censorship by government and, sometimes, by owners.

Protection of press personnel may best promote diversity and be most central to the press's obviously vital fourth-estate role—checking abuse by government. Press workers ferret out information and make analyses that help check government abuses. They create alternative visions that can help redirect, energize, or maintain society. To perform these tasks with distinction is often the personal and professional goal of members of this diverse group. Protecting these press personnel from censorship by owners when their stories and exposes are contrary to the owners' perceived interest could promote fourth-estate values.

Distinguished performance of these tasks is a less forceful incentive for many press owners. Often, the economic interests of the media's corporate owners, which include many nonmedia conglomerates, are so aligned with the government or with nonpress, commercial interests that they are served by censorship or suppression of particular stories. Moreover, even if owners do not represent a monolithic perspective, there is probably greater diversity in backgrounds, values, and perspectives among press professionals than among owners. The goal of informative presentations of diverse viewpoints is probably better served by protecting professional journalists from censorship by either government or private owners than by merely protecting owners from censorship by government.

Finally, there is another merit in protecting the freedom of those whose creative and productive efforts in their daily lives involve press activities. Although not particularly relevant to the instrumental considerations that should control the interpretation of the press clause, this protection may promote individual liberty by contributing to their self-actualization.[22]

Interestingly, this arguably novel claim that the press clause primarily protects the press personnel is not inconsistent with the case law. Most disputes in which courts consider special press rights concern activities of, and claims of rights for, press personnel.[23] Reporters claim the right not to disclose their sources or not to be searched. Authors, to the same extent as owners, are protected against libel actions. Editors, as much as owners, object to laws that attempt to mandate public access, thereby interfering with the job of editors. Although the disputes involve objections to government, not owners, this litigation most directly provides protection for those people whose work makes up the press. Moreover, this orientation is consistent with the decisions upholding government power to regulate the ownership structure of the press, an issue I will discuss later.

Freedom for Owners

The first amendment recognizes more than a person's right to decide what to communicate. In *Buckley v. Valeo*,[24] the Court emphasized that freedom of speech must include a person's right to use her wealth (if any) to communicate her political views.[25] This freedom, however, derives from the concept of individual autonomy inherent in the speech clause. Thus, it provides no direct argument for interpreting the press clause as protecting owners.

Chapter 10 argued that protection of the commercial press properly rested on an institutional rather than an autonomy-based interpretation of the press clause. That argument, however, did not consider who the "press" is. If the press clause is based on a broad conception of public interest, the apparent need is to identify the institutional form that best serves the press's checking and informational functions. The instrumentalist, fourth-estate interpretation of the press clause leaves "the owners" as an unlikely answer to the question: "Freedom of the press for whom?" Rather, the group most deserving of press clause protection may be the press professionals.

This determination, however, is certainly debatable and probably is contextually variable. Moreover, pragmatic arguments that militate against reading the press clause to protect the press personnel might suggest reading it to protect the owners. If the press personnel's claims were to prevail constitutionally, the courts would have to develop detailed rules precisely defining the powers and rights of the employees that could not be abridged by the owners, a task not well suited for principled constitutional analysis. In addition, the consequences of such holdings for the press as an institution are unclear. They might lead, for example, to withdrawal of capital and collapse of the industry, to decreased efficiency, higher costs, and lessened output, or to some other result directly contrary to the social interests supposedly justifying the holding.

These problems suggest an alternative interpretation: The press clause protects the decision-making freedom of whatever institution the society or the government recognizes as the press. The press clause, however, should leave the government considerable discretion in structuring the institution and its internal authority relationships.[26] Thus, the government should determine whether the press clause protects the owners or the press personnel when their claims conflict.

FREEDOM FROM WHAT

Even if press professionals were the immediate recipients of special constitutional protection for the press (and the people were the ultimate beneficiaries), the question "freedom for whom?" might make little difference for two reasons. First, if the first amendment restrains only the government (which is the traditional answer to: "freedom from what?"), freedom for these purposes would mean freedom from the government. Only those interests of press workers that are consistent with those of owners, such as the reporter's privilege of confidentiality of sources, turn out to be relevant. No matter how ruthlessly private owners exercise censorship powers, *they* could not abridge press freedom.*

Second, no matter what the theoretical content of "press freedom," initially it seems that owners' speech rights must prevail over any claims by press personnel for freedom from owner censorship. Private owners would argue that the legitimacy of the legal order depends on absolute protection for their autonomy-based speech rights. Therefore, their speech rights must be superior to merely instrumentally justified press rights.

Nevertheless, neither argument is conclusive. Crucial premises on which they are based do not withstand analysis.

State Action

The lawyer's argument that only the state, not the owners, can violate press workers' constitutional rights falters once state action is seen everywhere. State action is overt wherever power is based on property, contract, or tort rights that the state maintains and could change. For example, state action exists in the state court's recognition of a traditional defamation tort, which constitutes a property interest in a person's own reputation. This was sufficient state action for the Court in *New York Times Co. v. Sullivan*[27] to hold that the state's formulation of this tort violated the speaker's first amendment rights. Here, the first amendment compelled an assignment of private rights contrary to the assignment chosen by the state.

In disputes between press professionals and their employers, owners depend on state-recognized property rights in the same way that plaintiffs did in their tort action in *New York Times v. Sullivan*. In settling these disputes, the courts must determine whether the Constitution mandates recognition of either the employees' or the owners' claims, or whether the Constitution permits the government to formulate these property rules as it chooses. The traditional question and answer, "freedom from what?—the government," does not resolve this issue. Both sides want to be free from government rules that uphold the other side's claim. A resolution depends on the conception of the "press" whose freedom the government may not abridge. If the "press" is the owners, the Consti-

---

*Of course, the radical claim would be that owners only exercise power because government recognizes their property claims and, therefore, owner's censorship involves the government in abridgement of the employees' freedom.

tution may bar a state attempt to protect the freedom of press personnel. If the "press" is the press personnel, the Constitution may mandate assignment of property rights or establishment of legal rules that protect their freedom within the press enterprise.

Or there is a third possibility. The state may have some discretionary power to identify the press or define property rights and arrange decision-making authority therein. That is, if the "press" is an institution, and if the government has some power to formulate the legal rules that structure the institution, the state could decide whether to protect an owner's authority or protect the press personnel from censorship by the owner. The constitutional constraint, the press clause, would only forbid governmental control or censorship of the press-related decisions of whatever press institution the government recognizes, and forbid the government from choosing institutional structures designed to undermine the integrity of the press or its capacity to perform its constitutional functions.

Freedom of Speech Versus Freedom of the Press

To read the press clause as requiring or permitting protection of press personnel may create a conflict with the owner's speech rights. If so, since interpretations that lead to conflicts between constitutional provisions should generally be avoided, the obvious response is to reject this interpretation. Alternatively, given the conflict, the fundamental autonomy-based speech right should prevail over the merely instrumentally based press right.

A conflict is not inevitable. Certain interpretations of the scope of the speech right avoid the conflict. For example, suppose wealthy individuals—possibly the press owners or certain advertisers—have a speech right to use their wealth to communicate as they wish and to obtain the assistance of other individuals or institutions. Still, this right does not necessarily include a corollary right to use their wealth to suppress communication by others. Even if owners can affirmatively choose to print their own messages, their freedom does not necessarily include a right to suppress the press personnel's communications by conditioning employment on following the owners' mandates for editorial deletions.[28] Owners do not have a first amendment speech right, any more than they have a fifth amendment property right, to exercise complete control over the institution. Of course, the owners' lack of a constitutional right must not mean that the government gets to exercise control of the institution—the press clause rules that out. Rather, the owners' lack of right leaves the press employees as an alternative.

This interpretation of the press clause has three components. First, it protects the press as an institution by prohibiting various overt government interferences with press operations; thus, it provides for the defensive rights discussed in Chapter 10. Second, this interpretation does not mandate any particular delineation of property rights. Third, although it does not mandate, it does suggest the propriety and desirability of legislative rules that promote editorial and journalistic freedom and diversity, as long as these rules do not prevent persons from using wealth to say what they want.

GOVERNMENT INTERVENTION TO SUPPORT FREEDOM OF THE PRESS

Various legal regimes could counter the censorship and loss of freedom that can result from private ownership, ownership concentration, and competitive market forces. Without engaging in the needed policy analyses to determine the merits of various types of legal arrangements, this section will discuss the constitutionality of some obvious possibilities.

Government Ownership

Government ownership, either of all or some mass media outlets, is a conceivable form of industry organization.[29] The government could organize these publicly owned presses as government mouthpieces, as independent editorial entities insulated from government censorship, as public forums with rules guaranteeing nondiscriminatory public access, or as some combination of these forms. The constitutionality of this regime depends on its specific content.

First, government ownership combined with a total prohibition of private ownership, particularly, of the print media, violates the first amendment even if the government presses operate as public forums or provide guaranteed public access. No legitimate purpose explains the gratuitous prohibition on private ownership. Any affirmative government purpose would not require this prohibition.[30] Its most overt purpose, to suppress privately controlled means of expression, unnecessarily restricts the autonomy of the press. In addition, prohibiting persons from using their resources to purchase and operate presses directly abridges their freedom of speech.[31]

Some government ownership of presses, however, is constitutionally unproblematic. At present, the government can and does own presses and freely chooses how it will operate them. Some are operated as the government's own mouthpieces while others have independent editorial boards insulated from government content regulation. Different versions of government ownership or government financing could promote various aspects of freedom. For example, existing government support of public broadcasting as well as its support for the arts and humanities is intended, in part, to counterbalance some of the market's economic "distortions" of private media and promote the freedom of artistic and journalistic workers. Likewise, the government printing office sometimes increases the public availability of useful information.

Theorists have raised two general challenges to governmentally owned presses. First, the massive government involvement in the speech arena might itself be offensive—the government's involvement can distort the results of free debate. Second, some liberal theorists argue for ideological neutrality of government—that is, the government should not choose to favor one form of the good life over another.[32] Government speech inevitably violates this required neutrality.[33] However, neither problem amounts to a constitutional objection from the perspective of the liberty theory of the first amendment. Government expression does not stop people from speaking or choosing as they wish. Moreover, people's right of self-determination requires the opportunity to have government promote collectively chosen policies and values. Thus, at least from the perspective of the liberty theory, governmental speech is sometimes called for and certainly not inherently objectionable.[34]

An additional practical problem is that governmentally subsidized communication media could compete with and economically destroy the private press. Nevertheless, government action undertaken for legitimate purposes, even if it undermines the economic viability of private presses, does not necessarily violate either freedom of speech or freedom of the press. Certainly, this conclusion follows if people have no right to effective speech, only a right to use any resources they have for speech purposes. Like government-induced changes in advertising practices, labor costs, or costs of newsprint, the competition of government-subsidized media could dramatically affect the economics of the newspaper industry without violating freedom of the press or freedom of speech.[35]

Protection of the institutional integrity of the press does not mean that the government must preserve particular, favorable economic conditions or particular market rules. As long as the purpose of the subsidized government presses was not to drive the private press out of existence, the private press' claim that they be guaranteed economic viability or that governmental presses are impermissible would amount to a claim to obtain benefits from the government. This would resemble the constitutionally unpersuasive arguments for offensive rights more than for the defensive rights defended in Chapter 10. Here, the press' objection is not to the government "appropriation" of the press' legitimately obtained work product or to a breach of its institutional borders. No plausible first amendment theory shows that a particular social and industrial organization is mandated by the Constitution. The only important caveat to this conclusion is that if either economic conditions or government monopoly of necessary resources prevent the viable operation of private presses,[36] the government may be obliged to provide for nondiscriminatory public access to governmentally owned outlets.[37]

Governmentally Mandated Access, Coverage, or Balance

In *Miami Herald Publishing Co. v. Tornillo*,[38] the Court unanimously struck down legislation that required newspapers to print replies by political candidates it had attacked. This access legislation arguably responded to the monopolistic qualities and related distortions of the private media. Nevertheless, whether the press is identified with the owners or the press personnel, access legislation interferes with the integrity of the press' editorial decision making.

Despite this conclusion of *Tornillo*, the Court in *Red Lion Broadcasting Co. v. FCC*[39] unanimously upheld an almost identical access requirement, a right to reply to a personal attack if made on the broadcast media. Without accepting the reasoning or result in *Red Lion*, I will argue here that the first amendment permits some forms of content-oriented structural regulations, at least as applied to some media. I will develop this claim through a critical examination of the FCC's constantly controversial Fairness Doctrine.

The Fairness Doctrine, upheld by the Supreme Court in *Red Lion* but currently repudiated by the FCC,[40] has two parts. It requires broadcasters to adequately cover public issues—its *coverage* provision; and it requires that coverage of controversial issues adequately reflect the opposing views—its *balance* provision. Each component raises different issues.

Although possibly the major practical problem with the Fairness Doctrine is its manipulability and general ineffectiveness when applied, theoretically and sometimes in practice the "balance" requirement is a ideologically loaded, potentially highly restrictive, content regulation. To require balance on a controversial issue prevents any crusading "press" from pushing its views. For example, the network prevented Robert MacNeil, then an NBC correspondent, from presenting his factually based conclusions concerning the need for gun control in an hour-long documentary, "Guns of August," when NBC lawyers invoked the Fairness Doctrine's balance requirement.[41]

The ideology of the balance requirement is the mainstream view that truth or wisdom lies somewhere in the middle, that both (all?) sides have something worth saying.[42] (But don't be fooled, the FCC is hardly the heir of Aristotle.) Extremism in defense of liberty is not allowed by the FCC. For example, the FCC found that NBC's award-winning documentary "Pensions: The Broken Promise" violated the balance requirement. Fortunately, in a tortured opinion that shows most clearly the vacuousness of the Doctrine's inevitably subjective standards, the Court of Appeals reversed on the ground that pension reform was not a controversial issue.[43] Balance may often be good. But it is not the philosophy of a first amendment that protects liberty and dissent. And sometimes it is misguided. Sometimes, some positions are just wrong.

The ideological thrust of fairness reinforces other pressures on the media to adopt middle-of-the road positions and moderate presentations on potentially divisive issues. Dominant practices of mainstream journalism already strive for balance.[44] Likewise, commercial pressures generally push broadcasters toward either noncontroversial programing or balance in order to avoid offending potential purchasers.

As almost inevitably applied, the centrist ideology of fairness may be even more pronounced than it is in theory. Fairness only requires balance for programs that raise controversial issues. Usually this requirement will impose little burden on the broadcaster. And it applies only if governmental enforcers find the issue presented to be controversial. Predictably, views paralleling those held by people in power will usually not seem controversial, at least to those people, and, thus, presentation of those views need not be countered with alternatives. Dissent, however, will seem controversial, so it must be balanced by the presentation of the established view. Thus, after the government adopted the view that cigarette smoking is dangerous, cigarette ads were deemed controversial.[45] In contrast, during the Vietnam war, ads for the military draft were found not to be controversial.[46] Thus, I was wrong. Extremism in defense of liberty is acceptable—but only if the FCC finds the extremism uncontroversial.

Doctrinally, the balance requirement is inconsistent with standard anti-censorship premises of the first amendment. First, it imposes burdens, arguably penalties, on broadcasters on the basis of the government's characterization of their expression. Second, this content control directly prohibits deviation from a particular ideological perspective—an FCC enforced, middle-of-the-road moderation. Moreover, in practice, the balance requirement predictably stimulates caution. It reinforces market pressures and journalistic pressures toward centrist programing that does not threaten rich or powerful social interests. Rather than guaranteeing access for real dissent, it assures that any station wishing to air nonconsensus views must mute that presentation.

The constitutionality of the fairness doctrine's other requirement, coverage, is a different story. The coverage requirement mandates that broadcasters devote time to controversial issues of public importance. This theoretically forces the allocation of a portion of a station's broadcast time to a certain type of use. (Theoretically, because the coverage requirement has virtually never been enforced[47] and may be too vague to have any more than symbolic relevance.) The coverage mandate does not burden or punish broadcasters because of the viewpoints they present. In a sense, the rule segments the broadcast time, allowing for broadcasters' unimpeded control of the largest portion but making another portion available for governmentally determined uses, with an independent private party, the broadcaster, accepting editorial control and responsibility to supervise this second use. Presumably, this type of division of a media outlet would be impermissible if applied to newspapers. Thus, the issue becomes whether broadcasting can properly be treated differently.

Government regulation of the air waves is often said to have originally been required because of scarcity and chaos, although chaos both then and now was the key factor.[48] As the Court noted, "[b]efore 1927 the allocation was left entirely to the private sector, and the result was chaos. . . . Without government control, the medium would be of little use because of the cacophony of competing voices, none of which could be clearly and predictably heard."[49]

The government could have intervened by auctioning off the broadcast frequencies (and thereafter treating the frequencies as private property).* It could, and did allocate some frequencies to particular uses such as publicly owned educational channels or noncommercial public broadcasting; and, presumably could have made some of these channels available only for children's programming or current affairs programming. Alternatively, as some of the original commercial developers of radio expected, the government could have made broadcasting into a common carrier type of industry, much like it treats the telephone.[50] As with the telephone, the owners of the medium would have no right to censor private parties. Rather the owners would be required to make their communication facilities available on a nondiscriminatory basis. In fact, given the likelihood that cable operations will amount to a near natural monopoly in a given geographical area, or at least as much of a monopoly as its main potential competitor, the local telephone, cable should be treated as a common carrier type of public utility in respect to at least a portion of the channel capacity. If the government had likewise chosen this common carrier model when it created and allocated rights to use broadcast frequencies, then the *owner-carrier* would not have first amendment rights any greater than other users. Both would

---

*References are to spectrum space allocated for uses that are directed to the general public audience. The government's power to structure the medium is illustrated by its practice of allocating large portions of the spectrum to military, navigational, police, and other, often content-defined functions.

have only a right of nondiscriminatory access to the governmentally created forum.

This common carrier structure for broadcasting would not have then and, possibly, does not now raise any constitutional problem. In contrast, any attempt to turn the print media, or newspapers, into this form of common carrier would surely be unconstitutional. The difference, I think, lies less in abstract logic than in history or context.[51] Given the historical development of journalistic practices, newspapers and magazines exhibit a unity and organization that common carrier requirements could destroy. Given this reality, any attempt now to impose such a requirement on the print media should be seen as an attempt to destroy the integrity of an important element of our communication order. A similar analysis does not apply to the less shaped, presently contextually different, broadcast media.

Congress rejected a full-fledged common carrier option for broadcasting.[52] Still, the two extremes of common carriers and private "presses,"or the possibility of independent entities performing special functions, are not the only possibilities. A plausible structure would combine these three alternatives. The government could allocate one portion of time for broadcaster control and another portion for other uses, such as for common carrier uses or mandated coverage designed to provide at least minimum amounts of programming within categories, such as public affairs or children-oriented programming, that the government concludes might otherwise be inadequately supplied. As the Court argued, "nothing in the First Amendment . . . prevents the Government from requiring a licensee to share his frequency with other and to conduct himself as a proxy or fiduciary with obligations to present those views . . . which would otherwise . . . be barred from the airwaves."[53]

In fact, this mixed structure roughly describes what Congress, though the FCC, has created with doctrines like the coverage requirement. The government has asserted *some* but not comprehensive power to allocate a portion of broadcast time to uses other than those that the broadcaster might choose in its role as a private press. Still, if access or coverage and not censorship justifies the allocation of time, the broadcasters' responsibilities should not turn either on the content of its broadcast choices during its "own" time period or on the viewpoint of the broadcast during the specially allocated time period.

Thus, structural allocations of time, such as the Fairness Doctrine's coverage requirement, should not abridge the first amendment. Without here reviewing the policy considerations behind various possible structural regulations, I suggest that some of these type of regulations have substantial merit—but not because of scarcity of broadcaster stations but more because of the industry's economic structure.[54] Hopefully, the belated recognition of the constitutional flaws in the Fairness Doctrine's balance requirement will not lead to the conclusion that broadcasters must be treated just like the print media.

Protection of Employees

Is legislation that protects the journalistic freedom of press professionals against either censorship or retaliation by press owners consistent with the first amendment? The last section argued that the press clause leaves open whether the press should be identified with the press professionals or with the prerogatives of the owner. Moreover, since institutions are necessarily legally structured by property, contract, labor, and corporate law, the state's choice of laws inevitably will affect who controls what within these institutions.[55] In this circumstance, the press clause should only constrain this institutional structuring by outlawing rules designed to undermine the independence and integrity of the institutional press. In addition, the speech clause prohibits violations of peoples's speech rights. Various types of rules survive both constraints.

First, Congress could protect all employees from employer retaliation for their nonjob-related speech[56]—a principle already embodied to a limited extent in existing law.[57] For example, fully implemented, this principle could have protected Daniel Schorr, who leaked a Congressional committee report to the *Village Voice,* from retaliation by his employer, CBS.[58] Second, more dramatically, the government could develop rules or mandate practices that protect the press professionals' expressive activities within the media enterprise.

Various methods of achieving this result are possible. Legislation could limit the reasons for which an employer could fire a press professional. Or require lengthy severance pay if the employee were fired or quit under certain circumstances. Or require that owners give editors-in-chief a guarantee of editorial freedom for some specific, lengthy period. Alternatively, the government could enhance employee expression by regulating the structure of the enterprise. It could require that elected councils or worker committees have specific decision-making power, that is, to nominate the candidates from which the editor-in-chief is chosen, to veto the dismissal of the editor-in-chief, or to have similar roles in respect to all employees. Legislation could also empower these committees to participate in the operations and policy decisions of the enterprise.

Such contractual or structural rules could promote a socially desirable degree of freedom for press professionals. In contrast, the parties could not be expected themselves to bargain for an optimal degree of protection for the press personnel's decision-making rights, as some economists might wrongly suggest. The premise of the fourth estate or institutional integrity theory is that society, not merely the owner and employee, gains from the optimal institutional structure. In economic language, this societal gain is an externality—the direct parties to bargaining have no incentive to take this gain into account.[59] Sole reliance on bargaining to achieve optimal protection is predictably unwise. Legislatively structured protection is needed. Still, the question remains: would legislative protection of press personnel be constitutional? Possibly, the answer depends on whether the rules apply broadly to all economic enterprises or only to the press. Both possibilities will be considered.

General Rules

General rules that promote the worker's expressive freedom are arguably like government-imposed safety rules, environmental laws, or anti-discrimination laws that apply to all or a large category of enterprises. Each limits and structures the employer's power to bargain about or to control the employment relationship. The post-*Lochner* era uniformly recognizes the permissibility of this type of regulation. Nevertheless, application of these rules to the press arguably clashes with the plausible premise that the government cannot restrict unregulated private ownership of a press.

People frequently rely on other people, as well as on various physical equipment, to deliver or amplify their messages. Most prohibitions on the use of wealth to purchase the services of others to amplify the purchaser's chosen message can only be explained as an attempt, for whatever reason, to restrict people's communications. These prohibitions violate the first amendment. The difficult question is whether this argument necessarily applies to limits on owners' control of the press. Although lacking desirable clarity, I think a constitutionally relevant line can be drawn between hiring someone merely to amplify the employer's speech and controlling an entire media enterprise that involves employees' creative, investigative, and expressive efforts.

Certainly some individuals and families have used their wealth to develop distinguished newspapers.[60] Sometimes their control may have been directed toward amplifying their own values and visions. In these cases, limits on "owners" control of the enterprise could interfere with their expressive opportunities. Nevertheless, any institutional and economic arrangements that society makes available necessarily limit as well as create expressive opportunities. People, whether owners or workers, could hardly have a first amendment right to the structure that most benefits their expression given that some alternative inevitably would be better for someone else.

Moreover, as long as owners are able to have their own personally chosen messages included in the enterprise's presentation, protection of employee's expressive choices does not abridge the owner's speech. Rather protection of the employees relies on the premise that the first amendment does not protect people's use of their resources to control another person's expression.[61] The "sovereignty" aspect of property should be subject to legislative control.[62] Applying that premise here, as long as the government does not design the rules in order to stop speech—as it arguably would be if the rules totally prohibited hiring people to amplify a person's specific message—the rules relating to the institutional arrangement do not violate the speech clause. And as long as these rules do not undermine the integrity and independence of the press, they do not violate the press clause. Protection of employee decision making in the media enterprise passes these tests. Like all institutional arrangements, this protection will restrict some people's (here, the owners') capacity to control communications. But possibly because of the inevitability of such effects within any legal regime, "effect" cannot be the standard. The rules should be understood as furthering the legitimate purposes of promoting the employee's expression and promoting an independent press.

In other words, guild socialism, even though not constitutionally mandated, is not inconsistent with the constitutional guarantee of freedom of the press. It may even be the institutional form that would best promote that freedom under current historical conditions. In any event, the government should be permitted to promote workers' freedom through definition of property rights and regulation of market practices as long as it does so, as it presumably can, in a manner that preserves the right of people to use their resources to purchase communication opportunities.

Maybe my claim is too broad. What about the voluntary association that wishes to control its newsletter or journal of opinion? What about the person who wishes to present her views but needs help of others in their formulation, elaboration, and circulation? What about the I. F. Stones? In its efforts to communicate, the person or group has no right to particular economic forms being available. Rather they only have a right to use all available forms and a right to form and act as a voluntary association with its own rules. And even the most collectivist forms of guild socialism inevitably provide considerable scope for the individual speaker who organizes and remains immersed in a communications enterprise. Alternatively, these examples may suggest that the first amendment should specially protect the nonprofit group organized for particular political or cultural purposes.[63] In any event, the relevant rules regulating corporate or enterprise relations are likely to provide exceptions for small enterprises, possibly for nonprofit or individually owned enterprises.

Special Rules

Basically, there are two serious objections to rules specifically favoring press personnel and restricting the prerogatives of owners of media enterprises. First, these rules purposively discriminate against people's use of their wealth for speech purposes. Presumably, this should be impermissible. Second, any discrimination against the press is also objectionable. In *Minneapolis Star v. Minnesota Commissioner of Revenue,*[64] the Court invalidated a special use tax on ink and paper used in publishing newspapers even though, according to the dissent, the tax was less than the sales tax from which the press was exempted. The differential treatment of the press apparently required a better justification than the state offered.

Neither objection is entirely persuasive. In contrast to the almost automatic invalidity of laws that prohibit expressive conduct, the constitutionality of laws that merely make speech more difficult or more expensive usually depends on whether the law is supported by a legitimate purpose unrelated to suppressing expression. *Massachusetts Citizens for Life*[65] involved a general regulation restricting the independent campaign contributions of corporations. The Court found that concerns that justified applying this restriction to ordinary profit-making corporations did not justify its restrictive effects on voluntary political associations using the corporate form. In other words, the Court held that under certain circumstances failure to adopt special rules that treat the first amendment activity differently could be unconstitutional. Even though not constitutionally mandated, special rules protecting press personnel from censorship by owners should likewise be permissible. They are supported by significant, non-speech-suppressive justifications. Although they prevent some people from using their wealth within a generally available social form, these people are not prevented from using other social forms for speech purposes. The challenged regulations should be viewed not as an impermissible prohibition on speech but as a permissible allocation of speech opportunities. Likewise from the perspective of the press clause, differential treatment must be carefully examined. The real evil, however, is not the different treatment itself but the undermining of the press. Reporter shield laws or special press galleries, for example, amount to differential treatment but are not unconstitutional. As the Court explained in the context of a special tax on the press, "differential treatment, *unless* justified by some special characteristic of the press, *suggests* that the goal of the regulation is not unrelated to suppression expression."[66]

Here, "special characteristics of the press"—namely, the special importance of promoting the independent judgment of the press personnel—justifies some differential treatment. Although careful consideration is necessary and suspicion is justified, if regulation by general rules would have been permissible, similar regulation by rules directed only at the press should also be permissible if the rules can be seen as promoting a plausible legislative conception of press freedom rather than as being designed to undermine the integrity and influence of the press.

Regulation of Ownership

A final strategy for reducing the negative impact on press freedom caused by economic forces and ownership concentration is to regulate the distribution or structures of ownership. Antitrust laws and FCC cross-ownership rules, which prohibit certain combinations of ownership of different media outlets within the same markets, exemplify structural regulations of ownership upheld by the Supreme Court.[67] Here, I will primarily consider whether ownership regulations that focus specifically on media outlets should be upheld. The antitrust laws upheld by the Court were general provisions that apply to all businesses. And arguably some special status of the broadcast media and the government's role in allocating channels were crucial for justifying the FCC cross-ownership rules.[68] Still, I will suggest here that ownership rules directed specifically at the press should be upheld even if the regulations go much farther than existing laws in requiring deconcentration of the press ownership.

Structural regulation that reduces ownership concentration could advance several constitutionally permissible objectives that further, rather than frustrate, the functioning of the press. Arguably, regulations could: (1) increase the strategic power of press workers (editors, writers, reporters) to determine the content of their own work and control its use; (2) increase the diversity of the press's output and the number and diversity of the people making content decisions; (3) prevent large corporate owners, as well as government, from dictating the media's orientation or from squelching exposes; and (4) increase the possibility of individuals making editorial decisions that are independent of profit dictates. Goals such as these could serve as policy standards against which to evaluate the existing, or any proposed, rules that regulate the ownership structure.

An extreme case can set the issue of whether structural regulation of ownership would be constitutional. Consider whether the government could prohibit ownership of media outlets by nonmedia enterprises and whether, in addition, it could require a radical dispersal of ownership[69] by outlawing any individual or any media enterprise from owning more than one media outlet.[70] In this analysis, a media outlet means either a single newspaper, magazine, broadcast station, or cable system or a set of such entities closely connected editorially and in terms of content and image.

Obviously, determining the effects of these rules would require study. They clearly would increase the number of independently owned outlets. This increase would in turn probably increase the number of actors who could make editorial decisions, initiate program experimentation, or expand the range of offerings. This more dispersed ownership, however, might turn out to be even more socially and politically homogeneous than existing corporate management. Moreover, continued corporate control of advertising funds would allow business to retain considerable control over the media.[71]

This structure might push the distribution of decision-making power in two opposing, both arguably desirable, directions. First, it probably would lead to an increase in owner involvement in content and policy decisions. Second, the decrease in corporate "distance" between journalistic personnel and owners or corporate managers might give this personnel greater motivation and more favorable opportunities to bargain for some degree of journalistic freedom and for control over their work.[72] The smaller scale of the enterprise should also improve the technical opportunities for owners and press workers to use their limited financial resources or their labor to subsidize innovation and the presentation of their own particular views.

Even if the proposal had the suggested positive effects, potential detrimental aspects might justify preference for the existing structure. First, possibly only large corporations are able to finance desirable technical innovations. Alternatively, corporate financiers of innovation may not need to own media outlets— or owners of single outlets, either individually or in groups, may be able to raise the needed capital. Moreover, innovations, even profitable innovations, are not always desirable. Some consideration should be given to whether the predictably different innovations that would occur under each ownership structure would contribute to the concerns behind the press clause.

Second, large corporate owners might more readily subsidize expensive journalistic investigations and more willingly take the risks inherent in journalistic or artistic experiments. Or maybe not. The proposed ownership structure does not rule out network systems of financing investigations or programming, or wire-service reporting. It would only prohibit network entities from owning or controlling media outlets. For example, statutory changes caused the centralized Corporation for Public Broadcasting to lose considerable power to the Public Broadcasting Service (PBS), which was controlled by local stations. PBS set up the Station Program Cooperative in which local stations would select and then pool resources to fund programs that would be made available nationally. This procedure allowed each station to participate in the design, selection, funding, and use of programs.[73] Other devices, including syndication, also allow for financing projects beyond the budget of a single media outlet. Finally, the effect of the proposed structure on the likelihood of and types of risk taking, innovation, or undertaking of "checking function" activities is not obvious. Views on this sociological issue vary. In the 1950s, Eric Sevareid's observation was that "[t]he bigger our information media, the less courage and freedom of expression they allow. Bigness means weakness."[74]

Third, a proliferation of ownership might merely increase the dominance of local, wealthy individuals who will provide their communities with primarily local material evincing a consistently single-minded, parochial viewpoint. Alternatively, local ownership of newspapers has often been associated with more serious reporting, higher quality news, and coverage that stimulates and supports citizen involvement in political life. Offhand, the dangers appear overrated; a press divided into smaller independent units could probably perform the checking function and provide diversity of outlook and quality of output at least equal to that of the present press.

Beyond the merits of restructuring ownership, what about its constitutionality? The most significant difference between this and the last section's discussion of restructuring of decision-making authority is that here the ownership limitations directly block a person's use of wealth to purchase socially available means of communication. This limit must be evaluated from the perspective of both the press and the speech clauses.

The press clause requires that government not abridge the independence or institutional integrity of the press. The press might argue that it should generally be free from discriminatory press-specific restrictions, citing *Minneapolis Star*[75] and its holding that the state's tax on newspaper ink was unconstitutional. But mere "differential treatment" should not suffice to invalidate the law. Sometimes exemptions from otherwise valid, uniform restrictions may be constitutionally required and, othertimes, at least permissible. Arguably, failure to exempt the press from certain general practices (such as grand-jury inquiries or third-party searches) abridges its independence. There, as here, the constitutional issue turns on the laws' purpose and predictable effect on the press' institutional integrity.

Of course, the purpose of any regulation will include an intent to *affect* the regulated activity unless, possibly, its purpose was purely symbolic. Congress surely intended antitrust legislation to affect ownership, production, and sales, yet the Court has approved its application to the press. Having an effect on an institution does not equal undermining its integrity or limiting its freedom. Here, the regulation of ownership structure would not limit what the press could do when engaged in press activities. It would not appropriate the work product of the press. It hardly manifests a purpose to decrease the ability of the press to perform its checking, informational, and entertainment roles, nor is it likely to have that effect. Arguably, the proposal would increase institutional integrity by reducing private censorship that the state, through its property laws, presently permits. Thus, this form of special regulation would not abridge freedom of the press.

Chapter 2 criticized "market failure" theories, which called for government regulation to equalize speech opportunities by limiting the amount of wealth a person could use for speech purposes. That critique might also apply here and show that this regulation of ownership structure abridges speech. This argument, too, is unpersuasive.

I have argued that a person does not have a first amendment right to use wealth to suppress the speech of others. Given this premise, the speech clause is not necessarily violated even by a prohibition on individual ownership of enterprises that involve the expressive efforts of a group of people. Likewise, unless it has a constitutionally objectionable purpose, a restriction on owning more than one media outlet would also be valid. A person could still attempt to enter into agreements to have other outlets print or broadcast her specific messages, that is, to amplify her speech. The ownership restriction only prevents her from controlling the expression of people in these other enterprises.[76]

Existing case law is consistent with upholding radical structural regulation of press ownership. The Court has rejected first amendment challenges to the application of antitrust laws to newspapers and wire services and to FCC regulation of the ownership of broadcast stations.[77] For example, the Court upheld FCC rules restricting a single person or entity's ownership of both newspapers and broadcast stations within the same community.[78] Although these cases typically either involve the application of general laws (the antitrust laws) or rely on a perceived greater governmental power to regulate broadcasting, neither factor provides a principled ground for limiting the precedential value of the cases.

Over forty years ago, Justice Hugo Black set the tone for the Court's reasoning in this area when he claimed:

It would be strange indeed, however, if the grave concern for freedom of the press which prompted adoption of the First Amendment should be read as a command that the government was without power to protect that freedom.... That Amendment rests on the assumption that the widest possible dissemination of information from diverse and antagonistic sources is essential to the welfare of the public.... Surely a command that the government itself shall not impede the free flow of ideas does not afford non-governmental combinations a refuge if they impose restraints upon that constitutionally guaranteed freedom.... Freedom of the press from governmental interference under the First Amendment does not sanction repression of that freedom by private interests.[79]

Speaking for the Court, Justice Black upheld the application of the antitrust laws to the Associated Press. Unlike the structural regulation of ownership proposed here, the judicial order in that case required the Associated Press to make its "views" available, on nondiscriminatory terms, to those whom the AP would not choose to give them. Thus, AP was required to "speak" when it would choose not to. This "forced speech" would be unconstitutional if applied to an individual.[80] But Black found structural regulation of a media enterprise raises different issues. Given that the enterprise was speaking broadly to the world, it is implausible to think that its forced speech violated anyone's autonomy claim not to speak. Congress certainly had intended the antitrust law to restrict individual and corporate "freedom" to organize the press as they choose. Application of the antitrust laws to the Associated Press amounted to a government-imposed structural reform of this press enterprise's procedure for distributing information. The antitrust laws, however, did not prohibit speech and the purpose of the structural regulation was to increase diversity, competition, and availability of information. This regulation neither destroyed the press's ability to operate, nor prohibited it from communicating or from performing any of its functions, nor involved governmental appropriation of the press's work product. The antitrust laws were properly found not to violate the press clause.

The Court's holding prompted Justice Murphy to argue in dissent that "government action directly aimed at the methods or conditions of [the collection and distribution of the news and information] is an interference with the press."[81] If the press were equivalent to the owner, Murphy's dissent would be persuasive. By forcing the AP to speak to those with whom it would choose to exclude, the government would have violated the owners' speech rights. In contrast, according to the Court, the owner's economic interest in limiting others' access and use of its speech is not an aspect of an individual's speech meriting constitutional protection. The constitutional right to speak normally does not determine what the speaker's economic rights in the speech will be.[82] More broadly, as Black suggested, an owner has no constitutional right to use his or her wealth to stop others from speaking as they choose—which, the Court believed, was the consequence of the monopolistic practices challenged in the case.

CONCLUSION

Justice Hugo Black's theses in Associated Press were that: (1) the government can intervene to protect freedom of the press and promote a diversity of voices and (2) private interests have no constitutional right to stop speech or repress the freedom. These, as well as the general assumption that the government can apply neutral rules and regulations to the press unless they abridge freedom of speech, have presently prevailed. I hope my analysis extends this understanding.

In Chapter 10, I argued that the fourth-estate interpretation of freedom of the press required protection of the integrity of the press's separate institutional existence even to the extent of justifying certain special "defensive rights" against government. This chapter, agreeing with Black's conclusion that the first amendment does not sanction and is in fact undermined by "repression of [press] freedom by private interests," has argued that the government can engage in structural regulation to reduce this private censorship. I only added a caveat that government response to the private threat must not abridge individuals' freedom of speech.

The problem is that the theses of the two chapters seem in tension. Government power to structure the press seems contrary to assertions of constitutional protection against government interference. A key insight was necessary to resolve this tension. That insight, implicit in both this and the last chapter, was seeing the relevance of an institution's necessarily conventional nature. The structure of the press has no natural content but is a creation instrumentally justified as serving certain social functions. Of course, various different institutional forms, each permissibly established by law, could promote these functions. Still, constitutional protection of the press's integrity and autonomy of the press renders certain government purposes impermissible reasons for structuring the institution; likewise it requires that the government not invade the institutional boundaries of whatever institution the laws recognize.

Three further considerations show how this insight resolves the tension between the two chapters. First, any set of rules, whether specifically directed at the press or of general application, will limit someone's opportunity to use the press as she might choose. Thus, the mere fact that a law has this effect cannot determine the law's constitutionality. While the press clause protects the press as an institution, its institutional nature means that the government necessarily retains some discretion in deciding how the press is to be structured. Moreover, a desirable, although probably not mandated, interpretation of press freedom suggests that the institution should be structured to favor the press personnel's freedom so as to protect their ability to perform the checking and informational functions. Thus, neither general nor special rules should be held unconstitutional under the *press clause* unless they are designed to undermine the press's integrity as an institution or its independence from government.

Second, freedom of speech is a right of individuals, not market-oriented institutions or corporations. The individual's right relates to using opportunities that society makes available for a variety of instrumental reasons, not a right that society be structured in a particular way that would promote that individual's speech. Thus, ownership regulations restrict the owner, but not in her own speech but only in respect to the institution that the law makes available.

This claim that ownership regulation does not violate the speech clause is incomplete, however, without the third argument: The individual's constitutionally protected speech interest is not in the press as a profit-making unit, as a means of production, but as a consumption good, that is, as a means to communicate what the individual chooses. Moreover, that person's right of free speech does not extend to a right to use property to suppress other people's freedom to speak. Therefore, as long as general economic regulations or rules specially directed at the press are not designed to impede people's use of wealth to communicate their views (i.e., to impede consumptive expenditures for speech) and do not prohibit any communicative activity by individuals, these rules do not violate people's speech rights.

Acceptance of these arguments dissolves the tension between recognizing the press clause's guarantee of institutional integrity and independence (press freedom) and recognizing the permissibility, if not the constitutional necessity, of structural intervention by government to promote that freedom in the face of threats from private economic interests.

Conclusion:
The First Amendment
and Constitutional Interpretation

The liberty theory of freedom of expression claims general applicability as a proper standard for any legal order. Still, the liberty theory also claims more specifically to be the proper interpretation of the first amendment of the U.S. Constitution. This second claim must implicitly rely on some theory of constitutional interpretation. However appealing its general principles, whether the liberty theory is a proper formulation of constitutional law depends on whether it reflects a proper approach to constitutional interpretation. This chapter defends the theory of constitutional interpretation implicit in this book's presentation. It proceeds by first showing how correction of specific problems of various popular or intuitive approaches to constitutional interpretation help lead to the theory of interpretation defended here. Then, it comments further on this "conversation-with-a-justificatory-intent" theory of interpretation.[1]

Literalism claims to interpret the constitution on the basis of the meaning of its words. This can be quickly put aside. The reason a person born by Cesarian-section is still eligible to be President is that, in context, the provision that says: "No person except a natural born citizen . . . shall be eligible to the office of President"[2] does not refer to "natural" methods of birth. But the point is more general. Words by themselves are always susceptible to alternative interpretations. Although certain interpretations are often ruled out, they are not ruled out by the word itself.

If the words themselves cannot provide sufficient meaning, a plausible view is that the *context* of language use shows what the words really meant, that the context leads to a (relatively) determinant content. But the notion of "really meant" implies that the context is used to try to get at the speaker's intent, which provides the real, determinant meaning. Therefore, the relevant concern for constitutional interpretation is the "framer's intent."

Any attempt to interpret in line with framer's intent involves a series of practical problems that at best can only be resolved through value choices of people other than the original speaker(s). Putting aside the actually quite serious prob-

272

lem of a historical record that provides inadequate information about what various people intended, there is the problem of whose intent and which of their intents count. There is no logical reason why the intent of those who drafted the document or who approved it at the Constitutional Convention, the so-called founding fathers, are as relevant as the host of ratifiers at the state conventions. Or should the intent be of the people in the states who elected delegates to the state ratifying conventions partially on the basis of the candidates' announced or suspected views?

But assume we identify the category of people whose intent is relevant. Since ratification was not by a single person but by various majorities, the problem of conflicting intents within the group must be considered. If of the, say, 65% who supported ratification, 25% intended the provision to mean one thing, 22% intended another, and 18% intended a third thing, what is the relevant intent? Would this 25% of the ratifiers (or founding fathers), who are less than a majority of even those supporting ratification, have established their view as fundamental, binding law?

Even this simplicity is unrealistic. As to many provisions, most ratifiers probably had no intent—that is, they supported it on faith that some one else had thought adequately about the provision's meaning. For their part, their intent was to get home for supper or to finish debate.

And then there are the potential contradictions built into the problem of level of generality. A person may have different intents at different levels and these different intents are not necessarily consistent (even if the person on the basis of available information and insight thought they were). Certainly, as conditions and perceptions change over time, intents that once seemed consistent will begin to conflict. For example, some supporters of the fourteenth amendment's equality norm may have intended at a very general level to oppose inequality in society's respect for humans, inequality that is, most obviously, implicit in slavery and its remnants. Specifically, however, these supporters may not have seen any problem with nor intended to outlaw legally imposed racial segregation in public institutions. Given current understanding of both racism and equality, the interpreter's choice of level of intent on which to focus could determine whether racially segregated schools, discrimination against woman, or the failure to provide all citizens with at least minimal levels of food, shelter, and education is consistent with these framer's equality intent.

Further, there is the paradox of what to do if, as some evidence suggests, the framer's intent (or expectation) was not to have framer's intent control the interpretation of the constitutional provision.[3]

Each dilemma could be resolved, but only by value-laden choices. There are, however, two even more fundamental problems with the framer's intent approach. First, it misconceives the nature of understanding. An interpreter cannot be inside the head of someone else. She necessarily brings to the task her own experiences and understandings. This involvement of the concerns and experiences of the interpreter is essential to both the motivation for and the substance of any interpretation and, thereby necessarily makes the activity of interpretation something other than identifying a single, constant, objective, past intent of another person (or group of persons).

Even more fundamentally, a defender of the framer's intent analysis needs to explain why we should want to be ruled by what people did or intended 200 years ago. There is no answer in simple democratic theory. Democratic theory does not explain why the intent of a past majority should have a greater status than a present one.. Even less clear is why we should want to be ruled by the limited group of white, male property holders involved in the "framing." The reason we recently celebrated the 200th anniversary of "our" constitution cannot be a desire to follow the intents of men who intended their constitution to assure the continuance of slavery.[4] As a minimum, some explanation is needed. Surely, the fact that no twentieth century Supreme Court justice can be said to have consistently followed a framer's intent interpretation provides some evidence that this approach misconceives the relevant task. Some more "progressive" conception of the constitution and the activity of interpretation is needed to explain its worthiness of current celebration.

A third set of interpretive approaches takes to heart the critiques of literalism and framer's intent. Unable to find any "neutral" or natural law principles that could substitute as a basis for constitutional law, this third approach argues that any constitutional decision necessarily involves essentially ad hoc, personal political judgments of the interpreter. At this point, followers of this approach diverge into different camps—although some engage in camp hopping. First, those with strong faith in democracy and little willingness to see themselves as imposing values on the political order may attempt to opt out.* At the extreme, a legislator holding this view of constitutional interpretation would always ignore the constitution and base her vote on policy considerations. A judge would reject all constitutional challenges. Second, some would not completely abandon judicial review but would recognize it as a serious assertion of unjustified political power. Therefore, they would occasionally rely on the constitution to invalidate an exercise of legislative power,† but only when necessary to make an especially important contribution. This approach usually develops more as an approach to judging than to interpreting the constitution.[5] It practices judicial deference, the "passive virtues," and talks of building institutional good will to be spent on the rare but important cases in which it invokes the constitution. Third, others would make the most of the inability of textual documents to control interpretations. Usually commentators, not judges, these skeptics assert that constitutional law is only and could only be politics. The only thing for responsible judges (and lawyers and legislators) to do is always to try to achieve good political results. These skeptics claim that none of the pronouncements about deference or principle ever stopped or could stop those judges with whom they disagree from being political. Therefore, they argue, they

---

*This claimed avoidance is a misperception. Given a social position that allows the holder to decide in varying ways, the choice to reject invocations of the constitution clearly amounts to a value choice of the interpreter and not merely deference and avoidance. That role holder, not an exogenous, presumably democratic body, determines the outcome. The role holder must explain why she uses her discretion the way she does. Neither the notions of the rule of law, of democracy, nor other values *automatically* point this way.

†The application of this logic to executive power is often not discussed.

should not tie their own hands. Against the charge that their approach is not democratic, they note that other institutions of government are really not very democratic either. Indeed, powerful democratic forces ranging from the appointment process to the need to listen to and respond to the arguments and cases brought to them result in judicial *politics* being comparatively democratic. In any event, objection to their embrace of politics is really a criticism of the human condition, not their responsible choice to be honest about interpretation. Moreover, we will have a better society if people do not rationalize their actions as required by some role or external authority but, instead, accept responsibility for trying to achieve good results in whatever position they find themselves.

Certainly, this political approach to interpretation is consistent with this book's conclusions concerning the proper scope of the first amendment. The problem is that this political approach is consistent with any set of conclusions. The advice that says: "interpretation is impossible, therefore, do what you think best and take responsibility" is not a theory of interpretation but, at best, is proposed therapy given to a person who has asked the wrong question. But the question is not wrong. Interpretation exists. Moreover, judges engage in it. Some judges experience reaching results to which they at some level object. (Justice Frankfurter was fond of objecting to illiberal laws that he upheld.[6]) Although occasionally this practice of reaching disagreeable results may reflect a need for therapy, judges often do seem to rely on legal texts in their thinking. In using these materials, judges (and lawyers, legislators, and citizens) experience both giving interpretations of and taking guidance from the texts. Both judges and most others would think it improper for this not to occur. Hence, it seems appropriate to ask for a theory of interpretation that provides guidance as to what an interpreter should do with some mass of texts.

Although I will not argue the point here, our world is one where people both experience the existence of ethical norms and properly make claims on each other. That is, at least within our social practices, obligations exist. The legal order is a part of these practices that evaluate and "sponsor" claims some people make on other people. The assertion that these claims can be or can fail to be legitimate, not just in a sociological but in a ethical sense,[7] seems and, I would argue, is right. Legal interpretation attempts to describe the content of this legal order. Rejection of the possibility of interpretation would seem to correspond to rejecting the possibility of any such ethical order or the possibility of valid obligation. For this reason this third approach seems irresponsible. Thus, the problems with this third approach include: its failure to provide guidance for the actual practice of interpretation; its incorrect view of that practice; and its failure to recognize that legal obligation can be legitimate but that this legitimacy depends on appropriate legal interpretation, a practice this approach rejects as undesirable if not impossible.

Nevertheless, this third approach provides valuable insights. It rightly recognizes that interpretive conclusions are not mechanically or logically mandated. Therefore, the interpreter must take responsibility for her conclusions— recognize, for instance, that she is proposing and, if she is the judge, she is imposing the punishment or the denial of the right. It also recognizes that the contested aspects of interpretations are about values, not (mere) logic. Finally, those recommending deference, even if wrongly thinking that this avoids responsibility, correctly recognize the serious consequences of all legal and, especially, of constitutional interpretations. Some literary interpretations can appropriately be motivated by whimsical concerns. Legal interpretation, however, is about exercises of power and violence by some people against others, an issue of obvious ethical gravity.[8]

A fourth approach to constitutional interpretation is really merely a particularly influential response to the failure of literalism and framer's intent. Both literalism and framer's intent purportedly allow the interpreter to disavow responsibility for constitutional mandates. Certainly, this is an advantage for those troubled by the so-called counter-majoritarian difficulty. Holding an act of the legislature unconstitutional seems anti-democratic because it frustrates the legislative body's statement of the presumed will of the majority. John Marshall's answer[9] that invalidation was required by law may have once offered some consolation. But after the attack of the legal realists, or after recognition of the inadequacies of literalism and framer's intent described above, the problem of judicial imposition of value choices could seem intense. Justice Stone's *Caroline Products* footnote,[10] best developed and recently popularized by Dean John Hart Ely,[10] provides a partial response to these perceived problems.

The fourth approach accepts critiques of literalism and framer's intent and further asserts that judges cannot derive value choices from the constitution itself—except maybe the value of democracy. Moreover, a commitment to democracy means that judges are not justified in imposing their own value choices. But this does not mean there is nothing for them to do. Instead, the courts' constitutional responsibility should be seen as "reinforcing democracy." Two types of judicial intervention are proper. First, courts should intervene to maintain or establish a properly functioning democratic process. For example, it should assure one person one vote and protect at least political speech and assembly.* Second, courts should intervene when the democratic process breaks down. Here, courts should mandate outcomes that a properly functioning representative democracy would have legislated. Thus, courts should be particularly wary of situations where, because of prejudice against discrete and insular minorities, the normal processes of coalition building and political compromise are unlikely to work to adequately take in account the interests of these minorities.

For present purposes, three problems with this "representation reinforcing" approach to constitutional interpretation are important.[12] First, as usually elaborated, the theory does not have a precise enough account of democracy to be able to resolve most real constitutional conflicts. For example, if the majority wants to assure that rural areas are represented in a legislative body and chooses to deviate from the one-person one-vote standard to accomplish this result, but if that majority retains the power to use the initiative and referendum process

---

*The claim that the first amendment protects only or primarily political speech is often based on this interpretative approach. Thus, the critique of the political speech theory in Chapter 2 duplicates some of the points made here.

to mandate one-person one-vote, is the decision inconsistent with democracy?[13] Is failure to guarantee everyone the fulfillment of the basic material or resource needs as understood by our society inconsistent with assuring a properly functioning democracy?[14] To determine the implicit content of a commitment to democracy, the value basis of the commitment, as well as the social organizational implications of realizing those values, must be understood. But uncovering and implementing these value premises seems perilously close to the value-based, interpretative activism that this "representation-reinforcing" approach was designed to avoid.

Second, most common American understandings of democracy[15] would encompass a representational process that takes everyone's values or preferences into account and then reaches some summation or compromise that leaves no one's views without some influence on the final outcome. This process, however, is consistent with adopting overtly racist laws which, due to taking into account minority and nonracist views, are slightly less racist than they would have been if these people had been actually excluded from the political process.[16] These racist laws are unacceptable to American courts and most constitutional commentators. This observation suggests that we in fact prefer to see the constitution as placing value-based limits on, not merely perfecting, democracy. Certainly popular rhetoric within our constitutional tradition asserts that various constitutional provisions were purposefully designed and are properly implemented to protect rights of people against majority-imposed restriction.

Third, this "representation-reinforcing" approach to interpretation owes us an explanation of why democracy is so great. Why should democracy be viewed as so fundamental that it becomes the central constitutional task of the courts to reinforce it? This question is particularly acute since the constitution seems to be a document that, in addition to spelling out one version of a relatively democratic government, also quite clearly set limits on it. Of course, many apparently individual rights provisions can be interpreted as primarily specifying proper democratic "procedures" or "processes." But certainly these interpretations involve contestable value-choices that require some defense. That defense, however, would presumably require an answer to the question put above: What's so great about democracy. And again a greater part of our constitutional tradition, even as it has changed its view as to the anti-majoritarian rights meriting protection, has appeared to accept the notion that limits on democracy are part of what the constitution, and particularly what specific constitutional amendments, are about.

Combining insights implicit in the critiques of these four approaches to constitutional interpretation begins to provide an outline of a better approach. First, remember John Marshall's earlier response to the current nagging question: "Why should we allow ourselves to be ruled by decisions made 200 years ago by some white, male property holders?" Roughly, he said that we should because the constitution is (the supreme) law. Accepting Marshall's assertion that the constitution is law, the question does not go away. Instead, it becomes: Why should we allow ourselves to be ruled by law? Or, more fundamentally, why should a person ever be viewed as obligated to obey a law or governmental decision with which she disagrees (or which is contrary to her interests)? An inadequate answer is that democratic decision making justifies legal obligation. It is inadequate because, like the "representation-reinforcing" analysis, it never explains why majority rule justifies legal obligation. On the contrary, I would think that people should not view themselves bound by a majority's decisions to make them slaves, to deny them opportunities to obtain food, or to prohibit nonviolent, noncoercive religious or sexual practices that they consider necessary for expressing their identity.

Possibly the issue of legal obligation could more informatively stated: Given that people need collective arrangements, that people need law and obligation in order to fully develop and carry out human endeavors, what features must this collective order contain for the government (or the majority) legitimately to expect and demand that a person obey laws even when obedience is not in the person's immediate interest? To justify legal obligation, this question must be at least implicitly answered. And since legal obligations are the "output" of legal interpretation, if the justification of legal obligation depends on the obligation's content or on how it is created, the justification could determine the appropriate form of legal interpretation.

A fully defended answer is beyond the scope of this Conclusion.[17] Briefly, however, I would argue that a collective can justify legal obligation only if it treats all those who are obligated with equal respect and concern as autonomous persons.* Most fundamentally, the collective must exhibit overriding respect for human dignity. This required respect can be further elaborated as containing at least four more specific, universal elements:[18] (1) respect for people's autonomy or liberty; (2) respect for people's equality as humans; (3) democracy in contexts appropriate for collective decision making; (4) a structure of rights that systematically subverts structures of domination.

Of course, respect for people's autonomy is roughly the liberty theory of the first amendment elaborated in this book. Respect for equality is at the heart of the fourteenth amendment's equal protection clause. The first two elements, liberty and equality, require some form of and scope for democracy. Democracy embodies liberty in the sense that it expands the possibility of self-determination. Since many human objectives and many aspects of human flourishing require collective agreement or the maintenance of collective structures, democratic politics and government are necessary for self-determination. And democracy embodies equality in the sense that everyone has at least the same formal right to participate and control collective outcomes, a mandate the Court has properly interpreted "equal protection" to require.[19]

---

*A collectivist might disagree, arguing that obligation is justified merely because the person takes his or her being from membership in the group and the group's collective history. Disobedience, therefore, would be in some basic sense self-destructive. This view correctly recognizes that individuality or personhood and much of the specific content of a person's identity is a social or collective achievement but ignores the normative claims of autonomy that are central to this collective creation. The question remains why the person should not view her collectively created identity as oppressively imposed on her. Only if the collective order allows a member to affirm, to accept and, thus, also to deny or reject this identity, as well as presumably allow the member to participate in changing this identity and the collective traditions on which it is based, could the collectivist response meet the complaint of the person who asks why he or she should obey.

Any social or legal structure will, however, inevitably contain elements that embody and contribute to injustice and coercive domination. These elements will be partially reflected in many people's values and preferences, which will in turn "distort" further democratic decision making. Acceptance of and confidence in democratic decisions would be more rational if the social/legal order systematically subverted these structures of domination and weakened their deleterious, continuing influence on democratic decisions. Simple "majority rule" democratic decision making may effectively reflect all preferences, including those infected with injustice. If so, then fundamental constitutional provisions—those that invalidate legislation that embodies equality and liberty-denying values—operate to weed out some of the influence of these unjust structures. This partial purification of democratic choice at "time one" leaves the net set of laws, and hence the new structures that are then embodied in new preferences, somewhat more just than they would have been otherwise. By limiting the generative role of preferences reflective of injustice, these constitutional rights operate as levers to create a spiral in which over time we should be able to have increasing confidence in the preferences that generate democratic decisions.*

This description of minimal conditions for the justification of legal obligation answers the question addressed to the "representation-reinforcing" approach, namely: What is so great about democracy? Democracy is valuable as a partial embodiment of more basic values, as a means to give content to notions of equality and liberty. But these same values that require democracy also require specific limits. Democracy should have no authority to reach decisions contrary to the values by which it is justified. The representation-reinforcing approach had the derivation backwards. Rather than derive constitutional limits from the premise of democracy, democracy is the derivative conclusion based on fundamental constitutional values. The key dilemma posed for the representation-reinforcing approach was that the enterprise of constitutionalizing rights against majoritarian abridgement appears to limit democracy. This explanation of fundamental constitutional values resolves this dilemma. Both democracy of some sort and limits on democracy follow from the respect for liberty and equality that is necessary to justify legal obligation.

The above observations did not answer the question of how to interpret a constitution, a document that says nothing without an interpreter and, with interpretation, may not say all that it should. My claim is that viewing constitutional interpretation as a conversation between the interpreter and the text (and the related, relevant legal materials such as precedent and evidence of "framer's intent") provides a useful guide. "Conversation" is an apt metaphor because it avoids the image of interpretation as striving to find what is really there, the image implicit in literalism and framer's intent theories,† while still emphasizing the importance of texts, of the "objects" of interpretation, that are ignored by those who purportedly see interpretation as totally unconstrained by

---

*Various elements of the governmental structure that push toward value debate, and discursive value formation based on agreement—that is, effective implementation of "republican" ideals of government process—arguably provide another means to promote this result.

†Note that this notion of finding what is really there is a version of the belief in objective truth rejected in Chapter 1.

the texts. Moreover, the insights gained in the earlier critiques are deepened by examining ways in which interpretation is like conversation or, at least, like conversation aimed at agreement or understanding.

Interpretation is like conversation in that both parties bring something to the interaction. Thus, it makes a difference who the parties are. Both parties should be respected. Both can be wrong. Interpretation, like conversation, relies on the past and looks toward the future. It is "interested." That is, participation in either interpretation or conversation is oriented by values or is in pursuit of values. In addition, *legal* interpretation differs from other interpretation. These differences can be seen in its special "interested" nature, a particularity closely related to the role of official* legal interpretation in leading to the actual or threatened application of force or violence against those who deviate.

The parties to the conversation matter in that they both—the text and the interpreter—bring their own horizon and interests to the conversation. Intuitively, not only the very notion of law but also the attention continually lavished on texts (the constitution and judicial precedent and materials evidencing framer's intent) provide evidence that texts can and do matter. People continually experience being able to derive something from texts that they did not know before.

The specific task of constitutional interpretation is to arrive at conclusions that justify legal obligation. This task means that an objective of interpretation is to derive a legal order consistent with justice. Indeed, this is one special "interest" of legal interpretation. At first, this objective might seem to require the interpreter to ignore texts and rely solely on political theory. This view, however, has too abstract a view of the basis of obligation. Even if some aspects of justice can be determined abstractly, others are surely variable and a matter of historical development.[20] Part of what is justifiable depends on the past. Since the texts are the horizon of this history, the interpreter needs to look to them for this insight. And since obligation properly relates both to socially textured requirements of justice and variable aspects of group identity and group commitments, the texts properly play a role in determining the content of the legal order. Moreover, as long as this justificatory "interest" can plausibly be attributed to the texts, then they bring the wisdom of prior inquiries into the conversation. In itself that would be an adequate reason to rely on the texts unless a convincing case is made that these prior inquiries reach answers inconsistent with justice.

The interpreter also brings something to the conversation. First, a person only engages in interpretation with an interest. The interpreter brings questions, which vary with her project and her own values. The interpretive inquiry differs depending on whether the interpreter's project relates to writing a psychological biography, studying the role of particular theories of property or the influence of

---

*"Official" refers to the role of judges, legislative bodies, or law appliers. Other interpreters who attempt to determine the appropriate content of these official interpretations or to influence official interpretations have closely related "interested" qualities. There could be, however, other nonofficial interpretations, for example, an interpretation in aid of a psychological biography, an intellectual history, or a class analysis of society that have entirely different "interests." Unless otherwise noted, all references to legal interpretation will assume an orientation toward "official" use.

typically masculine perspectives, or justifying the application of force. The conversation, the inquiry, is always doubly interested in that the interpreter both wants to learn about particular things and the interpreter always has her own values or hypothesis at stake.

Legal interpretation, however, differs from conversation in that the central interest of the inquiry is given—namely, it is oriented toward justifying legal obligation. Thus, in legal interpretation, the interpreter should be assumed to bring this interest to the activity. In addition, the interpreter necessarily brings her own special interests and experiences to the conversation. The importance of the judges' identity is usually less a matter of integrity than of horizons. No notion of racial uniformity[21] is required to see that Justice Thurgood Marshall has brought an especially valuable, added voice to the Court. Not only is this variability of horizons inevitable and appropriate given the humanness of the activity of interpretation, but it suggests some more pointed conclusions. The centrality of justifying obligation to those who have apparent reason to resist, combined with the centrality of respect for equality and liberty in this justification, underline the importance of interpreters whose experiences and sensitivities make them particularly attuned to the concerns of dissidents and minorities, of outcasts and underclasses.

As noted, one reason why general theories of interpretation cannot be applied in a straightforward manner to legal interpretation is its specifically interested nature. It relates to the threatened or actual application of force or, equivalently, to obligation. Use of force or imposition of obligations requires justification. The justification must show that the enforcement of the obligation is consistent both with justice as well as with other aspects of who or how the collective is and wants to be. The constraint of justice is particularly central to portions of constitutional interpretation, which can override legislative decisions about self-definition. Here the interpretive enterprise directly intersects the project of this book. The general view of interpretation described here leads to interpreting the first amendment as protecting individual liberty of expression because respect for this liberty is fundamental to the justifiability of the legal order.

Legal interpretation differs from other interpretation in a second important way. The judge (or other official interpreter) appropriately recognizes that his or her official role necessitates greater acquiescence to past texts than is true in many conversations. This role requires following the law, which, even if aspiring toward legitimacy, may embody mistakes or human failings. Still, the judge also properly recognizes that the legitimate authority of that role depends heavily on the legitimacy of the legal order. And the interpreter's responsibility within that role is precisely to achieve legitimacy. Thus, the degree of acquiescence that the legal order can justly require of the interpreter varies. It varies with the legitimacy of that general legal order and with whether the specific decision that acquiescence requires would be consistent with a legitimate order. If the prior text is indubitably inconsistent, sometimes the judge can properly interpret her role as authorizing repudiation of the old answer. But sometimes not. Then, the judge has the "normal," but difficult, range of options varying from resignation to open civil disobedience to calculated dishonesty—the appropriateness of which will not be considered here. (But consider the argument of Chapter 5.)

The particular interested nature of the inquiry has other important implications for legal interpretation. Again the conversational image casts light on interpretive method. Conversation looks for insight wherever it can find it. Different statements of a conversational partner will vary in importance. But only momentary needs of the conversation, not abstract formula, can determine their differing import. Likewise, no mechanical formula can show the proper scope or weight to give particular constitutional texts, historical evidence of intent, or precedent. As illustrated by this book's selective use of each in formulating and defending a first amendment theory, their role in the conversation should vary depending on their capacity at any point to make a useful contribution. Since a motivating "interest" of interpretation aims at uncovering and creating an order that justifies legal obligation, a principled approach can be nothing other than value based.[22] Thus, it requires this selective, variable use of sources. The superficial neutrality of any mechanical approach that gives each element a specific force would be unprincipled.*

Sometimes legal texts represent conversational false starts that can be ignored or reinterpreted on the basis of their underlying proper concerns. This is certainly true of precedent but can even be true of constitutional provisions. At least, our constitutional history seems to show this. For example, the Court in 1934 did not challenge the dissent's characterization of the "contracts clause"† as "meant to foreclose state action impairing the obligation of contracts *primarily and especially* in respect of such action aimed at giving relief to debtors *in time of emergency*." But this Court, recognizing that "emergency may furnish the occasion for the exercise of power," used doctrinally unexceptional reasoning to reject a contracts clause challenge to a state mortgage moratorium law since the "reservation of essential attributes of sovereign power [is] read into contracts as a postulate of the legal order."[23]

Other times, a prior decision represents less a misunderstanding and more an overt transgression of norms necessary for legitimacy (or an overt deviation from persuasive accounts of collective self-definition). In these cases, the precedent should be repudiated as wrong. Thus, this conversational approach indicates that sometimes precedents should be transformed, other times they should be reversed. Of course, this conclusion leaves the problem of role responsibilities described above if the offending text is a constitutional provision where repudiation, not transformation, is called for.

This book has illustrated constitutional interpretation as "conversation with a justificatory intent." In this approach, the interpreter must recognize the contested nature of the discussion and the centrality of value issues. The interpreter must take responsibility for her conclusions, not externalize responsibility onto

---

*For example, "stare decisis" is a doctrine of respect for prior court decisions that asserts that once the court has decided an issue, later decisions of that court should be bound by the decision. Like other doctrines of interpretation, its justification lies not in neutral logic or anything inherent in the words "rule of law" but in its contribution to justice and legitimacy. Hence, the only principled application of this pragmatic doctrine would give it varying weight depending on its contribution, in the particular circumstances, to achieving justice.

†"No state shall ... pass any ... Law impairing the Obligation of Contracts." U.S. CONST., Art. I, Sec. 10.

some mechanical interpretive theory or assertedly neutral logic, even as she correctly recognizes that the correct resolution depends in part on what is brought by her conversational partner, the text. This understanding is evident in the book's measured reliance on text, its critical appropriation of tradition and precedent, and its eclectic use of philosophy, history, and social science. The interpreter's responsibility to arrive at decisions that contribute to the justifiability of legal obligation suggests that in determining the proper meaning of texts, the interpreter should, as this book did, draw heavily from political theory. Finally, the book's implicit understanding of the conversation's purpose is evident in its focus on liberty, and its attempt to formulate doctrines and premises that guarantee liberty from limitations based on collective decisions aimed at welfare maximization or at particular visions of collective self-definition.

The slogan of a recent national convention of the National Lawyers Guild was: "Justice Is a Constant Struggle." The view of constitutional interpretation presented here is similar: Constitutional interpretation is a constant struggle and, properly understood, is part of the struggle for justice. One claim of the book is that even the struggle for understanding cannot succeed merely by dialogue or rational inquiry. It requires embodiments in practices. Still, I would like to view the elaboration of the first amendment theory presented here as part of that struggle for justice.

Notes

INTRODUCTION

1. J. S. Mill, *On Liberty* (1956) (1st ed. 1859) [hereafter cited as *On Liberty*]. Mill's argument was made in a long chapter, "Of the Liberty of Thought and Discussion," *id.* at 19–67, which he intended to serve as an example of his defense of liberty in general. In fact, his argument for liberty in general rests on different assumptions and is not subject to the criticisms I will make of his defense of liberty of thought and discussion.

2. *Id.* at 64. *See also New York Times v. Sullivan*, 376 U.S. 254, 279 n.19 (1964); *On Liberty, supra* note 1, at 33–36, 41–43.

3. *On Liberty, supra* note 1, at 41; see *Dennis v. United States*, 341 U.S. 494, 584 (1951) (Douglas, dissenting).

4. As Mill explained:

> Were an opinion a personal possession of no value except to the owner, if to be obstructed in the enjoyment of it were simply a private injury, it would make some difference whether the injury was inflicted only on a few persons or on many. But the peculiar evil of silencing the expression of an opinion is that it is robbing the human race, posterity as well as the existing generation—those who dissent from the opinion still more than those who hold it.

On Liberty, supra note 1, at 21. For the same view, see Z. Chafee, *Free Speech in the United States* 33–35 (1964); A. Meiklejohn, *Political Freedom* 26–27 (1965).

5. The analogy between the perceived need to correct for failures in the economic market and the idea market is, I think, more than accidental. Most advocates of the market failure model of the first amendment would probably also advocate considerable governmental regulation of the economy. See, e.g., Fiss, "Free Speech and Social Structure," 71 *Iowa L. Rev.* 1405 (1986). This group typically is quick to identify negative externalities or oppressions that result from private exercises of power and sees great possibilities for intervention to promote fair, useful outcomes. In contrast, "conservatives" advocating decreases in government regulation recommend that "liberals" should have the same faith in economic markets that they have in the unregulated marketplace of ideas. See Coase, "Advertising and Free Speech," 6 *J. Legal Studies* 1 (1977); Coase, "The Market for Goods and the Market for Ideas," 64 *Am. Econ. Rev.: Pap. & Proc.* 384 (1974); Director, "The Parity of the Economic Market Place," 7 *J. Law & Econ.* 1 (1964). Chapter 9 argues that this analogy, accepted by both groups, should be rejected.

6. See, e.g., Barron, "Access—The Only Choice for the Media?," 48 *Texas L. Rev.* 766 (1970); Barron, "Access to the Press—A New First Amendment Right," 80 *Harv. L. Rev.* 164 (1967). See also *Columbia Broadcasting Sys. v. Democratic Nat'l Comm.*, 412 U.S. 94, 170–204 (1973) (Brennan & Marshall, dissenting).

7. Extending the concept of speech to cover nonverbal conduct will be controversial. Still, I will argue in Chapter 4 that nonverbal conduct that has the same uses as constitutionally protected verbal conduct and causes effects in a manner relevantly similar to the way speech causes effects should be treated as speech. Even if this conclusion is rejected, often the recommended protection of non-verbal conduct could be justified as an aspect of the free exercise of religion or of freedom of assembly. This book helps develop a proper interpretation of these clauses in that (1) it critiques the marketplace of ideas paradigm that currently improperly dominates the interpretations of freedom of assembly and (2) it develops distinctions and provides an alternative liberty paradigm that resolves difficulties in giving these clauses adequate meanings.

CHAPTER 1

1. J. Milton, *Areopagitica—A Speech For The Liberty of Unlicensed Printing* (1644). Despite continual invocations of Milton's striking vision, it is easy to forget the limitations of his time and not notice the quite constricted degree to which he espoused what today would be viewed as strong free speech claims. See L. Levy, *Emergence of a Free Press* 93–96 (1985).

2. Cf. R. Rorty, *Philosophy and the Mirror of Nature* (1979) (rejecting precisely the possibility of ever having such comparisons).

3. J. S. Mill, *On Liberty* 53 (1956) (1st ed. 1859) [hereafter cited as *On Liberty*].

4. These three assumptions are all explicit in *On Liberty*, note 3 *supra*. The first, that truth is objective, is clearly suggested by the language Mill uses to describe truth: persons "rediscover" truth, *id.* at 36; we should "give truth a chance of reaching us." *Id.* at 26. Second, human rationality is necessary. The "doctrine is meant to apply only to human beings in the *maturity of their facilities.*" *Id.* at 13 (emphasis added). See also *id.* at 25. Finally, a decrease in pluralism and an absence of intractable value conflicts are expected and applauded by Mill. In agreement with the "best of men," Mill concludes that "no belief which is contrary to truth can be really useful," *id.* at 28; and that "the well-being of mankind may almost be measured by the number and gravity of truths which have reached the point of being uncontested." *Id.* at 53. The result is that there is a "gradual narrowing of the bounds of diversity of opinion." *Id.* See also J. S. Mill, *Utilitarianism* 40–48 (1957). A person "still needs to be conscious that his real aim and theirs do not conflict." *Id.* at 43.

5. The Court's theoretical or explanatory references are usually either to its earlier opinions or to people, such as Jefferson, who may have influenced the drafters of the first amendment. Brandeis, for example, quoted marketplace of ideas notions found in Jefferson: "We have nothing to fear from the demoralizing reasonings of some, if others are left to demonstrate their errors and especially when the law stands ready to punish the first criminal act produced by the false reasoning." *Whitney v. California*, 274 U.S. 357, 375 (1927) (Brandeis, concurring). Mill, however, is occasionally cited. See, e.g., *Columbia Broadcasting Sys. v. Democratic Nat'l Comm.*, 412 U.S. 94, 189 n.25 (1973) (Brennan & Marshall, dissenting); *Furman v. Georgia*, 408 U.S. 238, 467, (1972); *Red Lion Broadcasting Co. v. FCC*, 398 U.S. 367, 392 n.18 (1969); *New York Times v. Sullivan*, 376 U.S. 254, 272 n.13, 279 n.19 (1964); *Poe v. Ullman*, 367 U.S. 497, 514–15 (1961) (Douglas, dissenting); *Barenblatt v. United States*, 360 U.S. 109, 151 n.22 (1959) (Black, Douglas, and Warren, dissenting). See also *Paris Adult Theatre I v. Slaton*, 413 U.S. 49, 68 n.14 (1973) (rejecting Mill's argument for liberty in general). I refer to Mill to exemplify the marketplace theory because he provides its best formulation.

6. Speech is unprotected when there is (or, in the case of attempts, when the speaker intends that there be) "a clear and present danger that [the speech] will bring about the

substantive evils that Congress has a right to prevent." *Schenk v. United States*, 249 U.S. 47, 52 (1919). The clear and present danger test originated as a criterion that Holmes thought was necessary for speech to amount to a prohibited *attempt* to commit some crime outlawing something other than words and, Professor Chafee to the contrary, appears to have had little connection with first amendment considerations. Cf. Chafee, "Book Review," 62 *Harv. L. Rev..* 891 (1949) with Rogat and O'Fallon, "Mr. Justice Holmes: A Dissenting Opinion—The Speech Cases," 36 *Stanford L. Rev.* 1349 (1984). Arguably, the clear and present danger test is an appropriate means to identify speech that constitutes an "attempt" to commit a crime not defined in terms of speech. See Linde, "'Clear and Present Danger' Re-examined: Dissonance in the Brandenburg Concerto," 22 *Stanford L. Rev.* 1163 (1970). Still, despite its origins, Holmes and Brandeis' theoretical and rhetorical elaboration and defense of the clear and present danger test in decisions starting with *Abrams v. United States*, 250 U.S. 616 (1919), relied on the marketplace of ideas theory of free speech much more than on a common law conception of attempts.

7. *Abrams v. United States*, 250 U.S. 616, 630 (1919) (Holmes & Brandeis, dissenting).

8. *Whitney v. California*, 274 U.S. 357, 375 (1927) (Brandeis & Holmes, concurring), *overruled, Brandenberg v. Ohio*, 395 U.S. 444 (1968).

9. *Id.*

10. *Id.* at 376. Cf. *On Liberty*, supra note 3, at 10. Mill referred to people's servility toward their masters and gods that leads them to "burn magicians and heretics."

11. *Id.* at 377.

12. Learned Hand's test, "whether the gravity of the 'evil', discounted by its improbability, justifies such invasion of free speech as is necessary to avoid the danger," was adopted in *Dennis v. United States*, 341 U.S. 494, 510 (1951). The test, implicitly for the majority and explicitly in Frankfurter's concurrence, involves "balancing" to determine the protection to be given speech. This judicial adoption of a legislative type balancing approach has been properly criticized. See, e.g., T. Emerson, *Toward a General Theory of the First Amendment* 53–56 (1966) [hereafter cited as *General Theory*]; Frantz, "The First Amendment in the Balance," 71 *Yale L. J.* 1424 (1962). However, balancing itself involves no theory of what, or why, speech is protected. Indeed, the Court made clear in *Dennis* that they continued to rely on the marketplace of ideas as the central concept of the first amendment, 341 U.S. at 503, 545–46, 549–50, 553. See note 54 *infra*.

13. *Gitlow v. New York*, 268 U.S. 652, 673 (1925) (Holmes & Brandeis, dissenting).

14. *On Liberty, supra* note 3, at 67–68. See also *id.* at 117 (when there is no time to warn another of danger, a person can temporarily stop the other from crossing the unsafe bridge).

15. 354 U.S. 476 (1957).

16. *Id.* at 484–85. See also *Memoirs v. Massachusetts*, 383 U.S. 413 (1966).

17. 354 U.S. at 484 (emphasis added).

18. See, e.g., *Chicago Police Dep't v. Mosley*, 408 U.S. 92 (1972). Licensing and other time, place and manner restrictions traditionally have been upheld only if they do not permit the government to discriminate among communications. *Shuttlesworth v. Birmingham*, 394 U.S. 147 (1969); *Cox v. Louisiana*, 379 U.S. 536 (1965); *Kunz v. New York*, 340 U.S. 290 (1951); *Cox v. New Hampshire*, 312 U.S. 569 (1941). The current Court may be abandoning its rejection of content discrimination. See *Young v. American Mini Theatres*, 427 U.S. 50 (1976); *Lehman v. Shaker Heights*, 418 U.S. 298 (1974). But cf. *Boos v. Barry*, 108 S.Ct. 1157, 1162–64 (1988). For a traditional analysis of this development, see Goldman, "A Doctrine of Worthier Speech: Young v. American Mini Theatres," 21 *St. Louis U. Law. J.* 281 (1977). Chapter 8 argues that some forms of content-based, time and place regulation arguably do not abridge certain types of expressive activities, e.g., commercial entertainment, while they would abridge other types, e.g., advocacy. Cf. *Paris Adult Theatre I v. Slaton*, 413 U.S. 49, 112–13 (Brennan, Stewart, &

Marshall, dissenting) (1973) (suggesting that unconsenting adults can be protected from obscenity) with *Cohen v. California*, 403 U.S. 15, 21 (1971) (in context of "advocacy" speech, state cannot protect unconsenting viewers).

19. *Roth v. United States*, 354 U.S. at 484.

20. *Roth* was unclear about whether obscenity was defined to be without redeeming social importance or whether a finding of its absence was crucial for labeling the material obscene. In *Memoirs v. Massachusetts*, 383 U.S. 413 (1966), Brennan made clear that the second was intended. But see *id.*, at 460–62 (White, dissenting).

21. *Kingsley Int'l Pictures Corp. v. Regents of New York*, 360 U.S. 684, 688–89 (1959).

22. *Ginzburg v. United States*, 383 U.S. 463, 489–90 (1966) (Douglas, dissenting).

23. *Id.* at 489.

24. F. Schauer, *Free Speech: A Philosophical Inquiry* 182 (1982). For a similar analysis but opposite conclusion, see H. Kalven, Jr., *A Worthy Tradition* 18, 33–34, 41 (1988).

25. *Miller v. California*, 413 U.S. 15, 34 (1973).

26. The Court emphasized this factor when it concluded that the method of advertising the publication constituted pandering and thereby provided evidence that it was designed for the pleasure, not the opinion, market. *Ginzburg v. United States*, 383 U.S. at 474–75.

27. The state interest lies in protecting the "community environment, the tone of commerce. . . and, possibly, the public safety itself." *Paris Adult Theatre I v. Slaton*, 413 U.S. 49, 58 (1972). See also *id.* at 63–64.

28. See, e.g., MacKinnon, "Pornography, Civil Rights, and Speech," 20 *Harv. Civ. Rights Civ.-Lib. L. Rev.* 1 (1985).

29. See Duggan, Hunter, and Vance, "False Promises: Feminist Antipornography Legislation in the U.S.," in *Women Against Censorship* 130 (V. Burstyn ed. 1985); Strossen, "The Convergence of Feminist and Civil Liberties Principles in the Pornography Debate," 62 *New York U. Law Rev.* 201 (1987). Studies have shown correlations between increased availability of "hardcore" pornography and a *decrease* in sex crimes and sex offenses against children. *Id.* at 205 n.25. One study found that the most important factor associated with low rates of unwanted pregnancy is "openness about sex (defined on the basis of four items: media presentations of female nudity, the extent of nudity on public beaches, sales of sexually explicit literature and media advertising of condoms)." E. Jones, et al., "Teenage Pregnancy in Developed Countries: Determinants and Policy Implications," 17 *Family Planning Perspectives* 53, 61 (Mar/Apr. 1985), cited in *Brief Amici Curiae of Feminist Anti-Censorship Taskforce, American Booksellers Ass'n v. Hudnut*, 771 F.2d 323 (7th Cir. 1985) (No. 84–3147), *aff'd*, 106 S.Ct. 1172 (1986), a brief opposing an Indianapolis ordinance that regulated pornography on the grounds that it is an offense against women. The *Brief*, joined in by over 70 prominent male and female feminists such as Roberta Achtenberg, Rita Mae Brown, Betty Friedan, Kate Millet, Adrienne Rich, and Barbara Smith, argued that not only was the ordinance unconstitutional but that it would in fact contribute to forces that oppress women.

30. 413 U.S. 49, 96 (Brennan, Stewart, & Marshall, dissenting).

31. *Miller v. California*, 413 U.S. at 34. The Court does explicitly reject Mill's argument for liberty in general. *Paris Adult Theatre I v. Slaton*, 413 U.S. 49, 68 n.14. However, Mill's argument for liberty in general rests on entirely different premises from those of his argument for freedom of speech.

32. *Id.* at 67.

33. *New York Times v. Sullivan*, 376 U.S. 254 (1964).

34. *Id.* at 280.

35. *Id.* at 269, 270 (quoting *Roth v. United States*, 354 U.S. 476, which quoted from Justice Brandeis's concurring opinion in *Whitney*).

36. *Id.* at 272 n.13.

37. *Id.* at 279 n.19.

38. *Garrison v. Louisiana,* 379 U.S. 64, 75 (1964).

39. The test, unless made "with knowledge that it was false or with reckless disregard of whether it was false or not," is best understood as derived from the marketplace theory, that is, as based on protecting all good faith participants in the marketplace of ideas. Still, several objections to the test are plausible even from the perspective of the marketplace theory. First, as the Court approvingly noted, Mill showed that falsehoods can serve a useful function in the marketplace. See note 37 *supra.* Mill even suggested that we should try to find people to contest all important truths. *On Liberty, supra* note 3, at 45–46. Thus, knowing falsehoods arguably should be protected. See T. Emerson, *The System of Freedom of Expression* 536 (1970). Nevertheless, Mill's argument that falsehoods "can" serve a useful function probably varies with context—and in the defamation context, where the speaker is unconcerned with truth, the effect may be both injury to the defamed and a discrediting of the media of communications. Second, according to the marketplace theory, the government generally is not the appropriate body to determine the truth of a statement—which this test would require. See *id.* at 536–37. Of course, courts do precisely this in many legal contexts. Finally, as a practical matter, the Court's test may not give the needed protection. *Id.* at 535–36. Goldberg, joined by Douglas, argued that the Court's analysis "is not responsive to the real issue presented by this case, which is whether that freedom of speech which all agree is constitutionally protected can be effectively safeguarded by a rule allowing the imposition of liability upon a jury's evaluation of the speaker's state of mind." 376 U.S. at 300. This danger is illustrated by the extent that people, at least during periods of hysteria, will conclude that their enemies, for example, the communists, should not be protected because they are not interested in truth. See *Dennis v. United States,* 341 U.S. 494 (1951). Following Goldberg, Emerson emphasizes the need to consider the systemic effects of the legal rules. T. Emerson, *General Theory, supra* note 12, at 16–46. Emerson notes: "Most of our efforts in the past have been seriously defective through failure to take into consideration the realistic context in which such limitations are administered." *Id.* at 16. In a very discouraging summary of convictions for speech during World War I, Professor Zechariah Chafee, Jr., reports a case where a jury "found the words, 'I am for the people, and the government is for the profiteers,' were a false statement, known to be false and intended and calculated to interfere with the success of our military and naval forces." Z. Chafee, *Free Speech in the United States* 53 (1941).

40. *Garrison v. Louisiana,* 379 U.S. 64, 75 (1964).

41. *Gertz v. Robert Welch, Inc.,* 418 U.S. 323, 348–50 (1974). One reason the Court gave for differentiating between public and private parties is their differential access to the media. *Id.* at 344. This explanation partially relies on the market failure model. See Chapter 2.

42. 418 U.S. 323 (1974).

43. *Id.* at 340.

44. *Id.* (emphasis added; citations omitted).

45. *Id.* (citations omitted).

46. Cf. *Dun & Bradstreet v. Greenmoss Builders,* 472 U.S. 749 (1985) (first amendment gives little protection to libel relating to a matter of merely private concern). The plurality opinion made little reference to marketplace theory. The case, however, should be understood less as indicating a view on the centrality of the marketplace of ideas to the first amendment than as contesting the relevant scope of that marketplace. See Chapter 2.

47. *Virginia State Bd. of Pharmacy v. Virginia Cit. Cons. Council,* 425 U.S. 748, 765 (1976).

48. *Id.* at 762. See also *Bigelow v. Virginia,* 421 U.S. 809, 826 (1975) (explicitly invoking the "marketplace of ideas" image in protecting advertisement concerning services related to obtaining a legal abortion).

49. See, e.g., articles cited in Chapter 9, n.134.

⌐ 50. *First National Bank of Boston v. Bellotti*, 435 U.S. 765 (1978). In *Federal Election Commission v. National Right to Work Committee*, 459 U.S. 197 (1982) the unanimous Court upheld a regulation of corporate political solicitations, contributions, and expenditures, suggesting that *Bellotti* may be limited to referenda campaigns. The two cases are arguably distinguishable. The law upheld was in a context that arguably involved a greater threat of real or apparent corruption, a factor the Court could employ in a balancing analysis. See *id.*, at 210 n.7. See also *Citizens Against Rent Control v. Berkeley*, 454 U.S. 290 (1981). Nevertheless, the Court emphasized the propriety of treating unions, corporations, and similar organizations differently from individuals. See also *FEC v. Mass. Citizens for Life*, 107 S.Ct. 616 (1986). This consideration, which did not appear in *Bellotti*, is explicitly contrary to the marketplace of ideas reasoning that dominated *Bellotti*. Apparently, the Court has not yet established a consistent approach to the first amendment in this context. In Chapter 9, I will argue that the *Bellotti* approach is misguided and should be abandoned.

51. 435 U.S. at 804–5, 812–21.

52. *Id.* at 777. The majority in *Bellotti* did not reject the importance of speech for individual self-expression. Instead, it argued that the first amendment protects both this individual autonomy interest and also the collective welfare interest in open and informed discussion. See, e.g., *id.* at 777 n.12, 783. Likewise, the dissent rejected neither rationale—but quite clearly it treated the first as more central and less abridgeable.

53. 341 U.S. 494 (1951).

54. *Id.* at 582, 588 (Douglas, dissenting).

55. *Id.* at 503 (citing *American Communications Association v. Douds*, 339 U.S. 382 (1950)). Frankfurter, concurring in the judgment, noted the "sobering fact that . . . we can hardly escape restriction on the interchange of ideas." *Id.* at 549. Frankfurter proceeded to elaborate and praise the theory that this interchange provides the best means for finding truth and displacing error. *Id.* at 550, 553–54.

56. R. Bernstein, *Beyond Objectivism and Relativism* (1983).

57. See T. Kuhn, *The Structure of Scientific Revolutions* (2d ed. 1970); M. Polyani, *Personal Knowledge* (1964).

58. For both a description of the modern view of knowledge and a discussion of the problems with it, see R. Unger, *Knowledge and Politics* (1975).

59. This assumption serves in my argument the same function served in Mill's argument by his assumption that nothing contrary to truth can be really useful. See *On Liberty*, *supra* note 3, at 28.

60. See J. Habermas, *Communication and the Evolution of Society* (1976); R. Unger, *supra* note 58, at 146–47, 234, 243–45, 248. But see *id.* at 230–31.

61. See Chapter 2.

62. R. Wolff, B. Moore, Jr., H. Marcuse, *A Critique of Pure Tolerance* 109–111 (1968).

63. See, e.g., P. Berger and T. Luckman, *The Social Construction of Reality* (1967); K. Mannheim, *Ideology and Utopia* (1954); C. Wight Mills, *Power, Politics, and People* (1967). See also P. Winch, *The Idea of Social Science and its Relation to Philosophy* (1958). Although now an established part of mainstream social science, this entire field owes a tremendous debt to the writings of Karl Marx.

64. One social science commentator observed:

The propagandist aware of the findings of the behavioral sciences no longer has as much confidence as his counterparts from the late eighteenth to the early twentieth century had in the ability of rational arguments or even of catchy slogans to influence human behavior. The evolution of psychoanalysis, clinical psychology, and experimental research on communication has made it clear that reactors' responses are affected not only by the immediate input of symbols but also (and often more powerfully) by three other sets of forces: (1) the stored residues of, and associations to, previous inputs of related symbols, which often give the reactor a predisposition and capacity to ignore or to rationalize away the current flow of symbols; (2) economic inducements . . . and coercive inducements. . .and (3) the coercive structures and processes in the surrounding social systems.

"Propaganda," *International Encyclopedia of the Social Sciences* 584 (1968) [hereafter cited as "Propaganda"].

65. A defense of the market model might suggest that, although not all people reason rationally all the time, progress results because some people are sometimes sufficiently insightful to reach an improved understanding and others recognize their gains and carry the insights forward. This defense, however, does not explain its last step, how people persuasively demonstrate their new insights to others. Given limited rationality, one might equally expect that existing "correct" insights would be abandoned—and the overall proportion of correct insights, existing plus newly found minus newly abandoned, would stay constant. Two explanations, however, might give reasons to believe that limited reason could produce gains. First, historical developments may make people desirous or in need of the new insights or perspectives. See T. Kuhn, *supra* note 57; Wallace, "Revitalization Movements," 58 *Am. Anthropologist* 264 (1956). Second, new insights that are put into practice might provide modes of interaction that people find more appealing or useful than dominant practices and, therefore, people would convert. Note that both explanations crucially depend not merely on the intellectual persuasiveness of the new viewpoints. Rather, both depend on the appeal of the implementation of the insights. This suggests that faith in the marketplace might be reasserted, but only if dissenting or minority groups are free to implement their perspectives. See Chapters 4 and 5.

66. On the notion of pure procedural justice, See J. Rawls, *A Theory of Justice* 84–87 (1971).

67. The power of dominant groups legally to restrict opportunities to practice alternatives, thereby restricting development of alternative perceptions or knowledge, can occur in two ways: (1) through legal prohibitions of certain behavior, but see Chapter 4; or (2) through legal control of economic resources enabling them to limit work experience, see Gintis, "Consumer Behavior and the Concept of Sovereignty: Explanations of Social Decay," 62 *Am. Econ. Rev., Papers & Proc. Supp.* 267, 271 (1972), or other consciousness forming experiences.

68. My critique of the marketplace theory, of course, does not stand alone. Particularly in the last ten years, numerous commentators have developed similar criticisms. See, e.g., F. Schauer, *supra* note 24, at 15–34 (1982) (particularly criticizing the rationality assumption). Others have pointed to additional problems. See, e.g., Ingber, "The Marketplace of Ideas: A Legitimizing Myth," 1984 *Duke L. J.* 1; L. Bollinger, *The Tolerant Society* 43–75 (1986). Bollinger describes as "Pollyannish [the] claim that truth will always win out as a natural result of evolutionary processes." *Id.* at 74. His main critique, however, is simply that often any marginal gain in truth that can be expected would not outweigh the extensive harm that certain speech can cause.

69. See Coase, "Advertising and Free Speech," 6 *J. Legal Studies* 1 (1977); Coase, "The Market for Goods and the Market for Ideas," 64 *Am. Econ. Rev., Pap. & Proc.* 384 (1974); Director, "The Parity of the Economic Market Place," 7 *J. Law & Econ.* 1, 6 (1964).

70. "Communications, Mass," 3 *Int'l Encyclopedia of the Social Sciences* 82 (1968).

71. *Id.* at 85.

72. Jaffe, "The Editorial Responsibility of the Broadcaster: Reflections on Fairness and Access," 85 *Harv. L. Rev.* 768, 769–70 (1972). Each of the conclusions in the text concerning the effects of the mass media is supported by Professor Jaffe's brief survey of communications theory.

73. E. Barnouw, *The Sponsor* (1978); B. Bagdikian, *The Media Monopoly* (1983). See generally Chapter 11.

74. Conflict could potentially arise between a class-conscious mass audience and power elites or dominant economic groups. In case of conflict, the second groups appear in effective control unless dissident groups can gain control of independent media. See Chapter 11. Generally, the most the mass audience can hope for may be the set of communications it most prefers that are also consistent with the interests of the power elite. (This hypothesis might be tested by considering the ways the media has responded, as it clearly has, to feminism.) To the extent dominant groups control the character and content of social experience, a congruence of mass desires and status quo promises can be expected. This congruence may be ruptured, however, if the system has important dysfunctional characteristics. See, e.g., J. Habermas, *Legitimation Crisis* (1975); C. Reich, *The Greening of America* (1970). Protected opportunities for people to develop alternative patterns of interaction could also contribute to change in the mass audience's perspectives.

75. In "Propaganda," *supra* note 64, at 587, the author first explained the ways in which people are not dominantly rational but are controlled by other factors. Then, with little explanation, the author expressed optimism that the marketplace would work:

> By definition, a healthily functioning democracy is a polity in which opposition to propaganda is habitually expressed primarily through peaceful counterpropaganda. It is assumed that a variety of propagandists will compete vigorously in "the marketplace of ideas," and it is hoped that the ideas best for society will find the most takers in the long run.

One wonders if faith in the marketplace is sustained precisely because the marketplace aids in preserving the existing order. Or is it because no meaningful alternative to the marketplace can be imagined? But see Chapters 4 and 5.

76. See Chapter 2.

77. See R. Wolff, B. Moore, Jr., H. Marcuse, *supra* note 61.

78. R. Unger, *supra* note 58, at 103, 242, 253, 255.

79. Mill implicitly approved this argument by explicitly rejecting its converse. Mill noted that authorities might defend suppression, not on the ground that they are infallible in their knowledge of truth but because the suppression is useful. Mill first responded that practices contrary to truth will not really be useful. But he also offered a practical argument unrelated to this assumption of objective truth. Mill claimed that the authorities' argument for suppression merely moves the authority's assumption of infallibility from a claim to know objective truth to a claim to know usefulness or, in modern terms, pragmatic truth. The authorities, however, have no better claim infallibly to know what is useful than to know what is true. Censorship is as likely to suppress views that will turn out to be useful as it is to suppress those that are true. *On Liberty, supra* note 3, at 27–28. Professor Bollinger, in contrast, notes that free speech advocates seldom examine the real harms speech can cause and, thus, finds this argument for the usefulness of suppression quite persuasive. L. Bollinger, *supra* note 68. At least as long as truth is not the only value and the marketplace is valued only instrumentally, as it is in marketplace theories, Bollinger's objections seem well made. In fact, Bollinger's point may explain precisely why marketplace theorists are so prone toward balancing.

80. Duval, "Free Communication of ideas and the Quest for Truth: Toward a Teleological Approach to First Amendment Adjudication," 41 *George Washington L. Rev.* 161 (1972).

81. *Id.* at 203.

82. *Id.* at 205–6.

83. See, e.g., R. Bernstein, *supra* note 56.

84. L. Wittgenstein, *On Certainty*; R. Rorty, *Consequences of Pragmatism* (1982).

85. "Usefulness" is indeterminant for reasons and in ways parallel to the indeterminacy of efficiency. See, e.g., Baker, "The Ideology of the Economic Analysis of Law," 5 *Phil. & Pub. Aff.* 3 (1975); Baker, "Posner's Privacy Mystery and the Failure of the Economic Analysis of Law," 12 *Georgia L. Rev.* 475 (1978).

86. Cf. Reisman, "Democracy and Defamation: Fair Game and Fair Comment I," 42 *Columbia L. Rev.* 1085 (1942). But see Baker, "Limitations on Basic Human Rights—A View from the United States," in *Limitations on Human Rights in Comparative Constitutional Law* 76, 93–102 (A. de Mestral et al., eds., 1986).

87. See note 85 *supra*.

88. See, Baker, "Sandel on Rawls," 133 *U. Pennsylvania L. Rev.* 895 (1985); Baker, "Outcome Equality or Equality of Respect: The Substantive Content of Equal Protection," 131 *U. Pennsylvania L. Rev.* 933, 949–59 (1983).

89. 343 U.S. 250 (1952). See *Collin v. Smith*, 578 F.2d 1197 (7th Cir.), *cert. denied*, 439 U.S. 916 (1978).

90. L. Bollinger, *supra* note 68, at 253–56 n.66 (describing the ban on racist speech in the Convention on Genocide and its implementation by many European countries).

91. See J. Habermas, *The Theory of Communicative Action, Vol. I* (1984); Cornell, "Toward a Modern/Postmodern Reconstruction of Ethics," 133 *U. Pennsylvania L. Rev.* 291 (1985).

92. A. Meiklejohn, *supra* note 4, at 26 (1965).

CHAPTER 2

1. Shiffrin, "The First Amendment and Economic Regulation: Away from a General Theory of the First Amendment," 78 *Northwestern L. Rev.* 1212, 1239 (1983). On the views of the colonists and framers as going beyond protection of political speech, see, e.g., Anderson, "The Origins of the Press Clause," 30 *UCLA L. Rev.* 455 (1983).

2. A. Meiklejohn, *Political Freedom: The Constitutional Powers of the People* (1965).

3. See, e.g., Kalven, Jr., "The New York Times Case: A Note on 'The Central Meaning of the First Amendment,'" 1964 *Sup. Ct. Rev.* 191.

4. See, e.g., Brennan, Jr., "The Supreme Court and the Meiklejohn Interpretation of the First Amendment," 79 *Harv. L. Rev.* 1 (1965).

5. Meiklejohn, "The First Amendment Is an Absolute," 1961 *Supreme Ct. Rev.* 245, 256–57.

6. Bork, "Neutral Principles and Some First Amendment Problems," 47 *Indiana L. J.* 1, 20, 29–30 (1971). Bork argued that "all other forms of speech raise only issues of human gratification, and their protection against legislative regulation involves the judge in making [illegitimate] decisions. . . ." *Id.* at 26. Thus, he could conclude that "constitutionally, art and pornography are on a par with industry and smoke pollution." *Id.* at 29. Although Bork, too, later broadened his conception of political speech to include, for example, scientific and moral debate, he long argued that since artistic speech does not "directly feed the democratic process," it should be subject to regulation. Bork, "The Individual, the State, and the First Amendment," unpublished speech, University of Michigan 1978, at 8. See also, BeVier, "The First Amendment and Political Speech," 30 *Stanford L. Rev.* 299 (1978).

7. *Connick v. Myers*, 461 U.S. 138 (1983); *Dun & Bradsteet v. Greenmoss Builders*, 472 U.S. 749 (1985).

8. 341 U.S. 494 (1951)

9. *Id.* at 545.

10. *Cohen v. California*, 403 U.S. 15, 25 (1971).

294

Notes for Pages 26–32

11. Chafee, "Book Review," 62 *Harv. L. Rev.* 891 (1949); Shiffrin, "Defamatory Non-Media Speech and First Amendment Methodology," 25 *U.C.L.A. L. Rev.* 915, 935–38 (1978).

12. See, e.g., Meiklejohn, *supra* note 5, at 262.

13. Shiffrin, *supra* note 1, at 1234. For example, since the Court first considered the issue in *Winters v. New York*, 333 U.S. 507 (1947), where even Justice Frankfurter in dissent agreed that "wholly neutral futilities" as well as Keats' poems are protected by freedom of speech, *id.* at 528, no Supreme Court Justice has accepted Bork's view that the first amendment does not protect artistic expression.

14. Redish, "The Value of Free Speech," 130 *U. Pa. L. Rev.* 591, 598–99 (1982).

15. The next paragraph follows critiques presented by others. See, e.g., Redish, *supra* note 14, at 599–601; Shiffrin, *supra* note 1, at 1233–39.

16. Bork, "Neutral Principles," *supra* note 6, at 26.

17. Other commentators will simply conclude that Bork is wrong to think that any uniform considerations distinguish protected speech from all other human activity. Instead, they will insist many overlapping, pragmatic concerns justify protection. See, e.g., Shiffrin, *supra* note 1.

18. *Whitney v. California*, 274 U.S. 357, 375 (1927) (Brandeis, joined by Holmes, concurring).

19. Bork appears to adopt this view when he claims that the one function of speech identified by Brandeis that merits constitutional protection is the "discovery and spread of political truth"— although Bork undercuts the relevance of this analysis by adopting an extremely relativistic notion of truth. Bork apparently identifies truth with whatever results from the process he chooses to protect. Bork, "Neutral Principles," *supra* note 6, at 26 (quoting Brandeis). Thus, his argument becomes circular since a different process, e.g., one that protected different speech or no speech, would merely produce different truths and Bork has given no reason not equally to value these alternatives for their contribution to those truths.

20. A. Meiklejohn, *supra* note 2, at 26.

21. *Id.* at 27 (emphasis added).

22. *Id.* at 27.

23. *Id.* at 59–60, 74–75.

24. Meiklejohn, *supra* note 5, at 263–64; Bork, "Neutral Principles," *supra* note 6, at 30.

25. C. B. Macpherson, *The Real World of Democracy* (1966).

26. *Whitney v. California*, 274 U.S. 357, 375 (1927) (Brandeis, joined by Holmes, concurring)(emphasis added).

27. Meiklejohn, *supra* note 5, at 263.

28. This interpretation, however, is in tension with other aspects of Meiklejohn's argument. An emphasis on people's participation in the activity of governing suggests that everyone must have the opportunity to participate. This would seem to reverse Meiklejohn's concern only that everything relevant be said.

29. Equality arguably plays a similar fundamental role. Elsewhere, I have examined the connection between liberty and equality and the content of this notion of equality. Baker, "Counting Preferences in Collective Choice Situations," 25 *U.C.L.A. L. Rev.* (1978); Baker, "Outcome Equality or Equality of Respect: The Substantive Content of Equal Protection," 131 *U. Pa. L. Rev.* 933 (1983).

30. Kennedy and Michelman, "Are Property and Contract Efficient?," 8 *Hofstra L. Rev.* 71 (1980).

31. See note 29 *supra*.

32. See, e.g., A. Meiklejohn, *supra* note 2, at 4, 19, 36–37, 75–76.

33. *United States v. Carolene Products Co.*, 304 U.S. 144, 152 n.4 (1938) ("It is unnecessary to consider now whether legislation which restricts those political processes which can ordinarily be expected to bring about repeal of undesirable legislation, is to be subjected to more exacting judicial scrutiny under the general prohibitions of the Fourteenth Amendment than are most other types of legislation.") Many, and most articulately Dean Ely, have argued that this and other portions of the footnote could provide a theory explaining most of modern constitutional law. J. Ely, *Democracy and Distrust* (1980). But see, Baker, "Neutrality, Process, and Rationality: Flawed Interpretations of Equal Protection," 58 *Texas L. Rev.* 1029 (1980).

34. See J. Ely, *supra* note 33.

35. *First National Bank v. Bellotti*, 435 U.S. 765 (1978). Protection of corporate political speech has been extensively criticized. See, *e.g.*, Marshall, "Book Review," 96 *Yale L.J.* 1687, 1697 (1987); Baker, "Realizing Self-Realization: Corporate Political Expenditures and Redish's The Value of Free Speech," 130 *U.Pa.L.Rev.* 646 (1982); Brudney, "Business Corporations and Stockholder's Rights Under the First Amendment," 91 *Yale L.J.* 235 (1981); Miller, "On Politics, Democracy, and the First Amendment: A Comment on First National Bank v. Bellotti," 38 *Wash. & Lee L. Rev.* 21 (1981); O'Kelley, "The Constitutional Rights of Corporations Revisited: Social and Political Expression and the Corporation after First National Bank v. Bellotti," 67 *Georgetown L. J.* 1347 (1979); Note, "The Corporation and the Constitution: Economic Due Process and Corporate Speech," 90 *Yale L. J.* 1833 (1981).

36. Meiklejohn, *supra* note 5.

37. Z. Chafee, Jr., *Free Speech in the United States* 53 (1941).

38. One fear is that the calculated political lie would be used, often at the last minute, to win elections. I am inclined to think that any attempt to forbid these lies, e.g., requiring a second election if a court concludes that a candidate's calculated lies significantly contributed to the candidate's success, would create more problems than it would solve. The legal solution is unlikely to reach the most offensive and distortive campaign propaganda— racist speech, unrealizable or inconsistent promises or merely massive doses of simplistic pandering. See *Brown v. Hartlege*, 456 U.S. 46 (1982). On the other hand, the danger of public exposure of overt lies is likely to be as effective as legal sanctions to deter this type of speech. Finally, any large category of prohibited lies would likely produce continual judicial challenges to election results.

Nevertheless, a possible doctrinal argument would be that setting aside the election because of a calculated political lie would not abridge freedom of speech. First, the government would only be setting up and enforcing the rules for determining when someone has won the election. Like rules to keep order in the court, certain speech would not be permitted in this governmentally set up practice. No punishment—jail or monetary liability—would follow from the speech. Since the "only" sanction would be a new election, no one would be stopped from saying anything. Dissident groups, unable to win elections, would not be threatened at all. Finally, popular will could still prevail. In the new election, voters could always re-elect the person the court found to have lied—as they re-elected socialist representatives whom legislative bodies refused to seat during the early twentieth century. Nevertheless, this argument may "prove" too much. The threat of requiring a new election is quite obviously a penalty for the speech. *Brown v. Hartlege.*

39. *Whitney v. California*, 274 U.S. 357, 375 (1927). (Brandeis, joined by Holmes, concurring).

40. Cf. R. Dworkin, "Civil Disobedience," *Taking Rights Seriously* 206–222 (1977).

41. After a thorough survey of political repression by the United States government, Robert Goldstein argues that an important variable affecting the degree of repression is the opposition or lack of opposition to repression by key elites—i.e., lower-level govern-

mental officials, intellectuals, journalists, lawyers, business executives and labor leaders. R. Goldstein, *Political Repression in Modern America: From 1870 to the Present* 559, 572–74 (1978).

42. A public-issue orientation can also cause an especially intense negative reaction to political speech that is thought to be misguided. Committed reformers (or revolutionists) who believe in a radical split between ends and means, a view I criticize in Chapter 5, may not find the argument for tolerance described in the text to be relevant. Their intense concern with creating a better society often provides a strong, public- spirited reason for seeking to suppress the Nazi's expression or the picketers and civilly disobedient protes- tors outside abortion clinics. When the protest activities violate laws, sometimes distinc- tions can be made between appropriate legal responses, e.g., the decision to prosecute, depending on whether the protest activities interfere with other people's, particularly the less powerful people's, ability to exercise their rights. See R. Dworkin, *Taking Rights Seri- ously* 206–22 (1978). Differential standards for treating actual civil disobedience depend- ing on the circumstances do not, however, justify restricting any demonstrator's first amendment rights.

43. "The guarantees for free speech and press are not the preserve of political expres- sion or comment upon public affairs, essential as those are to healthy government." *Time, Inc v. Hill*, 385 U.S. 374, 388 (1967), cited in *Dun & Bradstreet v. Greenmoss*, 472 U.S. 749, 777 (1985) (Brennan, Marshall, Stevens, dissenting). "Of course it is immaterial whether the beliefs sought to be advanced by association pertain to political, economic, religious, or cultural matters." *NAACP v Alabama*, 357 U.S. 449, 469 (1958). "Nothing in the First Amendment or our cases discussing its meaning make the question of whether the adjective 'political' can properly be attached to those beliefs the critical constitutional inquiry." *Abood v. Detroit Board of Educ.*, 431 U.S. 209, 231 (1977). *Id.* at 231 n.28 (quot- ing 13 more cases rejecting the political/nonpolitical line). "[E]ven though political speech is entitled to the fullest possible measure of constitutional protection, there are a host of other communications that command the *same* respect. . . .To create an exception for appellees' political speech and not for these other types of speech might create a risk of engaging in constitutionally forbidden content discrimination." *City Council v. Taxpayers for Vincent*, 466 U.S.789, 816 (1984) (emphasis added). "Above all else, the First Amend- ment means that government has no power to restrict expression because of its message, its ideas, its subject matter, or its content. . . . To permit the continued building of our politics and culture, and *to assure self-fulfillment for each individual, our people are guar- anteed the right to express any thought*, free from government censorship." *Police Dept. v. Mosley*, 408 U.S. 92, 95–96 (1972) (emphasis added) (citations omitted). "It is never- theless often true that one man's vulgarity is another's lyric. Indeed, we think it is largely because governmental officials cannot make principled distinctions in this area that the Constitution leaves matters of taste and style largely to the individual." *Cohen v. Califor- nia*, 403 U.S. 15, 25 (1970).

44. My textual claims apply best to the use of this type of dicta by certain Justices, for example, Justice William Brennan, Jr. Recently, the Court has, I think, misused this dicta in the context of giving lesser protection to commercial speech and "adult fare" enter- tainment. In Chapter 9, I argue that commercial speech should not be protected and in Chapters 4 and 8 I argue that "zoning" notions may properly apply to some entertainment activities—but these arguments are not premised on the greater constitutional status of political speech as compared to other protected speech.

45. See, e.g., B. Bagdikian, *The Media Monopoly* (1983).

46. See, e.g., E. Barnouw, *The Sponsor* (1978).

47. See, e.g., B. Owen, *Economics and Freedom of Expression* (1975) (arguing for struc- tural reform including antitrust enforcement); Cooper, "The Tax Treatment of Business

Grassroots Lobbying: Defining and Attaining the Public Policy Objectives," 68 *Columbia L. Rev.* 801, 841–59 (1968) (suggesting method of using tax laws as incentives for political speech of private groups, particularly relatively poor groups).

48. J. S. Mill, *On Liberty* (1956) (1st ed. 1859) at 46.

49. In *Red Lion Broadcasting Co. v. FCC*, 395 U.S. 367 (1969), the Court upheld the "fairness doctrine," which was considered to be a method of assuring that the electronic media would air views on the most important issue. In various cases the Court has suggested that it would assure that effective channels of communication exist for all positions. *Linmark Assoc., Inc. v. Township of Willingboro*, 413 U.S. 85, 93 (1977) (one of two grounds for decision); *Columbia Broadcasting Sys. v. Democratic Nat'l Comm.*, 412 U.S. 94, 122 (1973) (the Court, quoting Meiklejohn, suggests that assuring an effective forum for all viewpoints is constitutionally crucial: "'[W]hat is essential is not that everyone shall speak, but that everything worth saying shall be said'"); *id.* at 193–96 (Brennan & Marshall, dissenting); *United States v. O'Brien*, 391 U.S. 367, 388–89 (1968) (Harlan, concurring).

50. The Court, for example, has struck down laws restricting people's use of their money to continue speaking even after their view is "adequately" expressed in the market place. *Buckley v. Valeo*, 424 U.S. 1 (1976). The Court has also struck down laws requiring some access to the print media and rejected proposals that it assure some access to broadcast media as being contrary to, or at least not required by, the first amendment. *Miami Herald Publishing Co. v. Tornillo*, 418 U.S. 241 (1974); *Columbia Broadcasting Sys. v. Democratic Nat'l Comm.*, 412 U.S. 94 (1973). But cf. *Red Lion Broadcasting Co. v. FCC*, 395 U.S. 367 (1969) (upholding "fairness doctrine," requiring each side of public issues to be presented by the media). These decisions implicitly reject the market failure model. And although the Court continued to invoke marketplace language, see, e.g., *Miami Herald Publishing Co. v. Tornillo*, 418 U.S. at 529 (White, concurring), the decisions are best explained by a liberty theory. Baker, "Commercial Speech: A Problem in the Theory of Freedom," 62 *Iowa L. Rev.* 1, 41–42 n.144.

51. D. Ginsburg, *Regulation of Broadcasting* 556–612 (1979); L. Powe, Jr., *American Broadcasting and the First Amendment* 108–161 (1987).

52. This model develops difficulties if an information overload, too much "noise," decreases people's ability or willingness to assimilate messages. If even a minimal presentation of all viewpoints would produce dysfunctional levels of "noise," instead of guaranteeing presentation opportunities for all viewpoints, arguably speech should be left unregulated in the hope that the messages most often presented will be closer to truth than those not presented. Alternatively, limits on how much a given message could be presented could be imposed in the hope of reducing "noise" distortion. But cf. *Buckley v. Valeo*, 424 U.S. 1 (1976) (invalidating expenditure limits).

53. Federal Election Campaign Act of 1971, 2 U.S.C. §§431–456 (1976); 47 U.S.C. §§ 801–805 (Supp. II 1972), as amended by Pub. L. No. 93–443, 88 Stat. 1263 (1974).

54. *Harper v. Virginia Bd. of Elections*, 383 U.S. 663 (1966) (striking down poll tax). See also *Lubin v. Panish*, 415 U.S. 709 (1974); *Bullock v. Carter*, 405 U.S. 1344 (1972).

55. See Baker, "The Ideology of the Economic Analysis of Law," 5 *Philosophy & Pub. Aff.* 3, 32–41 (1975).

56. For example, this is accomplished by giving people full credit against their taxes for political expenditures (contributions) up to a certain level and, for people who do not pay taxes, by directly giving them rebates for political expenditures. Absent this second procedure, the law should succumb to an equal protection attack.

57. Baker, "Counting Preferences in Collective Choice Situations," 25 *UCLA L.Rev.* 381 (1978).

58. R. Dworkin, *supra* note 42, at 150–205; Baker, *supra* note 55, at 48–55.

59. Baker, "Sandel on Rawls," 133 *U. Pa L. Rev.* 895 (1985); Baker, "Outcome Equality or Equality of Respect: The Substantive Content of Equal Protection," 131 *U. Pa. L. Rev.* 933 (1983) [hereafter, Baker, Outcome Equality].

60. Michelman, "On Protecting the Poor Through the Fourteenth Amendment," 83 *Harvard L. Rev.* 7 (1969). Baker, Outcome Equality, *supra* note 59. See *San Antonio Independent School Dist. v. Rodriguez,* 411 U.S. 1, 23–24, 25 n.60, 36–37 (1973).

61. 391 U.S. 367 (1968).

62. This "passage [in the Court's opinion] does not foreclose consideration of First Amendment claims . . . [where a regulation] has the effect of entirely preventing a 'speaker' from reaching a significant audience with whom he could not otherwise lawfully communicate." 391 U.S. at 388–89 (Harlan, concurring).

63. Interestingly, the clearest example of the Court relying on this "adequacy of access" argument involved a situation where those excluded were not political dissidents but were presumably quite middle class. *Linmark Assoc., Inc. v. Township of Willingboro,* 431 U.S. 85, 93 (1977) (one ground for invalidating a ban on "For Sale" signs on homes was that the homeowners did not have "satisfactory" alternative means of communication). Cases protecting the expressive conduct of civil rights activists in the South might appear to contradict the generalization in the text. However, when these cases favored the dissidents, the Court usually relied either on discriminatory enforcement (content discrimination) or on statutory vagueness or overbreadth grounds to set aside the convictions—not "adequacy" arguments. Unless the Court fully adopts the perspective of the dissidents, these faults are more easily seen and more easily corrected by judicial decrees than is the inadequacy of access opportunities.

64. *Abrams v. United States,* 250 U.S. 616, 630 (1919) (Holmes & Brandeis, dissenting).

65. The Court noted that equality of input may produce a troublesome inequality of opportunity, for example, for those lacking name recognition before the campaign. *Buckley v. Valeo,* 424 U.S. 1, 56–57 (1976).

66. These objections to equalization are suggested by Winter, "Poverty, Economic Equality, and the Equal Protection Clause," 1972 *Sup. Ct. Rev.* 41. Mistakes in Winter's analysis, see, e.g., Baker, "Utility and Rights: Two Justifications for State Action Increasing Equality, 84 *Yale L. J.* 39, 44 n. 17 (1974), make these objections less persuasive if the subsidy is constitutionally required rather than legislatively chosen and if the subsidy attempts to achieve a minimal level of "merit good" availability rather than absolute equality.

67. Baker, Outcome Equality, *supra* note 59.

CHAPTER 3

1. T. Emerson, *The System of Freedom of Expression* 6–7 (1971) [hereafter cited as *Freedom of Expression*]; T. Emerson, *Toward a General Theory of the First Amendment* 3–15 (1966).

2. Since "*democratic* participation in change" focuses on individuals' freedom to participate, if the speech is not chosen by anyone and is not properly treated as a manifestation of the speaker's values, even though the speech may cause change or advance knowledge, it does not serve this liberty value and is not protected.

3. See R. Dworkin, *Taking Rights Seriously* (1977); J. Rawls, *A Theory of Justice* (1971); Baker, "Utility and Rights: Two Justifications for State Action Increasing Equality," 84 *Yale L. J.* 39 (1974).

4. See generally, J. Habermas, *The Theory of Communicative Action, Vol.I* (1984).

5. Scanlon, "A Theory of Freedom of Expression," 1 *Philosophy & Pub. Aff.* 204, 206–7 (1972).

6. Most thoughtful commentators agree with Scanlon's categorization. See, e.g., L. Tribe, *American Constitutional Law* 601, 605 (1978); Nimmer, "The Meaning of Symbolic Speech Under the First Amendment," 21 *UCLA L. Rev.* 29, 36 (1973). Professor Kent Greenawalt emphasizes that the free speech principle primarily covers "assertions of fact and value." K. Greenawalt, *Speech, Crime, and the Uses of Language* (1989) [hereafter cited as Greenawalt, *Uses of Language*].

7. G. Orwell, *1984* (1948).

8. Cf. *Stanley v. Georgia*, 394 U.S. 557 (1969) (statute banning private possession of obscene material held unconstitutional). This case led to the interpretation of the Court's decisions as protecting obscenity only to the extent that no communication between people, at least people outside the home, was involved. *United States v. Thirty-Seven Photographs*, 402 U.S. 363, 382 (1971) (Black & Douglas, dissenting) (Court's treatment of *Stanley* may only protect a person who "writes salacious books in his attic, prints them in his basement, and reads them in his living room"). Compare praying in a state that wants to promote atheism.

9. Compare Karl Marx's report that in ancient India the "poet . . . in some communities replaces the silversmith, in others the school master." K. Marx, *Capital* 357–58 (1967). A liberty theory recognizes both, the marketplace theory only encompasses the school master.

10. L. Wittgenstein, *Philosophical Investigations* §304 (3d ed. 1958).

11. *Id.* at §23 (emphasis added). After listing various uses, Wittgenstein continues: "It is interesting to compare the multiplicity of the tools in language and of the ways they are used, the multiplicity of kinds of word and sentence, with what logicians have said about the structure of language." *Id.*

12. *Genesis* 1:3 (emphasis added). See also *Psalms* 33:9 ("For he spoke, and it came to be"); *Hebrews* 11:3 ("By faith we understand that the world was created by the word of God"). Richardson explains that to the Hebrew mind: "Thought, word, and deed are not three separate processes or acts but are organic elements of the same single process, an act of volition." *A Theological Word Book of the Bible* 232 (A. Richardson ed. 1950).

13. H. Arendt, *The Human Condition* 25–26 (1958) (emphasis added).

14. *Id.* at 177. See also *id.* at 175–81.

15. *Id.* at 190.

16. A. Macleish, *Poems, 1924–1933* 123 (1933).

17. G. Bachelard, *The Poetics of Space* XVIII (1969).

18. *Id.* at xix–xx. Compare Pierre-Jean Jouve's statement that "[T]here is no poetry without absolute creation." Quoted in *id.* at xxviii.

19. See *Freedom of Expression, supra* note 1, at 338.

20. Of course, a rule utilitarian could view the Constitution as merely restricting governmental actions that, although possibly welfare-promoting or harm-preventing, are particularly prone to be mistaken.

21. Nozick, "Coercion," in *Philosophy, Science, and Method* 440, 459 (S. Morgenbesser, P. Suppes & M. White eds. 1969).

22. In developing this description of threats, I am influenced by Nozick, note 21 *supra*. See also Kreimer, "Allocation Sanctions: The Problem of Negative Rights in a Positive State," 132 *U. Pa. L. Rev.* 1293, 1352–59 (1984) and sources cited *id.* at 1353 n.220; and F. Haiman, *Speech and Law in a Free Society* 209–241 (1981). But I deviate from Nozick in two main ways. For reasons noted in the text, I conclude that the benchmark position cannot be merely the "normal and expected course of events," but must be events or

options that, under the circumstances, the person has a moral or legitimate right to expect. (Of course, often the normal course of events contributes greatly to what one has a right to expect.) Second, because in the context of blackmail the threatener may have a right or even a duty to give information to others (e.g., the police), Nozick viewed the blackmailer's statement that she would accept payment in return for making the disclosure to be an offer. *Id.* at 447. A better approach would be to treat the benchmark as defined not only by opportunities to which the threatened person has a rightful expectation but also by the rights of the threatener. If the speaker has no normative right to engage in her "proposed action," the positive law could prohibit her from engaging in the action for instrumental purposes, thus making the proposal a threat. See text accompanying note 25 *infra.*

23. The key problem in this second category is finding the theoretical limits on the extent to which the state can restrict the threatener's "rights" to use various means.

24. If an observer distinguishes more positive, conventional rights—rights that typically determine the instrumental significance of a person's acts—from rights essential to a person's autonomy, the autonomy rights must normally supersede (others') conventional rights. However, a person's autonomy rights cannot override another's autonomy. In this context, respect for a person's autonomy, for a person's speech rights, does not bar legal control of the person's speech. Speech that invades another's area of autonomy is coercive and can be regulated. Note, however, that reputation, which depends on the precise form of the social order and the attitudes of other people, is clearly conventional or instrumental, not an autonomy right in the sense described above.

25. Cf. *United States v. Ballard*, 322 U.S. 78 (1944). The defendants were charged with obtaining money by false representations. The Court held that the Constitution prevented conviction for making false religious claims—i.e., the truth of the religious claims could not be submitted to a jury. It did not decide, however, whether the defendants could be convicted for making religious claims that they believed to be false. In dissent, Justices Stone, Roberts, and Frankfurter concluded that the defendants could be and were properly convicted for making representations which they did not believe. *Id.* at 89–90. Note that although the effect on the listener would be the same whether or not the speakers believed their statements, the purpose or nature of the speaker's act would be different. In *Ballard*, to make knowingly false representations would disrespect the other's mental processes and, hence, would be the type of speech that I argue is coercive.

26. The distinction between the way the person uses information in blackmailing and whistle blowing corresponds in many ways to the distinction between the "use value" and "exchange value" of property, a distinction discussed in Chapter 9. For the speaker, exposure has only exchange value in blackmail but use value in whistle blowing.

27. K. Greenawalt, *Uses of Language, supra* note 6. See also Greenawalt, "Criminal Coercion and Freedom of Speech," 78 *Northwestern L. Rev.* 1081 (1983) [hereafter cited as Greenawalt, "Criminal Coercion"]. Professor Greenawalt's article is an extended comment on the leading case on the subject, *State v. Robertson*, 293 Or. 402, 649 P.2d 569 (1982), written by a major first amendment scholar, Judge Hans Linde.

28. Greenawalt recognizes that this expression will imply or involve some fact and value assertions, but suggests that this will be no more than is implicit in virtually any behavior. K. Greenawalt, *Uses of Language, supra* note 6, at 60; Greenawalt, "Criminal Coercion," *supra* note 27, at 1095, 1110.

29. K. Greenawalt, *Uses of Language, supra* note 6, at 95.

30. *Id.* at 63–65.

31. But see, Chapter 9 (many market-oriented or instrumental exchanges are subject to regulation). Greenawalt's conclusion also presumably rejects protection for associations that, typically, are based on at least implicit agreements. Likewise, note his relatively

dismissive treatment of first amendment objections to conspiracy law. This treatment is characteristic of marketplace theories but not of the liberty theory which not only would protect cooperative associations but also the offer and the agreement to associate. See Chapters 4 and 7.

In various ways, including his notion of distinguishing "assertions of fact or value" from "situation-altering utterances" as well as his argument that many factual statements simply are true or false (strongly suggesting "objective" notions of truth), Greenawalt implicitly adopts an epistomology radically dependent on a subject-object split, a view quite different from the one accepted here. Note that a dialogic theorist, see, e.g., Cornell, "Toward a Modern/Postmodern Reconstruction of Ethics," 133 *U.Pa.L.Rev* 291 (1985), would argue that a central function of speech is attempting "to come to agreement." Admittedly, Greenawalt would protect agreements about facts and judgments, claiming that only agreements about actions are situation altering. From a dialogic perspective, however, the difference between the two types of agreements in not obvious.

Possibly, for Greenawalt, agreements about facts and judgments are not situation-altering because in reaching agreement the subject does not act on the object but at most changes her perception of it, while agreements about actions involve commitments of subjects (one or both parties to the agreement) to do something to some object (even if the object is a person).

In contrast, to the extent knowledge exists within language and "ways of life," dialogue aimed at agrement on facts and values as well as agreements on actions or modifications of practices changes the world. Both similarly change the environment with which we are faced. Both can change our perceptions; both make the world different for us and change our options.

32. Of course, Greenawalt treats agreements and offers as situation altering. I have noted objections to that analysis of agreements, see note 31. In addition, even within Greenawalt's epistemology there should be a sense in which agreements change the situation while offers do not. An offer merely gives information, asserts facts, about what the speaker is prepared to do. But it does not change the situation, other than by providing the information about willingness to enter into an agreement, until someone takes whatever further step, required by recognized practices, that causes the two to have formed an agreement.

33. K. Greenawalt, *Uses of Language, supra* note 6, at 94.

34. Given Greenawalt's emphasis that the free speech principle covers all assertions of fact and value, he might be expected to find the speech covered even if he thought the second portion contained situation-altering elements. See *id.* at 61, 62.

35. It also seems genuinely communicative of information to offer to engage in an unnatural response like paying money.

36. At times, Greenawalt also emphasizes that the issue is *the way* the utterance changes the situation. *Id.* at 61. This recognition pushes the disagreement back to identifying the framework that best explains the difference between the protected and the unprotected *manner.*

37. *New York Times Co. v. United States*, 403 U.S. 713 (1971). See, Linde, "Courts and Censorship," 66 *Minn. L. Rev.* 171 (1981) (on the Court's unfortunate dicta in *Near v. Minnesota*, 283 U.S. 697 (1931), that the first amendment does not protect publication of ship's sailing dates).

38. *Freedom of Expression, supra* note 1, at 58–59.

39. See Linde, "'Clear and Present Danger' Reexamined," 22 *Stanford L. Rev.* 1163 (1970); Greenawalt, "Speech and Crime," 1980 *Am. Bar Found. Res. J.* 645.

40. Alternatively, the argument in the text might be taken as a reason to accept Emerson's categorizations if, for other reasons, it seems prudent to adopt his "systems" anal-

ysis—distinguishing between the "system of military operation" and "the system of freedom of expression." Still, Emerson's approach allows greater restrictions, e.g., where the espionage agent's acts are too far removed from any actual, attempted, or foreseen use of violence to justify prohibiting or punishing the speech act under my argument. If, however, courts are going to allow this behavior to be prohibited, Emerson's categorization might promote greater purity in overall doctrine, an important practical achievement.

41. *Cf.* 18 U.S.C. 794 (criminalizing giving national defense information to a foreign nation) *with* 18 U.S.C. 793 (criminalizing giving or receiving similar information if the recipient is unauthorized to receive it, presumably applicable even if the speech is public or the recipient is the press). See *United States of America v. Morrison*, 844 F.2d 1057 (4th Cir. 1988).

42. In protecting the privacy of involuntary listeners, the government cannot regulate in a way that would prevent the speaker from communicating with willing listeners or burden the listener's receipt of desired communications. *Erznoznik v. City of Jacksonville*, 422 U.S. 205 (1975); *Cohen v. California*, 403 U.S. 15 (1971); *Lamont v. Postmaster Gen.*, 381 U.S. 301 (1965); *Saia v. New York*, 334 U.S. 558 (1948); *Martin v. City of Struthers*, 319 U.S. 141 (1943). However, some content-neutral time, place, and manner regulations may be acceptable. *Kovacs v. Cooper*, 336 U.S. 77 (1949). See Chapter 8. Restraints that *only prevent* communications directed to unwilling listeners will be upheld. *Rowan v. Post Office Dep't*, 397 U.S. 728 (1970); *Martin v. City of Struthers*, 319 U.S. 141, 147–48 (1943) (dicta) (state can punish those who call on a home "in defiance of the previously expressed will of the occupant"). The listener's right to hear, read, or see when there is no willing speaker or when the speaker has no legal right to speak is, at best, weakly protected. Some cases apparently have recognized some status for this first amendment right, creating an issue that deserves more attention than it will be given here, although I would argue that some of these were wrongly decided and others are supportable on alternative grounds. See, e.g., *Richmond Newspapers, Inc. v. Virginia*, 448 U.S. 555 (1980); *First Nat'l Bank v. Bellotti*, 435 U.S. 765 (1978); *Virginia State Bd. of Pharmacy v. Virginia Cit. Cons. Council*, 425 U.S. 748 (1976); *Kleindienst v. Mandel*, 408 U.S. 753 (1972); *Zemel v. Rusk*, 381 U.S. 1 (1965). See also cases discussed in note 43 *infra*.

43. These cases are often cited to support an independent right to know: *Virginia State Bd. of Pharmacy v. Virginia Citizens Consumer Council, Inc.*, 425 U.S. 748 (1976) (invalidated prohibition of pharmacists' advertising drugs in suit brought by consumers); *Red Lion Broadcasting Co. v. FCC*, 395 U.S. 367 (1969) (upheld fairness doctrine in broadcasting); and *Lamont v. Postmaster Gen.*, 381 U.S. 301 (1965) (struck down regulation burdening receipt of communist political propaganda mailed from abroad). See L. Tribe, *supra* note 6, at 675–676 nn.7 & 8.

Nevertheless, these cases could mostly be given a different interpretation. Under *Virginia Board of Pharmacy*, once the Court concludes that the first amendment protects commercial speech, presumably the first amendment protects the pharmacist's speech. See *Bates v. State Bar of Arizona*, 432 U.S. 350 (1977). *Red Lion* arguably recognized the permissibility of the government's regulation of broadcast media as a partial common carrier (or partial public forum), not a right to know. See *Columbia Broadcasting Sys. v. Democratic Nat'l Comm.*, 412 U.S. 94 (1973). *Lamont* does not require a theory of special listener's rights since the first amendment, which limits government power rather than giving individuals' rights, should not permit the government to abridge the freedom of speech of foreigners. Clearly a willing speaker (with liberty interests) and a willing listener existed in *Lamont*. Moreover, unlike in *Kleindienst v. Mandel*, 408 U.S. 753 (1972) (foreigner not allowed to enter the United States even though he wished to engage in speech activities; his written or telephonic communications were allowed entry), the legal burden in *Lamont* was placed directly on the communication between willing speakers and listeners whose liberty interests were unquestionably involved. In *Mandel*, the burden was placed on unprotected activities of foreigners and the law merely had some limited effect on communications.

44. Of course, increased access to information is normally a desirable societal policy. The general allocation effects of policies increasing access to governmental and corporate controlled information may be to increase the egalitarian and democratic nature of society. See Baker, "Posner's Privacy Mystery and the Failure of Economic Analysis of Law," 12 *Georgia L. Rev.* 475 (1978).

45. Sometimes people may have a constitutionally based privacy right to have the government not provide sensitive personal information that the government possesses to interested "listeners." Cf. *Whalen v. Roe*, 429 U.S. 589 (1976) (dicta recognizing this right of informational privacy) with *Paul v. Davis*, 424 U.S. 693 (1976) (no constitutional violation for government to post information that person was suspected thief).

46. 17 U.S.C. §106. *Sony Corp. of America v. Universal City Studios*, 464 U.S. 417 (1984) (personal use of VCR to tape copyrighted material is not a copyright infringement).

47. See, e.g., *Richmond Newspapers, Inc. v. Virginia*, 448 U.S. 555 (1980).

48. *Nebraska Press Ass'n. v. Stuart*, 427 U.S. 539 (1976). See *New York Times Co. v. United States*, 403 U.S. 713 (1971). Of course, the argument in the text may have skipped a step. If the press as listener used illegal means to obtain the information, does that justify a limit on its use of the information? Although the courts have not unambiguously answered this question, protecting the person's rights as a speaker would require that the state only be permitted to punish the illegal acts involved in obtaining the information, not its later use. See *Nebraska Press Ass'n v. Stuart*, 427 U.S. at 598 (Brennan, Stewart & Marshall, concurring) (concluding that an injunction restraining publication would not be justified no matter how the information was obtained).

49. *Virginia State Bd. of Pharmacy v. Virginia Citizens Consumer Council, Inc.*, 425 U.S. at 781–82 (Rehnquist, dissenting).

50. In *Stanley v. Georgia*, 394 U.S. 557 (1969), the Court apparently recognized the importance of the liberty interest of the reader. Cf. L. Tribe, *supra* note 6, at 676–77 (interpreting *American Mini Theatres* as involving only the lesser right of the listener if the commercial speaker had no personal first amendment claim). But see *United States v. 12 200-Foot Reels of Film*, 413 U.S. 123 (1973). The commercial publisher or the distributor is the more typical defendant in an obscenity prosecution. Whether this defendant manifests a liberty interest or a market-enforced profit motive may be difficult to determine. However, the first amendment protects one particular industry—the press—from regulations relating to its product on a fourth estate theory and on the basis of the conclusion that generally its product, print or speech, contributes importantly to its recipients' liberty while not itself being coercively or violently destructive. See Chapter 10. Thus, the liberty interest of the reader and the special constitutional status of the press combine to protect both parties in the distribution or communication of obscenity.

51. The argument of this chapter and the book is not intended to denigrate reasons other than respect for individual liberty to protect speech—e.g., the allocational concerns that would justify protection of drug price advertising. These other concerns, however, usually have two problems as constitutional standards as opposed to bases for legislative action or common law development. First, they typically seem to concern the type of judgments and trade-offs appropriate for collective political bodies and concern utilitarian welfare values that usually do not require constitutional protection. See Fried, "Two Concepts of Interests: Some Reflections on the Supreme Court's Balancing Test," 76 *Harvard L. Rev.* 755 (1963). Second, and relatedly, pursuit of these concerns usually requires tradeoffs with other concerns and, thus, does not provide clear standards for constitutional decision making.

CHAPTER 4

1. *Stromberg v. California*, 283 U.S. 359 (1931).
2. This distinction between "expression" and "action" provides "[t]he central idea of a system of freedom of expression." That system "cannot exist effectively on any other foundation, and a decision to maintain such a system necessarily implies acceptance of this proposition." T. Emerson, *The System of Freedom of Expression* 17 (1971).
3. *Id.* at 18.
4. *Id.*
5. See J. Austin, *How To Do Things with Words* (1962).
6. Or the choice might be "logical" if logic is seen as conventional. See C. Wright Mills, *Power, Politics, and People* (1967). Mills quotes Ernest Nagel who argued that "the principles of logic are. . .conventional without being arbitrary." Mills then suggests that "laws of proof may be merely the conventional abstract rules governing what are accepted as valid conversational extensions." *Id.* at 428. In a separate essay Mills argues that "motives are the terms with which interpretation of conduct *by social actors* proceeds." *Id.* at 440 (emphasis original). Presumably, whether the motive attributed to the actor was "to do" or "to express" depends on the social context and on the needs of the interpreter.
7. The size of a demonstration hardly affects the logic of a demonstrators' views. Rather, the existence and size of the assembly are important because they suggest the power and willingness of people to promote the position. Likewise, a group boycott expresses ideas but, equally important, it exercises power. See Chapter 7.
8. *Freedom of Expression, supra,* note 2, at 293 (emphasis added).
9. *Id.* at 89.
10. *Id.* (emphasis added). Of course, those using coercion or pressure may believe that their acts will induce change by causing people to change their opinions. Indeed, they may only want to stimulate discussion, e.g., "raise consciousness," in these "action" cases.
11. Failing to carry a draft card presumably "interferes" or "obstructs" the working of the selective service system and for that reason apparently is classified as an "action" by Emerson. *Id.* at 86–87.
12. *Id.* at 84.
13. *Id.* at 445. This difference does not rely on Emerson's exclusion of commercial activities from the scope of the system of freedom of expression. *Id.* at 19–20, 447.
14. *Id.* at 445.
15. *Id.* (emphasis added).
16. *NAACP v. Claiborne Hardware Co.*, 458 U.S. 886, 921 (1982). The Court's description of this activity as coercive represents an unduly broad conception of coercion, at least if the concept is to play the role suggested in this book.
17. See *Organization for a Better Austin v. Keefe*, 402 U.S. 415 (1971); *NAACP v. Claiborne Hardware*, 458 U.S. 886 (1982).
18. J. S. Mill, *On Liberty* 13 (1956) (emphasis added).
19. See Baker, "Counting Preferences in Collective Choice Situations," 25 *UCLA L. Rev.* 381 (1978).
20. Cf. *New York Times v. Sullivan*, 376 U.S. 254 (1964) (invalidating state libel law that gave a person authority to control—or to demand compensatory damages because of—certain speech of others). Various constitutional provisions, including the first amendment, due process, equal protection, and the prohibition on involuntary servitude, may limit the way government can allocate decision-making authority concerning a person's body. The government cannot give another, e.g., a husband or parent, the right to prohibit or require a woman to have an abortion. See *Planned Parenthood v. Danforth*, 428 U.S. 52 (1976). Possibly more is required. The concept of a person as someone whose

dignity, integrity, and autonomy are respected generally requires that the person have decision authority over the purposes for which his or her body is used. One arguably has a right not to be required to use one's body over a long period of time to aid and support another, even though it is readily conceded that one may be required to forego claims to physical or economic resources needed to benefit another. This right would support the second of two arguments commonly invoked to support the claimed right not to be prohibited from having an abortion. The two arguments are: (1) A fetus is not a person, an issue which has no clear resolution; and (2) one cannot be forced involuntarily to use one's body to support the existence of another. See Thompson, "A Defense of Abortion," 1 *Philosophy & Pub. Aff.* 47 (1971).

21. A time, place, and manner regulation must be content neutral. If it is not, it becomes something else, usually an obvious case of prohibited censorship. See, e.g., *Police Dep't v. Mosley*, 408 U.S. 92 (1972). However, the issue is more complicated if the regulation, neutral on its face and applied according to its terms, will necessarily limit some groups or some points of view more than others. See, e.g., *Kovacs v. Cooper*, 336 U.S. 77, 102–3 (1949) (Black, Douglas, & Rutledge, dissenting) (total ban on sound trucks disadvantages poor and favors views of those who own the dominant forms of media communication). For a "facially neutral" statute that "deals with conduct containing elements of both expression and action, the First Amendment issue turns in part upon the question whether the legislation is directed at the expression or action." T. Emerson, *Freedom of Expression, supra* note 2, at 85 (objecting to the Court's failure to do this in O'Brien). For the court to invalidate only if it concludes that the government had a conscious desire to limit the expression of certain viewpoints provides insufficient protection if the first amendment requires the government to be careful not to restrict people's freedom of speech. This broader duty provides an explanation of least restrictive means tests in the area of time, place, and manner regulations. Failure to adopt a reasonable, but less restrictive, regulation is evidence of an implicit or "objective" purpose to ignore the first amendment mandate that the government be concerned with people's freedom of speech. On this reasoning, the Court in *Kovacs* should not have upheld the complete ban on sound trucks. See also Chapters 7 and 8.

22. See Chapters 2 and 3.

23. "I can imagine no more distasteful, useless, and time-consuming task." *United States v. Thirty-Seven Photographs*, 402 U.S. 363, 380 (1971) (Black & Douglas, dissenting).

24. See *Moore v. City of East Cleveland*, 431 U.S. 494 (1977) (invalidating a zoning ordinance that prohibited such living arrangements). But cf. *Village of Belle Terre v. Boraas*, 416 U.S. 1 (1974) (upholding zoning ordinance prohibiting certain types of living arrangements).

25. *Village of Euclid v. Ambler Realty Co.*, 272 U.S. 365 (1926).

26. See Mishan, "Pareto Optimality and the Law," 19 *Oxford Econ. Pap.* 225 (1967). See also *Young v. American Mini Theatres*, 427 U.S. 50 (1976) (upholding zoning ordinance regulating location of "adult" theatres). Cf. *Schad v. Mt. Ephrom*, 452 U.S. 61 (1981) (striking down exclusion of live, first amendment protected expressive entertainment from commercial zone where it was not available in nearby areas of the jurisdiction). But cf. *Renton v. Playtime Theatres*, 106 S.Ct. 925 (1986). In *American Mini Theatres*, the Court concluded that the regulation did not thwart or even greatly burden people in fulfilling their substantive desire to see adult films. 427 U.S. at 71–72 n.35. The case can be read to say that content restrictions in time, place, and manner regulations may be permissible if they do not limit the realization of the substantively valued aspects of the restricted activity. Thus, such a content-based restriction would never justify limiting advocacy or propaganda that restricted the location or manner of advocacy that the

speaker valued, e.g., because of wanting to reach the audience that could be reached there. This contrasts with the commercial entertainment context where the regulation did not stop but at most imposed an instrumental cost on the valued communication. See Chapter 7.

27. On this analysis, nudity could normally be prohibited in most public areas on the assumption that the nudist's substantive expression relates to style of life and is not dependent on location nor on exposure to those who find public nudity offensive. However, when nudity is a form of expression intended to confront the public and communicate a message, the argument for banning nudity from the public arena may be unpersuasive. See generally Chapter 8. But see L. Tribe, *American Constitutional Law* 680–81 (1978).

28. *Clark v. Community for Creative Non-Violence*, 468 U.S. 288 (1984).

29. P. Devlin, *The Enforcement of Morals* (1965); M. Sandel, *The Limits of Liberalism* (1982). But cf. Baker, "Sandel on Rawls," 133 *U. Pa. L. Rev.* 895 (1985) (group rights are ethically, although not historically, derivative of individual rights of autonomy and equality, and this view prevents group rights from being used to justify coerced establishment of oppressive, hierarchical, closed associations or communities).

30. See, e.g., *Wooley v. Maynard*, 430 U.S. 705 (1977); *Wisconsin v. Yoder*, 406 U.S. 205 (1972); *West Virginia State Bd. of Educ. v. Barnette*, 319 U.S. 624 (1943).

31. The arguments in this paragraph closely parallel some developed in Michelman, "Property, Utility and Fairness: Comment on the Ethical Foundations of 'Just Compensation' Law," 80 *Harvard L. Rev.* 1165 (1967). The "takings" Michelman discusses primarily involve resource allocations, not liberty of action. According to the analysis here, resource allocations are more legitimately subject to revision by majority decision.

32. Note that this rule utilitarian argument could be leveled against general prohibitions of both substantively and instrumentally valued behavior. Carried to an extreme, it could be applied to most cases of government decision making. See J. Buchanan, *The Limits of Liberty* (1975). Nevertheless, both abuses of the power and dissatisfaction caused by the abuses may be greater in respect to restrictions on substantively valued behavior.

33. See Chapter 3; R. Dworkin, *Taking Rights Seriously* (1977).

34. See Baker, "Sandel on Rawls," 133 *U. Pa. L. Rev.* 895 (1985).

35. Efficiency analyses must rely on both some assumed set of tastes and on some distribution of resources. Usually, the assumed set will not be justified but rather will show the bias of the analyst. See Baker, "Posner's Privacy Mystery and the Failure of the Economic Analysis of Law," 12 *Georgia L. Rev.* 475 (1978); Baker, "The Ideology of the Economic Analysis of Law," 5 *Philosophy & Pub. Aff.* 3 (1975). Tribe, "Technology Assessment and the Fourth Discontinuity: The Limits of Instrumental Rationality," 46 *So. California L. Rev.* 617, 635–41 (1973).

36. J. Mill, *On Liberty, supra* note 18, at 14.

37. Tribe, *supra* note 35, at 640.

38. R. Unger, *Knowledge and Politics* (1975). "[T]he spiral of domination and community progresses through constant experiments in association. Unless emergent groups are free to develop and are not disadvantaged in relation to existing ones, there is the danger that a partial vision of the good will be petrified and the spiral arrested." *Id.* at 287. See also, J. Habermas, *Communication and the Evolution Of Society* (1979).

39. Under this view, *Bowers v. Hardwick*, 106 S.Ct. 2841 (1986), narrowly upholding a prohibition on homosexual conduct, was wrongly decided.

40. 381 US 479 (1965).

41. *Id.* at 493.

42. *Id.* at 493, 48 (Goldberg, concurring); *id.* 500 (Harlan, concurring in the judgment)

(referring to his opinion in *Poe v. Ullman*, 367 U.S. 497); *id.* 505 (White, concurring in the judgment).

43. *Poe v. Ullman*, 367 U.S. 497, 546 (1961) (Harlan, dissenting).

44. *Ginzberg v. United States*, 383 U.S. 463, 489–92 (Douglas, dissenting).

45. Those calling for dialogic reciprocity as a foundation for ethics or politics should recognize not only that it implies an acceptance of individual autonomy as basic within dialogue but also that protection of this broader range of autonomy is itself foundational for the uncoerced dialogue. Cf. Cornell, "Toward a Modern/Postmodern Reconstruction of Ethics," 133 *U. Pa. L. Rev.* 291 (1985).

46. Cf. Chapter 9 (arguing that the market structure coerces or "dictates" the choice of speech messages by economic enterprises and, therefore, unregulated enterprise speech can undermine the process of democratic decision making). Generally, a more thorough and systematic analyses of the influence of various power structures on people's expression is needed.

CHAPTER 5

1. This function is recognized by, for example, the John Stuart Mill marketplace-of-ideas theorists, who focus on the role of speech in discovering truth and promoting human progress; the theorists who claim that the first amendment primarily protects the political speech essential for self-government; and the liberty theorists, who derive first amendment rights from the need to respect individual liberty and autonomy and who agree that one aspect of liberty is the right to participate in the process of change.

2. Probably the most common criticism of the liberty theory of the amendment is that it fails to take account of the central political role of first amendment rights. See, e.g., Jackson and Jeffries, "Commercial Speech: Economic Due Process and the First Amendment," 65 *Virginia L. Rev.* 1, 31–32 n.109 (1979). My presentations of the liberty theory, however, have always stressed that protection of individual, value-based action and of voluntary associations is necessary if we are to have any confidence in society's collective decisions.

3. A. Huxley, *Ends and Means* 10 (1937).

4. Liberals generally assume that this evaluative freedom is possible. It follows logically from an assumption of the subjectivity of value or from ethical relativism.

5. This paragraph's notion of interpretive possibilities resonates with Carol Gilligan's observations concerning typical gender differences in the ways people understand or interpret practical dilemmas. C. Gilligan, *In a Different Voice* (1982).

6. See J. Habermas, *Toward a Rational Society* 91–93 (1971). This dichotomy does not necessarily describe all conduct. Moreover, sometimes both categories apply to some extent to the same conduct. In his more recent work, Habermas has found the critique of instrumental reason to narrow. He describes the world as composed of both a lifeworld in which communicative rationality should dominate and separated off subsystems in which functional reason dominates. Oppression, alienation, distortion of communicative reason, and, potentially, resistance occur when systems and their related functional reason "colonize" realms of the lifeworld in which communicative reason ought to control. Although both lifeworld and subsystems and their corresponding communicative and functional reason are developmentally necessary, Habermas does not merely divide the world into separate realms, some appropriate for communicative reason and others for functional reason. Rather, as I read him, he argues that communicative reason or the lifeworld ought to retain power and authority to direct and reorganize the functional subsystems. For example, democracy properly asserts the primacy of the lifeworld in contrast

to capitalism's opposed grant of dominance to system's logic. J. Habermas, *The Theory of Communicative Action, Vol. 2—Lifeworld and System: A Critique of Functionalist Reason* (1987). Cf. Chapter 9.

7. See, e.g., J. Habermas, *supra* note 6, at 112–13, 121–22; M. Horkheimer, *Critique of Instrumental Reason*.

8. See R. Aron, "Max Weber," in 2 *Main Currents in Sociological Thought* 233, 250 (1967).

9. But cf. Hill, "Symbolic Protest and Calculated Silence," 9 *Philosophy & Pub. Aff.* 83 (1979) (noninstrumental justification of symbolic protest that is congruent with the liberty theory of freedom of speech). Ever since being a student in a large constitutional law class, I have found it curious that so many people find noninstrumentalist justifications for symbolic protest so inadequate. In law school, virtually no one defended the importance of first amendment rights of speech except in the instrumentalist terms of a right to effective speech. See also *Linmark Ass'n, Inc. v. Township of Willingboro*, 431 U.S. 85, 93 (1977); *United States v. O'Brien*, 391 U.S. 367, 388 (Harlan, J., concurring) (1968); Fiss, "Free Speech and Social Structure," 71 *Iowa L. Rev.* 1405 (1986).

The theory of a fundamental right to "effective" speech or a "properly" working marketplace, which I criticized in Chapter 2, embodies a ends-justifying-means view of the freedom. As I suggested earlier, it also tends toward justifying practices that embody this view. If people believe they have a right to effective speech and also strongly believe in the correctness of their views, their logic would imply that the state has violated their right to a properly functioning marketplace of ideas unless their view prevails. If illegal action, either as a means to more effective communication or as direct action remedying the "misguided" state practices, is a permissible or a predictable response to this perceived violation of a right to effective speech, then acceptance of this instrumental right would increase the likelihood of illegal, possibly violent action.

10. See J. Habermas, *supra* note 6, at 103, 106; Michelman, "Political Markets and Community Self-Determination: Competing Judicial Models of Local Government Legitimacy," 53 *Indiana L. J.* 145 (1978). Currently, the two views of politics are being debated by legal academics under the labels of "interest group politics" and "law and economics" on one side and "Republican politics" on the other.

11. See generally R. Unger, *Knowledge and Politics* (1975). See also H. Arendt, *On Revolution* 122–37 (1965) (discussion of public happiness).

12. H. Lefebvre, *La Somme Et Le Reste* 612 (1959) (quoted in W. McBride, *Fundamental Change in Law and Society* 133 (1970).

13. Rawls provides a good description of pure procedural justice. J. Rawls, *A Theory of Justice* 85–90 (1971). Liberals of varying sorts consistently find the notion of pure procedural justice alluring. See, e.g., J. Ely, *Democracy and Distrust* 87 (1980); R. Nozick, *Anarchy, State, and Utopia* 96–108 (1974). The theory, however, must find stronger value-based support than its defenders typically provide. See R. Unger, *supra* note 11, at 186–87; Baker, "Neutrality, Process and Rationality: Flawed Interpretations of Equal Protection," 58 *Texas L. Rev.* 1029, 1051 (1980); Tribe, "The Puzzling Persistence of Process-Based Constitutional Theories," 89 *Yale L. J.* 1063, 1064 (1980).

14. *Gitlow v. New York*, 268 U.S. 652, 672–73 (1924) (Holmes, dissenting).

15. See, e.g., R. Dahl, *A Preface to Democratic Theory* 3 (1956); R. Posner, *The Economic Analysis of Law* 404–8 (2d ed. 1977). But see, e.g., Michelman, *supra* note 10, at 201–06.

16. This chapter assumes that constitutional rights are respected in practice. This, of course is not necessarily true. Governments often lawlessly ignore and abridge people's legal rights. Likewise, even if certain expressive activities are not constitutionally protected and are in fact made illegal, people may still engage in those activities, and the

government may be unable or unwilling to enforce its restrictive laws. For example, consider the strikes of the workers in Poland in August 1980, political strikes that would be illegal under existing statutes if they had occurred in the United States. History provides examples of powerful uses of nonviolent, technically illegal means that are arguably more effective than the use of violence as a means to oppose state power, including violent state oppression. See generally G. Sharp, *Social Power and Political Freedom* (1980).

17. Robert Dahl suggests that the United States may have imposed more severe legal and social obstacles to political dissent than have European democracies. Dahl, "Preface," *Political Oppositions in Western Democracies* xiii–xiv (R. Dahl ed. 1966). Constitutional provisions are not adequate to make civil liberties a reality. Thus, Robert Goldstein not only documents an incredible pattern of one hundred years of violation of basic civil liberties of political and labor dissidents, but also suggests that our history may have been very different, that is, more progressive, had these violations not been so prevalent. R. Goldstein, *Political Repression in Modern America* (1978).

Evaluation of the likelihood that first amendment rights will be respected in practice is mostly beyond the scope of this book. Still, if the general claims made here concerning the unity thesis are correct, inadequate legal or societal protection of first amendment liberties should not lead those interested in fundamental, progressive change to turn to violent, instrumentalist means of change. Instead, radicals should continue to engage in those activities that should receive protection and should make increased protection for these liberties a high priority.

18. The debate is clearly evident in Thucydides' report of the speeches of the Greeks. See Thucydides, *The Peloponnesian War* bk. I, xxxii–xxxvi (c. 416 B.C.) (C. Smith trans. 1919). See also F. Schiller, "Letters Upon the Aesthetical Education of Man," in *Essays Aethetical and Philosophical* 25 (1875). My impression is that writers and people in the arts and humanities are more likely to hold the thesis of a unity of ends and means in politics and history than are social scientists and most political activists. If this unconfirmed bit of sociology of knowledge is accurate, it does not necessarily mean that one group is more naive than the other. Rather, it suggests a number of hypotheses including: (1) the alternative theses support the needs of the two groups—that is, justify their activities—in different ways; (2) differences in the objects of study of the two groups leave them sensitive to different aspects of the relation between events or to different types of events; (3) the two groups characteristically differ as to what they would count as change; and (4) the two groups characteristically focus on different aspects of the ends-means relationship.

19. From the perspective of the independent thesis, force, power, and violence are closely related or interchangeable instrumental concepts. For a criticism of this usage, see text accompanying notes 23–25 *infra*.

20. See, e.g., *Weatherman* 141–42 (H. Jacobs ed. 1970).

21. C. Wright Mills, *The Power Elite* 171 (1956).

22. H. Arendt, *The Human Condition* 139–40 (1958).

23. H. Arendt, *On Violence* 44–46 (1969).

24. H. Arendt, *The Origins of Totalitarianism* 124, 301–32 (1958).

25. Although this usage roughly reflects common usage, it is somewhat arbitrary, and better understanding may require both greater precision and the use of additional terms such as "force," "authority," and "might." Nevertheless, these distinctions suffice to help clarify the claims of the unity thesis.

26. Although people experience ends and means as separate, I argue that they are necessarily connected in that alienated means lead to alienated ends.

27. The classic development of this theme is in the works of Max Weber. See, e.g., M. Weber, *Economy and Society* (G. Roth & C. Wittich eds. 1978). See also J. Habermas, *Knowledge and Human Interests* (1971); M. Horkheimer, *Eclipse of Reason* 3–58 (1947);

R. Unger, *supra* note 11, at 63–142; Tribe, "Technology Assessment and the Fourth Discontinuity: The Limits of Instrumental Rationality," 46 *So. California L. Rev.* 617 (1973).

28. This view of values and individual desires is characteristic of traditional liberal thought. See, e.g., D. Hume, "Book II of the Passions," in *A Treatise of Human Nature* 275 (2d ed. L. Selby-Bigge 1978) (n/p. 1739–1740). See generally R. Unger, *supra* note 11. It remains prominent in recent liberal theory. See, e.g., B. Ackerman, *Social Justice in the Liberal State* (1980).

29. T. Hobbes, *Leviathan*, pt. 1, ch. XI, p. 80 (M. Oakeshott ed. 1962) (1st ed. 1651).

30. *Id.* at Ch. X, 72 (emphasis in original). Hobbes, like other liberals, uses "power" to refer to instrumental means as well as capacities based on consent and combination, as opposed to Arendt's usage, which is employed elsewhere in this chapter. See text accompanying notes 23–25 *supra*.

31. The best development of this argument is found in C. B. Macpherson, *The Political Theory of Possessive Individualism* 29–46 (1962).

32. M. Weber, *The Theory of Social and Economic Organizations* 337 (1964). For a slightly different translation, see M. Weber, *supra* 27, at 223.

33. M. Weber, *supra* note 27, at 989 (emphasis added).

34. *Id.* at 224.

35. R. Aron, *supra* note 8, at 250.

36. M. Weber, *supra* note 27, at 988.

37. But see Baker, "The Ideology of the Economic Analysis of Law," 5 *Philosophy & Pub. Aff.* 3 (1976); Gintis, "Consumer Behavior and the Concept of Sovereignty: Explanation of Social Decay," 62 *Amer. Econ Rev., Pap. & Proc.* 267 (1972).

38. Marx and Weber report the same "facts" concerning how the market treats people, although they disagree about the significance of those facts. Loewith, "Weber's Interpretation of the Bourgeois-Capitalistic World in Terms of the Guiding Principle of 'Rationalization,'" in *Max Weber* 101–22 (D. Wrong, ed. 1970).

39. M. Weber, *supra* note 27, at 225.

40. *Id.* at 975.

41. *Id.* at 637.

42. *Id.* at 731.

43. J. Rawls, *supra* note 13, at 119.

44. See, e.g., *id.* at 425.

45. Baker, "Outcome Equality or Equality of Respect: The Substantive Content of Equal Protection," 131 *U. Pa. L. Rev.* 933, 949–59 (1983). This objection to Rawls' argument for his two principles does not apply to his quite persuasive argument for his methodology for thinking about and deriving principles of justice. See *id.* at 959–72; Baker, "Sandel on Rawls," 133 *U. Pa. L. Rev.* 895 (1985).

46. See J. Rawls, *supra* note 13, at 13.

47. M. Weber, *supra* note 27, at 636.

48. This point is developed in Kelman, "Consumption Theory, Production Theory, and Ideology in the Coase Theorem," 52 *So. California L. Rev.* 669, 685–88 (1979).

49. I further discuss this point and the manner in which the ends are also independent of the reflective values of consumers in "Property and its Relation to Constitutionally Liberty," 134 *U. Pa. L. Rev.* 741 (1986).

50. R. Wolff, *The Poverty of Liberalism* 162–95 (1968).

51. See Chapter 9; Gintis, *supra* note 37, at 273–77.

52. See generally N. Machiavelli, *The Prince and the Discourses* (1950) (1st ed. 1513); note 58 *infra*.

53. J. Habermas, *Communication and the Evolution of Society* 165 (1970).

54. *Id.* at 166. See also note 6 *supra*.

55. See the section entitled The Failure of the Independence Thesis *supra.*

56. S. Avineri, *The Social and Political Thought Of Karl Marx* 238 (1971). See note 69 *infra.*

57. See text accompanying notes 26–43 *supra.*

58. This claim runs through liberal thought. Machiavelli presents an analysis that in this respect is almost identical to Hobbes' and Weber's. Like them, Machiavelli does not think that people are basically bad or naturally desirous of more power, wealth, or instrumental effectiveness. Yet he tells rulers that they must "learn how not be good." N. Machiavelli, *supra* note 52, at 56. He also suggests that many will prefer the life of the private citizen, apparently because that life allows the preferable, humane course of acting decently. See *id.* at 184. Even Rousseau's unpersuasive interpretation, that Machiavelli intended *The Prince* to expose the evil ways of the rulers to the common citizens, makes sense only if one assumes that the citizens are basically good. J. Rousseau, "The Social Contract," in *Social Contract* 237 (E. Barker ed. 1948). The very structure of the political realm and the fact that some political opponents will use "uncivilized" means, N. Machiavelli, *supra* note 52, at 64, requires that princes adopt the view that "the ends justify the means." *Id.* at 66. Machiavelli, Hobbes, and Weber all see a world where the instrumental and sometimes objectionable actions of some people require similar instrumental responses by others. And all three claim that escape from this situation is impossible. See notes 31–45 and accompanying text, *supra* (discussing Hobbes and Weber). The "revolutionary" described in the text implicitly accepts this conclusion. The more radical position, suggested by the unity thesis, claims that this conclusion of liberal social theory is precisely what the radical must challenge. And, this radical analysis argues that the frameworks and the instrumentalist mandates that these three have described will collapse or can be overcome by withdrawing support and generating collective "power" within alternatives.

59. See, e.g., C. Gilligan, *In a Different Voice* (1982).

60. See text accompanying notes 6–11 *supra.*

61. See generally G. Sharp, *Social Power and Political Freedom* (1980). Sharp makes arguments that parallel the analysis in this chapter, particularly that of the last three paragraphs. He argues that the use of violent sanctions leads to centralization, while the political use of nonviolent means leads naturally to the increased ability of people to resist domination and implement their own goals. He emphasizes that the human results of political struggle follow directly from the nature of the means used. Relying heavily on historical examples, he also argues that *nonviolent sanctions are consistently more successful* than violent sanctions for opposing and "defeating " either internal or external political forces that rely on violence to maintain or extend oppression.

62. H. Arendt, *supra* note 23, at 51–53, 56; H. Arendt, *supra* note 22, at 26.

63. J. Habermas, *supra* note 53, at 61. According to Avineri, Marx also adopts this thesis of the relation of ends and means: "The end-results of the revolution are thus historically formed and determined during and by its occurrence." See also S. Avineri, *supra* note 56, at 143. "[P]olitical power retained through terror would be unable to emancipate itself from its terroristic birth marks, and would certainly cease to implement those ends for which it had been instituted. The retention of political power would under such circumstances become an end unto itself." *Id.* at 193. See also *id.* at 142, 217, 218.

64. *See* note 37 and accompanying text *supra.*

65. This analysis is not new. It has had a continual following in the left and was a major strain in leftist thought in the United States during the late 1960s and 1970s. See note 102 *infra.*

Although Rosa Luxemburg would disagree with some of the arguments made here under the label of the unity thesis, her early review of the Russian Revolution perspicaciously forecast how reliance on hierarchical, instrumental, nonsocialist means would lead to future problems. Luxemburg, "The Russian Revolution," in *Rosa Luxemburg Speaks* 367–95 (M. Walters ed. 1970). Luxemburg concluded that failure to achieve "unlimited democracy," including freedom of the press and rights to assembly and association for opponents as well as supporters of government, and reliance on a dictatorship of a handful of leaders, "inevitably [leads to] a brutalization of public life: attempted assassination, shooting of hostages, etc.," id. at 389–91, and undermines socialist democracy. *Id.* at 393–95. Moreover, she described a situation in which "Draconian measures of terror are powerless," *id.* at 393, and "[t]he harshest measures of martial law are impotent against outbreaks of lumpenproletarian sickness." *Id.* at 392. Stalinism as well as social and economic stagnation seemed to be the outcome that she predicted in 1919.

66. If the revolutionary process decreases respect of the rule of law, the revolution could lessen the constraints on the use of instrumental means by revolutionary leaders. The hope and belief that the rule of law induces some restraint on the part of even political elites apparently led a major leftist historian to conclude that the rule of law is an "unqualified human good." E.P. Thompson, *Whigs and Hunters* 266 (1975).

67. For present purposes of mere illustrative uses of history, the immense problems of historical description and identification of causal relations will be ignored. Moreover, there is a constant need to recognize that neither historical choices nor outcomes are foreordained. See, e.g., Gordon, "Critical Legal Histories," 36 *Stanford L. Rev.* 57 (1984).

68. T. Skocpol, *States and Social Revolutions* (1979). See also, H. Arendt, *supra* note 23 (describing many events in a manner that provides historical support for the thesis); G. Sharp, *supra* note 61.

69. See T. Skocpol, *supra* note 68, at 14–18, 168–71, 291.

70. *Id.* at 47–51, 112.

71. *Id.* at 29, 161–62.

72. *Id.* at 161–64, 178–79, 196–202, 215–18, 226–30, 263, 285.

73. See notes 34–45 and accompanying text *supra*.

74. At least since 1957, China has not followed the Stalinist course and has partially resisted Western-style bureaucratic domination. T. Skocpol, *supra* note 68, at 286.

75. *Id.* at 252.

76. *Id.* at 253.

77. *Id.* at 270–71.

78. *Id.* at 267.

79. *Id.* at 268.

80. See S. Avineri, *supra* note 56, at 142–46.

81. T. Skocpol, *supra* note 68, at 275–80.

82. See *id.* at 29, 161–62.

83. See *id.* at 224.

84. *Id.* at 222–25.

85. *Id.* at 224.

86. *Id.* at 275.

87. *Id.* at 170.

88. The types of reasons justifying normally objectionable means vary. Sometimes, the claim will be that the act is not objectionable in this context; other times, even though the act is objectionable, important concerns will be said to justify engaging in it. We can distinguish the claim that in a particular case the principles underlying the justification for keeping promises do not support keeping the particular promise from the claim that other goals justify breaking the promise. These two possibilities apparently collapse into one from the consequentialist view of the relation of ends and means: keeping promises is only valuable as a means that is often, but not always, an instrumentally useful practice.

89. T. Skocpol, *supra* note 68, at 99, 154, 282.

90. *Id.* at 293.

91. *Id.*

92. See *id.* at 292. Skocpol refers to the possibility of the "working classes" becoming "politically self-conscious revolutionaries" in a possible future "working-class socialist revolution." *Id.*

93. *Id.* at 15–17, 291.

94. *Id.* at 293.

95. Skocpol does not offer a complete description of democratic means. Certainly, democratic means are not limited to or even necessarily focused on majority rule or electoral practices. For example, a dictionary definition of democracy is: "a state of society characterized by tolerance toward minorities, freedom of expression, and respect for the essential dignity and worth of the human individual with equal opportunity for each to develop freely to his fullest capacity in a cooperative community." *Webster's Third New International Dictionary of the English Language Unabridged* 600 (1966). Other definitions emphasize political, social, or economic equality and control by the rank and file. "Democratic" generally refers to "for or of the people." As used here, "democracy" refers to any process of collective decision making that fully respects the equality, worth, and autonomy of all members of the collective. In this sense, democracy would be a partial realization of liberal values. "Democratization" usually refers either to change in the political process, i.e., increased popular control, or to material results, i.e., resources and opportunities made available to everyone. See generally C. Macpherson, *The Real World of Democracy* (1966). See also Michelman, *supra* note 10.

96. T. Skocpol, *supra* note 68, at 292.

97. See J. Habermas, *supra* note 53, at 120–29. Habermas analyzes the process of change as a matter of building institutions that are then relied on in the new order; and as a learning process that he describes both in terms of developing societal capacities that are then embodied in new institutions and practices and in terms of new normative conceptions or orientations.

98. See note 1 *supra*.

99. This paragraph follows points developed in Chapters 1 and 4.

100. For an explanation of this terminology, see text accompanying notes 24–25 *supra*.

101. This illogical conclusion has represented the dominant legal view until recently. See, e.g., *Reynolds v. United States*, 98 U.S. 145, 164 (1878) ("Congress was deprived of all legislative power over mere opinion, but was left free to reach actions which were in violation of social duties or subversive of good order.") See also *Cantwell v. Connecticut*, 310 U.S. 296 (1940). But see *Wisconsin v. Yoder*, 406 U.S. 205, 215–19 (1972); Baker, "Scope of the First Amendment Freedom of Speech," 25 *UCLA L. Rev.* 964, 1035–39 (1978).

102. See, e.g., H. Arendt, *supra* note 32, at 49. See generally G. Sharp, *supra* note 61. This general perspective, which assumes the unity thesis, was basic to one of the two major strands of leftist thinking in the 1960s and 1970s. For an excellent presentation by a member of the student left, see D. Harris, *Goliath* (1970). See also C. Reich, *The Greening Of America* (1970); Seeley, "Remaking the Urban Scene," 97 *Daedalus* 1124 (1968); *The Port Huron Statement* (1962) (adopted by the Students for a Democratic Society). Central elements of the women's movement— suggested by the slogan that "the personal is political" and by the broadside critique of "male" manipulative, hierarchical, instrumental practices—can be viewed as elaborations of the above analysis. In contrast, a second strand of leftist thinking criticized these "nonviolent, pacifist, countercultural" views as being unrealistic, naive, and insufficiently political. For a relatively extreme version of this second view, see *Weatherman*, *supra* note 20. If the argument of this chapter is cor-

rect, it is this second strand that is insufficiently radical in that it accepts the key alienating aspects of liberal thought and practice. See text accompanying notes 26–43 *supra*.

103. For a doctrinal argument for a counter view, see Berle Constitutional Limits on Corporate Activity, 100 *U. of Pennsylvania L. Rev.* 933 (1952).

104. J. Habermas, *supra* note 53, at 121–22.

105. *Id.* at 120, 184–86. Many of our important institutions and practices, including our "democratic" political order, assume, although they usually do not achieve, this justificatory process. The assumption that this type of justificatory process is legitimate is implicit in many of the best recent additions to liberal political theory. See, e.g., B. Ackerman, *Social Justice and The Liberal State* (1980). Rawls' original position can be seen as an attempt to describe an undistorted justificatory decision-making process for constructing fundamental structural principles of justice. See J. Rawls, *supra* note 13, at 120. The process tries to accomplish this by eliminating biases that reflect unjust arrangements. Nevertheless, its exclusion of information leads to irrationality. See Baker, *supra* note 45, at 946–49. But see J. Rawls, *supra*, at 139–40.

106. J. Habermas, *supra* note 53, at 122. Habermas argues not merely for institutions that embody particular values but for value-based methods of considering and resolving value questions.

107. Habermas' emphasis on the need for a "milieu favorable to the stabilization of successful attempts" corresponds to Skocpol's emphasis on the importance of the international context and the dampening of military rivalries. *Compare* J. Habermas, *supra* note 53, at 122, *with* T. Skocpol, *supra* note 68, at 293.

108. Professor Emerson usefully employed the speech/action dichotomy to distinguish coercive practices, which the first amendment does not protect, from noncoercive practices, which it should protect. See T. Emerson, *The System of Freedom of Expression* 17–18 (1970). The speech/action dichotomy, however, provides inadequate scope for first amendment rights because the first amendment, to fulfill its functions, must protect activities that involve people living their values, either through speech, religion, assembly, or association. See Chapter 4. On the other hand, the first amendment should not protect even speech where the choice of speech content has no intrinsic connection with individual value choices. For example, although the marketplace of ideas theory offers first amendment protection for commercial speech, Chapter 9 argues that this speech is not intrinsically connected with individually valued choices and, therefore, should not be protected. See also, T. Emerson, *supra*, at 460–61.

109. This consideration requires a strong interpretation of freedom of association that goes beyond protecting association merely as a means for propagating speech. Compare *Griswold v. Connecticut*, 381 U.S. 479 (1965), and *Wisconsin v. Yoder*, 406 U.S. 205 (1972), with *Runyon v. McCrary*, 427 U.S. 160 (1976). See Chapters 6–8.

110. Protection of practices that are not welfare maximizing is essential if the community is to break from goals that reflect and embody the distortion of people's values caused by existing forms of domination and subordination. This consideration is the "political" version of the normative argument that the first amendment rights must not be limited by a utilitarian criterion.

111. Commercial speech only receives protection under a marketplace of ideas theory and not under a liberty theory of speech. See, e.g., *Consolidated Edison Co. v. Public Serv. Comm'n*, 447 U.S. 530, 533–35 (1980); *First Nat'l Bank of Boston v. Bellotti*, 435 U.S. 765, 783 (1978). Marketplace theory's instrumentalism, however, permits the conclusion that commercial speech should receive less protection than other speech. In fact, in the commercial context, the Court appears to approve any regulation that it thinks makes a real welfare contribution—only striking down regulations that are both inefficient and have a perverse distributive impact. Likewise, the Court justified its refusal to protect

obscenity or pornography in *Paris Adult Theatre v. Slaton*, 413 U.S. 49 (1973), principally on the assumption that public sale or exhibition of pornographic materials does not contribute to the general welfare. *Id.* at 57–60. The Court's willingness to accept limits on commercial speech (which it views as protected) and its failure to protect obscenity illustrate the marketplace theory's inability to provide convincing justifications for protecting conduct that is not welfare maximizing. See also, *Gertz V. Robert Welch, Inc.*, 418 U.S. 323 (1974).

112. See *United States v. O'Brien*, 391 U.S. 367, 388–89 (1968) (Harlan, J., concurring). See also, Chapter 2, section entitled "Market Failure Model."

113. See Baker, "Sandel on Rawls," 133 *Pa. L. Rev.* 895 (1985) (defense of the universalism implicit in the assumption in the text).

114. Of course, this protection does not guarantee such a result. The protection may be necessary but surely it is not sufficient. This caveat follows because the change that does occur depends on people's actual choices and actions. The first amendment also protects distorted, alienated choices such as allowing the Nazis to march in Skokie, even though people would not make those choices in a truly liberated society. Moreover, this protection does not guarantee that people will be motivated to attempt the escape from present conditions. Finally, the choices available to people will also depend on the resources available to them. Thus, distributive practices will influence the content of change.

115. See generally J. Mill, *On Liberty* 14 (1956) (1st ed. 1859). By emphasizing interests as "a progressive being," this somewhat "utilitarian" standard has the interesting feature of not assuming existing preferences as the standard, a common but objectionable feature of typical market-oriented utilitarian or law and economics reasoning. See Baker, "Posner's Privacy Mystery and the Failure of the Economic Analysis of Law," 12 *Georgia L. Rev.* 475, 480–83, 487–88, 493 (1978).

CHAPTER 6

1. Even first amendment absolutists accept something like a balancing or reasonableness standard in most time, place, and manner contexts. Justice Black, a leading advocate of an absolutist approach, saw no alternative to balancing in this context. See, e.g., *Martin v. City of Struthers*, 319 U.S. 141, 143–144 (1943); *Barenblatt v. United States*, 360 U.S. 109, 141–42 (1959) (Black, dissenting); *Konigsberg v. State Bar of California*, 366 U.S. 36, 68–69 (1961) (Black, dissenting); Kalven, "The Concept of a Public Forum: Cox v. Louisiana," 1965 *Supreme Court Rev.* 1, 28. Professor Thomas Emerson, the preeminent scholarly proponent of first amendment absolutism, recognizes that in allocating the use of physical facilities for the exercise of the right of expression, "[t]he governing principle can only be a fair accommodation of opposing interest. . . [that is] . . . a kind of balancing test." T. Emerson, *The System of Freedom of Expression* 359 (1970); see also, *id.* at 345.

2. "Congress shall make no law . . . *abridging* the freedom of speech, or of the press; or the right of the people peaceably to assemble, and to petition the Government for a redress of grievances." U.S. Const. amend. I (emphasis added).

3. L. Tribe, *American Constitutional Law* 583–84 (1978) ("quagmire of ad hoc judgment" is unavoidable in the context).

4. Linde, "'Clear and Present Danger' Reexamined: Dissonance in the Brandenberg Concerto," 22 *Stanford L. Rev.* 1163, 1184–85 (1970).

5. See Kalven, *supra* note 1.

6. Assuming that the balancing invalidates some restrictions on first amendment conduct, balancing is more protective of expression than the arguably most obvious alter-

native doctrine, namely automatically upholding any governmental regulation that is not aimed at restricting ideas or information. L. Tribe, *supra* note 3, at 682 (our system rejects this alternative). Justice Black accepted this balancing in order to give added protection to speech where the law only "indirectly" burdened speech. See *supra* note 1.

7. This section is derived from arguments of Justice Hans Linde, in particular Linde, *supra* note 4.

8. Cf. T. Emerson, *supra* note 1, at 18. Emerson here appears to adopt the individual rights/effects perspective.

9. This last point obviously requires the formulation of some theory that will identify what resources the government must make available and when it must do so. Mostly, the next two chapters will develop certain contextual principles to perform this task. Other clauses of the constitution, most prominently the equal protection clause, may also mandate some resource allocations.

10. Justice Linde observed:

> [T]he antiabsolutist position generally confuses a claim that the first amendment states an 'absolute' prohibition against making such laws with a claim that the amendment gives individuals an 'absolute' right to speak regardless of circumstances.

Linde, *supra* note 4, at 1183 n.66. Linde used this observation in making an absolutist objection to laws directed at specific speech content. *Id.* at 1183. He does not make clear whether he would extend it, as is suggested here, to laws directed more generally at speech or assembly.

11. The observations in the text do not imply any necessary disagreement with Professor Emerson's own use of his expression/action dichotomy, which may be focused primarily on distinguishing coercive or physically violent conduct from protected conduct. See Chapter 4.

12. Cf. *Cox v. Louisiana*, 379 U.S. 559, 578 (1965) (Black, concurring in No. 24 and dissenting in No. 49) ("picketing . . . is not speech, and therefore is not of itself protected by the First Amendment").

13. The apparent conservatism of the general public could reflect either "false consciousness" resulting from, for example, inadequate consciousness of alternatives, or the often structurally based, disproportionate influence of the more conservative elements in society. For a useful analysis of the notion of ideology and false consciousness, see R. Guess, *The Idea of a Critical Theory* (1981).

14. See Marcuse, "Repression Tolerance," in R. P. Wolff, B. Moore & H. Marcuse, *A Critique of Pure Tolerance* 81, 109–11 (1965).

15. Another way to put this is that utilitarianism must take some set of preferences at some point in time as its evaluative criterion, but it has no criteria for determining which set of preferences or which time period is relevant. This dilemma makes it inapt for evaluating dissent that critiques values—or for addressing any dynamic issue.

16. *Abrams v. United States*, 250 U.S. 616, 630 (1919) (Holmes, dissenting).

17. See Chapter 1.

18. An interesting, and possibly ideologically telling, practice of the Supreme Court is its focus on "speech" and expression in cases in which it has the option of using either a speech or an assembly analysis. See, e.g., *Shuttlesworth v. City of Birmingham*, 394 U.S. 147, 152 (1969) ("our decisions have also made clear that picketing and parading may nonetheless constitute methods of expression, entitled to First Amendment protection"); *Edwards v. South Carolina*, 372 U.S. 229 (1963) (arrest and conviction of demonstrators who "peaceably assembled" and refused to disperse when ordered by police to do so unconstitutionally punished the demonstrators for their "speech").

The Court often treats the status of both assembly and association as deriving from their contribution to the marketplace of ideas. See, e.g., *Buckley v. Valeo*, 424 U.S. 1, 15 (1976) (right of association protected because it enhances effective advocacy); *Runyon v. McCrary*, 427 U.S. 160, 175–76 (1976); *NAACP v. Alabama*, 357 U.S. 449, 460 (1958) (a first amendment right "to engage in association for the advancement of beliefs and ideas"); *DeJonge v. Oregon*, 299 U.S. 353, 365 (1937) ("rights of free speech, free press and free assembly [preserved] in order to maintain the opportunity for free political discussion"). But see *Roberts v. United States Jaycees*, 468 U.S. 609, 622 ("protection [of] collective effort on behalf of shared goals"). This subordination of assembly to speech provides the most obvious explanation of how the Court can conclude that picketing and parading, which are rather obvious and important forms of assembly, are not "afford[ed] the same kind of freedom . . . [as is] pure speech," *Cox v. Louisiana*, 379 U.S. 536, 555 (1965), but nonetheless do receive some protection since parading and picketing "constitute methods of expression." *Shuttlesworth v. City of Birmingham*, 394 U.S. at 152.

19. "What is essential is not that everyone shall speak, but that everything worth saying shall be said." A. Meiklejohn, *Political Freedom* 64 (1960). Constitutional objections to some "reasonable" time, place, and manner regulations could appear plausible from a market failure perspective. On closer examination, however, the goal of equalizing speech opportunities fails to provide useful constitutional guidance. See *infra* note 23 and accompanying text.

20. On several occasions during demonstrations in the 1960s, I heard demonstrators demand that an official or university administrator appear, explain policies, and listen to and respond to criticisms. The demands were rejected explicitly on the ground that useful, rational dialogue or interchange could not take place in the context of large groups.

21. *Attorney General of Canada v. Dupond*, 84 D.L.R.3d 420, 439 (S.Ct. Canada 1978) (rejecting a claim that parades and street meetings are aspects of the fundamental freedom of speech and assembly).

22. See Chapter 7. In contrast, from the perspective of the liberty theory, the capacity of assembled people to "do something," *peaceably* to take "collective action," is a major reason to protect the right to assembly.

23. This paragraph exemplifies the problems of market failure versions of the marketplace of ideas theory of the first amendment. See Chapter 2.

24. See *supra* note 18.

25. Occasionally courts that view the issue as a matter of liberty will place primary emphasis on the value of the parade to the participants. They will recognize the parade as a method of carrying out the parader's objectives. Only secondarily will they consider the parade's communicative function. Thus, one court noted:

> These processions for political, religious, and social demonstrations are resorted to for the express purpose of keeping unity of feeling and enthusiasm, and frequently to produce some effect on the public mind by the spectacle of union and numbers. They are a natural product and exponent of common aims, and valuable factors in furthering them.

Frazee's Case, 63 Mich. 396, 404, 30 N.W. 72, 75 (1886). The court proceeded to emphasize that spectators are often important. The spectators' importance could be, however, as much for their contribution to the parader's enthusiasm, unity, and self-definition as for their relevance to some goal of spreading a message.

26. An adequate conception of "non-peaceable" or "coercive," of course, still must be developed for this context. See Chapters 7 and 8.

27. Kalven, *supra* note 1, at 25. Kalven called this an "unbeatable proposition" while describing *Cox v. New Hampshire*, 312 U.S. 569 (1941), as a "great precedent." But see Chapter 7.

28. Vince Blasi concludes that "[e]ven absolutists must retreat in the face of Harry

Kalven's 'unbeatable proposition.'" Blasi, "Prior Restraints on Demonstrations," 68 *Michigan L. Rev.* 1481, 1486 (1970).

29. *Paris Adult Theatre I v. Slaton,* 413 U.S. 49, 67 (1973); L. Tribe, *supra* note 3, at 680. Some passersby will find the nude display seriously disturbing, arguably invading their privacy and injuring them almost as severely as a physical blow. This injury, however, occurs in a different manner than a physical blow. The injury results because of the cultural and personal norms and values the observers hold and that the demonstrator may be challenging. I suspect that, for most offended observers, the invasion and the injury are no greater than the invasion and the injury of seeing a public display of Nazi insignia and demonstrators would be for many residents of Skokie. See *National Socialist Party v. Skokie,* 432 U.S. 43 (1977); *Collin v. Smith,* 447 F.Supp. 676 (N.D. Ill.), *aff'd,* 578 F.2d 1197 (7th Cir. 1978). *See* L. Bollinger, *The Tolerant Society: Freedom of Speech and Extremist Speech in America* (1986).

30. This fear plays a part in many conservative arguments concerning the need for law as a means to prevent moral decay. See, e.g., P. Devlin, *The Enforcement of Morals* (1965).

31. Rather than adopting a theory that mechanically favors the present or the past or the future set of values, the liberty theory implies that those values that result from a legal order that respects people's liberty and equality should be favored. In turn, that suggests the propriety of presently accepting the existing preferences depends in part on the extent that challenge and change are not impeded and on the extent that those present preferences do not reflect systems of domination or repression.

32. Cf. Tribe, "Structural Due Process," 10 *Harvard Civ. Rts.- Civ. Lib. L. Rev.* 269 (1975).

33. "Black argued that balancing . . . left too much discretion to judges. . . . That argument has carried the day." Tushnet, "Anti-Formalism in Recent Constitutional Theory," 1985 *Michigan L. Rev.* 1502, 1509. "It is difficult to recapture the intensity of the balancing debate because Justice Black's position overwhelmed the balancers." *Id.* at 1518. But see *id.* at 1531,

34. Aleinikoff, "Constitutional Law in the Age of Balancing," 96 *Yale L. J.* 943 (1987).

35. Judge Hans Linde, a proponent of an absolutist approach, forcefully criticized this tendency. Linde, *supra* note 4.

36. Shiffrin, "The First Amendment and Economic Regulation: Away from a General Theory of the First Amendment," 78 *Northwestern U. L. Rev.* 1212 (1983).

37. Baker, "Sandel on Rawls," 133 *U. Pennsylvania L. Rev.* 895, 920–928 (1985).

CHAPTER 7

1. See *Cox v. New Hampshire,* 312 U.S. 569 (1941).

2. See *id.*

3. According to Professor Abernathy, during the last quarter of the nineteenth century state courts generally struck down challenged parade permit ordinances. Then, after a 35-year period in which no cases involving parade permits are reported, a 1934 case, *Sullivan v. Shaw,* 6 F.Supp. 112 (S.D. Cal. 1934) upheld a permit system and a denial of a permit. After *Shaw,* there was general acceptance of those permit requirements that do not allow for discriminatory enforcement. G. Abernathy, *The Right of Assembly and Association* 94–98 (1961).

4. *State v. Cox,* 91 N.H. 137, 146, 16 A.2d 508, 515 (1940).

5. *Cox v. New Hampshire,* 312 U.S. at 576.

6. Abernathy indicates that all but one of "the reported parade cases prior to 1900

occurred in the period 1885–1900 and dealt with rather obvious attempts ... to circum-scribe the ambulatory religious services of the Salvation Army." G. Abernathy, *supra* note 3, at 84. The sole exception was not a permit case, but rather a nuisance case in 1875. See *id.* at 85–93.

Nevertheless, it is not entirely clear when the permit system was invented and then regularized. Professor Gutman reports that in 1874, which is 10 years earlier than any of the permit requirement cases found by Abernathy, New York City required that parades be approved by the Police Board and that public meetings in the parks be approved by the Department of Parks. Gutman, "The Tompkins Square 'Riot' in New York City on January 13, 1874: A Re-Examination of its Causes and its Aftermath," 6 *Labor History* 44, 48 (1965) [hereafter cited as Gutman, Tompkins Square Riot]. Gutman reported an incident that has become typical of a troublesome pattern in the governmental use of parade permits. During 1873, large public meetings of unemployed people and occasional marches occurred in many cities. Gutman, "The Failure of the Movement by the Unem-ployed for Public Works in 1873," 80 *Political Science Q.* 253 (1965). See also F. Piven and R. Cloward, *Poor People's Movements: Why They Succeed, How They Fail* 43–44 (1977) (noting major nineteenth-century unemployment demonstrations). In January 1874, the Committee of Safety (an organization of the unemployed) sought approval of a parade route to City Hall. The police turned down the proposed route and prohibited demonstrations at City Hall—although a demonstration had apparently been held there a week earlier. The Committee decided to cancel the parade and only hold an assembly at Tompkins Square, for which they had a permit from the Parks Department. The night before the assembly, the Parks Department, at the request of the police, cancelled the permit. Apparently the Committee or, at least, most of the people coming to the assembly were not notified of the cancellation. At the meeting, the police went into the peaceful crowd, ordered people to go home, and, then, without waiting, began an onslaught, using clubs indiscriminately. A general police riot ensued. Gutman, Tompkins Square Riot, *supra*, at 48–55.

7. With one exception, see *supra* note 6, the Salvation Army cases are the first point where I find reference to parade or assembly permit procedures in the United States. The permit requirements were often adopted as a direct response to local antagonism toward the Salvation Army. A leading case striking down a parade permit requirement, *Frazee's Case*, 63 Mich. 396, 30 N.W. 72 (1886), provides a good example. The ordinance was adopted in September 1886, immediately after the latest attempt to convict Salvation Army marchers as a public nuisance had resulted in an acquittal. As soon as the ordinance went into effect, Salvation Army marchers were arrested. Likewise, in *Anderson v. City of Wellington*, 40 Kan. 173, 19 P.719 (1888), the court struck down a parade permit require-ment that was enforced against the Salvation Army the first day it became effective.

The Salvation Army was born in England in 1878 under the anti-liquor leadership of William Booth. Its Sunday processions drew up to fifty thousand participants. Local crowds—the Skeleton army, usually supported by "brewers and publicans"—often tried to stop these marches. Local governments also gave the Salvation Army mixed responses, sometimes protective but sometimes repressive. These responses generated significant English legal opinions protective of the right to assemble and parade. See D. Richter, *Riotous Victorians* 73–85 (1981).

Nevertheless, the first English permit requirement to which I have found reference apparently did not involve the Salvation Army. The Metropolitan Board of Works in London established a permit requirement in 1877 and applied it to public speaking in the parks. *Id.* at 91–93. This provision apparently was a restrictive response to a multitude of groups holding outdoor public meetings, "a social phenomenon that achieved a sort of apogee in late Victorian England." *Id.* at 87. The permit requirement, however, was fought by the Home Office during the tenure of Sir William Harcourt, who viewed the repression of freedom of assembly as likely to lead to discontent and disorder rather than public peace. *Id.* at 93–94.

8. 92 Mass. 510, 39 N.E. 113 (1895).

9. G. Abernathy, *supra* note 3, at 93. The situation in England was similar. Despite adoption by London Metropolitan Board of Works of a permit requirement, see *supra* note 7, the parliamentary government at that time generally recognized the right to assemble and parade. Harcourt, the Home Office Secretary, was opposed to the marches of the Salvation Army. Still, he was generally sympathetic to assemblies and recognized that the Salvations Army's "processions, not being illegal in themselves, cannot, in the absence of other circumstances, be legally prevented." Harcourt, however, thought the processions could be prohibited on the basis of sworn information that the processions would lead to a breach of the peace. D. Richter, *supra* note 7, at 80. The English courts repudiated even this limitation on assembly. In apparent disagreement with the reasoning of the later, infamous American hostile audience decision, *Feiner v. New York*, 340 U.S. 315 (1951), the English court found no legal authority for the proposition that "a man may be convicted for doing a lawful act [assembling] if he knows that his doing it may cause another to do an unlawful act [attack the assembly]." D. Richter, *supra* note 7, at 81, quoting Justice Field in *Beatty v. Gillbanks*, 9 Q.B.D. 308 (1882).

10. Although courts in these early parade permit cases frequently emphasized the arbitrary power placed in the hands of the mayor or chief of police, the courts routinely approved this same power in the context of permit requirements for meetings in the street or parks. See G. Abernathy, *supra* note 3, at 64–66, 85–92.

11. In addition to the Massachusetts cases, which have consistently upheld all permit requirements, see, e.g., *Commonwealth v. Davis*, 162 Mass. 510, 39 N.E. 113 (1895), Abernathy reports that the majority view was to uphold permit requirements for street *meetings*. G. Abernathy, *supra* note 3, at 64–66. See also *City of Bloomington v. Richardson*, 38 Ill. App. 60, 74 N.E.2d 48 (1890); *Love v. Phalen*, 128 Mich. 545, 87 N.W. 785 (1901); *Fitts v. City of Atlanta*, 121 Ga. 567, 49 S.E. 793 (1905). Still, some decisions in the early 1920's struck down permit ordinances for not having standards.

12. In upholding a permit requirement for street meetings, the court in *Love v. Phalen*, 128 Mich. 545, 87 N.W. 785 (1901) distinguished *Frazee's Case*, 63 Mich. 396, 30 N.W. 72 (1886), on the ground that the permit requirement there raised an entirely different question, namely "who may travel in the highways [rather than] who may occupy the public spaces in the city." *Love v. Phalen*, 128 Mich. at 548, 87 N.W. at 787. See also *Commonwealth v. Surridge*, 265 Mass. 425, 164 N.E. 480, 481 (1929); *People ex rel. Doyle v. Atwell*, 232 N.Y. 96, 133 N.E. 364 (1921) ("Public streets are primarily for public travel. . . . Any obstruction . . . may be declared unlawful"); Goodhart, "Public Meetings and Processions," 6 *Cambridge L. J.* 161 (1937).

13. G. Abernathy, *supra* note 3, at 91. Abernathy, a strong proponent of the right of assembly, sees modern conditions relating to traffic as increasingly justifying restrictions on parades. He reads the Court's decision upholding the permit requirement in *Cox v. New Hampshire*, 312 U.S. 569 (1941), while striking down restrictions in *Hague v. CIO*, 307 U.S. 496 (1939), to suggest that by the late 1930s the Court had reversed the prior tradition and now favored street meetings over parades. Abernathy finds this increased restriction of parades predictable and reasonably acceptable. His conclusion follows for two reasons. First, Abernathy concludes that modern parades create greater traffic problems. Second, Abernathy believes that, in contrast to parades, street meetings are particularly important to less popular or unpopular groups. Therefore, according to Abernathy, restrictions on parades will involve relatively little suppression of ideas. Given his reliance on the dominant marketplace of ideas theory of the first amendment, Abernathy can

conclude that the regulation of parades does not create a serious infringement. G. Abernathy, *supra* note 3, at 105–7.

14. Generally, there is little evidence that providing police protection was either a purpose of the permit requirement or that police protection was routinely provided after a permit request. Obviously, as will be developed below, when the paraders fear danger and desire police protection, the mandatory permit process does not improve their situation. The paraders can, even without a permit requirement, give the police notice and request protection. Richter describes how the requests of the Salvation Army in the 1880s in England for police protection were resisted by the local governments, which only had limited police personnel, but were supported in principle by the English Home Office. D. Richter, *supra* note 7, at 75–83.

15. The courts' approval of the requirement that groups obtain permits for meetings in the parks before they were willing to accept similar permit requirements for parades suggests that traffic control was not their major concern. Application of the permit requirement to small groups that obey traffic signals and walk on the sidewalks also belies this traffic control interpretation.

16. During both this and later periods, violence was seldom initiated by paraders or by assemblies to which mandatory permit requirements apply. The more common occurrence is for violence to result from police attempts to interfere with assemblies or parades. Sometimes the violence results specifically from the government's attempt to enforce permit requirements. Many examples are collected in R. Goldstein, *Political Repression in Modern America from 1870 to the Present* (1978). See, e.g., *id.* at 93 (unemployment demonstrations attacked by police in 1913–1915); *id.* at 145 (May Day celebrations attacked by police, soldiers, and bystanders in various cities in 1919); *id.* at 203–04 (many police attacks, some extraordinarily vicious, on peaceful demonstrations of unemployed workers in 1930–1933); *id.* at 223 (fifteen hundred police and deputy sheriffs broke up strike parades in a California agricultural region in 1936). See also R. Murray, *Red Scare: A Study in National Hysteria, 1919–1920* at 74 (1964) (riot ensued in Boston in 1919 when police tried to enforce parade permit requirement to stop parade of fifteen hundred socialists); Gutman, "Tompkins Square Riot," *supra* note 6 (enforcement of permit cancellation lead to police riot); Leab, "United We Eat: The Creation and Organization of the Unemployed Councils in 1930," 8 *Labor History* 300, 306–7 (1967) (scores injured when on International Unemployment Day, May 6, 1930, police charged crowd after refusing to allow 35,000 persons meeting in Union Square in New York City to march on City Hall). Chicago's denial of various permits to political demonstrators and to Yippies during the Democratic National Convention in 1968 came after prolonged attempts by the groups to secure the permits. See D. Walker, *Rights in Conflict* 59–75 (1968). This denial was a factor reducing the number of demonstrators coming to Chicago, *id.* at 92, but it is very possible that, if the city had allowed the planned demonstrations, those deterred from coming by the lack of permits would have been peaceful, as most of those who did come had intended to be. According to the remarkably informative Walker Report, the "clearing of demonstrators from Lincoln Park," for which a permit had been denied, "led directly to the violence. . . . [L]iterally, it forced the protestor into confrontation with police in Old Town and the adjacent residential neighborhoods." *Id.* at 4. See also J. Skolnick, *The Politics of Protest* 68 (1969).

17. Today many cities usefully rely on permit systems for these and other legitimate purposes. I will argue below, however, that these legitimate functions do not necessitate the use of a mandatory permit system. Here, the claim is only that these legitimate functions do not persuasively explain the political origins or the original judicial approval of the permit requirements.

18. *Lochner v. New York*, 198 U.S. 45 (1905).

19. *West Coast Hotel v. Parrish*, 300 U.S. 379 (1937).

20. *Cox*, 312 U.S. at 574. Cf. *West Coast Hotel*, 300 U.S. at 391: "But the liberty safe-guarded is liberty in a social organization which requires the protection of law against the evils which menace the health, safety, morals and welfare of the people. Liberty under the Constitution is thus necessarily subject to the restraints of due process and regulation which is reasonable in relation to its subject matter . . . is due process."

21. Decisions shortly after *Cox* provide arguable grounds to object to the Court's analysis. *See* text accompanying notes 60–64 *infra*. Moreover, some relevant development of first amendment doctrine had occurred during the five years before *Cox*, including several cases in other contexts striking down permit requirements. The Court in *Cox* distinguished these cases on various grounds, most importantly on the grounds that official discretion was not controlled as it was in *Cox* by making "comfort or convenience in the use of streets the standard of official action." 312 U.S. at 577. Still, at the time of *Cox* these recent precedents could have been read more broadly as amounting to "an appreciation of the character of the evil inherent in a licensing system." *Thornhill v. Alabama*, 310 U.S. 88, 97 (1940). See also *Near v. Minnesota*, 283 U.S. 697 (1931) (state statute directing court to enjoin a person from further publication or circulation of malicious, scandalous, or defamatory, newspaper or periodical is an unconstitutional prior restraint). Possibly the difference between publication and street activity, and the theoretical possibility of avoiding content discrimination in *Cox* while content evaluation was the focus of the law in *Near*, could lead a court to ignore the analogy.

22. *Commonwealth v. Hessler*, 141 Pa. Super. 421, 15 A.2d 486 (1940). See G. Abernathy, *supra* note 3, at 96.

23. The Court in a closely related context two years earlier had clearly indicated that a person whose behavior might be subject to regulation could challenge an improper, overbroad regulation. See, e.g., *Thornhill v. Alabama*, 310 U.S. 88, 97–98 (1940).

24. In practice, a sympathetic court consistently finds some basis to strike down a local ordinance as unreasonable or discriminatory. Courts find either that a permit procedure requires application too long before the event, that the appeal process for a denial is non-existent, inadequate, or too slow, that insurance requirements are improper, that ordinance lacks standards to limit official discretion, or, most often, that the procedure is administered discriminatorily. Nevertheless, even a very narrowly drawn permit system is subject to relatively great abuse that will be virtually beyond possible judicial oversight. See *infra* text accompanying notes 67–70.

25. See *San Antonio, Texas Code* §§38–100.12, 38–100.14 (1983). The Code defines a parade as "any parade, march, demonstration, public assemblage, ceremony, show, exhibition, pageant, or procession of any kind, or any similar display, in or upon any street, park, alley, or plaza or other public thoroughfare in the city." *Id.* §38–100.12. In Omaha, "[n]o parade or procession shall be allowed upon any street or public way, nor shall any open-air public meeting be held upon any street, public way or other public place . . . until a permit . . . shall be obtained from the public safety director." *Omaha, Nebraska, Code* §20–292 (1982); and "[i]t shall be unlawful for any person . . . to make any public speech in any park, except upon written permission from the director of parks . . ." *Id.* §21–10. For similarly broad definitions and permit requirements, see, e.g., *Atlanta, Ga., Code* art. E, §11–2072 to –2083 (1981); *Columbus, Ohio, City Code* §2111.01 (1977); *Denver, Colorado, Code* §54–357(2)(1973).

26. *Martin v. Struthers*, 319 U.S. 141 (1943); *Schneider v. Irvington*, 308 U.S. 147 (1939).

27. A better analysis would emphasize that these regulations of door-to-door canvassing and leafletting on the street are invalid because the state must not prohibit expressive conduct at least when the expressive conduct is not itself the evil. A possible explanatory

principle is that the government must always direct its restrictions at the real evil. The government could prohibit unwanted invasions of privacy by enforcing privately posted No Trespass signs and could prohibit littering by acting against the person who drops the pamphlet on the ground. Whenever the law does not point directly at the evil, there necessarily will be an alternative, although the alternative will not necessarily be as convenient, practical, or cheap. Thus, an honestly applied balancing analysis will not always require the less restrictive, but sometimes less effective or more expensive, alternative. In contrast, the less restrictive alternative requirement follows from the premise that the government cannot choose repression of speech and assembly as its means to further its legitimate ends.

The permit requirement raises a different issue. The government claims that the evil is the existence of the assembly under circumstances in which the government does not have notice or an opportunity to prohibit the assembly because of conflicting uses of the space or other serious inconveniences. Thus, the permit requirement appears aimed directly at the evil.

28. Parade permit requirements can also be described as unconstitutional conditions. The permit system conditions a person's use of the street on giving up the right to be free of government supervision in the exercise of the right of free assembly.

29. See *Metromedia, Inc. v. City of San Diego*, 453 U.S. 490 (1981) (plurality indicates regulation of commercial billboards would be proper). A liberty theory of the first amendment would not protect such parades. See Chapter 9. See also Jackson and Jeffries, "Commercial Speech: Economic Due Process and the First Amendment," 65 *Virginia L. Rev.* 1 (1979). But see Redish, "The Value of Free Speech," 130 *U. Pa. L. Rev.* 591 (1982). Some cities presently *prohibit* parades by commercial groups. See, e.g., *San Diego, California, Code* §22.0207 (1981) (prohibits "parade which is to be held for the primary purpose of advertising any person, product, goods, wares, merchandise, or event, and is designed to be held primarily for private profit or a charitable purpose"). Even if the government can regulate commercial speech, San Diego's ordinance appears to prohibit some protected activities, e.g., fund raising parades by charitable groups. *Village of Schaumberg v. Citizens for a Better Environment*, 444 U.S. 620 (1980). If so, it unconstitutionally discriminates among protected activities and also is unconstitutionally overbroad. See *Metromedia, Inc. v. City of San Diego*, 453 U.S. 490 (1981).

30. *Sacramento, California, Code* §38.150 (1982); *San Diego, California, Code* § 22.0207(a)(1)(1981). See also *Seattle, Washington, Municipal Code* 11.14.410, 11.515.010 (requires parade permit only if the organized movement "requires the closure of streets to prevent a conflict with the regular flow of vehicular traffic")(1982). Despite broadly written ordinances that would cover "parades" that only involve small groups that walk on the sidewalks and obey traffic lights, many local governments may not apply the ordinance in those circumstances and possibly are not even aware that the language of their ordinance covers these "parades."

31. An alternative argument would be to show that the permit requirement has an impermissible purpose. Given that historically permit requirements consistently have been used to harass and to limit the parades and assemblies of dissident and unpopular groups, this argument would seem plausible. Both the claim that the mandatory permit requirement provides relatively little gain in the city's attempt to supply adequate policing and traffic control while imposing serious restrictions on the right of assembly, see *infra* text accompanying notes 39–70, and the observation that the restrictive consequences of the permit requirement, even when fairly administered, fall most heavily on certain dissident groups, see *infra* text accompanying notes 60–66, support this interpretation of the objective or contextual purpose of the requirement. Nevertheless, the contribution that permit requirements presently make to legitimate traffic and safety concerns argues

against this interpretation of the condition as having a constitutionally impermissible purpose.

32. 307 U.S. 496 (1939).

33. *Id.* at 515. Justice Roberts then says the right is "not absolute, but relative." *Id.* at 516.

34. Mishan, "Pareto Optimality and the Law," 19 *Oxford Economic Papers* 255 (1967).

35. Kalven, "The Concept of the Public Forum: Cox V. Louisiana," 1965 *Supreme Court Rev.* 1, 12.

36. Obviously, any set of rules will favor some uses over others. Nevertheless, the general purpose of traffic laws is to further individual's capacity to achieve their individual aims safely—except that the traffic laws can properly prohibit an individual's valued use if that use would determine the nature of the space in a way that undermines the values of almost all the other users—for example, it can prohibit reckless driving or speeding. See Baker, "Counting Preferences in Collective Choice Situations," 25 *UCLA L. Rev.* 381 (1978). In contrast, parades, which are inherently limited in time and can be conducted with little threat to safety, do not create the constant interference with others' uses or the continuous threat to safety. Nor does a parade necessarily even temporarily create serious disruption unless the parade includes a large number of participants.

37. In some cities, the city council has either initial or final authority to approve some or all permit applications. Typically, park and recreation departments have authority over park property. The police officer in charge of issuing permits in a medium-size city reported that the police initially will refuse permission for parades to travel on a certain major downtown street. The police believe that parades on this street require greater use of police resources and create more traffic problems. But sometimes parade leaders (presumably of a popular group) go to the mayor. Since the mayor believes that parades on this street help business, the mayor will indicate support. The police department will then grant permission, but only with respect to that specific parade.

I wrote to twenty-eight large and medium sized cities in all regions of the country asking for copies of parade ordinances and some additional information, and received replies from eighteen. For seven cites—Atlanta, Georgia; Columbus, Ohio; Des Moines, Iowa; Madison, Wisconsin; Omaha, Nebraska; San Diego, California; and Seattle, Washington—in order to gain information on the actual operating process I made follow-up telephone calls on July 20 and 22, 1983 to the person identified in the reply as knowledgeable, usually a police officer in charge of issuing permits or monitoring parades. These replies and notes on these conversations are on file with the author [hereafter cited as *Inquiries to Cities Regarding Parade Permits*]. The information in the paragraph above resulted from one of these phone conversations.

38. Conversations with local authorities, see *Inquiries To Cities Regarding Parade Permits, supra* note 37, lawyers, and dissident marchers, as well as historical reports, lead to my tentative conclusion that route and time agreements are particularly controversial and difficult to reach in the case of controversial political marchs. See, e.g., *Houston Peace Coalition v. Houston City Council*, 310 F.Supp. 457 (S.D. Tex. 1970); cases cited *infra*, Ch.8, note 59.

39. *Inquiries to Cities Regarding Parade Permits, supra* note 37 (conversation with officials from Omaha, Seattle, Madison, and Atlanta).

40. See Chapter 8, note 7.

41. Local governments cannot, however, distinguish funerals from other processions on the ground that funerals will be less disruptive, less political, or even that they will not lead to violence. Many of the largest, most political parades take the form of funeral processions. See Chapter 8, note 10.

42. See *Police Dept. of Chicago v. Mosley*, 408 U.S. 92 (1972). Forcing the government to reach more general conclusions, with the expectation that the government will discover that the legitimate need to restrict expression is not as great as it first seemed, is a major function of a liberally interpreted prohibition on content discrimination.

43. The police in one city reported that they almost always had advance knowledge of parades independently of the permit process. *Inquiries to Cities Regarding Parade Permits, supra* note 37.

44. Lack of standards typically makes these waiver provisions appropriate targets for constitutional challenge. The text claims more broadly that the absence of provision for waiver should also make the ordinances unconstitutional.

45. The ordinance appears to have been greatly influenced by the analysis of Professor Vince Blasi. Compare "Sacramento Parade Ordinance," *Sacramento, California, Code* §§ 38.150–157 with Blasi, "Prior Restraints on Demonstrations, 68 *Michigan L. Rev.* 1481 (1970).

46. *Sacramento, California Code* §38.155 (1982).

47. In practice, the Sacramento approach may often prevail. See text accompanying note 46 *supra*. Many police forces exercise discretion and do not enforce the permit requirements and traffic laws when faced with a parade in progress; they handle spontaneous parades in the same way as parades with permits. Some police forces will, however, inform the leaders of nonpermitted parades of the permit requirement and, if the police conclude that there was an intentional decision by the parade leaders to ignore the requirement or if violence or serious damage to property occurs, the police will issue a citation to the leaders of the parade if they can be found. *Inquiries to Cities Regarding Parade Permits, supra* note 37. The occasionally chosen alternative, enforcing the permit requirements, often results in violence between the police and demonstrators—an ironic result given that the permit requirement is designed to give the police notice so that they help prevent violence. See *supra* note 16.

48. See note 6 *supra*.

49. See note 16 *supra*.

50. See note 16 *supra*.

51. Relatively spontaneous marches are not solely the response of fringe dissidents. During the 1968 Democratic Convention in Chicago, some convention delegates decided after midnight to parade that night in response to the police riots and the defeat of Eugene McCarthy's presidential nomination. Nearly 600 delegates engaged in the march between 3:00 and 4:00 A.M., culminating in speeches to the demonstrators. D. Walker, *supra* note 16, at 333–36. In a different vein, the police in Columbus, Ohio, report that if Ohio State wins the Ohio State/Michigan football game, a large, "spontaneous" parade erupts for which often there has been no permit granted. (Sometimes, optimistic groups from the school will have obtained a permit, but the police prepare for the parade whether or not a permit is obtained.) See *Inquiries to Cities Regarding Parade Permits, supra* note 37.

52. Some ordinances make it illegal to participate in a parade for which no permit has been issued. Others make it illegal to participate if one knows that no permit has been issued. In either case, a parader's proper exercise of the first amendment right may be made illegal because of the inaction of someone else. Cf. *NAACP v. Claiborne Hardware Co.*, 458 U.S. 886 (1982)(state cannot impose liability on a "guilt for association" theory).

53. See, e.g., F. Piven and R. Cloward, *supra* note 6, at 297–98.

54. See F. Schauer, *Free Speech: A Philosophical Enquiry* 201–3 (1982).

55. *Dennis v. United States*, 341 U.S. 494, 577 (1951) (Jackson, concurring).

56. G. Abernathy, *supra* note 3, at 83. Abernathy, at this point abandoning reliance on the marketplace of ideas theory, thinks the parades should receive protection since the Constitution does not require an interchange of ideas as a precondition of protection. *Id.*

57. See Chapter 8, text accompanying notes 94–97.

58. The Court decision most obviously recognizing this aspect of liberty and most difficult to rationalize within a marketplace framework is *NAACP v. Claiborne Hardware*, 458 U.S. 886 (1982). But see *Frisby v. Schultz*, 108 S.Ct. 2495 (1988).

59. See Chapter 4.

60. 312 U.S. 569 (1941).

61. *Minersville School Dist. v. Gobitis*, 310 U.S. 586 (1940).

62. *West Virginia State Bd. of Educ. v. Barnette*, 319 U.S. 624, 642 (1943) (emphasis added).

63. See, e.g., *Wooley v. Maynard*, 430 U.S. 705 (1977).

64. Since a person's claim to property wealth, as opposed to liberty, must depend on collectively adopted allocative practices or rules, see Baker, "Property and Its Relation to Constitutionally Protected Liberty," 134 *U. Pa. L. Rev.* 741 (1986), compulsory taxes do not properly raise the issue discussed in the text. See, e.g., *United States v. Lee*, 455 U.S. 252 (1982) (Old Order Amish can be compelled to pay Social Security taxes).

65. But cf. *Bowen v. Ray*, 106 S.Ct. 2147 (1986) (five justices, Blackmun, O'Connor, Brennan, Marshall, and White, apparently conclude that government cannot deny child benefits because the parents do not apply for a Social Security number for the child if the parents' religious convictions prevent them from applying).

66. Compare *Sherbert v. Verner*, 374 U.S. 398 (1963)(conditioning the availability of unemployment benefits on the applicant's willingness to work on Saturday in violation of personal religious beliefs is an unconstitutional interference with free exercise of religion) with *Braunfeld v. Brown*, 366 U.S. 599 (1961)(statute prohibiting commerce on Sunday did not prohibit the free exercise of the Orthodox Jewish faith). In *Thomas v. Collins*, 323 U.S. 516 (1944), the Court argued:

> If the exercise of the rights of free speech and free assembly cannot be made a crime, we do not think this can be accomplished by the device of requiring previous registration as a condition for exercising them and making such a condition the foundation for restraining in advance their exercise.... So long as no more is involved than exercise of the rights of free speech and assembly, it is immune to such a restriction.

Id. at 540. See also *id.* at 539. The dissent found the permit requirement in *Thomas* indistinguishable on principle from that in *Cox v. New Hampshire*, see *id.* at 556 (Roberts, J., joined by Stone, C.J., Reed, and Frankfurter, JJ., dissenting). Thus, the dissent apparently read the majority as treating *Cox* as wrongly decided. The majority, however, might argue that the parade in *Cox* involved speech plus conduct, or, maybe, assembly *on the street*, not mere assembly. Hence, the majority could distinguish the cases by employing a "speech plus" theory. See *id.* at 540. Nevertheless, the dissent seems correct that *Thomas* and *Cox* are fundamentally inconsistent.

67. The easiest ground for a court to invalidate a permit system is to find that the ordinance, on its face, does not contain adequately clear standards. Courts face more difficult proof problems when the ordinance on its face or as interpreted limits official discretion. Still, these courts often properly find these ordinances discriminatory as applied. See, e.g., *Shuttlesworth v. City of Birmingham*, 382 U.S. 87 (1965); *Cox v. Louisiana*, 379 U.S. 536 (1965); *Houston Peace Coalition v. Houston City Council*, 310 F.Supp. 457 (S.D. Tex. 1970). For a discussion of the equal access principle in other first amendment contexts, see N. Dorsen, P. Bender, and B. Neuborne, *Emerson, Haber & Dorsen's Political and Civil Rights in the United States* 287–88 (4th ed. 1976).

68. Except for the government and its officials, all the parties to parade- or assembly-related litigation cited in this chapter are civil rights groups, dissident political groups, religious minorities, or labor activists. The typical practice of adopting permit systems in

response to the presence of religious or politically oriented street activity is suggestive both of local attitudes and the way these permit systems are enforced.

69. A flagrant example of this normally low visibility form of abuse occurred during the 1968 Democratic Convention in Chicago. See *State v. McFetridge*, 484 F.2d 1169 (7th Cir. 1973); D. Walker, *supra* note 16, at 59–75.

70. See *supra* text accompanying note 7.

71. The police have responsibilities that give them incentives to restrict parades even by popular groups, although counterincentives operate there that do not operate in respect to unpopular groups.

72. See Handler, "Dependant People, The State, and the Modern/Postmodern Search for the Dialogic Community," 35 *UCLA L. Rev* 999 (1988) (showing how the incentives on officials by structured design of system can be crucial for promoting values that liberal legalism often tries to establish by creating legal rights).

73. Vince Blasi's balancing leads him to interpret the first amendment "to mean that a demonstration must be allowed whenever the probable number of demonstrators exceeds the number of citizens who would be seriously inconvenienced by the march or rally." Blasi, *supra* note 45, at 1503. This interpretation reverses the proper notion that the first amendment protects liberty from majority suppression. It should particularly protect liberty to dissent and engage in expressive activity in ways that upset normal routine. An instrumentalist version of a liberty theory, which values our power to exercise liberty in order to change or redefine ourselves, might hold that people's capacity peacefully to impose some costs on the majority is a benefit, not a cost, of freedom of assembly. In contrast, a marketplace of ideas theorist might defend Blasi's rule. The disruptive assembly implicates primarily the use of public resources and the personal satisfaction of the users, not the survival of an idea. *Id.* at 1491. This argument, however, is unpersuasive on its own terms given the real dynamics by which ideas come to prevail. It is also irrelevant from a liberty perspective, which asserts that a function of the first amendment is to protect expression from rules justified merely as a means of maximizing welfare satisfaction.

74. But see *San Diego, California Code*, discussed *supra* note 29 (prohibits commercial parades).

75. See Chapter 5.

CHAPTER 8

1. See Baker, "Outcome Equality of Equality of Respect: The Substantive Content of Equal Protection," 131 *U. Pa. L. Rev.* 933, 969–72 (1983).

2. *Id.* See J. Rawls, *A Theory of Justice* 48–50 (1971).

3. See, e.g., Redish, "The Content Distinction in First Amendment Analysis," 34 *Stanford L. Rev.* 113 (1981). Cf. Stone, "Content Regulation and the First Amendment," 25 *William & Mary L. Rev.* 189 (1983) (properly defined content distinction makes sense); Stone, "Restrictions of Speech Because of Its Content: The Peculiar Case of Subject-Matter Restrictions," 46 *U. Chicago L. Rev.* 81 (1978).

4. See, e.g., *Young v. American Mini Theatres*, 427 U.S. 50 (1976) (plurality opinion).

5. Karst, "Equality as a Central Principle in the First Amendment," 43 *U. Chicago L. Rev.* 20 (1975).

6. See, e.g., *Anderson v. City of Wellington*, 40 Kan. 173, 19 P. 719 (1888) (ordinance passed in 1887 exempted funerals, fire companies, and government troops); *Frazee's Case*, 63 Mich. 396, 30 N.W. 72 (1886) (court noted exemption for funeral processions in 1886 ordinance). For the origin of permit requirements, see Chapter 7, notes 6 & 7.

7. I wrote to twenty-eight large and medium sized cities in all regions of the country asking for copies of parade ordinances and some additional information, and received replies from eighteen. For seven cites—Atlanta, Georgia; Columbus, Ohio; Des Moines, Iowa; Madison, Wisconsin; Omaha, Nebraska; San Diego, California; and Seattle, Washington—I made follow-up telephone calls on July 20 and 22, 1983, to the person identified in the reply as knowledgeable, usually a police officer in charge of issuing permits or monitoring parades. [hereafter cited as *Inquiry to Cities Regarding Parade Permits*].

Nine of the eighteen ordinances, after apparently defining the parade permit requirement broadly enough to include funeral processions, explicitly exempted them. Internal features of other ordinances, such as a requirement to apply for the permits 30 days before the procession, made it relatively clear that these ordinances were not intended to apply to funerals. Other information, such as the number of permits issued a year, suggest that none of the surveyed cities regularly applied their ordinance to funeral processions, even though by their terms, most ordinances would appear to cover them.

The historical pattern of applying parade ordinances to harass dissent would predict that sometimes they would be applied to funerals. Thus, a permit was sought and secured from Jackson, Mississippi, authorities in June 1963 for Medgar Evers's funeral procession in which about 5,000 people participated. See *NAACP v. Thompson*, 357 F.2d 831, 836 (5th Cir. 1966). The city apparently did not regularly require parade permits for funeral processions, or for many other events. During the three years ending in June 1965 only thirteen parade permits were applied for and issued— about half for civil rights marches. See *Guyor v. Pierce*, 372 F.2d 658, 660 (5th Cir. 1967). But when civil rights activists marched in large groups, even on the sidewalks, they were likely to be arrested for parading without a permit. See *NAACP v. Thompson*, 357 F.2d at 836.

8. *Chicago Police Dept. v. Mosley*, 408 U.S. 92 (1972).

9. See Chapter 7, note 16.

10. Memories of Pericles and Mark Antony should warn us of the possible significance of funerals. See also R. Ellison, *The Invisible Man* 385–98 (1952).

American history continually presents examples of large funeral processions that constitute large political demonstrations. These processions can result in any problem, from traffic disruption to physical violence, that surround other parades. During the 1913 Paterson, New Jersey, strike, after two workers were killed, allegedly by private detectives hired by the mill owners, 15,000 workers marched in a ten block procession, with IWW leaders making speeches at the grave. J. Kornbluth, *Rebel Voices: An IWW Anthology* 200 (1964). In 1914, after a bomb killed Arthur Carron, a free speech activist, the IWW, led by Alexander Berkman, planned a funeral parade in New York. When the Health Department denied permission for the parade, 20,000 people gathered peacefully at Union Square for a memorial service. J. Jaffe, *Crusade Against Radicalism: New York During the Red Scare, 1914–1924*, at 43–44 (1972). In 1913, in Calumet, Michigan, deputies hired by the owner-controlled local government and deputized gunmen supplied by the companies murdered two strikers. During the funeral procession, the mourners cursed the police who responded with gunfire, wounding one woman. V. Jensen, *Heritage of Conflict* 282 (1950). The only time the police allowed an outdoor demonstration planned by the Communists in Chicago in 1930 to proceed until its end, the demonstration was a funeral procession. H. Lasswell and D. Blumstock, *World Revolutionary Propaganda* 168–69 (1939). In March 1932, after police fired point blank into the group of 3,000 workers who had marched from downtown Detroit to the Ford plant in Dearborn, killing four of the demonstrators, the Communists organized a memorial service and a five mile march of 30,000 people to the cemetery. I. Bernstein, *The Lean Years* 432–34 (1966); *American Violence: A Documentary History* 179–84 (R. Hofstader ed. 1971). Special treatment of funeral processions continues both in the United States and worldwide. Countries that repress political dissent constantly either decide or are effectively forced to allow funeral "assemblies" and "parades" even though other meetings with similar speakers would be banned.

11. See *Kime v. United States*, 459 U.S. 949 (1982) (Brennan, dissenting from denial of certiorari). See also *Schacht v. United States*, 398 U.S. 58 (1970).

12. But cf. *Godwin v. East Baton Rouge Parish School Bd.*, 408 S.2d 1214 (La.) (upheld rule prohibiting all hand-held signs in school board office building), *appeal dismissed*, 103 S.Ct. 31 (1982).

13. *Grayned v. City of Rockford*, 408 U.S. 104, 107–08 (1972) (upholding quoted ordinance).

14. *Martin v. Struthers*, 319 U.S. 142 (1943); *Minneapolis Star & Tribune v. Minnesota Commissioner of Revenue*, 460 U.S. 575 (1983); *Schneider v. Irvington*, 308 U.S. 147 (1939). But see *Los Angeles City Council v. Taxpayers for Vincent*, 466 U.S. 789 (1984).

15. Nonprotection of speech that purposefully creates a clear and present danger is consistent with a full protection theory to the extent that the unprotected speech constitutes an *attempt* to engage in crime. See, e.g., Linde, "'Clear and Present Danger' Reexamined," 22 *Stanford L. Rev.* 1163 (1970); Rogat and O'Fallon, "Mr. Justice Holmes: A Dissenting Opinion—The Speech Cases," 36 *Stanford L. Rev.* 1349 (1984). From this full protection view, the issue is whether or not the *law* amounts to an abridgement of the relevant right or freedom—and a law against attempts does not. In contrast, from a balancing perspective, the relevant issue is the extent of the restriction of protected conduct versus the societal interest in the regulation.

16. Contained as part of Draft VIII of the University of Oregon's proposed *Rule on Posters, Placards, Signs and Banners* (Memorandum to author, March 2, 1981). The proposed restriction, which had also been in earlier drafts, for example, Drafts VI and VII, was finally removed from Draft IX. I was a spokesperson for the local chapter of the Oregon Civil Liberties Union and the local chapter of the National Lawyers Guild in negotiating with the University in respect to the proposed rule between November 1978 and April 1981. During this period, the University devoted considerable time of numerous employees in its apparent attempt to determine the maximum degree to which it could require prior approval of, or could ban from the University, all signs, posters, and banners.

17. Other accepted first amendment approaches similarly reject apparently welfare-maximizing restraints on speech. The clear and present danger test means that, as long as there is time for others to respond to the evil counsels, restraint is impermissible even though others are unwilling to offer wiser counsels or would be unsuccessful. Thus, the test permits the evil counsels to prevail. More generally, the refusal to allow guilt by association in the first amendment context, see e.g., *NAACP v. Claiborne Hardware Co.*, 458 U.S. 886 (1982), means that the basis of regulation as well as punishment must be actual prohibitable conduct, not welfare-maximizing use of accurate statistical likelihoods.

18. See, e.g., *Carey v. Brown*, 447 U.S. 555 (1980); *Police Dept. of Chicago v. Mosley*, 408 U.S. 92 (1972). See also *Consolidated Edison Co. v. Public Servs. Comm'n*, 447 U.S. 530, 537 (1980) ("The First Amendment's hostility to content-based regulation extends not only to restrictions on particular viewpoints, but also to prohibition of public discussion of an entire topic").

19. *Erznoznik v. City of Jacksonville*, 422 U.S. 205 (1975).

20. *FCC v. Pacifica Foundation*, 438 U.S. 726, reh'g denied, 439 U.S. 883 (1978).

21. *Papish v. Board of Curators*, 410 U.S. 667 (1973).

22. *Cohen v. California*, 403 U.S. 15, 25–26 (1971).

23. *Metromedia, Inc. v. City of San Diego*, 453 U.S. 490 (1981).

24. See *Cohen v. California*, 403 U.S. 15, 25–26 (1971). In terms of lifestyle, if not in

terms of traditional notions of "rational" debate, the medium will often be crucial to the values expressed or practiced.

25. The constitutionality of a complete ban on residential picketing was left open in *Carey v. Brown*, 447 U.S. 455, 459 n.2 (1980) and again in *Frisby v. Shultz*, 108 S.Ct. 2495 (1988).

26. According to the dissent in *Brown v. Louisiana*, 383 U.S. 131 (1966), "[s]hort of physical violence, petitioners could not have more completely upset the normal, quiet functioning of the . . . Library." *Id.* at 163 (Black, joined by Clark, Harlan, and Stewart, dissenting). The plurality found that "there was no disturbance of others, no disruption of library activities, and no violation of any library regulations." *Id.* at 142. This disagreement can be understood if the plurality implicitly agreed with the state (and the dissent) that the symbolic expression of the assembled blacks was "enough to unnerve a woman in the situation Mrs. Reeves [the assistant librarian] was in," *id.* at 140, but viewed the reaction of observers, including Mrs. Reeves, to the expressive demonstration to be an impermissible basis on which to attribute the disruption to the demonstrators. See also *id.* at 133 n.1. This conclusion would reflect the principle that people's dislike of other people or other people's choices and their exercises of liberty does not justify imposing restraints— that respect for people's equality and autonomy rules this out. This principle has been accepted by the Court in various contexts. For example, it seems implicit in the unanimous decision that in applying the proper standard, "the best interests of the child," a state cannot consider the "reality of private [racial] biases and the possible injury that they might inflict" in its decision about removal of the child. *Palmore v. Sidoti*, 466 U.S. 429 (1984). See also *Caban v. Mohammed*, 441 U.S. 380 (1979). It would, as well, arguably undermine the Court's holdings in several discredited decisions. See, e.g., *Palmer v. Thompson*, 403 U.S. 217 (1971); *Feiner v. New York*, 340 U.S. 315 (1951).

27. *Grayned v. City of Rockford*, 408 U.S. 104, 107–08 (1972).

28. *Brown v. Louisiana*, 383 U.S. 131 (1966); *Cox v. Louisiana*, 379 U.S. 536 (1965). Cf. *United States v. O'Brien*, 391 U.S. 367 (1968). Similarly, the Court has recognized that some generally applicable laws cannot be used to require behavior contrary to a person's expression of religious values. See *Wisconsin v. Yoder*, 406 U.S. 205 (1972) (cannot require Amish child to attend high school); *Bowen v. Roy*, 476 U.S. 693 (1986) (several opinions indicating that government cannot require Indians to obtain Social Security number in order to obtain welfare benefit if this activity would violate the person's religious beliefs). See also Stone, "Content-Neutral Distinctions," 54 *U. Chicago L. Rev.* 46, 105–114 (1987) (suggesting an effect analysis of these "incidental effects" cases and argues that they should be treated like direct restrictions of communication, at least, where the law "has a highly disproportionate impact on free expression or directly penalizes expressive activity").

29. 307 U.S. 496 (1939).

30. *Id.* at 515.

31. *Id.* at 516.

32. Cf. *Schneider v. State*, 308 U.S. 147 (1939) (invalidating ordinance prohibiting leafletting); *Martin v. City of Struthers*, 319 U.S. 141 (1943) (invalidating ordinance prohibiting door-to-door distribution of leaflets). If, as the second proposed principle claims, the first amendment prohibits the adoption of statutes that are specifically directed at restricting assembly or expression, these restrictions would be disallowed. The thesis of the third principle is that even a general rule could not prohibit some of this first amendment conduct.

33. The Supreme Court upheld the right of the public and the press to attend criminal trials in a decision that is generally taken to be the first Supreme Court victory for a first-amendment-based right of access. *Richmond Newspapers, Inc. v. Virginia*, 448 U.S. 555

(1980). Nevertheless, the plurality opinion was written as if the Court were invalidating an unreasonable limitation on a particular place that tradition had made into a public forum or, at least, into a place that must be open to the public to exercise its first amendment right to assemble in order to listen. See *id.* at 576 n.11, 577–78, 581 n.18. See also *id.* at 599–600 (Stewart, concurring in the judgment) ("a trial courtroom is a public place" and relying on analogies to reasonable time, place, and manner restrictions).

34. 408 U.S. 104 (1972).

35. *Id.* at 116.

36. *Id.* at 115–16.

37. See, e.g., *Jamison v. Texas*, 318 U.S. 413, 416 (1943) ("But one who is rightfully on a street which the state has left open to the public carries with him there as elsewhere the constitutional right to express his views in an orderly fashion.") But cf. *Frisby v. Shultz*, 108 S.Ct. 2495 (1988) (state can prohibit picketing directed at specific residence).

38. The discussion of principle four will give meaning to the phrase "in a manner that prohibits substantially valued first amendment conduct." Basically, the third principle permits restrictions that merely involved instrumental burdens—for e.g., increased costs—on expressive conduct. It prohibits, however, restrictions that prevent a person from expressing certain messages or embodying her values in her conduct or engaging in communicative interactions with willing listeners.

39. The third principle as well as Marshall's formulation amount to a requirement to adopt less drastic alternatives. One can interpret this requirement either as an aid to balancing, see Note, "Less Drastic Means and the First Amendment," 78 *Yale L. J.* 464, 467–68 (1969), or as an aid in characterizing the purpose of the law, the interpretation adopted here.

40. These results are properly avoided. See Baker, *supra* note 1, 131 *U. Pa. L. Rev.* at 949–59.

41. The various principles are often duplicative attempts to interpret a few basic value commitments. Therefore, it is not surprising that the third principle will in some ways duplicate the results of several other principles.

42. See *Board of Educ., Island Trees Union Free School Dist. v. Pico*, 457 U.S. 853 (1982).

43. See, e.g., Jarrett and Mund, "The Right of Assembly," 9 *New York U. L. Rev.* 1, 19–30 (1931) (Eight out of forty-five cities responding to an ACLU study require permits for meetings held in *privately* owned meeting halls. In other places, the hall-owners' licenses are implicitly subject to obtaining the informal approval of the police for all meetings; in these cities, hall-owners informally submit all programs to police departments for approval. The local governments clearly used this process to censor speakers on basis of their views.) See also *CIO v. Hague*, 25 F.Supp. 127, 144 (D.N.J. 1938) (plaintiffs offered to prove that the unavailability of "private places in which [to hold meetings] . . . [was] due to coercion by the City officials"); J. Jaffe, *supra* note 10, at 40 (police in New York in 1914 "took steps to insure that owners of public halls would not rent to [the IWW]"; R. Goldstein, *Political Repression in Modern America* 89 (1978) (during Paterson, New Jersey, strike of 1913, police closed "every hall in town to strikers").

44. See discussion of principle four, *infra* text accompanying notes 60–83.

45. For a particularly useful discussion of this issue, see Neisser, "Charging for Free Speech: User Fees and Insurance in the Marketplace of Ideas," 74 *Georgetown L. J.* 257 (1985).

46. See I. Horowitz, *The Struggle Is the Message* 58 (1970) (confrontation increased the cost of the Vietnam war; the two-day march on the Pentagon cost the government $1 million).

47. During the first 10½ months of 1967, Montreal, Canada, reported having 97 dem-

onstrations, not including parades held for religious, ethnic, or commercial purposes; the demonstrations cost the city an estimated $7,000,000. *Attorney General of Canada v. Dupond*, 84 D.L.R.3d 420, 431 (S.Ct. Canada 1978).

48. San Diego reported costs in March 1983 of $1118 for police time and $194 for equipment to cover eight road runs; $773 for police time and $218 for equipment to cover two parades. A St. Patrick's Day parade cost San Diego about $900 while an elementary school commemoration of Martin Luther King was listed as costing the city $254. Costs of no greater magnitude were noted by police department representatives in Columbus and Seattle. The Seattle officer in charge of policing parades commented that political parades tend to be cheaper to manage than other parades because they were more likely to occur at times the city would not need to pay police overtime. *Inquiry to Cities Regarding Parade Permits, supra* note 7.

49. Many ordinances impose either insurance requirements, clean-up fees, policing fees, or costly facility requirements. See, e.g., *San Francisco Municipal Code*, pt. II, ch. VI, art 7, 7.06(d)(provides exemption for first amendment protected conduct where expenses would be so burdensome as to prevent activity); *Madison Wisconsin, Vehicle Code*, 12.87(11)(n); *Columbus, Ohio, City Code*, 2111.04 (1982 amendment). Columbus reported charging police costs, not referred to in the ordinance, to paraders except for regular civic parades like Veterans Day and Columbus Day parades. Due to litigation, Columbus did not charge a recent anti-war parade or gay pride parade. *Inquiry to Cities Regarding Parade Permits, supra* note 7. Seattle, lacking authorization in any ordinance to charge for policing, presently does so on an ad hoc basis. It does not, however, charge those parades that it identifies as protected by the first amendment, a rather interesting interpretive practice that apparently excludes commercial-oriented parades. Seattle, however, does report to the organizers of "first amendment" parades the cost of the policing and sometimes receives donations of that amount. *Id.* See generally, Neisser, *supra* note 45, at 352–62 (sampling of fee requirements for public events in 66 jurisdictions).

50. But see *Cox v. New Hampshire*, 312 U.S. 569, 576–77 (1941) (poorly reasoned analysis upholding as reasonable a charge of up to $300 as a means for the city to meet expenses incident to administration of parade ordinances and to maintain public order). Cf. T. Emerson, *The System of Freedom of Expression* 310 (1970) (there is no justification for fees; they should be invalid, although cases go both ways).

51. 308 U.S. 147 (1939).

52. *Id.* at 163.

53. *Id.*

54. 427 U.S. 50 (1976).

55. *Id.* at 71 n.35. See also *id.* at 77–79 (Powell, concurring). Although the reasoning was much less persuasive, both the Court and Justice Powell invoked the same concern with access to the speech in *FCC v. Pacifica Foundation*, 438 U.S. 726, *reh'g denied*, 439 U.S. 883 (1978). In a more recent case again involving zoning of adult theatres, while claiming to apply *American Mini Theatres*, the Court followed a standard requiring only "reasonable alternative avenues of communication" and generally seemed much less concerned about the effect of the ordinance on availability of alternative locations. *Renton v. Playtime Theatres*, 106 S.Ct. 925 (1986).

56. 452 U.S. 640 (1981).

57. The crucial "ample alternative" criterion was not properly implemented in *Heffron*. Justice Brennan pointed out that the fair officials' restriction on distribution of literature outside the booths, a restriction upheld by the Court, "sharply limit[ed] the number of fairgoers to whom the proselytizers and candidates can communicate their messages." *Id.* at 660 (Brennan, Marshall, and Stevens, concurring in part and dissenting in part). See also *infra* note 59. Any rule that prevents an "advocate" from reaching a

potentially willing listener in a place where, except for the communicative activity, they both have a right to be, fails to leave ample alternatives available—a valued interchange has been prevented. See also *Metromedia, Inc. v. City of San Diego*, 453 U.S. 490, 516 (1981) (ample alternative channels not available); *Linmark Assoc., Inc. v. Township of Willingboro*, 431 U.S. 85, 93 (1977) (alternatives unsatisfactory).

58. 452 U.S. at 648, quoting *Virginia Bd. of Pharmacy v. Virginia Citizens Consumer Council*, 425 U.S. 748, 771 (1976). The other two criteria are that the restrictions "are justified without reference to the content of the regulated speech [and] that they serve a significant governmental interest." *Id.*

Of course, the Court's references to "communication of information" manifests the dominant marketplace of ideas focus. From the perspective of the liberty theory, the Court should refer to the broader category of "expressive conduct" or "speech and peaceable assembly."

59. See *Dr. Martin Luther King, Jr. Movement v. City of Chicago*, 419 F. Supp. 667 (N.D. Ill. 1976). A civil rights group requested permission to march to a park in a white neighborhood and then to have a protest meeting. The city denied the request but offered an alternative route to an alternative park in a predominantly black neighborhood. The city pointed out that on a previous march by the group, bystanders had resorted to violence resulting in property damage, injury to police officers, and 52 arrests. The court rejected the city's argument. One reason that it found the proposed alternative unacceptable was that it would have placed the demonstrators before an audience that did not need persuasion to the demonstrators' views.

Lower courts frequently have invalidated time, place, and manner regulations that restrict access to relevant audiences. See, e.g., *Albany Welfare Rights Org. v. Wyman*, 493 F.2d 1319 (2d Cir. 1974), *cert. denied*, 419 U.S. 838 (1974). *Collin v. Chicago Park Dist.*, 460 F.2d 746 (7th Cir. 1972); *Wolin v. Port of New York Authority*, 392 F.2d 83 (2d Cir. 1968), *cert. denied*, 393 U.S. 940 (1968); *Sixteenth of September Planning Comm. v. City of Denver*, 474 F.Supp. 1333 (D. Colo. 1979); *Unemployed Workers Union v. Hackett*, 332 F.Supp. 1372 (D.R.I. 1971).

60. *Heffron v. International Soc'y for Krishna Consciousness*, 452 U.S. 640, 600 (1981) (Brennan, joined by Marshall and Stevens, concurring in part and dissenting in part).

61. See *Young v. American Mini Theatres*, 427 U.S. 50, 79 n.3 (1976) (Powell, concurring).

62. *Id.* at 78 n.2. Powell contrasted the expression that Detroit regulated with certain other expression that the Court has protected. The contrasting examples of protected expression included protests against segregation at the site of the segregated facilities, as well as other, more general, political demonstrations. (Justice Powell also noted that the theatre owners did "not profess to convey their own personal messages," *id.*, but that point seems irrelevant to any proper analysis).

63. See *Carey v. Brown*, 447 U.S. 455, 468 n.13 (1980) (discrimination between labor and non-labor picketing cannot be distinguished on the ground that nonlabor picketing could as meaningfully occur elsewhere since a residential audience might be key for the purposes of the nonlabor picketing). In *Carey*, Justice Brennan's majority opinion left open the possibility that the Court would uphold a content neutral regulation. *Id.* at 470. See also *Frisby v. Shultz*, 108 S.Ct. 2495 (1988); *Organization for a Better Austin v. Keefe*, 402 U.S. 415 (1971).

64. See, e.g., *Schneider v. State*, 308 U.S. 147.

65. See, e.g., *Martin v. City of Struthers*, 319 U.S. 141 (1943).

66. Some demonstrators certainly choose demonstration tactics with an eye toward media coverage. Nevertheless, the hypothesis that the prevalence of television has played a huge role in the rise of demonstrations as a major political tool in this country and that

the frequent occurrence of demonstrations only began with the rise of the civil rights movement beginning about 1960, see A. Etzioni, *Demonstration Democracy* 12–14 (1970), seems far-fetched, possibly manifesting a myopia created by the relative calm of the 1950s or an excessive tendency to attribute everything to television. Any reading of history will reveal that labor groups, radicals, religious sects, the unemployed, political activists, and other social groups and moral reformers have constantly resorted to rallies and demonstrations throughout our history.

67. In a dissenting opinion, Justice Douglas emphasized that "when [the jailhouse] houses political prisoners or those who many think are unjustly held, it is an obvious center for protest." *Adderley v. Florida*, 385 U.S. 39, 49 (1966) (Douglas, joined by Warren, Brennan, and Fortas, dissenting). Despite an arguably content-neutral practice of prohibiting assemblies at the jail grounds, Douglas argued that the first amendment protected the demonstration because, as he read the facts, the demonstration did not interfere with the dedicated use of the facility, thereby illustrating the third principle, and because the jailhouse was a uniquely meaningful place to engage in the expression, thereby illustrating the fourth principle.

68. See, e.g., *Columbia Broadcasting Sys. v. Democratic Nat'l Comm.*, 412 U.S. 94 (1973).

69. 383 U.S. 131 (1966).

70. *Id.* at 141–43.

71. The argument in the text accepts and sometimes requires permitting expression in otherwise restricted contexts if there is a special connection between the content of the expression and the location of the expression. The Court's opinion could, but should not, be read to accept a different type of content discrimination—a discrimination that protects expression aimed at achieving the constitutionally mandated result of desegregation, but that does not protect other expression.

72. *Brown v. Louisiana*, 383 U.S. at 142. An alternative basis for the 5–4 decision is that the demonstrators did not actually violate any valid time, place, or manner regulation.

73. 468 U.S. 288 (1984).

74. *United States v. Abney*, 534 F.2d 984, 985 (D.C. Cir. 1976) (regulations violated first amendment by giving officials standardless discretion to permit sleeping in the park).

75. The government might be concerned with other harmful behavior that it predicts will be associated with the lengthy presence of the demonstration. Predictions of evils associated with expressive conduct, however, are not a proper basis for prohibiting the expressive conduct. The government must direct its regulations at the evil, not the correlated expression. See, e.g., *Martin v. Struthers*, 319 U.S. 141 (1943); *Schneider v. State*, 308 U.S. 147 (1939). But cf. *New York v. Ferber*, 458 U.S. 747 (1982) (one reason for prohibiting the circulation of child pornography is to prevent the evils of its exploitation of children during its production). If the law must be directed at the evil, those engaged in assembly and speech can modify if necessary, rather than abandon, their expressive activity. Moreover, often the government will conclude that it does not really want to prohibit all occurrences of the often minor evil. Thus, the standard better protects expressive conduct.

76. Obscenity laws dramatically raise a similar problem. See *Paris Adult Theatre I v. Slaton*, 413 U.S. 49, 73–114 (1973) (Brennan, joined by Stewart and Marshall, dissenting).

77. Cf. *United States v. Ballard*, 322 U.S. 78 (1944) (truth or falsity of religious beliefs cannot be issue in fraud case but relevance of sincerity left open). Laws concerning conscientious objection also obviously raise this issue.

78. Chapter 7 explains why a voluntary but not a mandatory permit system would be permissible.

79. *Cox v. Louisiana,* 379 U.S. 559 (1965) (police permission implicitly showed that location of demonstrators was not statutorily "near" the courthouse).

80. See J. Rawls, *supra* note 2, at 204 (1971) (distinguishing liberty from the worth of liberty).

81. See *Buckley v. Valeo,* 424 U.S. 1 (1976).

82. But see Chapter 11.

83. Although the dichotomy is often misunderstood, Professor Emerson's illustrations of his proposed expression/action dichotomy suggest that operationally the dichotomy is quite similar to the principle described in the text. See T. Emerson, *supra* note 50.

84. The point is made, for quite different reasons, by theorists of quite different persuasions. See Kennedy and Michelman, "Are Property and Contract Efficient?," 8 *Hofstra L. Rev.* 711 (1980); Coase, "The Problem of Social Cost," 3 *J. of Law & Econ.* 1 (1960). See generally Horwitz, "The Doctrine of Objective Causations," in *The Politics of Law* 201 (D. Kairys ed. 1982).

85. *Whitney v. California,* 274 U.S. 357, 377 (1927) (Brandeis and Holmes, concurring).

86. P. Maier, *From Resistance to Revolution: Colonial Radicals and the Development of American Opposition to Britain, 1765–1776* at 22 (1972) (quoting New York newspapers of 1768 and 1770, and also citing various uses of this argument in the 1740s and 1760s).

87. *Id.* at 24.

88. *Id.* at 23.

89. *Id.* at 21. See also D. Hoerder, *Crowd Action in Revolutionary Massachusetts, 1765–1780* at 84 (1977) ("riots were recognized as part of the contemporary social and political institutions, their commonly accepted guidelines as part of the political tradition").

90. P. Maier, *supra* note 86, at 24.

91. An important aspect of the right of assembly may be its protection of the power of people who feel oppressed and ignored to impose costs on government and society. A key democratic feature of peaceable assemblies, as opposed to the instruments of violence, is that their capacity to cause disruption and inconvenience is directly related to the number of supporters and participants. Historically, it seems that mass action, including some degree of the usually restrained and usually rationally directed violence typical of the "riot," usually occurs only when other channels of effective political action are undeveloped or atrophied. See, e.g., J. Skolnick, *The Politics of Protest* 336 (1969). If protection of peoples' power peaceably to engage in disruption is recognized as one of the rationales of the right of assembly, a general welfare, balancing analysis must be quite unsatisfactory. The capacity of the assembly to impose inconveniences and disruption on the community would in the welfare calculus be a significant cost that would appear to justify regulation and in the constitutional analysis would be a major benefit that regulation could undermine.

92. Professor Skolnick concludes that an appropriate government response would be to reduce the resources devoted to domestic force while increasing those devoted to redressing social grievances. *Id.* at 344–45. He suggests "as a general rule that a society which must contemplate massive expenditures for social control is one which, virtually by definition, has not grappled with the necessity of massive social reform." *Id.* at 344.

93. See T. Emerson, *supra* note 50, at 7 (lists "achieving a more adaptable and hence more stable community" or a proper "balance between stability and change" as one of four functions of freedom of expression that justify its constitutional protection; expressing dissent allows societal or governmental response before pent-up dissatisfaction erupts in major violence).

94. G. Le Bon, *The Crowd* (2d ed. 1969) (original published in 1895). See R. Nye, *The Origins of Crowd Psychology* (1975) (very critical evaluation of Le Bon's thought). Although social science has advanced beyond Le Bon, even many of the better, more sophisticated versions continue to treat the group as secondary, less rational, and more primitive. See, e.g., N. Smelser, *Theory of Collective Behavior* (1962).

95. R. Brown, *Social Psychology* 709 (1965).

96. See, e.g., Note, "Restrictions on the Right of Assembly," 42 *Harvard L. Rev.* 265, 269 (1928): "The right of assembly thus appears more restricted than many other elements of personal liberty. This is inevitable, for in the misuse of concerted group action lies the most powerful menace to public peace."

97. The major scholarly impetus for the rejection of Le Bon's views and of the psychologists' and sociologists' disparaging treatment of the crowd or mob, see *supra* note 94, has resulted from historians' study of actual crowds. The foundational work is that of George Rude. See, e.g., G. Rude, *The Crowd in History* (1964). See also Thompson, "The Moral Economy of the English Crowd in the Eighteenth Century," 50 *Past & Present* 76 (1971). Although these historians generally avoid broad generalizations and emphasize the need to study the behavior of crowds in their social and historical context, their studies repeatedly find the crowd to be rational in its choice of both ends and means and consistently find its behavior to be oriented around some legitimizing norm. See, e.g., G. Rude, *supra*, at 252–57; Thompson, *supra*, at 78. In the years since these ground-breaking studies, these conclusions and the rejection of Le Bon's view of the crowd have been both affirmed and extended in a rich body of historical literature focusing on Great Britain and the United States. See, e.g., D. Richter, *Riotous Victorians* (1981); M. Feldberg, *The Turbulent Era: Riots and Disorder in Jacksonian America* (1980); J. Stevenson, *Popular Disturbances in England 1700–1870* (1979); D. Hoerder, *supra* note 89.

98. See J. Skolnick, *supra* note 91, at 71–73.

99. See treatment of causation in articles cited *supra* note 84.

100. A. Meiklejohn, *Political Freedom* 64 (1960).

101. But cf. *Abernathy v. Conroy*, 429 F.2d 1170 (1970) (upholding as reasonable an ordinance prohibiting parading after 8 P.M.) Demonstrators contended that working people could not get off work, eat, take care of children, assemble, receive the required instruction in nonviolence, and march four blocks to the park to pray before 8:00 P.M. *Id.* at 1173.

102. The concern with the need for amplication is typical of market failure version of the marketplace of ideas theory. In addition to other problems (see Chapter 2), this theory lacks any adequate conception of what degree of amplication is necessary. Likewise, until the rationale for the group right theory is developed, it will be unclear whether allowing a reasonable number of the group to celebrate their values is an adequate version of the right to assemble.

103. *The Conduct of the Paxton Men* (1764 Philadelphia) (quoting a 1737 speech in Parliament), cited in D. Hoerder, *supra* note 89, at 79–80 (1977). This early view both as to the times when riotous assemblies will occur and the appropriate response has the modern ring of a study of the causes and appropriate responses to riots. See, e.g., *supra* notes 91–92.

104. See, e.g., *Adderley v. Florida*, 385 U.S. 39 (1966) (Douglas, dissenting) (rejecting state claim that protesters blocked passage); *Shuttlesworth v. City of Birmingham*, 382 U.S. 87 (1965); *Cox v. Louisiana*, 379 U.S. 536 (1965) (reversing conviction for obstructing public passage). Cf. *United States v. Jones*, 244 F. Supp. 181 (S.D.N.Y.) 1965) (sustaining disorderly conviction for blocking entrance in "chain-in").

105. *NAACP v. Claiborne Hardware Co.*, 458 U.S. 886 (1982). The distinction between the demonstrators who purposefully stop the movement of another person, which would

not be protected under principle five, and those whose presence merely occupies space that is normally less crowded, thereby "necessarily" causing disruption, is similar to the Court's distinction in *Claiborne Hardware* between the boycotters who did and did not employ violence. The Court's refusal to impute to all members of the group responsibility for those who acted illegally parallels a conclusion that the government can only outlaw, that is, enjoin or punish, the individual behavior of stopping another's movement and cannot enjoin the assembly itself or punish all members of the group.

106. P. Maier, *supra* note 86, at 114–22. "The enduring arguments for nonimportation were, then, above all political. It offered the 'wisest and only peaceable method' for Americans to recover their liberty, one, moreover, that was legal and seemed to promise success." *Id.* at 119. Illustrating the typical response to group action, opponents charged that it was an "unlawful confederacy," in effect, a conspiracy. *Id.* at 131–33.

107. See Baker, "Property and its Relation to Constitutionally Protected Liberty," 134 *U. Pa. L. Rev.* 741 (1986); Cohen, "Property and Sovereignty," 13 *Cornell L. Q.* 8 (1927). Use of property to exercise power over others should be subject to legislative control. In contrast, the personal, substantive expression of values involved in the refusal to deal, at least, for noncommercial reasons, should make the social or political boycott a constitutionally protected aspect of liberty.

108. A close reading of *NAACP v. Claiborne Hardware Co.*, 458 U.S. 886 (1982), clearly shows it to depend on a liberty rather than a marketplace of ideas theory.

109. Any follower of the news will have seen many examples of this tendency to restrain expression of dissent in the streets not only in the United States but all over the globe, whether from the Soviet Union, Poland, South Africa, Philippines, Burma, Mexico, Latin America, or Western Europe—and will sense the democratic importance of keeping this right in the hands of the people. In country after country, this form of "democratic people power" has been a major force in bringing down governments and producing democratic change. For a well-documented, modern example from Australia, see F. Brennan, *Too Much Order with Too Little Law* (1983).

110. 307 U.S. 496 (1939).

CHAPTER 9

1. *Cammarano v. United States*, 358 U.S. 498, 513–14 (1959) (Douglas, concurring).

2. 316 U.S. 52, 54 (1942). The brief opinion in *Chrestensen* sustained a New York City ordinance prohibiting distribution of "commercial and business advertising matter" in the streets and other public places. *Id.* at 53–55. The ordinance had been invoked to prevent Chrestensen's distribution of handbills soliciting paying customers to tour his submarine. *Id.* at 53. After Chrestensen's initial attempts to advertise were frustrated by the city ordinance, he changed his handbill so that the commercial message was printed on one side, with the reverse side carrying a protest against the city's denial of permission to dock his exhibit at a city pier. *Id.* In deciding whether this application of the ordinance to these handbills constituted an unconstitutional abridgment of freedom of expression, the Court remarked:

> This court has unequivocally held that the streets are proper places for the exercise of the freedom of communicating information and disseminating opinion and that, though the states and municipalities may appropriately regulate the privilege in the public interest, they may not unduly burden or proscribe its employment in these public thoroughfares. *We are equally clear that the Constitution imposes no such restraint on government as respects purely commercial advertising.*

Id. at 54 (emphasis added).

3. The attempts to define or restrict the category of commercial speech have focused on: (1) the self-interested motive of the speaker; (2) the context or form of the speech; and (3) the content of the speech or its expected effect on the listener.

The first identifying principle—speech "made for the primary purpose of commercial gain" or speech that relates to a "profit motive"—was rejected in *Bigelow v. Virginia*, 421 U.S. 809, 818–21 (1975); *Pittsburgh Press Co. v. Human Relations Comm's*, 413 U.S. 376, 385 (1973); and *Virginia Bd. of Pharmacy v. Va. Citizens Consumer Council*, 425 U.S. 748, 761 (1976). See also *Cammarano v. United States*, 358 U.S. 498, 513–14 (1959) (Douglas, concurring). It was assumed that the profit motive was equivalent to self-interest, a view this chapter critiques. Therefore, since in most cases of clearly protected speech (e.g., political speech) the speaker is self-interested—often even monetarily self-interested, a profit motive could not be the basis for denying protection. "[N]either profit motive nor desire to influence private economic decisions distinguish the peddler from the preacher, the publisher, or the politician." Note, "Developments in the Law, Deceptive Advertising," 80 *Harvard L. Rev.* 1005, 1027 (1967). See also Redish, "The First Amendment in the Marketplace: Commercial Speech and the Values of Free Expression," 39 *Geo. Wash. L. Rev.* 429 (1971). Commentators have also been unable to explain the anomaly that the "same speech," possibly having the same effects, would in some cases be protected and in others not, depending only on whether it was profit motivated.

The Court wisely rejected the identification of commercial speech by the context in which it appears—e.g., the paid advertisement or other commercial form. *Virginia Bd. of Pharmacy*, 425 U.S. at 761; *Bigelow*, 421 U.S. at 818–19; *Pittsburgh Press*, 413 U.S. at 384–85; *New York Times v. Sullivan*, 376 U.S. 254, 266. Paid advertisements are often the most effective way of reaching a large audience with a political or religious message. Concluding that a form of expression, such as the leafletting in *Chrestensen*, is unprotected merely because it is sometimes used to deliver commercial messages would be entirely unacceptable. *Schneider v. State*, 308 U.S. 147 (1939); *Martin v. City of Struthers*, 318 U.S. 141 (1943). The Ohio Supreme Court distinguished *Peltz v. South Euclid*, 11 Ohio St. 2d 128, 228 N.E.2d 320 (1967) (ban on political signs unconstitutional abridgement of first amendment) from *Ghaster Properties, Inc. v. Preston*, 176 Ohio St. 425, 200 N.E. 328 (1964) (ban on signs near interstate highway) on grounds that *Ghaster* involved commercial speech.

If the content of speech is the proper constitutional focus—and, according to the court in *Virginia Bd. of Pharmacy*, 425 U.S. at 761, it must be—any speech attempting to influence private economic decisions would be unprotected. The Court has interpreted *Chrestensen* and *New York Times* as being consistent with this approach: "The critical feature of the advertisement in *Valentine v. Chrestensen* was that . . . it did no more than propose a commercial transaction." *Pittsburgh Press*, 413 U.S. at 385; *see Bigelow*, 421 U.S. at 821–22. Cf. *Matter of R.M.*, 455 U.S. 191 (1982) (commercial speech is speech that relates solely to the economic interests of speaker and audience); *Central Hudson Gas & Elec. Corp. v. Public Serv. Comm'n*, 447 U.S. 557, 561 (1980) (same).

But given this definition, the Court decided to protect the speech:

> Our question is whether speech which does "no more than propose a commercial transaction" . . . is so removed from any "exposition of ideas" . . . that it lacks all protection. Our answer is that it is not.

Virginia Bd. of Pharmacy, 425 U.S. at 762. This conclusion is right. The fact that the speech is aimed at influencing private economic decisions should not exclude protection. Surely, the appeals of the politicians, conservationists, or priests to conserve or not to buy oil, or sugar, or meat, or Coors beer are protected. Adding the motivational or involvement factor—e.g., the speech of the person who proposes a commercial transaction—did not provide a solution for the Court because no court or commentator had shown that a profit motivation or personal involvement could be relevant to the value of the speech. Thus, no constitutional justification for the category was found.

4. One commentator noted that "no court has undertaken to explain why commercial advertising does not deserve the title 'speech' which ennobles and protects political, social, and religious advocacy." Note, "Developments in the Law, Deceptive Advertising," 80 *Harv. L. Rev.* 1005, 1027 (1967).

5. See, e.g., DeVore and Nelson, "Commercial Speech and Paid Access to the Press," 26 *Hastings L. J.* 745 (1975); Freedman, "Bulls, Bears, Fat Cats and Consumerism," 1 *Civ. Lib. Rev.* 125 (1974); Redish, "The First Amendment in the Marketplace: Commercial Speech and the Values of Free Expression," 39 *Geo. Wash. L. Rev.* 429 (1971); Note, "The Commercial Speech Doctrine: The First Amendment at a Discount," 41 *Brooklyn L. Rev.* 60 (1974); Note, "Commercial Speech—An End in Sight for *Chrestensen*," 23 *De Paul L. Rev.* 1258 (1974), Comment, "The Right to Receive and the Commercial Speech Doctrine: New Constitutional Considerations," 63 *Georgetown L. J.* 775 (1975), Comment, "The First Amendment and Consumer Protection: Commercial Advertising as Protected Speech," 50 *Oregon L. Rev.* 177 (1971); Comment, "The First Amendment and Commercial Advertising: Bigelow v. Commonwealth," 60 *Virginia. L. Rev.* 154 (1974) (objects to application of commercial speech doctrine in *Bigelow*).

6. Observers could not help but note that by the time of *Bigelow v. Virginia*, 421 U.S. 809 (1975), most Justices had indicated a willingness to reject the commercial speech exception and provide protection under the first amendment. See, e.g., *Lehman v. City of Shaker Heights*, 418 U.S. 298, 314 n.6 (1974) (Brennan, joined by Stewart, Marshall, and Powell, dissenting); *Pittsburgh Press Co. v. Pittsburgh Comm'n on Human Relations*, 413 U.S. 376, 393 (1973) (Burger, dissenting); *id.* at 398 (Douglas, dissenting); *id.* at 401 (Stewart, joined by Douglas, and substantially by Blackmun, dissenting); *Dun & Bradstreet, Inc. v. Grove*, 404 U.S. 498, 513–14 (1959) (Douglas, dissenting from denial of certiorari); *Cammarano v. United States*, 358 U.S. 498, 513–14 (1959) (Douglas, concurring).

7. 421 U.S. 809 (1975).

8. 425 U.S. 748 (1976).

9. *Virginia Bd. of Pharmacy*, 425 U.S. at 761–62; *Bigelow*, 421 U.S. at 825–26. The Court in *Virginia Bd. of Pharmacy* concluded that "commercial speech, like other varieties, is protected." 425 U.S. at 770. The *Bigelow* Court, in dicta very troublesome to civil libertarians, stated that "[a]dvertising, like all public expression, may be subject to reasonable regulation that serves a legitimate public interest." 421 U.S. at 826.

10. Redish, *supra* note 5.

11. See *id.*, at 432–47.

12. See P. Berger and T. Luchmann, *The Social Construction of Reality* (1966).

13. See, e.g., *Virginia State Bd. of Pharmacy*, 425 U.S. at 763–65; *Bigelow*, 421 U.S. at 828–29; *First National Bank of Boston v. Bellotti*, 435 U.S. 765, 776–77 (1978).

14. T. Emerson, *The System of Freedom of Expression* 311, 414–417, 561 (1970); Emerson, "First Amendment Doctrine and the Burger Court," 68 *Calif. L. Rev.* 422, 458–61 (1980).

15. A. Meiklejohn, *Political Freedom* 87 (1965). See also F. Schauer, *Free Speech: A Philosophical Enquiry* 103 (1982); Cox, "Forward: Freedom of Expression in the Burger Court," 94 *Harvard L. Rev.* 1, 28, 33 (1980).

16. This unraveling is well described in the one of the best and most theoretically interesting articles on the subject, one that reaches very different conclusions from those offered here but that agrees that most commercial speech claims for protection should lose. Shiffrin, "The First Amendment and Economic Regulation: Away from a General Theory of the First Amendment," 78 *Northwestern U. L. Rev.* 1212 (1983).

17. *Schneider v. State*, 308 U.S. 147 (1939); *Martin v. Struthers*, 319 U.S. 141 (1943).

18. 425 U.S. at 759.

19. 453 U.S. 490 (1981).

20. The majority was composed of seven judges. 453 U.S. at 513 (White, Stewart, Marshall, and Powell); *id.* at 543 (Stevens, dissenting in part); *id.* at 563–69 (Burger, dissenting); *id.* at 569–70 (Rehnquist, dissenting).

21. See, e.g., *Virginia Board of Pharmacy*, 425 U.S. at 770.

22. 447 U.S. 557 (1980).

23. 106 S.Ct. 2968 (1987). The ground for the decision in *Posadas* was laid in *Central Hudson Gas & Electric Corp. v. Public Services Commission*, 447 U.S. 557 (1980), where the Court indicated that a state interest in conservation could justify content regulations designed to prevent presumably truthful advertising that promoted energy use if the energy use was inconsistent with the state's conservation goals.

24. *Freedman v. Rogers*, 440 U.S. 81 (1979).

25. *Pittsburgh Press*, 413 U.S. 376.

26. *Virginia Bd. of Pharmacy*, 425 U.S. at 771 n.24.

27. *Virginia Bd. of Pharmacy*, 425 U.S. at 759.

28. Consideration of the merits of any legislative decision as to the desirability of any particular regulation is beyond the scope of this Chapter. For a sampling of materials arguing the merits of regulation versus freedom for advertising, see Millstein, "The Federal Trade Commission and False Advertising," 64 *Columbia L.Rev.* 439 (1964), and sources cited therein; and G. Robinson & E. Gellhorn, *The Administrative Process* 352–371 (1974), and sources cited therein.

29. As used here, "motivation" refers to the purposes or aims analytically attributable to the person or corporation, given the structure of the situation in which the person acts. No attempt is made to reconstruct the person's actual internal thoughts and wishes.

30. See *Lynch v. Household Finance Corp.*, 405 U.S. 538 (1972). In *Lynch* the Court stated that "the dichotomy between personal liberties and property rights is a false one." *Id.* at 552. *See also* Coase, "Advertising and Free Speech," 6 *J. Legal Studies* 1 (1977); Coase, "The Market for Goods and the Market for Ideas," 64 *American Economic Rev., Pap. and Proc.* 384, 389 (1974) (concluding that the reasons or lack of reasons for government regulation apply equally to both the "market for goods and the market for ideas"); Director, "The Parity of the Economic Market Place," 7 *J. Law & Economics* 1 (1964).

31. Jackson and Jeffries, "Commercial Speech: Economic Due Process and the First Amendment," 65 *Virginia L. Rev.* 1 (1979) (critiquing protection of commercial speech as a move toward economic due process).

32. See note 13 *supra.*

33. See generally Chapter 1. The classic statement of this marketplace of ideas theory is in J. S. Mill, *On Liberty*, Ch. 2 (A. Castell ed. 1947). Justice Holmes provided an eloquent judicial statement of the theory in his dissent in *Abrams v. United States*, 250 U.S. 616, 630 (1919):

> [W]hen men have realized that time has upset many fighting faiths, they may come to believe even more than they believe the very foundations of their own conduct that the ultimate good desired is better reached by free trade in ideas—that the best test of truth is the power of the thought to get itself accepted in the competition of the market, and that truth is the only ground upon which their wishes safely can be carried out. That at any rate is the theory of our Constitution.

See also *Whitney v. California*, 274 U.S. 357, 375–78 (1927) (Brandeis, concurring).

34. *First National Bank of Boston v. Bellotti*, 435 U.S. 765, 777 (1978). Emphasizing this marketplace of ideas approach, the Court concluded that "[t]he proper question therefore is not whether corporations 'have' First Amendment rights. . . . Instead, the question

must be whether §8 abridges expression that the First Amendment was meant to protect."
Id. at 776.

35. *Virginia State Bd. of Pharmacy*, 425 U.S. at 761–70; *Bigelow*, 421 U.S. at 826. Balancing may be the only alternative if first amendment coverage is extended to an area where the Court or society is unwilling consistently to give protection, but is unable to find a principled basis to explain when protection will or will not be given. The Court is unlikely to allow complete freedom for false, misleading, or offensive advertising practices; it may continue to allow the government to impose disclosure and labelling requirements as well as to allow some bans on advertising of certain disapproved products such as cigarettes; and it may possibly permit continued enforcement of Green River ordinances while protecting noncommercial door-to-door solicitations or bans on commercial billboards while allowing noncommercial billboards, despite the obvious content discrimination. Cf. *Metromedia, Inc. v. San Diego*, 453 U.S. 490 (1981). Thus, as long as the Court views commercial speech as included within the first amendment, it almost inevitably will accept "[*t*]*he task of balancing the interests at stake*." *Bigelow*, 421 U.S. at 826 (emphasis added). This balancing, in turn, predictably leads to decreased and more eclectic constitutional protection.

36. *Pittsburgh Press Co. v. Pittsburgh Comm'n on Human Relations*, 413 U.S. 376, 385 (1973); *Cammarano v. United States*, 358 U.S. 498, 514 (1959) (Douglas, concurring); *Holiday Magic, Inc. v. Warren*, 357 F. Supp. 20, 25 (E.D. Wis. 1973); Note, "Developments in the Law, Deceptive Advertising," 80 *Harvard L. Rev.* 1005, 1027 (1967); Note, "Freedom of Expression in a Commercial Context," 78 *Harvard L. Rev.* 1191, 1205 (1965). But compare the rather unusual argument of Justice Jackson, concurring in *Railway Express Agency, Inc. v. New York*, 336 U.S. 106, 116 (1949):

> [T]here is a real difference between doing in self-interest and doing for hire, so that it is one thing to tolerate action from those who act on their own and it is another thing to permit the same action to be promoted for a price.

I assume Jackson was not making the Marxist point of distinguishing self-reliant practices of a small scale farm society or a socialist society from those of the capitalist market.

37. Cf. *Lochner v. New York*, 198 U.S. 45, 75 (1905) (Holmes, dissenting).

38. The discussion below will make use of Max Weber's analysis in M. Weber, *Economy and Society*, vol. *1–3* (G. Roth & C. Wittich eds. 1968). Weber's categories are useful and his historical observations suggestive. Weber describes the principal historical forms of appropriation and indicates in which cases and to what degree the economic activity was carried on for a profit. 1 *id.* at 144–50. He categorizes the principal historical forms of profit-making activity, 1 *id.* at 164–66, and describes the development and structure of the capitalist form of profit-oriented market activity, which he views as part of an historically irreversible process of rationalization. 1 *id.* at 223–23; 3 *id.* at 987–88. See also R. Aron, *Main Currents in Sociological Thought* 214, 248–52 (1967). In this chapter, the term "profit orientation" will be used only in reference to a specific form of profit-making activity: that of the profit-making enterprise—which is "to a large extent peculiar to the modern Western World." 1 M. Weber, *Economy and Society* 165. Following Weber, the term, "profit-making enterprise" refers to "types of acquisitive activity which are continually oriented to market advantages, using goods as a means to secure profits." 1 *id.* at 99. Generally, for descriptions of different historical forms of economic activity and their implications, see 1 *id.* at 63–211.

39. See L. Fuller, *The Morality of Law* 171 (rev. ed. 1969); C.B. Macpherson, *Democratic Theory: Essays in Retrieval* 181 (1973). Macpherson argues:

> [It is] very unhistorical to equate capitalism with laissez faire. . . . [C]apitalism . . . [is] the system in which production is carried on without authoritative allocation of work

or rewards, but by contractual relations between free individuals . . . who calculate their most profitable courses of action and employ their resources as that calculation dictates.

Such a system permits a great deal of state interference without its essential nature being altered.

Id.

40. See 3A W. Fletcher, *Private Corporations* §1039 (perm. ed. rev. repl. 1975).

41. C.B. Macpherson, *The Political Theory of Possessive Individualism* 46–70 (1962).

42. M. Weber, *The Protestant Ethic and the Spirit of Capitalism* 17 (T. Parsons transl. 1958).

43. Capital accounting is peculiar to rational economic profit making. 1 M. Weber, *supra* note 38, at 91. Weber discusses the principal conditions necessary for maximum formal rationality of capital accounting: these include, market freedom and appropriation of non-human means of production, free labor, substantive freedom of contract, mechanically rational technology, rational (predictable) legal administration, a rational monetary system, and the complete separation of the enterprise from the household or private budgetary unit. *Id.* at 161–62.

The presence of these factors generally increases both the possibility and the necessity of rational pursuit of profits. Still, the absence or incomplete development of some factors usually does not make a profit orientation less likely but merely transforms the conditions for its realization or the range of its application.

44. See A. Alchian, "The Basis of Some Recent Advances in the Theory of the Management of the Firm," in *The Economics of Legal Relationships* 487 (H. Manne ed. 1975). In contrast to market-enforced profit orientations, legal enforcement of a profit orientation is sometimes attempted but is usually ineffective.

45. H. Arendt, *The Human Condition* (1958). Legal commentators often note the variable placement of these categories of the political, economic, and personal for purposes of distinctions between public and private realms. See, e.g., Olsen, "The Family and the Market: A Study of Ideology and Legal Reform," 96 *Harvard L. Rev.* 1497 (1983) (critiquing the distinctions and their uses).

46. See 1 M. Weber, *supra* note 38, at 98, 162.

47. For example, unless not unprofitable because owning and operating the store is considered a form of consumption, the "unprofitability" of a family store may be hidden by the subsidy provided by cheap family labor.

48. *See id.* at 163–64, 378–80; M. Weber, *supra* note 42, at 21–22.

49. See 1 M. Weber, *supra* note 38, at 164; Baker, "The Ideology of the Economic Analysis of Law," 5 *Philosophy & Pub. Aff.* 3, 32–41 (1975). The resulting form of life is criticized by both the romantics and radicals. One either is admonished to return to old forms of life where no separation has occurred or is exhorted to take control of one's own history and make oneself the subject of one's own will—a process called "freedom"— now that humanity has reached a stage of rational self-consciousness.

50. See 1 M. Weber, *supra* note 38, at 98.

51. *Bell v. Maryland*, 378 U.S. 226, 265–66 (1964) (Douglas and Goldberg).

52. *Id.* at 253.

53. *Id.* at 245–46, 265–67.

54. *Id.* at 246.

55. See *id.* at 246, 263. Cf. *Griswold v. Connecticut*, 381 U.S. 479 (1965).

56. *First National Bank of Boston v. Bellotti*, 435 U.S. 765, 804–5 (1978) (White, Brennan, and Marshall, dissenting). See also *Roberts v. United States Jaycees*, 468 U.S. 609, 631–40 (1984) (O'Connor, concurring in part and concurring in the judgment).

57. Cf. C. Cole, *Microeconomics: A Contemporary Approach* 450–52 (1973). While the economic model described in the text does not completely or uniformly describe our world, for purposes of this analysis the only relevant criticism would be to show that the

choices or decisions of successful enterprises are neither determined by nor necessarily congruent with this profit orientation. Such a critique could take two forms. First, it could be argued that the enforced profit orientation does not occur within any important realm of economic activity. My underlying assumption is that, as applied to modern American society, the model's accuracy suffices to overcome this criticism. Second, it could be argued that the profit orientation does not occur within certain identifiable types or arenas of economic activity. The truth of this criticism should be admitted, and to the extent that the household and the enterprise are not separated and the profit orientation does not rule, this first argument for denying protection to commercial speech does not apply.

58. Tribe, "Technology Assessment and the Fourth Discontinuity: The Limits of Instrumental Rationality," 46 *So. California L. Rev.* 617, 618 (1973) (emphasis in original). Frequently, instrumental rationality is said to be the only form of reason recognized in liberal thought, for within liberal thought, reason is distinguished from and subordinate to will or desire. See R. Unger, *Knowledge and Politics* 36–46, 52–54, 152–54 (1975).

59. 1 *M. Weber, supra* note 38, at 24–25.

60. See generally, J. Brehm and A. Cohen, *Explorations in Cognitive Dissonance* (1962); L. Festinger, *A Theory of Cognitive Dissonance* (1957).

61. Dissonance theory, by focusing on consequences of behavioral commitment would, for example, predict that an individual will be receptive to or search out information favorable to his or her occupational commitments and block out critical information. J. Brehm and A. Cohen, *supra* note 60, at 300. Change toward attitudes congruent with those manifested in the occupational role would be expected the more the occupational role was viewed as a matter of free choice (prediction from dissonance theory), but even if the role is not perceived as freely chosen, the positive attitude change would be predicted when reinforced by significant occupational rewards (prediction from reinforcement or learning theory). See Linder, Cooper and Jones, "Decision Freedom as a Determinant of the Role of Incentive Magnitude in Attitude Change," 6 *J. Personality & Soc. Psych.* 245, 247 (1967). Socialization and role theories could also be invoked. However, any general analysis, which is far beyond the scope of this book, must also note the occurrence and discuss reasons for noncongruence of private beliefs and occupational behavior—i.e., alienation—and alternative responses, such as protest or rebellion. This disassociation is more likely the more the job performance is viewed as forced or as merely instrumental for the achievement of other goals. Of course, other coping mechanisms are possible, including a complete psychological divorce between a person's occupational and private life. For a most chilling example of this type of separation, see H. Arendt, *Eichmann in Jerusalem* (rev. ed. 1965).

62. In this discussion, I wish neither to defend nor criticize the market. This Chapter's claim that the market enforces a profit orientation is a conclusion shared by conservative economists, Marxists, as well as the Weberian account invoked here—even if each group evaluates the conclusion differently. Note, however, that market champions often mistake profit maximation for an efficiency orientation. See Baker, "Property and Its Relation to Constitutionally Protected Liberty," 134 *U. Pennsylvania L. Rev.* 741, 788–89 n.89.

63. Cf. Heymann, "Problem of Coordination: Bargaining and Rules," 86 *Harvard L. Rev.* 797, 802–4 (1973). This system of coordination takes the present distribution of wealth as given. If the content of that distribution is in dispute, as it always is in cases of disputes about the content of the legal rules, there is no "given" to be assumed and the economic or efficiency analysis is inherently indeterminate. Or if the distribution is objectionable, the results of a perfectly operating free market may likewise be objectional. See, e.g., Baker, *supra* note 49.

64. It should be surprising that truly "value neutral" speech either needs or deserves protection. Moreover, the second half of this chapter notes additional reasons for denying protection.

65. See Gintis, "Consumer Behavior and the Concepts of Sovereignty: Explanations of Social Decay," 62 *American Economic Rev., Pap. & Proc.* 267, 273–77 (1972); Tribe, "Ways Not to Think about Plastic Trees: New Foundations for Environmental Law," 83 *Yale L. J.* 1315, 1315–16 (1974).

66. Of course, both moderate and radical critics have continually asserted this point. Cf. E. Fromm, *The Sane Society* 200–08, 355–57 (1955); H. Marcuse, *One Dimensional Man* 56–83 (1964). Popular interpretations of the youth culture of the late 1960s indicate mass awareness that increasing material welfare and market satisfactions do not lead to happiness or personal fulfillment. See, e.g., C. Reich, *The Greening of America* 265–98 (1970). The best evidence for this claim, as Hobbes knew, is finding that it is so with oneself. See T. Hobbes, *Leviathan* 34 (Oakeshott ed. 1946).

67. In *Wisconsin v. Yoder*, 406 U.S. 205 (1972), both issues were in dispute. However, in deciding for the Amish, the Court principally protected their right to make choices about how they wanted to form their society and themselves, given that the resulting process did not destroy equivalent rights of others.

68. See, e.g., *Central Hudson Gas v. Public Service Comm'n*, 447 U.S. 557 (1980) (dicta suggesting the permissibility of prohibiting certain advertising that encourages inefficient energy use, which has negative environmental externalities).

69. See V. Packard, *The Hidden Persuaders* (1957). See also 1 M. Weber, *supra* note 38, at 99–100.

70. C. B. Macpherson, *supra* note 39, at 182.

71. *Id.* at 183.

72. Macpherson argues:

Since profits will increasingly depend on creating ever more desire, the tendency will be for the directors of the productive system to do everything in their power to confirm Western man's image of himself as an infinite desirer.

Id. at 38. Note that although the market dynamic may result in satisfying a particularly large *number* of desires compared with some other systems, there is no reason to expect that it satisfies a particularly high *percentage* of existing desires, since it also works to increase the number of unsatisfied desires. Of course, numbers may not be of prime importance. Some observers argue that both the kind and quality or diversity of desires, and the process whereby desires are created or chosen and then satisfied, are of greater importance for human flourishing. See *id.* at 18–21.

73. The foremost concern of the enterprise's commercial speech is the creation of demand for the firm's products. But often this demand depends on particular images of masculinity or femininity, of youth and beauty, of patriotism or maturity, that are created or reinforced by advertising but that may be even more value laden (and objectionable) than the products themselves. To create demand, firms may relate their product to idealized, although usually stereotyped, heroes or exemplary people and their asserted success. Because the advertisement's effectiveness depends on both the causal connection and the importance of the associated "ideal" objects being believed or felt at some level by the potential consumer, this commercialization process tends to confuse, develop, repress, or modify, in a possibly objectionable manner, both our causal and value orientations.

74. See *Lehman v. City of Shaker Heights*, 418 U.S. 298, 317–18 n.10 (1974) (Brennan, Stewart, Marshall, & Powell, dissenting) (suggesting comparisons between advertisements of a cigarette company and a cancer society, a lumber company and a conservation group, an oil refinery and a pollution control environmental group, etc.).

75. *Federal Election Comm'n v. Mass. Citizens for Life*, 107 S.Ct. 616, 628–29 (1986) (relying on this contrast in invalidating a prohibition on corporate political spending as applied to a nonprofit, nonstock corporation).

76. See, e.g., C.B. Macpherson, *supra* note 70, at 38, 61–63, 182–83 (1973); Baker, *supra* note 49, at 32–41; Gintis, *supra* note 65 at 273–77; Sagoff, *On Preserving the Natural Environment*, 84 *Yale L. J.* 205, 210–12, 219–25 (1974); Tribe, *supra* note 65, at 1315–17.

77. See Tribe, *supra* note 65.

78. This counterargument must claim that the choice can be successfully made *within* a competitive market setting. In contrast, people's ability to resist profit dictates by adopting legal regulations that further their nonprofit-maximizing values is consistent with this chapter's argument. In fact, the claim here is precisely that only the possibility of this political regulation of commercial practices provides for freedom because a market economic structure prevents nonprofit-maximizing choices be enterprises within its domain.

79. See text accompanying notes 117–21 *infra*.

80. Of course, if the enterprise is profitable, the owner could consume the profits in realizing her substantive values. However, to the extent that the household or budgetary unit has been separated from the enterprise, this pursuit of substantive values is not realized within the context of the commercial enterprise. The separation is least complete, and thus the conclusion least valid, in enterprises of almost opposite types: (1) the family business where underpaid labor subsidizes unprofitable aspects; and (2) monopolies or quasi-monopolies which, because competition does not force strict pursuit of profits, can modify economic decisions in accord with the personal desires of relevant groups within the enterprise.

81. T. Hobbes, *Leviathan* 64 (Oakeshott ed. 1946) (emphasis added). See C. B. MacPherson, *supra* note 41, at 9–106. Weber also notes that a fully developed market system presupposes "the battle of man with man." 1 M. Weber, *supra* note 38, at 93.

82. The relevant sense of coercion is discussed in Chapter 3. Despite the concept's centrality in the liberty theory of the first amendment, definition is difficult. Different usages relate to different conceptions of the social world as well as different normative theories. See, e.g., C. Bay, *The Structure of Freedom* 92–94 (1958). Bay defines coercion as "actual physical violence" or "application of sanctions strong enough to make the individual abandon his *strong and enduring wishes*," *id.* at 274 (emphasis added), a definition closely tied to his conception of freedom. A slightly different concept of freedom may have changed the notion of coercion. Cf. C. B. MacPherson, *supra* note 39, at 95–119 (1973) (critiquing Isaiah Berlin).

83. 425 U.S. 748 (1976).

84. *Id.*

85. Compare *Scientific Mfg. Co. v. FTC*, 124 F.2d 640 (3rd Cir. 1941), with *Perma-Maid Co. v. FTC*, 121 F.2d 282 (6th Cir. 1941) (FTC has power to enjoin distribution of pamphlets by business trying to influence customers to buy their product, but no power to enjoin distribution by author not materially interested in sale of goods); *Koch v. FTC*, 206 F.2d 311 (6th Cir. 1953) (sustaining order to cease false and misleading advertising; in dicta, noted that a ban on Dr. Koch's book, which developed the same theme as the advertisement, would violate first amendment).

86. Cf. *Andrus v. Allard*, 444 U.S. 51 (1979) (no fifth amendment taking of property where person prohibited from selling certain Indian artifacts but could continue to possess them or give them away).

87. The distinction between substantive and instrumental values has more general importance in the first amendment area. For example, it helps explain the apparent conflict between *Braunfeld v. Brown*, 366 U.S. 599 (1961) (orthodox Jew can be prohibited from operating his business on Sunday), and *Sherbert v. Verner*, 374 U.S. 398 (1963) (person cannot be denied unemployment benefits for refusing to work on Saturday). The

desire to work was of instrumental importance (for business success) while the refusal to work represented a substantive value. Likewise, if conscience is the key to one's eligibility for draft classification as a conscientious objector, the substantive-instrumental value distinction would be the organizing principle. In *Welsh v. United States*, 398 U.S. 333 (1970) the distinction is drawn between those whose objection rests "upon moral, ethical, or religious principle" and those whose objection rests "upon considerations of policy, pragmatism, or expediency." *Id.* at 342–43.

88. Cf. Drekmeier, "Knowledge as Virtue, Knowledge as Power," in *Sanctions for Evil* 192, 194 (N. Sanford and C. Comstock eds. 1971):

> The fabric of social interaction, of nondominative communication in which legitimacy is rooted and in which the self is negotiated as it comes to recognize and define itself in relations with others, wears thin as instrumental action preempts the human stage.

Commercial speech differs from other speech precisely because it is the archetype of a *purely* instrumental activity.

89. Coercive activities are an important subcategory of instrumental activities and a type the state is generally conceded the right to regulate or prohibit. See J. S. Mill, *On Liberty* 13 (A. Castell ed. 1956). But the dominantly *instrumental* quality of market-oriented activities may explain why Mill concluded that "the principle of individual liberty is not involved in the doctrine of free trade"—and further concluded that the legitimacy of regulating commercial practices "is in principle undeniable." *Id.* at 116.

90. See R. Tawney, *Religion and the Rise of Capitalism* 114–15, 250–53 (1962); M. Weber, *supra* note 42, at 155–83.

91. In the history of constitutional law, this conclusion is illustrated by the demise of substantive due process. However, some recent theoretical writing may be taken to recommend the revival and expansion of *Lochner*-type economic due process. See, e.g., R. Epstein, *Takings: Private Property and the Power of Eminent Domain* (1985); R. Nozick, *Anarchy, State, and Utopia* 26–53 (1974); Coase, *supra* note 30, at 384–90 (1974).

92. See C. B. Macpherson, *supra* note 39, at 40–52, 92, 146–47. Macpherson argues that capitalist market practices involve the use of extractive power—and hence capitalist commercial practices are not only instrumental but also coercive. He contrasts extractive power with developmental power which should be maximized. See also Gintis, *supra* note 65, at 267–87 (1972).

93. T. Emerson, *The System of Freedom of Expression* 311 (1970) ("Such activities fall within the system of commercial enterprise and are outside the system of freedom of expression").

94. Linde, "'Clear and Present Danger' Reexamined", 22 *Stanford L. Rev.* 1163 (1970); Rogat and O'Fallon, "Mr. Justice Holmes: A Dissenting Opinion—The Speech Cases," 36 *Stanford L. Rev.* 1349 (1984).

95. In the rest of this section, references to liberty will mean the formal conception central to the liberty theory developed in this book. Obviously, regulation of commercial practices could promote substantive conceptions of liberty; hence, any claim that liberty requires protection of these practices must rely on a more formal conception. For a defense of reliance on this more formal conception, see Baker, *supra* note 62, at 775–85.

96. See, e.g., *Griswold v. Connecticut*, 381 U.S. 479, 485 (1965) (contraceptives); *Moore v. East Cleveland*, 431 U.S. 494 (1977) (house or apartment).

97. Collective decisions inevitably affect the "exchange value" of different forms of such qualities as intelligence, beauty, and strength. This societal role provides one of several justifications for collective regulation of the use of these qualities in the context of market exchanges. Outside this context, however, direct restrictions on the use of these personal qualities in a person's chosen activities seems more obviously to be an objec-

tionable collective interference with liberty than an interference with the use of wealth to which a person has no natural ties.

98. But consider the strange case of chastity. Even here, society most severely disapproves of its alienation in overtly market transactions.

99. "It is a purpose of the ancient institution of property to protect those claims upon which people rely in their daily lives." *Board of Regents v. Roth*, 408 U.S. 564, 577 (1972).

100. Radin, "Property and Personhood," 34 *Stanford L. Rev.* 957 (1982).

101. Cohen, "Property and Sovereignty," 13 *Cornell L. Q.* 8, 11–14 (1927). *Cf.* Kessler, "Contracts of Adhesion—Some Thoughts About Freedom of Contract," 43 *Columbia L.Rev.* 629, 640 (1943).

102. Baker, *supra* note 62, at 742–74 (1986) (discussing the various functions of property and the notion of disaggregating them).

103. Although he did not disaggregate the notion of property, and although he had other objections to inequality, Rousseau, like Marx, recognized that property exchanges could be exploitive and destructive of liberty. See J. Rousseau, "The Social Contract," in *Social Contract* 217 n.11 (E. Barker ed. 1947) ("Where [millionaires and beggars] exist public liberty becomes a commodity of barter. The rich buy it, the poor sell it").

104. Cf. J. Rawls, *A Theory of Justice* 78 (1971) with Baker, "Outcome Equality or Equality of Respect: The Substantive Content of Equal Protection," 131 *U. Pennsylvania L. Rev.* 933. See also, Kronman, "Contract Law and Distributive Justice," 89 *Yale L. J.* 472 (1980) (both liberals and libertarians should share the view that the law of contracts should have some egalitarian redistributive function); Baker, "Utility and Rights: Two Justifications for State Action Increasing Equality," 84 *Yale L. J.* 39 (1974) (both a utilitarian and a rights analysis require some societal intervention in the market to increase equality).

105. Robert Nozick has suggested that the two are indistinguishable. R. Nozick, *Anarchy, State, and Utopia* 169 (1974).

106. Baker, "Counting Preferences in Collective Choice Situations," 25 *UCLA L. Rev.* 381, 398 (1978).

107. In addition, I suspect that reports of workers disliking governmental regulations, such as safety rules, often reflect a context in which management's organization of the work activity, the equipment it provides, and the productivity that it demands make the rule burdensome. These workers do not (necessarily) dislike the practices required by the rule. Rather, they dislike how the rule is implemented. That is, the dislike reflects management's ability to transfer all or a portion of the instrumental cost of the rule to the workers. See Baker, *supra* note 62, at 788–89 n.89.

108. This conduct, when not engaged in as a profession, should constitute protected freedom of speech and association.

109. Cf. *United States v. O'Brien*, 391 U.S. 367 (1968).

110. In *Southwestern Elec. Power Co. v. FPC*, 304 F.2d 29 (5th Cir.), *cert. denied*, 371 U.S. 924 (1962), the court upheld a determination that, for accounting purposes, grassroots lobbying and advertising concerned with the superiority of private power over public power should be charged as a deduction from income rather than as an operating expense. The rule was intended to force owners to pay for the speech and prevent passing the costs on to consumers. In effect, this rule prohibited "commercial political speech" (which would be a business expense) while allowing speech that is attributed to and paid for by the owners. See note 127 *infra*. The same effect and rationale applies for *Cammarano v. United States*, 358 U.S. 498 (1959) (upholding tax regulation providing that money spent for defeat of legislation could not be deducted from income as a business expense). See also *Consumer Power Co. v. United States*, 427 F.2d 78 (6th Cir. 1970); *Southeastern Elec. Power Co. v. United States*, 312 F.2d 437 (Ct. Cl.1963).

111. Examples are collected in: *Citizens Against Rent Control v. City of Berkeley*, 454 U.S. 290, 307–08, & nn. 2–4 (1981) (White, dissenting); Baker, "Realizing Self-realization: Corporate Political Expenditures and Redish's *The Value of Free Speech*," 130 *U. Pennsylvania L. Rev.* 646, 647–48 & n.8 (1982).

112. See *Pittsburgh Press Co. v. Pittsburgh Comm'n on Human Relations*, 413 U.S. at 385.

113. The exercise of power argument also justifies regulation. Of course, the corporate use of wealth to engage in political speech may seem no different from an individual's use of wealth to engage in political speech. However, a corporation's speech that is oriented toward profits is valued, and its influence is valued, purely instrumentally. Moreover, the reason artificial entities are allowed to amass property and power in the economic sphere is to achieve society's allocative objectives. Therefore, these entities' use of this property and power could properly be limited to their economic role. See *Federal Election Comm'n v. Mass. Citizens for Life*, 479 U.S. 238 (1986); *First National Bank v. Bellotti*, 435 U.S. 765 (1978) (Rehnquist, dissenting); Brudney, "Business Corporations and Stockholders' Rights Under the First Amendment," 91 *Yale L. J.* 235 (1981). Society could reasonably limit corporations' use of property-for-power to their economic roles, reserving the constitutionally protected use-value roles to individuals, voluntary associations, and democratic political bodies. *Federal Election Comm'n v. Mass. Citizens for Life*. Cf. *Anderson v. City of Boston*, 380 N.E.2d 628 (1978), *appeal dismissed*, 439 U.S. 1060 (1979).

114. See *Int. Rev. Code* of 1954, §61(a); cf. *James v. United States*, 366 U.S. 213, 218–21 (1961).

115. See generally 3A W. Fletcher, *Private Corporations* §§1102–12, at 130–58 (perm. ed. rev. repl. 1975).

116. See 1 W. Fletcher, *Private Corporations* §§3–7, at 28–49 (perm. ed. rev. repl. 1974); cf. C. Israel, *Corporate Practice* §§2.01–2.05, at 8–12 (rev. ed. 1974).

117. When the competitive market structure allows only efficient firms to survive, a profit orientation is structurally required and speech is properly assumed to be profit motivated. If the economic structure does not require efficient behavior, the attribution of the speech to a profit motive must rely on guesses about psychological processes. Since there is no principled manner to make such guesses, any attempted regulation would be unconstituionally overbroad. Nevertheless, if the enterprise is legally required to be profit oriented or if it makes a legal claim—e.g., a tax claim—that its practice was profit oriented, the enterprise could not also claim first amendment protection, at least if the first amendment is based on protecting personal liberty.

118. *FEC v. Massachusetts Citizens for Life, Inc.*, 479 U.S. 238 (1986) (federal ban on use of corporation's treasury funds for influencing elections unconstitutional as applied to nonprofit, nonstock corporation).

119. It is undoubtedly the orthodox view that the function of the business corporation is profit and that it is therefore improper for it to spend money or engage in activities not entered into with a view toward profit. W. Cary, *Cases and Materials on Corporations* 60 (4th ed. 1969). But cf. *SEC v. Medical Comm. for Human Rights*, 404 U.S. 403, 409–10 (1972), where Justice Douglas remarked in dissent:

> The philosophy of our times, I think, requires that such enterprises [(the modern "super-corporations")] be held to a higher standard than that of the "morals on the marketplace" which exalts a singleminded, myopic determination to maximize profits as the traditional be-all and end-all of corporate concern.

120. The Court has explained the constitutionally legitimate purpose of 18 U.S.C. § 610 (1970) as the prevention of the corporate contribution without the consent of shareholders, *United States v. CIO*, 335 U.S. 106, 113 (1948), and the protection of dissenting

members of labor unions from involuntary political contributions. *Pipefitters Local Union No. 562 v. United States*, 407 U.S. 385, 414–15 (1972). Dicta suggest that prohibiting political contributions from funds generated by the voluntary donations of union members, or allowing contributions from funds made up of involuntary assessments on union members' salaries may both violate first amendment rights. Compare *Pipefitters*, 407 U.S. at 404–9, with *International Ass'n of Machinists v. Street*, 367 U.S. 740, 749, 765–70 (1961). Cf. *Communications Workers of America v. Beck*, 108 S.Ct. 2641 (1988) (avoiding consititutional question). This may explain the framework for the legislatively created structure of PACs.

121. The analysis in this section follows closely that of Justice White's dissent, joined by Brennan and Marshall, in *First National Bank v. Bellotti*, 435 U.S. 765, 802–22 (1978).

122. See L. Overacker, *Money in Elections* 234–36, 294, 303, 337 (1932); E. Sikes, *State and Federal Corrupt-Practices Legislation* 107–8, 127–28, 188–92 (1928); G. Thayer, *Who Shakes the Money Tree?* 38–41, 53–54 (1973).

123. *Testimony Taken Before the Joint Committee of the Senate and Assembly of the State of New York to Investigate and Examine into the Business Affairs of Life Insurance Companies Doing Business in the State of New York* (Armstrong Committee) 397 (1905), quoted in E. Sikes, *supra* note 122, at 110.

124. E. Sikes, *supra* note 122, at 108–13; see also, L. Overacker, *supra* note 122, at 177–88. Prohibitions on corporate political participation also may be justified on the ground that, in light of their massive concentration of resources, allowing these special-interest collectivities to participate in the political process would give them a huge comparative advantage over other interest groups because, in preparing for their economic role, corporations have already borne the heavy organizational expenses inherent in collective action. See M. Olson, *The Logic of Collective Action* 46–47 (1971). Compare the half billion dollars spent on all political campaigns during 1972, a presidential election year, with business' ability to budget nearly $60 billion a year for advertising and sales promotion during the late 1960s. C. Lindbloom, *Politics and Markets* 195, 214 (1977). Although I have not found explicit reliance on this "transaction cost imbalance" argument in the reform literature, but see C. Lindbloom, *id.*, at 194–98, it has frequently been suggested that, because corporations are artificial creations of the state, the state may properly limit them to the specific functions for which they were created. See, e.g., *First National Bank v. Bellotti*, 435 U.S. 765, 825–27 (1978) (Rehnquist, dissenting); *id.* at 809 (White, dissenting).

125. Although not mentioned in the reform rhetoric of the time, one wonders whether some corporate interests quietly supported some of this legislation as a means to avoid the pressure to contribute created by fear of political retaliation. See G. Thayer, *supra* note 122, at 46. Cf. *Capital Broadcasting Co. v. Mitchell*, 333 F.Supp. 582, 587–89 (D.D.C. 1971) (Wright, dissenting), *aff'd mem. sub nom. Capital Broadcasting Co. v. Acting Att'y Gen.*, 405 U.S. 1000 (1972) (federal prohibition on cigarette advertising on electronic media enabled tobacco industry to avoid conflict between their need to advertise to maintain brand loyalty and their desire to discontinue television and radio advertising to avoid the effective antismoking messages that under the FCC's fairness doctrine resulted from this advertising).

126. *Int. Rev. Code of 1954*, §162(e); Treas. Reg. §1.162–20(c)(4).

127. Since the tax laws do not allow private individuals to deduct their political expenditures, disallowing a deduction for corporate political speech has been justified as a means of placing "everyone in the community . . . on the same footing" with regard to purchasing political publicity. *Cammarano v. United States*, 358 U.S. 498, 513 (1959) (upholding disallowance of ordinary and necessary business expense deduction for grass-roots lobbying). This equal footing argument is quite clearly wrong. For example, a non-

business individual will spend $1.00 on lobbying or a campaign to the extent that she values the expenditure at or more than $1.00; the person spends up to the point where the value of lobbying equals the cost or expense of lobbying. For that person, lobbying is merely one possible consumption good to be compared with other consumption goods. The purported inequality that presumably justifies denial of a deduction for corporate lobbying is that if lobbying expenses are deductible when profit motivated, a business person in a 50% tax bracket can obtain $1.00 of lobbying for 50¢. If the corporate lobbying expenses are valued only for their contributions to profits, that is, if they are properly described as business expenses, this purported inequality vanishes. Note that a $1.00 increase in earned income resulting from a $1.00 lobbying expenditure is only worth 50¢ (after taxes) to the business person who is still in the 50% tax bracket. Thus, the business person who can deduct her profit-oriented lobbying receives 50¢ for 50¢ while the non-business individual received $1.00 for $1.00. Since the gain from lobbying for the business person is increased taxable income, and the gain for the nonbusiness person is not taxable (if the expenditure is treated as a consumption expenditure, the "gain" presumably is a consumption good comparable to other consumptions of income), equality requires a deduction for the business expense and requires its denial for the nonbusiness political expenditure. Thus, the law upheld by the Court does not create equality but rather discriminates against the business' political speech. Of course, equality is only required if corporate political speech is constitutionally protected. However, denial of the business deduction in effect forces the enterprise to treat the expenditure as a consumption item and creates equality among entities as consummers.

For an elaboration of this and other arguments showing that the equality assumption of *Cammarano* is wrong, see Cooper, "The Tax Treatment of Business Grassroots Lobbying: Defining and Attaining the Public Policy Objectives," 68 *Columbia L. Rev.* 810, 810–13 (1968). Although Cooper proceeds to argue that creating an inequality was the apparent and possibly *desirable* purpose of this provision of the tax law, he manifests considerable doubt about its constitutionality. *Id.* at 813–16, 830–41. Its justification requires the view argued here, that corporate political speech should be treated as unprotected commercial speech.

128. See, e.g., *Grosjean v. American Press Co.*, 297 U.S. 233, 250 (1936) (tax on gross receipts of periodicals of a certain circulation violates first amendment).

129. See 2 U.S.C. §441b, *replacing* 18 U.S.C. §610 (repealed 1976). The Supreme Court has studiously avoided deciding the constitutionality of bans on contributions as applied to profit-oriented corporations (or labor unions). See *FEC v. Mass. Citizens for Life*, 107 S.Ct. 616, 631 (1986); *FEC v. National Conservative PAC*, 470 U.S. 480, 496 (1985). See also *Pipefitters Local Union No. 562 v. United States*, 407 U.S. 385, 442 (1972); *United States v. UAW*, 352 U.S. 567, 589–93 (1957); *United States v. CIO*, 335 U.S. 106, 107–10 (1948); cf. *Cort v. Ash*, 422 U.S. 66, 80–85 (1975); *International Ass'n of Machinists v. Street*, 367 U.S. 740, 746–50 (1961). Commentators report finding no reported convictions for corporate contributions from the time the ban originated in 1907, Act of Jan. 26, 1907, ch. 420, 34 Stat. 864, until the 1973 convictions involving contributions for reelection of President Nixon. See Comment, "The Constitutionality of the Federal Ban on Corporate and Union Campaign Contributions and Expenditures," 42 *U. Chicago L. Rev.* 148 (1974). But see *Egan v. United States. 137 F.2d 369*, 378, 381–83 (8th Cir.), cert. denied, 320 U.S. 788 (1943) (upholding conviction for political contributions by registered public utility holding company; first amendment issues not considered).

130. See 2 U.S.C §441 b.

131. 435 U.S. 765 (1978).

132. *Id.* at 805, 806. The dissent added a note at this point suggesting that this relation to self-expression distinguishes the regulation of corporations from the issues involved in *Buckley v. Valeo*, 424 U.S. 1 (1976).

133. *Id.* at 825–27.

134. See, e.g., Baker, *supra* note 111; Brudney, *supra* note 113; Note, "The Corporation and the Constitution: Economic Due Process and Corporate Speech," 90 *Yale L. J.* 1833 (1981); Miller, "On Politics, Democracy, and the First Amendment: A Comment on *First National Bank v. Bellotti,*" 38 *Washington & Lee L. Rev.* 21 (1981); O'Kelley, "The Constitutional Rights of Corporations Revisited: Social and Political Expression and the Corporation After *First National Bank v. Bellotti,*" 67 *Georgetown L. J.* 1347 (1979).

135. 459 U.S. 197 (1982).

136. *Village of Schaumburg v. Citizens for a Better Environment,* 444 U.S. 620 (1980).

137. 459 U.S. at 207–8. The Court also emphasized the importance of preventing the appearance and reality of corruption. *Id.* at 208–9. Cf. *Myer v. Glenn,* 108 S.Ct. 1886, 1894 n.7 (1988) (rejecting equalizing-of-political-resources rationale in noncorporate context). Earlier, in overturning an application of a ban on independent electoral expenditures by political committees, the Court emphasized that because of the law's broad coverage, this "is not a 'corporation' case." The Court explained that the groups involved, which were "designed expressly to participate in political debate, are quite different from the traditional corporations organized for economic gain." *FEC v. National Conservative PAC,* 470 U.S. 480 (1985).

138. *Id.* at 210 n.7 (the Court unpersuasively noted that *Bellotti* related to referenda while this case relates to candidate elections).

139. *Id.* at 496 (noting that neither here nor in *Bellotti* does the Court decide whether Congress can restrict a corporation from "making independent expenditures to influence elections for public office").

140. See note 111 *supra.*

141. Lydenberg and Young, "Business Bankrolls for Local Ballots," 33 *Business & Society Rev.* 51, 53 (1980).

142. L. Overacker, *supra* note 122, at 197.

143. The Court appears to treat them differently but to favor the corporate. Cf. *Bellotti,* with *Abood v. Detroit Bd. of Educ.,* 431 U.S. 209 (1977). In contrast, there are a variety of reasons to conclude that unions should be treated more like governmental units, with the collective power to engage in speech that some members do not accept but also with an obligation not to abridge the speech and associational rights of members. Baker, *supra* note 111, at 656 n.35.

144. *Thornhill v. Alabama,* 310 U.S. 881 (1940). Pope, "Labor and the Constitution: From Abolition to Deindustrialization," 65 *Texas L. Rev.* 1071 (1987). Other considerations may justify some regulation of some union activities. It is often suggested that in some situations speech may be properly classified as partaking of the qualities of action. For example, speech may be coercive without leaving a realistic possibility of a person exercising her own will or judgment, an argument that suggests that a union's use of a "signal" for application of economic force may not be protected. See T. Emerson, *The System of Freedom of Expression* 315–16, 423–24 (1970); but see Pope, *supra.* Moreover, unions may be quasigovernmental bodies within which members *must be* guaranteed democratic rights. If they are, arguably the union should be no more prevented from using dues (taxes) to promote visions of the good than are governments. But see *Abood v. Detroit Bd. of Educ.,* 431 U.S. 209 (1977).

145. Justice Jackson in *Dennis v. United States,* 314 U.S. 494 (1951), recognized this in arguing that the Court was wrong to treat *Dennis* as a speech case and to use the clear and present danger test that had been developed to deal with speech issues. Jackson argued, "The highest degree of constitutional protection is due the *individual* acting without conspiracy." *Id.* at 570 (emphasis added). However, "[t]here is no constitutional right to 'gang up' on the government." *Id.* at 577. He explained, "[A] combination of persons to commit a wrong, either as an end or as a means to an end, is much more dangerous

[than an individual acting alone], because of its *increased power* to do wrong, because it is more difficult to guard against and prevent the evil designs of a group of persons than a single person." *Id.* at 573-74 (citation omitted) (emphasis added). Alternatively, as argued in Chapters 6, 7, and 8, freedom of peaceable assembly and association should be protected precisely because they properly embody a fundamental right of people to generate power to do things, even to "gang up" on the government.

CHAPTER 10

1. Confidence in reasoning and analysis should increase when the resulting conclusions are relatively congruent with the more fixed aspects of the reasoner's judgment. The analysis is most powerful when it gives coherence to areas of doubt in judgments or values. However, human reasoning often misleads; and when analysis appears to contradict fixed points in our values and judgments, we should not be too quick to abandon those values and judgments. For a development of this notion of reflective equilibrium, see J. Rawls, *A Theory of Justice* 20-22, 48-51, 120 (1971). See generally Dworkin, "The Original Position," 40 *U. Chicago L. Rev.* 500, 509-19 (1973).

2. Stewart, "Or of the Press," 26 *Hastings L. J.* 631, 634 (1975). Examples of the press ferreting out governmental abuses, both at the local and national level abound. The press's role in the Watergate scandal and the downfall of a president is a particularly dramatic example of this fourth estate role.

3. E. Barnouw, *The Sponsor* 70-73 (1978). For example, "Gunsmoke" was dropped while still high in the ratings because it reached too old and rural an audience. *Id.* at 73.

4. Justices Brennan and Marshall, dissenting in *CBS v. Democratic Nat'l Comm.*, 412 U.S. 94 (1973), argued that:

> [I]n light of the strong interest of broadcasters in maximizing their audience, and therefore their profits, it seems almost naive to expect the majority of broadcasters to produce the variety and controversiality of material necessary to reflect a full spectrum of viewpoints. . . . [I]n the commercial world of mass communications, it is simply 'bad business' to espouse—or even to allow others to espouse—the heterodox or the conroversial.

Id. at 187.

5. To the extent media forms such as movies or magazines are situated so that specialized attention to small population subsets is economically feasible, this criticism may be different and less severe. Cable and VCRs may eventually serve this role for video.

6. N. Eberstadt, "Myths in the Food Crisis," *New York Review of Books*, Feb. 19, 1976, at 32-37.

7. Both the concern and this type of solution were suggested by Varrow, "The Fairness Doctrine: A Double Standard for Electronic and Print Media," 26 *Hastings L. J.* 659, 622-69, 679 (1975), wherein the author notes concerted attempts to limit "fairness" or "access" regulation of cable television and concludes: "If the current policy move is successful, cable television will be limited to serving business, professional, entertainment, and other profit-making institutions. This limited use would waste a valuable asset." *Id.* at 707.

8. *Miami Herald Publishing Co. v. Tornillo*, 418 U.S. 241 (1974). See generally, J. Barron, *Freedom of the Press for Whom?* (1973). In discussing access proposals, Jerome Barron, the lawyer in *Miami Herald*, concludes that: "Blandness in our time has an overt commercial motivation: the pursuit of the largest audience." *Id.* at 84. See also Barron, "Access to the Press—A New First Amendment Right," 80 *Harvard L. Rev.* 1641 (1967).

9. See *CBS v. Democratic Natl's Comm.*, 412 U.S. 94, 171-78 (1973) (Brennan & Marshall, dissenting); *Red Lion Broadcasting Co. v. FCC*, 395 U.S. 367, 388-96 (1969). But

see *Miami Herald Publishing Co. v. Tornillo*, 418 U.S. 241, 247–54 (1974); *CBS v. Democratic Nat'l Comm.*, 412 U.S. at 110.

10. This access argument was rejected by the Court in *CBS v. Democratic Nat'l Comm.*, 412 U.S. at 127, and in *Miami Herald Publishing Co. v. Tornillo*, 418 U.S. at 258.

11. 418 U.S. 241 (1974).

12. The basic analysis does not change if the media is supported by advertising, although the concern is with the audience "accepting," not "purchasing," the message. The advertisers can, however, provide an additional source of constraint.

13. Many alternative media fit this account. See, e.g., D. Armstrong, *A Trumpet to Arms: Alternative Media in America* (1981); J. Downing, *Radical Media* (1984).

14. For example, Professor Bagdikian claims that no existing, distinguished newspaper, except perhaps the *Philadelphia Inquirer*, was developed by a chain and he notes that one small study indicates that nonchain papers have more of every type of serious news (local, state, national, and international) and more stories written by staff (rather than the cheaper, syndicated stories) than the chain papers. His implicit explanation is that the local owners have subsidized those results—a type of investment in which the chain organizations were uninterested or which they were unable to make. Bagdikian, "Conglomeration, Concentration, and the Flow of Information," in *Proceeding of the Symposium on Media Concentration* 6, 15–17 (FTC 1978).

15. In marketplace theory, the content (and circulation) of the speech, not its source, is the key concern—and, thus, the media's product and other industry's commercial speech often would not be relevantly different. Under the preferable liberty analysis, the product of a commercial enterprise (e.g., the publication) would appear to have no special constitutional status as compared to other commerical products.

16. See, e.g., Bezanson, "The New Free Press Guarantee", 63 *Virginia L. Rev.* 731, 732 (1977).

17. The phrasing in the religion section of the first amendment adopted by the House on August 24, 1789, indicates concern with the rights of conscience: "Congress shall make no law establishing religion or prohibiting the free exercise thereof, nor shall the rights of conscience be infringed." Madison's proposal read: "The civil rights of none shall be abridged on account of religious belief or worship, nor shall any national religion be established, nor shall the full and equal rights of conscience be in any manner, or on any pretext, infringed." 1 *Annals of Cong.* 434 (Gales ed. 1789) (emphasis added), quoted in *New York Times Com. v. United States*, 403 U.S. 713, 716 n.2 (1971) (Black & Douglas, concurring). See also D. Richards, *Toleration and the Constitution* 114–16, 141–46 (1886).

18. See, e.g., *Lynch v. Donnelly*, 465 U.S. 668 (1984) (O'Connor, concurring).

19. In the marketplace theory the proper goal is, to use economic language, an efficient or desirable production and distribution of speech. Under certain circumstances unimpeded markets are assumed to lead to an efficient, and possibly desirable, production and distribution of goods. However, market failures or breakdowns occur. For various reasons such as the high cost of market transactions, of obtaining accurate information, and of enforcement of agreements, or because of undefined or nonexclusive property rights, a more efficient or desirable production and distribution will result from some degree of nonmarket decision making—e.g., governmental regulation. In addition, since market allocations depend on the given distribution of resources and tastes, critiques of these existing patterns may justify government interventions. Given market failures, unequal distribution of wealth, and concern for the dynamic development of values or preferences, the government could attempt to restructure or regulate the marketplace in order to achieve the desired production and distribution of the appropriate types of expression.

The theoretical objections to this approach are, first, that governmental intervention may well violate the liberty of other speakers. See *Tornillo* and *Buckley*. Second, the government has no criteria by which to determine what changes would be considered improvements. Without such criteria, governmental restructuring to correct for what it views as market failures is liable to amount to promotion of particular, governmentally endorsed positions—a result hardly consistent with the marketplace of ideas theory. See Chapter 2.

20. For purposes of this chapter, I equate the press with at least print, broadcast, and film media. In the next chapter I will consider the possibility of treating the broadcast and cable media, but not newspapers, more as partial common carriers.

21. *Herbert v. Lando*, 441 U.S. 153, 181 (1979) (Brennan, dissenting).

22. *Id.* at 183 n.l (emphasis added).

23. *Id.* at 184.

24. *Id.* at 187.

25. Blasi, "The Checking Value of the First Amendment," 1977 *American Bar Found. Res. J.* 521 (one very important value of the first amendment is its contribution to discovering and deterring abuse of official power).

26. 441 U.S. at 185. Although Justice Brennan, when speaking of censuring the state or exposing its abuses, explicitly referred only to the protection given by the first amendment, not the press clause, the context of the discussion suggests that he had the press especially in mind. The footnote accompanying the quoted passage makes continued references to "the press," and in the text immediately following the quoted statement Brennan quotes an historical passage praising freedom of the press.

27. An emphasis on the instrumental value of speech, combined with the failure to recognize that this value is superfluous for justifying protection, can lead to improper limitations on people's speech rights. Brennan's rejection of a merely instrumentalist approach to analyzing the fourth amendment exclusionary rule reflects a parallel concern. See *Herbert v. Lando*, 441 U.S. 153, 188 n.7 (citing the Court's analysis of the exclusionary rule in *Stone v. Powell*, 428 U.S. 465 (1976). The exclusionary rule may be a required aspect of the government's respect for individual autonomy and not merely an instrument to the attainment of a right; if so, it should be enforced even if instrumental considerations such as deterrence would not justify enforcement. See Baker, "Utility and Rights: Two Justifications for State Action Increasing Equality," 84 *Yale L. J.* 39, 53 n.46 (1974).

28. See Linde, "Due Process of Lawmaking," 55 *Nebraska L. Rev.* 197, 254 (1976).

29. Stewart, *supra* note 2. Justice Potter Stewart believes that the press clause embodies different values than the assembly and speech clauses because its foundation is the institutional checking function of the organized press. He argues that the free press guarantee is a structural provision. Justice Stewart implicitly assumes that the framers were specially concerned with protecting this particular profit-oriented business from governmental regulation. Stewart notes that "[t]he publishing business is, in short, the only organized private business that is given explicit constitutional protection." Moreover, he concludes that protection of "the institutional autonomy of the press . . . was the purpose of the Constitution to guarantee." Stewart, *supra* note 2, at 633, 634 (1975). Professor David Anderson persuasively shows that this special role of the press and its protection as an institution that could criticize and check governmental power was an important aspect of the framer's original conception of the press clause. Anderson, "The Origins of the Press Clause," 30 *UCLA L. Rev.* 455 (1983). Professor Nimmer makes a distinction similar to the one developed in this chapter concerning the difference between the free speech and free press guarantees. Nimmer argues that speech performs a "self-fulfillment" function that does not have much applicability to the press. (This argument corresponds to the conclusion here to the extent that the press is found to be profit oriented.) Nimmer argues that the press performs another function, the "democratic dialogue" function, which often

does not apply to speech. Nimmer, "Introduction—Is Freedom of the Press a Redundancy: What Does It Add to Freedom of Speech?," 26 *Hastings L.J.* 639, 653 (1975).

30. See Blasi, *supra* note 25, at 565 n.146.

31. See *id.* at 521, 528, 548, 565 n.146, 649 n.416.

32. Blasi does note that he is merely elaborating the checking value and that other strands of first amendment theory might change some of his conclusions. See Blasi, *supra* note 25, 528, 632.

33. Blasi, *supra* note 25, at 634–35. Cf. T. Emerson, *The System of Freedom of Expression* 587–92 (1970).

34. Another possibility, occasionally suggested by the Court opinions but not pursued here, is that various instrumental first amendment values justify judicial balancing or rule formulation to extend protection of speech beyond that which respect for individual autonomy absolutely demands.

35. Blasi, *supra* note 25, at 547.

36. *Herbert v. Lando*, 441 U.S. 153, 183 n.1 (1979) (Brennan, dissenting).

37. Blasi, *supra* note 25, at 547.

38. Although the Court has rejected a statute granting a right to reply to newspaper attacks, *Miami Herald Publishing Co. v. Tornillo*, 418 U.S. 241 (1974), Blasi would rely on the checking function to override the claim of the newspaper if the right of reply was only given to challengers, not incumbents, in elections. See Blasi, *supra* note 25, at 621–22, 627–28.

39. See note 33 *supra*.

40. The Court restricts recovery for libels of "public figures" to cases where the libel was made with "reckless disregard" of its falsity. *Curtis Publishing Co. v. Butts*, 388 U.S. 130, 164 (1967). Blasi would narrow this protection to situations where the libel concerned the official actions of "public officials." Blasi, *supra* note 25, at 581. Although never yet permitted by the Court, see, e.g., *Nebraska Press v. Stuart*, 427 U.S. 539 (1976), Blasi would also permit gag orders on press reporting of criminal trials to protect the defendant's sixth amendment right to a fair trial. Blasi, *supra* note 25, at 636–37. The better first amendment view is that since both the right of speech and the right to a fair trial are rights against the state, a private speaker could not violate the defendant's right and the two rights cannot be in conflict. Linde, "Fair Trials and Press Freedom—Two Rights Against the State," 13 *Willamette L.J.* 211 (1977). See also *C.B.S. v. United States District Court for C.D. of California*, 729 F.2d 1174, 1184 (Godwin, concurring) (1984) (adopting Linde's reasoning). The state's authority to prosecute is limited both by the requirement that the trial be fair and that the state only use legal means to pursue the prosecution. Its desire to prosecute no more justifies the state in gagging speech than it justifies illegal searches.

41. Blasi, *supra* note 25, at 547.

42. *Id.* at 541.

43. See *id.* at 564. See also *id.* at 602–7 (arguing for reporter's privilege).

44. See *id.* at 529–38.

45. See *id.* at 620–21.

46. *Mills v. Alabama*, 384 U.S. 214, 219 (1966) (striking down statue banning election-day newspaper endorsements or criticisms of candidates).

47. Since Blasi and I adopt different doctrinal approaches, our specific conclusions about the content of special press rights differ. Blasi's other interesting claims, which often unduly limit the protection offered to speech, should be analyzed using traditional speech theory. When his balancing approach contradicts traditional first amendment doctrine and limits protection of liberty, one should reject his balancing analysis as unnecessary and inappropriate to his key insight into the importance of the checking function.

48. *Herbert v. Lando*, 441 U.S. 153, 180 (1979) (Brennan, dissenting).

49. In a fundamental sense, the instrumentalist fourth estate theory is dependent on the liberty theory for its normative grounding. As argued in Chapter 2's discussion of political speech theories, without the liberty theory's premise of the centrality of equality and autonomy, there would be little reason to think the "distrusted" government should be checked rather than enhanced. Except for these values, why should not the goal be to insulate the government from exposure and restraint?

50. Writing for the majority in *Saxbe v. Washington Post Co.*, 417 U.S. 843 (1974), Justice Stewart stated: "[N]ewsmen have no constitutional right of access to prisons or their inmates beyond that afforded the general public." The proposition "that the Constitution imposes upon government the affirmative duty to make available to journalists sources of information not available to the public generally . . . finds no support in the words of the Constitution or in any decision of this Court." *Id.* at 850 (quoting *Pell v. Procunier*, 417 U.S. 817, 834–35 (1974)) (citations omitted).

51. 376 U.S. 254 (1964).

52. Anderson, "The Origins of the Press Clause," 30 *UCLA L. Rev.* 455, 458 n.20 (1983). See generally, Shiffrin, "Defamatory Non-media Speech and the First Amendment," 25 *UCLA L. Rev.* 915 (1978).

53. Stewart, *supra* note 2, at 635 (1975).

54. Justice Stewart states, "the Court has never suggested that the constitutional right to free speech gives an individual any immunity from liability for either libel or slander." *Id.* But cf. *New York Times Co. v. Sullivan*, 376 U.S. 254 (1964) (directing verdict for private, nonmedia defendants). Indeed, many commentators read *Gertz v. Robert Welch, Inc.*, 418 U.S. 323 (1974), to limit protection to media defendants. See, e.g., Nimmer, "Introduction—Is Freedom of the Press a Redundancy: What Does It Add to Freedom of Speech?" 26 *Hastings L. J.* 639, 649 (1975). But see Lange, "The Speech and Press Clauses," 23 *UCLA L. Rev.* 77, 116–17 (1975).

55. *Dun & Bradstreet, Inc. v. Greenmoss Builders, Inc.*, 472 U.S. 749 (1985).

56. I use "speaker" to refer to anyone who communicates, whether it be an individual talking to a friend or the press publishing a story.

57. 418 U.S. 241 (1974).

58. 412 U.S. 94 (1973).

59. See Nimmer, *supra* note 54, at 644–45.

60. See Lange, *supra* note 54.

61. See Bezanson, *supra* note 16, at 754–62. Here, Bezanson relies on, I believe, a mistaken version of the analogy to the establishment clause.

62. *Id.* Although the plurality in *Branzburg v. Hayes*, 408 U.S. 665 (1972), apparently rejected a qualified testimonial privilege for reporters, Justice Powell's concurrence is often read along with the dissents to find support for such a privilege. See, e.g., Goodale, "*Branzburg v. Hayes* and the Developing Qualified Privilege for Newsmen," 26 *Hastings L. J.* 709, 716–18, 742–43 (1975).

63. See *Saxbe v. Washington Post Co.*, 417 U.S. 843 (1974); *Pell v. Procunier*, 417 U.S. 817 (1974).

64. See *Press-Enterprise Co. v. Superior Court*, 478 U.S. 1 (1986); *Richmond Newspapers v. Virginia*, 448 U.S. 555 (1980); *Gannett Co. v. DePasquale*, 443 U.S. 368, 397 (1979) (Powell, concurring). Two issues are implicit: whether there is any right of access and, if so, whether it is a right of the press or of the general public.

65. *Prahl v. Brosamle*, 98 Wis.2d 130, 295 N.W.2d 768 (1980) (no first amendment right for news reporters to trespass to gather news). See also *Dietemann v. Time, Inc.*, 449 F.2d 245 (9th Cir. 1971).

66. This situation would occur if *Nebraska Press Ass'n v. Stuart*, 417 U.S. 539 (1976),

applies only to the press. See *Landmark Communications, Inc. v. Virginia*, 435 U.S. 829, 848 (1978) (Stewart, concurring).

67. See *Branzburg v. Hayes*, 408 U.S. 665 (1972).

68. See *Herbert v. Lando*, 441 U.S. 153, 157 (1979).

69. See *Zurcher v. Stanford Daily*, 436 U.S. 547 (1978).

70. See *Associated Press v. NLRB*, 301 U.S. 103 (1937); *FCC v. National Citizens Comm. for Broadcasting*, 436 U.S. 775 (1978).

71. See *Miami Herald Publishing Co. v. Tornillo*, 418 U.S. 241 (1974); *Red Lion Broadcasting Co. v. FCC*, 395 U.S. 367 (1969).

72. The task of identification assumes that we have a clear definition or conception of the press—which is not true. The focus of concern in protecting the press centers on people's continuing role in uncovering and communicating information to a public usually as large as is willing to receive (pay for) the communication. This role suggests that the lecturer as well as the print publisher should receive protection if (1) she consistently devotes a large proportion of her time to this role and (2) she makes her communications available to the general public and (3) her claim for protection relates to the performance of this role. Protection would not, then, extend to the private detective. Arguably, the investment newsletter in *Lowe v. Securities and Exchange Comm'n*, 472 U.S. 181 (1985), merited the label of press—it was not individualized and was directed at whoever would buy the publication—while the credit report in *Dunn & Bradstreet v. Greenmoss*, 472 U.S. 749 (1985) was somewhat more individualized and more a provision of a specific service and, therefore, should be subject to regulation to the same extent as are other "speech" service businesses, e.g., lawyering and psychiatry. Nevertheless, rather than fully develop and defend this approach, I take the usual "out" of a person who does not want to think through the issue, by suggesting that a definition of "press" be developed through case-by-case adjudication.

73. This problem was suggested by Lange, *supra* note 54, at 105–6.

74. *Branzburg v. Hayes*, 408 U.S. 665, 682–85 (1972); cf. *Nebraska Press Asso. v. Stuart*, 427 U.S. 539, 588 n.15 (1976) (Brennan, concurring in the judgement) ("does not necessarily immunize [the press] from civil . . . or criminal liability for transgression of general criminal laws during the course of obtaining that information").

75. 449 F.2d 245 (9th Cir. 1971).

76. *Id.* at 249.

77. State courts also sometimes construe custom to give the press an implied consent to entry in certain situations. *Florida Pub. Co. v. Fletcher*, 340 So.2nd 914 (Fla. 1977), *cert. denied*, 431 U.S. 930 (1977).

78. For a good introduction to the issues raised in this paragraph, see M. Franklin, *Mass Media Law*, 3rd ed., 597–621 (1987).

79. Both Watergate and Oliver North's conduct in the Iran-Contra scandal exposed during Congressional hearings in 1987 provide illustrations of attempts to destroy crucial evidence even though both also involved some disclosure when judicially ordered. Judicial aid, however, cannot be considered certain even when timely—i.e., before the shredding. Cf. *McGehee v. CIA*, 697 F.2d 1095 (D.C.Cir. 1983). Judge Bork, in dissent, argued that illegally lengthy delays in giving information for which there was a statutory right of access under the Freedom of Information Act and examples of illegal noncompliance evidence bureaucratic inefficiencies, not bad faith, and therefore would have granted summary judgment in favor of the government. *Id.* at 1115.

80. The purely instrumental qualities of organizational or institutional claims for secrecy can be contrasted with the claims made by individuals, which can derive from premises of liberty, autonomy, or equality. See Baker, "Posner's Privacy Mystery and the Failure of Economic Analysis of Law," 12 *Georgia L. Rev.* 475 (1978).

81. This concession, by itself, does not provide an argument that government should be able to stop the communication of information once the press or anyone else has obtained it.

82. Freedom of Information Act, 5. U.S.C. §552; Privacy Act of 1974, 5 U.S.C §552a.

83. Cf. *United States v. Richardson*, 418 U.S. 166 (1974) (federal taxpayer lacked standing to demand that Congress provide constitutionally mandated disclosures).

84. This discussion may also apply to defensive rights. Legislatures can, and often do, respond with shield laws. In fact, reliance on the judiciary is particularly problematic in the case of many claims for defensive rights. The claim is often for defense against inquiries imposed by the judiciary. As a party in interest, the judiciary may be particularly insensitive to defensive claims. Some courts have even impulsively struck down shield laws as improper legislative interference with their judicial power. See *Farr v. Superior Court*, 22 Cal. App. 3d 60, 99 Cal. Rptr. 342 (1971) *cert. denied*, 409 U.S. 1101 (1972); *Ammerman v. Hubbard Broadcasting, Inc.*, 89 N.M. 307, 5512 P.2d 1354 (1976). See generally Goodale, "Courts Begin Limiting the Scope of Various State Shield Laws," *Nat'l Lawyer* Dec. 11, 1978, at 28, col. l.

Nevertheless, most courts recognize a nonstatutory, qualified privilege for newspersons. In 1979, Goodale found that nine federal circuits have adopted a qualified privilege while one, the Fifth Circuit, has apparently rejected it; and the states, either by court decision or legislative action, have split 16 to 4 in favor of a qualified privilege. Goodale, "Review of Privilege Cases," *Communications Law* 431, 491–507 (1979).

85. In the interesting interchange between Nimmer and Lange on the personal fulfillment press people obtain from their work, Lange argues that "a sense of self-fulfillment continues to provide a substantial portion of the raison d'etre of the so-called 'working press'." Lange, *supra* note 54, at 104.

86. See Blasi, *supra* note 25, at 589–91.

87. But see *Nebraska Press Ass'n v. Stuart*, 423 U.S. 1327, 1333–34 (1975). In his published opinion, Justice Blackmun temporarily prohibited the press from reporting the facts of the case, including some of the facts recited in his opinion. Presumably publishing his opinion in Nebraska while the opinion was current would have been illegal.

88. *Nebraska Press Association v. Stuart*, 427 U.S. 539, 588, 604, 612 (1976) (Brennan, Stewart & Marshall, concurring); *id.* at 570 (White, concurring); *id.* at 617 (Stevens, concurring).

> Settled case law concerning the impropriety and constitutional invalidity of prior restraints on the press compels the conclusion that there can be no prohibition on the publication by the press of any information pertaining to pending judicial proceedings or the operation of the criminal justice system, no matter how shabby the means by which the information is obtained.

Id. at 588.

89. The legitimacy of restraints may be different for the prosecution and maybe for plaintiffs than for those involved involuntarily in the court proceedings. The speech of prosecutors and other public employees may be restricted in order to promote the proper performance of their jobs. *Pickering v. Bd. of Educ.*, 391 U.S. 563 (1968). In contrast, those involuntarily involved in trials should not be required to forego the exercise of their speech rights—although the court might condition its order gagging the prosecutor on the defendant's acceptance of similar restraints. Cf. *Seattle Times v. Rhinehart*, 467 U.S. 20 (1984). Moreover, a gag order would interfere with the asserted right of defendants to make their defense, in part, to the public.

90. Cf. *Seattle Times v. Rhinehart*, 467 U.S. 20 (1984) (in appropriate cases, court can

condition use of discovery on using information only for purpose of the law suit even though party is a newspaper).

91. For a summary and analysis of data, see A. Bezanson, G. Cranberg, J. Soloski, *Libel Law and the Press* (1987).

92. *New York Times v. Sullivan*, 376 U.S. 254, 278 (1964).

93. *Id.* at 295 (Black and Douglas, concurring). See also *id.* at 294 ("the state libel laws threaten the very existence of an American press viable enough to publish unpopular views on public affairs").

94. For a discussion in a slightly different context of the relevance of demoralization costs to utilitarian calculations, see Michelman, "Property, Utility and Fairness: Comments on the Ethical Foundations of 'Just Compensation' Law," 80 *Harvard L. Rev.* 1165, 1214–24 (1967). See also Franklin, "Winners and Losers and Why: A Study of Defamation Litigation," 1980 *American Bar Found. Research J.* 455.

95. G. Calabresi, *The Costs of Accidents* (1970).

96. See generally, Shiffrin, "Defamatory Non-Media Speech and First Amendment Methodology," 25 *UCLA L. Rev.* 915 (1978).

97. See, e.g., Aleinikoff, "Constitutional Law in the Age of Balancing," 96 *Yale L. J.* 943 (1987).

98. *Herbert v. Lando*, 441 U.S. 153, 183–84 n.1 (1979) (Brennan, concurring).

99. I am indebted to Professor Thomas Emerson and Justice Hans Linde for stimulating the analysis in this paragraph.

100. Professor Vince Blasi exhibits a similar concern, although he reaches different conclusions concerning balancing. Blasi, "The Pathological Perspective and the First Amendment," 85 *Columbia L.Rev.* 449 (1985).

101. *Bransburg v. Hayes*, 408 U.S. 665 (1972).

102. See H. Linde and G. Bunn, *Legislative and Administrative Processes* 644–45 (1976) [quoting *Hearings Pursuant to H.R. Res. 802 Before the House Comm. on the Judiciary*, 93d Cong., 2d Sess., bk. VIII, 321–23 (1974) (excerpts of Nixon's conversation concerning the *Washington Post*)].

103. *Fed, R. Evid.* 501.

104. For example, confidentiality of communications between an attorney and a client will not be judicially recognized should the conversations entail some joint criminal exploit. The fifth amendment may, however, prevent forced testimony.

105. But see *Pittsburg Press Co. v. Pittsburg Comm'n on Human Relations*, 413 U.S. 376, 388 (1973). In dicta, the Court said that it had "no doubt that a newspaper constitutionally could be forbidden to publish a want ad proposing a sale of narcotics or soliciting prostitutes." One wonders why. Certainly, the press should be able to publish the information in a news story. Moreover, the state's interest in law enforcement would seem well served by publication, therby giving the police knowledge of the location of a proposed crime. Only the interest in suppressing information about a person's willingness to engage in consensual criminal activity, i.e., suppressing truthful information, justifies the ban.

106. Given the importance of stopping crime, promoting communication about the crime within the counseling scenario is arguably desirable, giving counselors a chance to dissuade the potential wrongdoer. Or such a privilege could be limited, imposing a duty to divulge the contents of the communication if the attempted dissuasion fails.

107. Recognizing the privilege may weaken law enforcement very little. The absence of a privilege does not guarantee that reports about future crime will actually be made to government officials. People often conceal prior knowledge of forthcoming crime; they are sanctioned only in the rare cases that the authorities both discover their prior knowledge and decide to prosecute them for their noncooperation.

108. 408 U.S. 665, 725 (1972) (Stewart, Brennan, & Marshall, dissenting). Justice Stewart would adopt the following qualified privilege for reporters:

> [T]he government must (1) show that there is probable cause to believe that the newsman has information that is clearly relevant to a specific probable violation of law; (2) demonstrate that the information sought cannot be obtained by alternative means less destructive of First Amendment rights; and (3) demonstrate a compelling and overriding interest in the information.

Id. at 743 (footnotes omitted). Justice Douglas, on the other hand, recognized a more absolute privilege on two grounds: as a specific right of the press and as a general privilege for anyone engaged in first amendment activity. *Id.* at 712–17.

The lawyers' decision not to argue for an absolute privilege could reflect lawyers' almost instinctual tendency to advocate the apparently narrowest ground for reaching the proper result—a practice that sometimes misdirects doctrinal development and can even backfire to prevent reaching the result the advocate desires in the case at hand. This can occur, for example, when a principled justification exists for the broader but not the narrower ground.

109. *Id.* at 783–43.

110. See *Gibson v. Florida Legislative Investigation Comm.*, 372 U.S. 539 (1963); *Koningsberg v. State Bar*, 366 U.S. 36 (1961); *Braden v. United States*, 365 U.S. 431 (1961); *Wilkinson v. United States*, 365 U.S. 399 (1961); *Barenblatt v. United States*, 360 U.S. 109 (1959); *Watkins v. United States*, 354 U.S. 178 (1957).

111. The analysis of purpose here would be the same as in other areas of constitutional law, e.g., equal protection, establishment clause, negative implication of the commerce clause.

112. *Smith v. Arkansas State Highway Employees Local 1315*, 441 U.S. 463 (1979).

113. See, e.g., *Keyishian v. Board of Regents*, 385 U.S. 589 (1967). See generally, Kriemer, "Allocational Sanctions: The Problem of Negative Rights in a Positive State," 132 *U. Pennsylvania L. Rev.* 1293 (1984).

114. This was essentially Douglas' second argument in *Branzburg*. See note 108 *supra*.

115. *Branzburg v. Hayes*, 408 U.S. 655, 728–36 (1972) (Stewart, dissenting).

116. In addition to the first amendment analysis, Justice Stevens offered a quite persuasive argument that the fourth amendment does not allow a search warrant for an unannounced search of the property of a citizen not suspected of criminal conduct, without reasonable grounds for a "fear that, if notice were given, he would conceal or destroy the object of the search." *Zurcher v. Stanford Daily*, 436 U.S. 547, 582 (1978) (Stevens, dissenting).

117. Brinkley, "Nicaraguan Rebel Tells of Killings as Device for Forced Recruitment," *The New York Times*, A10, Sept. 12, 1985. 125. 436 U.S. 547 (1978).

118. Generally, the Constitution can be viewed as providing standards for the behavior of government, in which case it should control wherever the government acts, or as providing rights to Americans (and maybe people who are present within our territory). The issue is controversial, but the better view, which is receiving increasing scholarly and case law support, is the first. See *Foreign Relations Law of the United States, 3rd Restatement* §721 comment b; §722 comment m and reporter's note 16 (1987).

119. See generally, Shiffrin, "Government Speech," 27 *UCLA L. Rev.* 565 (1980).

120. In his Zurcher dissent, Justice Stewart argued that police should use a subpoena rather than a search warrant to secure material from a newspaper office unless "[a] search warrant application should demonstrate probable cause to believe that a subpoena would be impractical." *Zurcher v. Stanford Daily*, 436 U.S. at 575 (Stewart, dissenting).

121. 408 U.S. 665 (1972); see note 108 *supra*.

CHAPTER 11

1. For an introduction to the literature on these points, see B. Bagdikian, *The Media Monopoly* (1983); E. Barnouw, *The Sponser* (1978).

2. At least one commentator has suggested that our European allies have drawn this conclusion. See R. Homet, *Politics, Cultures and Communications* 98–99 (1979); Homet, "Communications Policymaking in Western Europe," 29 *J. Communications* 31, 34 (1979).

3. Barron, "Access to the Press: A New First Amendment Right," 80 *Harvard L. Rev.* 1641 (1967). J. Barron, *Freedom of the Press for Whom?* (1975). Although I appreciate his question, it should be clear that I do not adopt his answer.

4. See, e.g., DuVal, "The Occasions of Secrecy," 47 *U. Pitt. L. Rev.* 579 (1986).

5. In *CBS v. Demo. Nat. Comm.*, 412 U.S. 94, 122, 124 (1973), after claiming "that the interest of the public is our foremost concern," the Court allowed broadcasters to refuse proposed editorial advertisements, concluding that "editing is what editors are for."

6. 395 U.S. at 390.

7. *Id.*

8. *Miami Herald Publishing Co. v. Tornillo*, 418 U.S. 241 (1974).

9. Even at present, considerable diversity exists within the entire range of media output. The degree of diversity in the content of communications emanating from any particular segment of the communications industry results in large part from the interaction between the public's "desires" and the legal, economic, and technological contexts within which the segment operates. Our multitude of special interest magazines, in contrast to lesser diversity in television programming, results, in part, from the different ways in which the enterprise can capture economic return from the "benefited" audience—i.e., whether it can more successfully sell advertising space or sell the "publication" directly to the audience. Potentially, a variety of legal and technical changes, including greater use of cable, a large increase in the number of channels, and a system of consumer (audience) payment for individual programs, could dramatically increase the diversity of programming in the audiovisual industry, making it more like the magazine industry.

10. See *A Public Trust: The Report of the Carnegie Commission on the Future of Public Broadcasting* (1979).

11. But see *id.* at 275–80. Arguably, having a small audience for specific programs but a large audience for the entire set of offerings is consistent with the proper goals of broadcasting. Measured by this standard, public broadcasting may be increasingly successful.

12. For example, in a market with three broadcasters, if 66% of the audience wanted programming of type "X," 19% wanted programming of type "Y," and 15% wanted programming of type "Z," market pressures would encourage each of the three stations to broadcast "X," getting an average of 22% of the audience apiece. However, legal regulations that required one station (or each station part of the time) to broadcast "Y" and another to broadcast "Z" would result in 100% of the audience having its desires satisfied, presumably a preferable result. Moreover, under a system paid for by advertising, the broadcaster is only able to capture the value of the programming to the advertiser. Very high transaction costs (but consider subscription or pay TV) prevent the broadcaster from internalizing the value to viewers (who presumably would be willing to pay for desired programming). Thus, the market will underproduce at least some types of programming. See, R. Noll, M. Peck, and J. McGowan, *Economic Aspects of Television Regulation* 20–57 (1973). Both problems may be reduced somewhat by greater use of cable.

13. A form of public access in which members of the public designate agents for broadcast purposes might be effective. The Netherlands have developed a procedure of this

type. See R. Homet, *supra* note 2, at 25–27 (concludes system is not presently living up to promise). Moreover, the suggestion in the text that a mandated public forum approach may have little impact on audiences does not rule out the possibility of either commercial or nonprofit, subsidized stations allocating some time to this format if they conclude that audience response would justify it.

14. It may be possible to distinguish, in a legal sense, the facilities of communication (printing presses, broadcast facilities, etc.) from the communications enterprise that puts together newspapers or television or radio programs. If so, then access to the facilities could be distinguished from access to someone else's communication enterprise. This conceptualization would justify treating the communications *facilities* as utilities and regulating them as common carriers. Nevertheless, I leave this possibility aside for now.

15. For an elaboration and critique of this argument, see Chapter 2. The Court is often viewed as accepting this argument in *Red Lion* and unanimously rejecting it in *Miami Herald.*

16. See, e.g., *Buckley v. Valeo*, 424 U.S. 1 (1976); *Miami Herald Publishing Co. v. Tornillo*, 418 U.S. 241 (1974); *CBS v. Democratic Nat'l Comm.*, 412 U.S. 94 (1973). See also Chapter 2.

17. See Linde, "Fair Trials and Press Freedom—Two Rights Against the State," 13 *Willamette L. J.* 211 (1977).

18. Note the suggestion in *San Antonio Ind. School Dist. v. Rodriguez*, 411 U.S. 1, 35–36 (1973), that some level of education might merit constitutional protection to provide for a person's meaningful exercise of her speech or electoral franchise rights. Assuming state action, a similar argument could be made for access rights. See *Linmark Assoc., Inc. v. Willingboro*, 431 U.S. 85 (1977); *United States v. O'Brien*, 391 U.S. 367 (1968) (Harlan, J., concurring). See generally Michelman, "On Protecting the Poor Through the Fourteenth Amendment," 83 *Harvard L. Rev.* 7 (1969).

19. Any full development of the argument in this section would require a method of resolving the conflicting claims of superiors (i.e., the editor-in-chief) and subordinates (i.e., a reporter).

20. See McDonald, "The Media's Conflict of Interests," *Center Magazine*, Nov./Dec. 1976, at 15, 19–20.

21. See, e.g., *Bell v. Maryland*, 378 U.S. 226, 242 (1964) (opinion of Douglas); Berle, "Constitutional Limitations on Corporate Activity," 100 *U. Pa. L. Rev.* 933, 942 (1952).

22. Of course, this argument is more a general claim that control by workers usually promotes individual liberty than a special consideration relating to the press, unless journalists stake more of their personal identity on their professional creativity and discretion to make on-the-job decisions than most workers do.

23. But see *Minneapolis Star v. Minnesota Comm'r of Revenue*, 460 U.S. 575 (1983) (tax on the press); *Grosjean v. American Press Co.*, 297 U.S. 233 (1936) (same). Governmental attempts to stop or force publication presumably can interfere with the decisions of both owners and editors. E.g., *Miami Herald Pub. Co. v. Tornillo*, 418 U.S. 241 (1974); *New York Times Co. v. United States*, 403 U.S. 712 (1971) (the Pentagon Papers case); *Near v. Minnesota*, 283 U.S. 697 (1931). But remember Burger's famous dicta: "editing is what editors are for." *Columbia Broadcasting System v. Democratic National Committee*, 412 U.S. 94 (1873).

24. 424 U.S. 1, 39–59 (1976).

25. But see Wright, "Politics and the Constitution: Is Money Speech," 85 *Yale L. Rev.* 1001 (1976).

26. This approach obviously describes many aspects of the government's present involvement in structuring the broadcast industry. But it suggests that both government

supervision to insure that broadcasting be in the public interest and government restrictions on broadcast choices are unconstitutional.

27. 376 U.S. 254 (1964).

28. See Baker, "Property and its Relation to Constitutionally Protected Liberty," 134 *U. Pa. L. Rev.* 741 (1986) (restraint on the sovereignty role of property is proper use of legislative power and sometimes is constitutionally required).

29. In many democracies, the state owns all the broadcast media. This is not true of newspapers, although in 1928, Leon Blum, a French socialist leader, proposed that the state take over the finances of political newspapers, but allow the political parties to maintain publishing and editorial control. F. Terrou and L. Solal, *Legislation for Press, Film and Radio* 80–81, 157–91 (1972).

30. Cf. *Board of Education v. Pico*, 457 U.S. 853 (1982). Unlike the affirmative purposes justifying choices for a school curriculum, taking books out of the library in order to suppress their message is impermissible.

31. See *Buckley v. Valeo*, 424 U.S. 1 (1976).

32. B. Ackerman, *Social Justice and the Liberal State* (1980); R. Dworkin, *Taking Rights Seriously* (1978).

33. One problem with this theory is that all government action or inaction inevitably violates this premise.

34. See generally M. Yudof, *When Government Speaks* (1983); Shiffrin, "Government Speech," 27 *UCLA L. Rev.* 565 (1980); Shiffrin, Book Review, 96 *Harvard L. Rev.* 1745 (1983).

35. To the extent regulation of advertising is constitutionally permitted, regulation of advertising could greatly affect the economics of various communications enterprises. Nevertheless, this effect should not be constitutionally relevant. See *Capital Broadcasting Co. v. Mitchell*, 405 U.S. 1000 (1972) (upholding ban on cigarette advertising on the electronic media). The application of the National Labor Relations Act to the press could conceivably increase the press's cost of labor, yet the Court held such application valid in *Associated Press v. NLRB*, 301 U.S. 103 (1936). See also *Associated Press v. United States*, 326 U.S. 1 (1945); *P.A.M. News Corp. v. Butz*, 514 F.2d 272 (D.C. Cir. 1975).

36. This situation would occur, for example, if newsprint became a "scarce resource" that the government controlled and allocated. At times, countries such as England, France, Italy, Sweden, India, and Mexico have chosen central, sometimes public, ownership or control of newsprint and its allocation instead of relying on market mechanisms. F. Terrou and L. Solal, *supra* note 29, at 108–13.

37. See T. Emerson, *The System of Freedom of Expression* 712–14 (1970). Obviously, the doctrinal foundations and the specific rules relating to this conclusion need development. Cf. Chapter 8. Because they are not central concerns here, I will put those issues aside for now.

38. 418 U.S. 241 (1974).

39. 395 U.S. 367 (1969). Douglas did not participate in their 8–0 decision and later said he would have dissented.

40. *Syracuse Peace Council v. WTVH*, 867 F.2d 272 (D.C. Cir. 1989).

41. E. Epstein, *News from Nowhere* 65–72 (1973), excerpted in D. Ginsberg, *Regulation of Broadcasting* 557 (1979).

42. The identification of relevant sides is obviously a subjective, valued-based task. Watching MacNeil-Lehrer, I had expected that the side opposing the Reagan administration's support for the contras, the "freedom fighters," could be nothing other than a defense of the popular, democratic government of Nicaragua. Instead, balance was achieved by presenting the factually misguided view that the Nicaraguan government was

dangerous, oppressive, and antidemocratic—but that we should not use military means to oppose it. Good conclusion, but balance? Or am I just discovering why authority laden definitions will always be problematic.

43. *National Broadcasting Company v. FCC*, 516 F.2d 1101 (D.C. Cir 1974), vacated as moot, *id.* at 1180, *cert. denied*, 424 U.S. 910 (1976).

44. See, e.g., H. Gans, *Deciding Whats News* 175–76 (1979).

45. *Banzhaf v. FCC*, 405 F.2d 1082 (D.C.Cir. 1968), *cert. denied*, 396 U.S. 842 (1969). But see *Public Interest Research Group v. FCC*, 522 F.2d 1060 (1st Cir. 1975), *cert. denied*, 424 U.S. 965 (1976) (ending application of Fairness to most product advertisements). Although withdrawal of the balance requirement from the product advertising context makes lots of sense on a number of grounds, it overtly forswears attempts at balance in relation to some of the most powerful forces shaping our society.

46. *Green v. FCC*, 447 F.2d 323 (D.C.Cir. 1971).

47. The only case commonly cited as applying the coverage requirement is *Rep. Patsy Mink*, 59 FCC 2nd 987, 37 R.R.2d 744 (1976) (failure of West Virginia station to cover strip mining violated coverage requirement).

48. L. Powe, Jr., *American Broadcasting and the First Ammendment* (1987); E. Barnouw, *The Tube of Plenty* (1982) (history of broadcasting). Scarcity is typically observed in respect to goods for which no price is charged. To the extent there is a market in broadcast frequencies, their scarcity will parallel that of newspapers, an item that most people also will not have the resources to buy or initiate.

49. 395 U.S. at 375–76. "Because of this chaos, a series of National Radio Conferences was held between 1922 and 1925, at which it was resolved that regulation of the radio spectrum by the Federal Government was essential." *Id.* at 375 n.4. After commenting on the problem of massive interference that would limit the number who could use the spectrum, the Court indicated that "[i]t was this fact, *and chaos which ensued* from permitting anyone to use any frequency at whatever power level he wished, which made necessary the enactment of the Radio Act of 1927." *Id.* at 388.

50. See *Red Lion Broadcasting Co. v. FCC*, 395 U.S. 367, 390–91 (1969).

51. Context and history provide the basis of meaning and I think this is the key to why a government attempt now to impose common carrier status on newspapers would be offensive. An alternative, thoughtful, pragmatic argument is that mandatory access opportunities and editorially independent media serve somewhat different values, that we need both, and that, therefore, the propriety of imposing access requirements on one medium (e.g., broadcasters) follows precisely from the fact that we do not impose it on other media (e.g., newspapers). See P. Chevigny, *More Speech: Dialogue Rights and Modern Liberty* 137–40 (1988) (preferring government-promoted balance in only certain, concentrated media); Bollinger, "Freedom of the Press and Public Access: Toward a Theory of Partial Regulation of the Mass Media," 75 *Michigan L. Rev.* 1 (1976).

52. *CBS v. Democratic Nat'l Comm.*, 412 U.S. 94, 105–14 (1973).

53. *Red Lion Broadcasting Co. v. FCC*, 395 U.S. 367, 390–91 (1969).

54. Another possible structural rule would be to require that when the broadcaster treats time not as a product it chooses for delivery to the public but a product to be sold to others, that it engage in the sale as a common carrier. Thus, during the time in which it devotes to advertising, it could be required to accept any noncommercial advertisements on a nondiscriminatory basis. Cf. *CBS v. Democratic Nat'l Comm.*, 412 U.S. 94, 105–14 (1973). Although the Court found that the first amendment did not require access for the political advertisers, dicta suggested that the issue would be different if Congress or the FCC had found that access ought to exist.

55. These legal frameworks specify who has what decision-making authority in what circumstances. Although there are few constitutional constraints on legislative choices in

this regard, the first amendment may require some allocations of "property" rights. The idea of expressing oneself, of a person having freedom of speech, may require that a person have those rights essential to her identity as a person. This may require that a person have rights over her "own" body and her speech decisions. See, e.g., *New York Times Co. v. Sullivan*, 376 U.S. 254 (1964).

56. Deciding on the appropriate content of this protection may be difficult. Where the government is the employer, the first amendment directly restricts employers. In this context, the best formulation of the rule is that a person should have a right to speech unless the speech interferes with the job performance that the person was hired for. Obviously, this standard will be hard to apply, but at least it seems to move in the right direction if applied with real concern for the people's speech rights and a willingness to limit management's claims concerning what interferes with job assignments. Cf. *Pickering v. Board of Education*, 391 U.S. 563 (1968) and *Rankin v. McPherson*, 107 S.Ct. 2891 (1987) *with Connick v. Myers*, 461 U.S. 138 (1983). See also *Branti v. Finkel*, 445 U.S. 507 (1980); *Elrod v. Burns*, 427 U.S. 347 (1976).

57. See, e.g., 29 U.S.C. §158(b)(4) (1973). The uniquely American doctrine of "at-will" employment allowed an employee to be fired for a good reason, no reason, or a bad reason. Recent inroads on this doctrine have included the notion that a person cannot be fired for reasons contrary to public policy, which potentially could include protection of the exercise of first amendment freedoms. *Novosel v. Nationwide Ins. Co.*, 721 F.2d 894 (3rd Cir. 1983) (wrongful discharge for refusal to engage in company's lobbying campaign).

58. D. Schorr, *Clearing the Air* (1977).

59. To some extent a function of the journalists' standards of professionalism is to give them a special incentive to value the presumably desirable social consequences of their freedom, and these standards could effect the bargaining.

60. See B. Bagdikian, *supra* note 1, at 15–17.

61. Cf. *Pruneyard Shopping Center v. Robins*, 447 U.S. 74 (1980) (having opened shopping center to the public, the state could require that owners allow people at the center to engage in free expression subject only to reasonable time, place, and manner regulations).

62. Baker, "Property and its Relation to Constitutionally Protected Liberty," 134 *U. Pennsylvania L. Rev.* 741 (1986); Cohen, "Property and Sovereignty," 13 *Cornell L. Q.* 8 (1927).

63. *Federal Election Commission v. Massachusetts Citizens for Life*, 479 U.S. 238 (1986).Split Rings and Shear Plates

64. 460 U.S. 575 (1983) (noting that the government can subject newspapers to generally applicable economic regulations but that the tax challenged here "singled out the press for special treatment;" alternative ground of decision was that law targeted a small group of newspapers).

65. 479 U.S. 238 (1986) (could not constitutionally apply a political expenditure restriction, which was permissible as to ordinary profit-making corporation, to corporations that were "more akin to voluntary political associations").

66. *Minneapolis Star and Tribune Co. v. Minnesota Comm'r of Revenue*, 460 U.S. 575, 585 (1983) (emphasis added).

67. See *FCC v. National Citizens Comm. for Broadcasting*, 436 U.S. 775 (1978) (upholding rule prohibiting ownership of both a newspaper and a radio or TV station in the same community); *Citizen Publishing Co. v. United States*, 394 U.S. 131 (1969) (joint ownership agreement between the only two newspapers in Tucson violates Sherman and Clayton Acts); *United States v. Storer Broadcasting Co.*, 351 U.S. 192 (1956) (upholding regulation limiting the number of stations that an applicant for a new license may own);

Associated Press v. United States, 326 U.S. 1 (1945) (agreement prohibiting distribution of news to nonmembers of a news association stifles competition and violates Sherman Act); *National Broadcasting Co. v. United States,* 319 U.S. 190 (1943) (upholding rule prohibiting the granting of a license when applicant too closely related to a network).

68. See, e.g., *FCC v. National Citizens Comm. for Broadcasting,* 436 U.S. at 794–95; *National Broadcasting Co. v. United States,* 319 U.S. at 216. Commentators have severely criticized various proposed rationales for the constitutionally special status of the broadcast industry: rationales such as the scarcity of channels, the great power of the broadcast media, and the intrusiveness of the broadcast media. See, e.g., Powe, "Or of the [Broadcast] Press," 55 *Texas L. Rev.* 39 (1976); Powe and Krattenmaker, "Televised Violence: First Amendment Principles and Social Science Theory," 64 *Virginia L. Rev.* 1123 (1978).

69. For these purposes, ownership would mean the legal power (through equitable title, contractual rights, or other means) to choose or otherwise control media content.

70. Media outlet would not include, or the proposal would exempt, media internal to a corporation or organization, such as employee newsletters, and media outlets operated on a nonprofit basis by nonprofit organizations that are not controlled by profit-based enterprises.

71. For a good introduction, see E. Barnouw, *supra* note 1. Complex institutional structures, however, produce anomalies belying simplistic expectations. Despite its control over a huge amount of advertising funds, Mobil Corporation took out a full-page advertisement in the *Wall Street Journal,* complaining that CBS denied Mobil access to television when Mobil wanted to respond to CBS News' allegedly inaccurate, prefabricated story about Mobil's corporate profits. *Wall St. J.,* Nov. 6, 1979, at 24.

It may be that Mobil did not face a corporate monolith; John Bache, President of CBS, argues that diversity can and does exist under a single corporate mantle. He cites among other examples a condemnation of a CBS news documentary on hunting, "The Guns of Autumn," by *Field and Stream,* a part of CBS. Bache, "Size and Competition: The Danger of Negative Thinking," 28 *J. Communication* 48, 50 (1978). This intramural competition may, however, further the overall corporate interests of CBS. In contrast to Bache's report of corporate pluralism, Donald McDonald cites an incident in which *Field and Stream* fired its conservation editor after he began to rate U.S. Senators and Representatives according to their environmental voting records and criticized the Forest Service's Environmental Program for the Future. McDonald, *supra* note 20, at 20. McDonald also reports that CBS officials, when criticized for broadcasting an eighth rerun of "The Real McCoys" rather than the Senate Foreign Relations Committee hearings on Vietnam, replied that CBS shareholders will not accept a decrease in net profits. *Id.*

72. The basis for this expectation is the hypothesis that it would be harder for a large, dispersed group of employees to agree on the form or extent of their interest in participating in policy or editorial decision making than on their interest in direct monetary benefits. Likewise, it would be harder for owners or managers to evaluate the risks of giving up decision-making power to a dispersed, diverse group than to a smaller group with whom they have more direct and constant contact. Accordingly, either formal or informal bargaining over decision-making authority, in contrast to material benefits, will more likely occur within the single outlet operation than within the multioutlet enterprise. Other factors may, however, point the other way.

73. *A Public Trust, supra* note 10, at 45–48, 155–56, 157.

74. McDonald, *supra* note 20, at 24. Sevareid also argued, "Courage in the realm of ideas goes in inverse ratio to the size of the establishment." *Id.*

75. 460 U.S. 575 (1983).

76. The split between production and consumption goods helps illustrate this conclu-

sion. The government's power to regulate market-controlled, profit-oriented economic enterprises suggests the power to require that ownership of these enterprises be separate from ownership of protected consumption goods (the purchase of speech amplifications, for example).

77. See note 67 *supra.*

78. *FCC v. National Citizens Comm. for Broadcasting,* 436 U.S. 775 (1978). In upholding FCC regulations that limit individual ownership of several media outlets, even through the use of separate corporations, the Court approved a drastic structural regulation of ownership of the press. The regulation is justified, however, on the ground that: (1) a person's freedom to use her wealth to communicate does not protect using wealth to stop others from communicating and (2) ownership of press outlets that engage a number of people in composing the communications messages, that is, where there is something more than mere broadcasting of the owner's speech, would involve the owner asserting rights to control others' speech. This is the same argument that justified regulations protecting press personnel from owner censorship. The ownership regulation still leaves the owner of one outlet free to contract to have her own messages appear in other outlets and, in that way, does not prohibit her speech. Some discussion by the Court suggests this reasoning. *Id.* at 800 n.18. Other portions of the opinion rely instead upon the view that government has a special power to regulate broadcasting. See *id.* at 798–801.

79. *Associated Press v. United States,* 326 U.S. 1, 20 (1945).

80. *Wooley v. Maynard,* 430 U.S. 705 (1977); *West Virginia State Bd. of Educ. v. Barnette,* 319 U.S. 624 (1943).

81. 326 U.S. at 51. France responded with legislation to an analogous problem in 1947. Before World War II, one company controlled newspaper distribution and arguably discriminated against some newspapers. The new legislation guaranteed all press enterprises the right to distribute their own papers but required that any organization that distributed more than one paper be a cooperative company. Only owners of newspapers or periodicals could own the capital of this cooperative and each owner was allowed only one vote. Moreover, the cooperative had to permit any press enterprise to join and its charges could not be discriminatory. F. Terrou and L. Solal, *supra* note 29, at 116–18. Such legislation would be constitutional in the United States under the analysis developed herein.

82. As Justice Black explained:

> It is argued that the decree interferes with freedom "to print as and how one's reason or one's interest dictates." The decree does not compel AP or its members to permit publication of anything which their "reason" tells them should not be published. It only provides that after their "reason" has permitted publication of news, they shall not, for their own financial advantage, unlawfully combine to limit its publication.

Associated Press v. United States, 326 U.S. at 20 n.18 (1945).

CONCLUSION

1. There is a massive literature on the issue of interpretation. Without specific citation, this Conclusion draws on three somewhat separate traditions. First, *constitutional* interpretation has generated its own, detailed literature. The piece here that I find most resonate with my own thinking is: Brest, "The Misconceived Quest for the Original Understanding," 60 *Boston U. L. Rev.* 204 (1980). Second, there is a vast general literature on legal interpretation, much of the best of which, during the last ten years, has to a large degree been written by members of, or has been stimulated as a response to, the Conference of Critical Legal Studies. Some of this has reached a very high level of theoretical

sophistication. See, e.g., Cornell, "Institutionalization of Meaning, Recollective Imagination, and the Potential for Transformative Legal Interpretation," 136 *U. Pa. L. Rev.* 1135 (1988). Third, there is more general philosophical literature on interpretation, particularly by hermeneutic theorists and some of their critics. See, e.g., H. Gadamer, *Truth and Method* (1975); J. Habermas, *The Theory of Communicative Action, Vol. 1*, 102–41 (1984); Habermas, "A Review of Gadomer's Truth and Method," in *Understanding and Social Inquiry* 335 (F. Dallemayer and T. McCarthy, ed. 1977).

2. U.S. Const., Art. II, Sec. 4. The example is adapted from J. Ely, *Democracy and Distrust* 13 (1980).

3. See Powell, "The Original Understanding of Original Intent," 98 *Harvard L. Rev.* 885 (1985).

4. See Bell, Book Review, 92 *Harvard L. Rev.* 1826 (1979).

5. See Linde, "Judges, Critics, and the Realist Tradition," 82 *Yale L. J.* 227 (1972).

6. See, e.g., *Dennis v. United States*, 341 U.S. 494 (1951) (Frankfurter, concurring).

7. See Hyde, "The Concept of Legitimation in the Sociology of Law," 1983 *Wisconsin L. Rev.* 379.

8. R. Cover, *Justice Accused* (1975). It always seemed to me that the first thing to object to about Captain Vere's judgment was that it was a poor statement of the law and that a proper *legal* conclusion would not have resulted in punishment.

9. See *Marbury v. Madison*, 1 Cranch 137 (1803).

10. *United States v. Caroline Products*, 304 U.S. 144, 152 n.4. (1938).

11. J. H. Ely, *supra* note 2.

12. Like most powerfully developed, influential theories, Ely's "representation-reinforcing" theory has drawn a large set of equally significant critiques. See, e.g., Tribe, "The Puzzling Persistence of Process-Based Constitutional Theories," 89 *Yale L. J.* 1063 (1980); Tushnet, "Darkness on the Edge of Town: The Contributions of John Hart Ely to Constitutional Theory," 89 *Yale L. J.* 1037 (1980). Similar to many of these other arguments, I have developed the criticisms summarized in the text in much greater detail in Baker, "Neutrality, Process, and Rationality: Flawed Interpretations of Equal Protection," 58 *Texas L. Rev.* 1029 (1980).

13. See *Lucas v. Forty-Fourth Gen. Assembly*, 377 U.S. 713 (1964) (invalidating this scheme as adopted by Colorado voters) (Stewart and Clark, dissenting, arguably were more consistent with the Stone/Ely approach).

14. C. Michelman, "Welfare Rights in a Constitutional Democracy," 1979 *Washington U. L. Q.* 659.

15. Our understandings of democracy are certainly not universally accepted. See, e.g., C. B. Macpherson, *The Real World of Democracy* (19xx).

16. Although I once criticized Ely's approach for being susceptible to this objection, Baker, *supra* note 12, Ely's own development of his conception of democracy would exclude giving any scope to these racist preferences. Ely, "Professor Dworkin's External/Personal Preference Distinction," 1983 *Duke L. Rev.* 959, a normative conclusion that I share, even if I would arrive at it by slightly different means. Baker, "Counting Preferences in Collective Choice Situations," 25 *UCLA L. Rev.* 381 (1978).

17. Elsewhere I have accepted and defended Rawls' basic methodology while criticizing his own elaboration of conclusions. Baker, "Sandel on Rawls," 133 *U. Pa. L. Rev.* 895 (1985); Baker, "Outcome Equality or Equality of Respect: The Substantive Content of Equal Protection," 131 *U. Pa. L. Rev.* 933 (1983).

18. Even if I am right that these elements are universal, justice may also require additional, historically more specific elements. Moreover, the content of the more universal elements may be historically or contextually variable. See, Baker, "Sandel on Rawls," *supra* note 17.

19. *Baker v. Carr*, 369 U.S. 186 (1962); *Reynolds v. Sims*, 377 U.S. 533 (1964).

20. Baker, "Sandel on Rawls," *supra* note 17.

21. *Castaneda v. Partida*, 430 U.S. 482, 503 (1977) (Marshall, concurring) (noting social science research on members of minority groups adopting majority's negative attitudes toward the minority and objecting to decision based on stereotyped assumptions).

22. Herbert Wechsler's famous call for neutral principles did not refer to the self-deluding notion of principles without value content but was much more a call for universality and consistency. Wechsler, "Toward Neutral Principles of Constitutional Law," 73 *Harvard L. Rev.* 1 (1959). In that sense, his call, as opposed to the understanding of many of his followers, is fully consistent with the type of value-based principles seen here to be necessary. The needs of the judicial role, also recognized here, may result in the implementation of the principles not being as perfect as Wechsler would like.

23. *Home Building & Loan Ass'n v. Blaisdell*, 290 U.S. 398 (1934). See Baker, "Property and Its Relation to Constitutionally Protected Liberty," 134 *U. Pa. L. Rev.* 741 (1986).

Index

Abernathy, Glen, 138, 139, 140, 153, 318*n*3, 320*n*13
Abortion, 305*n*20
Abridgement
  conditions identifying, 181
  interpretation of, 127–28, 161, 165, 175–76, 181–82, 192
Absolutist approach
  abridgement of freedom of assembly and, 163, 165–69
  caveats to, 162
  cost-benefit analysis of mandatory permit system and, 157, 159
  institutional rights and, 232
  interference with others and, 183–90
  mandatory parade permit requirements and, 143–44
  press protection and, 242, 245, 248–49, 360*n*108
  procedural conditions and, 191–92
  versus reasonableness standard, 136–37
  six principles of, 162–63
  terminology and, 125
Abuse of government power, and the press, 233–34, 246–47. *See also* Fourth estate theory
Abuse of permit system, 155–57, 322*n*24, 326*n*67–327*n*70
Access to information, right of, 303*n*44
  government secrecy and, 238–39
  press claims and, 237–38
Access to marketplace of ideas
  adequate, for all viewpoints, 37–38, 39, 41, 42–44
  equal, for all individuals, 38, 39–40, 41, 44–46
  equal, for all viewpoints, 37–38, 39
Access to media
  access requirements and, 227–28, 364*n*51
  rights of public and, 251–53

Action, communicative versus instrumental, 94–96, 107–8. *See also* Expression/action dichotomy; Nonverbal conduct
Adequcy of access. *See* Access to marketplace of ideas
Advertisers, censorhip by, 253–54
Advertising. *See* Commercial speech
Agreements, protection for, 300*n*31, 301*n*32
Air pollution, and general prohibitions, 76, 77–78, 83
Allegiance, compelled symbolic affirmation of, 154
Allocation rules. *See also* Resource allocation
  coercion and, 81
  general prohibitions as, 78–80
  liberty and, 74–75
  permit requirements as, 148
  property for use versus power and, 214
Ample alternative criterion, 174–75. *See also* Zoning restrictions
Anderson, David, 354*n*29
Antitrust law, and the press, 269–70
Arendt, Hannah, 53, 99, 110
Aristotle, 260
Artistic expression, 26, 294*n*13
Assembly, right of
  absolutist principle prohibiting abridgement of, 163, 165–69
  as group right, 186–87
  liberty theory and, 187–88
  marketplace theory and, 186
  peaceable disruption and, 183–84
  permit requirements and, 141, 143–44, 152–55
  principles for interpretation of abridgement and, 161
  restrictions on, 127
  size of assembly and, 132–33

371

Collective decision making
by behavioral voting, 78
individual rights and, 48–51
Collectivism, and legal obligation, 278*n*
Columbia Broadcasting System (CBS), 366*n*71
Columbia Broadcasting System v. Democratic National Committee, 235, 297*n*49–50, 352*n*4
Columbus, Ohio, and parades, 325*n*51, 332*n*49
Commercial speech, 68. *See also* Press rights
argument against protection of, 197–206, 296*n*44
arguments favoring protection of, 206–10
as category, 223, 338*n*3
constraints on, 21
as embodiment of individual values, 207–10
first amendment values and, 52
general argument for regulation of, 210–18
history of protection of, 194–96
individual liberty and, 197–206
marketplace theory and, 11, 314*n*111
misleading, 196, 203, 341*n*35
parades and, 323*n*29
versus personal beliefs, 201–2
political, 218
profit-motive as value in, 200–206
regulation of, and property as power, 210–18
social economic order and, 198–200
speaker's values and, 207–8
as subject to control, 59
wisdom of nonsuppression and, 21
Common carrier
broadcasting industry and, 261–62
regulation of media and, 227
Commonwealth v. Davis, 139, 320*n*11
Communication
equality of access and, 45–46
listener's uses of, 67–69
self-fulfillment and, 54
as use of speech, 51–52
Communications facilities, distinguished from communications enterprises, 362*n*14
Communications industry. *See* Broadcast media; Cable television; Freedom of the press; Media; Newspapers; Press rights; Television
Communicative action. *See also* Expression/action dichotomy; Nonverbal conduct
instrumental action and, 94–96
progressive change and, 110

Community, first amendment values and, 47, 48. *See also* Voluntary associations
Competition
independence of ends and means and, 102
profit-oriented behavior as required by, 206–7
Confidentiality, 359*n*104
Conscience, rights of, 353*n*17
Conscientious objectors, 346*n*87
Consensus, and liberty, 31
Consolidated Edison Company of New York, 222
Conspiracy, and freedom of association, 224
Constitutional interpretation
as conversation between interpreter and text, 279–83
counter-majoritarian difficulty and, 276
framer's intent and, 272–74
literalism and, 70, 272
mechanical approach to, 282
political approach to, 274–76
problems with framer's intent view, 272–74
representation-reinforcing approach to, 276–77, 279
role of interpreter in, 280–81
value issues in, 276–77, 279–81, 282
Consumer protection, 196
Content discrimination, 8–9, 287*n*18
absolutist approach and, 162, 163–65, 166, 167–68
civil rights activists and, 298*n*63
commercial speech and, 341*n*35
content-relevance of context and, 334*n*71
exceptions to ban on, 163
forms of, 167–68
funeral processions and, 164–65
by local governments, 331*n*43
parade ordinances and, 152–53
in time, place, and manner regulations, 178, 287*n*18, 305*n*21, 305*n*26
Coyright law, 68
Corporate political speech, 218–23
constitutionality of bans on, 305*n*129
corporate shareholders and, 348*n*120
expenditures on referendums and, 222–23
interest groups and, 349*n*124
legislative tradition on, 221–22
restrictions on speech and, 32, 295*n*35
transaction cost imbalance and, 349*n*124
Corporations, value-based activity by, 343*n*57, 345*n*80, 348*n*119

Freedom of the press (*continued*)
    private economic threats to, 250–71
    for the public, 251–53
    and state action, 256–57
French Revolution, 112, 113, 114
Fulbright, William, 239
Funeral processions
    parade permits and, 149, 164–65, 328*n*7
    as political demonstrations, 328*n*10

Gag order, 241
General prohibitions
    arguments for, 81–88
    ban on, and marketplace of ideas theory,
        88–91
    choice and, 77
    instrumental versus substantive value
        and, 77–80
    justifiable, 76, 77
    liberty and, 75–81
    objectionable nature of, 76–81
Gertz v. Robert Welch, Inc., 11
Gilligan, Carol, 307*n*5
Goldstein, Robert, 295*n*41, 309*n*17
Goodale, James, 358*n*84
Governmental intervention, criteria for, 42–
    43
Government property. *See* Public property
Government regulation, trend toward
    acceptability of, 139
Gravity of the evil test, 8, 287*n*12
Grayned v. City of Rockford, 169
Greenawalt, Kent, 62–65, 299*n*6
Griswold v. Connecticut, 88
Group rights, 306*n*29
Guerilla theater, 154
Guild socialism, 264–65
Gutman, Herbert, 151, 319*n*6

Habermas, Jürgen, 86, 107, 110, 120,
    307*n*6
Hague v. CIO, 145, 145–47, 169, 192
Hand, Learned, 287*n*12
Handbills, commercial distribution of,
    337*n*2
Hand-held signs, 165, 166–67, 329*n*12
Harlan, John Marshall, 43, 44, 88
Harm. *See also* Coercion
    caused by protected versus unprotected
        conduct, 71–73
    criteria for determination of, 73–74
    as justification for restriction of liberty,
        73–74
    legal restriction of speech and, 55

Hatch Act, 231
*Heffron v. International Society for Krishna
    Consciousness,* 173–75, 332*n*57
History
    constitutional focus on speech and, 27
    error of suppression and, 18–20, 21
    relation between instrumental and
        communicative action in, 95–96
    relation of ends and means and, 111–17
Hitler, Adolf, 19
Hobbes, Thomas, 101–2, 206
Holmes, Oliver Wendell, 7–8, 97, 198
Homeless persons, and expressive activity,
    178–80
Homosexual conduct, 306*n*39
Household/enterprise distinction, 200–202,
    220, 221, 343*n*57, 345*n*80
Human development, as value, 13*n*
Human dignity
    coercion and, 58–69
    elements of respect for, 278
    methods of causing harm and, 55–56
    respect for, and legal obligation, 278
    values of liberty and equality and, 41–42
Human fallibility, 18, 20, 21–22
Humphrey, Hubert, 239
Hutchinson, Thomas, 183

Ideology
    of balance requirement, 260
    marketplace theory and, 16–17
    time, place, and manner regulations and,
        128–31
Independence thesis, 92
    bases of, 98–104
    failure of, 104–8
    liberalism and, 99–104
Individual autonomy. *See also* Human
        dignity; Self-fulfillment
    caveats to absolute protection for, 162
    checking function of press and, 230–33
    collective decision making and, 48–51
    commercial speech and, 197–206
    community-defining rules and, 82
    control of own speech and, 58–59
    and conventional rights, 300*n*24
    dialogic reciprocity and, 307*n*45
    general prohibitions and, 77, 81
    incommensurate respect for freedom of
        speech and, 230, 231
    intentional interference with others and,
        185
    market exchange and, 214
    methods of causing harm and, 55–56
    respect for, 50, 278